THE COMMUNIST
PARTY
IN SPAIN

THE COMMUNIST PARTY IN SPAIN

VÍCTOR ALBA

Translated by Vincent G. Smith

Transaction Books
New Brunswick (U.S.A.) and London (U.K.)

Library of Congress Catalog Number: 82-19339
ISBN: 0-87855-464-5 (cloth)
Printed in the United States of America

Library of Congress Cataloging in Publication Data
Alba, Víctor.
  The Communist Party in Spain.
  Bibliography: p.
  Includes index.
  1. Partido Comunista de España—History.
I. Title.
JN8395.C6A7413 1983   324.246075'09   82-19339
ISBN 0-87855-464-5

Contents

Preface

Why this book? Why just now? The PCE is not an organization of the past, already deceased, but rather one that functions and operates in Spanish politics. Must not writing about it, then, be a form of politics?

For reasons the reader will soon see, the PCE is an unusual party. It has stronger international connections than other parties, more rigid systems of organization, stricter platforms, its own modus operandi—all of which is not apparent at first sight. It can only be understood by observing the evolution of the party and how its peculiarities come about and are expressed.

Neither the internal documents of the party, the minutes of the meetings—when they were taken—the internal bulletins, nor correspondence are available. Printed documents are in abundance. But we are dealing with propaganda which reflects the various lines of the party, not the means by which they were arrived at, the debates which gave birth to them, nor the discrepancies which could have arisen from them.

The memoirs of party members are not very valid, because they reflect official positions of the party at the time when they were written and are an attempt at self-justification. For another part, they are few in number and do not contain material which could be called human, but rather political. There are few anecdotes, portraits of militants or leaders, transcriptions of private conversations, personal opinions, but only carbon copies of the party "line."

Leaders' statements are not any more valuable, because they change with the changes of the line. There are instances in which an individual gives one version of certain details of an event, and years later there is a different version according to changes occurred in the meantime in the party line or party leadership.

Memoirs and commentaries from members who have been expelled from the party are not only self-serving but also differ among themselves. An ex-Communist leaning toward the Right gives one version of a particular action or meeting and an ex-Communist leaning toward the Left gives another. Of course, something can be learned from the reports.

Finally, there are few serious studies on the history of the party and a good deal of material on it must be sought in books which only tangentially refer to the PCE. This book brings together a mosaic of disperse fragments from which the image of the party with all its ups and downs finally emerges, sometimes in clear lines, other times in a blurred profile.

As to the interpretation, it has almost always had to be personal, often based on interpretations of the international Communist movement or that of other countries, since aside from two or three Spanish scholars, almost no one in Spain up to now has been concerned with making a serious analysis of the PCE and its lines. On one hand, this is due to lack of political education, a consequence of forty years of dictatorship; on the other hand, to the propaganda of that very dictatorship which, blaming the Communists for all action against it (and thereby departing from the truth), made the PCE taboo for all opponents of the dictatorship, who could be the only ones possibly interested in objectively analyzing the PCE.

Add to these difficulties those arising from the fact that much of both the clandestine and legal press about the party is available only in incomplete collections (partially destroyed by Francoist fanaticism); and besides there are no reports of certain events important to the PCE, information about which can only be gotten from the commercial press—not always impartial or well informed—or from personal recollection. Nor has it been easy to write the book once all the essential documentation had been collected. When the time came for it to be typed, three obstacles were to be faced.

First and foremost, a psychological one: to get the reader to see what is written and not what he wants to see, to get the anticommunist reader to find documentation and not just encouragement of his sentiments, and to get the procommunist reader to also find information rather than proof of "systematic anticommunism" of which he has heard so much. One must not forget the difficulty which faces every author who writes about something he has lived; he must use his own experience as a source of information and does not want his prejudices and convictions to influence—or at least overly influence—his memories and approach to the subject.

The second difficulty is of another nature. Given that the facts are disperse and that there is no precedent for a book like this, and taking into account the very nature of the Communist movement (secret, using language with double meanings and with its own jargon), the job that the researcher performs is like that of a detective. He does not work with clear and direct facts, but rather with traces and clues, and he must tie them together to construct his hypotheses and to later see if they match the known facts and explain the behavior of the PCE better than other hypotheses or than the defense the PCE makes. In this task of reporting the facts, personal points of view run the risk of getting in the way. There the reader must distinguish, once again, between information and interpretation and try to relate the facts for himself to arrive at his own conclusions.

Finally, there is the difficulty of style. Purely academic researchers are in the habit of paying part of the price of being "disinterested spirits" by boring their readers. But whoever writes with a specific purpose—to inform people and make them think—and addresses himself not to the specialist but to the general public, must try to be anything but boring. The political journalist—which fundamentally I am—knows that one of his greatest problems is to make exciting what, by its very nature, is monotonous, without detracting from the objectivity of the information nor the clarity of the interpretation. The difficulty increases when one considers that the prose Communists use (which must be frequently quoted) tends to be ponderous, repetitious, interminable, and without any personal wit or imagination. This is due to the very nature of the Communist movement, which requires that whatever its members say be a carbon copy of what its leaders say.

Having stated that, I indirectly point to another reason for deciding to write this book now. The "now" does not refer to the political situation, but to my age. Within a few years, I probably will have decided to stop writing, considering that I will not have anything new or interesting to contribute and I will be on "the sidelines" simply because of the passage of time. If the people who lived a large part of the events which I present and analyze had published books on the PCE, I would not be the one writing now. My ideological stance would advise me to let people learn from those other books. But those other books do not exist. Nor, as far as I know, are they in the process of being written. Nor is any group of researchers preparing something along these lines.

Of course, there is always the hope that a young researcher will deal with the topic. After my book about Andreu Nin was published, others, more academic and documented, appeared. Similarly, there is the likely hope that in time other books on the PCE will appear. But, as in the case of Nin, they would be cold and bland because their authors would not have lived what they were analyzing. In politics nothing can replace the climate, the atmosphere, the collective emotions, all of which are decisive factors.

I use here material from several of my previous books. But this volume is new and different, and brings the subject up to the present. One bit of advice before starting to read: the reader must not forget that in political books the meatiest parts are often in the footnotes.

Kent, Ohio
1981–1982

1.
Impatience of the Young

Like many other Communist parties, that of Spain was born under the sign of the Russian Revolution. Unlike other countries, it arose from two splits, one in the Socialist movement and another in the Anarcho-Syndicalist movement. Aside from Spain, only in Brazil and Portugal did the Communist party have this double origin, even though in some countries, like France, the revolutionary trade unionists felt attracted to the Communist movement.

Russia and Spain

The year 1917 saw not only the overthrow of Czarism in February and the triumph of the Bolsheviks in October, but also the strongest anti-monarchic and revolutionary movement ever in Spain. In 1917, the Assembly of Parliamentarians met; but a general strike broke out when it failed in its attempt to impose a constituent assembly. The Socialist-led General Union of Workers (UGT) and the Anarcho-Syndicalist National Confederation of Labor (CNT), united by a transitional pact, acted in the strike which produced strong, almost insurrectional tremors in Asturias and Vizcaya. In August 1917, the Spanish monarchy was about to follow the path which Czarism had taken months before. But it held on.

This caused many Socialists to be disillusioned with their leaders whom they considered to be too united to the Republican parties which had failed in 1917. This disillusion persisted despite the fact that the Socialist leaders landed in jail and were released when they were elected representatives in the following elections.

News of events in Russia, which was fragmentary and partisan, excited many and aroused a great deal of sympathy inside the labor movement. Similarities between the two countries were evident. In both, there was a semifeudal regime with capitalist enclaves in a state of decomposition. In both the peasant was reduced to almost servile status, despite laws which had put an end to serfdom. An oligarchy of aristocrats and political bureaucrats exercised political power. The bourgeoisie vacillated between

1

the desire to make its own revolution and the fear that the labor movement would drive it further than it wished to go.

In Russia as in Spain, the labor movement had been organized primarily by the Anarchists but it was more powerful in Spain than it was in Russia. In both countries the peasants' organization derived from a tradition of terrorist acts; in Spain they were the responsibility of commoners, but of sons of the nobility and the bourgeoisie in Russia.

In both countries there was a certain amount of industrial development; in Russia it was more advanced before World War I, while in Spain it accelerated during the war years. In Spain there was more political consciousness, more ideological education, and the political parties and labor organizations were stronger.

To the frustration of 1917 was soon added, at the end of World War I, the problem of economic crisis and the consequent increased aggression of management, which resisted demands for salary increases because in only a few months it had lost the easy markets of the belligerent nations.

These frustrations made the similarities between Spain and Russia more noticeable than the differences. Many believed that what had been done in Russia could be done in Spain. In the Spanish Socialist Labor Party (PSOE) there were those who hoped that the party would become radical and be converted into an equivalent of its Bolshevik counterpart. In the CNT there were those who considered it possible for the Anarcho-Syndicalist organization (in which there was room for people of all ideologies, not only anarchists) to play the same role in Spain as the Bolshevik party had in Russia.

Very little was known in Spain about Russian history and still less about its Socialist movement. Except for some Marxists—the few that existed in the country—no one knew anything about Lenin or his ideas. At best, the very informed in the PSOE knew of Lenin's polemics with Bernstein and Rosa Luxemburg. Trotsky's traveling through Spain did not stir any particular interest, for no one knew of him. A few, perhaps, remembered his role in the Russian Revolution of 1905.[1] In Spain no one knew what a soviet was. The press did not even mention that this word means in Russian what the term *asamblea* does in Spanish. Soviet, therefore, assumed a kind of magic power, like a political incantation.[2]

Sympathy for the Russian Revolution, of which so little was known, was common in the working-class movement, independent of ideologies. There were many union protests and also by some socialist parliamentarian or other when they suspected that the Spanish government would accede to the petition of the French and join the blockade against Russia.[3] The Congress of the National Federation of Farmers congratulated the Russian peasants in December of 1918 "for having put into practice our slogan:

the land for those who till it." The steel unions of Vizcaya (UGT) asked the government to establish diplomatic relations with Russia.[4]

A social historian has summed up the mood of the people—those who read the press and were interested in politics: "The certainty that capitalism had collapsed in a great nation and that wage earners were governing caused indescribable enthusiasm in all working-class sectors."[5]

The Berne Conference

The Socialist party was growing but its unions in the UGT were less powerful than those of the CNT. There were few Marxists in the party and Marxism was certainly not the orientation of its politics. Before World War I, the Socialists, probably influenced by constant contact with the Republicans, proved to be more pro–Allied powers than internationalist. They did not send representatives to the international conferences at Zimmerwald and Kienthal.

But social tension provoked the radicalization of certain socialist groups, especially among the young. They criticized the leaders of the party who, they said, followed the Republicans in tow. The Russian Revolution attracted numerous Socialists. Their lack of information prevented them from learning of the warnings of Rosa Luxemburg and others regarding the dangers of a dictatorship by a workers' party. Had they learned of the warnings, they probably would have rejected them.

On January 24, 1919 the first direct contact between the Russian Revolution and the Socialists was established. Trotsky had a radiogram sent signed by the Russian Communist party with an invitation for delegates to be sent to a founding congress of a new International. The same invitation had been extended to thirty-eight other parties and labor organizations. The radiogram, written in apocalyptic terms, was not directed to the PSOE but rather to "the leftist elements of the PSOE" who did not dare publish it in their weekly *Nuestra Palabra* [6] (*Our Word*) because it suggested not only the relentless struggles against the "conservative leaders of the party," but also secession by revolutionary elements. The unity of Spanish socialism had been an untouchable axiom from its origins and nothing could jeopardize a platform more than the appearance of divisionism. *El Socialista,* the official organ of the PSOE, published the call perhaps to undermine the potential supporters of the future International. The same day an assembly of the Socialist Youth of Madrid unanimously pledged allegiance to the new International.

The Socialist leaders were busy in those days preparing a delegation to the conferences in Berne, one Socialist and another unionist, which were to reorganize the Second International and create an international organization of unions. Julián Besteiro and Francisco Largo Caballero were representatives of the PSOE and UGT respectively. The Bolsheviks did not attend and harshly criticized such a meeting for the harm it might cause their own International.

At the conference, held in February 1919, the moderate Socialists presented a resolution stating that the organization of postwar Europe ought to be based on democracy, universal suffrage, and fundamental liberties. Despite the fact that this position corresponded to the one traditionally supported by his party, Besteiro voted against it because, he said, it could be prejudicial to the Russian Revolution and the decisions of the International which was to reappear. Besteiro voted for the resolution of the leftist Adler-Longuet, who refused to judge the Russian Revolution prematurely and invited "all revolutionary parties from all countries conscious of class interests"[7] to join the Socialist International.

This indicates that the differences between the Center and the Left in the PSOE were more nominal than actual. Both camps wanted a republic as well as nonparticipation in bourgeois governments and the retaining of revolutionary objectives as a foundation for their propaganda. The Left differed from the Center in its rejection of the alliance with the Republicans and its sympathy for the Russian Revolution. Neither group opposed electoral and parliamentary activity, and neither was ready to go out into the streets to raise barricades.

In Russia but Not in Spain

The first preparatory documents of the Third International's founding congress had a spontaneous, libertarian, and antiparliamentarian tone, and the revolution was forecast for the near future. This tone must have indeed alarmed the Center of the PSOE which was fundamentally parliamentarian. Those in the Center were not considered reformists since they had opposed the revisionism of Bernstein. Representatives in the Parliament like Besteiro, Pablo Iglesias, Largo Caballero, and Andrés Saborit were considered by their colleagues in the traditional parties to be dangerous subversives. In short, they were revolutionary reformists, the latter in practice and the former in propaganda and convictions. When in May 1918 the writer José Ortega y Gasset said that the Socialists and regionalists were the only honest elements in politics and called on them to govern, Besteiro, speaking in the name of the party, answered that the Socialists would not take part in a monarchic government, that they would be confined to being watchdogs as it should be, given the weakness and "diffuse" quality of party members in many parts of the country.[8] Besteiro stated that he understood the "need for proletarian dictatorship" in Russia, but not in Spain or in Western nations,[9] and he even went so far as to say that, had he been in Lenin's place, he would have done what Lenin did. The Socialists in the Center had no faith in the workers who, they said, were wards of the church and who, while in the army, fired against men of their own class when ordered to. To think of setting up soviets in Spain, then, was to dream. The lack of mass political consciousness rendered the country unprepared for revolution. "Let's talk less about Russia and see to it that more people read our newspapers and join our party," Saborit said to the young socialists.[10]

The Solitary Pérez Solís

The right wing of the party was shrinking to such an extent that one could say it was reduced to a single important figure, Óscar Pérez Solís. Indalecio Prieto and Remigio Cabello could also be considered rightists, but they generally moved with the Center of the party, while Pérez Solís acted as a free agent.

He was the frankest and often the only spokesman for reformist positions. He had been a captain of artillery and came from the agricultural region of Valladolid. He maintained that the PSOE ought to concern itself, above all, with practical measures and try to understand and capitalize on national sentiments and not become involved in the dilemma of republic or monarchy.[11]

He was a romantic sort, a bachelor who, having lost faith in God, looked for him in the people, as he himself said. Influenced by his military experiences in Morocco, he collaborated on the Socialist weekly *Adelante,* in Valladolid. He left the army in 1911.

At the beginning of his time with the PSOE Pérez Solís was a supporter of the alliance with the Republicans, but the provincial and agricultural atmosphere of Valladolid gradually swayed him and he ended up criticizing the antimonarchism of the party and devoted himself to stamping out local bossism, personified in his province by Santiago Alba who exiled him from the city. He was not attracted to the Russian Revolution and in the PSOE he supported the Second International.

The "Thirdists"

The Socialist Left was increasing in size. Its newspaper *Nuestra Palabra* was gaining new readers. The training ground for the Left was the Escuela Nueva (New School) founded in Madrid by Manuel Núñez de Arenas, son of a highly-placed public official in the House of Representatives who joined the party after the antimilitarist, antiwar Tragic Week of 1909. It had militants like typographer Ramón Lamoneda, Virginia González, journalist Mariano García Cortés (chief editor of the Germanophile daily *España Nueva*), and César R. González.

In 1919 García Cortés was elected president of the Agrupación Socialista of Madrid with a committee of leftists. This group wanted a purged and reorganized Second International in which there would be room for Bolsheviks. It received the call for the Third International with caution. As was the case with all Socialists, party unity was held above all else: its meetings in defense of Russia were not attacks on the party's leadership. In addition to those already mentioned, Andrés Ovejero, Ramón Merino Gracia, and José Antonio Balbontín spoke at these meetings. The demonstration on May 1, 1919, was punctuated with shouts of "Long Live Russia!" and the French Embassy was stoned to protest the intervention of that country against the Bolshevik government.

That left wing was not homogeneous. The elements in the Escuela Nueva were considered at once Fabian and revolutionary. Many who had sided with the allied countries now sided with Russia. Among them were Julio Álvarez del Vayo, Luis Araquistáin, and Leopoldo Alas. Disappointed by Wilson and the Allies, they placed their hopes in Lenin. Leopoldo Alas said that the news about the violence of the Bolsheviks should not be believed and that, in any case, violence and revolution could not be separated.[12] The person who was to have the most influence was Núñez de Arenas. He had been a follower of Bernstein. During the war he collaborated with supporters of the Allies on the journal *España* and was a member of the Spanish section of the Association of Friends of the League of Nations. In the party congress of 1918 he defended the Republican-Socialist alliance and approved the party's new program because, he said, "even a thoroughly liberal government could adopt it."

The disillusionment that the Versailles peace treaty of June 1919 caused among the left-wing Socialists was expressed in July by a call by the Socialists in Madrid for the new International. The war, instead of freeing countries, had "subjected Europe to bourgeois imperialism," which made impossible the fulfillment of Wilson's ideas (which Spanish Socialists had welcomed with enthusiasm). The future Communist International would see to recovering Europe for the people.

Thus began a struggle between the Left and the Center which occupied the entire life of the party for more than two years and which destroyed friendships and modified ideas and postures. The pages of *El Socialista* welcomed letters from members on the subject and it could be seen that the majority were inclined toward the Third International. Veterans of the Center felt sympathy for the Second International, to which the PSOE belonged since its founding, but they did not believe it would be possible to confront the Left. *El Socialista* came out in the defense of Lenin and the Bolsheviks and provided a good deal of information on Russia. Iglesias opposed the idea of a plebiscite in the party because, he said, party decisions were always adopted in congresses where there is less danger of division than in a plebiscite whose sole purpose is voting, not debating. Finally, the national committee convened a special congress in order to avoid a plebiscite.

Meanwhile the Asturian Federation proved in its congress to be a staunch supporter of the Third International and was about to approve a proposal in favor of immediately joining it. Local leader Isidoro Acevedo at the last moment persuaded the congress to approve a resolution in favor of rebuilding the Second International with the ideology of the Third. The ideological confusion was comparable only to the expert maneuvering.

Intellectuals and Students

Spanish intellectuals had always been elitists, which explains why the Russian Revolution itself did not attract many writers. There was no role for them in something similar in Spain. Miguel de Unamuno, for example, said that anyone who saw the Bolshevik Revolution as an "anarchist" phenomenon was mistaken. "Lenin is like a prophet of Israel and what he preaches is a new religion," he said, adding that religion would end up like a kind of Buddhism and that, like Christianity, which in order to triumph had to ally itself with paganism and Hellenism, Bolshevism would have to ally itself with bourgeois economic philosophy.[13] Besteiro called "second-hand Bolsheviks" socialists who thought Bolshevism had something to do with the weakening of the state. Ortega y Gasset also criticized Bolshevism.[14]

A few placed their hopes in the Russian example. They were, more than anything else, men who at the time aspired to a less centralized and more libertarian order and believed that the Russian Revolution was achieving just that. Manuel Pedroso, in defense of Bolshevik terror, said that "revolutions are not made with white gloves and madrigals." He said that everything was justified by the fact that the Bolsheviks were breaking down old concepts including the "fictitious concept of popular sovereignty."[15] Like Pedroso, Julio Álvarez del Vayo had been a correspondent in Germany during the war and both men knew Rosa Luxemburg. Nonetheless, her warnings about Lenin did not dash their dreams. It is worthwhile to remember these points of view because in Stalin's time they would be repeated by intellectuals of subsequent generations.

This same confusion about the nature of Bolshevism is found among militant workers. So, Daniel Anguiano, secretary of the railroad union of the UGT, Socialist representative and a simple man, highly respected for his honesty and loyalty, believed that the Russian Revolution was fundamentally syndicalist. He was a supporter of the alliance of Socialists and Anarchists and of moving speedily to an uprising, counting, he said, on the proletarians in the army. The young Socialists, with their weekly *Renovación*, were perhaps the only other Socialists to maintain that hope.

At the beginning of the century, young members of the Socialist Circle of Bilbao created a youth group directed by writer Tomás Meabe. In 1905 the Federación de Juventudes Socialistas (Federation of Socialist Youth—FJS) was established, with few more than a thousand members, three hundred of whom were from Bilbao. The FJS was devoted above all to the fight against the war in Morocco and it took form in the left wing of the party. During World War II it enthusiastically supported the Allies. In 1920 there were 5,000 members and in some places the young were more numerous than the adult members of the party. It was essentially made up of clerks and laborers with few students (at that time education was very classist and students tended to be extremely nationalist and Catholic). The FJS was the first group of the Socialist movement to openly demand joining the Third International. For the young, the Russian example was associated with August 1917 and embodied their hopes and dreams. Another nucleus of partisans of the Third International was the Grupo de Estudiantes Socialistas (GES) founded in Madrid just before the strike of 1917. In 1918 the dominant group was that of José Antonio Balbontín who was a fervent supporter of the Allies and more a devotee of Nietzsche than of Marx.[16] Many years later he wrote: "When the Russian Revolution broke out, every socialist student became, like Lenin, an inflexible Marxist. . . . The first communists in Spain were the students of our group." They were dedicated to spreading propaganda for the Russian Revolution but found sympathetic audiences only among some young socialists. "We weren't aware of the coldness [of the audience] nor did we know how to interpret the profound silence—which seemed to us reflective—of the young listeners," recalls Balbontín. He relates that at one meeting in Segovia, where the people looked like Roman shepherds to him, in the front row were several women breastfeeding their babies. One of them asked him not to speak so loudly so as not to wake up her baby who would start to cry if he were frightened by the speaker's shouting.[17]

Among the student socialists active in the FJS were Eduardo Ugarte (who preached terrorism and who later went to Russia to fight in the Red Army), Ramón Merino Gracia, Ernesto Giménez Caballero, and Manuel Cardenal. Juan Andrade and Gabriel León Trilla were only members of GES. In October 1919 GES, with Ugarte presiding, decided to support the Third International.

From Wilson to Lenin

A good part of the Socialist Left was formed by people who once were supporters of the Allies and who had faith in Wilson's Fourteen Points. Few had belonged to the Socialist Left before 1917.[18] Disillusionment with the movement of 1917, frustration over Wilson's failure in the discussion for a peace treaty, and the absence of new ideas and perspectives in the postwar European Socialist movement, all radicalized those who had held these dreams. In the same way that there is no "worse enemy than a scorned woman," there is no one more radical than a disillusioned moderate.

Thus arose the paradox that those who would have been accused by Lenin before the war (had he been aware of their existence) of being traitors and renegades actually headed in 1919 the Socialist wing which supported entry in the Third International.

Eduardo Torralba Beci put it very clearly when he said that the same idealism which brought so many socialists to the side of the Allies forced them to recognize that the peace of Versailles was not "a peace of the people nor a peace of justice and reconciliation which they thought they had been promised, but rather an imperialist and capitalist arrangement which would unfold over a terrifying vision of new wars."[19]

The liberal daily *El Sol* observed that the former most radical supporters of the Allies were those who wanted a change of Internationals.[20] Leftist militants were more patient; they knew that what was needed was constant and quiet work to strengthen the party and its unions. They were not looking for spectacular gestures nor did they feel any inclination toward the millenial prophecies found in Trotsky's calls for a Third International.

The favor that the Third International found was increased by the failure of a conference convened in Lucerne in August which was unable to reestablish the Second International. The Socialist Association of Madrid, despite the warnings of Besteiro and Largo Caballero, approved a resolution demanding preparation of a new revolutionary movement as well as support of the Third International and the breaking off of alliances with petit-bourgeois parties.

Since there was also a strong "Thirdist" current in the CNT, the Socialist Left insisted on the need for an alliance with the Anarcho-Syndicalists. In 1917 there had already been an alliance between the CNT and UGT, and if a revolutionary movement was to be repeated, it was essential to revive the alliance. This position got reinforcement from the disillusionment of Socialists in Barcelona who were unable to channel or attract workers who were becoming more and more active. They had voted for Largo Caballero in the elections of 1918, and if in Madrid they had thought it was because of sympathy for socialism, they were mistaken; they elected him to get him out of jail. Because the Socialists were unable to penetrate Catalonia and because the Catalonian proletariat was essential to the revolution, an alliance had to be sought with the organization which represented the Catalonian proletariat: the CNT.

The national committee of the UGT, reflecting these sentiments, put one of its Catalonian members in charge of initiating negotiations with the CNT. In the CNT there were supporters of an alliance, Salvador Seguí and Ángel Pestaña, for example, while others like Emilio Boal and Manuel Buenacasa, were skeptical about the revolutionary fervor of the Socialists and hoped that the rapidly growing CNT would eventually replace the UGT. They said that only a congress of the CNT could debate matters regarding unity and that consequently, precongress negotiations were unnecessary. It was paradoxical that the adversaries of unity were the most passionate Thirdists, while the advocates of unity reacted cautiously toward the Bolsheviks.

The PSOE Congress of 1919

The PSOE congress, which the Thirdists had been requesting, finally convened. At that moment the UGT had some 200,000 members and the PSOE some 25,000.[21] The congress was convened in Madrid from December 10 to 15, 1919. The center had not changed its position; it continued to be parliamentarian, gradualist, and "Secondist." In order to pacify the Left, Besteiro eulogized the Russian Revolution and even accepted the fact that proletarian dictatorship might be essential for a socialist victory but with different forms according to the country and without imitations. In Spain proletarian dictatorship could be a powerful parliament dominated by the workers. The best way to defend the Russian Revolution was to strengthen the existing International. A revolution in Spain could not even be considered until workers were in power in Great Britain.[22]

Prieto spoke frankly against the idea of a proletarian dictatorship. He described defense of the Third International as "Byzantinism and literary dilettantism in the style of Madrid." In Madrid where the revolutionary spirit was "pale" there were more supporters of the new International. He concluded by defending the Russian Revolution, but he did not accept the idea that the ideologies of Lenin and Trotsky took precedence over socialist doctrine.

Pérez Solís said that the Bolsheviks were more nationalist than socialist and the possibility of the triumph of socialism in Russia was in the distant future. The Russian Revolution of October had been an "aberration," a result of discontent and famine, a "gesture of rage against Czarist tyranny." He asked whether the Russian workers were educated enough to control production, and to the affirmative shouts of those in attendance he answered with a stentorian "No." After reading a few fragments from Engels which said that political revolution cannot lead to economic revolution, he stated that in Spain there would never be conditions for a revolution until the workers were capable of replacing the capitalists. "I belong to the Second International and I want my party to remain in it," he concluded.

The Left explained its points of view in a declaration signed by García Cortés, José Verdes Montenegro, and Núñez de Arenas. They considered the Second International a failure because it did not throw out the prowar socialists, it supported the "disgraceful sham" of the League of Nations, and it did not represent the same spirit that the International had before the war. Its leaders failed to understand that humanity had entered into a definitive phase of the Socialist Revolution during which the proletariat would take power and impose its "saving dictatorship." The Third International would replace the second, and Spanish socialism would support it. This would involve the struggle for unity of workers in Spain and continual action against the bourgeoisie, without excluding the electoral fight but without the dream that a victory for the workers could be achieved in the ballot box either. Parliament would not be the model for a socialist regime based on committees of workers in charge of production.

The Right as well as the Center and the Left wanted to maintain unity in the party at all cost. Pérez Solís and Antonio Fabra Ribas proposed a resolution in which, it was said, the congress declared that since there was only one proletariat, there should be only one International; that the duty of the Socialists was to fight, nationally and internationally, for the unity of all forces hostile to capitalism. Therefore, the congress decided that the PSOE should continue to support the Second International and send a delegation to the next congress in Geneva with the mission of asking that measures be adopted to arrive at a merger of the Second and Third Internationals. Isidoro Acevedo, from Asturias, proposed an amendment according to which, at the next congress of the Second International, the Spanish delegation would suggest the union of all Socialist parties in the world. If that were not possible because of fundamental differences of opinion between the Third International and supporters of the second, then the PSOE would join the Third International. The Pérez Solís-Fabra-Acevedo Resolution was approved by a small margin: 14,010 to 12,497. The congress approved the dissolution of the alliance with the Republicans which had begun in 1910. Besteiro, Largo Caballero, and Prieto opposed this break but it won nonetheless by a vote of 14,435 to 10,040.

The Young Socialists

Obsession over party unity was not as strong among young Socialists as it was among militant adults. The FJS included members up to thirty-five years of age. It was headed for years by Andrés Saborit but it had not called a congress in quite some time and its operation was bureaucratic and dictatorial. The association of youths in Madrid which was beginning to show discontent pressured the group into finally convening a congress which took place in Madrid immediately after that of the "adults" (December 14–19, 1919). It showed sympathy for the Third International and displeasure at the PSOE's playing for time on this matter. The Asturians Questo and Loredo proposed immediately joining the Third International; Núñez de Arenas was opposed, proposing that entry to the new International be adopted in principle, but that this decision not take effect until after the congress in Geneva, so that the party and its youth acted together. Nonetheless the vote favored the proposal for immediate membership.

The FJS congress was oriented by the group in Madrid which had become quickly radicalized with the help of the Basque and Asturian sections. The congress elected a national committee composed exclusively of members of the group in Madrid. Among those elected were Ramón Merino Gracia, Manuel Ugarte, Luis Portela, and Rito Esteban. No one knew at first if the decision of the congress would involve separation from the PSOE or if the leaders of both organizations would find a way to arrive at an agreement. At any rate the congress in Geneva would meet in scarcely a month and in so little time no categorical measures could be taken.

Borodin's Visit

Spain was of marginal interest to the Bolsheviks. They believed that to make a success of the global revolution or at least a European one, it was necessary for the proletariat to take power in some industrial nations. Spain did not figure among them. There was no reference to Spain in the works of Bolshevik theorists. In keeping with their fondness for drawing parallels to their own revolution, they believed that Spain had not even arrived at the 1905 phase.[23]

Trotsky visited Spain because of the French police. The first agent of the new International visited Spain because of his itinerary. He was Mikhail Borodin who later became famous as representative of the Comintern in Canton in the first phase of the Chinese Revolution. He had spent many years in the United States where he was director of a business school. Moscow sent him to Mexico to try to gain recognition from the Mexican revolutionary government, which he failed to do, and to organize communist parties in Latin America in which he met little success. He returned to Russia by way of Spain accompanied by a native of India, M. N. Roy, who had lived in Mexico as an exiled Indian nationalist and by a Chicano (in those days they were called "pochos") who was traveling under the name of Ramírez.[24]

Moscow ordered them to take advantage of their trip through the Iberian peninsula to investigate the situation. They arrived in La Coruña and immediately left for Madrid. Ramírez was interpreter since Borodin spoke no Spanish. The first contact they made, in the Ateneo (club of intellectuals and university professors), was with the Socialist Fernando de los Ríos who introduced them to several centrists and Thirdists with whom they met several times in their hotel room. He met Ángel Pestaña but made no attempt to establish contact with the CNT. His utterly Slavic appearance, his culture, and conspiring mannerisms made a profound impression.

Everyone interpreted his words the way they wanted. The Thirdists thought he was advising them to stay in the party and work for entrance in the Third International. The young Socialists thought he was advocating a split. As for Borodin he said later that nothing could be expected from those "leftist loudmouths" (i.e. the Thirdists).[25] Borodin proposed the creation of a daily newspaper favoring the Bolsheviks which would be financed by the Third International.[26] He seemed to have already made a decision by then: the Communist party must emerge from the young. When he left Spain in mid-January 1920 after only a fifteen-day stay he left Ramírez in charge of working with the young.[27]

The First Party

Ramírez stayed in Madrid three or four months meeting with young Socialists in a café on Fuencarral Street. The decision to postpone by six months the conference in Geneva, which was to rebuild the Second International, helped him in his efforts because the young Socialists were growing impatient over the prospect of having to wait not until January, as they had thought in their congress in December, but until July. The Third International was already in existence, having been founded in March 1919, and it seemed absurd to the young Socialists to wait any longer to join it.

Renovación was proving, with each weekly issue, to be more aggressive in its criticism of the leadership of the PSOE and its parliamentarianism. It also criticized "Thirdists" like Núñez de Arenas and García Cortés, those whom it considered "timid democrats." Ramírez promised Comintern money for a Communist newspaper and finally in late February 1920 the national committee of the FJS decided that the time had come to create a Spanish Communist party not by means of a congress but rather as a fait accompli. The national committee of youth notified every local association so they could convene local assemblies on April 15, 1920, albeit without specifying an agenda. Assemblies of youth organizations throughout the country met on that date and a communiqué from the national committee declaring that the FJS was going to become the Communist party as well as a manifesto of introduction of the new party were presented in each assembly. These documents had been sent in a sealed envelope to the secretaries of each federation with the order to open them on April 15. Undoubtedly many were opened before that date but the secret was kept. It stated that the desire for unity at all cost was reactionary. "Let there be division. We're only sorry for the time we've lost." The manifesto stated:[28] "The Communist party has as its only purpose social revolution; it rejects all minimum programs; by use of political action it establishes a platform of propaganda and attack against the bourgeoisie. Upon the ruins of parliamentarian regime and middle-class democracy, discredited forever, will be established the Soviet regime, the only one able to bring about the dictatorship of the proletariat."[29]

At the assembly in Madrid before some 100 members César R. González objected and finally, seeing that he would be defeated, left the hall followed by about 25 others. In the provinces the associations which voted in favor of the change became sections of the new party.[30] The

FJS had about 5,000 members. About 1,000 votes were cast from the various sections in favor of the change.[31] The Asturian section, thanks to Saborit, rejected the conversion which was a blow to the new party. Even though young people in Vizcaya were supporters of the Third International, they refused to break with the party.

López y López and others immediately reorganized the FJS out of the group which rejected the conversion. The new Communist party was left with about 1,000 members here and there and about 100 in Madrid. Those who had made the split were young people, generally between the ages of 20 and 25. As a result the newly formed Communist party looked like an adventure of a handful of adolescents from Madrid who carried along some youths from the provinces who had not dared face a congress or the debate which should have preceded it, who had been leaders of the FJS scarcely five months, and who had been used by an envoy of the Comintern bearing promises of aid. Much of this was exaggerated but that was the image the PSOE succeeded in giving of the first Communist party. It set up headquarters in a basement on Álvarez de Castro Street. The title *Renovación* was changed to *El Comunista* (*Renovación* continued publication a little later as an organ of the reorganized FJS). And so there was a Communist party in Spain.

Notes

1. Trotsky, *Ma vie,* Paris, 1953, p. 266 ff.
2. It was Fernando Durán, M.D., at a conference at the Ateneo in Madrid who, according to Portela, provided the best information about what was happening in Russia. The professor of the junior college in Alicante, José Verdes Montenegro, succeeded him at the rostrum. Those two conferences constituted all the ideological documentation the socialists had on the Russian Revolution.
3. It is an exaggeration to say that "the working masses rose up in an impressive movement which caused the government to back down," as stated in *Historia del Partido Comunista en España* (by "a commission of the central committee of the party formed by comrade Dolores Ibárruri, who presided over it, as well as comrades Manuel Azcárate, Luis Balaguer, Antonio Cordón, Irene Falcón, and José Sandoval"), Paris, 1960, p. 20. It will be necessary to refer to this book often and the abbreviation *Historia del PCE* will be used.
4. *Historia del PCE,* p. 21.
5. J. Díaz del Moral, *Historia de las agitaciones campesinas andaluzas,* Madrid, 1923, p. 174.
6. This weekly had begun to be published in 1918 and the principal leftists of the PSOE collaborated on it. In 1919 it was replaced by *La Internacional,* which Antonio Fabra y Ribas founded upon his return to Spain after being thrown out of Cuba. Later Núñez de Arenas was editor of this weekly.

16   The Communist Party in Spain

7. Pierre Renaudel, *L'Internationale à Berne*, Paris, 1919, pp. 7 ff., 35 ff., 133–35.
8. Quoted by Gerald H. Meaker, *The Revolutionary Left in Spain, 1914–1923*, Stanford, 1974, p. 197.
9. Andrés Saborit, *Julián Besteiro*, Mexico City, 1961, p. 171 ff.
10. Quoted in *Renovación*, Madrid, November 15, 1919.
11. Óscar Pérez Solís, *Mi amigo Óscar Perea*, Madrid, 1929. His points of view at that time are summed up in *El Partido Socialista y la acción de las izquierdas*, Valladolid, 1918.
12. *El Sol*, Madrid, January 20, 1919.
13. *El Liberal*, Madrid, July 3, 1920.
14. José Ortega y Gasset, *España invertebrada*, Madrid, 1922, p. 83 ff.
15. *El Sol*, Madrid, January 25, 1919.
16. José Antonio Balbontín, *La España de mi experiencia*, Mexico City, 1952, p. 119. Portela, in a letter to the author in 1979 states that the Socialist students did not play as large a part and that in the meetings there was a great deal of enthusiasm.
17. Balbontín, pp. 144–45.
18. Meaker, p. 210 ff., underlines these Wilsonian antecedents.
19. Eduardo Torralba Beci, "Fin del ensueño wilsoniano," *El Sol*, Madrid, May 9, 1919.
20. *El Sol*, Madrid, July 21, 1919.
21. There are estimates which raise that figure to 42,000. Actually, in the first months of 1919 the number of members had increased by 50 percent which would give a total of 22,000 members.
22. At this time the majority of foreign capital invested in Spain was British and the Royal Navy was impressive.
23. Meaker, p. 250.
24. Consult the following texts on Borodin's mission in Latin America: Víctor Alba, *Politics and the Labor Movement in Latin America*, Stanford, 1968; and Robert J. Alexander, *Communism in Latin America*, New Brunswick, 1957.
25. "Cómo juzga Borodin el socialismo español," *El Comunista*, Madrid, April 1, 1920.
26. There are marginal references to Borodin's stay in Spain in M. N. Roy, *Memoirs*, Bombay, 1964, p. 223 ff. Meaker (pp. 511–12) provides personal recollections from people who lived during that period. M. N. Roy was also in Madrid and Barcelona in December 1919 and had an interview with Pablo Iglesias who "with a kind smile, not without a certain degree of sadness, took pity on the victims of the recent wave of fanaticism." He called several meetings with half a dozen young workers who "assured me that Iglesias had no influence in the Socialist party in which there was a majority who would follow them to join the Third International" (Roy, *Memoirs*, Bombay, 1964, pp. 234–35).
27. Ramírez lived many years in Moscow under the name of Manuel Gómez. Later he said that Borodin, in order to find out whom it was advisable to attract, put him in charge of reading what was being written in the Spanish press in order to identify sympathizers. That is how poorly informed the International was about Spain. Upon his departure he left Ramírez a little

money. The Chicano lived at the home of a shoemaker without paying rent (he must have been a sympathizer). Borodin sent him a little more money from Berlin and Ramírez formed a committee for the Third International with about 20 young socialists from Madrid. This group published a weekly journal, *El Obrero,* which Ramírez directed from the shoemaker's home. When the second congress of the International met, Ramírez decided to leave for Moscow as a representative of the Mexican Communist party (Manuel Gómez, "From Mexico to Moscow," *Survey,* London, October 1964). One man who met him said, "Manuel Ramírez, about 30 years old, of medium height, very dark complexion, rarely spoke. His wide, Aztec face looked like a mask. He was a laborer who had worked several years in the tobacco industry in Tampa, Florida where he learned English and received an education about unions which gave him a certain prominence when he returned to his country. Of average intelligence and lacking a theoretical foundation, he approached communism more for emotional than ideological reasons. He became secretary of the Mexican Communist party, but lacking in common sense, in 1924 he committed a grave political error and lost his leadership which he never regained. . . . Being completely unaware of the art of clandestine operations, he made blunders in Madrid which, once discovered, did not help increase his limited prestige" (Maurín, *Revolución y contrarrevolución en España,* Paris, 1966, p. 270).

28.   Published by *Renovación* on the same April 15, which indicates that its approval by the local assemblies was taken for granted. The *Historia del PCE* says that the manifesto appeared in *El Comunista.* That is erroneous. This weekly began publication shortly after, when *Renovación* changed its title. Andrade says that "with the collaboration of some members of the Group of Socialist Students . . . the printing of the sentimental chronicles of Tomás Meabe as well as the articles of a purely laborist nature by the sons of the Pablist family [reformist Socialists, thus called because of their leader Pablo Iglesias] disappeared from the columns of the organ of the youth group." He also remembers that "the maneuver to create the Communist party was what might be called a coup d'état by the National Committee of Youth with the consent, of course, of the majority of militants. All but two of the members of the National Committee (who were not invited to the meetings), together with the committee of Madrid in its entirety, agreed to adopt the secret resolution which would transform the Federation of Young Socialists into the Spanish Communist party" (Juan Andrade, "La fundación del Partido Comunista de España," *Tribuna Socialista,* Paris, May-July 1977).

29.   The members of the national committee which had made way for the conversion were: Vice-president José Illescas, Secretary Ramón Merino Gracia, Assistant Secretary Luis Portela, *Renovación*'s director Tiburcio Picó, Recording Secretary Vicente Pozuelo, and committee members Emilio Agudo, Eduardo Ugarte, Rito Esteban, and Eleuterio Rodríguez. President José López y López alone refused to assist in the plan. Portela, in a letter to the author, said that neither Rodríguez nor Agudo was part of the national committee. The quotes from Portela, unless otherwise indicated, come from that letter.

30.   Portela, who was on the committee of the FJS, does not know who proposed

the novelesque idea of the sealed envelope. He approved of it when his companions presented it to him in the visiting room of the prison where he was detained. He supposes that the idea must have been Ramírez's or Merino Gracia's. Anguiano had had dealings with the young people, but he changed his mind.

31. Portela thinks there were about 2,000.

2.
Seduction of the Anarchists

In the name of the Communist International, Trotsky extended an invitation for membership only to the Socialists. It is paradoxical that among the Anarcho-Syndicalists there was more enthusiasm for the Russian Revolution than among the Socialists, which shows how poorly informed Moscow was about life in Spain, for it neglected to send an invitation to the CNT.

The undercurrent of controversy going on between the Russian Social Democrats and the Anarchists must also have had something to do with it. Contributing to that oversight—if indeed that is what it was—must have been the fact that the weak Russian unions were to a great extent founded and led by Anarchists. The Bolsheviks, who naturally wanted to control the labor union movement, therefore had to confront the Anarchists. In 1919 there were quite a few Russian Anarchist prisoners although the majority of their people, led by Kropotkin, were free and still had certain means of self-expression. The plight of the Russian Anarchists was little known in Spain.

The "Sovietists"

Just as the supporters of the Third International in the Socialist movement were called "Thirdists," the Anarchist and Anarcho-Syndicalist admirers of the Russian Revolution were commonly called "Sovietists." The word is significant because it reveals their enthusiasm. It surely was not the Bolshevik party or Lenin's ideology that attracted so many Anarchists and Anarcho-Syndicalists but rather the concept of soviets.

Seen from afar and with the scanty amount of information that was available, the soviets looked, in the eyes of the CNT people, like the ideal instrument to run both society and the economy without resorting to the authority of government. They were not seen simply for what they were—that is, assemblies—but rather as instruments of working-class consensus, as means of leading and controlling without displaying authoritarian attributes.

The Russian Revolution was unexpected and conspiratorial in nature.

The Bolshevik takeover was not the result of action by the masses, but a sudden coup prepared militarily and in secret. This was encouraging to those who did not see any other alternative for Spain except a total break with the past and present. They rejected elections, parliamentary action, and politics, and placed their faith in the coming of the "great night" which would put an end to the society of exploitation. "The people in the CNT were completely taken with the Russian Revolution to the extent of seeing in it the revolution which they had been dreaming of. . . . For many of us—the majority of us—a Bolshevik was a demigod, bearer of freedom and happiness for all. . . . What anarchist in Spain ever shrank from calling himself a Bolshevik?"[1]

"In this case desire was the mother of invention and . . . each individual was determined to see in Russia what he hoped to see in his own country."[2] At the outset the Third International "tried to resemble not so much the Second, made up of the Socialist parties, but rather the First which joined the whole labor movement regardless of unions and parties."[3]

A witness at the time[4] later pointed out that "what mainly appealed to the Anarcho-Syndicalists about the Bolshevik Revolution was the agrarian revolution and the intention of ending the war. The Anarcho-Syndicalists adopted as their own the Bolshevik slogan 'bread, peace, and land.' Andalusian peasants in 1918–19 felt as Bolshevik as Catalonian workers if not more so. . . . Anarcho-Syndicalist support of the Russian Revolution was intuitive and sentimental. Lenin captivated them because they saw in him echoes of the Jacobins and Bakunin."[5]

Second Congress of the CNT

History is often unjust due to the myopia of historians. The Catalonian regional congress of the CNT called in Sants, Barcelona, in 1918 went almost unnoticed. In it "a construction painter, Salvador Seguí, defended a revolutionary thesis which was later approved: the conversion of the trade unions into industrial unions. That agreement was going to change the bases of the country's political and economic stability radically and quickly. . . . The National Confederation of Labor which was just beginning in 1910 had already become a giant by 1919 capable of shaking institutions. The big leap was made in a couple of years due mainly to the industrial union."[6]

The second congress of the CNT assumed monumental importance. It was called "de la Comedia" after the name of the theater in Madrid where it met on December 10–18, 1919. Its main purpose was to decide whether the CNT would join the Third International. There were 437 delegates representing 714,000 members (more than three times the number the UGT had at the time); 128 delegates represented the 427,000 Catalonian members alone. The majority of delegates were under 35 years of age. A witness described the assembly in this way:[7]

> In its second congress the CNT had to solve two fundamental problems: (1) what tactic to follow, and (2) what relationship to establish with the other labor organization, the UGT.
>
> The congress resolved the first one successfully but it erred in its approach to the second. Instead of seeking unity of labor within manageable dimensions, it adopted an absurd resolution: absorb the UGT. . . .
>
> The delegation that fought the "absorption" harder than the others was the Asturian of which Eleuterio Quintanilla, José María Martínez, Avelino González, Aquilino Moral, and Jesús Rodríguez were members. The Asturian labor movement has always had a great sense of responsibility both in the CNT and UGT, and it has always been the first to take up arms when the battle call was sounded.

In one of its first sessions the congress reaffirmed the anarchist character of the CNT, since its ultimate objective was the establishment of "anarchic communism" or, as it would be called decades later, libertarian communism.

Unionists and Anarchists

Seen in retrospect and in light of this affirmation of principles, it would seem absurd to suppose that the CNT would join the Third International. Nonetheless, it happened. To understand the apparent contradiction it must be kept in mind that the Russian Revolution was understood as it has been stated and not as it actually was and that, in addition, information was lacking. Despite its anarchic principles the CNT was an open organization to which people of diverse ideologies belonged— not only Anarchists. Although the Anarchists held the majority of delegations to the congresses there were also Socialists who did not want to belong to the UGT. In addition there were revolutionary syndicalists and unaffiliated Marxists not only among the members and militants but also in positions of leadership in the unions and on regional and national committees. One participant recalls the congress in its non-political aspects this way:[8]

> The format for discussion was always the same: first a project would be discussed exhaustively, without rhyme or reason, touching the most serious of matters with utter naiveté. When the president would get tired of hearing

such nonsense he would propose that a committee be formed to prepare a report. The committee was built around the four or five names that repeatedly "came up" in the discussion. The committee would retire to deliberate and the congress would take up another topic on the agenda and the same procedure would be repeated. When the members of a committee would return to the hall with their report, the discussion would be interrupted and someone would read the report . . . which generally was approved unanimously or nearly so. This singular procedure led to the approval of contradictory reports.[9]

The Catalonian delegation, often supported by the Asturian, was the pivot for the Anarcho-Syndicalists, while the Andalusian delegations played the same role for the Anarchists. Valencia, Aragón, and Madrid, as well as Galicia, fluctuated and were split between both tendencies. The delegates from the Center often attempted to be mediators.

The Anarchists (especially Catalonians)[10] were the most numerous supporters of the Third International and the Anarcho-Syndicalists were the most mistrustful of Moscow. Thus arose the paradox in which Anarcho-Syndicalists spoke of the "sacred (anarchist) principles" in order to present opposition to membership, and the Anarchists spoke of efficiency, encouragement, and revolution to advocate membership and did not resort to ideological arguments.

Provisional Membership

It was the second to the last day of the congress and the most pressing problem had yet to be discussed. The most "Bolshevik" of all was the marble-cutter from Valencia, Hilario Arlandis, who was determined not to win the congress's sympathy for the Russian Revolution, sympathy which already existed, but rather to back proletarian dictatorship, the Leninist vision of the revolution. He said the advances of capitalism had left the idea of "spontaneous production by small groups" in the lurch and that centralization of production was necessary. His platform was not favorably received, for those concepts were contrary to those held by the majority. Nor was the Asturian Jesús Ibáñez any more successful. Many others spoke in favor of joining the Third International; there were some who said that the Bolsheviks had achieved the ideals of revolutionary syndicalism and others who recognized that the ideas of the Bolsheviks were in opposition to the antiauthoritarian principles of the CNT, but that it was necessary, even so, to join while waiting for a libertarian International. Among those who spoke in favor of membership was Andrés Nin, a Catalonian schoolteacher and one-time member of the PSOE. (Nin's presence was an indication of the open nature of CNT membership.) He said: "I am a fanatic for action and revolution. I believe more in action than in an ideology for the distant future and in abstract matters. I am a supporter of the Third International because . . . it goes beyond ideology, it represents a principle of action, a principle of coexistence of all the purely revolutionary ideologies which strive to establish communism at once."[11]

The secretary of the national committee of the CNT, in recalling the congress, recorded that "in spite of the fact that not a single one of the 400 anarchist delegates in Madrid was willing to give an inch regarding our ideological convictions, it is indisputable that nearly all of us acted like true Bolsheviks."[12] Opposition was persistent, despite the fact that it represented only a minority. Eleuterio Quintanilla, the Asturian who enjoyed great prestige and who earlier had lost a battle trying to persuade the congress to adopt a more flexible attitude toward the UGT, said of the International: "The Russian Revolution does not embody our ideals. . . . Its direction and orientation do not include the participation of workers but rather of political parties. It is all well and good to try to prevent the Central and Western nations of Europe from cordoning off and choking the Russian citizenry, a maneuver which requires an understanding with the rest of the workers of the world. However, because I consider the Third International a political body, I believe that the CNT has no reason to be represented in it."[13]

The unions "which had nothing to do with the revolution" subordinated themselves to the decisions of those in power offering themselves to them unconditionally. The Bolshevik dictatorship "constitutes a serious threat and if we are not in a position to combat it, at least we must not applaud it."

Eusebio Carbó, who later became secretary of the AIT, the Anarchist International, came out in favor not only of membership but also of proletarian dictatorship saying: "We praise it, we cherish it if it is to help establish definitively the reign of justice in the world." He then made a distinction between a dictatorship of the state or government and a dictatorship of the people.[14]

Seguí sided with Quintanilla even though he accepted membership in principle "so as not to remain isolated from workers in the rest of the world until the day when the true International of the workers is organized." He emphasized the lessons of the Russian Revolution. For example, in order to carry out the revolution workers must prepare themselves to take charge of production without the need to resort to the dictatorial measures of the Russians. "Therefore it is necessary for the workers in industry, agriculture, and intelligence to really see the uniqueness of this moment in the history of the world which we are now experiencing. They must also see the need to do everything possible by means of willpower and intelligence to better themselves, to foresee, or rather to have resolved all those things which, at a given time, could guarantee the transfer of power from capitalism to the proletariat."[15]

By no means did membership, adopted with great acclaim, constitute surrender; membership was provisional, until another International was organized. The approved decision said the following: "First: that the CNT declare itself a steadfast defender of the principles of the First International upheld by Bakunin. Second: declare provisional membership in the Communist International because of its revolutionary character while the CNT of Spain organizes and convenes the universal workers' congress to determine the guidelines which the true workers' International is to follow." The congress also decided to send a delegation from the CNT to Russia. Quintanilla and Pedro Vallina were considered but finally (probably because they themselves withdrew from the mission) Ángel Pestaña, Eusebio C. Carbó, and Salvador Quemades were named.[16]

Aid to Russia

The congress resolved to defend the Russian Revolution which was at that time threatened by the Allied blockade as well as by the Civil War. The congress approved a resolution proposed by the national committee which said: "First: that Spanish arms and ammunition factory workers should refuse to build equipment to be used to fight the Red Army, and second: that the confederation agree to declare a general strike the moment the government tries to send troops to Russia."[17] Naturally the second part of the resolution never stood a chance to be put into practice. As for the first, it remained merely a gesture, since Spain was not an exporter of arms nor was the control or destination of arms in the hands of the workers.

By unanimously voting for this resolution the congress followed its anti-Socialist sentiments which were revealingly expressed by Buenacasa: "Since the Socialists have not done so, we who are not socialists must unanimously agree to aid the Russian Revolution—but with actions more than words."[18] Carbó was even more lyrical. He, among others, had a special motive for fomenting sympathy toward the Russian movement, something which "spontaneously rises in my veins," something which told him that "the Russian movement has great merit, even if documents to judge it appropriately are lacking." That motive was his "having seen Spanish socialists for three years shamelessly and ignominiously denigrate it [the Russian movement]."[19] Finally, Seguí told Joaquín Maurín, who was attending the congress dressed as a soldier (he was doing military service in Madrid): "Thanks to you we're holding a congress of workers, peasants and . . . a soldier."[20]

Pestaña in Moscow

Ángel Pestaña was the only one of the delegation of three who was able to get to Moscow. Someone who knew him well said of him: "A watchmaker by trade. More than a worker, strictly speaking, he was an artisan. Until he was named editor of *Solidaridad Obrera* in 1916 . . . he lived with a certain degree of independence, working at home. He had spent several years in Algeria in direct contact with the French workers' movement. He was personally modest and austere. His ascetic, withdrawn nature was in contrast to Seguí's which was open, generous, Mediterranean. He had read a lot and had a great capacity for assimilation. He wrote with ease and expressed his thoughts clearly. And he was a good speaker."[21] In a sense he considered himself a pure anarchist, even though he might coincide with Seguí's style of action. Once while in Russia after absorbing on the trip what such non-Spanish anarchists as Malatesta and Rocker had written about the Russian Revolution, he found himself torn between Catalonian Anarchists' enthusiasm for the Third International, the doubts he had arising from his own anarchism, and the practical experience of his participation in unions.

The sessions of the second congress of the Comintern began on July 22, 1920. Since the first congress fifteen months earlier Bolshevik hopes for a European revolution had been frustrated. Germany and Hungary had both been failures. Moscow interpreted this as an indication of the need for greater discipline and centralization in the Communist movement. The second congress must commit itself to integrating and disciplining the movement. Lenin's book *Extremism, a Childhood Disease of Communism* was published in April and fought against the antiparliamentarian, workers' councils, and insurrectional trends in many Communist parties. With its victories in the Civil War Russian Communists had gained a good deal of self-confidence considering the Russian model as universal. The International would take charge of enforcing it.[22] It would thus lose the open character it had assumed at the outset and would become an organization of political parties. That posed a problem for an antipolitical individual like Pestaña.

In Berlin Pestaña had learned of the convocation of the second congress and had waited in the German capital for authorization from the CNT to represent it. Previously he had gone as a delegate of the CNT simply to visit Russia. His colleagues in the delegation were unable to get there; Carbó was arrested in Italy and Quemades did not make it past Paris. In those days police all over Europe tried to obstruct passage to Russia.

By rail and car Pestaña went from Berlin to Russia via Reval accompanied by the French revolutionary syndicalist Alfred Rosmer who listened with amazement as the Spaniard described the situation in Spain as ripe for the overthrow of the monarchy.[23] In Russia he was moved by the air of sadness and suffering of the people. He was aware of that sadness throughout his entire visit.[24]

Zinoviev, president of the International, received the group of delegates in Petrograd and accompanied them to Moscow by train. Once there they were invited along with other unionists to a meeting of the executive committee of the Comintern to discuss the founding of a Red Trade Union International to oppose the Amsterdam Trade Union International led by Socialists. Pestaña knew nothing of this project and believed that his mandate did not include any decision about it. His doubts were intensified when a manifesto directed to "unionists the world over" was read. Prepared by Losovsky in consultation with Lenin, it took for granted submission of the unionist movement to the Communist movement, affirming the need for a proletarian dictatorship and a "close and indestructible alliance" between unions and Communist parties.

Syndicalists were opposed to these concepts. Pestaña adopted an ambiguous position; he pointed out the antiauthoritarian nature of the CNT but indicated that since the CNT congress had decided to support the Third International, he was forced to sign the manifesto. He added that anything referring to a proletarian dictatorship—assumption of power and collaboration of the unions with the parties—would be subject to any reservations the CNT might have. He proposed amending the manifesto. However, he was unable to achieve his goal and signed it nonetheless.[25]

From experience he learned a trick which later gained general acceptance in the Communist movement. With Rosmer's help he removed from the original text of the manifesto a sentence condemning the "treachery of the unionists during the war." It alleged that many unionists—those of the CNT among others—had not betrayed their internationalist principles. However when the manifesto was published the sentence, whose removal Radek had approved, appeared word for word.[26]

Meetings with Trotsky and Lenin

The two "stars" of the congress were Trotsky and Lenin. Pestaña had a confrontation with the former, a pleasant talk with the latter. Pestaña disagreed with the congressional recommendation that Communist parties be formed in every country. Nor did he agree with the supposition that there could not be revolution without Communist parties. This idea, he said, "seeks to negate the history and genesis of every revolutionary movement man has generated." Addressing himself to Russian Communists, Pestaña said: "You did not make the revolution in Russia, you collaborated on its making and you were luckier for having gained the power." Trotsky and Zinoviev replied—the former for 45 minutes and the latter for 30—but the CNT delegate was not able to return to the floor. Trotsky said:

> Comrade Pestaña, secretary of the great labor organization in Spain, has come to Moscow because there are among us friends who more or less directly belong to the syndicalist family; others are "parliamentarians," so to speak; others, well, are neither parliamentarians nor unionists, yet they are supporters of action by the masses, etc. But what can *we* offer them? We can offer them an international Communist party, that is, the unification of the progressive elements in the working class who have brought their experience, their mutual confrontations; they criticize one another and after discussion make decisions. When Comrade Pestaña returns to Spain taking the congress's resolutions with him people will ask him, "What did you bring us from Moscow?" He will present the fruits of our labor and will bring our resolutions to a vote and the Spanish unionists who unite around our theories will make up the Spanish Communist party. . . . Who will resolve matters in Spain? The Spanish Communist party will, and I hope that Comrade Pestaña will be one of the founders of the party.

Pestaña refused to vote for any of the resolutions on the relationship between unions and Communist parties or on the proletarian dictatorship, and along with other Anarcho-Syndicalists (Emma Goldman, Agustín Souchy, Alfred Rosmer, Jack Tanner, and the Russian Shapiro) he proposed that the Red Trade Union International be declared independent of all political movements. This proposal never even reached discussion. In this way Pestaña learned about the procedures by which Communist meetings were conducted and toward the end of his participation in the congress he pointed out that while in the CNT the chairman of a meeting was confined to leading debates, in the International or the Russian Communist party the Presidium exerted decisive influence over the debates; it was like a parliament in which the head of the government was the chairman.

Pestaña was part of the unionist commission of the congress, where he had several confrontations with Karl Radek, whom he referred to as a "raving antiunionist." When he realized that he was not being listened to he stopped attending the commission's meetings. In the last session of the congress Pestaña went up to Lenin to say goodbye and Lenin asked him to come visit him. After chatting and arguing a while on the subjects of dictatorship, centralism, and revolution, Lenin asked Pestaña: "By the way—What opinion do you have of the delegates who attended the congress as revolutionaries?"

"Shall I be frank with you?"

"That is why I asked."

"Well then, even though you may be disillusioned or think I am not able to recognize man's worth, the opinion I have of the majority of delegates attending the congress is deplorable. Save for a few rare exceptions, everyone is of bourgeois mentality. Some because they are self-seeking and others because such is their temperament and upbringing."

"And what basis do you have for expressing such unfavorable judgment? It certainly must not be what they said in the congress!"

"On the basis of that alone, no; I base my opinion on the contradiction between the speeches which were given in the congress and the common way of living I observed in the hotel. The little things one does every day reveal more about men than all their words and speeches. How do you expect us, Lenin, to believe in the revolutionary, altruistic, and emancipatory sentiments of many of those delegates who in their daily lives act, quite simply, like perfect bourgeois? They grumble and complain about how little and mediocre the portions of food are, forgetting that we foreign delegates are receiving the best meals; and most important of all: they forget that millions of men, women, children, and elderly go without the barest essentials, not merely the frills. How can one believe in the altruism of those delegates who bring miserable, starving girls to the hotel for dinner in exchange for their favors in bed, or who give presents to women whom they later take advantage of? What right do those delegates have to talk of brotherhood who insult and abuse hotel employees who are not quick to attend to their most insignificant whims? They consider men and women of the people servants and lackeys, forgetting that perhaps some of them have fought and risked their lives for the defense of the revolution. . . . And, finally, those lucrative arrangements which those of us who are sickened by such moral defection have to witness; that constant placing a price on their support; all of this smacks of deception of the vilest, most despicable sort. How can we believe in the revolutionary spirit and in the honesty of such people? You say they want revolution in their respective countries? They do, but they want it without endangering their lives and they want it in the exclusive interest of their lustfulness. This naturally does not mean that in the Communist parties and the masses there are not hundreds of individuals of good faith, willing to make sacrifices and who are worthy of all respect and esteem. Those people are different.

These are purely personal criticisms regarding the delegates attending the congress. This is my opinion, sincerely expressed."

"Fine, Pestaña, fine . . . although your judgment might be slightly exaggerated!"

"And with these words Lenin stood up. The interview had ended."[27]

The topic which interested Lenin the most, the adoption of the 21 conditions he had drawn up for membership to the International, did not seem to interest Pestaña who abstained from voting on them, alleging that the CNT was apolitical. After the congress Pestaña stayed a few days longer to attend the meetings of the organizational committee of the Profintern (Russian abbreviation which they began to use for the future Red Trade Union International). The Anarcho-Unionists had courted for years the idea of a revolutionary unionist international and the congress of "la Comedia" served to revive it. Would the Profintern be that International? The syndicalist delegates proposed, to make more evident its autonomy, that headquarters be located outside of Russia, but the response they got was that the Russian delegates would have trouble getting visas.

The Bolshevik experience which had turned unions into instruments of the party and the state in the area of production was irreconcilable with the theory of syndicalists who saw the unions as means to change society and manage production without bowing to anyone. Souchy and Tanner left one committee session angrily but Pestaña remained. Losovsky, who was chairman, proposed that polemical matters be left for the founding congress of the Profintern which would meet in 1921. Tomsky, who was more flexible, replaced Losovsky and accepted that the invitation to the congress be addressed to all unionist organizations which practiced "class struggle" and made no reference whatsoever to political questions. This enabled Pestaña to persuade Tanner and Souchy to return to the meetings.

From Sadness to Prison

While he was in Russia Pestaña wrote for *Pravda* several articles about the CNT[28] as well as a report for the Third International on the "situation of each of the social forces in Spain." He also had many meetings with other syndicalist delegates from several European countries. Victor Serge, whom Pestaña knew from the time he was in Barcelona, took care of orienting and guiding those delegates, especially Pestaña; and Serge did not conceal from them the revolution's problems and shortcomings.[29]

He spent a month traveling through Russia where he discerned in the people an overall sadness; he did not let himself be dazzled by the hospitality of the Bolsheviks nor did he allow their hospitality to make him forget his anarchic perspective, made stronger probably by the reports from the American anarchist Emma Goldman (who spoke Russian) about the imprisonment of some Russian colleagues. In everything he wrote about Russia Pestaña underlined the incompatibility of the libertarian spirit of the Russian Revolution and the dictatorial spirit of the Bolsheviks, which seemed to him to come from Lenin's personal nature which he called "Germanic."

The way Pestaña saw it, the revolution, if left to itself, would establish a new order, but the Bolsheviks were corrupting and deforming it. The party, not the people, was the master of all and it gave to each individual, not according to his needs, but rather according to his productivity. The Russians seemed apathetic, slow, and lazy. Lenin, being very different from his countrymen, wanted to transform Russia into a "Taylor system where every motion, gesture, and action would be determined beforehand." Human instinct, however, would cause that experiment to fail. During his trip to Moscow Pestaña was afraid that reality would cause him to deny his own convictions but, as he told Lenin, his visit to Russia helped strengthen them. Lenin whispered to him, "You are wrong, Pestaña, you are wrong." This did not keep Lenin from saying later privately that Pestaña was "an intelligent and puritanical worker who had a great gift for observation; he also had a critical sense which set the principle of freedom as the cornerstone of his ideology."[30]

Upon his departure from the USSR he headed first for Berlin where with other European syndicalists he helped organize a conference which was to take place in December in order that they might formulate a common platform to be presented to the upcoming founding congress of the Profintern. In the German capital he saw De los Ríos and Anguiano who were en route to Russia. He went to Italy where factories were being occupied by workers, there to discuss the Berlin congress with Italian syndicalists. Police arrested him immediately and they confiscated the documents and notes he was carrying in his luggage. He was held two months in a Milan prison and was eventually shipped to Barcelona after the Spanish police were alerted. Police were waiting for him at the harbor and he was taken to Montjuich prison.

This development prevented Pestaña from writing his report. Moreover, documents had been confiscated by the Italian police. Finally in November 1921, while still in prison, he managed to finish the report and send it to the national committee. In this way the CNT, in spite of the negative impressions of its delegate, continued to be a member of the Third International.

Notes

1. Manuel Buenacasa, *El movimiento obrero español,* Barcelona, 1928, p. 64 of the Paris reedition, 1966. The author was secretary of the national committee of the CNT in 1918–19.

2. Diego Abad de Santillán, *Contribución a la historia del movimiento obrero español,* Puebla, 1965, vol. II, p. 284.

3. Joaquín Maurín, "Hombres e historia: La CNT y la III Internacional," *España Libre,* New York, November, 6, 1960.

4. Joaquín Maurín, "Apéndice sobre el comunismo en Espana," in *Revolución y contrarrevolución en España,* Paris, 1966. This book is a reedition with appendix and epilogue of the one published in 1935, *Hacia la segunda revolución.*

5. This is confirmed by J. Díaz del Moral (p. 173) when he says that following the first news about the Russian Revolution, "there was stronger agitation by the workers than the history of our country records. As always Andalusia took the lead."

6. Joaquín Maurín, "Hombres e historia: El II Congreso de la CNT," *España Libre,* New York, April 1, 1960.

7. Ibid.

8. Adolfo Bueso, *Recuerdos de un cenetista,* Barcelona, 1976, pp. 128–29.

9. A full report on the debates in congress appears in: *Confederación Nacional del Trabajo. Memoria del congreso celebrado en el Teatro de la Comedia de Madrid, los días 10 a 18 de diciembre de 1919,* Barcelona, 1932.

10. On May 25, 1917 *Solidaridad* of Barcelona (CNT's daily) published a manifesto signed by Seguí, Pestaña, and Miranda which showed admiration for the February revolution, and on November 10 the CNT daily stated in an editorial that "the Russians show us the road to follow" (speaking about the decision for the distribution of land). Catalonian anarchist groups published several pro-Bolshevik pamphlets. But one of their thinkers, Federico Urales, expressed his suspicions in a pamphlet entitled *Dictatorship or Freedom?* Syndicalists and some unaffiliated intellectuals like Manual Bueno collaborated on a newspaper almost exclusively specializing in Russian topics, *La Cuestión Social.*

11. Víctor Alba, *El Marxisme a Catalunya, 1919–39,* Barcelona, 1974, vol. III, pp. 49–50.

12. Buenacasa, p. 89.

13. The complete text of Quintanilla's participation is in Ramón Álvarez, *Eleuterio Quintanilla,* Mexico City, 1973, p. 240 ff.

14. Ibid., p. 251.

15. Manuel Cruells, *Salvador Seguí, el Noi del Sucre,* Barcelona, 1974, p. 133.

16. Santillán, *Contribución a la historia,* vol. II, p. 286.

17. Buenacasa, p. 89.

18. *Memoria del congreso,* p. 344.

19. Ibid., p. 367.

20. Maurín, "Hombres e historia: El II Congreso de la CNT."

21. Maurín, *Revolución y contrarrevolución en España,* p. 249.

22. "The Russian model—Lenin wrote in his book—demonstrates something to every nation, something essential to its near and inevitable future." This "something" was the need for "an absolute centralization and the strictest discipline."

23. Alfred Rosmer, *Moscou sous Lénine,* Paris, 1953, p. 54.

24. Ángel Pestaña, *Setenta días en Rusia,* Barcelona, 1924. This book was published in two parts, one about "What I Saw" and the other about "What I Think."

25. Ángel Pestaña, *Memoria que el Comité de la Confederación Nacional del Trabajo presenta de su gestión en el II Congreso de la III Internacional,* Madrid, 1921, p. 34 ff. It is reproduced in Ángel Pestaña, *Trayectoria sindicalista,* Madrid, 1974, p. 440 ff.

26. Rosmer, p. 61.

27. Ángel Pestaña, *Setenta días en Rusia,* p. 202 ff.

28. Meaker (p. 517) notes that one of those articles advocated that "Spanish revolutionary forces and the new Communist party march arm in arm in the fight for the liberation of the Spanish proletariat." Meaker believes that this sentence was not Pestaña's; he thinks instead that it was added when his article was translated into Russian as published in *Pravda,* July 25, 1920.

29. Pestaña stated in his report to the national committee of the CNT, previously cited, that with respect to his trip to Russia he was only referring to his actions regarding union matters. He later wrote a report about the Third International. Afterwards, during the Spanish dictatorship, he wrote his book of impressions, *Seventy Days in Russia.*

30. Quoted by Meaker, p. 298.

3.
Division of the PSOE

At the beginning of 1921 there was a Communist party in Spain, formed by the split in the Federation of Socialist Youth, and a unionist organization, the CNT, "provisionally" affiliated with the Third International. Discussion continued in the PSOE about the affiliation, while doubts about the desirability of maintaining support for the International was increasing in the CNT. The position of the Spanish Communist movement was fluctuant. The events of the next two years would make it even more uncertain.

The PCE versus the Thirdists

While Pestaña was actively participating in the International's congress, Ramón Merino Gracia, secretary general of the newly formed PCE, was traveling to Moscow; he could not reach the Russian capital until after the congress was over. Once in Moscow he was invited to attend the meetings of the International's executive committee. Merino spoke about the situation in Spain and underlined what he considered incompetency in the Socialist left wing. The new party wanted to boost its stature at the cost of gaining potential new Communists. He said that there was not the slightest tactical or ideological difference between the PCE and the Bolshevik party. It seems that only Bukharin insisted on having more information and inquired about Spanish unions.[1]

Merino had gone to Moscow specifically to get the financial aid which Borodin had promised during his trip through Madrid and which was necessary to sustain and develop *El Comunista*. He spoke of this in the meeting of the International's executive committee in which it was promised that Borodin would return to Madrid and in which the PCE was recognized as the Spanish section of the International. Someone who would soon learn of those anecdotes by Victor Serge said of Merino Gracia while he was in Moscow: "On the door of his room in the Hotel Lux was an ostentatious sign which said in Spanish, Russian, French, German, and English: 'Ramón Merino Gracia—General Secretary of the Spanish Communist Party.' Its occupant grew a Trotsky-like beard. He ran into Pestaña and spoke to him authoritatively. Pestaña burst out laughing."

On his return to Moscow after a trip to Baku, Merino visited Lenin who was interested in the Spanish peasantry and the agricultural system and, according to the schoolteacher, "did not raise the slightest objection" to the principles and tactics of the PCE. Lenin also told him that proletarian dictatorship had been "predicted by scientific Marxists" and not invented by the Bolsheviks. Merino met and spoke with De los Ríos and Anguiano in Moscow. He later stated that the document which the delegates of the PSOE were taking to Moscow had caused "stupe-faction" in the International.[2]

Conditions of the PSOE

Although the secession of young people from the Socialist party had appeased the impatient Socialist Left, leaving it in a bad position, the postponement of the Socialist conference in Geneva was encouraging to the Thirdists. They published a manifesto saying that the PSOE ought to send a delegation to the second congress of the Communist International. They were supported in this by the Asturian federation. In an effort to pacify the Thirdists the executive committee decided to send Besteiro and Anguiano to a Socialist meeting to take place in Rotterdam in March, with instructions to work for the unification of the Internationals. But nothing very concrete was achieved in Rotterdam.

The PSOE and the UGT had grown a great deal. This caused many to believe that the revolution was close at hand and, therefore, that it was necessary to join the revolutionaries of the Third International and not the reformists of the Second or the Austro-Marxist conciliators of the Working Union of Socialist Parties or Vienna International (or, as Lenin called it, the Second and a Half International). This International had been formed shortly before and had failed early in its attempt to create an organization in which the Russians would be members but not supreme leaders. Pablo Iglesias, very ill at this point, wrote an article asking delegates to be sent to the congresses of the Second International as well as the Vienna International but not the Third.[3]

When the party congress met in June, Lenin's 21 conditions still had not been approved in Moscow. There were no great debates in the congress. Pérez Solís stated that the party should not let itself be led by its feelings because "the disillusionment will be awful." The Bolsheviks had no greater importance in Russia than the Jacobins had had in the French Revolution. "Support for the Third International would not automatically imply revolution in Spain." The Thirdists were revolutionaries in name only, not action.

De los Ríos had joined the PSOE two years before, having come from the monarchic reformism of Melquiades Álvarez. He said that since the PSOE had pulled out of the Second International, it could only go to the Third despite its "nebulous nature" and despite the danger that this support might accentuate the tendency of the Spanish people to look for a messiah who would do what they could not do for themselves.

At the time of the vote only a few hands were raised in favor of remaining in the Second International. More were in favor of "unconditional support" for the Third, proposed by García Cortés, Anguiano, and others. The resolution proposed by those in the center, signed by Isidoro Acevedo, José María Suárez, and Fernando de los Ríos, finally won. After pointing out the excessive but understandable influence the Bolsheviks had on the doctrines of the Third International, thus leading to a doctrinal exclusivism which impeded the unification of socialist forces, it proposed supporting the Communist International, but on the following conditions: (1) that the PSOE ask the Third International to recognize its full autonomy in whatever tactic it adopted in the class struggle; (2) that the PSOE have the right to revise in its own congresses whatever doctrine the Third International adopted as well as the agreements it decided upon; (3) that the PSOE work for the unification of all Marxist parties without exclusion and that it participate in all unifying congresses that could be convened. To Iglesias's proposal was added the promise of the PSOE to continue to work in city halls and Parliament and to carry on with its mutual and cooperative work with the unions.[4]

The Thirdists tried to eliminate the conditions. García Cortés called the second condition "grotesque" in view of the small number of Spanish socialists who had a deep understanding of Marxist doctrine. Fabra Ribas spoke in favor of the Vienna International and Besteiro and Largo Caballero gave speeches which did not clearly show their position, although it was evident that it did not coincide with that of the Thirdists. Despite his moralistic airs, Besteiro did not hesitate to praise them:

> The importance which the working masses give the Russian Revolution and the enthusiasm which they display for Soviet Russia are fully justified. . . . The Spanish Socialist party had no choice but to approve the action of the proletarian organizations which have been in power in Russia since the October revolution. The shortcomings attributed to the Soviet government of workers and peasants are not the fault of their own organization but of the total state of decomposition in which the Czarist regime has left the country. Because they are aware of the principles which govern

the conduct of Russia's revolutionary government, the Spanish Socialist party declares these principles to be the same socialist principles on which the actions of all militants of the International are based.

The two resolutions merged into one for the sake of sacrosanct unity. The Thirdists allowed "unconditional entrance" to be replaced by "immediate entrance" and the Centrists accepted the removal of the condition referring to attendance at unifying congresses (which is to say, the International of Reconstruction). The vote took place on June 19. There were 8,269 votes cast in favor of the common proposal, 5,016 against and 1,616 abstentions. Even though the PSOE had 55,000 members, only those who had paid their dues had the right to be represented in the congress. These numbered no more than 15,000.

The congress took place without impassioned dialectical bouts. Good manners and camaraderie were not forgotten. The only incident was provoked by a group of ex-Socialist youths who publicly demanded the firing of the exiled Menshevik journalist Tassin (translator into Spanish of the majority of works of Lenin and Trotsky). The chairman refused and there were blows and exchanges as significant as the one between Fabra Ribas and Juan Andrade, editor of *El Comunista*. In the course of their struggle, when Ribas asked Andrade who he was, Andrade answered, "The one who insults you in *El Comunista* and who now insults you to your face. You shameless traitor!"[5] A few years later the same insults would be directed at Andrade by his one-time comrades.

The congress elected a national committee with a Thirdist majority: Antonio García Quejido, Daniel Anguiano, Ramón Lamoneda, César González, Andrés Ovejero, Manuel Núñez de Arenas, Luis Araquistain. Those in the minority were Fernando de los Ríos and Antonio Fabra Ribas. Besteiro and Largo Caballero were also elected but did not accept. Anguiano and De los Ríos were sent to Moscow to present the conditions for membership.

Skepticism in the UGT

There also was a Thirdist camp in the UGT; its existence was inevitable given that members of the PSOE were also members of the unions of the UGT (211,000 in 1920). There was very little discussion at the 14th congress of June 1920, meeting only a few days after the PSOE had met. A conciliatory proposal in favor of unity of action with the CNT was approved in spite of the exclusivist tone of the CNT's resolution in the congress at "la Comedia" on the same topic. Not even the debate about international affiliation was impassioned. The UGT had become a member of the International Labor Federation (the International of Amsterdam) which was organized toward the end of 1919.[6]

The Centrists who had been half defeated in the PSOE congress thought that they could make headway in the UGT congress. And they succeeded. The Centrists dominated the leadership of the unions. Unlike the CNT, the UGT had salaried leaders who formed a bureaucratic network.[7] But this alone is not enough to explain why they did not join the Third International. Despite differences in their situation, the majority of the other great union federations of Europe did not join it either. Rather, the way to look at it is that the bulk of the European working class was not attracted to Bolshevik concepts or events in Russia.

Be that as it may, the Thirdists were able to stir up neither its members before the congress nor the congressional delegates once it was in session. Francisco Largo Caballero, a construction worker in his youth, had been elected secretary general by the congress of 1918 and, in view of the events in the PSOE, had prepared resistance to the Thirdists. This group had lost members due to the fact that by 1920 the Third International had still not created its trade union International. Yet the socialists, who did not have a political International, had a trade union organization in the International of Amsterdam. Largo Caballero did not have much faith in the Russian Revolution and thought that conditions in Spain were very different from those in Russia.[8]

The Thirdists were facing one other handicap: joining the Third International would logically bring about the fusion of the UGT and CNT; given the difference in strength between the two groups, it would cause the absorption of the UGT by the CNT. Neither the leaders nor the members of the UGT viewed this prospect with satisfaction. For this reason, after failing in their attempt to pass a resolution favoring the creation of workers' councils, the Thirdists were unsuccessful once again in proposing a pull-out from the International of Amsterdam in order to join the Third International. Manuel Llaneza, a leader of the Asturian miners, and Largo Caballero argued that the Spanish proletariat was not ready for revolution and that joining the Third International would mean a commitment to a revolution which the workers did not want yet.

The vote was 110,919 in favor of remaining in the International of Amsterdam and 17,919 for joining the Communist International. Largo Caballero was reelected secretary general, Iglesias (following tradition) president, and Besteiro vice-president. There was not a single Thirdist on the executive committee. This situation necessarily influenced the delegation sent by the PSOE to Russia. It arrived in Moscow after Pestaña's appearance with his great Anarcho-Syndicalist movement, without the support of the Socialist unions and facing Merino Gracia's highly skeptical report regarding the Thirdists in the PSOE.

Twenty-One versus Three Conditions

The trip Anguiano and De los Ríos took to Moscow is known mainly as the De los Ríos Mission because Anguiano kept a low profile. They spoke with Pestaña in Berlin. Naturally they did not get along. It was there that the two Socialists learned that the International's congress had approved the 21 conditions; these were in opposition to the conditions for joining the International which had been voted in by the PSOE congress. So the mission of De los Ríos and Anguiano was pointless. They consulted Paul Levi, chief of the German Independent Socialist party and a Thirdist who thought that there was not even a basis for discussion, but he advised them to go to Moscow anyway. Once there, they had to wait for the return of Zinoviev from Germany in order to meet with the executive committee of the International. This is how Zinoviev remembered De los Ríos years later: "This professor was, after all, a professor, and in political matters, he was very naive. And this professor told us with touching naiveté: 'Comrades, you know that personally I am a reformist, but Spanish workers wish to be admitted to the Communist International and they have sent me here for that purpose.' This professor was almost a saint, for he said everything with utter candor."[9]

At the beginning of November the executive committee interrogated the Spanish delegates during two of its sessions. Anguiano, a railroad worker, a former federal Republican, and secretary to Iglesias, spoke only Spanish. The majority of the responses were given by De los Ríos in French. De los Ríos recognized that the conditions put forth by the PSOE were incompatible with the 21 conditions and that, while Anguiano accepted the latter, he was opposed to democratic centralism, the creation of an illegal parallel party, and the compulsory nature of the Comintern's decisions. Even Anguiano insisted that reformism and revolution were not incompatible in the eyes of the PSOE.

Later the two delegates traveled through Russia[10] and at the end of the same month they had another meeting with the executive committee. De los Ríos, unlike Anguiano, stated at that time that he disagreed with the International's opinion that the revolution was already in progress in Europe. The way he saw it, there was no chance of a successful insurrection of workers. The victory was far off and would be more difficult to achieve than the leaders of the Communist International were predicting.[11]

With these statements the chiefs in the International no longer paid any attention to the professor and turned their attention to the railroad worker. On December 10 the executive committee of the International delivered a letter to the delegates which was aimed at the PSOE. It criticized the PSOE's positions as well as its "lack of clear ideals" and it called on party members to join the Third International and let the reformists remain in the Second.

The evening before the delegates' departure, Lenin arranged for them to meet with him in his office at the Kremlin where they had a pleasant chat. Anguiano, in response to Lenin's questions, said that the 21 conditions would make the PSOE's entrance to the International difficult, and De los Ríos asked him how long he thought it would take for the proletarian dictatorship to make way for complete freedom in Russia. Lenin answered:

> We have never spoken of freedom, just of proletarian dictatorship . . . which we exercise in the name of the proletariat. Since the Russian proletariat, strictly defined, is a minority, dictatorship is exercised by that minority and will last as long as the other elements of the society do not surrender to the economic conditions which the Communists impose. . . . The period of dictatorship will be a long one for us, perhaps 40 or 50 years. Because of their industrial status, other countries, like Germany and England, will be able to abbreviate that period. . . . Yes, yes, our problem is not freedom, and in reference to this we always reply: "Freedom? For what purpose?"[12]

He recognized that the concessions made by the Bolsheviks to foreign capitalism for the purpose of obtaining investments could draw out the period of dictatorship, but "we cannot overcome foreign capitalism which is kept going by the working-class masses." It can only be achieved through world revolution "which we are sure—added Lenin—is beginning, although it is developing more slowly than we would wish."

Anguiano's report for the PSOE was in favor of joining the International, but contained one reservation: it rejected the need for proletarian dictatorship to be that of a party. He said that in Russia government would not be so cruel if it were in the hands of the masses and not a party. In his report De los Ríos complained that Moscow did not distinguish between support for the Russian Revolution and submission to Bolshevik ideology, and he pointed out that the conditions fixed by the congress of the PSOE had been categorically rejected by Moscow. After all was said and done, it was a question of freedom, and he opposed joining the Third International because he opposed all dictatorships. Freedom was not bourgeois or proletarian; it was human. These reports greatly distressed the Thirdists. They would have to choose between renouncing freedom of action as a party or estranging themselves from the Bolsheviks.

Anguiano's report was rejected by the national committee; the only votes in favor of it were cast by Acevedo and García Quejido. Núñez de Arenas and César González voted against it, not because they rejected the 21 conditions but rather because they disagreed with Anguiano's reservations. De los Ríos's report was also rejected, the only votes cast in favor of it being those of Francisco Azorín, Remigio Cabello, Antonio Fabra Ribas, Francisco Giner, and Iglesias. Rejected, too, was the letter of the International's executive committee; it was supported only by Darriba, Núñez de Arenas, and César González. Since no decision was made by the national committee, it resolved to convene an additional congress to settle the dispute.

The Party of the "Hundred Kids"

One of the leaders of the PCE said later: "If the proselytizing results of the first split [that of the Socialist Youth] were indeed of little interest, the international report and indoctrination carried out [by the young ex-Socialists], especially in *El Comunista,* were of great merit and use. Their work greatly helped disseminate the theoretical and tactical foundations of Bolshevism and the Communist International."[13] Another leader recalled: "That party was insignificant because of the small number of members it had; but because of the fervor of some of its constituents who thought it would be possible to bring about an awesome revolution in a wink . . . and because it had available material means of propaganda the source of which was not difficult to guess, the party managed to be quite active among the ranks of Spanish workers, mainly because of its pamphlets and periodicals. It would violently attack us Socialists who supported the Third International."[14] Those "material means" must have been the aid promised by Borodin and later by the executive committee of the International to Merino Gracia. It must have come through because *El Comunista* did not suspend publication.[15]

According to one of the founders of the PCE of youth,[16] the party started out with about 2,000 members. To it "were added without delay militants from the Socialist party, many of whom were men of great value. In Alicante there was Rafael Millá, who had consistently maintained an internationalist position; in Salamanca Fernando Felipe, teacher at the normal school; in Madrid Vicente Arroyo, the active labor militant, Gerardo Ibáñez, the brilliant, tactful, and honest leader, along with Arroyo and Chicharro, of the carpenters' union; also in Madrid Joaquín

Ramos, president of the organization of salesclerks, and Fernando Durán, a physician and excellent writer; in Bilbao there was Leandro Carro." Also joining were those coming from an anarchist background such as Hilario Arlandis, from Valencia, who "in a moment of distress helped us financially with funds from his trade union." Germán Alonso and Ángel Pumarega, with backgrounds in the CNT, were added to the ranks of the PCE in Madrid. The Thirdists in the PSOE viewed "with consternation and resentment" the formation of the PCE of youth but "on the whole the Socialist party valued the romanticism of our gesture and did not think that we were moved by personal ambition." The PCE was jokingly called the party of the "hundred kids."[17]

The press did not pay any attention to the birth of the first PCE. Perhaps because it was a party of young people, of "hotheads." "This was both its strength and its weakness," said Portela. "Its strength because of its enthusiasm, altruism, self-denial, and the dynamism of its militants; its weakness because we were missing a quality which is only developed with time: political experience."

The national committee of the PCE was made up of Ramón Merino Gracia who was secretary general, Juan Andrade,[18] editor of *El Comunista,* L. Buendía, Luis Portela, and Vicente Arroyo.[19] "Save for a few exceptions those with intellectual inclination dominated among the founders of the party. They did not win over the masses; but they interpreted mass sentiment." This group wielded a certain degree of influence over the carpenters', printers', and clerks' unions in Madrid.

If the press paid the PCE no attention, the authorities devoted themselves to censoring the columns of *El Comunista,* and there were plenty of "preventive arrests" of some of its militants. A police inspector named Badenas was in charge of keeping an eye on and making life difficult for the PCE. Badenas looked everywhere for "Moscow gold." "What he could not have guessed was that the secret 'treasurer' of the party, from time to time, was none other than the distinguished writer Gregorio Martínez Sierra, the heart and soul of the great actress Catalina Barcena's famous theatrical company." Another example of "Moscow gold" was that of a German delegate of the Comintern who, accompanied by several comrades from Madrid, visited Madrid one day when the streets were lined with petitionary tables. At the end of their tour the German delegate took a handful of bills from his pocket and handed them to one of the Spaniards. "The contribution of some duke or marquis had found its way from one of the tables, where perhaps a princess or duchess was in charge, to the delegate's pocket. The "gracias a Dios" for this unexpected and providential assistance must have been given by the owner of some printing house."[20]

There were differences of opinion in the new party. When elections were held the party was divided between parliamentarians and antiparliamentarians (the latter headed by Andrade), but no split occurred. This problem was a source of annoyance for the party during its brief existence.

Special Congress of the PSOE

With the special congress in mind, both factions of the PSOE redoubled their propaganda. Pablo Iglesias and Pérez Solís were the most active. Iglesias favored the Vienna International and Pérez Solís the Second International; both were against any split whatsoever. The Thirdists were anxious. In Madrid where the latter were in control, opposition to the 21 conditions began to appear. García Cortés and his friends were replaced in an assembly by Largo Caballero and his men. The assembly voted 247 to 147 in favor of the Vienna International. The Thirdists forecast a defeat in the congress. What they did not foresee was that their bitterest enemy, Pérez Solís, would join their forces. Pérez Solís had always said that Spaniards were weak-willed, that the working class was not ready for the revolution, and that was why it was reformist. But in one article he wrote shortly before the special congress[21] he showed himself to be overtly voluntarist. In his writing he wanted the PSOE to be closer to the tactics of Blanqui, and the Blanquists at that time were the Bolsheviks. Doubtless he had been radicalized by his stay in the Basque region. One might also suspect that he had begun to lose patience over "the lack of conscience of the Spanish people" and that in the Bolsheviks' model he found a rescue from the pit of collective indifference. Prieto's influence, which had taken him to Bilbao after the authorities had thrown him out of Valladolid, was not enough to counteract the atmosphere in Bilbao where he felt at home because the workers in that city paid attention to him. Pérez Solís allied himself with the Thirdist Facundo Perezagua in the latter's fight against Prieto and ended up being more important than Perezagua. At the bottom of it all, then, Pérez Solís's conversion to thirdism was in accordance with his elitist ideas and temperament. The only thing was that he changed his elite, because the Bolsheviks seemed more efficient to him than the reformists.

The Thirdists had other supporters in the Asturian Socialists. Isidoro Acevedo, a printer, was representative of this change in the Asturian Socialists. In the past he had been in the Center but was an Internationalist instead of a supporter of the Allies, and when it came to the International he always tried to remain between the two camps. It was he who proposed the resolution approved by both in which the three conditions which

Moscow rejected were put forth. Led by his comrades, he now declared himself a Thirdist.

The supporters of the Comintern could rest on some triumphs outside of Spain: the German Independent Socialist party's joining the Third International, likewise the majority of the French Socialist party, and the split in the Italian Socialist party with some 50,000 members going to the Comintern. The 21 conditions had not "frightened" those three great groups; why should they frighten the Spanish Socialists? They had against them not only the fact that the 21 conditions worried many, but also that the unions of the UGT were opposed to joining the Third International, and finally that Moscow paid no attention to the congress (neither letters nor delegates were sent by the Comintern) perhaps because of the contempt with which Merino Gracia had spoken of the Thirdists.

The special congress met in Madrid April 9–13, 1921. It was impassioned and there were insults and even blows. The anti-Thirdists took the initiative because De los Ríos was the first to report on his trip to Russia. He emphasized the lack of liberties in Russia as well as the decadence of workers' councils. Naturally, he harshly criticized the 21 conditions. When it was time for his report Anguiano explained the facts given by his travel companion citing as its causes the resistance to the revolution, the Civil War, and the country's backwardness. He concluded by pointing out that the Russian system had a fundamental defect: the preponderance of the Communist party. He warned that if something similar occurred in Spain, he would not join the Communist party.

Virginia González[22] was the most passionate defender of membership in the Third International, attacking the party leadership for its behavior in 1917 and during World War I. Saborit, who had been an Internationalist during the war, came out against the Comintern because of the 21 conditions, but he insisted that there were not any real differences between supporters and adversaries of membership in the Third International since both groups were "class collaborationists," while he was for class struggle.

Largo Caballero, who declared himself reformist and said he would be ashamed to make revolutionary statements and act in a "self-seeking" way, raised two questions which were on the minds of many: the exclusion of the reformists required by the 21 conditions (which would leave the party without most of its founders, starting with Pablo Iglesias), and going underground. If the party went underground, it would not last because of lack of strength, said Largo Caballero amid accusations of being a "spineless coward." Largo, who was secretary general of the UGT, also raised the problem of the unions. The UGT was on the side of the International of Amsterdam. In accordance with the 21 conditions, if the PSOE joined the Comintern, it ought to fight for the UGT's alliance with the Profintern which was in the process of being established.

Besteiro said that it was absurd to set up differences between revolutionaries and nonrevolutionaries and that what was happening was "a mutiny of sergeants against generals." In other countries the fight was over ideals; in Spain it was over insults. The Thirdists might be able to win over the party but the masses would not follow them. The logical thing would be for the supporters of the Comintern to leave the PSOE and join the PCE but, he added, this was not done "because the truth is that the Communists do not want you," and in the midst of applause from the young ex-Socialists in the gallery he finished by saying, "And they do not want you because they think you are insincere."[23]

Ramón Lamoneda, a printer, member of the group at the Escuela Nueva, an Internationalist during the war, and editor of *Nuestra Palabra,* was the last one to speak on behalf of the Comintern. He denied that thirdism was a result of ambition and he said that De los Ríos had not understood what he had seen in Russia. From the galleries came cries of "Long Live Russia!"

The matter was then voted on, being presented in the following way: "In view of the response given by the executive committee of the Third International to the resolution of our congress: (a) Does the party agree to join the Third International, accepting the 21 conditions? (b) If not, does it agree to instead support the Vienna International? (c) If the above resolutions are rejected, what stance should the party adopt?"[24] The vote was 8,088 in favor of the Vienna International to 6,025 for the Third International. Verbal as well as physical violence during the voting was such that Andrés Ovejero, exasperated by cries of "traitors" and "frauds," said that whatever the outcome he would not remain in the PSOE nor would he side with the Thirdists but rather would fight on his own. Verdes Montenegro and Luis Araquistáin adopted a similar decision and many less-known militants imitated them.

Founding of the PCOE

The Thirdists were never certain of victory. Many questioned it in their meetings every night at the Escuela Nueva in order to discuss the progress of the congress. Acevedo and Perezagua supported staying in the party. Núñez de Arenas and especially Pérez Solís wanted to leave and were the ones who worked hardest among the Thirdists to get this proposal adopted. Having García Quejido, prestigious founder of the PSOE, on their side allowed them to persuade almost everyone that party unity was mere fiction. Pérez Solís himself admitted[25] that he adopted the more radical position to dispel all doubts about the sincerity of his conversion. Besteiro's diatribe, which questioned the Thirdists' motives, forced them to take steps to show their ideological honesty.

A manifesto written almost entirely by Pérez Solís was drawn up just in case of a negative vote. When the results were made known, Pérez Solís approached the rostrum, surrounded by some of his comrades from Bilbao, and stepped up to read the document. The gist of it follows:

> The end of the debate about membership in the Communist International necessarily demands us to publicly make known our incompatibility with those elements who have declared themselves in favor of the theses upheld by the working union in Vienna. We cannot and must not collaborate with them or aid them in their actions which we consider counterrevolutionary and antisocialist. . . .
>
> We would not honorably be able to coexist with those who, through conclusive displays by some of their most representative leaders, have accused us of being immoral and self-seeking, thus debasing a discussion which we would have liked to hold on a doctrinal level. . . .
>
> With the serenity of one who has fulfilled a debt of conscience, we leave the congress, for there is nothing left for us to do. We want to join—indeed we had already joined in spirit—the Communist International which cannot be separated from the Russian Revolution despite all the subtleties and dialectical sophisms which attempt to distinguish between the two and which try to hasten the collapse of capitalist society. We do not want to remain any longer with the indolent and weary legions who seem to wait for time to consummate an act for which they feel incompetent. . . .
>
> We believe with unyielding faith that the Spanish proletariat will not follow you along the gentle paths which lead from Vienna but rather along the rocky road, the road of salvation nonetheless, which is called the Communist International beneath whose banner we take refuge from this day on.

When the speech was over, having been interrupted by shouts, applause, and boos, García Quejido got up and left the building followed by 34 of those who had signed the document as well as by some young Socialists who had stayed in the PSOE through the split with the FJS. They went to the Escuela Nueva where, meeting with others who were waiting for them and who were not delegates, they founded the Partido Comunista Obrero Español (Spanish Communist Workers' party—PCOE), joined to the Third International.[26] They immediately elected an executive committee which would function as an organizational commission and which was made up of García Quejido, Anguiano, Perezagua, Núñez de Arenas, and Virginia González. They decided to start a weekly journal, *La Guerra Social (The Social War)*, under the direction of Torralba Beci.[27]

Not every Thirdist went to the Escuela Nueva after the founding of the PCOE. "There were quite a few who claimed they had been deceived and turned back, on the pretext that they placed party unity, which they did not want to see broken, above everything else."[28] But most Thirdists did not let themselves become obsessed with the myth of unity and actively participated in the new party. They were "old militants who were denied good faith and unselfishness, unjustly so in every instance."[29] The press and politicians paid little attention to the birth of the second Communist party. Outside the PSOE few realized that an event which would have continual impact on the future of the country had just taken place.

Notes

1. Meaker, p. 299 quoting from *El Comunista,* Madrid, November 27, 1920.
2. The account of this visit to Russia appears in *El Comunista,* March 5, 1921. The quote about Merino Gracia in Moscow belongs to Maurín, *Revolución y contrarrevolución en España,* p. 271.
3. *El Socialista,* Madrid, June 19, 1920.
4. *El Socialista,* Madrid, June 23, 1920.
5. As told by Meaker, p. 271 quoting Andrade himself who, according to the author, recalled the entire matter with relish.
6. Amaro del Rosal, *Historia de la UGT de España,* Barcelona, 1977, vol. I, p. 197.
7. Juan Andrade, *La burocracia reformista en el movimiento obrero,* Madrid, 1935, analyzes the mentality of this bureaucracy.
8. Francisco Largo Caballero, *Mis recuerdos,* Mexico City, 1954, pp. 40–41.
9. Meaker, p. 302. These observations were made before the 4th congress of the Comintern and appear in its minutes.
10. Fernando de los Ríos summed up the impression of this visit in *Mi viaje a la Rusia sovietista,* Madrid, 1922, dedicated "to the Spanish Socialist party with the deepest respect."
11. The report of these meetings appears in *El Socialista,* January 18, 1921.
12. This poorly-translated phrase of Lenin's, taken out of context, became "Liberté pourquoi faire?" (Liberty? What for?) Lenin and De los Ríos spoke to each other in French. De los Ríos was not responsible for this distortion since he provided the accurate translation of the sentence in *El Socialista.*
13. José Bullejos, *La Comintern en España,* Mexico City, 1972, p. 19.
14. Óscar Pérez Solís, *Memorias de mi amigo Óscar Perea,* Madrid, 1929, p. 94.
15. Around this time police uncovered a group of Germans in Barcelona who were accused of being Bolshevik agents. They were probably militant workers who fled their country because of repression against Communists. There was also talk of some Russian agents expelled by the government (Manuel Burgos Mazo, *El verano de 1919 en Gobernación,* Madrid, 1921, quoted by Eduardo Comín Colomer, *Historia del Partido Comunista de España,* Madrid, 1967, vol. I, pp. 53–54).

16. Portela.
17. Amaro del Rosal and Luis Portela recall this epithet.
18. Juan Andrade had been a follower of the Republican demagogue Alejandro Lerroux until 1918 and had collaborated on the youth organ of the radicals in Madrid, *El Bárbaro*. And later he became a functionary in the Treasury. Andrade (ch.1, n. 28) lists the following as constituents of the first national committee of the first PCE: secretary general, Merino Gracia; assistant secretary, Luis Portela; members, José Illescas, Eduardo Ugarte, Emeterio Chicharro, Ricardo Marín, Rito Esteban, Tiburcio Picó, and Juan Andrade who was also editor of *El Comunista*. Andrade himself wondered after 60 years "if the creation of the Spanish Communist party was not a mistake," since with the votes the young people could have gathered in the PSOE plus those of the Thirdists, they might have achieved a majority in the PSOE congress which would have then become the Communist party.
19. The *Historia del PCE* (p. 27) gives the names of Buendía, Arroyo, Millá, and Merino Gracia and indicates in a footnote that Merino Gracia "later left the party's ranks and the workers' movement." At the end of the list, "and others" was modestly added. Those others, Portela and Andrade, are the ones who in time left the PCE. Later on the PCE severely harassed them. Portela says that neither Buendía nor Arroyo was on the committee.
20. Amaro del Rosal, "Anécdotas y recuerdos," *Nuestra Bandera*, no. 66 (1970–71). Portela says that this is mere fantasy on the part of Rosal.
21. *El Socialista*, Madrid, April 12, 1921.
22. Virginia González was born of a worker's family from Valladolid. An anarchist in her youth, she became a socialist in Bilbao. She soon distinguished herself as an orator. She emigrated with her family to Argentina but returned in two years and later went into exile in France. In 1915 she was a member of the executive committee of the PSOE and the following year of the UGT. She collaborated on the founding of the Escuela Nueva (Aurora de Albornoz, "Virginia González, mujer de acción," *Tiempo de Historia*, Madrid, July 1977).
23. Reports on the congress in *El Socialista*, Madrid, April 12, 1921 and in *Congreso Extraordinario del PSOE, 1921*, Madrid, 1974.
24. Quoted by Comín Colomer, vol. I, p. 64.
25. Pérez Solís, *Memorias de mi amigo*, p. 275 ff.
26. The text of the decision follows: "The delegates to the Socialist congress signing the declaration read by Óscar Pérez Solís in which they announced their separation from the party agreed: first, immediately proceed with the organization of working-class forces which, in full understanding of their revolutionary duty, join the Communist International in order to form a party with the name of Partido Comunista Obrero Español; second, name an organizational commission composed of comrades Virginia González, Antonio García Quejido, Daniel Anguiano, Eduardo Torralba Beci, Manuel Núñez Arenas [no longer Núñez de Arenas], Luis Mancebo, and Evaristo Gil; third, send out a call to all workers and associations to send notice of their membership from now on to the Organizational Commission, Box 873, Madrid" (reproduced by Comín Colomer, vol. I, p. 105).
27. Maximiano García Venero, *Historia de las Internacionales en España*, Madrid, 1957, vol. II, p. 394. This is the list that García Venero gives and

which Meaker reiterates. But Bullejos (*La Comintern en España*, p. 23) lists the following: Antonio García Quejido, Virginia González, Daniel Anguiano, Eduardo Torralba Beci, Manuel Núñez de Arenas, and Evaristo Gil. Amaro del Rosal lists the same names as García Venero but says the name of the new party's publication was *La Antorcha (Torch)*. Actually the publication of the PCE was *Guerra Social (Social War)*.

28. Pérez Solís, *Memorias de mi amigo*, p. 279 ff.
29. Portela. His moral appraisal has special value because after a few years Portela disagreed with the party line and later joined BOC and POUM which, as we will see, were viciously persecuted by the PCE.

4.
Unification by
the Communist International

The Spanish Communist movement began under the sign of division. In 1921 there were three organizations related to the Third International: the PCE, the PCOE, and the "Sovietist" groups of the CNT. For a while all the volleys were wasted on internal fighting. This went on until finally the International intervened, ordered unification in Moscow, and sent an agent to Madrid to see it through. To the sign of division was added, in its initial stages, the guardianship of the Comintern.

An Unpropitious Moment

The Thirdists and young socialists had been radicalized in the heat of the sympathy the people felt for the Russian Revolution, which reached only the most politicized and organized strata of the working class as well as a small part of the peasantry. This sympathy was shrinking noticeably, although the Thirdists did not seem to notice. The PCE was born when this sympathy was still growing but it was not in a position to capitalize on it politically because it was a "moderate" kind of sympathy. Enthusiasm for a social experiment, for the destruction of an unjust order, but without the inclination to imitate the Bolsheviks or to run the risks that this would have involved in Spain's situation. Because of its radicalism the PCE lost the sympathy that could have been aroused among those who sided with the Russian Revolution.

The PCOE, embracing individuals of greater experience, came into being at a time when that sympathy was already declining, when doubts began to arise about the path the Bolsheviks were following. In CNT circles details about the persecution of Russian Anarchists were being discovered and of course this caused not only doubt, but mistrust and protest as well. The Socialists learned even more about the persecution of the Mencheviks. Naturally the anxiety this caused was reflected in the reaction to Soviet Russia.

Internal conditions in Spain were worsening. In 1919 Spaniards were still living off the prosperity of World War I; in spite of 1917 the workers had faith in their own strength and one had the general impression that Spanish society was in a state of complete disintegration. But things had changed. In Catalonia union leaders were hunted down by gunmen, Martínez Anido's police force harassed strikers, the employers' union mobilized the "somatenes," and unionist terrorism could only respond to that offensive, not stop it. In the rest of Spain the peasants, who had agitated a great deal in years past, were pacified by the presence of troops and the civil guard. The unions acted cautiously, especially those of the UGT, because the recession was nationwide, a reflection of the European recession and a consequence of the end of the lucrative contracts of the war-making powers. The workers' movement was in a holding pattern. Besides, now that the revolutionary wave was past, conservatives prevailed throughout Europe. Portela, who lived through those times, saw things differently and describes the situation of the workers' movement at the time in a letter to the author:

> The Communist party was born in Spain in 1920, not when its founders wanted to create it, but when they were able to, and it still can be said that it was a difficult birth. In 1920 the revolutionary wave began its decline: social democracy toppled the Spartakists in Germany and with them fell the revolution in that country; and with help from the outside the revolution was drowned in blood in Bavaria as well as in Hungary. The Red Army failed in Poland. In Italy the great strikes characterized by the occupation of factories found the proletariat at a dead end because of the lack of political vision on the part of Socialists, for places of employment were being occupied but prefectures and ministries were not. Nonetheless, the possibilities for revolution were not yet exhausted: in 1923 in Bulgaria and Germany there were revolutionary situations which neither the International nor the Communist parties were capable to take advantage of, for in their ranks there were more theorists—not all of them good, far from it—than men of action. Lenin was only one of them and by 1923 he was already seriously ill. Regarding Spain, the working class was already beating a retreat. In industrial areas as well as in the countryside the harsh battles of 1917, 1918, and 1919 had exhausted the working class and repression had decimated it. Neither was the sympathy of the Spanish proletariat for the Russian Revolution moderate (on the contrary, the cry of "Long live Russia!" came spontaneously from every voice and any allusion to the country of revolution was vigorously applauded), nor did the radicalism which has been attributed to the Spanish Communist party alienate any sympathy "which might have been aroused." Without a doubt the Communist party was born too late but it could not have been born any sooner. And it was not possible for its founders to change a given situation to their liking. We worked under circumstances determined by time and place and we had no other material than what we are made of.

And when all is said and done, it was the best material there was in those days and even after.

Neither of the two parties had either funds or headquarters. The PCOE used the Escuela Nueva on Madrazos Street from which premises the school eventually moved. The PSOE kept *El Socialista,* its Casas del Pueblo, as well as its representatives in Parliament.

If these conditions seemed hardly propitious, they could not be considered totally adverse either. In times of crisis revolutions do not take place, but repression does. But times of crisis politicize some and radicalize others. With a skillful, agreeable, unresentful policy, the PCOE could expect to attract elements from the Socialist party who had vacillated and voted against the Thirdists more out of support for the myth of unity than for ideological reasons. Portela said of relations with the PSOE: "No matter how skillful their policy was, the Communist Workers' party could not attract the Socialists. Not only could it not attract those who voted against joining the Third International in an effort to maintain unity in the old party, but it could not even attract those who voted in favor of it yet preferred to remain in the old party. Among them were Araquistáin, Álvarez del Vayo, Pedroso, Cordero, Galarza, and Ovejero."

The Socialist Crisis

The Communist movement in its initial stages looked far from inviting. Its appearance could be summed up in two phrases: a constant struggle against the competition (instead of trying to win it over) and confusion of reality with aspirations. Those two traits would characterize the PCE for decades. They were peculiar to many Communist movements and not only to Spain's. The 21 conditions which alienated a good number of traditional and experienced members—albeit undramatic revolutionaries—from the Third International did not attract individuals who were impatient, out of touch with reality, doctrinaire, given more to attacking adversaries than to analysis of the situation—men whose principal argument was to brand as traitors those who did not follow them. The PCE and PCOE devoted a large part of their efforts to attacking the Socialists (between the two they could not have had more than 7,000 nominal members, some 500 militants).

The division among the Thirdists threatened to break up the PSOE because the two factions' struggle was so charged with slander that many Socialists went home disgusted with both groups. Of the 45,477 members it had in 1920 there remained 23,010 after the division, although few of those 22,000 members they had lost went to the PCOE.[1] At Iglesias's proposal the executive committee came forth with a manifesto calling Socialists to stay in the party with the assurance that the Thirdists could also remain to defend their viewpoints and that the rejection of the 21 conditions did not mean the rejection of the Russian Revolution: "We are not in agreement with the conditions which the Third International of Moscow is imposing; but we affirm today, as we have since the first day of the Russian Revolution, that we do fully identify with that revolution . . . and to our party we say, as always, that we consider ourselves dedicated to its defense."[2]

Iglesias and his colleagues had to wage the bitterest battles in Vizcaya and Asturias. The workers in the North were anxious and impatient. Forty percent of the Asturian miners were unemployed due to the decrease of coal exports.[3] The miners left the unions and the struggle between Socialists and Communists contributed to their disenchantment. Because the Socialist union leaders did not want to stir up any conflicts, and being fearful that companies would not be able to increase salaries in the face of profit losses after the war, the Communists accused them of being on the companies' payrolls. Quite a few young miners believed them.

Triumphs and Failures

In Asturias the PCOE had some councillors elected as Socialists. One of them, Enrique García of Mieres, persuaded the miners' union's congress of August 1921 to remove the traditionalist leader Manuel Llaneza and to elect an executive committee made up of Communists. However, there was a referendum for all members on this removal from office and Llaneza was reinstated. In spite of everything the PCOE continued to have influence among the miners.

In Vizcaya many Socialists criticized Pérez Solís and Perezagua for their participation in the division, since their mandate made no mention of it. Pérez Solís had to give up hopes of carrying the Vizcayan federation. From then on, Bilbao's Communist group was very active but aggressively anti-Socialist.[4] Nonetheless the relative success of Asturias and some partial triumphs in several isolated unions in Madrid (led essentially by members of the PCE) as well as in some other cities gave the PCOE hopes of effecting a change of attitude in the UGT. They thought that to avoid a repetition of the split which had taken place in the PSOE the leaders would be agreeable to what they had turned down a year before, that is, joining the Profintern which had been established meanwhile in Moscow.

The 15th congress of the UGT met in November of 1922. In one year membership had fallen from 240,000 to 208,000. In the face of a worsening economic crisis the PCOE had proposed to the PSOE, UGT, and CNT the formation of a United Workers' Front. Some unions of the UGT supported it despite the fact that the leadership forbade its members to form alliances with "elements which promote divisions in the workers' movement." Discussion at the congress was violent. But spirits improved with the appearance of two representatives of the International Labor Federation of Amsterdam, Oudegeest and Leon Jouhaux. Jouhaux was the "arch-devil" of the French Communists for his stance during World War I and his attitude toward the Russian Revolution. The Thirdists printed some leaflets attacking Jouhaux, the Socialists opposed their dissemination, there were blows and shots, and a Socialist militant died of a gun wound. The emotional reaction to all this made a change in international affiliation unlikely. But there was indeed the opportunity for the expulsion from the UGT of any section or union which did not accept the congress's positions. The Vizcayan miners' union, seven unions from Bilbao, the Asturian transportation union, the employees' association of Oviedo, three lesser unions in Madrid, three in Vigo, four in Pontevedra, and one in Crevillente[5] were all expelled. The elected executive committee was made up of only Socialist centrists, with Largo Caballero as secretary general. The Communists had lost the opportunity of remaining and working in the UGT.[6]

The PCOE had one distinct success: immediately following the PCOE's congress it attracted a large part of the FJS which had been reorganized after the split which brought about the PCE. Concerning the composition of the PCE at the time, Portela said:

> Laborers were barely represented in the party ranks. The social composition of the Communist party was no different from that of the Socialist party. Even though it was more natural for the young people to feel attracted to the new party as opposed to those who were deeply rooted in the old, the Communist party was not an organization exclusively for the young. From the very beginning a certain number of militants who could no longer be considered young joined those who were coming from Socialist youth groups. And once they were unified, the imbalance which might have arisen in favor of the young people in the Spanish Communist party was checked by the contribution of the militants of the Workers' Communist party.

Three months after its founding the PCOE had 6,500 members of which there were 500 in Vizcaya, 1,500 in Asturias, and about 500 in the Juventudes Comunistas Obreras (Communist Working-Class Youth).

It was organized in federations like the PSOE—the Asturian federation being the strongest. The party had about 80 sections, about 50 councillors, and three provincial representatives; all of them were elected, to be sure, as Socialists and, upon leaving the PSOE, did not resign their posts gained in the ranks of the PSOE.[7]

Young against Old

The PCE had hardly grown at all. It did not trust parliamentarianism nor the spontaneity of the masses. It believed the revolution was just around the corner and that it must be carried on by the party since the masses were ignorant and passive. Communist youth were convinced that the worse the economic situation became, the better the prospects for revolution. Therefore they refused to join a campaign such as one against increases in railroad fares. "Fortunately the class struggle in Spain is taking on the character of a civil war," they would say.[8] By the end of 1920 the PCE decided not to take part in the parliamentary elections.

According to the PCE, the UGT "was in the hands of the counter-revolutionary party." Therefore "the duty of the Communists is not to divide the unions but rather to throw out the reformist elements from the committees and take over their leadership." Toward this end, the PCE must "create revolutionary union groups" to "form a federation of minority unions within the UGT."[9] Curiously, the PCE proved to be more realistic and aware of the facts in dealing with unions than with politics. Regarding the unionist activity of the PCE, Portela recalls, "indeed, several unions in Madrid under Communist leadership were in the hands of men in the Spanish Communist party. Outside of Madrid there were unions led by members of the Spanish Communist party. One day we received a very modest donation, five pesetas, for *El Comunista* from the organization of stone masons in Pontevedra. This was a touching gesture since those workers had been on strike for fourteen months."

In the eyes of the PCE the Thirdists in the PSOE almost looked like reformists and opportunists. The special congress of the PSOE was deserving of contempt. To the PCE Anguiano's report at the congress seemed "irresponsible in theory, lacking in practical information, and essentially manipulated by Fernando de los Ríos." With regard to the Thirdists, they are "without a policy of their own" and therefore the only recourse they have is to "join us, a decision which will not prevent us from accepting Moscow's 21 conditions."[10] The Thirdists were the object of some ruthless caricatures in the pages of the PCE's periodical:[11]

Anguiano: he's afraid of everyone and hides from himself. He doesn't fool himself and his conscience accuses him of cowardice. He went to Russia to see yet he saw nothing; to listen, yet he heard nothing; to study, yet he learned nothing. He curses the time he wrote the report of his trip.

Núñez de Arenas: as changeable and versatile as a butterfly. He needs the compliments of others to tell him who he is. With a cigarette between his fingers, he talks endlessly. He criticizes, elucidates, comments, recounts, and smiles. A reformist yesterday, he talks with this one and that one, and today is a Thirdist—but always in style, fashionably, if need be. In him there is neither shrillness nor strength of speech. If he's attacked he turns pale. Instead of responding to his adversary he answers him with academic politeness.

Ovejero: supporter of the allies, Germanophile, neutral, white, red, yellow; a socialist, communist, unionist, anarchist, Lerrouxist; art, the masses, the proletariat, the future, the past, culture; men's rights, women's rights, children's rights; democracy, the people, legislators, the French Revolution. He is the most diversified man in the Socialist party.

Lamoneda: young, reflective, moderate, calculating. Forever a frustrated self-seeker, the more daring man beats him out. . . . He has always mingled his personal beliefs with the most sacred tenets of idealists. His golden dream of being a member of the Spanish Parliament was becoming increasingly unlikely.

As was to be expected, they were not any more kind to the old socialist leaders:

Iglesias: he lost sight of the social struggle long ago. He is a spirit which speaks to us from the past. . . . This man, had he died before the day when Jaurés was assassinated, would have lived on eternally in the hearts of the people. He has survived, but in raising his already indistinct silhouette against the Moscovite giant, he tosses the last shovelful of dirt upon his grave. . . .

Largo Caballero: when he speaks he is insulting; when he is silent he poisons the atmosphere with his silence; when he observes he forecasts insults. He makes accusations with innuendos and silences of refined hypocrisy and malice. He is never sincere. Always on guard, he collects figures and information on individuals for his own use. He fights against anecdotes, not ideas. Utilitarian and egotistical, he thinks the time has come for him to reap the harvest. . . .

Besteiro: when the masses were ignorant he was taken for a scholar. Today they have learned through the Russian Revolution and it took them by surprise to see that the man they considered to be king is only a stick figure. He is neither intelligent nor passionately devoted to ideals of justice, nor did he ever burn the midnight oil reading Marx. . . .

Fernando de los Ríos: he is the poisonous quintessence of bourgeois ideology. For him, socialism means nothing more than writing articles full of eloquent details from bourgeois periodicals. . . .

Prieto: he considers himself a socialist because he is capable of slapping a face. Socialism for him is personal braggadocio. He despises the party and its members. He has a bourgeois sense of humor. Sarcastic and cynical, he said in the previous Socialist congress that the subject of the International was unimportant. His socialist label does not prevent him from feeling representative of the interests of the middle class in Bilbao.

The Weight of the Old Party

"The majority of those who split from socialism brought to the new organization practices derived from a long period of coexistence with the PSO[E]. What was originally a split in the masses ended up inevitably as a split in personalities."[12] Their supporters discovered that they were such as a reaction to the leadership of the PSOE and that in the new party there appeared the same figures they had seen for years next to Iglesias, Besteiro, and Largo Caballero. The same thing happens in political divisions as in marital separations in which the ex-spouses devote themselves more to mutual criticism than to looking for new partners. Those who had split dedicated the best part of their energies to attacking their former colleagues. The PCOE's actions took place almost entirely in the ranks of the PSOE and the UGT. The PCOE did not try to open new doors, to attract nonorganized workers, or to work within the CNT or the autonomous unions. In this sense the former Socialist leaders managed to install the new party in an area in which it could not succeed. They immobilized the PCOE in the Socialist ring.

The PCOE had included in its name the word *obrero* (worker) so as not to be anything less than the PSOE and to distinguish itself from the PCE as well, which it considered to be a group of loud-mouthed insignificant students. To distinguish itself from the PSOE the Communists had to adopt new attitudes. Since they did not have a great deal of support from unions they fell into the conspiratorial mood.

In the summer of 1921 the national leadership of the Communist party decided to organize an armed insurrection (this episode has never been publicly mentioned), an insurrection which would begin in Bilbao and whose greatest blow would be delivered by the Communists in the Basque mining region. In our revolutionary infantilism we considered everything possible. And we dedicated our efforts to organizing the insurrection. In the meetings where the possibility of insurrection was discussed, a single voice, the sanest, that of an old miner, José Sánchez, spoke in opposition. With great political sensitivity he made us see that neither were conditons permitting nor did we have the necessary strength and influence to carry the working class to armed insurrection. . . . We thought he was wrong, that he was still working under social democratic reformism.[13]

Portela, who during that time was living the life of the party intensely, refuted this version of the facts:

> The story that Dolores Ibárruri tells is false from beginning to end. It is as stupid as that other story the detective Fenoll pulled from his sleeve at the end of 1923 to justify repression of the party: an insurrectional plot organized by the Communist parties in Spain and Portugal and for which a Portuguese soccer team which played a match in Seville acted as a link. Our supposed insurrectional plot was also referred to by Pérez Solís at a time when he had been back to his beginnings for some time and by Tuñón de Lara who had taken on "La Pasionaria's" version without quoting the source. But because the man is not overly endowed with imagination, in every lie there tends to be a particle of truth. In this case there is too. Ugarte took a trip to Vizcaya, either in the summer of 1920 or 1921. And this is where the truth of the account ends. Ugarte was clearly a hothead, yet too intelligent to order, propose, or suggest an armed insurrection in one of Bilbao's neighborhoods or in a small town in the mining basin. Such an absurd project was never discussed either in the party or at meetings of any of its organizations or in private conversations. On the other hand, if Ugarte had gone overboard we would have known it since we would have been asked for specific explanations and instructions. And no one ever said a word about it to us. Because of "La Pasionaria" this story is a fiendish trick, a low blow; its only objective might have been to discredit those of us who had for years been her party colleagues and whose presence both in and out of the workers' movement was annoying to her.

The masses did not understand the division in the PSOE, aside from a few points for which they had political training and unionist tradition. In one small town, Baltanás, for example, the peasants

> did not comprehend that change; they were only able to see it gradually through our communist solidity. For this reason the Agrupación Socialista was dissolved. Of the original twenty-two of us, along with some sympathizers, there remained only seven, who joined the Communist party. The others dropped out. In 1921 it was very difficult to be called a communist in a provincial town . . . because the whole town was against communism. We did not have the peasants' support, or anyone's support for that matter, since the sympathizers we had counted on in the Socialist party were also against us; besides, the socialists who separated from us created a very bad atmosphere for us. We could scarcely leave our homes. They called us "dirty communists" and at night they would stone our houses.[14]

Failed Negotiations

The existence of both Communist parties created a confusing and dangerous situation for the very development of the Communist movement.[15] The working class did not realize the Communist parties existed, but the few Communists there were, were undoubtedly disconcerted and disappointed by the division which accompanied the birth of the movement. The leaders of the PCOE took the initiative of looking for ways to unify the two parties. Perhaps to look good in the eyes of the International, and so that it could not be said that they were against unity, the young people in the PCE were willing to negotiate. Yet they were hardly enthusiastic about being absorbed by a larger party even though it was less dynamic.

The differences between the two parties were more temperamental and generational than ideological. The PCE was made up of young people who were not "warped" by the PSOE, feeling the pride of having been the first to form a Communist party and having the conviction that the revolution was within reach and that they would be the ones to lead it. The PCOE was made up of adults who had been with the PSOE longer and who until recently had not thought the revolution in Spain was just around the corner. Many were coming from the Socialist right wing or center. Therefore there were reasons for mistrust of the PCOE on the part of the PCE.[16]

In spite of it all there were negotiations. Andrade, Chicharro, and Portela, who reportedly saw a lack of "revolutionary daring" in the PCOE, were in charge of negotiations for the PCE. They added that certain militants in the PCOE would have to be thrown out to achieve unification in accordance with the seventh of the 21 conditions. They were Anguiano, García Cortés, Pérez Solís, Acevedo, López y López, Perezagua, and Lázaro García. The PCE claimed two-thirds of the national committee and the editorial staff of the publication of the future unified party. The national committee ought to have the right to throw out questionable ideological elements. It was obvious that the PCOE would not accept those conditions and one might think that they were formulated so they would be rejected and the PCOE would therefore be held responsible for the failure of the endeavor.

The delegation of the PCOE, Núñez de Arenas, Torralba Beci, and César González, did not fall for it. It proved itself to be conciliatory and showed that the scission of young people did not prevent the FJS from being revived while the division among the adults had disintegrated the PSOE (which was an exaggeration). It added that the statutes of the

Third International stated that positions of leadership in Communist party mergers ought to be conferred on the various factions according to their membership. The expulsions ought to be decided not by a committee, but by the party congress. A merging of the two national committees was proposed which would constitute a single committee to lead the party until a unification congress met.

Andrade replied for the PCE. He emphasized that members of the PCE were superior both individually and collectively because they knew enough to separate from the PSOE at the right time.[17] As could be expected, negotiations broke down and Andrade blamed the PCOE. Meanwhile the Comintern had sent an invitation to send a delegation to the congress of the Communist International made up of five members of each faction.[18]

Two Delegations in Moscow

The first phase of unification had not led anywhere. The second phase took place in Moscow where "the recommendations of the Communist International helped to overcome this anomalous situation and to unify the two parties."[19] The PCE sent a delegation made up of Merino Gracia, Millá, Pumarega, Gonzalo Sanz, and Joaquín Ramos. The PCOE followed suit with Torralba Beci, César González, Virginia González, José Rojas, and Evaristo Gil.[20]

The International's third congress met in June and July of 1921, two months after negotiations broke down in Madrid. The rebels in Kronstadt had just been squelched by Trotsky. The congress was much less argumentative than its predecessor because the 21 conditions had eliminated the most rebellious and spontaneous elements. But some unionists and anarchists did attend. The NEP (New Economic Policy) had been proclaimed shortly before and this was disconcerting to many delegates (certainly to those in the PCE). The revolution in Europe had failed. This provoked a lot of talk against "revolutionary adventures" and brought about the need for propaganda, organization, and a winning over of the unions. The 7,000-odd Spanish Communists were few compared to the 300,000 Germans or Czechs, the 150,000 French, the 70,000 Italians, and the 95,000 Norwegians. In his reports Trotsky did not even mention Spain. Of all the Spanish delegates only Torralba Beci of the PCOE had the chance to speak to the congress; the rest had to be satisfied with merely participating in the commissions (this perhaps was due to the fact that the delegation from the PCE arrived in Moscow after the congress had already begun).[21]

Torralba certainly struck a discordant note. He said that Spanish

Communists and workers had gotten used to the theses of the International's second congress and that they ought to be allowed to continue adhering to them instead of following those of the third congress. He stated falsely that the Communists were in control of a large number of unions and asked the executive committee of the Communist International to intervene in the unification of the two Spanish parties. In the congress's daily newspaper, Merino Gracia wrote an article criticizing the PCOE and Torralba.

The statutes of the International did not allow for the existence of more than one party in each country. Delegates from both parties were called to the office of the director of the Latin section of the Comintern, the former Swiss pastor Jules Humbert-Droz, who pointed out that the differences between the two parties were not fundamental and he allowed that there might be some expulsions. Zinoviev suggested an emissary be sent from the International to direct negotiations for the merger. They thought of Nicola Bombacci (who later converted to fascism) but finally decided to send the Italian count Antonio Graziadei.[22]

While the congress was in session the disaster of Annual in the Moroccan War occurred. The International's executive committee referred to it in a manifesto which said that "Spanish imperialism had suffered total defeat" (Zinoviev's words). Millá, one of the delegates from the PCE, returned to Spain by way of Rome where he interviewed Graziadei. Perhaps this influenced him in favor of the young people's party.[23] Graziadei spent two weeks in Madrid, almost constantly in hiding, because repression of Communists had begun again due to their stance on the Moroccan War. For ten days in November of 1921 the Italian delegate would meet each evening with the same delegates from both parties: Gonzalo Sanz from the PCE and Núñez de Arenas from the PCOE, although he also had separate interviews with other leaders. Graziadei found Núñez to be "somewhat of a centrist" and Sanz to be very intelligent and not at all intimidated by talking with an intellectual.[24]

The Merger

An agreement was finally reached: the PCE got two-thirds of the committees to be formed until the time when the unifying congress met, and it waived the requirement of expulsions, although Graziadei believed the requirement to be "generally well founded." During that interval the party's publications would be directed by Millá with Andrade and Núñez de Arenas as assistants. The organ of the unified party-to-be would be called *La Antorcha*. No declaration of principles was made; instead it was decided that theory and practice of the new party would be the same as those of the Third International.

When Graziadei left, Merino Gracia returned from Moscow. He had been converted to the positions of the third congress. He accused his friends in the PCE of being venturesome and he arrived at an agreement with members of the PCOE in the temporary national committee, winning over a couple of his comrades with the result that the majority of the committee left the antiparliamentarian stance of the PCE. In December the committee decided to present candidates for the upcoming municipal elections.

Merino Gracia wrote an article criticizing the PCE in *La Antorcha* which had just begun publication, and when the newspaper refused to print replies from those referred to in the article, they formed a Grupo Comunista Español which in January 1922 published a manifesto against party leadership, while still expressing loyalty to the International. The merger, they said, had been a step backward because it stifled the country's only revolutionary voice. Zinoviev ordered the group to dissolve. The group replied by letter explaining its position and affirmed its loyalty to the International. The national committee suspended those who had signed the group's manifesto until the unifying congress could meet to pass judgment on them.

The congress met secretly in Madrid in March 1922.[25] The entire session was spent discussing the positions taken by the antiparliamentarian Left. There was a majority from the PCOE, aided by friends of Merino Gracia, and it decreed that members of the group be suspended for a year and the group itself was to be dissolved. Ugarte, Andrade, and Chicharro respected this decision, but Ángel Pumarega did not and left the party. In obedience to the International, the group was dissolved. They appealed in vain to the executive committee of the Comintern to annul the congress's decision of suspension.

The congress elected García Quejido as president of the executive committee of the new PCE (changing the title to Communist Party of Spain, not Spanish Communist Party as in the "hundred kids"). Lamoneda filled the post of secretary general, and Virginia González, Antonio Malillos, Evaristo Salmerón (son of the president of the First Republic in 1873), Núñez de Arenas, Evaristo Gil, and Ignacio Ojalvo were secretaries.[26] The two merging parties' youth organizations also merged. Their organ was the weekly *El Joven Comunista*. The congress was the first of the new PCE. There was now a single PCE, but not every Spanish communist belonged to it.

Notes

1. M. Martínez Cuadrado, *Elecciones y partidos políticos en España, 1868–1931,* Madrid, 1969, vol. II, p. 487.

2. *El Socialista,* Madrid, April 15, 1921.

3. Meaker, p. 371.

4. Andrés Saborit, *Asturias y sus hombres,* Toulouse, 1964, p. 184 ff.; David Ruiz, *El movimiento obrero en Asturias,* Oviedo, 1966, p. 178 ff.; Juan Pablo Fusi, *Política obrera en el País Vasco, 1880–1923,* Madrid, 1975, p. 446 ff. (the latter talks of Perezagua, p. 298 ff.).

5. Javier Aisa and V. M. Arbeloa, *Historia de la Unión General de Trabajadores (UGT),* Madrid, 1975, pp. 94–95; and Amaro del Rosal, *Historia de la UGT de España,* vol. I, p. 249 ff.

6. *La Antorcha,* Madrid's Communist weekly, published in its January 12, 1923 issue a communiqué by the executive committee of the Profintern about the UGT's congress. It said that "its expulsion is the most important event in the history of the UGT. Supporters of the Profintern should remain calm and not imitate the tactics of the social-democratic bureaucrats. They must oppose divisional maneuvers with unified strength. Despite the fact that they have been the object of great humiliation, they must remain in the ranks of the UGT. Reformists fulfill their role of servants of the bourgeoisie when they work for division among unions; fulfill your role of servants of the working class as you work for the merger and the Frente Único [United Front]. . . . And achieve the merger with the CNT by working against the professional petty politicians who divide you in order to maintain their sinecures; work on behalf of autonomous unions, of all Spanish workers, in order to later join the Profintern and thus to contribute to the formation of a block made up of all revolutionary workers throughout the world."

7. *El Comunista,* Madrid, May 21, 1921.

8. *El Comunista,* Madrid, November 21, 1920.

9. "Los comunistas en la UGT," *El Comunista,* Madrid, July 23, 1921.

10. "Un miserable profesor burgués calumnia a la Revolución Rusa," *El Comunista,* Madrid, April 16, 1921.

11. "Figuras del congreso socialista," *El Comunista,* Madrid, April 16, 1921.

12. García Venero, *Historia de las Internacionales,* vol. I, p. 394.

13. Dolores Ibárruri, *El único camino: Memorias de La Pasionaria,* Mexico City, 1963, p. 84 ff.

14. Santiago Rodríguez, "Cómo conquistamos la primer alcaldía de España," *Nuestra Bandera,* no. 63, April 1970.

15. *Historia del PCE,* p. 33.

16. Meaker (p. 379) points out that the facts supported this mistrust. Pérez Solís converted to catholicism while in jail, Merino Gracia went over to the "free" unions, and García Cortés joined the Partido Liberal of Romanones and ended up being a supporter of Franco. Núñez de Arenas left for France in 1923 to avoid arrest and abandoned his militant activities. González and Lamoneda returned to the PSOE and Anguiano quietly withdrew from the party at the beginning of the dictatorship but kept fairly active in the UGT. Examples of the polemics between both parties are found in Joan Estruch, *Historia del PCE (1920–1939),* Barcelona, 1978, appendices III and IV.

17. *El Comunista,* Madrid, issues of May 14–25, 1921.

18. Comín Colomer (vol. I, p. 113) says that Bela Kun, who had been leader of the Hungarian Commune in 1919 and worked in the Comintern, was in Madrid to work for unification. But Colomer does not provide any reference in support of this statement which appears nowhere else. Portela denies that Bela Kun was ever in Spain.
19. *Historia del PCE,* p. 33.
20. Amaro del Rosal indicates that Virginia González was delayed en route by illness.
21. Meaker, p. 406.
22. Antonio Graziadei (1873–1953) was professor of economics, a Socialist of long standing, and one of the founders of the Italian Communist party. He was a representative of both the Socialist and Communist parties. He was considered a right-wing deviationist because of his stance on the economy. Nonetheless he did not leave the Communist party. In his *Memorie de trent'anni* he does not mention his mission in Madrid, for the memoirs go only as late as 1920. Nor is it mentioned in *Piccola Enciclopedia del Socialismo e del Comunismo* of Giulio Trevisani (Milan, 1958, p. 308) which provides this information.
23. Meaker, p. 407.
24. Meaker (p. 410 ff.). The corresponding documents and reports of Graziadei are found in the archives of Humbert-Droz. These are in the International Institute of Social History of Amsterdam. Andrade does not share the Italian delegate's opinion of Sanz. Since the executive committee and many militants were in jail because of the campaign against the war in Morocco, "our representation fell to a comrade who was not the most suitable but he had to obey instructions sent to him from jail."
25. Amado del Rosal erroneously gives the date of the congress as 1923 and alters the reasons for dissension, saying they were due to the fact that the dissidents thought Graziadei "had been deceived." The *Historia del Partido Comunista en España* (p. 33) does not speak of the merging congress but rather takes the merger for granted in what it calls a "merging conference" which took place on November 7–14, 1921. Actually this was nothing more than a series of conversations between Graziadei, Núñez, and Sanz from November 5 to 15. Some documents on the merger are in Estruch (appendices V and VI). Andrade says that the PCE had 2,050 members and the PCOE 4,500 at the time of the merger. The former had two newspapers, the latter six. He also points out that the crises in the party were due to the fact that five of the nine members of the PCE who were part of the executive committee of the new party soon "began to identify almost completely with the former leaders of the PCOE" which resulted in the other four members forming a "Spanish Communist Opposition" within the party.
26. These are the names which Amaro del Rosal gives. García Venero (*Historia de las Internacionales,* vol. II, p. 395) gives another list which is erroneous because it mixes names of successive executive committees and even includes Maurín who at the time was not a member of the PCE. Portela recalls that the presidency did not exist then.

5.
Loss in the CNT

The PCE had about 6,000 members. But the International in Spain had an organization a hundred times stronger: the CNT. Even though the PCE might have had the Communist International's seal, its members were only a small minority among members of the International, at least as far as figures go. Politically speaking, things were different.

Doubt in the CNT

The evolution of the Soviet regime made many in the CNT suspicious, and for those who had opposed the CNT's joining the Comintern, it confirmed their doubts about the true nature of Bolshevism. Pestaña's return from Russia, after being in an Italian prison, aggravated these suspicions. When Pestaña wrote his report it was not the Anarchists who were leading the CNT but rather the syndicalists, and among them some who were considered more or less Marxists or Communists. The experience Pestaña told about had no impact on them.

The police had put the majority of the leaders of the CNT in jail—those who made up the Catalonian regional committee as well as the national committee. Evelio Boal, secretary of the national committee, had been arrested and was later assassinated, and Andrés Nin was chosen as his replacement. The Catalonian regional committee was forced to reorganize. As a representative from Lérida, Joaquín Maurín, a fervent "Sovietist," participated in this committee.

The assassination of Eduardo Dato, head of the government, brought about fierce repression. But two of the three assailants managed to flee the country. One of them, Ramón Casanellas, went to Moscow. Nicolau and Mateu were arrested and tried. The national committee decided to call a plenary meeting. One of the participants described it in this way:

> In attendance were Andrés Nin, Jesús Ibáñez (from Asturias), Arena (Galicia), Hilario Arlandis (Valencia), Arturo Parera (Aragón), and Joaquín Maurín (Catalonia). The Northern and Central regions, as well as Andalusia, were not represented. The meeting began early in the morning and lasted four hours. . . . There was a discussion of repression to which the CNT

65

throughout all of Spain and in particular in Barcelona was subject. There were two positions: that of the national committee and the Catalonian regional which opposed the use of terrorism, and that of the Aragonese regional which supported continuous and systematic terrorism. Arturo Parera's thesis did not receive support. The position of the national committee and the Catalonian regional was adopted.

Next Nin reported on an invitation extended to the CNT to send a delegation to the third congress of the Third International in Moscow which was to meet in June. It was accepted. Then they went on to name the delegates. Chosen were: Andrés Nin, Jesús Ibáñez, Hilario Arlandis, and Joaquín Maurín.

Hilario Arlandis proposed that the Federación de Grupos Anarquistas (the Federación Anarquista Ibérica had not yet been established) be invited and that it name a fifth man to the delegation. The proposal was accepted and the Grupos Anarquistas designated Gaston Leval. The delegates were between 25 and 33 years of age, Maurín being the youngest and Arlandis the oldest.[1]

The trip was eventful.

Nin and Maurín come in contact with Pierre Monatte, editor of the pro-Communist syndicalist weekly *La Vie Ouvrière*. . . . Through his contacts in Metz, Monatte helped Nin and Maurín get across the French and German border without documents. Arlandis and Leval went from Paris to Berlin on their own with help from their contacts in Anarchist groups. Ibáñez was fortunate for he was traveling with a passport.

When they arrived in Berlin at the beginning of June, Maurín and Nin went to the home of Fritz Katter, one of the leaders of the German Anarcho-Syndicalist organization with which the CNT shared fraternal relations. Katter notified them that Jesús Ibáñez, who had arrived in Berlin a few days before, was being held prisoner. The German police excitedly went about searching for the Spanish suspects since the Spanish government had promised a reward of a million pesetas for the capture of the terrorists who in March of that year had killed Eduardo Dato in Madrid. . . .

During their stay in Madrid they talked extensively with Rudolf Rocker, the highly esteemed Anarcho-Syndicalist theoretician. His doctrinal position differed considerably from that of Pierre Monatte. He severely criticized the actions of the Communists saying that "dictatorship of the proletariat," the Bolshevik slogan, was dictatorship over the proletariat.[2]

Profintern Congress

The CNT delegation attended many sessions of the Comintern's third congress, but its real reason for being in Moscow was to take part in the founding congress of the Profintern. The delegates of both Spanish Communist parties participated in the debates of the International's congress. Members of the CNT, representing an organization infinitely more powerful than the Communist party, felt a certain contempt for those new Communists.[3] Maurín explained it later:

> We delegates of the CNT . . . discovered that the CNT had become a second-class guest. First place was taken by a hypothetical Spanish Communist party whose chief leader was Merino Gracia. Our delegation did everything possible to avoid a break with the early bird Spanish Communist party which was better known in Moscow than in Spain. Our delegation also tried to make the Russian leaders understand that the future of Communism in Spain was intimately linked to the CNT. One must recognize that Lenin and Trotsky, with whom we exchanged ideas, understood perfectly well that indeed such was the case. But neither Lenin nor Trotsky was concerned about Spain which was abandoned like a distant province where more or less unknown and intelligent revolutionaries would experiment.[4]

The Profintern's founding congress met in Moscow from July 3 to 19, 1921.

> The chief leader of the Russian unions was Tomsky who made up part of the party's Politburo together with Lenin, Trotsky, Bukharin, Zinoviev, Kamenev, and Stalin. Tomsky was the one who should logically have been the head of the Profintern since Zinoviev was the chief leader of the Communist International. But Tomsky spoke only Russian and that constituted a serious drawback in an organization of international stature. As a replacement the Bolshevik leaders chose Arnold Losovsky who had lived in France. . . . He had been a Menshevik and had gone over to Bolshevism like so many others as a result of the October Revolution. Not a brilliant intellectual, he was always a second-class figure within the Bolshevik hierarchy. He was familiar with the international workers' movement, spoke several languages, and having been a worker, he felt psychologically closer to the delegates from proletarian backgrounds than did the other Bolshevik delegates, intellectuals with a middle-class background—in other words, the majority of them. . . .

> The delegates of the CNT played a leading role in the development of the congress of which Nin was one of the leaders. Arlandis participated actively on the commissions; Ibáñez collaborated discreetly and Maurín performed the duties of the delegation secretary. From the outset Gaston Leval assumed an attitude of mistrust or indifference depending on the situation and almost always kept to himself. . . .

> The item which was most discussed in the congress was the relationship which ought to exist between the two internationals: the political Comintern and the unionist Profintern. There were two opposing camps: the one supporting the stance that there should be no organic relationship between the two, and the one in favor of such a relationship. The fundamentally syndicalist delegations, like that of France, were divided internally over the issue. In the Spanish delegation Arlandis opposed the relationship in

principle; Nin, Ibáñez, and Maurín supported it; Arlandis yielded to majority opinion.

The congress of the Profintern did not get very far off the ground. Besides being eclipsed by the congress of the Comintern, the truth is that there were no congressional members capable of raising the level of discussion. One of the few participants whose name took on international importance years later was the Bulgarian Georges Dimitrov who distinguished himself in the congress, not by his participation in the plenary session but by his uncompromising coarseness on the commissions. . . .

With the exception of scarcely a half-dozen delegations, including the Spanish CNT, the majority of delegates represented minority groups. And what the congress was ultimately looking for had a negative thrust: how to infiltrate the unionist movement of the large organizations in order to take them over or divide them.[5]

In Defense of the Russian Anarchists

Many Anarchists who had influence upon the weak Russian unions before the revolution came out as its supporters. But when they saw that it was drifting toward dictatorship they opposed it. Guerrilla warfare under Machno in the Ukraine was an expression of opposition to the revolution as were, to a certain extent, the green rebellions of the Volga peasants and finally the insurrection in Kronstadt shortly before the congress of the Profintern which Trotsky ruthlessly squelched in March 1921. At the time of the congress there were hundreds of imprisoned Anarchists, although their principal figures were free such as Kropotkin, now quite elderly.[6] Delegates in the Anarcho-Syndicalist camp (among them the Spaniards) made several moves in favor of those who were pursued by the Bolsheviks. Maurín gave the following account:

> They agreed to name a commission which would interview Dzerzhinsky, chief of the Tcheka (political police) in order to present the problem openly. This commission was made up of five delegates one of whom was Maurín representing the CNT. . . .
>
> Since Dzerzhinsky spoke only Russian and Polish, Manuilski served as interpreter. Whether Manuilski, who later played a major role in the "Bolshevization" phase of the Communist parties, was an agent of the Tcheka is not certain.
>
> Dzerzhinsky . . . listened to the explanation being presented to him and said that the Anarchists were not being pursued as Anarchists but rather as active adversaries of the regime and as perpetrators of criminal acts. "It is possible," he said, "that some errors have been made, but if you point them out to us we will correct them."

The commission was ready: it had a list of some fifty names of imprisoned Anarchists.

When Dzerzhinsky read the list his face became distorted, his nostrils flared and he said something probably very strong which Manuilski translated as, "You have been deceived. On this list I see names of thieves and murderers. Others I have never heard of. Some are the names of men who are not imprisoned but are fugitives and some of them are planning assaults and robberies."

The commission had failed in its interview with Dzerzhinsky. When it gave its negative account, a second commission was agreed upon to interview Lenin.

Lenin received the delegates in his office at the Kremlin and as always behaved with cordial camaraderie. He said that the Anarchists had collaborated admirably in the first phase of the revolution; but they began to fail as the revolutionary process grew more difficult. He understood the significance of there being imprisoned Anarchists from the point of view of propaganda from outside Russia. "I will present the matter," he summed up, "to the Politburo. But do not forget that that's where Trotsky is."

Lenin took the matter to the Politburo. Some time later a revision was made in the case of the imprisoned Anarchists, and those who had not been involved in thefts, holdups, murder attempts, murder, and sabotage were freed.

The delegates of the CNT had another mission: "The national plenary meeting of the CNT had given the Spanish delegation the job of raising a 'critical' question: 'Could the Soviets send arms to the CNT for the purpose of revolution?' Trotsky answered: 'To carry out a revolution it is necessary to have won the sympathy of the majority of the population and so you naturally depend on soldiers who have the arms. The arms which are necessary for a Spanish revolution are in Spain. Win the trust of those who have them and you will have the arms you need.' "[7]

Plenary Session in Zaragoza

When the CNT found out that its delegation in Moscow had voted in favor of a link between the Profintern and the Comintern there was a lot of commotion. The delegates who returned to Spain met with an atmosphere of hostility. Nin had stayed in Moscow in the Profintern.[8] Part of the uproar was caused by the voluminous correspondence of the French anarchist Gaston Leval (whose real name was Pierre R. Pileer) who had been living in Barcelona since 1914. Leval said he was convinced that his colleagues in the delegation were Communists. Rudolf Rocker, the German Anarchist whom the delegation visited in Berlin, concurred. He wrote: "This delegation which was not elected by any congress and whose traveling expenses were paid by Russia was determined to hand over the CNT to the Comintern from the outset. The only honorable exception among the members was the French Anarchist Gaston Leval."[9]

On his way back to Spain Leval wrote a pamphlet about his impressions of Russia which appeared in Valencia's *Solidaridad Obrera*.[10] While the delegation was in Moscow the anarchistic members in the CNT had been winning ground from the syndicalists. Those who previously had been the most enthusiastic "Sovietists" were now the staunchest adversaries of the Comintern. In August of 1921 a national plenary session of the CNT took place in Logroño. This session was requested by the CNT of Guipúzcoa (where the Communists were very active and aggressive toward the CNT). The plenary session in Logroño "unanimously disallows the meeting in Lérida [which actually took place in Barcelona], as well as its resolutions and the delegation which is in Russia without anyone's warrant."[11] In spite of this statement there is no doubt that the Lérida-Barcelona plenary was legitimate, since the secretary of the national committee was in attendance as were delegates from various regions. At any rate it was no less legitimate than the plenary in Logroño which the secretary of the national committee did not attend.

Years later Nin would defend the delegation with these words: "The anarchic members who so viciously fought us know as well as we that there was nothing illegitimate in appointing the delegation. . . . It would have been much more logical to say that the congress of 1919 had operated out of sentimentality and that Spanish anarchism was returning to its traditional position without at all taking into account the lessons of the war and the Russian Revolution and acting accordingly."[12] When the delegation returned there was another plenary in October, this time in Lérida, "which delegates from a majority of regions attended, according to Maurín's report which was unanimously approved."[13] Maurín acted as provisional secretary of the national committee. He was arrested in February 1922 and so the skillful defender of the Comintern was absent from the other meetings of the national committee.

The CNT found itself in a quandary. The repression by General Martínez Anido had destroyed its leadership and its unions were almost memberless. But when the conservative José Sánchez Guerra who was considered an enemy of the workers' movement set up government in March 1922 the situation improved. He reestablished constitutional rights, replaced the authorities in Catalonia, and freed social prisoners. This of course was not enough to convince the Anarchists that the political struggle made sense, but it allowed them to reorganize the CNT which began to regain strength. The return of the imprisoned leaders undermined the "Sovietists" who had taken over their jobs in many places. *Lucha Social* (*Social Struggle*), a weekly journal managed from Lérida by Maurín, and *Nueva Senda* (*New Path*), written by Anarchists from Madrid, printed polemics on a weekly basis.

A formal gesture was needed for their words to be translated into action. Manuel Buenacasa, using an alias, got the governor of Zaragoza to authorize the celebration of a "meeting of workers from several locations." This "meeting" was a national plenary of the CNT which began in the Aragonese capital on June 11. Buenacasa was pressed because on June 16 the founding congress of the AIT (International Association of Workers) was scheduled to meet in Berlin, the purpose of which was to assemble both the Anarchist and Anarcho-Syndicalist movements. The plenary meeting took place in the Workers' Center in Zaragoza, and when the police discovered the true nature of the meeting and tried to dissolve it, the threat of a general strike in the city forced them to allow the meeting to continue.

Juan Peiró, secretary of the national committee, opened the session. Pestaña spoke about his experiences in Russia. On the second day of the meeting, before hearing the delegation sent to Moscow, the plenary elected Galo Díez and Avelino González as the delegates who would go to the conference of the AIT in Berlin. Arlandis was the only "Sovietist" to speak, defending the legitimacy of the delegation; he tried to make people believe that the CNT had maintained its autonomy in Moscow. After an impassioned debate, during which the Anarcho-Syndicalists questioned whether a plenary could revoke a congress's decision (the one referring to membership in the Third International), a commission wrote a long and confusing conciliatory resolution which stated that membership in the Comintern reflected sympathy for the Russian Revolution more than an ideological identification and that it could not commit the CNT to membership. As a result the plenary, in the hope that a congress would make a definitive decision, resolved "in principle" that the CNT should separate from the Profintern. Since a session of a congress was difficult under the political situation then prevailing, the decision would be submitted to a referendum in the ranks of the confederation. The referendum, which was also to decide on membership in the AIT, never took place. But the CNT, which had "provisionally" joined the Third International, separated from it "in principle" and joined the AIT.[14] The "Sovietists" had lost their influence in the leadership of the CNT. Yet despite the decisions of Zaragoza they did not believe that the CNT was lost for Communism.

Revolutionary Syndicalist Committees (CSR)

The Anarchists had stated that "if Communists were able to attain positions in the confederation (CNT), it was because those who had held them previously had been decimated" and "they took advantage of the occasion which caused the disasters referred to [repression] in order to attack the leaders of the confederation in Catalonia. There were times when the national committee itself was guided by agents in Moscow" who came out with "a famous manifesto against the Anarchists whom they accused of being cowardly and dogmatic."[15] These were false accusations. Neither the delegates to Moscow in 1921 nor their friends were unknown to the police (who were looking for Nin and who shortly after wounded Maurín before arresting him), but they were surely not as popular as the imprisoned leaders they replaced.

The "Sovietists," who had been relieved of their posts and defeated in the plenary meeting in Zaragoza, tried not only to clear themselves of these accusations but also to regain influence in the CNT. They were not confined to Catalonia. They were also to be found in Asturias, Valencia, the Basque region, and some in Castille, although their main strength—still very much a minority—was in Barcelona and Lérida. They published *Acción Sindicalista* in Valencia and the already cited *Lucha Social* in Lérida. The editorial staffs of these two weeklies decided to suspend publication in order for both of them to support a new periodical, *La Batalla* (*The Battle*), which began publication on December 21, 1922,[16] six months after the plenary session in Zaragoza. Three days later representatives from these various groups met in Bilbao in a conference in which the Comités Sindicalistas Revolucionarios (CSR) were established. Their mission was to fight within the unions in the CNT against Anarchic influence and in favor of membership in the Comintern.

The committees were inspired by the example of several French revolutionary syndicalist groups such as the Vie Ouvrière of Alfred Rosmer and Pierre Monatte and, to a lesser extent, by Marxism as Lenin interpreted it. They were critical of any dogmatism in the CNT which, they said, was meant to welcome workers of every revolutionary ideology and they wanted to oppose "the doctrine of collective violence against all."[17] The conference of Bilbao agreed that the CSR must join the Profintern and they named Andrés Nin as their own delegate. In Moscow Maurín and his colleagues had grown to accept Lenin's tactical ideas. Despite rejection of the CNT's requests for aid, they doubtless received some financial support from the Profintern, especially in light of the fact that Nin was in Moscow. Yet this aid, if it did indeed exist, must have been very modest since *La Batalla* always had problems keeping afloat and its 3,000 readers were not enough to cover expenses. "The Bolshevik sectors [of the CNT], now clearly in the ultraminority, had to fight from marginal sectors."[18] In spite of everything, they won leadership in several unions and made their voices heard in many of them. Three very important unions in Barcelona, the transportation, mining, and textile unions, were in their hands.

The CSR could only operate publicly, out in the open. They had to derive their strength from propaganda, from the prestige of those who defended their positions and from their participation in assemblies. These were essential elements of their tactic. Without union assemblies there was no hope of reaching the active working masses or of winning them over. When the dictatorship was established in September 1923 and the CNT's unions were dissolved, the CSR found themselves like fish out of water, without a milieu in which to operate. Although some members of the CSR were also members of the PCE, the majority of them did not join the party. Sympathy for the Comintern did not mean sympathy for its Spanish party. Maurín himself at that time was not a member of the PCE. The dictatorship was bound to modify the relationship between Communists in the party and those in the CSR.

Notes

1. Joaquín Maurín, *Revolución y contrarrevolución en España,* p. 255 ff.
2. Ibid., p. 256 ff.
3. Scorn for both Spanish Communist parties became apparent in the Profintern congress when the committee of credentials under Bolshevik control agreed to allow Sanz, one of the PCE's delegates, to participate on the pretext that he was a leader of the carpenters' union in Madrid. The delegates of the CNT energetically opposed and managed to have him accepted only as an observer (Meaker, p. 398).
4. Joaquín Maurín, *El Bloque obrero y Campesino,* Barcelona, 1932, p. 7.
5. Arlandis was the only one to die while in the Communist party (during a bombardment of Figueras at the end of the Spanish Civil War). The others left the party at one point or other in their lives. Nin defended his position in 1921 and that of this two colleagues in this way: "[The Spanish delegation] could not act in any other way since it was linked to the Third International by an agreement of membership approved by the second congress of the CNT" (Andrés Nin, *Las organizaciones obreras internacionales,* Madrid, 1933, p. 79).

6. Kropotkin's last document was a letter to Lenin written shortly before Kropotkin's death in February 1921 in which he said that the Bolsheviks had returned to the Middle Ages when they decided to take as hostages revolutionary Socialist leaders in order to prevent another attempt on Lenin's life like the one he had sustained shortly before, albeit without serious consequence, at the hands of a revolutionary Socialist. The letter, dated December 21, 1920, is found in P. A. Kropotkin, *Selected Writings on Anarchy and Revolution,* Cambridge, Mass., 1970, pp. 338–39.

7. Maurín, *Revolución y contrarrevolución en España,* p. 261 ff.

8. It had been decided that Nin should remain in Moscow because the Spanish police had implicated him in the attempt on Dato's life, and it was absurd to leave him open to retaliation. At the end of a few months he tried to return; he was arrested in Berlin but the Soviet Embassy managed to get him out of jail. On his way back to Moscow he was given a job in the Profintern Secretariat where for several years he held a position of some power, in which capacity he visited Italy, France, and Germany and received the Spanish delegations sent to the USSR and intervened in problems with the PCE. In addition to serving as functionary he represented the "Sovietist" sector of the CNT in the Profintern and was elected by foreign residents in Moscow as member of that capital's city countil. (For more details on Nin's stay in the USSR see Pelai Pagés, *Andreu Nin: su evolución política (1911–1937),* Madrid, 1975; and Víctor Alba, *El marxisme a Catalunya, 1919–1939,* vol. III.)

9. Rudolf Rocker, *Revolución y regresión,* Mexico City, 1967, p. 398.

10. Xavier Paniagua, "La visió de Gaston Leval de la Rússia Soviètica en 1921," *Recerques,* no. 3, Barcelona, 1974.

11. Manuel Buenacasa, p. 105.

12. Andrés Nin, *Las organizaciones obreras internacionales,* pp. 79–80.

13. Maurín, *Revolución y contrarrevolución en España,* p. 265.

14. On the plenary session in Zaragoza see Buenacasa, p. 106 ff. Communists and some of Seguí's Marxist biographers have said that Seguí supported the CNT's return to the Comintern and that he received an invitation to go to Moscow shortly before his assassination and was willing to accept it. This invitation had been written by Nin who attached a personal message to it. Seguí knew his organization well and must have realized at any rate that the winds were blowing against Moscow and he must have thought that nothing as marginal as this, once the emotionalism of the issue was overcome, was worth risking the majority held in the plenary. The plenary meeting, indeed, defended Seguí and Pestaña from the accusation the Anarchists had made in connection with the pact of the CNT–UGT in 1920. The plenary likewise approved one of Seguí's proposals which infuriated the Anarchists: the unions were to salary their elected secretaries in order to make them full-time employees. They elected a national committee in which Seguí's friends formed the majority: Pestaña, J. M. Martínez, Carbó, and the Anarchist Galo Díez in addition to Seguí himself.

Following Seguí's assassination Nin wrote an obituary in *La Correspondance Internationale* (Moscow, April 11, 1923) which, following Seguí's biography, said that "in the course of the last two months our comrade began to see clearly; he understood that his position was completely in error; he had made clear to many friends his desire to go to Russia and upon his return to work to firmly straighten out the Spanish workers' movement with an orientation toward Moscow. We firmly believe that Salvador Seguí would have soon been completely on our side." It is difficult to say whether this article was the basis of the legend which had Seguí supporting Communism or whether, on the contrary, echoes of this legend, spread by pure Anarchists, had gotten as far as Nin in Moscow.

15. This manifesto was published in Sant Feliu de Guixols, in *Acción Social Obrera*, one of the few surviving CNT periodicals. The quotes are from Buenacasa, p. 94.

16. Luis Portela, "Presentación" to *Los hombres de la Dictadura,* by Joaquín Maurín, Barcelona, 1977.

17. *La Batalla,* Barcelona, December 30, 1922. Maurín reported in *La Correspondance Internationale* (February 2, 1923) on the conference in Bilbao as well as on the formation of the CSR. He said that the conference showed representations by "syndicalists in the CNT and Communist-syndicalists in the UGT." Actually the CSR operated only in the CNT and no reference was made to the UGT in Bilbao.

18. Josep Termes, "Repercussions de la revolució d'octubre a Catalunya," *Serra d'Or,* Barcelona, December 1967.

6.
The United Front

At the end of 1922 there was a unified Communist party in Spain which was a member of the Third International. The CSR were members of the Profintern and operated within the CNT. There was a great deal of agitation over the Moroccan war and the recent disaster at Annual, and the possibility of dictatorship could be seen off in the distance. The Catalonian bourgeoisie was alarmed by the resurgence of the CNT which it thought it had crushed through terrorism. Although the socialists seemed to have recovered from their division they suffered a serious crisis, sustaining losses in total strength and beleaguered by the constant fighting with the Communists in the UGT.

The Morocco Problem

The first news of the disaster in Morocco came in July 1921. People immediately held the king responsible because they knew he enjoyed giving orders directly to his generals in the Protectorate. Later on the Parliament appointed a commission to begin an inquiry—the so-called Picasso Inquiry for the name of the general who investigated the matter. There was talk of demanding that the king take responsibility for his actions. After the crisis of 1917 which almost put an end to the monarchy, the king's entourage foresaw a new crisis and preparations were made to deal with it, at first with a national government headed by the old conservative Antonio Maura. This was constituted in August.

The PCE protested against the war in Morocco in meetings and demonstrations, and there were always Communists in the demonstrations whenever there were shipments of troops. The PSOE and the CNT also protested, yet with much less fervor than the Communists, perhaps because they thought that the protests would have no effect, perhaps because they were debilitated by recent events (namely the division among the Socialists and official terrorism against the CNT). The Communists protested most energetically against the war in Morocco. Consequently they were subject to relatively strong repression (imprisonment, closing of headquarters, and shutting down of newspapers).[1]

The battle was not easy for anyone inexperienced, the young for example, neither for some adults who were more accustomed to dialectical rather than organizational combat. The campaign was to be waged with several goals in mind: to take away members from the PSOE, win over unions, attract new recruits, and win elections. The Communists were not successful in any of those areas. The only success, and a relative one at that, was the winning of several unions in Barcelona by the CSR. The CSR looked upon the PCE with contempt because they believed that the CNT was the potential revolutionary force of the nation and that it was necessary to win it over instead of trying in vain to deplete the PSOE. As for the PCE it preferred to devote itself to the UGT and its members' mistrust of the CNT carried over from their membership in the PSOE.

Apocalyptic Behavior

In Asturias and Vizcaya the unions had to face an offensive on the part of employers to reduce salaries. While they fought against this threat, the battle between Socialists and Communists was developing in their midst. It was not always a verbal bout since there was fighting and gunfire too. In Bilbao for example, there were encounters in which workers were killed.[2] In Vizcaya and Asturias Pérez Solís attributed the fact that the Communists lost their influence to the lack of leadership and to the "infection of unionist methods" in miners coming from the first PCE which alienated many potential Communists by their "eve of the Apocalypse" policy.[3]

Strikes were organized to denounce the "treachery" of Socialists and members of the UGT. This brought about fierce warfare. Bilbao followed Barcelona in the number of assassination attempts. But, as Prieto pointed out, in Bilbao they were all attempts on the lives of workers, not bosses.[4] Although there were various assaults on the Socialist headquarters, not a single one was made on the aristocratic Yacht Club. And when Pérez Solís tried to publish a Communist daily, Las Noticias, he managed to have it printed at the press of Euzkadi, the organ of the Comunión Nacionalista Vasca which attempted to uplift Communists in order to weaken the Socialists. The owners of the printing company consulted with the Bishop of Vitoria and got his approval before printing the Communist sheet. One small triumph that Pérez Solís achieved at that time was the "conversion" of Ramón Casanellas, one of Dato's assailants. After hiding out in Madrid, his colleagues in the CNT took him to Bilbao and it was there that Pérez Solís took him under his protection to shuttle him to France and indoctrinated him while hiding him for two months in his office at *Las Noticias*. Casanellas arrived in Moscow, served in the Red Army a few years, and took Russian citizenship.[5]

Another triumph was the winning over of the mining union of Vizcaya by the Communists in their congress of November 1921. José Bullejos, a telegram delivery man who had just arrived from Madrid, was elected president of the miners' union in this congress. (A little later during a general mining strike there was an attempt on Bullejos's life. He survived but was badly wounded.) The minority ended up separating and founded its own union which in a few months was as strong as the Communist union. The Socialists, seeing that the industrial mining crisis was not a mere ploy of employers, preferred to accept salary reductions rather than lose their jobs. And the workers ended up following the Socialists' advice.

This was a time when "there were mixed ideological discussions . . . with conflicts of a personal nature acting as negative factors and distorting the focus and analysis of the basic problems."[6] In the opinion of the Communist who wrote this, such a situation arose from "the profound crisis which faced the leaders of Spanish Socialism prior to this new situation in the workers' movement and which had been carried over in part to the new parties." The party propaganda was intense but reached very few; *La Antorcha* printed some 5,000 copies. The other weeklies which printed fewer than 1,000 copies were: *Bandera Roja*, Bilbao; *Aurora Roja*, Oviedo; *Nueva Aurora*, Pontevedra; and *El Comunista Balear*, Palma de Mallorca.[7]

The Elections and Fractionalism

The problem of parliamentarianism arose once again. Was the party going to participate in the municipal elections set for 1922 and in the legislative elections of the following year? Many militants coming from the first PCE as well as a considerable number from Vizcaya were opposed to participating. Those who had resorted to terrorism[8] were not interested in elections. And these groups were the party's muscle and formed its strongest bulwark.

Unification had been administrative and bureaucratic and was imposed by the Communist International but it did not reflect unified points of view. "Although intergroup fighting should have ended with the first congress . . . it is evident that it really never stopped or even diminished. The internal crisis finally appeared along with the corresponding threat of division." It was brought about by the decision to participate in the municipal elections.[9] Four of the members of the central committee and the majority of the central committee of Juventudes Comunistas (Communist Youth) disagreed with it. They published a manifesto explaining how they differed from the PCE leadership which they labeled as "opportunist." *La Antorcha* in turn labeled those in disagreement as "undisciplined" and "enemies of the Communist International." The protesters formed a Grupo Comunista Español which appealed to Moscow for its intervention. Moscow sent to Madrid one Jules Humbert-Droz, a member of the executive committee of the Communist International. It was Humbert-Droz's first time in Spain but it would not be his last. He was in charge of the Latin countries in the Communist International.

Bullejos[10] said that "the conciliatory action of the international delegate broke down the intransigence of the two rival groups thereby solving the crisis at least temporarily." Those who had been excluded by the central committee because of their "fractional activities and lack of discipline" both in the party and in the Juventudes were readmitted and assumed their former positions of leadership on the condition that the Grupo Comunista be dissolved and the central committee's decision with regard to elections be accepted. Besides, they would have to make a public retraction. This was the first instance in Spain of what was called "self-criticism." According to Bullejos "this resolution was accepted by the leftists, if reluctantly, but it did not solve the crisis in the Communist party."

The resolution could not solve the crisis because it did not center around discipline or elections but rather a completely new concept of the party. Those in the majority—almost all of whom were coming from the PCOE—saw the party as a long-term instrument for revolution and they ranked propaganda, organization, and parliamentary action as top priorities. Those coming from the old PCE placed the organization of insurrection as top priority and wanted to push for action by the masses. These were two different approaches within the same elitist system. The adults wished to expand the elite to attract the masses; youth believed that the elite which they themselves formed was all that was needed to attract the masses. In his report to Moscow, Humbert-Droz said that "this retrocession [in the PCE] has origins which are general and independent of the party. The Spanish workers' movement is going through an obvious period of depression. . . . The repression which followed the unsuccessful strikes has dealt a serious blow to our organizations in Asturias and Vizcaya. Many militants have had to emigrate. The period of attraction which the Russian Revolution enjoyed is over. . . . Between reformism and syndicalism which share influence over the masses, the party is forced to make its way with insufficient means."[11]

The municipal elections confirmed Humbert-Droz's pessimism. The PCE won few victories. Yet it claimed the first Communist mayor in Spain—in Baltanás, in the province of Palencia. There all seven members of the party declared themselves as candidates for the seven seats on the council.[12] In the elections for representatives in April 1923 a third of the seats in Congress (146 representatives) were proclaimed without an election since there were no opponents. Prieto won in Bilbao; Llaneza, in Asturias. The Republicans and Maurists lost in Madrid where Socialists won the majority by a margin of 700 votes. Besteiro received the greatest number of votes with 21,417. The Communists received 2,476 votes for Núñez de Arenas.[13]

The Second Congress

The second congress of the PCE began on July 8, 1921 shortly after a series of disturbances in Vizcaya in addition to a general mining strike. The congress "was not as important as it should have been neither for the quality of its debates nor for the accords reached given the extraordinary gravity of the coming events. For this reason it failed to cause a stir in proletarian and democratic circles."[14]

The debates echoed the fourth congress of the Communist International which initiated the slogan of United Front. But there was passion in the issues which separated the different camps: electoral participation, the "opportunistic orientation" of the central committee, and the isolation of the party from the Left in general. Humbert-Droz came to the rescue once again in the name of the International. He realized that the party's influence had diminished. What he did not realize was that the number of its militants had also decreased, perhaps because its leaders misrepresented the figures to him. At the time party membership did not reach more than 1,200,[15] which is to say a fifth of what it had at the time of the merger. Humbert-Droz said in his report to the Comintern:

The small Spanish Communist party was very much affected by childhood disease and its members have still not gotten rid of their leftism. Polemics between the two parties prior to the merger were extremely lively and very personal; there is still a great deal of resentment in one area or another. Unity has not created the atmosphere of camaraderie which ought to exist in a small party. . . . These incessant polemics have discouraged many militants who have returned to the old Socialist party. . . . They have cast a certain amount of discredit upon many militants and indeed upon the party. . . .

The congress discussed the measure taken by the central committee as well as the party's general policy in several secret sessions so that I could participate. (In Spain the police must be notified of all congresses, assemblies, etc. so they can send an observer.)

Finally the congress approved a proposal by Humbert-Droz which read:

1. The party will continue with its previous policy approved and explicitly stated by the Fourth Worldwide Congress.
2. It will intensify its political activities.
3. It will give greater attention than it has up to now to work inside the CNT.
4. It will strengthen its inner discipline.
5. Two permanent salaried positions will be created: those of secretary general and editor of the periodical.
6. Internal fighting will cease and all efforts will be channeled to the constructive work of the party.
7. A consolidated central committee will be created, made up of comrades who are most suited for the task regardless of their tendency.

This consolidated central committee elected an executive committee formed by: César R. González, secretary general; Ramón Lamoneda, trade union secretary; Luis Portela, secretary of the interior; José Baena, foreign secretary; Joaquín Ramos, administrative secretary; F. Alonso, agrarian secretary; and José Rojas, organization secretary.[16] Juan Andrade was editor of *La Antorcha* and Pérez Solís had been elected secretary general but declined.[17]

In its first printing in 1926 the *Great Soviet Encyclopedia* said that this congress "expressed great dissatisfaction over the passivity of party leadership and the fractional fighting which prevailed in it. The delegates from industrial centers who were also workers called for an end to internal struggles. However these revolutionary members who were trying to rehabilitate the party were not yet strong enough to demand changes in the leadership. The resolution and decisions which the congress adopted remained on paper and the party was isolated from the masses just as it was in the beginning."[18]

The United Front

What caused the "opportunists" in the central committee to triumph in the congress along with Humbert-Droz's help was the fact that they had put into practice the policy of united front. Although they did not achieve success with it because none of their proposals to other workers' organizations was accepted, it revealed their obedience to the International which was what really mattered.

Nonetheless the PCE did not stand whole-heartedly behind the united front tactic. Although the tactic seemed appropriate in Spain from the point of view of propaganda, its delegate in Moscow joined the French and Italian delegates to oppose the slogan in an extended meeting of the executive committee of the Communist International in March 1922.[19]

During the mining events in Vizcaya the PCE organized a united front committee made up exclusively of Communists who declared a strike which only the few members of the CNT in that region of the country joined. Instead of a united front, what resulted was shooting between Socialists and Communists. In Asturias the UGT declared a mining strike which lasted almost two months and which was successful thanks to the mediation of the conservative "premier" Sánchez Guerra. Following the strike Llaneza expelled from his union thirteen Communist-led sections which formed an independent mining union.

None of this seemed to set the ground for the proposal which the PCE sent in an open letter to the PSOE, UGT, CNT, and Anarchist groups on June 15, 1922 suggesting "the formation of a united front based on a program which [will] denounce salary decreases and a lengthening of the work day and advocate the dismissal of Martínez Anido y Arlegui from [official functions in] Barcelona and of Regueral in Bilbao, amnesty for all political prisoners, elimination of the death sentence, and the end of the war in Morocco."[20]

The executive committee of the UGT refused to "dignify members who have only divided and debilitated the strength of organized labor." The CNT responded that since the PCE "could not represent the Spanish proletariat," its proposal did not deserve a reply. When the PCE formed a united front in Madrid in order to support a strike by carpenters, the UGT expelled every union which answered the call including the strikers' union itself (led by the PCE). Largo Caballero in a meeting said that the slogan of a united front verified the failure of the PCE, whose members would be better off returning to the PSOE.[21]

Less scornful were some bourgeois politicians who, using the war in Morocco as a pretext, spoke with Pérez Solís, on July 13, 1923 in a ceremony at the Ateneo of Madrid. Next to the Communist leader "a Carlist representative participated as did a Maurist aristocrat who desperately wanted to be mayor of Madrid and who would do anything to gain popularity."[22]

Crisis in the Dictatorship

The coup d'état of September 13, 1923 which established the military dictatorship of General Miguel Primo de Rivera gave the PCE another occasion to emphasize the united front tactic. On the afternoon of the coup delegates from the PCE, the local federation of the CNT, and Anarchist groups met in Madrid and made public a joint declaration condemning the coup because, they said, it would strengthen the Moroccan campaign and it threatened the "Spanish proletarian vanguard" and "the very life of the unions." They formed a "Committee of Action against the war and the dictatorship." They went to the UGT and the PSOE to organize "a common struggle to defend rights which are to be respected even in times of the most brutal repression."[23] This manifesto was only a gesture. There was no unity of action simply because there was no action. Exhausted, the country resigned itself to dictatorship.

The dictatorship was a time of confusion for the PCE. Spanish Communists did not realize that dictatorship was approaching. Even Maurín who was keener and, living in Barcelona, was closer to the source of the coup d'état, two months prior to it wrote a study on "La España actual" ("Modern-Day Spain") in which he analyzed the different parties and unions as if nothing were threatening their future.[24]

Moscow did not lend much importance to the dictatorship. Nin, for instance, in an article in *La Correspondance Internationale* (September 26, 1923) said that the new power could never last. "Its main foundation, the industrial bourgeoisie, is small in number and poorly organized. It will fail in Morocco for better reasons than any other government. . . . The situation will be favorable to the development of the Spanish workers' movement." In the same issue R. A. said that if instead of spending their time slandering the Spanish Communists, the Anarchists and Socialists had made a united front of the revolutionary forces "to achieve systematic propaganda using the principles of class struggle in the army," the dictatorship never would have come about because the soldiers would have opposed it. And on December 28 when the dictator had already been in power for three months, Nin wrote that "from the revolutionary point of view, after all is said and done the coup might possibly benefit us." He saw the end of the dictatorship thanks to the divorce of the dictator from Catalonian industry on the one hand and from the agricultural bourgeoisie on the other. "This divorce will create a situation favorable to the revolutionary movement." For this reason "the military government will not be able to last very long." The only one of these observations which was at all realistic was Nin's statement that Primo de Rivera's coup "cannot be considered a fascist coup d'état but rather as only one of the countless pronunciamentos with which the history of the nineteenth century in our country is filled."

The PCE had not overcome its fractional crises. They were aggravated by the position which the military government adopted regarding the party. While the CNT dissolved itself and the dictatorship respected the

UGT and the PSOE, it ignored the PCE. The party placed two police across from its headquarters in Madrid but took no other measures. In December 1923 the Military Directory announced that a conspiracy had been discovered and many Communists were jailed. But there were no further developments.[25] The PCE operated only in those places where local authorities did not think it dangerous (Madrid, cities of Castille, Andalusia). You could not even breathe in Asturias and Vizcaya where police surveillance of the entire workers' movement was acute. *La Batalla* continued publication although subject to censorship as did *La Antorcha* in Madrid, *El Comunista Balear* in Palma de Mallorca, *Nueva Aurora* in Pontevedra, and even *La Bandera Roja* in Vizcaya.[26]

Members of the PCE had never been underground and the party was not ready for it. Although it was just a case of minor illegality, it knocked the party pretty much out of joint. There would soon be a serious setback when César R. González left his position as secretary general and, together with Lamoneda, García Cortés, Rodríguez Vega, and others, returned to the PSOE. Anguiano withdrew from all militant activity. One might think that this decision was not determined by the establishment of the dictatorship but rather by discussion in the second congress, although César R. González and Lamoneda did not appear to be irresolute during the session since they accepted positions in the executive committee.[27]

The Communists tried to pass off these defections as a product of fear of repression.[28] Regarding those who purchased a round-trip ticket to the PSOE, the Communists said that "in the face of the severe persecutions by Primo de Rivera, they tried to impose on the party an opportunistic policy which would give in to the struggle. In support of their posture they argued that 'it was necessary to save their strength for the decisive moment,' 'wait for better times.'"[29]

In 1924 the party had barely 500 members. Since the CSR were not able to operate with the unions dissolved, a segment of their components formally joined the PCE. Maurín was one of them.[30] These were the members who, together with others from Valencia and the North, most assiduously criticized the passivity of the leaders of the PCE. Maurín had returned to Moscow around the middle of 1924 to attend a congress of the Profintern with a delegation made up of leaders from the transportation union (Desiderio Trillas and José Grau Jassans) and the steel union (José Valls and José Jover) of Barcelona who were supporters of the CSR. "The delegation's general impression [of Moscow] was one of displeasure. None of the four workers felt attracted to communism"[31] despite the warm welcome which Nin gave them as a member of the secretariat of the Profintern.

The First Triumvirate

The group of communist exiles in Paris (Portela, Gorkín, and Trilla) joined the Vizcayan, Catalonian, and Balearic federation in pressuring for a change in the party's orientation. This pressure coincided with the position adopted by the fifth congress of the Comintern for the Bolshevization of the parties. These pressures came to the fore in a party conference which took place in Madrid in November 1924. The executive committee resigned and the conference elected another with Maurín from Catalonia, González Canet from Valencia, and Martín Sastre from the North. It agreed to move executive committee headquarters to Barcelona. The first thing the committee did was to publish a new periodical, albeit an illegal one, called *Vanguardia* which strongly opposed the dictatorship. The passivity of the PCE had ended.[32] Official tolerance also ended. In January 1925 González Canet and Sastre were arrested in Madrid. Maurín and the leadership of the CSR met the same fate in Barcelona.[33]

Several of these arrests were made as a result of a breakdown in the secret service of the French Communist party which was under the direction of Suzanne Girault at the time. The delegation of the Comintern in France decided to send the Parisian Communist councilman Louis Sellier on a fact-finding trip to Spain. Upon his arrival in Madrid he was arrested and found with the addresses of leaders in the PCE and an appointment with Maurín. Gorkín, who was in Paris at the time, believed there was a slip-up somewhere in the organizing of the trip and that Sellier was tailed once he crossed the border.[34]

After the arrest of the first triumvirate, the Communist International named Pérez Solís secretary general. In Bilbao he tried to reorganize the party leadership and went to Paris to speak with the delegate from the Comintern[35] who endorsed his decisions. He later settled in Perpignan and with Roberto Fresno, another member of the Juventudes, soon after went secretly to Barcelona where in no time he was arrested by the police. Pérez Solís converted to Catholicism after long conversations in jail with the Dominican priest José Gafo.[36] Merino Gracia, also arrested, converted to "free syndicalism" (company unions) to which he lent his services during the dictatorship. They were soon set free.

The party had been decapitated. Maurín, from jail, as well as others, wrote the Comintern demanding the reorganization and greater activity of the party and called for the appointment of leaders with revolutionary spirit. They did not see that the problem lay not in Spain but in Russia.

Notes

1. The police linked the fact that the recruits in the Regiment of Garellano were from Bilbao and that the regiment rebelled when they were shipped off Malaga in August 1922. Corporal José Sánchez Barroso, the leader of the insurrection, was condemned to death by a court martial but his death sentence was commuted.

2. "Our lack of political training brought us to hate our former comrades to the point of considering as a great revolutionary act having shootouts in the streets with "social reformists" who rejected the 21 conditions of Lenin. There were months and years of bloodshed and fratricidal stupidity," recalled Jesús Hernández (*Yo fui ministro de Stalin,* Mexico City, 1953, p. 358).

3. Pérez Solís, *Memorias de mi amigo,* p. 280. Portela attributes this loss of strength to the policy of Pérez Solís and Bullejos.

4. Indalecio Prieto, *Yo y Moscú,* Madrid, 1955, p. 10. This book is a pirate summary of articles published by Prieto in Mexico during his exile, edited in Spain to provide propaganda for Franco's regime.

5. Pérez Solís, *Memorias de mi amigo,* p. 295 ff. "Generally good relations existed between Basque nationalists and Communists for two reasons: both hated the Socialists, and Communism had adopted the principle of self-determination" (Julian Gorkín, *El revolucionario profesional,* Barcelona, 1975, p. 69). So, for example, Pérez Solís took advantage of the offer of a Basque nationalist mayor to provide Gorkín with documentation under an alias when he had to escape from the police to France.

6. Amaro del Rosal.

7. Bullejos, *La Comintern en España,* Mexico City, 1972. Bullejos does not list *Lucha Social* in Lérida or its successor *La Batalla* in Barcelona, both of which were CSR organs, among those periodicals. This shows the rivalry that existed between the syndicalist and administrative branches in the Spanish Communist movement.

8. "When the masses cannot act collectively in defense of their interests or against their enemies, it is common for a group of heroic individuals to try to take over by resorting to terrorism and assassination attempts. Even though Communism condemns individual terrorism and considers it useless and destined to failure, Basque Communists, deeply influenced by Anarcho-Syndicalist tactics, made use of it from 1921 to 1923. As in Barcelona, the results of such a tactic were totally negative." Bullejos, p. 34.

9. Ibid.

10. Ibid.

11. Jules Humbert-Droz, *De Lénine à Staline,* Neuchâtel, 1971, p. 63.

12. Santiago Rodríguez. The Communist city council expropriated communal property stolen from the people and divided it among the peasants. The dictatorship removed this council from office as it did with all the other councils throughout the country.

13. García Venero, *Las Internacionales en España,* vol. II, p. 409.

14. Bullejos, p. 44.

15. Guy Hermet, *Les communistes en Espagne,* Paris, 1971, p. 24. Also in Spain at that time was the Italian Dino Tranquilli (who later became famous

as Ignazio Silone) who tried to organize the Socorro Obrero Internacional (International Workers' Aid). He was arrested and from his prison cell wrote several articles in *La Batalla*.

16. There is a great deal of confusion about this executive committee. The names I have given were provided me by former militants including Luis Portela, a committee member. However Bullejos adds to the list the names of Evaristo Gil, Fernández Mula, José Rodríguez Vega, but excludes Alonso (p. 47). The party was organized in federations.

17. Luis Portela, conversation with the author, Barcelona, April 1978.

18. Quoted by Eduardo Comín Colomer, *Historia del Partido Comunista de España*, Madrid, 1965, vol. I, p. 137. This book sticks to the police's conspiratorial vision of Communism yet provides many documents which probably come from police archives where they were filed after searches and arrests.

19. Jane Degras, *The Communist International*, London, 1956, vol. I, p. 308.

20. *Historia del PCE*, p. 36.

21. Meaker, pp. 435–36. There was a gap between what people knew in Moscow and how people were living in Spain which even someone as tuned-in as Nin knew nothing of. For example, in the January 30, 1923 issue of *La Correspondance Internationale* Nin wrote an article about the constitutional congress of the AIT, the Anarchist International, in which he stated that "the tendency of the Profintern was beginning to have an effect on the CNT and that it would not take much for it to prevail," while on June 1 of the same year in the same magazine Hilario Arlandis, writing from Spain, referred to "the dawn of the Catalonian workers movement," but did not mention at all the influence the CSR supposedly had on it. This did not prevent the executive committee of the Profintern from advising the Spanish workers a week later to create, in the face of white terrorism, "the system of worker centuries as was created in Germany"—yet without pointing out that the centuries had no effect whatsoever in that country.

22. Pérez Solís, "Un vocal español en la Komintern," *El Español*, Madrid, January 30, 1943. In the same article the author states that Jacques Doriot, leader of the French Communist party at the time, attended the second congress of the PCE. Portela says that Doriot did not attend this congress but went instead to the congress of Juventudes Comunistas in the summer of 1923.

23. *Historia del PCE*, p. 40.

24. *La Correspondance Internationale*, July 20, 27, August 4, 1923.

25. The *Historia del PCE* (p. 42 ff.) tries to pass that first year of dictatorship off as a year of persecution of the party. The truth of the matter is that members of the CNT were the main victims of repression and that the Communist party was not the object of special "attention" on the part of police until 1924 as a result of what will soon be explained. Bullejos (p. 54) says that "there were attempts to obtain party cooperation especially in those places where the party was particularly strong such as in Vizcaya." The governor of this province proposed to Bullejos and Pérez Solís the reopening of the unions in exchange for the PCE's neutrality. The offer was rejected. Andrade recalls (loc. cit.) that even though party headquarters were shut down, the police allowed the room where *La Antorcha* was written to remain open but they managed to have mail opened and to make note

of correspondents, subscribers, etc. Andrade asked the leaders of the party on several occasions if it was wise to continue legal publication of the paper, and he was always told that propaganda was worth the risks taken with the police. There were times when because of arrests "*La Antorcha* was written in jail, having to resort to all kinds of ingenuity to pass the manuscript to the comrades outside and to get information and documentation from outside."

26. Hermet, p. 24.
27. Nevertheless González went in October to Perpignan for a few days to visit Francesc Macià at the Hotel Victoria where he met with union delegates, Catalonian nationalists, Basques, and Communists (Macià, *La seva actuació a l'estranger,* Mexico City, 1952, vol. I, pp. 26, 30).
28. Amaro del Rosal.
29. *Historia del PCE,* pp. 45–46.
30. They entered the Catalonian-Balearic federation of the PCE which soon fell into the hands of the members of the CSR and increased its membership. For the history of the Catalonian-Balearic federation see Albert Pérez Baró, *Els "feliços" anys vint,* Palma de Mallorca, 1974, p. 160 ff.
31. Maurín, *Revolución y contrarrevolución en España,* p. 266.
32. The *Historia del PCE* sums up this attempt at making the party more dynamic in this way (p. 46): "The incorporation of Maurín and a group of syndicalists from Barcelona which could have supposed the strengthening of the party with new forces linked to the Catalonian proletariat, contributed instead to increasing difficulties. Maurín turned out to be a political self-seeker and not a revolutionary militant. He planned to take over party leadership, to turn it into a nationalistic, petit-bourgeois organization at the service of suspicious causes." Andrade (loc. cit.) indicates that the conference was called by an order from Moscow, transmitted by Jacques Doriot, the Communist International's delegate for Spain. The order called for a campaign with the slogan "Long live Abd-el Krim!" This slogan was approved by the conference, if unenthusiastically out of a sense of discipline, yet it was never implemented because of a lack of funds. On the other hand the two opposition factions, one which wanted to move executive offices to Bilbao and another which preferred Barcelona, took advantage of the meeting to take over the leadership which first moved to Bilbao and following several arrests there moved to Barcelona.
33. Bullejos was court-martialed because of the events in Bilbao of the previous summer. González had been sentenced to a year in prison by another court-martial. Both were released because in order to free General Dámaso Berenguer and others imprisoned because of the disaster at Annual the government granted an amnesty which also benefited the Communists and others who had been court-martialed. The governor of Vizcaya gave Bullejos the option of continually being arrested or leaving the country. He consulted with the party which decided he should go to Paris, and from there to Moscow where he acted as substitute delegate of the PCE in the Comintern. The regular delegate was Pérez Solís who spent only a short time in the USSR. (Bullejos, p. 53 ff.) Portela also had to emigrate. "The reason for Luis Portela's flight from Madrid was this: the Spanish press, in accordance with the Portuguese, had spread far and wide the discovery of a revolutionary plot on the occasion of a soccer game played in Seville by teams of both

countries. This plot was a figment of the imagination of the police" as a pretext to carry out numerous governmental arrests. Portela, who was accused of organizing the nonexistent plot, had managed to make it to Paris (Gorkín, *El revolucionario profesional,* p. 93).

Maurín was arrested as he fled in Barcelona having seen several police waiting for him. He was shot and wounded. He was taken from the hospital to the castle of Montjuïc from which he tried to escape. In November 1927, on the occasion of a diplomatic meeting in Paris between France and Spain regarding Morocco, a campaign was begun in favor of Spanish political prisoners and so as not to create an environment hostile to the conference, the government freed Maurín and other prisoners (Alba, *El marxisme a Catalunya, 1919–1939,* Barcelona, 1974, vol. I, p. 32 ff.).

34. Gorkín, *El revolucionario profesional,* p. 114. Portela said that Sellier openly arrived in Spain in 1924 carrying as his cover a letter from the mayor of Paris for his counterpart in Madrid. Marcel Cachin also visited Spain. "They both returned deeply impressed by the enthusiasm and self-denial of those militants who in defiance of repression each day devoted long hours to their party's work after finishing their own daily jobs." Sellier was arrested and expelled. Cachin was asked to leave the country.

35. At the time the delegate was the German Klein whose personality and horrifying death in China is described by Gorkín in *Caníbales políticos* (Mexico City, 1941, p. 81) years later when kidnapped by terrorists. In 1925 Klein ordered "the suppression of Primo de Rivera." Gorkín suggested that, given the seriousness of the matter, the Comintern should be consulted. Moscow rejected the idea without even discussing it (Gorkín, *El revolucionario profesional,* pp. 119–20, 140). Actually Klein was not German (although he passed as such) but Russian, and his name was Guralsky.

36. Pérez Solís was given a job in CAMPSA (the state oil monopoly), later wrote his memoirs, collaborated intermittently on the rightist daily *El Debate,* and fought in the Civil War on the side of Franco. He took advantage of this to try to help some of his former comrades imprisoned under the Franco regime (Pérez Baró, p. 191).

7.
Bolshevization

The first congress of the Communist International was open to all. The second congress approved the 21 conditions which alienated a good number of the International's organizations (including the PSOE and the CNT). The third congress marked a turn to the Right which was a parallel to Lenin's NEP in Russia with its tactic of a united front. The fourth congress passed almost unnoticed. But the fifth in 1925 signaled important changes. The tactic which some called "revolutionary adventurism" prevailed and brought with it greater discipline in the parties—in other words, Bolshevization. Bolshevization meant the establishment of democratic centralism of the Russian Communist party in every party, the prohibition of factions, giving the Comintern systematic participation in local decisions, leaving to the Comintern the selection of leaders (the parties would later "elect" these leaders), and finally, having the parties depend on financial help from Moscow.[1] Many of the founders who accepted the third congress's turn to the Right resisted Bolshevization. They withdrew or, if they opposed Bolshevization, they were expelled. Maurín and his friends in Spain were more concerned about radicalization and a political line which required greater activity, which was what they demanded from the party in Spain. In the long run Bolshevization had greater influence over the PCE.

The Second Triumvirate

The first triumvirate was formed by a decision of party organs, responding to feelings of the majority in the party. The second was, in effect, appointed by Moscow. It marked the end of democracy and the independence of the PCE. From their prison cells, Maurín and his friends kept at Moscow for a more active policy. Bullejos reports that Maurín suggested him as secretary general, but Maurín's version was that they were seeking an active and aggressive secretary but that there were no nominations.[2] Bullejos had been one of the leaders in the strikes in Bilbao and in the confrontation with the Socialists. His thinking matched his actions perfectly; he was the image of the Bolshevized leader whom

91

the International's fifth congress was looking for. To a certain extent it was logical for Moscow to trust Bullejos. Once in Moscow, Bullejos saw the beginnings of the struggle for Lenin's succession in Trotsky's attacks against Zinoviev and Kamenev regarding the International's policy as well as in the conciliatory position of Stalin and Bukharin.

The International formed a commission to study the problem of Spain, made up of Humbert-Droz from the Communist International; Losovsky and Nin from the Profintern; Doriot, Marty, and Semard from the French Communist party; Gramsci and Verti from the Italian Communist party; Almanza from the Mexican; Smeral from the Czechoslovakian; Maslow from the German; Piatnisky and Vasiliev from the Russian; and Codovila from the Argentine. Bullejos, Ibáñez, and Gorkín represented the Spanish Communist party. The end result of the commission's efforts was to name Bullejos secretary general in the spring of 1925 with "full power to reorganize the party and reconstruct the central committee." Thus party members had no say in the appointment.[3]

Once he was back in Paris Bullejos began to reorganize the party. He sent three liaisons, only two of which made it to Spain. They finally managed to convene a meeting in Ivry of representatives of the federations in the party. There they chose a second triumvirate which Bullejos proposed. Bullejos was secretary general, Gabriel León Trilla was secretary of agitation and propaganda (despite the fact that French Communists considered him a Trotskyite),[4] and Portela was the organization secretary. Andrade, who came out in support of the new line, continued as editor of *La Antorcha*. Gorkín worked with this triumvirate.

There was discontent among party members. They could not accept leadership being imposed upon them without asking at least for their opinion. Nin was sent to Paris to help overcome this discontent, but he could be of little help since he was arrested by French police only a few days after his arrival, having just joined the party secretariat, and was later expelled from France.[5] This discontent on the part of party members was subsequently expressed between 1925 and 1927: "Our party could have taken advantage of the period of military dictatorship to win the sympathy of the working masses and to strengthen the groups of militants. The decomposition of Anarcho-Syndicalism and the open collaboration of the social democrats with the dictatorship created a situation highly favorable to the development of the PCE. Nonetheless the only activity of any importance or persistence which its leaders pursued was the factional fighting in what was left of the party, thereby destroying all those nuclei which did not identify with the total incapacity and the narrow and petty functionary attitude of the leading bureaucrats."[6]

Nevertheless these bureaucrats scored two triumphs. At the end of 1925 Bullejos helped the former colonel and representative from Catalonia Francesc Macià get to Moscow to seek aid for his plans for insurrection in Catalonia. The trip was a failure since leaders in the International refused to help. Bullejos went to Moscow to prepare for this visit in which Nin also took part. Regarding Macià's trip to Moscow, "the general impression . . . was that the Communist International wanted to take advantage of the so-called period of pre-revolutionary propaganda to jointly sign manifestos with two organizations as powerful and prestigious as the CNT and [Macià's] Estat Català. The purpose was to win supporters for the Communist cause in Spain where little headway had been made."[7] The second success, more substantial, occurred in 1927 when a strong nucleus of transportation, dock, steel, and bakery workers in Seville joined the PCE. Some of its members such as José Díaz, Manuel Adame, Manuel Delicado, and Antonio Mije would go on to have important roles in the party.

Communist propaganda, in particular propaganda against the war in Morocco, must not be overlooked either. Although it may not have reached the masses, it did have an impact on the police and the dictator. On August 22, 1925 he issued one of his colorful and officious notes making reference to "clandestine, pacifistic leaflets about Morocco which were fervent in their hostility toward the classes of national leaders, bankers, and employees." Propaganda about the war in Morocco was directed by Klein and a joint committee of French and Spanish Communist parties. The slogan for the propaganda was "Long live the fraternization of French and Spanish soldiers with the Arabs!" This was later replaced by another slogan: "Immediate settlement of peace."

Russian Oil

The party did not make its operations known to the people. It was a closed circle within which endless fighting went on among its factions. Moscow thought that first the party had to be purged of all those who were not in agreement with the line taken by the fifth congress of the International. "The policy of massive expulsions . . . spanned the years of 1926 and 1927. First the majority of members who had made up the central committee which came about in the second congress [of the PCE] were expelled. Subsequently important militants from Asturias, Catalonia, and Valencia would be thrown out."[8]

In many federations there was opposition to this policy which was slowly but surely doing the party in and was asphyxiating its most independent members: Loredo Aparicio in Asturias, Maurín in Catalonia, and Arlandis in Valencia. This opposition was not a reflection of the struggle for power in the USSR. The protesters at the time were neither anti-Stalin nor pro-Trotsky but rather anti-Bullejos.[9] Moscow always sided with Bullejos. In 1927 when Bullejos accused Maurín, who had just arrived from Paris, of being a police informer, and when Maurín appealed to the control commission of the Comintern which backed him up and censured Bullejos, Maurín logically called for Bullejos's dismissal, but Moscow kept him on.[10]

Bullejos created a strong party mystique and "consequently party militants saw their existence exclusively and strictly in terms of the party. And the party, in practice, soon became identified with its leaders.[11] Bullejos spoke of 'iron discipline' and of the 'interior regime of dictatorship' [in the party]."[12] Those in opposition made the mistake of seeing in all this a policy of Bullejos and not the result of Bolshevization undertaken by the International. To strengthen discipline the executive committee decided to move to Spain. But prior to that, in December 1925, the central committee met in Bordeaux to reorganize the executive committee. Portela had reservations about Bullejos's tactics and he was replaced by González Canet (who was going by the name of Martín Zalacaín); Méndez and Daniel Martín from Bilbao were also added, thereby strengthening Bullejos's position. On the Comintern's request Trilla[13] was sent to Moscow and Luis García Palacios from the youth group Juventudes was sent to the seventh enlarged plenary meeting along with Bullejos. Bullejos's home base was in Bilbao and he chose this city as headquarters for the executive committee. Jesús Hernández and Agapito García Atadell were in charge of a small, clandestine printing plant, although La Antorcha continued to be published legally. But the PCE participated neither in the unrest in the army nor in the conspiracy on the night of St. John's Day just as it had not taken part in previous activities against the dictatorship.

The seventh enlarged plenary meeting of the International reaffirmed the struggle against Trotskyism and established the theory of socialism in a single country, thus marking the triumph of Stalin as Lenin's successor. It was the last time Zinoviev, Trotsky, Rikov, and Kamenev spoke at the International. In a meeting between leaders of the Comintern and the Spanish delegation the latter was asked what position the party would adopt regarding the advisory National Assembly which Primo de Rivera was proposing. Moscow wanted the PCE to appoint candidates and develop propaganda. The Spanish delegates were opposed. They knew that if this were done they would be left without a single member. Bullejos said: "The pressure placed upon me to change my position and accept the directives of the Communist International was strong and they even threatened in an overt way to hold me in Moscow for an extended period of time. There must not have been unanimity in the commission or in the executive of the Comintern on the practicality of such a tactic since no definitive action was taken and I was allowed to return to Spain."

At that time the Soviet government was negotiating with Primo de Rivera (even though it did not have diplomatic relations with Spain) a considerable and continuous sale of Russian oil for the newly-founded Spanish state monopoly of CAMPSA. The Soviets thought that the PCE's participation in the farcical National Assembly would soften the Spanish negotiators. Moscow did not stop pressuring the executive committee. The committee vacillated. The Catalonian-Balearic federation was in firm opposition. A national conference was called in Durango to discuss the matter which a delegate of the Comintern, the Pole Veletsky, attended. Although Bullejos claimed that Catalonia was represented at the conference by a man named Llopis, the Catalonian federation refused to send anyone. Llopis was just a friend of Bullejos. There was a long period of discussion since many did not dare disobey Moscow's wishes, but finally a sense of politics prevailed and it was decided not to support the Assembly. When Primo de Rivera organized the Assembly on the basis of direct nomination, without elections, he saved the PCE from an embarrassing situation.[14]

While indifference toward the PCE and the USSR was common among workers, there was sympathy toward the USSR among intellectuals and students, a phenomenon which has been repeated throughout the years. Rodolfo Llopis, a teacher and a socialist, visited the USSR and on his return wrote *Cómo se forja un pueblo: la Rusia que yo he visto (How a Nation Is Created: The Russia That I Saw)*. The attorney Diego Hidalgo also traveled throughout the USSR and wrote a dithyrambic volume called *Un notario español en Rusia (A Spanish Notary in Russia)*. If indeed the dictatorship exercised severe censorship of the press, there was no censorship of books. Probably at no other period prior to the 1970s has there been in Spain such an abundance of books on social and ideological themes and in particular about Marxism, the USSR, and communism.

The practice of forming fellow traveler organizations began around that time and became common years later. The Antiimperialist League was created in 1929 under Communist leadership, yet gained the membership of personalities like Nehru, Haya de la Torre, and many others, and convened in Berlin a congress of intellectuals called by Romain Rolland, Maxim Gorki, Albert Einstein, and Henri Barbusse. Along with Gorkín, also representing Spain were the Anarchist Orobón Fernández, who lived as an exile in Berlin, and the Socialist Rodolfo Llopis. Unamuno was unable to attend but sent a message. Orobón Fernández was one of the few who dared to dissent, asking about the persecution of the Anarchists and Trotsky in the USSR. Barbusse, who was a friend of Gorkín, ordered him to "expose Orobón." Since he refused to do it Barbusse then asked him to sign a receipt for seventeen Spanish delegates (when there were only seven in the delegation.) Gorkín suspected that it was a trap and refused. He was excluded from the French Communist party shortly thereafter.[15]

The PCE participated in a general strike in Vizcaya in October 1927 and in a mining strike in Asturias in November of the same year. They were sponsored by the UGT which was trying to gradually separate itself from the dictatorship and create an image of opposition. This would reflect the antidictatorial sentiment which was developing among the workers who up to this time had been rather passive. The PCE provided much aid to militants. Although the strike in Asturias lasted forty days it failed in its immediate objectives.[16] The triumvirate's reports to Moscow must have been exaggerated because they received congratulations from the executive committee of the International. Repression caused by the strikes was severe and it was considered a good move to organize a substitute executive committee. The Sevillian Adame first appeared on the scene in this committee. Bullejos had time to visit Pérez Solís, who had already converted but had not yet made it public, but failed in his attempt to reintegrate him into the party.[17] Shortly after, Bullejos was arrested in Madrid where he spent two years in prison.

The Third Congress

When Bullejos was arrested Trilla returned from Moscow to Spain and formed a provisional triumvirate with Adame and Luis Arrarás. *La Antorcha* was closed down. Yet repression continued and it was decided that an executive committee should be formed in Paris. The International determined that it would be composed of Arroyo and two delegates from the French Communist party. This executive committee called the third congress of the PCE which met in Paris in August 1929. Several delegates sent from the interior of the country were arrested crossing the border. The congress elected a new executive committee made up of Bullejos, Trilla, and Adame but, for the time being, leadership remained in the hands of Arroyo and the delegates of the Comintern, especially an Italian named Greco. It was he who insisted on calling the congress because a year earlier in 1928 the sixth congress of the Comintern had met and adopted a new line, the so-called third period (of definitive decomposition of capitalism), and established the tactic of class against class. Part of the new strategy was the theory of social fascism, that is, the accusation that the Socialists (as well as Anarchists wherever there were any) were the predecessors of fascism and the tactics of a united front from below. Moscow wanted all parties to openly acclaim the new line which marked the triumph of Stalin over his opponents in the USSR. The congress in Paris accepted the line without ado, although it expressed a good deal of criticism of Spanish leadership of the party.

The congress was important because it determined the separation of two groups. Maurín and Pedro Bonet, the delegates of the Catalonian-Balearic federation who were leaders of the opposition to "Bullejos and his camp" were rejected by the congress on the pretext that, living in Paris by order of the International, they must stay in the French Communist party and therefore could not be members of the PCE. Maurín later pointed out that "in spite of the fact that the delegations (from Spain) which opposed the leadership fell into the hands of the police 'by chance' and that Bonet and I were not admitted, the congress condemned the policy followed by the troika."[18] The congress nevertheless rejected the thesis of the Catalonian-Balearic federation which favored the PCE's temporary struggle for a Federal Democratic Republic since the congress categorized it as "rightist." It adopted the slogan "Democratic Dictatorship of Workers and Peasants" which, given that a dictatorship existed in Spain, promised two cups of the same broth, even though they might contain different ingredients.

On the other hand the congress led to the crystallization of the position of party members, both in Spain and in exile, who sympathized with Trotsky in the battle over Lenin's succession and who did not agree with the line adopted by the sixth congress of the Comintern. Trotsky's expulsion from the USSR in 1929 facilitated this crystallization since it was now possible to maintain correspondence with him. The strange part is that none of the first Spanish Trotskyites knew him personally except for Andrés Nin. After working for a short while with Bukharin in Moscow, Nin sided with Trotsky, got himself expelled from the Profintern, and for several years was not permitted to leave the USSR where he lived off translations and collaborated in the Trotskyite faction with men who would be influential in the history of the PCE such as Stepanov and Antonov-Ovseenko.[19]

The Troika

The committee of the PCE which remained in Paris was surprised when Primo de Rivera fell from power on January 28, 1930. However, it would not be fair to blame the only Spanish leader who was part of the committee. Actually most of the responsibility fell to the executive of the Comintern who, as on other occasions, was not in a position to understand or appreciate what was going on in Spain. Ignorance of the situation was such that one of the greatest leaders, Manuilski, called the collapse of Primo de Rivera's dictatorship an accident devoid of importance. "Even this—he said in a meeting of the central committee of the Soviet Communist party—is less important than the most insignificant strike in France."[20]

The amnesty of 1930 freed Bullejos who managed to meet in Bilbao with Arroyo who had come from Paris with the Frenchman Claude Rabaté and the German "Federico." Since the delegates of the Comintern and the Spaniards saw things differently they decided to call a national conference. It was called the Conference of Pamplona yet it took place in Dos Caminos near Bilbao in March 1930. Bullejos[21] reported that delegates from all federations attended. Maurín reported that no delegate was sent by the Catalonian-Balearic federation because it considered itself detached from the PCE; he also said that Bullejos credited the delegation to a friend of his. The Catalonian-Balearic federation said that the conference was called hastily, without time to study the agenda and that "it was rigged so that the leading faction would come out on top." He was also sure that they "forgot" to call some members of the central committee and delegates of the Madrid local federation since "the communist organization in Madrid had come out by an overwhelming majority against the factional policy of the executive committee."[22]

The German delegate had written the political theses which stated that Spain was a country with a developed system of capitalism which had entered its third period, the period of decomposition. Bullejos makes no mention of the discussion of these theses, but they were described by the Catalonian-Balearic federation in this way: "The theses presented by the executive committee were discarded. Rejected first and foremost was the division of the trade union movement entailed in the formation of a Unitarian Confederation of Labor." Although the foreign delegates stated over and over that factionalism in the party must be overcome, actually everything possible was done to maintain those in power despite the criticism this engendered. The central committee which had been nominated in the third congress met after the conference, for the first time since its election, to appoint the executive committee. Yet the delegates from Valencia as well as others who opposed the leaders were not invited to the meeting of the central committee. The elected executive committee was made up of Bullejos as secretary general, José Silva as organization secretary, Manuel Adame, union secretary, Vicente Arroyo, secretary of agitation and propaganda, and Trilla, Etelvino Vega, Luis Arrarás, and Jesús Hernández in other secretariats. It was decided that the executive committee would have its headquarters in Madrid. Dolores Ibárruri, the delegate from Vizcaya, was named a member of the central committee.[23] The militants immediately became aware of who really was in charge, and so in keeping with the Russian custom, they spoke of the Bullejos-Trilla-Adame troika. The conference of Pamplona-Bilbao confirmed the separation of the Catalonian-Balearic federation; some prominent members of the federation of Valencia and later the association of Madrid followed suit.

The Conference of Reconstruction

Moscow realized that the PCE had not been completely Bolshevized. It called Bullejos and Arroyo to Berlin, headquarters of the European office of the Comintern and it was there that the Bulgarian Georgi Dimitrov, head of the office, demanded that the decision of the Profintern on trade union policy be honored. Bullejos said that "after considerable discussion which lasted for two days, we reached a settlement which essentially satisfied our position."[24] In the conference in Pamplona-Bilbao the delegates agreed that it was necessary to rebuild the CNT "on a foundation of the most extensive sort of trade union democracy." Yet following the trip to Berlin "it was decided that a union controlled by Communists, a goal which was given to the stevedores of Seville, call of its own initiative a national conference of all unions in favor of rebuilding the CNT". . . . The maneuver had limited results, as it led the local Sevillian CNT federation to expel unions favoring reconstruction and the CNT systematically cast from its ranks anyone who was in agreement with the Communists."[25]

The conference took place in June 1925 in the midst of a strike declared in Seville to protest police aggression against a worker. Adame headed it under Rabaté's supervision. Rabaté was sent by the Profintern which wanted a "unitarian CNT" to be born of the meeting. The Catalonian-Balearic federation sent Arlandis but did not agree with the decisions of the conference. The conference did not dare to create a new national federation, but it formed a National Committee Reconstruction of the CNT so as not to displease Rabaté. In Moscow this committee was considered a federation, member of the Profintern. The Committee of Reconstruction presented itself as the true CNT because, according to a declaration of the Profintern, "it represents for the workers the only center of leadership where power emanates from the workers themselves and therefore the only center authorized to speak in the name of the CNT. The Pestañas, Peirós, and company, leaders by the grace of the so-called anarchistic CNT, are nothing more than representatives of the Spanish bourgeoisie of which they form one of the detachments against the working classes."[26]

The Separations

Perhaps to console themselves after this defeat, the troika decided to expel Maurín and the Catalonian-Balearic federation. Maurín had returned from Paris and once again began publication of *La Batalla*. The troika demanded his public self-criticism but he refused. The federation solidified around him and found itself automatically out of the party. But Maurín kept sending his reports to Moscow; he had not lost hope that the Comintern would bring order to the PCE. Moscow did not confirm the expulsion (for the sake of "liberalism" and "Menshevism") until July 1931 when the federation had already merged with a Partit Comunista Català (Catalonian Communist party) secretly founded in 1928 by Joan Farré, Jordi Arquer, and others, and which never became a member of the International. Nonetheless according to Portela Arquer was in Paris negotiating affiliation with the Comintern which was rejected because Moscow believed that there ought to be only one party per nation and that the nation should be independent in order to have its own Communist party. The product of this merger, formalized in March 1931, was the Bloc Obrer i Camperol (BOC) of which Joaquín Maurín was secretary general.[27]

Meanwhile in August 1930 the weekly *Mundo Obrero* had begun publication as the party organ, even though it was subtitled "organ of the workers and peasants." Appearing in the September 13, 1930 issue was the following: "Comrades who still believe that those individuals [the ones involved in *La Batalla*] have something in common with the Communist party must have convinced themselves that they have nothing in common with us and the International. . . . They are following an utterly right-wing and conciliatory policy; the very policy all Trotskyites are currently following."

Mimicry of Moscow was evident. There could still be active Trotskyite nuclei in the USSR but they did not exist in Spain although there were militants in the Communist party who sympathized with Trotsky in his battle against Stalin. The first Trotskyite nucleus was organized in exile by a Spanish worker from Brussels, Francisco García Lavid, who had been exiled in the USSR and who began writing articles in the Trotskyite *La Verité* of Paris about the situation in Spain. He signed his articles

Lacroix (the name he continued to use after returning to Spain following the amnesty of 1930). Berenguer, Juan Andrade, and Luis García Palacios, all from Madrid, José Loredo Aparicio, from Asturias, and Esteban Bilbao, from the Basque country, began to consider themselves Trotskyites. On February 28, 1930 Lacroix organized in Liège, Belgium the first National Conference of Spanish Communist Opposition. In keeping with Trotskyite tactics of the time, it was not a matter of leaving the party but rather of remaining in it, coordinating action against the Stalinist leadership and changing the party from within.[28]

The only place where the few Trotskyites that existed were able to accomplish anything at all, thanks to the fact that their criticism of the troika was echoed by other Communists, was in the Communist Association of Madrid, which on several occasions supported the Catalonian-Balearic federation and jointly signed with them declarations and protests. In July 1930 the association held a secret assembly at the Dehesa de la Villa. Adame was present on behalf of the executive committee and they called him to account for the economic situation of the party, which he refused to do. There was harsh criticism of the executive committee and its behavior, and in August the executive committee dissolved the association's committee. The one hundred members of the association supported its committee and expelled two members of the executive committee who formed part of the association. Then the executive committee expelled the association and created a new one. The association was confident that the executive committee would be displaced either by Moscow or a congress, but as time went on and this did not happen, many of its members went from tactical to strategic criticism and related the policy of the executive committee to the International. They were following in the footsteps of the Catalonian-Balearic federation. The association rejected the executive committee's charge of being Trotskyite. Gradually, however, the attraction of the executive committee and its "official" nature had an effect on some of the less seasoned members and when the executive committee made an offer of individual reentry it was accepted by some. The association dissolved itself in December 1931.

The federation of Valencia sided with its Catalonian-Balearic counterpart and went so far as to sign a declaration which it worked out in conjunction with the association in Madrid, but the executive committee managed to have the protesters defeated in a secret assembly toward the middle of 1930. There were also expulsions in Asturias and elsewhere. Meanwhile the masses on the streets were full of hope, the unions were reorganizing themselves, students were protesting, parties were forming and merging, militants were agitating, soldiers revolted in Jaca, and there were general strikes throughout the country. But the party was concentrating on those internal disputes. The party propaganda did not reach beyond militants and some sympathizers, it was held in contempt in workers' political circles, and it passed unnoticed in Republican circles.[29] When the Socialists came out in favor of the Republic, the Communists, following the tactic of social fascism, accused them of selling out to the bourgeoisie. When the workers called for unity, the party, on Moscow's suggestion, considered organizing a new trade union federation.

All this expense of energy and insults, stratagems, dismissals, expulsions, replacements, and meetings, the coming and going of delegates—all of this took place in a closed little world scarcely made up of 500 people. The Catalonian-Balearic federation concluded: "The decay of the military dictatorship which could be traced step by step all during the previous year caught unawares the leaders of the PCE who acted as if they had just seen a ghost, astonished that something like that could have actually happened. Neither during the weeks which preceded the fall of Primo de Rivera nor during those which followed was our party anywhere to be seen. Arroyo, the party's secretary, in a political article published in the official [Communist] press, maintained that Primo de Rivera's replacement by Berenguer was of no importance. . . . This political blindness on the part of the leading faction pushed the party to the brink of suicide."[30]

At that time the "instructor" of the Communist International summed up the situation of the party in this way:

> National leadership, made up of five members, lived and worked in secrecy with help from a few militants and with exasperating sluggishness. The number of party members in Barcelona was theoretically placed at forty. But I only saw a dozen. It was the first time I had to start up a nonexistent party. . . . Our party continues to live in absolute passivity without daring to go out into the light of day. . . . The number of members in Madrid increased four-fold and in Barcelona five-fold, but to start out with, there were only twenty in Madrid and ten in Barcelona. In Bilbao there were fourteen members. . . . Since our branch is utterly detached from the world of politics and labor, one remains unaware of what is happening, even within the city itself. Thanks to *Berliner Tageblatt* we learned of the strike at the university.[31]

Notes

1. In the International's fifth congress which Pérez Solís attended as delegate of the PCE, a refugee in Moscow, and appointee to the executive committee of the Comintern, Lenin (who had died in 1924) was praised with these words which became the basis of the campaign of Bolshevization which

Zinoviev had initiated: "The loss has incited the Communist parties to arm themselves with the powerful weapon of Leninism, it has helped to present the problem of Bolshevization on a large scale, and it has given a new impulse to the fight for unity and homogeneity among the Communist ranks." In addition Bolshevization established that a certain percentage, indeed a majority, of leaders should be from blue-collar backgrounds, and it also set up organizations by cells. There were some in the PCE who were at odds with these two conditions, believing that everyone within the party ought to be equal regardless of social background, and that cells were not preferable—at least in situations of legality—to assemblies (Andrade, loc. cit.).

2. Bullejos, p. 59. Maurín in a conversation with the author in New York in September 1972. Portela says that Bullejos had gone to Paris with a passport because the police gave him the option of either leaving or spending his life in prison. Because he was crippled and spoke no French, it was difficult for him to find work in France and for this reason his friends in Paris decided to send him as a refugee to Moscow.

3. Bullejos, p. 61. Bullejos proposed sending Nin to strengthen the PCE. The commission refused because Nin was under investigation for having written "Trotskyite" letters to friends of his in France. As can be seen, Bolshevization implied censorship of correspondence. Gorkín said he did not take part in that commission (Bonamusa, *El Bloc Obrer y Camperol, 1930–1932,* Barcelona, 1974, p. 23).

4. "Gabriel León Trilla was a young intellectual who joined Bullejos's corps of leaders as secretary of agitation. Son of a coronel, he studied in Valladolid and Madrid earning a degree in humanities. In 1921 he emigrated to France to avoid being sent to fight in Morocco. In Paris, together with Gorkín and Portela, he was the strength behind the Spanish Communist group. He was a Trotskyite sympathizer and even later when he recognized his "error" was never able to overcome the stigma (Maurín, *Revolución y contrarre-volución en España,* p. 277). Portela says that Trilla went to Africa in 1921. He served in the Quartermaster Corps and while on leave deserted and went to Paris where in 1924 he began to work as a functionary in the French Communist party, taking charge of the secretariat of the Spanish Communist groups in France.

5. Pelai Pagés, *Andreu Nin: su evolución política, 1911–1937,* p. 117. Portela gives a rather different version. He says that the executive committee appointed in Moscow was composed of Bullejos, Ibáñez, and Nin. Nin went to Paris where he was arrested scarcely a month after his arrival and was deported. Bullejos proposed Portela as his replacement. "Ibáñez was sent to Moscow because of his personal behavior, which nearly caused a serious incident with a militant in the French Communist party who had lent us his home to serve as party office and Bullejos's residence." Bullejos nominated Trilla as his replacement, but the French Communist party vetoed him, "and it only gave in when I promised to see to it that there would not be any attempt to fractionalize from within party leadership."

6. "Manifiesto del Comité Regional de la Federación Comunista Catalano-Balear y de la Agrupación Comunista de Madrid," *La Batalla,* Barcelona, September 19, 1930.

7. *Macià, La seva actuació a l'estranger*, vol. II, pp. 63-65. To Moscow Bullejos reported that there was only a slight chance for success for insurrection in Spain. The trip was a result of the establishment among exiles in Paris of a committee made up of the Estat Català, the CNT, and the PCE. In his above-mentioned visit to Paris, it was Nin's responsibility to have a manifesto for a single front signed by this committee. Vidiella, who at the time was the CNT's delegate on the committee, saw the first draft which he found to be "a true reflection of Bolshevik literature." Nin's arrest prevented the document from being signed. The CNT withdrew shortly after from the committee, which was dissolved because they believed it to be manipulated by the PCE. Portela said that negotiations with Macià and Vidiella "took place after Nin's expulsion from France. Vidiella did not tell the truth" (Rafael Vidiella, *De París a la cárcel de Madrid*, Barcelona, 1932, pp. 72-73).

8. Pelai Pagés, *El movimiento trotskista en España, 1930-1935*, Barcelona, 1977, p. 19. The June 18, October 22, and November 5, 1926 issues of *La Antorcha* list these expulsions, which are always flavored with insults and unfavorable epithets.

9. Pagés, p. 19.

10. Bonamusa, pp. 24-25.

11. Pagés, pp. 19-20.

12. "Resolución del CE contra la política de destrucción de la derecha y por el establecimiento de la disciplina en el Partido," *La Antorcha*, Madrid, February 12, 1926.

13. Bullejos, p. 76 ff. Portela said that "the meeting of the central committee took place in Bordeaux in December 1925. There was no disagreement in the executive committee; we had essentially done nothing but begin to reorganize the party. Yet without a doubt there would have been discord at a later date. Returning from a trip to Madrid which I took in November to negotiate with some officers who were conspiring against the dictatorship, namely Galán, Perea, and Jesús Rubio, I faced an overwhelming list of charges. I was being accused of every sort of misdeed and crime: negligence, incompetence, inefficiency . . . you name it. The perpetrator of the deceit was Trilla and Bullejos was his accomplice (Trilla exercised considerable yet negative influence over Bullejos). González Canet was public prosecutor in the trial. As a matter of fact that central committee had no choice but to politically execute me. Canet replaced me, but for just a short while. From that point on I broke off all relations with the Spanish Communist party even though I did continue to militate in the French Communist party until my return to Spain in 1931.

"The party did not participate in the so-called conspiracy of the evening of Saint John, but it did take part in planning the military uprising which Galán and Perea were preparing for November 1925. These officers had asked for the party's cooperation through Andrade with whom they had been put in contact by friends of theirs in the Ateneo. The project was abandoned because they were becoming discouraged. . . . I believe that after my return to Paris contacts between conspiring officers and the party had pretty much disintegrated."

14. Bullejos, p. 76 ff. The *Historia del PCE* does not make the slightest reference to this stance taken by Moscow. Portela disagreed with those who attributed

this position of the Comintern to the sale of Russian oil to Spain. He said: "The International tried to mechanically put into effect in Spain the policy which the Bolshevik party had adopted under Czarism in which it had some of its militants elected to the Duma. This was the same policy it imposed on the Italian Communist party. The International played this card for all it was worth. Valetzky called me in Paris and we had a long interview. The International was aware of my position regarding the Spanish Communist party with which I had broken off all relations. People must have thought that this would lead me to support the International's position. But Bullejos and I were in complete agreement about this. The International believed, of course, that the worker representatives in the National Assembly would be named by a vote of the members of its organizations. I, for one, never believed it. But I think that this posture of the International has nothing to do with the oil supplies to CAMPSA. The creation of CAMPSA did not please the large companies which dominated the petroleum market. Their response was to boycott oil supplies to Spain. The dictatorship was forced to purchase oil from whomever would sell it. . . . The Russians always separated politics from business."

15. Gorkín, *El revolucionario profesional,* pp. 259–61.
16. Around this time after the student strike of March 1929 a boy who in time would be important in the history of the PCE made his first appearance. He was Santiago Carrillo. In *Aurora Social,* the Socialist weekly from Oviedo (November 1 and 29, 1929 issues), Carrillo wrote two articles advocating the formation of a socialist student group whose members, he said, must belong simultaneously to the FJS and some union (David Ruiz, "Escritos juveniles de Santiago Carrillo," *Historia 16,* Madrid, July 1977).
17. Bullejos, p. 89.
18. Joaquín Maurín, "A propósito de mi exclusión del Partido Comunista," *La Batalla,* Barcelona, August 13, 1931. In this article Maurín says that the leaders were deposed "even though months later the International would reappoint them all." Actually they were not removed from office but rather replaced by Arroyo while Bullejos and Arrarás were in prison.
19. For more information on the third congress see Alba, *El marxisme a Catalunya,* vol I, p. 41 ff., and Bullejos, p. 91 ff. The *Historia del PCE* also devoted a few lines to the subject (p. 48). After saying that the third congress considered "the nature of the revolution being waged in Spain as democratic-bourgeois," he points out that the congress agreed that it was urgent "to strengthen discipline in its ranks." He does not indicate that Dolores Ibárruri was a delegate to the congress; she could not get across the border as she herself mentions in her memoirs (p. 104).
20. Bullejos, p. 97.
21. Bullejos, p. 98.
22. A document of the Catalonian-Balearic federation and the communist association of Madrid, cited in Bonamusa, pp. 29–30.
23. Bullejos, pp. 99–100. A curious anecdote shows how blindly instructions were carried out: "While Bullejos says that it was the delegates from the Communist International who maintained the capitalist nature of Spanish society, and consequently the perspective of a socialist and not a democratic-bourgeois revolution, the editing staff of *Historia del PCE* says just the opposite: [Bullejos and Trilla] rejected the bourgeois stage of the revolution

106 The Communist Party in Spain

and identified the crisis of the monarchic regime with the crisis of the capitalist system. At any rate the resolution made in the conference continued to be orthodox: the democratic and bourgeois nature of the Spanish revolution was reaffirmed, as was the proletariat's role of leadership, etc" (Estruch, p. 57).

24. Bullejos, p. 100.
25. Miguel Artola, *Partidos y programas políticos, 1808–1936*, Madrid, 1974, vol. I, pp. 592–93.
26. Quoted by Estruch, p. 62.
27. About this episode *Historia del PCE* says (p. 53): "In Catalonia Maurín used foul play to win over part of the Catalonian-Balearic Communist Federation. This upheaval had painful consequences for the development of the party in Catalonia even though, despite the temporary setback, a nucleus of staunch militants reorganized the ranks of the party." Actually this nucleus was composed of no more than 50 people. There are two interesting quotes on the federation's separation in Estruch, appendix IX.
28. Pelai Pagés, *El movimiento trotskista en España*, pp. 22, 42. The *Historia del PCE* in reference to this says (p. 50): "In addition to this offensive on the part of police [by the general director of security Emilio Mola, not specifically against Communists but rather all 'subversive elements'], there was the attack of the Trotskyites on party unity. . . . In Spain, the Trotskyites opened fire on the party's policy on all fundamental problems of the revolution in an attempt to control party leadership and to carry out their counterrevolutionary goals."
29. Not even the police had a clear idea of what the PCE was or what it did. This comes to light in a fantastic story which General Emilio Mola tells (*Lo que yo supe*, Valladolid, 1940, pp. 263–64) about an alleged international Communist conspiracy to set up "the regime established in the USSR" in Spain.
30. "A las Federaciones Regionales del PCE," *La Batalla*, September 19, 1930.
31. Humbert-Droz, *De Lénine à Staline*, Neuchâtel, 1971, pp. 403, 457.

8.
Down with the Bourgeois Republic!

The years of the dictatorship were the PCE's infancy. They were spent in rivalries, quarrels, and stratagems without having any impact on events and, more seriously, without providing an understanding of the situation in Spain. The years of the Republic were just as sterile from the point of view of influence and doctrine. Moscow viewed life in Spain with blinders and consequently the PCE was out of touch with it. But when the "Dictablanda"[1] began, which was a period of transition, the party was already completely Bolshevized. Those who did not give in were expelled or simply left. The troika reigned over the 500 members the party had when the dictatorship collapsed.

The Wasteland of the "Dictablanda"

Moscow finally seemed to realize that something was going on in Spain but things had changed in Moscow by then. Nin was no longer in the Profintern and he was finally allowed to leave Russia. Humbert-Droz had lost favor and had been replaced by the Russian-Bulgarian Stepanov. In spite of everything Spain continued to be of only marginal interest for Moscow as shown by the fact that they decided to send once again Humbert-Droz as "instructor" for the Profintern in the same way that someone gets retired with a good pension because he is no longer in favor.[2] But prior to his arrival in Barcelona where he took up residence in December of 1930 the Comintern had sent to Spain the Frenchman Jacques Duclos who was later joined by the Swiss Edgard Woog, who went by the name of Stirner and who was a functionary in the International. Duclos spent two years at the top of the delegation of the Comintern assisted by Rabaté even though he lived most of the time in Paris where he performed his duties as leader of the French Communist party.

The mission of the delegates of the International primarily involved making sure the Comintern's line and decisions were strictly applied. It was up to Duclos to see to it that the PCE followed the line of class against class which had been adopted by the congress of Moscow in 1928. He was required to do this at a time when the monarchy was on

107

shaky foundation, when Socialists, Republicans, and even Anarcho-Syndicalists as well as those associated with *La Batalla* were jointly signing manifestos and were at the time allying with one another. The Pact of San Sebastián (among Republicans and Catalonian nationalists) and the formation of the Comité Revolucionario (of Republicans and Socialists) were fruits of popular pressure to unite all antidynastic forces. The PCE had no part in all this because its policy of class against class kept it isolated from the people's desires and the political reality of the time. Even though the PCE was still illegal, it could move with relative ease although later on the Communist leaders pretended to be victims of a special repression which actually did not exist.[3]

The arrest in the fall of 1930 of Bullejos and other leaders left the party at the mercy of the international delegation. Trilla, the only one who was free, was threatened with having to join the army for being a deserter, which was why he had been sent to Moscow as representative of the PCE in the Comintern. So there was not a single leader of prominence left to head the party. The effect of Bolshevization was clear: it tended to promote men of mediocre quality and thereby undermined the formation of strong personalities among the rank and file. Moscow did not allow the PCE to have alliances or contacts with other forces, particularly not with the Socialists. It is true that some Communists took action on their own regarding the circumstances.[4] For example Ramón Martínez Pinillos helped his friend Fermín Galán in preparing his unsuccessful "coup" of December 1930. But nowhere in any of the manifestos of the period does there appear the signature of any Communist.

At the beginning of 1931 there were no fewer than four "instructors": Humbert-Droz, Rabaté, Stirner, and a recent arrival, Pierre. "Overstepping their authority, they—Humbert-Droz in particular—usurped the responsibilities which corresponded to the party's Politburo and acted in its name."[5] They transferred their headquarters to Barcelona, doubtless in an attempt to counteract on the spot the BOC which was in the process of being formed and which already had more members than the PCE. Moscow thought that the failure of the "revolution of December 1930" (the revolt in Jaca of Galán) saved the monarchy and that the PCE ought to prepare itself for a period of political stability. But every Spaniard realized that what happened in December simply precipitated the collapse of the monarchy.

The delegation of the Comintern's error in perspective could have had serious consequences when the Berenguer government decided to call legislative elections in February 1931. The opposition which included the liberal monarchists decided to abstain from participating. The delegation of the Communist International decided that the PCE ought to take advantage of the elections and even began to make up lists of candidates. Humbert-Droz wrote to Moscow about it: "The party's executive committee received from Bullejos (still in prison in Madrid) a political letter signed also by Arroyo and Vega in which Bullejos came out against the party's tactic regarding the elections. He says that the situation here is close to revolutionary, that the party's main duty is to foment armed insurrection and that consequently the party ought to declare, as did the Republicans and reformists, electoral abstention. He attacks the party's leaders for having decided upon a tactic without first calling a party conference."[6]

Bullejos wrote to Moscow, which he was entitled to do since he was a member of the executive committee of the Comintern, and that exempted him from having to follow "prescribed procedure," that is, going through the delegation of the Communist International in Spain. And the executive committee of the Comintern decided that the PCE would not participate in the elections. It was already known by then that all the democratic opposition would abstain. Berenguer had to resign. His replacement, Admiral Juan Aznar, decided to call municipal elections in hopes that they would not be politicized. In the midst of the electoral campaign, when the country was thoroughly caught up with politics, it occurred to the PCE to organize a campaign of protest against unemployment. Only in Seville were they able to carry off a demonstration. The unemployed hoped for and were confident of the establishment of the Republic. The PCE could not understand this nor could the two remaining delegates, Humbert-Droz and Rabaté (meanwhile Pierre had been sent to Latin America and Stirner was expelled by the police).

When the entire country was in favor of the Republic and saw it as the solution to its problems, the PCE's position could be summed up in the words of an article of the weekly journal launched by Humbert-Droz, *Heraldo Obrero,* of Barcelona, published in the March 14, 1931 issue (exactly one month prior to the proclamation of the Republic) and written by the "instructor" of the International as was most of the weekly:

> The Communists are against the Republican movement, denouncing it as a trick on the working class and exhorting workers and peasants to fight for their own worker and peasant republic out of their own class interests. For this reason there cannot be any alliances or commitments between us and the Republicans. In spite of their fight against the monarchy and the country's most reactionary forces, the bourgeois Republicans stand next to the monarchy, on the other side of the barricade in the camp of the exploiters when it comes to combating the workers. They are the enemies

of the proletariat, its most dangerous enemy, because they sow democratic dreams in their rank and file and thereby divert the workers' movement from its struggle for its own interests and class goals in order for it to serve the interests of the bourgeoisie.

When Bullejos et alii were released from jail shortly before the municipal elections, leadership returned to Madrid. The PCE presented its own candidacy without any alliances. "No compromises!" was the slogan. There were a few electoral rallies, and the Republic's proclamation on April 14 "found the party leaders divided and scattered in Barcelona, Seville, and Bilbao."[7]

At the time the PCE had 800 members, 300 more than when the dictatorship had collapsed. It was a period when parties were growing rapidly, when the CNT would again exceed the membership it had in 1919, and the UGT and PSOE tripled its membership.[8]

All Power to the Soviets

To what extent did the PCE respect the rule of "no compromise" during the electoral campaign? According to Bullejos it was unanimously observed and in Seville, Bilbao, and Oviedo Communists were not allowed to become candidates in Republican and Socialist lists. The *Historia del PCE* nonetheless states that "some regional committees, including those of Euzkadi and Andalusia, did not agree with the tactic adopted by the executive committee. In Seville, Málaga, and other places Communists managed to establish electoral pacts with other parties."[9] It is not known for sure how many votes the candidates of the PCE mustered. In Madrid there were some 200 votes, slightly over 1,000 in Seville, and some Communist candidates running for city council were voted in in Vizcaya and Asturias.[10]

It was apparent on election eve that something important was going to happen. The Republicans were the only ones not sure of victory as proved by Azaña's statement to a French journalist: "It would be naive to hope for anything from the elections." The PCE's executive committee apparently was not that naive and it had a plan which was revealed in a report by Humbert-Droz in which he said that Bullejos and his comrades "recognized that their tactic of actively boycotting the elections and their proposal to call for immediate insurrection were erroneous and that the party's tactic (that is, the one imposed by Moscow) was the only correct one."[11]

The delegate from the Comintern made the following comments about the outcome of the campaign: "The municipal elections revealed the extreme weakness of the party, its complete isolation, and the little influence it had on the masses. . . . We were forced to admit that we were indulging in wishful thinking and that we do not have the influence we thought we had. . . . [In Barcelona] we did not even get 100 votes, while the supporters of Maurín, whose propaganda was much more intense than ours, gathered more than 3,000."[12]

So how can there be armed insurrection? With whom and with what? In this case the International stopped the Communists from making fools of themselves. But when the Republic was proclaimed, instead of stopping them, it ordered them to go out into the streets in a truck covered with red flags only to have the whole city of Madrid boo at them. The truck carried a picture of Lenin and slogans like "All the power to the soviets!" "Government of workers and peasants"; and "Down with the bourgeois republic!" at a time when few people in the country knew what soviets were, when there was not, of course, a single soviet, and when what the people wanted was all power for the Republic. So it was logical that "the reception we received from Republican groups which protected the Palacio de Oriente (royal palace) where a demonstration of 100 or so Communists (with Bullejos, Etelvino Vega, and Jesús Hernández) was headed, was decidedly hostile to our demands and slogans. This attitude lasted several days provoking attacks on our Communist flags, propaganda posters, and newspapers. In those days we were totally isolated. Nevertheless we did not change our position nor did we modify the tone of the propaganda. We took pride in sailing against the current."

The delegate from the Comintern reported: "You have to take into account this atmosphere of a folk festival in order to understand the phenomenon which resulted: the Communists who tried to organize demonstrations, hand out manifestos, or speak to the crowds met with catcalls and threats."[13] The attitude persisted until May 1. On that day the Communists organized their own separate demonstrations in Seville, Madrid, Oviedo, Bilbao, and Barcelona. They were successful only in Seville. Every Communist meeting "approved with acclaim" the following demands: diplomatic recognition of the USSR, a minimum salary of 10 pesetas, 75 percent subsidization of the daily minimum wage for all those who were laid off, abolition of the monarchy's law on public order, prohibition of governmental arrest, disarmament of the police, a government of workers and peasants, the right of Catalonia and the Basque country to self-rule, and the evacuation of Morocco.[14]

The Instructions of May 1931

Trilla returned from Moscow with new instructions from the Comintern as well as with the order for Bullejos and Adame to go to Moscow. Humbert-Droz was already in the Russian capital. When Bullejos undertook the trip, the PCE was being accused by both Monarchists and Republicans of being responsible for the events of May 10 in Madrid and other cities when people, indignant over demonstrations on the part of Monarchists, began to burn convents. The executive committee of the PCE published a manifesto when it learned what was going on. It was written the day after Bullejos and Adame's departure. It read: "Workers of Madrid! The contemptible behavior of the government of the republic, its benevolence and weakness have allowed bands of monarchist gunmen . . . to again commit their outrages and crimes against the people. Once again the government of the republic has used the odious civil guard to gun down the people who wanted to and still want to carry out justice with their own hands. This repression has led the people of Madrid to mass action in an attempt to impose revolutionary justice. The Communists enthusiastically welcome this virile behavior on the part of workers from Madrid."[15]

In Moscow Bullejos discovered that Spain had suddenly assumed a position of prime importance. Since all hope was lost for Germany and France, Spain "might be the long-awaited prologue of the 'third period' which had been announced three years before in the sixth congress [of the Communist International]." The Spanish delegates met for several days with a group formed by Manuilski, Kuusinen, Piatnisky, Martynov, Losovsky, and Stepanov representing the executive committee of the International, and by Togliatti from Italy, Pieck from Germany, Bela Kun from Hungary, and Thorez from France. While Martynov affirmed that Spain was going through a democratic-bourgeois revolution, the others believed that things were similar to the way they were in Russia in February 1917 and, for that reason, complete power should be asked for the soviets as well as the formation of a worker and peasant government. The group criticized the PCE saying: "The party . . . should have called the Socialist, Anarchist, and Republican workers to form a vast united front of workers to build the soviets and a revolutionary tribunal under its leadership as well as factory councils, and a worker and peasant militia to fight against the return of the monarchy, etc."[16]

Bullejos summed up the new stance saying: "In the immediate future the Communist party ought to devote itself above all to prolonging by all means available the crisis caused by the collapse of the monarchy and thereby prevent the Republican regime from stabilizing in its original form, since that would stop the revolution from continuing and radicalizing its goals. Therefore it was necessary to intensify and multiply the social struggles at once, giving them fundamental political objectives such as the establishment of soviets and the creation of workers' militias." On the way back to Madrid the delegates received some written instructions from the Comintern: "The Communist party should under no circumstances make pacts or alliances even of a temporary nature with other political forces. . . . In no way should it defend or support the Republican government."[17]

The Militants and *Mundo Obrero*

"From the outset the position of the Communists was one of unveiled opposition to the provisional government of the republic. . . . The strength of the Communist party at the time was very weakened given the fact that it barely had 3,000 members. The strength of its unions which had fallen off noticeably in Vizcaya was negligible outside of Seville. In Madrid there were a hundred or so militants, poorly organized and with deficient political training. In spite of everything, the policy drawn up in Moscow advocated causing and maintaining a state of permanent agitation, utilizing all kinds of opportunities to develop the revolution."[18]

Bullejos was exaggerating. The International estimates that the strength of the Communists rested on the efforts of 800 militants. Whatever their number was, those militants were astonishingly tenacious, fervent, and fanatical. Since the bulk of the working class was already incorporated in the PSOE, CNT, FAI, BOC, or the UGT, there was not much room left for the PCE to make an impression. Therefore, and because of the nature of its propaganda which seemed to attract the impatient, the resentful, the frustrated, or temperamentally fanatic in particular, the PCE made a particular impression among marginal strata of the working class, people lacking political experience who were awakened by the Republic and who therefore tended to act with the ardor of a neophyte and let themselves be led—indeed they wanted to be led—without ever discussing the orientation of those who led them.

So the PCE was a party with a lot of turnover. The phenomenon would be repeated several times in its history. I say this without intending to be pejorative—yet it must be said—since nonpoliticized workers have the same right (and perhaps even a greater right) as others to become politicized and organize. But what happened, on this occasion and on future occasions, was that they were politicized and organized, that is, the initiative did not come from them but rather from the PCE in accordance with the Leninist conception of party role.

When one speaks of the Communist party, in Spain or elsewhere, one must always distinguish between rank and file and its leaders. The leaders are trained, informed, and oriented. Nothing escapes them, not even the half-truths of propaganda or the consequences of their orders; nor are they unaware of their rivals for power within the party, power which means also a salary. The rank and file, on the other hand, are more naive. Politically they receive only that information which its leaders feed it, nor do they desire more since any other information coming from outside the party is seen, by definition, as false and biased. Those neophytes (the majority of them were such in the literal sense of the word in Spain of 1931) showed themselves able to endure solitude, of being capable of "swallowing snakes," and of being able to put up with rejection from other workers. This can only be explained by the combination of their political inexperience and, as a result, their image of themselves as a select group which holds the truth (the "right line") and "knows" that the future belongs to it. In Spain that small corps of militants had to make considerable sacrifices because their policies not only isolated them but also forced them to get involved in every instance of political agitation and action and therefore made them the target of constant repression.

Whether it was to keep intact enthusiasm among the neophytes or to avoid rubbing their own militants the wrong way, the central committee of the PCE, in receipt of the above-mentioned letter from the Comintern, neither published it nor circulated it among its militants. Carrying out those orders from Moscow required much effort and sacrifice on the part of the militants. Time, money, imprisonment, fighting, ridicule from fellow workers, and loneliness were the daily bread of the Communists. More than anything else, they were constantly being asked for money— for various reasons: giving builds loyalty, it reinforced in the rank and file the false feeling of being the party's owners, it covered the International's subsidies, and these subsidies were not large enough to be able to scoff at the nickels and dimes of the workers.

One leader of the Juventudes Comunistas at the time provided some figures on the "Moscow gold" of the period. These are the only statistics available during the entire history of the PCE. The following amounts in pesetas arrived monthly from Russia helping to fill the gaps in dues, subscriptions, and donations from militants and sympathizers to cover the cost of rent, propaganda, and the salaries of "full-time leaders" such as members of the executive committee, some secretaries of fairly important local or regional committees, but not the salaries or expenses of the Comintern's "instructors" which were paid by the Comintern:

Communist International, for the party	12,000
Profintern, for the Communist trade union movement	10,000
Communist Youth International, for the	
Spanish Communist Youth	5,000
International Red Aid, for the Spanish section	5,000
International Workers' Aid, for the Spanish section	2,000
Red Sports International, for the Workers'	
Sports and Cultural Federation	1,000
Press section of the Communist International,	
for the party newspaper	10,000
Total	45,000[19]

One of the greatest efforts required of the militants was conversion of the weekly *Mundo Obrero* into a daily. Subscriptions were taken in neighborhoods and in plants, wages were contributed, and collections were taken in meetings and on the streets. One naive militant received modest contributions from the Socialist Fernando de los Ríos and Bugallal, the Monarchic ex-minister. When the local committee of Madrid saw those names on the list of donors, it returned every cent and made it public in *Mundo Obrero*.[20]

Seventy thousand pesetas were collected. Although at the time it was relatively easy to start a four- to six-page journal such as *Mundo Obrero*, that amount was of course not sufficient. Up to 1935 *Mundo Obrero* never printed more than ten thousand copies of which scarcely half were sold. It always ran on a deficit which was covered by contributions and subscriptions from militants (each of whom had to buy two copies in order to give one away). Yet *Mundo Obrero* was an artificial creation.

"The Socialist party needed several decades before it could transform its weekly into a daily. One recalls with admiration the days when the daily *El Socialista* was a two-page publication. The CNT was able to transform the weekly *Solidaridad Obrera* into a daily only after the great syndicalist avalanche of 1916–17. The Communist party of Spain with a couple thousand members published its daily without any difficulty. It is evident that *Mundo Obrero* was sustained, just as was the party's bureaucratic machinery, by funds supplied by Moscow. *Mundo Obrero*, edited underhand by the Peruvian journalist César Falcón, was the Spanish edition of *Pravda*."[21]

The paper's first issue was printed on November 14, 1931. It had a proxy editor, Manuel Santana, who would go to jail if the paper were prosecuted (a procedure which a lot of leftist papers had followed in the past). The real editor was José Silva, from the executive committee, who was soon replaced by Manuel Navarro Ballesteros. The staff were Miguel González, Vicente Arroyo, Ceferino R. Avecilla, the cartoonist Helios Gómez, Dolores Ibárruri, Enrique Matorras, and Ángel Pumarega. Among the regular contributors were Francisco Galán, who wrote as KAS, José Díaz, Manuel Adame, and Etelvino Vega. Fernando Antón was the business manager. The daily operated out of no. 8 Concepción Jerónima Street, Madrid. *Juventud Roja,* the organ of Juventudes Comunistas, under the editorship of Etelvino Vega, was also published.[22]

The militants' economic endeavors did not stop here. They also had to support the International Workers' Aid as well as the International Red Aid (eventually the former was abandoned). The lawyer for Red Aid was the Radical Socialist representative José Antonio Balbontín. Isidoro Acevedo was its president, and its organ was *¡Ayuda!* The Society of Friends of the Soviet Union was self-supporting or received direct assistance from Moscow according to circumstances. As in many countries, figuring among its sponsors were well-known intellectuals such as Joaquín Arderius, Ramón del Valle-Inclán, Roberto Novoa Santos, Victorio Macho, Ricardo Baroja, Luis de Tapia, José Díaz Fernández, and others. Among them were the men who in 1930–31 published a biweekly journal called *Nueva España,* edited by Antonio Espina, which welcomed a great deal of Soviet propaganda. But for the time being the number of intellectuals attracted by the PCE was minuscule.

The Elections of 1931

Election campaigns were another of the militants' considerable responsibilities. The party viewed elections as a means of propaganda and knew it would not be able to come up with a candidate who could win. It took advantage of the campaigns by distributing manifestos, holding meetings, and putting up posters. All this was done and paid for by the militants, although the expenses were always greater than the party's resources and it was necessary to fall back on supplementary assistance from Moscow.

Up to 1936, the elections proved disappointing. The militants swallowed hook, line, and sinker what they read in the party press about its progress and triumphs, yet when the votes were tallied, there were fewer than even the most pessimistic would have expected. The disparity between reality and propaganda never was so apparent as at election time.

The republic's first parliamentary elections for the Constituent Assembly on June 28, 1931 must have shown the Comintern just how disoriented it was. In spite of an intense campaign which gave the impression that the PCE was much more important than it actually was, and participation in many events of the French Communist representatives Jacques Duclos and André Marty (who shortly before the elections were expelled from Spain by the police), 60,000 votes were culled in all of Spain, although party sources said that there were 190,000 (from almost 4 million voters).[23]

In Madrid, in addition to the official list of PCE candidates, which received 2,700 votes, there was a list headed by Joaquín Maurín and put forward by the Communist group of Madrid which continued to rebel against the political executive committee and collaborated with the Catalonian-Balearic Federation. It received 800 votes.[24] Bullejos and Adame headed the PCE's list of candidates in Madrid.[25] In Barcelona the PCE culled 312 votes and Maurín's Bloque Obrero y Campesino (BOC, Bloc of Workers and Peasants) received 1,250. What was written about the French Communist party can be applied to its Spanish counterpart of the time:

Once it was judged that the party had reached a certain degree of Bolshevization, it underwent merciless gymastics. Always on Moscow's orders, the leadership unleashed constant "mass action." For—or without—any reason whatsoever, and under favorable or unfavorable conditions, they fomented strikes and movements which were almost always destined to failure. . . . They tried to maintain a constant state of agitation and, at the same time, to select and put to test both the higher-ups and the rank and file. Employers seemed delighted with this tactic, for, thanks to it, they were able to discover members of the cells—and their sympathizers—and fire them. In this way the most active and disciplined cells were nearly destroyed. And some thousand militants temporarily lost their livelihood. Many of them became skeptical watching functionaries from Moscow, Paris, or Berlin—while they tinkered with their children's sustenance. . . . Parties as such were going to end up being reduced to a single maneuvering group, disciplined and faithful to a concrete and mythical goal: the unconditional defense of the USSR as the fatherland of the proletariat, waiting for the hypothetical international revolution.[26]

The Central Committee vs. the Executive Committee

There is one history of the PCE written in the streets and secretariats of unions and organizations and reflected in the press, and another written in meetings of the central and executive committees and only for the International's archives. The first is that of the militants; the second, that of the leaders. The militants were facing an exhausting task. They tried to be everywhere there was agitation in order to take credit for it even though it was provoked by others. The collection of *Correspondencia Internacional* provided proof of that "usurpation of glory." For example Catalonian Communists (scarcely a hundred of them) evaded the problem of voting for or against the autonomy statute project, proclaiming the "right of Catalonia to independence" (which only few were demanding);[27] on the other hand in Euzkadi the PCE, along with the Socialists and Republicans, did not support the preparation of the autonomy statute. In June Seville's unions, under Communist leadership, declared a general strike which really became general when there was police brutality in María Luisa Park which took the lives of four Communists; in all there were twenty deaths in the four-day strike.

The PCE grew slowly. It increased from 3,000 to 7,000 members. It absorbed the Party of the Revolutionary and Antiimperialist Left (founded by César Falcón and Graco Marsal) as well as the group of independent young socialists called Rebelión (with Navarro Ballesteros, Fernández Checa, Encarnación Fuyola). It was successful in forming a nucleus in the Ateneo of Madrid composed of Francisco Galán, Wenceslao Roces, Jiménez Siles, Joaquín Arderius, and Ricardo Baroja.[28]

The publishing company Europa-América which Maurín had managed in exile and which belonged to the Comintern, moved from Paris to Barcelona. The publishing company Cenit, although apparently a private firm, signed contracts with the Marx and Engels Institute in Moscow to publish books which the institute found to their liking. Visits to the USSR began to be organized and two Soviet journalists visited Spain. They were the editor-in-chief of *Pravda,* Mikhail Koltzov, and the novelist Ilya Ehrenburg who recorded his impressions in a book with the sarcastic title of *Spain: A Workers' Republic.*

The party could not prevent Communist (Trotskyite) opposition from being organized or its publishing journals and pamphlets, especially after Nin's return to Barcelona in 1930. But it put up a constant barrage of insults and accusations aimed at the Trotskyites (following instructions of the International's fourth congress). On the other hand the executive committee prevented any infiltration of Trotskyites in the party. The Trotskyites who worked within Madrid's Communist group were not able to gain control of it. This group finally broke up because "an organization is lost when it disagrees with the party, worships the International, takes everything from the party (name, method of agitation and propaganda, and structure), and only differs from it on relatively minor matters."[29] The demise of the Madrid group meant the death of its organ which had adopted the name of the old weekly of the early

PCE, *La Antorcha*. Therefore there was no longer any public opposition to party leadership among its members. Nonetheless there was opposition from outside the party. The party, keeping the slogan of "social fascism" devised by the International in 1928, never tired of attacking the Socialists and calling them the "anteroom of fascism" (and it did the same with those it called "anarcho-fascists"). This irritated the Socialist leaders, accustomed to being accused of reformism but not of fascism. Luis Jiménez de Asúa expressed this anger in a rally in Madrid: "The clear waters of Socialism run between two banks: the bourgeois and the Leninist. . . . If some day we come to power, the first thing we would have to do would be sweep out those Communist sympathizers."[30] Attacks such as this were just what the executive committee of the party wanted, for they used them to appease Moscow which had begun to worry.

The anxiety was not a result of the country's situation, of the party's isolation, or of its lack of influence. It resulted from the constant quarrels and rivalries among its leaders and from the headaches which all of this gave the Comintern's "instructors." The team of "instructors" continued to be led by Humbert-Droz. As he himself said: "My two colleagues took pleasure in increasing the number of meetings with the leaders of the Spanish party to the point that they became completely overwhelmed . . . for they did not understand Spanish, nor were they aware of either the country's situation, the party, or its work. The German Stroeker, head of the delegation, pretended to be better informed than the Spaniards themselves and would accept no briefing. He complicated matters infinitely and our meetings at times would last an entire day, going into the evening and not ending until six the following morning. The conflicts between Stroeker and the Spaniards were more violent than those between them and me." Bullejos relates that Stroeker wanted to "discuss" so many things (he would say in his broken Spanish) that they called him "Comrade Discuta," a nickname which was later given to other delegates.[31]

At times those "instructors" would act on their own. For example Humbert-Droz reestablished contact with some members of BOC, "but my efforts did not bring about renewed unity." Then he returned to publishing in Barcelona "my newspaper *Heraldo Obrero* for which I was the chief editor."[32] On Moscow's orders *Mundo Obrero* in late June 1931 published a call to members of BOC:

> On different occasions the Communist International and the party tried to bring an end to the situation which so heavily damaged the development of the Communist movement in Spain. Recently the International asked the chiefs of the bloc to send a delegation to Moscow to discuss the

conditions of its reintegration in the party and consequently the unification of all Communist forces. Maurín, who had already begun with determination his policy of alliance with the Catalonian bourgeoisie, capitulating shamelessly to Macià, and who attacked the Communist International from the rostrum of the Ateneo of Madrid, refused the invitation extended him, thereby revealing both his divisionist intentions and the hypocrisy of all his statements regarding Communist unification in Catalonia. The Central Committee of the Communist party fervently calls you to return to our ranks and it says that it is willing to admit you as a bloc provided you unreservedly accept the program and political line of the Communist International and its Spanish action.[33]

The discussions with the "instructors" were not the only ones which were to sustain the members of the executive committee. In effect "an internal struggle existed within the central committee. On the one hand it was fueled by José Bullejos, Manuel Adame, Etelvino Vega, and Gabriel León Trilla; on the other by Manuel Hurtado, Antonio Mije, Manuel Roldán, and José Díaz."[34] It was a battle between North and South or of neophytes against veterans. More than anything else there were rivalries for power within the party. Only the executive committee had relations with the International, it set the party line, and, relaying instructions from Moscow—real or imagined—it kept in line the members of the central committee who regretted having no influence in the party and being unable to go to Moscow.

In February 1931 this matter was brought up and the "instructors" from the Comintern, to avoid there being cracks in the so-called monolith of the party, proposed that Hurtado and Mije as well as Ramón Casanellas, who had just returned from Moscow and who had assumed the role of arbiter, all join the secretariat. Casanellas was devoted to Moscow (he was a Russian citizen by virtue of having been an officer in the Red Army) and without a doubt as arbiter he would follow whatever line the Comintern indicated. Shortly after that, in June, José Díaz was accepted into the executive committee,[35] so as to allow the minority in the central committee to have a voice in that organism. It seems that Dolores Ibárruri did not take sides in the fighting.

Actually what happened was that the troika, though very disciplined and loyal to the Comintern, was anxious about the line that Moscow required it to follow and which prevented the party from making any kind of progress. It did not want independence but rather a certain amount of autonomy. For this reason there were continual disputes with the "instructors." Realizing this, the troika's rivals, who actually did not disagree with the troika line, tried to lean on the "instructors" who in turn made use of the Andalusians to force the troika to renounce its modest designs for autonomy.

Notes

1. "Dictablanda" is a pun in Spanish. The word *dictadura* (dictatorship) contains the suffix *-dura* which by itself is an adjective and means "hard, harsh." The world *blanda* is its opposite, meaning "soft, mild" (translator's note).
2. Everything quoted from Humbert-Droz, written during his stay in Spain, comes from his memoirs: *De Lénine à Staline,* Neuchâtel, 1971.
3. One of the few successes, although minor, was the formation of a section in the Balearic Islands which in January 1931 began publishing the weekly *Nuestra Palabra (Our Word)* (Pere Gabriel, "Socialisme, sindicalisme i comunisme a Mallorca," *Recerques,* Barcelona, 1972).
4. Galán was a man of uncertain ideology, a temperamental nonconformist. Later the Communists tried to pass him off as one. One of his brothers, Francisco, joined the PCE after having flirted, as did other soldiers of the time, with the CNT and even with BOC (C.M. Lozano, *¡Hasta nunca! (Fermín Galán),* Barcelona, 1976, passim). Portela says that Martínez Pinillos never belonged to the PCE.
5. Bullejos, p. 112.
6. Humbert-Droz, p. 413, dated February 10, 1931.
7. Bullejos, p. 119.
8. In the fourth congress of the Communist International it was said that there were 5,000 members of the PCE in 1922. The seventh congress (1935) reported that in 1931 the PCE had 8,000 members. Humbert-Droz (p. 409) indicates that in January 1931 in all of Catalonia there were scarcely 50 members of the PCE while BOC, in the process of being established, had 700 (Branko Lazitch, *Les Partis communistes d'Europe,* Paris, 1956, p. 183).
9. *Historia del PCE,* p. 60.
10. Bullejos, pp. 60, 122.
11. Humbert-Droz, p. 446 dated April 10, 1931.
12. Humbert-Droz, p. 430.
13. Bullejos, p. 123. Humbert-Droz, pp. 431–32.
14. Neither the *Historia del PCE* nor the *Memoirs* of Dolores Ibárruri make reference to the slogans of April 14 or to those of May 1.
15. Bullejos, p. 127ff.
16. Bullejos, p. 133.
17. This letter, dated May 21 from Moscow, is found in its entirety in Comín Colomer, vol. I, pp. 287–301.
18. José Bullejos, *Europa entre dos guerras,* Mexico City, 1945, p. 135.
19. Enrique Matorras, *El comunismo en España,* Madrid, 1935. Matorras was the leader of Juventudes Comunistas and was replaced when there was a change of leadership in 1932. Following the figures provided, he notes: "This amount is in addition to the allocations for the delegates' support and is sent for the express purpose of fomenting activities of the party and its diverse organizations. All members of the political executive committee of the party and Juventudes are paid monthly salaries of 400 pesetas; in addition, they are given 10 pesetas per diem while traveling outside of the

city where they reside and all expenses are covered as well. There are several procedures for bringing the money into Spain. Sometimes men or women trained in the area bring it; on other occasions it is received through publishing houses connected with the party. That is how for more than two years the publishing company Cenit has been receiving these allotments."

20. Matorras, p. 71.
21. Maurín, *Revolución y contrarrevolución en España,* p. 282. Matorras (p. 66) says that the Comintern contributed U.S. $10,000 (100,000 pesetas at the exchange rate then). Bullejos (*La Comintern,* p. 157) explains that he went to Paris to ask for a loan (he does not say for what amount) from the French Communist party which, after consulting the Comintern, granted it; it was clear that the money came from Moscow. To understand the meaning of the figures given to the newspaper as well as the subsidies from the Comintern, it is important to remember that in 1931 a skilled laborer's salary did not exceed 10 pesetas a day, that a member of Parliament made 1,000 a month, and that the editor of a newspaper received between 500 and 1,000 a month.
22. Matorras, p. 65.
23. Matorras (pp. 45–46) lists the distribution by province. The "official" figures of the PCE were in reality much lower, as Manuel Tuñón de Lara showed (*El movimiento obrero en la historia de España,* Madrid, 1972, p. 884ff.). In many instances there is exaggeration because votes for the far Left were added to Communist votes, or because the figures were simply altered. It might even be an error of Matorras's. Or he may have taken the figures from party documents where they were inflated to look good to Moscow and justify receiving more aid. This supposition is based on the fact that Bullejos (op. cit., pp. 141–42) lists the same inflated figures as Matorras and even comments on the most implausible ones without questioning them. Bolshevization had the same effects in other countries. Why not in Spain? The electoral program of the PCE appears in Estruch, Appendix X.
24. Bonamusa, p. 83.
25. Javier Tusell Gómez, *La segunda República en Madrid: elecciones y partidos políticos,* Madrid, 1970, p. 56. Tusell gives 2,700 and 1,700 votes for the Communist party candidates in Madrid who culled the most and the fewest votes (in other words, the results are almost identical to 1923). Bullejos was a candidate in a by-election, also in Madrid, which was held on October 4, 1931. The party of the Revolutionary and Antiimperialist Left, which soon after would unite its few dozen members with the PCE, supported him. Bullejos received 6,027 votes. José Antonio Primo de Rivera (later a Fascist), who was a first-time right-wing candidate, culled 28,560 votes (Tusell, ibid., p. 73).
26. Gorkín, *El revolucionario profesional,* p. 247.
27. In a letter it sent in May, the executive committee of the Comintern censured the PCE for not taking a more active stance in the nationalities issue.
28. Bullejos, p. 156. I suspect that the figure of 7,000 members is exaggerated.
29. Luis Portela, "Vida y muerte de la Agrupación Comunista de Madrid," *La Batalla,* Barcelona, May 12, 1932.
30. Comín Colomer, vol. I, p. 351. The rally took place in December 1931.
31. *Discuta:* Fractured Spanish for the word *discuss* (Humbert-Droz, p. 455; Bullejos, p. 152).

32. Humbert-Droz, p. 457.
33. Regarding the document of the PCE, Jaume Miravitlles, who at the time belonged to BOC, said in a meeting: "The Communist party of Spain, the Spanish Section of the Communist International, honored its subtitle." The call was enough to bring half a dozen members of BOC, coming from the Catalonian-Balearic federation, back to the party. Some of them went on to be leaders: Arlandis, Sesé, and later on Ardiaca (Alba, *El marxisme a Catalunya*, vol. I, p. 172).
34. Matorras, p. 121.
35. Bullejos, p. 140. Also joining the executive committee was the secretary of the group in Madrid. Also, the leadership of Juventudes was reorganized to allow some members of the group Rebelión to enter it.

9.
Stalinization

The USSR was no longer what it had been in 1925 when the campaign of Bolshevization was begun. Nor was it what it had been in 1928 when the purging of its enemies and dissidents was stepped up (all of them were labeled Trotskyites). What was later called a "personality cult" was already fairly deep-rooted by 1932. There was no tolerance of personal opinion whatsoever nor was there any flexibility in the application of ukases coming from above. Bullejo's PCE therefore was behind the times regarding the International's new modes of procedure. Zinoviev had been removed from the International as was later Bukharin; in 1932 it was being directed by Manuilski, a Ukrainian of little prominence.

The "instructors" who had been "exiled" in Spain wanted to make themselves deserving of Manuilski's favor. The PCE had not met with any success in the application of the Communist International's instructions. They needed scapegoats for those failures. The troika was perfectly suited for that role. By eliminating it they could kill three birds with one stone: blame it for the failures of the PCE, replace the leaders with more "disciplined" ones, and fulfill the ambitions of those within the PCE who aspired to positions of leadership.

For three years, from 1932 to 1935, the party was subjected to an intense campaign of Stalinization which paralleled that which took place in the USSR after both the forced collectivization of agriculture and the first five-year plan had failed. Communist parties, from the very beginning, had reflected the interests of the USSR, but precisely because Russia's economy and international situation were ailing, the "Soviet patriotism" of the Communist parties was strengthened. All its policies were oriented toward defending the "fatherland of the proletariat." The PCE could not be an exception.

Against the Troika

Successors to the troika gave their own explanation, 35 years later, of the supposed motives for its displacement: "The group [made up of Bullejos, Adame, and Trilla] had not understood the nature of the

125

democratic bourgeois revolution before April 14. Their error stemmed from a false appreciation of the power held by the monarchy; their eyes were closed to the traces of feudalism which still existed in the country as well as to the political clout which the landed aristocracy still held, considering that within the governing bloc it was the bourgeoisie and not the landowning aristocracy which held leadership. This helps to understand the attitude of the group (that the revolution ought to be directed against the bourgeoisie) and its spontaneous slogan of April 14: 'Down with the bourgeois Republic!'"[1]

The very men who wrote this were, for a good quarter of a century, more sectarian than the troika. That is precisely why they managed to stay in leadership for so long. What the troika was truly criticized for was that it was sectarian against its will. According to Moscow's way of operating, those things could not be accomplished all of a sudden; it was necessary to justify them first. The "instructors" took charge of this, underhandedly maneuvering sections of the party. That is how, for example, workers' militias were formed in spite of the fact that the executive committee questioned, given the weakness of the party in that particular situation, what it considered mere showing off. The "instructors" made use of the enthusiasm of Juventudes to force the executive committee's hand.[2]

Another tactic to pull the rug from under the feet of the troika was the decision of San Sebastián's local federation of unions under Communist control, to propose a meeting of "union unity." This was in accordance with what Manuilski had laid down in his letter of May 1931 in which he entreated "all of us to start working on transforming the committee of [trade unions] reconstruction into the committee of unity."[3]

In November 1931 Manuilski had written another letter which began with the attack: "Our debates may give the impression that we are living in the period of the second congress of the Communist International, when we were discussing the problems of the revolutionary movement with some anarchist members who had come from Spain." He stated that "the Spanish revolution is of great international importance. It threatens French imperialism." He reprimanded the leaders of the PCE who had not undergone true self-criticism and took the following inventory:

Economic struggles: we have not participated at all. Agrarian movement: it has developed outside of our camp. The soviets: not created. . . . Party reorganization: no one has done anything. And yet when our delegation criticizes the party that is when the rebellion begins. . . . If we were dealing with a mature party that did not have that ["anarchist"] beginning, it would have been necessary to take drastic measures; but we are dealing with a young party . . . and it is necessary to be very patient in order to be convincing to comrades. . . . The main obstacle to the Bolshevization of the party is the executive committee which still has not understood the meaning of our change of line. . . . We are willing to go on as long as you would like, but you must not play with the Communist International. . . . We must call a party congress and speak to all the issues.

There was no longer any doubt. Moscow was looking for new leaders. *El Sol,* the daily of the intelligentsia, printed the letter—to the surprise of the troika which wanted to keep it secret. It seems that the Communist cartoonist Helios Gómez gave a copy of it to that newspaper.[4]

The Comintern's motives began to be seen clearly when Bullejos, Adame, and Vega were called to Moscow to prepare for the congress. They met with a delegation of the Comintern composed of Manuilski, Stepanov, Losovsky, and Piatnisky. Also in attendance were Piek and Ulbricht from Germany; Togliatti from Italy; Bela Kun from Hungary; Kuusinen from Finland; Smeral from Czechoslovakia; and Doriot and Barbé from France. Also invited as observers were the twelve Spanish students, among them Jesús Hernández, from the Leninist school of Moscow, where the future leaders were prepared. Manuilski harshly criticized the actions of the PCE and its executive committee. He blamed them for not having formed soviets and factory committees, for not having won over the CNT, and for not having "exposed Maurín's group." Piatnisky, Losovsky, and Togliatti tried to temper the criticism: Manuilski asked the Spanish delegates to make their self-criticism but they refused because "we feel that our party line is fundamentally on target" and because "we are revolted by a means of retraction which we consider unworthy, even though it had begun to be used in international discussions."[5] Bullejos pointed out that many of the errors attributed to the executive committee had been made while carrying out orders from the International, and Adame reiterated the same point with regard to the party's trade union policies.

The meeting ended by deciding that the executive committee of the Communist International would send a letter to the party's militants presenting what Manuilski had said. The letter would also state that the delegation from the Comintern should be changed, that the fight against Trotskyism (a tendency which was almost nonexistent in Spain at the time) would be heightened, that militants from BOC would be invited to return to the party (with the exception of Maurín and Gorkín who would be asked to make their self-criticism), and that the committee of reconstruction would be replaced by one of trade union unity. Following several parties in honor of the Spanish delegation, Manuilski invited its members to witness a ceremony of self-criticism performed by the delegates of another Communist party. Then something significant happened: Piatnisky introduced Professor Mayowsky to Bullejos. He was director of the Tass agency and would go to Spain secretly where he would serve as a direct link between Bullejos and Stalin. So then, the Comintern communicated without going through the Spanish executive committee with its sections and militants, and at the same time Stalin wanted to communicate with the Spanish executive committee without going through the International.

Bullejos believed that Manuilski's stance was inspired by the "constant intrigues of Humbert-Droz and Codovila" in Moscow. Perhaps for this reason the Spanish executive obeyed the order from the Comintern to send Trilla to Moscow to work in the International where he would be able to counteract those intrigues. "They wanted to separate Trilla from Spain's activities because it was mistakenly believed that our line of constant disagreement with the Comintern and its delegates was a result of the great influence it had on us."[6]

To put more pressure on the troika, Moscow decided to establish a journal dealing with theory (*Bolchevismo*), of which only three issues were printed. They were devoted to texts provided by Moscow and the "instructors," in addition to some articles written by party members. "*Bolchevismo* was organized directly by the party's central committee," which was "responsible for the party's political leadership." It printed 3,000 copies and was under the administration of José Moreno and directed by the central committee. In other words it was more or less a theoretical counterbalance of the executive committee. Moscow also decided to publish in Madrid a Spanish-language edition of its official weekly, *Correspondencia Internacional.* Two technicians were sent with 50,000 pesetas to train those who would be in charge of the edition, and offices were set up at 18 Pi y Margall Street in Madrid. It had a circulation of 7,000, the bulk of which was in Latin America. Eugenio Mejías was in charge of administration and Vicente Arroyo was editor in chief. Their work consisted of "translating French manuscripts sent to them from Moscow and choosing the ones that were to appear in each issue, since the Communist International communicated on a weekly basis a summary of what each issue should contain."[7]

These decisions were made in Moscow and approved by the plenary of the central committee which met in February 1932 secretly in Madrid (so the "instructors" could attend). The plenary agreed to call the fourth party congress (and the second of Juventudes). The proposal to call the congress was made by the secretariat. What had determined the calling of the plenary was another letter from the executive committee and the Communist International. This time the troika did not dare keep it secret. Since that letter was going to set PCE policy until 1935, it is important to reproduce its main points despite the heaviness of its style.

The Letter of January 1932

The letter, written in Berlin, had been sent by the Western bureau of the Communist International for Europe and the American continent, headed by Dimitrov. It was not addressed to the central committee but "to party members."[8] The following is a summary of the most noteworthy points of the document:

> The Spanish proletariat has great revolutionary potential. But, influenced in doctrine by Socialists and Anarcho-Syndicalists, the proletariat did not know enough to continue its task immediately after April 14 when they overthrew the monarchy. They did not know how to win over the peasants who were the revolution's second fighting force, and that is why the opportunity slipped through their fingers and fell into the hands of the bourgeoisie in the form of timid legal projects which can resolve nothing. . . .
>
> The objectives of the democratic-bourgeois revolution were not met. But the proletariat will be able to achieve them given a situation in which the proletariat is in charge of the revolution, guiding the peasants toward a democratic revolution in which they will win complete victory and create the conditions for the rapid transformation of that revolution into a socialist one. For that to happen we must have a Communist party aware of the fundamental problems of the revolution and which knows how to achieve through such a revolution hegemony for the proletariat.
>
> The proletariat, established as the leader of the bourgeois revolution and guided by the Communist party, will ensure the transformation of the revolution into a socialist proletarian one. The role of the Communist party is to direct the organization of the working masses since only under its leadership have they always achieved the maximum revolutionary daring which has brought them victory. . . .
>
> The party's weakness . . . lies in that the Communist party was, and unfortunately still is, bound by sectarianism and Anarchist traditions.
>
> The Communist party has withdrawn into itself, has wanted nothing to do with the working class, has ignored the peasants, has isolated itself from the masses, has not felt their pulse, and has scorned their aspirations, claims, and will to fight. And when things began to happen, when the Republic was proclaimed as a result of strong pressure from the masses who took to the streets, the party gave orders which were not only erroneous but incomprehensible to the masses.
>
> The Spanish Communist party has too many Anarchic vestiges; it is not

a purely proletarian organization but rather is made up of a group of sectarian propagandists weakly linked to the masses, lacking a clear policy and a definite perspective. The Spanish Communist party is a small circle of friends crystallized within a retort.

The regional organizations lead a listless life, without concern for the masses; they merely sit back and wait for instructions from the center. This has already reached intolerable proportions. Numerous instances can be cited in which experienced revolutionary workers have not been admitted into the party "in order that the quality of the Communist elite does not decline." This denotes a petit bourgeois revolutionary spirit which tends to create the "hero," a reflection of caciquism. . . .

The change of policy necessary for the Spanish Communist party is still not perceived because certain leading comrades are resisting it. The Fourth Congress of the Spanish Communist Party will pose very seriously the problem of the change in policy and its practical application.[9]

The Fourth Congress

Preparations for the congress were made on the basis of the Comintern's letter, although the executive committee tried to bring up in addition other issues, perhaps because it considered them more important or perhaps because it mollified the criticism from Moscow. "The regional congress produced no results and abounded with intrigues among the international delegates who tried every means to have elected to the congress a group of delegates hostile to us even though they might be disguised Trotskyites [cartoonist Helios Gómez, for example], such as happened in Madrid."[10]

As the day of the congress approached, the open letter from the Comintern to the militants arrived and the troika informed the "instructors" that it had decided irrevocably to resign during the congress and refuse other positions. The executive committee branded as Trotskyite every proposal not to its liking, for instance the one from the Sotrondio sector in Asturias which suggested calling together the dissidents, or the one from the eastern sector of Madrid which demanded the suspension of the executive committee.[11] The executive committee made some tactical errors. Bullejos said in a meeting at the Maravillas Theater in Madrid that the militants were to be blamed for the failures of the party. Such a statement infuriated many and he lost the sympathy of quite a few. This probably would not have happened had the situation been explained clearly as he did many years later when he wrote: "The Communist party . . . wanted to modify its political orientation, placing a priority on the fight against the monarchist and right-wing reaction. That was not possible given the inflexibility of the International, in particular its delegation in Spain, which, as a prisoner of the Fourth World Congress's resolution, could not agree to consider the monarchists and reactionaries as the true enemies of democracy. As far as Moscow was concerned, any softening of the position against the Socialists was a departure from the revolutionary line."[12]

The congress was inaugurated on March 17, 1932 in "Red Seville," as it was referred to in Communist newspapers. Paradoxically the sessions met in the U.S. pavillion of the Iberoamerican Exposition of 1929.[13] The congress was attended by 285 delegates representing 12,000 members (201 party delegates, 29 delegates of Juventudes, and 55 from "factories and unions representing more than 90,000 workers").[14] It lasted seven days. Although there was a delegation from the Comintern and another from the French Communist party, only the latter spoke publicly. The delegates from the Comintern had the responsibility of persuading the troika to withdraw its resignation and accept reelection. From Russia Vega sent his support of this action.

All theses prepared by the central committee—political, trade union, agrarian, and organizational—were read and approved at the congress. "There were several outbursts occasioned by the unfortunate intervention of some Trotskyite delegates whom the audience tried to throw out."[15] It was there that Dolores Ibárruri, who presided over one of the sessions, made her first national appearance. In the words of someone attending the congress, "it was of great importance for the Communist movement because not only was it held a good number of years after the last one which was illegal and after the central committee had been dormant for almost two years, but was also under direct control of the International whose delegates attended every meeting incognito, indicating to the leaders the position they ought to adopt."[16]

Bullejos presented an interminable political report which went on for five hours. He said he was aware that Spain was going through a democratic revolution at whose core was the agrarian revolution, but that the Communists had shied away from it because they did not understand its true nature. In April 1931 Spain did not have a duality of power like Russia had in 1917. The party had to spend its time setting up soviets and factory committees as well as exposing Trotskyites, Maurinists, and "social-fascists and anarcho-reformists." He criticized the speeches of the delegates for "their low political standards." In his report on the trade unions Adame attacked "syndicalists [who had just been expelled from the CNT] as well as the UGT, and said that it was necessary to maintain a position which was critical of and yet attracted the Federación Anarquista Ibérica (FAI). Communist factions ought to be organized in every union where there were militants or sympathizers in order to form "revolutionary opposition."[17] The congress put the central committee in charge of wording the final political theses using the approved letter from the Comintern as a guide.

In order to include the changes in policy, the party statutes were modified. The first article stated that "the Communist party is fighting to win over the working class and peasants, to establish proletarian dictatorship, to create the Iberian Union of Soviet Socialist Republics, to eliminate classes and bring about socialism, the first step toward establishing a communist society." The expression "democratic centralism" was included in the statutes, which meant that "party decisions can be discussed only by its members and organizations until the appropriate party organs made a decision." Article 4 allowed "under certain [unspecified] conditions" the chief organs to appoint leaders for the lesser ones and to coopt their own members. The chief organs had the right to take part in all meetings of the lesser organs and to annul or modify its resolutions.[18] The executive committee's name was changed to Executive Political Bureau or Politburó. The bureau's eleven members chose a secretariat made up of five members. These statutes "will transform the party into a powerful instrument in which the likelihood of the rank and file's orienting the line of action is as remote as is intense its identification with decisions made by the higher-ups."[19]

The troika had decided not to persist in its resignation. The secretariat was made up of José Bullejos as secretary general, Manuel Hurtado as organizational secretary, Manuel Adame as union secretary, José Silva as secretary of agitation and propaganda, and Dolores Ibárruri as secretary for the women's sector. That is how Ibárruri moved to the party's front lines while Díaz and Hernández were relegated to the second line of the political bureau.[20] In spite of some criticism of the leadership, the troika dominated the congress. Doubtless the troika would have been able to get a majority for a central committee which would be in complete favor of it and thereby be in a position to control the political bureau as well as the secretariat. The troika was satisfied with three of the eleven positions of the political bureau and two in the secretariat (Trilla was in Moscow working in the Comintern); one would think this was due to the "instructors" who tried to maintain some positions for the troika because they must have considered a rupture to be untimely. At the same time they tried to put the most submissive individuals in other organs of leadership.[21] One of the victors wrote that "the discussions and resolutions of the fourth congress constituted a serious blow to sectarian tendencies which had slowed down the development of the party and its process of consolidation. Nonetheless many of the problems at the core of the crisis, a crisis which existed in a latent state within the party, were not entirely resolved in the congress and they had to be resolved later on."[22]

Three Subsidiary Systems

The troika had been imposed by the Comintern between 1926 and 1928. To this administrative subsidiary system would be added two new kinds of dependence. Policy itself did not change because the International's line had not changed. What had previously been put into effect with reluctance, in the future would be carried out enthusiastically and without complaint. The Comintern no longer met with resistance from leaders in the PCE which, by the way, was transformed into a drive belt and would continue to be so for decades.

The first move had lasting consequences. It was the formation, not by decision of Catalonian members but of the Central Committee of the PCE, of a Communist Party of Catalonia (Partit Comunista de Catalunya—PCC) whose organ would be *Catalunya Roja (Red Catalonia)*. To complete this face-lifting the executive political board moved its headquarters for a while to Barcelona, capital of Catalonia and main bulwark of the CNT.[23] Having made the move, the board intended not only to transform the Catalonian-Balearic federation into the PCC, but also to undo the unfavorable effect the formation of the Committee of [trade union] Reconstruction had had in circles of the CNT. They made no progress in achieving the latter, but they met their goal concerning the former: building the skeleton of a party with Catalonian guise but totally dependent on the PCE. The PCC's fundamental objective was to fight BOC.

Ramón Casanellas was "elected" secretary general of the PCC by the "instructors," not only because he was totally devoted to the Comintern but also because, having been an Anarchist and one of those responsible for the attempt on Dato's life, he had had personal friendships in the past with some leading members of FAI. The truth is that those friendships were of no avail to him because he was considered a turncoat. The PCC made no gains regarding BOC. Not a single one of its militants went over to the PCC. Among the PCC's leaders were several men—Sesé and Arlandis, for example—who in their early days had belonged to BOC. One last attempt was made in spite of the fact that "Maurín's group" had already been expelled, and the Central Committee of the PCE issued a new call to BOC members.[24]

The PCC was "integrated within the PCE." There is no doubt about it, especially since the Soviet historian who affirms it is probably the only person who had access to the archives of the PCE and the Communist

International.[25] The PCC had a delegate on the political bureau of the PCE. The Soviet historian states that the PCC "was not very important numerically. Under its influence were some unions, the strongest of which was the Workers' Federation of the Gastronomic Unions of Catalonia (FOSIG). Arlandis, Matas, Sesé, and Valdés were at the head of the central committee of the PCC." Also included in that group were Francisco and José del Barrio, although the Russian historian does not mention José because he later became a supporter of Tito. Strangely, Casanellas is not referred to either.

Casanellas had been a pilot in the Red Army during his stay in Russia. He returned secretly to Spain in 1931, was arrested, and later retrieved his Spanish citizenry. His female companion, acting as secretary, was part of the delegation of "instructors" of the Comintern. On October 25, 1933 Casanellas and Francisco del Barrio (José's brother) were on a motorcycle en route to Madrid. The cycle crashed into a car coming from the opposite direction and the cyclists were mangled. *Mundo Obrero* said that Casanellas had been killed by order of the government. The party appointed a commission to investigate the case but did not publish any conclusions.[26] Miguel Valdés became the new secretary general of the PCC.

The issue of Catalonia put the PCC in a tight spot. In his letters Manuilski had criticized the troika for not understanding the importance of the problem of nationalities. When the statute of autonomy for Catalonia was voted on, the PCE had come out with the slogan "Right to Separate." It criticized BOC for having recommended voting for the statute in spite of its inadequacy. The PCC affirmed that the statute "marks Catalonian submission to Spanish imperialism with the complicity of Macià."[27] Maurín made the following remark on the Catalonian policy of the PCE-PCC: "Believing that the truly revolutionary position, a one hundred percent Communist one, was at all times the most extreme position, that is, one of stridence, the PCE-PCC has always lived on the fringe of reality. Thus it appeared crafty. Of course it has not had any impact at all."[28]

A quaint aspect of the Communist treatment of the problem of nationality is found in a book signed I. Kom (apparently, the Communist International),[29] which says that BOC and Maurín were in the service of the Catalonian bourgeoisie, while the Trotskyites were in the service of the Spanish imperialist bourgeoisie. On the issue of unions the system of subsidiaries did not relate to Madrid but to Moscow. The "instructors" had written Manuilski: "Here in Barcelona the Communist workers are forever asking for an explanation of what this committee [of reconstruction] is, owing to the fact that the question of unions is at the center of its discussions with Anarchists and Maurinists, and they do not know how to defend the party's trade union policy. . . . In Asturias where Gijón's unions are dominated by Anarchists and the majority of the region's unions are held by Socialists, our comrades say that they cannot even bring up the question of membership in the Committee of Reconstruction."[30]

What was being said about Barcelona and Gijón could also be said of the rest of Spain. In spite of this Moscow held to its line. Consequently the local federation of unions of San Sebastián, which the "instructors" had used as a battering ram against the troika a few months earlier, took the initiative—on orders from above—and called a conference for June 30. At the conference it was agreed to create a national committee of trade union unity which would work for unity of the CNT and UGT.[31] The only voice that dared dissent belonged to the Communist union leader from Guipúzcoa Juan Astigarrabía, who commented, "this is the situation of Spain as seen from Moscow." The "instructors" forbade him from participating unless he withdrew his opposition.[32]

The militants continued to participate in strikes, demonstrations, and protests. Yet rarely could they initiate action of their own. On May 1, 1932, for example, the PCE decided to stage demonstrations since the UGT, so as not to feed the provocateurs, had agreed to call off theirs. The Communist party was successful only in Seville. Moscow switched its "instructors," sending Victorio Codovila, an Argentine (who went by Medina), and Erno Gerö, a Hungarian (known as Pedro). The Argentine settled in Madrid and was not welcomed by the survivors of the troika who considered him an intrigant and an enemy. Gerö stayed on in Barcelona as an "advisor" to the PCC. Both delegates remained in their jobs until 1939.[33]

They arrived in Spain a few days before the military coup of General José Sanjurjo. In the August 10, 1932 issue of *Mundo Obrero* the full-page headline read: "The Azaña Government is the Center of the Fascist Counterrevolution." That very day Sanjurjo rebelled against the Azaña government in Seville. Workers of the Communist party and of the other organizations in Seville understood that there were certain differences between Azaña and Sanjurjo; they declared a general strike, demonstrated in the streets, and isolated the rebels. The troops sent by the government arrived on the 12th. Sanjurjo fled but was captured and arrested. The streets now belonged to the masses who burned down the landowners' club as well as the home of Luca de Tena and the clubhouse of the Mercantile Union. There was an assembly of all the unions in the bullring with speakers from the CNT, UGT, and the local Communist unions.

In Madrid the secretariat was disconcerted. Bullejos managed to impose on the party the slogan "revolutionary defense of the Republic." The slogan had been proposed before by the political bureau but was rejected by the "instructors" who, like Moscow, considered the Republican-Socialist government the most dangerous enemy of all. Bullejos was able to impose the slogan because only he, Vega, and Astigarrabía were in Madrid. Ibárruri was under arrest and the "instructors" Hurtado and Adame were still in Barcelona packing to complete the move of the political bureau back to Madrid. The bureaucratic spirit of collecting and keeping papers played a dirty trick on the delegation from the International.[34] But the latter got even: after the coup Moscow called the slogan "revolutionary defense of the Republic" "right-wing opportunism" and censured the political bureau. The demise of the troika began with this violation of the system of subsidiaries.

Expulsion and Abduction of the Troika

The replacement of the Bullejos-Trilla-Adame troika by another has all the ingredients of a novel. "At the end of the summer [of 1932] and following the events of August 10 in Seville, which were largely protagonized by the Communist party, the question of a change in leadership was discussed thoroughly on the initiative of the Communist International," said a Communist historian.[35] The "instructors" met with the political bureau on August 18 to establish the position to be adopted by Bullejos who, as a member of the Executive Committee of the Communist International, was going to Moscow to attend the next full plenary meeting of that body. Bullejos said that the events which took place in Seville had surprised the party, which allowed the CNT and the Republicans to take over the leadership of the anti-Sanjurjo movement. This was not the fault of the Sevillian Communists but rather of "the mistaken orientation of the political bureau which did not see the dangerous maneuvers of the counterrevolution in time." The "instructors" insisted that what had happened in Seville proved that Azaña was the worst enemy, not the reactionaries or monarchists. The events in Seville were not as serious as people thought, they said. With the exception of Hurtado and Mije, the political bureau backed Bullejos's point of view.

The following day the bureau met again without informing Bullejos. He found out about it and attended, only to find that the "instructors" were submitting a resolution to the bureau which called the troika counterrevolutionary and demanded that it yield to the Communist International's line. So the bureau had to break with the Communist International or condemn three of its members whom just the day before it had approved. Bullejos resigned. He received the support of Casanellas from Barcelona and Ibárruri from prison. Díaz was in jail in Seville and did not attend the meeting but "would have voted, as usual, for the delegation of the International, for he sincerely believed—and had said so—that the Communist International could make no mistakes." When Bullejos went to visit Dolores Ibárruri in the women's prison in Madrid, she asked him "not to change his vote regarding the Comintern under any circumstances" nor to agree to any compromise.[36]

Although at the previous day's meeting it had been agreed that the party's delegation to Moscow would be composed of Hurtado and Mije, both of whom were antitroika, it was later decided that there should be more delegates.[37] Adame and Vega were nominated but declined to accept. One of the "instructors" went in advance to Moscow to "inform" the Executive Committee of the Communist International that everything revolved around the fact that they had discovered the troika's plans to separate the PCE from the Communist International, which had to quickly make arrangements to cancel the enthusiastic reception planned for the "heroic Spanish fighters." The "instructors" tried to take advantage of Bullejos's resignation to call a national conference, but being far from expert in Spanish techniques of secrecy (the meeting had to be secret so that the "instructors" could attend), they were unable to prevent the police from finding them out and making some arrests before the session ever began.

With the exception of Trilla, the troika was still in Spain. In light of the arrests it decided to create a new leadership taking on Zapiraín and Mateos. The party found itself with two sets of leaders: the troika which had resigned but which was taking advantage of the arrests in an attempt to return to power, and those under arrest as well as those who were scattered about and who regrouped when Mije and Hurtado returned from Moscow and reorganized the secretariat, without the troika, of course. The first thing the secretariat did was to annul everything the troika had done in its "emergency regime," and then it adopted a resolution which said: "After a lengthy discussion of self-criticism during which the opportunity to state exactly their position was extended to comrades who, following the August 18–19 meeting of the political bureau, vacillated in putting their resolutions into effect or who unconsciously consented to the fractional tactics of Bullejos, Adame, and Vega . . . the secretariat of the party has unanimously passed the following resolutions: (1) the secretariat vigorously condemns the fractional position of Adame, Bullejos, and Vega . . . (2) the secretariat reports with satisfaction that the fractional and despotic position of Adame, Bullejos, and Vega has not found favor in the party, which has remained unanimously faithful to the political line of the Communist International."

The troika no longer had any work to do in Madrid and it went to Moscow hoping to regain power. Meanwhile Adame and Vega had received a telegram from the Executive Committee of the Communist International inviting them to accompany Bullejos to Moscow, which they were persuaded to do by the very affability of the invitation. When they arrived in the Russian capital, the enlarged plenary session of the Comintern's Executive Committee had already ended, having adopted a resolution condemning the troika. In the private discussions that followed there was a "climate of mutual hostility." What is startling is that the troika was unaware that it was not Madrid but Moscow that had decided to do away with it and that it was not the "instructors" who had taken the initiative but rather the Comintern which needed to "blame" someone for their failures in Spain. The discussions were attended by the Spanish students of the Leninist school—Hernández, Modesto, and Líster.

"The debates went on for several weeks since there did not seem to be any hurry to achieve definitive results." First there was a period of scathing criticism, followed by one of less severity during which an attempt was made to persuade the troika to withdraw its resignation. This made Bullejos think that the Russian delegation, which would make the final decision, was divided on the matter. Manuilski made the proposal that Bullejos go back to being secretary general and that Trilla, Adame, and Vega go to the USSR to work. Bullejos accepted the invitation to be on the political bureau and work with the PCC in Barcelona but declined the position of secretary general, which met with general approval.[38] As the Spanish delegates were packing their bags, they were given a copy of *Frente Rojo (Red Front)* in which there appeared a resolution of the political bureau adopted on October 5 during the troika's absence. The resolution ended:

Considering the ideological and political position hostile to the Communist International and the sectarian, despotic, and fractional work which the members of the group have attempted, the political bureau agrees to propose to the central committee, which will meet soon, the exclusion of comrades Bullejos, Adame, Trilla, and Vega from the bureau and from the central committee. . . . Likewise, given that comrade Trilla does not represent the party, and that ideologically and politically he is not in agreement with the platform of the Communist International and the party but rather with that of the sectarian group of which he is a preeminent member, the political bureau has decided to propose to the Executive Committee of the Communist International that said comrade discontinue at once as a representative of the party before the Executive Committee.

In view of this resolution, the Presidium and the Executive Committee of the Comintern, in a joint meeting, agreed to expel Bullejos, Vega, Trilla, and Adame. They were accused of sectarianism, nonexecution of the Comintern's instructions, and contempt of the Comintern and its delegates whom they had called "lackeys." Political motives were not mentioned.[39] The Comintern's organ reported:

> In the midst of this growing struggle of the masses, four former members of the Communist party of Spain—Trilla, Adame, Vega, and Bullejos—having contemptuously shown their lack of faith in the peasants and workers, broke with the Communist International. For many months they fought to prevent the creation of a true mass party in Spain . . . thereby supporting the policy of Spanish counterrevolution. . . . If the party has grown, it has not been because of, but rather in spite of Adame, Trilla, Vega, and Bullejos. . . . Whether they join the divisionary Trotskyites or go directly to the side of Spanish fascism is a secondary consideration. What is certain is that the Spanish counterrevolution has won four more recruits.[40]

On November 1 Duclos called the four men together and informed them of their expulsion. The French Communist warned them that they would be subject to Soviet penal laws if they attempted any move or tried to contact members of a Spanish delegation which had come for the October celebrations. Furthermore the Communist International would not take care of arrangements for their return to Spain. They would have to negotiate their departure permits with the Soviet authorities who held their passports. They realized that efforts were being made to keep them in Moscow so as to allow the new leadership time to establish full power. So they waited nervously. They continued to stay at the Lux hotel and to collect their per diem allowance, but were not allowed to receive visitors, mail, or the Spanish Communist newspaper.

In Spain rumors had it that the troika had been imprisoned in Russia. Those rumors reached Moscow while a petition signed by the four men asking for their release was being sent to the political bureau of the Russian Communist party. According to Bullejos, Manuilski and Stepanov wanted to retain them until they "repented for their misdoings." Losovsky and Piatnisky supported freeing them. It was finally decided to return their passports, give them an exit visa, and allow them to purchase return tickets. Vega, who did not have a Spanish passport, would remain in Moscow until he could be furnished with a Russian one. Actually he stayed on as a hostage to guarantee that the other three would not take any steps against the new leadership of the PCE. It was the end of December when the ex-troika arrived in Madrid.

Notes

1. *Historia del PCE,* pp. 77–78.
2. In a conversation with the author in Mexico in 1955, Bullejos himself acknowledged that he did not support forming Communist militias.
3. Artola, p. 686. The harshest criticism of the troika came from Seville as did later a good portion of the members of the team of leaders which replaced the troika. It is interesting that Sevillians also criticized the alliance of the CNT with Balbontín's party, since his party would join the PCE when those who found fault with it in 1932 were at the head of it (Manuel Tuñón de Lara, *Luchas obreras y campesinas en la Andalucía del siglo XX,* Madrid, 1978, p. 230ff.).
4. The complete text is found in Comín Colomer, vol. I, pp. 355–65.
5. Bullejos, p. 162.
6. Idem, pp. 164–65.
7. Matorras, pp. 95–96.
8. The complete text is found in Comín Colomer, vol. I, pp. 368–82, and in *La Correspondance Internationale,* January 15, 1932, which includes Matorras's summary, p. 82ff.
9. This letter was published later in pamphlet form with the title "La lucha por la bolchevización del Partido," although it omitted the parts critical of the troika.
10. Bullejos, p. 164.
11. Artola, p. 687.
12. Bullejos, *Europa entre dos guerras,* p. 139.
13. There is a significant disparity between the number of members which the executive committee (which exaggerated) gave and the figures provided by *Bolchevismo* of the central committee, which tended to play them down to make the troika look bad. For example, the first source listed 5,600 members in Andalusia while the second gave 4,750. The journal provided the following figures in addition to those for Andalusia: Basque-Navarre federation, 1,335; federation of Levante (Valencia), 750; federation of Madrid, 703; Asturian federation, 700; federation of New Castile, 400; Catalonian-Balearic federation, 400; federation of Castile and León, 326. Additional figures were: Barcelona, 326; Galicia, 265; Canary Islands, 203; Morocco, 159 (*Bolchevismo,* Madrid, no. 2). It seems strange that Almería did not send delegates "due to lack of funds."
14. *La Palabra,* the Communist party organ after the suspension of *Mundo Obrero,* mentioned 257 delegates and rounded off the 90,000 workers to 100,000. It also said that the sessions took place in the Brazilian pavillion and not that of the United States, which Bullejos reiterated. The local trade union federation (Communist) took charge of housing and feeding the delegates. To help with expenses, the Communist International sent 75,000 pesetas (Matorras, p. 97).
15. Bullejos, *La Comintern,* p. 156.
16. Matorras, p. 97.
17. Extracts from the theses on organization are found in Matorras, p. 97ff.
18. For information on the congress see Artola, pp. 688–89, and Tuñón de Lara, p. 888ff.
19. Artola, p. 988.

20. Bullejos, pp. 166–67. There is confusion regarding the names of the leaders. Tuñón (p. 889) says that the secretariat "continued under the direction of Bullejos, and included Adame, Hurtado, Vega, Trilla, Casanellas, and Astigarrabía."

21. To elect the central committee "the procedure of naming an extensive commission during the congress was followed. The commission was in charge of nominating a list of candidates to the assembly. This commission met separately with the delegates of the Communist International and finally named the actual central committee" (Matorras, p. 103).

22. Dolores Ibárruri, *El único camino,* p. 131. The *Historia del PCE* reproduces word for word these lines in its conclusions about the congress (pp. 76–77).

23. If we remember that the political bureau was composed of eleven members and that it seems unimaginable that all eleven of them would leave their jobs and look for others in Barcelona with the hope of finding one at a time of unemployment, one must presume that the eleven members were receiving salaries from the party. The PCE at the time, despite its frail economic position, had proportionately more functionaries on salary than any other labor organization in Spain. This does not mean that fighting within the party leadership was over those salaries. Any one of the leaders of the PCE would have been able to make as much, or more, working in his own profession. The struggle was not for money but for power, power over a small and weak political machinery, yet considerable power (greater than that of the leaders of any other oganization) over a disciplined rank and file. If the fascination for power at the center of the party is not understood, it will not be possible to understand the constant factional fighting in which the ideological motives tend only to mask the real motive.

24. Bullejos, p. 187.

25. L.V. Ponamariova, *La formación del Partit Socialista Unificat de Catalunya,* Barcelona, 1977, p. 33.

26. A friend of Casanellas who collaborated with him in the early days of the PCC said that Casanellas was becoming more independent of the "instructors" and even of his Russian friend Maria Schipora, his "controller" as he called her. "Because of the secrets he knew from his work in Latin America, especially in Mexico, he would be assassinated if he continued to free himself from Soviet influence." Prior to his imprisonment early in 1933 he gave a file of documents not to his wife but to his friend, who also said that Schipora belonged to the Russian police and he pointed out that attesting to her importance in the Soviet hierarchy was the fact that she was part of the Russian delegation at the Seventh Congress of the Communist International in 1935. This friend of Casanellas also added that only Maria Schipora and the secretary of the central committee knew about the motorcycle trip Casanellas and Francisco del Barrio took to Madrid to attend a meeting of the Central Committee of the PCE. He maintains that the faces of the dead men did not show the kind of injuries that a head-on collision would cause, no matter how violent it might be; rather the wounds were like those inflicted in order to disfigure or make identification impossible. That friend took it upon himself to make investigations, independent of the commission named by the PCC, without letting it interfere with his association with the party; he finished by saying: "Today I can assure you that the man from the GPU who headed Casanellas's assassination

served as intellectual leader in Trotsky's assassination in Mexico" R. Cabrer Pallás, "Ramón Casanellas: la rebotiga comunista,"*Xáloc,* Mexico City, July-August, 1977.

27. *Catalunya Roja,* Barcelona, November 9, 1932. This was the first issue of the PCC's organ which replaced *Las Masas,* "organ of the Communist party (Spanish section of the Communist International) in Catalonia, Aragon, and Levante." As was indicated, the PCE had fluctuated on the national question. Following the criticism from the Communist International, it published in 1932 the pamphlet "La cuestión nacional y el movimiento nacional-revolucionario en España," which condemned the underestimation of the nationalist movements by the Communists and pointed out a double error they committed: that of acknowledging the right of self-determination only for workers and peasants of the nationalities, which it called leftist deviation, and that of demanding the restoration of a sovereign Catalonian republic, which it called rightist deviation (Albert Balcells, *Marxismo y catalanismo, 1930–1936,* Barcelona, 1977, p. 62).

28. Quoted in "Quaderns d'Alliberament," *Questió nacional i lluita de classes,* Barcelona, 1977, p. 110.

29. I. Kom, *La revolución española,* Barcelona, 1932, passim.

30. Quoted by Bullejos, p. 183.

31. The organizers of the conference said that in attendance were representatives of 267,264 workers, 100,000 of whom belonged to "Red unions." "The conference . . . brought to light the failure of the Communists to penetrate the Socialist and CNT unions. In cases where there was penetration, the result had always been the exclusion of the penetrated union, which deprived the party of the necessary base to develop the program to win over the masses. . . . As a tactic the formation of a series of committees was proposed (the committees of struggle, strike, factory and, on the local level, of unity) with the objective of attempting to bring about among the labor rank and file the unity which had failed among the militants" (Artola, pp. 689–90). On the preponderant participation of the Andalusians at the meeting, see Tuñón de Lara, *Luchas obreras y campesinas en la Andalucía del siglo XX,* p. 245ff.

32. Comín Colomer, p. 434. Astigarrabía was finally thrown out after the Civil War because of his habit of saying what he thought.

33. For information about Codovila, see Bullejos, p. 197ff. "He had successively betrayed Trotsky, Zinoviev, and Bukharin and his political protectors from Nin to Humbert-Droz and Togliatti." For information on Gerö see Enrique Castro Delgado, *Hombres made in Moscú,* Mexico City, 1960, p. 139ff. Codovila returned to Argentina following World War II and became one of the leaders of the local Communist party. In 1956 Gerö, in the name of the Hungarian Communist party, asked the Soviet military command to squelch the people's revolution of October and November of that year. "Codovila was known for his sweaty corpulence, his thick skull of wavy hair, his vanity of considering himself a person of importance, and for his primarily obliging spirit. Having been named permanent delegate for Latin America, he filled out the most diverse commissions and invariably voted the way he was expected to. Whenever it was necessary to cover up a dirty deal, no matter what it was, he was the one sent, and only on special occasions did Humbert-Droz or Klein go. When Zinoviev fell into disfavor,

Codovila stopped talking about their physical resemblance and became one of his most vicious detractors. Later he did the same to Bukharin on orders from Dimitrov and Manuilsky. . . . Several years later Albert Vassart informed me that he was there when Manuilski made this promise to Codovila: "If you carry out our policy correctly in Spain, I'll reward you by personally introducing you to comrade Stalin" (Gorkín, *El revolucionario profesional*, pp. 157, 159–60).

34.   Bullejos, p. 189ff. In her memoirs Ibárruri makes no mention of the Sanjurjo rebellion. *Historia del PCE* gives it half a page without referring to the PCE's slogan (p. 81).

35.   Manuel Tuñón de Lara, p. 889.

36.   Bullejos, p. 200. Ibárruri makes no reference to any of this in her memoirs nor does *Historia del PCE*.

37.   The political bureau's resolution read: "In view of the fact that, contrary to the decision of the political bureau, the three men did not follow party discipline and persisted in their hostility toward the party and the Communist International and threatened to promote fractionalism, the political bureau, in its meetings of the 19th, resolved to separate Adame, Bullejos, and Vega from all responsibility in the party and to forbid Adame and Vega from traveling to the provinces. The political bureau is awaiting the decisions of the Communist International in order to make a final resolution." As far as the delegation of the Comintern was concerned, it said: "In the present crisis, which Bullejos and Adame systematically planned with the support of Vega, it is not a matter of a battle against the Communist International's way of operating or against maneuvers of the Comintern, as the three comrades claim; it is a matter of a constant struggle against the policy of the Comintern, a struggle which attacks even the fundamental principles of the Communist International. . . . This struggle of Bullejos, Adame, and Vega and the crisis in the leadership of the party, planned and carried out by those men, is a crime against the party, the Communist International, and the revolution. We are calling on the comrades to reject the policy of Bullejos, Adame, and Vega and defend the sound Leninist line of the Communist International" (Matorras, pp. 124–25).

38.   Bullejos, p. 204. Neither Ibárruri nor *Historia del PCE* make reference to any of this. Nor does Líster in his memoirs mention those debates which he attended. Tuñón (p. 289) gives the semiofficial version.

39.   *Correspondance Internationale,* November 8, 1932. Bullejos tried to form a Communist party after a couple of years, but failing to do so joined the PSOE as did Adame. Trilla and Vega managed to be admitted to the PCE later on, once they had recognized their "errors."

40.   *Correspondencia Internacional* printed a summary of the resolution against the troika in its November 4, 11, and 18, and December 2 and 9 issues of 1932; also printed was condemnation of the troika by various Communist parties.

10.
The Shadow of Hitler

In the twelve years the PCE had been in existence, the following men had been its leaders: Merino Gracia in the PCE, Pérez Solís-Lamoneda in the PSOE, Bullejos and Arroyo, Maurín's triumvirate, Arroyo and the delegates of the Communist International in Paris, Pérez Solís's second reign, and the troika made up of Bullejos, Trilla, and Adame. Seven leadership teams in twelve years. The team that Moscow designated and which the central committee of the PCE approved in November 1932 held office for ten years, although there were cooptions and changes of a secondary nature, and this team produced the two which succeeded it.

A Socialist who would later become a Communist sympathizer wrote the following at the time: "Almost everyone who was prominent in the Spanish Socialist movement and who separated from our Socialist party in 1921 . . . to join the Communist International has been thrown out of their own ranks: Anguiano, Torralba Beci, etc. were no longer part of the Communist party in Spain, having been branded as traitors of the Communist cause. . . . But shortly after, those who had 'purged' the Spanish Communist membership in time became victims of another 'purge.' And those who came along later also effected 'purges,' calling their predecessors to account. And thus ad infinitum."[1]

Public Confessions

The secretariat of the Comintern named the following officers in December 1932: José Díaz, secretary general; Manuel Hurtado, organizational secretary; Jesús Hernández, secretary of agitation and propaganda; Antonio Mije, trade union secretary. In addition, forming part of the political bureau were Vicente Uribe, Adriano Romero, Dolores Ibárruri, and Juan Astigarrabía.[2] Obviously it was not a team of newcomers. All of them had collaborated with the troika and had expressed opposition only when the delegation of the International decided to do away with it.

Moscow also changed its delegation. Codovila, an Argentine, was now the main personality, and Humbert-Droz no longer participated in Spanish affairs. In an attempt to bolster the Argentine, Heinz Neumann was sent. He was an exciting personality of the apparat who had fallen out of favor in Moscow and who spent a short while in Spain where he did nothing more than write a few articles.[3] The head figure of the new troika was Díaz who "although he had inherited the vivacity of his Andalusian background had no taste for drama. He was a prudent and modest man with good political instincts."[4] He had been an Anarchist, had spent a year at the Leninist school in Moscow, and was in jail when he was promoted to secretary general. The new leaders were facing a fragmented party. "The [Bullejos] group's expulsion finished the job begun by the fourth congress [of the PCE]: the completion of this particular stage of the fight against sectarianism. Yet it was not able to definitively root out this disease in the party."[5]

The first task of the new team was to consolidate its power. The team was composed of second-rank individuals, many of whom came from the sickly Communist union movement and lacked experience in political leadership. Therefore they clung to "chubby" or "the banker," as they used to call Codovila, and followed all his suggestions, the first of which was for all who could sympathize with Bullejos to undergo, in accordance with the model put into practice by the Communist International, public confession and self-criticism. Those who did so were, among others, Arrarás, Pascual Arroyo, Miguel Caballero, Manuel Roldán, José Silva, Pedro Fernández Checa, Zaparaín, and Dolores Ibárruri.[6]

Only two leaders refused to make a confession. One of them, to everyone's surprise, was Casanellas, who soon after would die before measures could be taken concerning him, and the other was Olmos, a member of the Executive Committee of Juventudes who had gone to Moscow and returned very disillusioned. It was in Juventudes that the first self-criticism took place. On October 20 its executive committee adopted a resolution which said that "the group formed by Bullejos, Adame, Vega, and Trilla have no political influence either over the secretariat or any of its members with the exception of comrade Olmos because of his questionable and indecisive behavior."[7] Most self-criticisms were written one or two days after the decision to expel the troika in October 1932. They looked like variations of a single rough draft. Some fragmentary examples will help to understand their significance. They were published almost immediately in the pamphlet "La lucha por la bolchevización del Partido."[8] Miguel Caballero's read:

> After having reflected, examining the entire discussion which had occurred, and after having reviewed the history of my political activity which was

always consistent with the sectarian and despotic political line of which I
have been perhaps the most characteristic provincial governor; having
reflected seriously the value of the discussion and my stance with relation
to it, and in view of the fact that I was practically a supporter of the
counterrevolution, as a result of the attitude I developed during the long
time devoted to that political line, I fully condemn that deceitful political
line and am ready to work for the revolution in the only place where this
is possible: in the Communist party and within the political line in the
International. . . .

I recognize that just as the political line of the International is right, its
delegation in Spain is its worthy representative, working hard to transform
our party into a true Bolshevik party of the masses, for which reason it
finds itself involved in the intrigues of those individuals who at any cost
wish to hamper the party's development.

Tiburcio Pascual Arroyo wrote: "I ask that the party put me under
every test it thinks appropriate and that it judge my conduct according
to the attitude it observes in my work in the future. I also ask that I
be relieved of all responsibility in party leadership and that I be sent
to work in the rank and file, effective immediately." One of the troika's
most enthusiastic supporters, Zaparaín, had to sign this text which, like
the others, was filled with Gallicisms: "I declare that, due to my lack
of understanding of the political substance of the crisis at hand and
because I was influenced by the policy of the group, I helped the group
take over party leadership. . . . I accept all measures the political bureau
deems necessary in the face of errors I have committed out of political
weakness and I am willing to fight with all the energy I can muster to
do the work assigned me toward the complete application of the political
line of the party and of the Communist International."

The case of Dolores Ibárruri was unique. She resisted for a short
while until an article by Jesús Hernández in *Frente Rojo*, reminding her
that the interest of the party was above one's feelings, caused her to
give in. Then after repeatedly attacking the very men whom she had
advised not to give in, she tried to pull the rug from under the new
leadership in which she participated only conditionally—in exchange for
her self-criticism—and in a secondary capacity. With this end in mind
she wrote the following as the crowning touch to her attacks on the
fallen troika: "Now then, are the members of the group, that is, Bullejos,
Adame, Trilla, and Vega, the only ones to be blamed for the fact that
the party has not been directed toward the revolutionary movement,
thereby delaying the demise of the regime and therefore strengthening—
although only momentarily—the position of the bourgeoisie and landowners? With all Bolshevik frankness I say no . . . although the greatest

responsibility falls to the group, I myself, along with the members of the central committee . . . share some of the responsibility for having been weak and cowardly, for allowing ourselves to be accomplices of the sectarian executive committee."

All committees, both local and of the federations, also declared their support for the new leaders. For example, the provincial Balearic committee proclaimed the "justice of the change of policy" and stated that "for a while now the party has not increased its membership . . . in a word, we have not been equal to the task."[9] They even attempted to get former members who had been expelled to confess. One of them was Julián Gorkín, to whom a delegate of the Comintern offered "the editorship of a newspaper against Trotsky and Trotskyism, against Maurín and Maurinism, and against myself in exchange for a thorough self-criticism." Naturally the offer was refused.[10] Within a couple of months the new leaders had the party well under control.

The German Catastrophe

The new leaders of the PCE were enthroned at a time when the Communist International was going through its worst setback and when the worldwide working-class movement was facing a catastrophe: Hitler's rise to power. Outside of Russia, the German Communist party was the most powerful in the Communist International. It had gone from 124,000 members and 4 million electors in 1930 to 360,000 members and 6 million electors in 1932 when Hitler's National Socialist party seemed to have begun its decline. But the fact that Socialists and Communists fought separately gave power as well as the strongest minority to the Nazis. All told, the Communist and Socialist votes were 1.5 million more than Hitler's.[11] But they were not added together. They were often subtracted. For example, in 1925 there were elections for president of the republic, and the Communists, knowing that their candidate Thaelmann could not win, ran him anyway instead of searching for a common candidate with the Socialists; this is how Marshal Paul von Hindenburg, who eventually would hand over power to Hitler, gained victory. Another example is when in 1930 Hitler managed to get a referendum against Prussia's Socialist government and the Communists voted with the Nazis against the Socialists. This is how the Communist International's policy of "social-fascism" opened the door for Hitler. It was not exclusively the Communists' fault, yet without them the Nazis would not have been able to win over the chancellory.

Germany, the masterpiece of Comintern strategy, fell into the hands of the enemy. Things began to change in Moscow. Yet the change was slow. For a period of two years, in spite of the fear which the image of Hitler with his "Eastward march" inspired (promised in *Mein Kampf*), the Communist International still emphasized the strategy put forth in the sixth congress: social-fascism, class against class, third period, united front from below. A more abrupt change of policy might have helped stop the Nazis in their tracks and would have prevented war. The slowness of the change of policy gave Hitler time to consolidate his power and destroy the German labor movement—which is why the change was doomed to fail.

In Spain those in the labor movement had traditionally shown little interest in anything happening outside the country. The Communist leaders considered whatever went on outside of Spain to be of primary importance if it affected the USSR. For this reason those in the labor movement called them Chinamen and "pigtails," because toward the end of the dictatorship and after the Republic had been proclaimed, whenever there was a debate either in the USSR or the Communist movement regarding Stalin's position on the Chinese Revolution, the Communist press filled its pages with articles about a far-off China.

The information provided by the Communist press is not really information. It is enough to see what *Correspondencia Internacional* was saying about Spain and compare it with the facts to understand that what it said about Germany was not any closer to reality. This explains why Hitler's victory surprised Spanish Communists. The truthfulness of the news was jeopardized by the fact that the delegations of the Communist International wanted to "show off" and therefore distorted reality, presenting it the way Moscow wanted to see it and not the way it really was. Furthermore, no one dared to analyze the strategy of the Communist International.

The German Communist periodical in exile in Switzerland said just a few days after Hitler's becoming chancellor that "after Hitler we will follow," because Hitler would destroy "the masses' dreams for democracy." Given this state of mind, it is easy to understand why the change of policy took so long.[12] For the new Spanish leaders Hitler's rise to power changed nothing. They were even more dogged because no longer was there any question about "advice" of the "instructors," the policy of "social-fascism," the united front from below, or of class against class.

It is true that beginning in March 1933 the PCE advocated an Antifascist Front, composed of the PCE, Juventud Comunista, the Tobacco Federation, the tiny Federal party, and the Radical Socialist Left. Neither the PSOE, UGT, nor CNT accepted the invitation to join it. The front publicly came out at a rally on July 8 at the Teatro Español in Madrid at which the famous French novelist Henri Barbusse spoke. A plenary meeting of the central committee on April 7, 1933 ratified this policy.

A New Kind of Sectarianism

Stepanov had stated the principles for the new leaders in a series of articles published under a pseudonym, S. Chavaroche, in which he said that the Spanish revolution had entered the "phase of [political and organic] preparation of the workers and peasants for the takeover of power." Nevertheless "conditions are not ripe . . . because although the masses are moving away from the Socialists, Anarcho-Syndicalists, Radical-Socialists, Republicans, and Radicals, they have yet to complete their separation." The party's mission, then, is to "undertake the political and organic preparation of the masses for the takeover of power." This could be done by organizing peasant occupation of land, creating factory and peasant committees, and "committees of national and social liberation" in Catalonia, Galicia, and the Basque country. Finally, Stepanov reminded them of what the Twelfth Plenary of the Communist International had said: "In Spain the movement of the masses is accelerating with a tendency to develop into popular armed rebellion."[13]

Sectarianism continued but in a different direction: the planning for takeover of power. However, it had to coexist with the Communist International's new task, the fight against fascism. This strengthening of sectarianism was due to the party's internal needs to counteract the confusion and demoralization caused by the manner in which the crisis of the troika was resolved. But it also reflected the desire of the Communist International to use it to absolve itself of the German catastrophe. It more or less said: "We were so right that despite Hitler's victory we did not have to change our policy."

It is easy to see why other oganizations did not want to be part of the Antifascist Front: they were wary not only of the continuing tactics of "social-fascism" and "anarcho-fascism" but also of the policy of the united front from below which invited "sincere" workers from other organizations to join the Communists in their fight against the leaders of those other organizations, leaders whom those "sincere" workers had elected. Although that tactic was unsuccessful, it discredited the slogan of the united front by linking it, in the spirit of the militant workers, to the divisionist maneuvers of the Communists.

The new leaders scored one small victory: in February 1933 the congress of a phantasmagoric Social-Revolutionary party was held; it was led by Representative José Antonio Balbontín (elected in 1931 as a Radical Socialist). This party which claimed to have 8,000 members and which only operated in Andalusia—on a limited basis—decided at that congress to join the PCE.[14] It is not known how many members of the PSR joined the PCE. Balbontín, as representative, managed to recite from his seat the positions and manifestos of the PCE. The first Communist representative in Spain, then, was not elected by Communist but rather Republican votes. Balbontín did not stay in the PCE for very long, for in March 1934 he resigned from the party (which hastened to expel him) because he was not in agreement with Communist attacks against Socialists and Anarchists "while Spanish fascism was advancing at an alarming rate and already had a foothold in the government and will inevitably gain monopoly of power if we do not hasten to stop it by means of a sincere antifascist unity."[15]

Historia del PCE does not even mention this "round-trip" representative, but attributes the triumph of the Communist candidate from Málaga, Cayetano Bolívar, in the elections of November 1933, to a so-called Popular Front. Bolívar was defeated in the first round. The executive board "ordered him to run with the list of candidates the Socialists and Radical-Socialists" had put together to check the advance of the right-wing candidates. This is how it got the certificate of election, with Republican and Socialist as well as Communist votes. In Madrid the Communist candidates garnered 16,311 votes and in Seville 14,000.[16] It was during the 1933 electoral campaign that Santiago Carrillo, then leader of the FJS and in constant controversy with the Communists, devised the idea of putting up posters which, as a parody of the CEDA slogan, said: "If you want to free Spain of Marxism, vote Communist."

The PCE waged an intensive campaign with a great display of propaganda which centered around the program of the workers' and peasants' government the party was advocating. This government was to confiscate large landholdings, nationalize large industry, introduce a seven-hour workday and unemployment insurance, recognize the right of regions to secede, free the colonies and Morocco, do away with the civil guard, police guard, and the army, arm the workers and peasants, create a Red army, and finally, sign a "fraternal alliance" with the USSR.

The PCE candidates received 400,000 votes according to *Historia del PCE,* but historians put the figure at 200,000 (there were 8.7 million voters; women were allowed to vote for the first time). The gains were in Asturias, Andalusia, and Madrid, while losses were suffered in Vizcaya and things remained unchanged in Catalonia.[17] The PCE became more active than it had been under the troika and tried to reach social groups previously ignored by the troika. For instance it organized a congress of young miners in Asturias in addition to one for peasant youths. In 1933 it created the Union of Communist Students of which Fernando

Claudín, Manuel Tuñón de Lara, Manuel Azcárate, and Luis Sendín were members. In May 1933 it established the Pioneers, the children's section of Juventudes Comunistas. In Catalonia Juventudes Comunistas did not begin operation until April 1934 when the first congress of the Partit Comunista de Catalunya was held.[18]

The new "instructors" reorganized *Mundo Obrero*. The publishing house Cenit lent the paper 80,000 pesetas, and this amount along with a public collection enabled them to buy an old printing shop on Andrés Mellado Street which had belonged to *El Socialista*. The printing shop was where Cenit's books were also printed, which allowed the party to prepare a large part of its propaganda with fewer expenses. Ángel Pumarega was the manager for the entire operation. Foreseeing possible suspension of the operation by the government, they had registered the title *Frente Rojo* which was used when *Mundo Obrero* was suspended. The editorial office was located on 9 Cardenal Cisneros Street. Arrarás was its administrator and he was succeeded by Manuel Delicado; Vicente Uribe was the editor. The editorial staff included, among others, Luis Sendín, Miguel González, and Manuel Navarro Ballesteros.[19]

In addition to the party's press in the provinces there were some publications inspired by the party such as *Los sin Dios* (*The Godless*), which was the organ of the Atheist League, a letterhead organization. There were also relatively luxurious magazines like *Octubre,* for intellectuals, and *Nuestro Cinema*. These two were relatively high-quality magazines and some intellectuals who would later distinguish themselves got their start writing for them. They did not have wide circulation but were read by professionals and students. Among the magazines' patrons were Rafael Alberti, César M. Arconada, Joaquín Arderius, César Falcón, Irene Falcón, María Teresa León, Ramón J. Sender, Emilio Prados, Juan A. Cabezas, Angel Gaos, Pascual Pla y Beltrán, and José Renau.[20]

There was increasing influence among intellectuals. This is how the Asociación de Escritores y Artistas Revolucionarios (AEAR) was formed. In addition to the above-mentioned individuals connected with *Octubre* and *Nuestro Cinema,* others participating in AEAR were Armando Bazán, Arturo Serrano Plaja, and Pedro Garfias. Ramón del Valle-Inclán and Francisco Galán were delegates in the International Union of Writers. Rosario del Olmo was in charge of operations for the association whose office was in the Ateneo in Madrid. *Octubre* was its magazine. A similar association was formed in Catalonia but lacked prominent writers. In Valencia José Renau, Ángel Gaos, Pla y Beltrán, and others founded the journal *Nueva Cultura*. With help from the PCE a proletarian theater and cinema club were in operation, inspired by César Falcón and María Teresa León, as part of the AEAR.

In April 1933 the Asociación de Amigos de la Unión Soviética was founded. Its members included Eduardo Barriobero, Eduardo Ortega y Gasset, Luis Jiménez de Asúa, Juan Negrín, Victoria Kent, Ramón J. Sender, Augusto Barcia, Luis de Tapia, Roberto Castrovido, Luis Bagaría, Marcelino Pascua, María Lejáraga (María Martínez Sierra), Federico García Lorca, Julián Zugazagoitia, Wenceslao Roces, Rodolfo Llopis, Amaro del Rosal, and Ezequiel Endériz.[21] On July 14 a group of members of the newly founded fascist Falange assaulted the headquarters of Amigos de la Unión Soviética. They destroyed furniture, stole records, and gagged the secretary and Wenceslao Roces, who was in charge of the association.

The party was touching all bases. On June 21, 1933 Balbontín, as Communist representative, introduced a bill to the Parliament calling for "class amnesty." Pro-amnesty committees were created. "The PCE had never as much support for any of its campaigns," but when it proposed a 24-hour strike in favor of amnesty, it was rejected by labor organizations. This campaign was organized by "instructor" Neumann who knew from experience how to make an impact in circles which had previously been indifferent: he simply appealed to sentiments.[22]

At that time Neumann "drafted for the PCE a new program of action to seize power and establish a workers' and peasants' government."[23] Perhaps it was Neumann, a charming and well-educated man, who won over for the PCE two valuable allies who never openly appeared as such but who always acted in the service of the PCE (or, more probably, of the Communist International). One of them was the Socialist representative Margarita Nelken and the other Julio Álvarez del Vayo, also a representative as well as a socialist writer.[24] It will soon be apparent how on numerous occasions they came to the party's aid or served as messengers. As far as we know, they began to have dealings with Communists in 1932 or 1933, although del Vayo had already gone to Russia and written a dithyrambic book about his trip called *La nueva Rusia.*

The CGTU

From 1932 to 1936 the PCE did not hold a congress, in spite of the fact that according to statutes there should have been four. The fifth congress, the first since 1932, was held in 1954. The party had been totally Stalinized. Neither the Russian party nor the International had held congresses for many years. The apparat ran everything and the leaders coopted each other for promotions in Spain as well as in the USSR. But the party grew considerably and ran better than it had in the past, since there was no longer tension between the executive board and the delegation of the Communist International.[25] "The regular get-togethers of colleagues were replaced by provincial, neighborhood, and cellular organizations. The party rented an office on the first floor of a house on Estrella Street in Madrid. Yet the main activity of the party did not take place there: it was carried out in neighborhoods, unions, leftist political parties, military quarters, universities, among the unemployed who congregated in places which were like hunger markets. The party finally began to be a party. Moscow was pleased."[26]

But there were some defects. Jesús Hernández, speaking before the thirteenth plenary of the Communist International in December 1933, said that "many workers forsake the Anarchists but do not join the PCE. The party has not yet convinced them that it is the only force capable of stopping fascism. . . . There are powerful movements in cities and in the country, but unfortunately their leadership is not in the hands of our party save in a few cases."[27] To build up the image of the party emergency rallies were organized everywhere. "It gave the impression of having many members even though it did not. . . . The machinery was set up. Each man was a part whose only connection with the other parts was his daily performance."[28] At that time the party had no more than 3,000 members.[29] There were workers among the militants in the PCE, but as the new leaders went about strengthening discipline and organization, those workers were joined by intellectuals, students (the Communists began to infiltrate the FUE), and by individuals from the middle class.

The new leaders realized that a labor party must gain support from the working classes and unions. So far the party had not been able to do so. In June 1932 it tried to organize a General Unitarian Labor Confederation—CGTU, but it never got off the ground. It never developed into anything more than an organizing committee.[30] The troika had resisted pressure from the "instructors," knowing that formation of another labor confederation would isolate the Communists among the workers to an even greater extent. The workers wanted unity, not division. But there was no longer any resistance from the new leaders. Moscow wanted a Spanish Communist labor confederation for the Profintern and it would get it.

The organizing committee of the CGTU (whose name was a direct translation of its French "sister") came out with a manifesto supporting the Communist candidates in the elections of November 1933. From April 25 to 29, 1934 the first congress of the CGTU met to officially and publicly shape the new labor confederation. In attendance were 135 delegates representing 180,000 members (as opposed to the 221 delegates and 267,000 members at the conference in Madrid in 1932). It appears that the CGTU actually had about 100,000 members, most of them from Andalusia and Asturias.[31] The platform the congress approved "was nothing more than a repetition of every position—united front, attacks on the UGT and CNT, demands for salary increases, shorter workday, social security, disarmament, etc.—which more or less characterized the party's operation since the Republic was proclaimed."[32] Neither *Historia del PCE* nor Dolores Ibárruri in her memoirs makes reference to the establishment of the CGTU.

The CGTU resembled the party in many ways: Andalusia, Vizcaya, and Madrid predominated in the leading teams, the leaders were relatively young, the majority of the members were workers, yet there was increasing influence from professionals such as doctors, lawyers, teachers, and even retired military personnel. In 1933 the ratio of members to voters was 1 to 20, that of members to union affiliates, 1 to 5. Naturally the teams of leaders "as a rule during those years kept within the guidelines set up by their International with maximalist focus." Following the "serious upheavals of 1932," the gap between those in leadership and the rank and file was narrowed, but "the impression remained that, unlike other sectors [of the labor movement], the greatest impetus as far as practices were concerned came from the top; yet local initiative was evident in the multiple instances of agitation in Andalusia (not only by farmers, but also, for example, in Seville's port), in the mines of Asturias, and so on."[33]

The Workers' Alliance

The large union and political labor movements were involved in local squabbles and underestimated the dangers of Nazism. The minor organizations which did not have to deal with the headaches of power reacted first. It was in Barcelona that this reaction produced concrete results.[34] In a private meeting in which the secretary general of the Unió Socialista de Catalunya, Joan Comorera, made a proposal to Joaquín Maurín of BOC calling for the unification of both organizations, it was agreed that since such unification was not feasible at the moment, it would be better to call the whole labor movement to unify against fascism in the form of a workers' alliance. The Popular Ecyclopedic Atheneum (led at the time by members of BOC) was asked to put out the call. A rally of several organizations was held, and in light of the enthusiastic reception of the initiative, a document was negotiated and signed on December 16, 1933 which established the Alianza Obrera and said: "The organizations whose signatures appear below, of varied doctrinal tendencies and aspirations, yet united by a common desire to safeguard the conquests won so far by the Spanish working class, constitute the Alianza Obrera; we oppose triumph of the reactionaries in our country to avoid any attempt at a coup d'état or the establishment of dictatorship and to preserve intact the benefits achieved to date which represent the heritage of the working class."

Neither the CNT nor PCE was in the Alianza. That did not prevent it from being immediately acclaimed throughout Spain. First in Valencia, then in parts of Andalusia and the center of the country local committees of Alianza Obrera were formed with local support of the PSOE and UGT. When Largo Caballero was elected secretary general of the PSOE, he leaned toward Alianza Obrersa, although he did not want the Socialists to join on a national scale before the CNT was also ready to join. There was considerable discussion in the CNT. In Madrid Orobón Fernández supported the Alianza and also the Regional Committee of Asturias, to the extent that he forced a plenary meeting of the CNT to accept the Asturian CNT's becoming a member of the Alianza. But the rest of the CNT remained aloof.

The Alianza did not come about simply because two leaders happened on an "ingenious idea." It was the product of a long Catalonian experience. In 1933 despite the strength of the CNT, the strikes which it declared mostly came to naught. As a reaction, trade union fronts were formed, first to aid in the struggle of the unemployed, then for the negotiation of a contract for utility workers, and then for a strike (the first in the history of the Spanish labor movement) of retail and office workers. They succeeded where separate unions had failed. With this proof that the concept of alliance was well received by the working masses and effective in practice, it could then move on to the political arena and this is what Alianza Obrera did. The Alianza existed in Catalonia and Asturias as well on a local level in many other places in Spain, particularly in Valencia. It had also formed in Madrid:

> The experience of two years with a Republican regime has shown the working class that nothing can be expected of the bourgeoisie or its coercive organizations except repression if it rebels, or famine and hardship if it does not give in. This experience has convinced the proletariat of the necessity of creating the effective weapon to defend itself against the increasingly brutal attacks of the reactionaries and the bourgeoisie and at the right moment to fight the final battle. That weapon can only be the unity of all those who are exploited. In agreement are several political and union organizations in Madrid: the Socialist party (Madrid Chapter), Tobacco Workers' Union (local of Madrid), Agrupación Sindicalista, Communist Left, and Socialist Youth—all constitute the Alianza Obrera, a body whose ultimate goal is to fight fascism in all its manifestations and enable

the working class to implant a socialist, federal peace in Spain, an essential condition for its complete liberation.[35]

A few weeks later, Juventudes Comunistas made a proposal of unification to Juventudes Socialistas which responded by inviting them to join Alianza Obrera. This sounded like anathema to Communist ears. Francisco Galán wrote: "If I had to sit at the same table with the Socialist leaders, I would blush like a virgin among prostitutes."[36] While trade union fronts were being formed in many places, the PCE created its CGTU. At the first congress of the Partit Communista de Catalunya which the Hungarian "instructor" Gerö attended, Vicente Uribe, who had been sent by the political bureau, underlined the fact that

> in putting into practice our policy of united front, there has been hesitation and doubt both among the leaders of the Catalonian party and in a certain number of organizations. The hesitation and doubt were expressed by the tendency to conceive the united front as a bloc of organizations, blotting out the personality of the Communist party. There has been great criticism and self-criticism regarding this, and all the delegates have come out in complete agreement with the policy of the Communist International and the Communist party of Spain in the establishment of the united front from below. We must not forget that it is in Catalonia where the Alianza Obrera was born, that malformed creature fathered by the renegades of the Bloque Obrero y Campesino, syndicalists, and Socialists—an alliance against the united front and the revolution. The correct policy of united front allows us to thwart the counterrevolutionary plans of the Alianza Obrera and, more importantly, to win for our battle thousands of Anarchist workers and achieve unity in combat among the Catalonian proletariat and peasant masses under the leadership of the Communist party.[37]

Other quotes will help to understand the tone of the party's reaction: "The lapdogs of the bourgeoisie who make up Alianza Obrera. . . . As part of Alianza Obrera, a caricature of the United Front, they try to deceive the workers who sincerely want the United Front."[38] Three months later things changed. Moscow decided to give the green light to the French Communist party to carry out some surveys and tests which might help determine the possibilities for success of a change in policy, which, at long last, the Comintern and Stalin had begun to develop. The PCE supported the tests of its French "brother." In a special meeting of the Central Committee of the PCE on September 11 and 12, 1934 the change took official form:[39]

> There was only one item on the agenda: United Front and Alianzas Obreras. The Central Committee of the PCE has discussed this matter before thousands of workers and has unanimously approved the political bureau's

proposition of joining Alianzas Obreras on one condition: "To have the freedom to raise and discuss fraternally all problems regarding the revolution." This agreement was a tremendous step forward along the way to unity of action and the road to victory. . . . Our party within the alliances will work to transform them from conglomerates of party leaders into active bodies of united front. As the party secretary said in his report: "The delegates to the Alianzas must be elected democratically in assemblies made up of unions, organizations, factory committees, peasants, and the unemployed."

Without making a retraction, the PCE forgot about the comments it had made in previous months against Alianza Obrera. But since there was a change of policy, it took as much advantage of it as it could. This is what Codovila, who visited Largo Caballero, tried to attend to. Largo Caballero related: "An individual called Medina—I don't think that is his real name—who spoke correct Spanish, was in the country and he was an agent of the Third International. Medina was introduced to me by Margarita Nelken, who at the time was a member of the Socialist party, for the purpose of speaking to me about Alianzas Obreras. He was trying to have his name changed (I don't recall to what—one that was more in harmony with Russian vocabulary) to facilitate Communist entry in the alliances. We spoke for several hours. He finally was convinced that it was neither opportune nor practical to import exotic-sounding names into Spain. The next day the Communist press reported that the members of their party had agreed to be part of Alianzas Obreras."[40]

The intent was evident: to have the name changed so that it would not look like the party accepted what it had criticized and so that the public would believe that the Alianza, with a different name, was a Communist invention. In spite of this failure, which prevented the PCE from getting the credit of having begun Alianza Obrera, *Historia del PCE* states:[41] "The Communist party, acting out of a deep sense of national responsibility, voted to participate in Alianzas Obreras. . . . This resolution constituted a bold tactical turnabout."

Mundo Obrero reported that Alianzas Obreras "are the fundamental body of the struggle for power,"[42] which makes them fit right in with the policy outlined by Stepanov. Nonetheless nearly a month passed before the PCE formalized its entrance into Alianza Obrera. It did so in Catalonia on October 4, when an assembly of Alianza was held to make decisions regarding events which had been seen coming, unleashed by the entry of CEDA (a rightist non-Republican party) in the government of the Republic. The assembly admitted the PCE without discussing the matter nor wasting any time to welcome it. In Asturias the PCE joined

Alianza at a time when fighting in the streets had already begun. Nowhere else was the PCE part of local alliances prior to October 4.[43]

The October Surprise

Historia del PCE devotes three pages to the movement of October 1934. A good portion of them are spent emphasizing the PCE's efforts to convert the alliances into "acting organs of the United Front," since upon entering Alianza "the party proposed establishing unity and permanent contacts with Socialist and UGT workers"—in other words, using Alianza as a field for united front tactics from below.[44] There is no mention made anywhere of the participation of the PCE which in both Catalonia and Asturias lagged behind Alianza. It had valiant militants who took part in the armed struggle and gave up their lives in it. And its militants, like those in the other labor organizations, suffered imprisonment, torture, and harsh prison sentences.[45]

We are dealing with a party which, in accordance with instructions from the International, must ready itself as well as the masses for the taking of power. According to Leninist doctrine, the party is considered the only qualified representative of the proletariat, indeed its incarnation, its vanguard, which history has charged with carrying out the proletarian revolution. And we are dealing with events in the course of which the proletariat in Asturias not only took power but administered and defended it for two weeks.

The party called by history to lead the revolution led nothing. The Leninist theory of the right line which, when the time came, would be supported by the people, failed in Spain in 1934, unless we suppose that the PCE did not have the right line. The PCE intervened only when Alianza ordered a withdrawal when the fighting in Asturias was through and when the Communists seized control of what was left. "The ardor of proselytizing carried the most disoriented to the extreme of falsifying the news to suit themselves, and they formed a committee behind Alianza Obrera's back in order to make useless sacrifices of lives."[46]

This committee announced immediately that the USSR would send fighter planes and went so far as to affirm that some Soviet ships were in Spanish waters. It tried to organize a Red army to replace the workers' militias which had been used up to that point. It even unveiled a plan to drill the militiamen and teach them to play the bugle and mark time. In the proclamations of this Communist committee Alianza Obrera was now called Alianza Obrera y Campesina (Workers' and Peasants' Alliance) in accordance with party policy, in spite of the fact that Asturian peasants did not take part in the fighting, and the name UHP (Union of Proletarian

Brothers) was replaced by PP (Proletarian Power). The revolution no longer belonged to everyone; now it was solely Communist. This committee barely lasted twenty-four hours. The Alianza committee was forced to negotiate the surrender since there was no longer any real possibility of continuing the battle and since neither the planes nor the ships which the Communists had promised had arrived.[47]

Neither the memoirs of La Pasionaria nor *Historia del PCE* makes reference to this Communist committee. Once the insurrection had been squelched, the PCE and the PCC came out in the international Communist press taking credit for the accomplishments of others. For example they said that in Lérida, a city dominated by BOC and in which the PCC had fewer than a dozen members, "barricades were put up beneath the furls of our red flag,"[48] when actually they were referring to the red flag of the hated BOC. The organs of the press on the far Right and official government propaganda were the only elements which attributed a leading role in the movement to the PCE.

The Comintern took quite a while in making its own analysis. It appears in the preparatory materials of the Seventh Congress of the Communist International: "The revolutionary miners of Asturias tried to establish soviets. As a result of Anarchist treason, the sabotage of most Social-Democratic leaders, and the inadquate training of the proletariat and peasantry—a consequence of the previous Social-Democratic policy—the Spanish proletariat was forced to withdraw."

In October the Executive Committee of the Communist International proposed to the Socialist International a joint action in defense of the Spanish proletariat. By that time an attempt at a new tactic had already been initiated and repression in Spain was a good excuse to see how the Socialists would react. The reaction was not favorable because, as Adler and Vandervelde told Cachin and Thorez (who delivered the Communist International's letter to the two men), there would be no reason, after twelve years of attacks, to expect people to believe it was not a ploy.[49]

Dolores Ibárruri attended a meeting in Paris in 1935 in defense of the Spanish workers. In her memoirs[50] she relates that she had to cross the border on foot and return the same way. If such was the case, it would indicate that the PCE had a pathetic illegal apparat. In those times to illegally cross the border was not difficult.[51] *Historia del PCE*[52] does not go into any analysis as to whether the PCE also had shortcomings. In perspective, the main shortcoming of the PCE was that it was surprised by the events of October as it had been by the Sanjurjo uprising of 1932. Different teams of leaders, but the same mistakes, because they did not rely on themselves but on the International.

The account of the events in Asturias which the PCE authorized was not made public until a year and a half later. We are talking about a book by Manuel Navarro Ballesteros (editor of *Mundo Obrero*), edited under the pseudonym Maximiliano Álvarez Suárez and titled *Sangre de Octubre: UHP*. It was published by Cenit in 1936. Curiously, the minister of war in October 1934, the moderate Republican Diego Hidalgo, was one of Cenit's stockholders and appeared in the *Anuario Financiero de Sociedades Anónimas de España* (*Financial Yearbook of Corporations in Spain*) of 1933 as a creditor of Cenit for 239,000 pesetas, which at the time was a considerable amount.

Notes

1. Antonio Ramos Oliveira, *Nosotros, los marxistas: Lenín contra Marx,* Madrid, 1932, p. 26.
2. Four Andalusians, three Basques, and one man from Madrid. Six workers, one peasant, and a housewife. Five former students of the Leninist school in Moscow (Enrique Castro Delgado, *Hombres made in Moscú,* p. 143).
3. Margarete Buber-Neumann, *L'Internationale Communiste,* Paris, 1971, p. 317ff. Neumann's widow who was in Moscow when the Nazi-Soviet pact of 1939 was being signed and who was then handed over to the Gestapo by the NKVD, relates that in 1932 she was sent as a liaison to Madrid with documents belonging to the Comintern for its delegation. By mistake she delivered them to Díaz and Uribe and the "Spanish Communists must have been more than mildly surprised at the considerable sum of dollars earmarked for the emissaries in Moscow." According to his wife, Neumann replaced the Pole Prumann in Spain. Prumann was in Madrid under surveillance of the Comintern and upon his return to Moscow committed suicide.
4. Buber-Neumann, p. 329.
5. *Historia del PCE,* p. 79.
6. In the same way that Dolores Ibárruri in her memoirs hushed up the advice given to Bullejos not to make any concessions, she kept quiet about her self-criticism. All she said was (p. 148) that a comrade from the political bureau went to see her in prison and informed her of the crisis in the party, and that she expressed "agreement with the measures taken to ensure the leadership and continuity of the party and to rectify the rigid and sectarian policy which had transformed the party into a group of self-denying, heroic propagandists whom workers admired for their courage but whom they did not follow."
7. Matorras, p. 138. Aside from Olmos, who left immediately, each member of the executive committee (Arévalo, Lafora, and Matorras) was replaced soon after by Rosado, De Grado, and Montalvo. Medrano was the only one to attain a position in the new youth leadership.
8. Quoted in Matorras, p. 139ff.
9. Pere Gabriel.
10. Gorkín, *El revolucionario profesional,* p. 286.
11. Claudín, *La crisis del movimiento comunista,* p. 97.

162   The Communist Party in Spain

12. More examples of this blindness: "The fascist dictatorship destroys hopes for democracy and frees the masses from the influence of Social-Democracy, and thereby helps speed Germany on its way to proletarian revolution. One would have to be an ignorant fool to say that the German Communists have been vanquished," wrote the German Communist representative Heckert in *Rundschau,* the German Communist party journal in exile. Heckert sought refuge in the USSR where he was later executed. In 1932 Stalin, in a meeting of the political bureau of the Russian Communist party, said: "Hitler will not win. General Schleicher will crush him." In 1934 Hitler crushed General Schleicher. In December 1933 Korin, a Russian leader of the Communist International, was still saying: "Fascism's success is a result of the fascination which Social-Democracy holds." And in February 1934 the French Communists were side by side with the fascist groups trying to attack the parliament in Paris (Víctor Alba, *Historia del Frente Popular,* Mexico City, 1959, pp. 40–41).

13. J. Chavaroche, "Las tareas fundamentales del PCE en la etapa actual del desarrollo de la revolución en España," *Correspondencia Internacional,* Madrid, April 21, 28, May 5, 1933.

14. The insignificant Partido de Izquierda Revolucionaria y Antiimperialista (Revolutionary Left and Anti-Imperialist Party) had previously joined the PCE.

15. Artola, p. 691.

16. These figures are from Matorras (p. 170). Tusell (p. 105) gives 12,610 votes for Madrid.

17. Tuñón de Lara, p. 891.

18. Ramón Castera, *Las JSUC ante la guerra y la revolución (1936–1939),* Barcelona, 1977, p. 72ff.

19. Comín Colomer, vol. I, p. 512.

20. *Nuestro Cinema,* Madrid, October 13, 1933.

21. Comín Colomer, vol. I, p. 524ff.

22. Buber-Neumann, p. 327.

23. Ibid., p. 330.

24. Hugh Thomas, *The Spanish Civil War,* New York, 1961, p. 72.

25. At the beginning of 1933 there was talk in political circles of negotiating the reestablishment of diplomatic relations between Spain and the USSR, and apparently Moscow had taken steps in this direction. At that same time an Anarchist insurrection broke out, the most dramatic outcome of which was a massacre in the village of Casas Viejas. The PCE ordered its militants not to get involved in the insurrection. *Historia del PCE* does not even mention Casas Viejas. The intense campaign of protest over Casas Viejas failed to gain the support of the PCE which always joined in any protest against the Republican government. Dolores Ibárruri does not speak of Casas Viejas in her memoirs either. Moscow was at that time negotiating its recognition by Madrid.

26. Castro Delgado, *Hombres made in Moscú,* p. 146. Tagüeña described one of the most anonymous, second-rank leaders of the period: "Velasco, editor of this journal (*Juventud Roja*), was the most perfect embodiment of a Communist functionary that I have ever met. He never expressed opinions which differed from those of his superiors, he worked endlessly for a pittance, and he carried out with great zeal every order he was given. Although he

was an employee and not a manual laborer, he looked on me with the same mistrust Stalin held toward the intellectuals of his time" (Tagüeña, p. 46).

27. Degras, *The Communist International,* vol. II, p. 293.

28. Ibid., p. 192.

29. The plenary meeting of the PCE which took place in April 1933 came out with the figure of 20,000 members, but the Thirteenth Plenary of the Communist International in December of the same year mentioned 30,000 plus 11,000 in Juventudes. A year later the Communist International said that the PCE had exactly 20,223 members (Tuñón de Lara, pp. 891–92). Anyone who has lived during those times and who has had contact with the PCE knows that the figure of 3,000 (given by Hugh Thomas, *The Spanish Civil War,* p. 71) is close to the truth. The PSOE had 80,000 members.

30. This attempt was probably the basis for many historians' dating the foundation of the CGTU in 1932, a time when it had only been talked about. The fact that the Profintern regarded this organizing committee as a confederation belonging to the Profintern doubtless contributed to the error.

31. Tuñón de Lara, p. 893.

32. Artola, pp. 691–92. See also *Hacia el congreso de la CGTU* and *Plataforma de lucha aprobada por el primer congreso de la CGTU,* Madrid, 1934.

33. Tuñón de Lara, pp. 894–95. This author, after working out the already mentioned ratios, says that the figure of 20,000 for the PCE membership is accurate.

34. For this entire section see Alba, *El marxisme a Catalunya,* vol. I, p. 227ff.

35. *El Socialista,* Madrid, March 6, 1934.

36. Quoted by G. Munis, *Jalones de derrota, promesa de victoria,* Mexico City, 1948, p. 112.

37. *Correspondencia Internacional,* Madrid, June 3, 1934.

38. Estruch, p. 79.

39. Report of Vicente Arroyo in *Correspondencia Internacional,* Madrid, September 23, 1934.

40. Francisco Largo Caballero, *Mis recuerdos: cartas a un amigo,* Mexico City, 1954, p. 224.

41. *Historia del PCE,* p. 88.

42. *Mundo Obrero,* Madrid, October 4, 1934.

43. In her memoirs (p. 155) La Pasionaria says that Largo Caballero opposed the "Trotskyist Alianzas Obreras" to those alliances of the United Front proposed by the Communists. "By means of this stance the leadership of the Socialist party, headed by Largo Caballero, tried to meet several objectives: counteract the obvious gains made by the United Front; apparently satisfy desires for unity among Socialist workers; and saddle the Communists with the responsibility of not having established unity if indeed they refused to join Alianzas."

44. *Historia del PCE,* pp. 89–92. Ibárruri, *El único camino,* pp. 158–61.

45. The Socorro Rojo Internacional (International Red Aid) was a good instrument for propaganda for it played on emotions. Its accounts, published in its organ *Aurreará* (Comín Colomer provides a photostat of it, vol. II, p. 429) indicate that the SRI distributed to prisoners and their families 850,000 pesetas and that it came to the aid of 353 political exiles, among

whom were 92 Socialists, 142 Communists, 9 individuals from the SRI, 7 from BOC, 25 from the CNT, 25 Republicans, and 54 unaffiliated. I do not know about the rest, but I do know that no member of BOC received aid from the SRI and that, had it been offered, it would not have been accepted since their own organization was looking after them.

46. *El Socialista,* Madrid, January 25, 1936.
47. B. Díaz Nosty, *La communa asturiana,* Madrid, 1974, p. 291ff.
48. *L'Humanité,* Paris, October 23, 1934, in an interview with anonymous leaders of the PCC.
49. Degras, *The Communist International,* vol. III, p. 330. Other Communist interpretations of October 1934 are found in Jesús Hernández's report to the Seventh Congress of the Communist International and in a document dated March 1935, signed by Díaz, Togliatti, and André Marty, addressed to "all Socialist, Communist, Anarchist, and union workers of Spain." Both texts place particular blame on the Socialists. (The texts appear in Comín Colomer, vol. II, pp. 437–55.)
50. Ibárruri, *El único camino,* p. 117.
51. A personal recollection illustrates this disorganization in the party following October 1934. At the beginning of 1935 the French Communist leader Gabriel Péri (who was later executed by the Nazis) came to Barcelona to interview local Communist leaders. He did not know where to find them since the addresses he had been given proved useless. He did not know what to do. Having recalled meeting me in Paris when I was there as a journalist, he called me and I put him in touch with Rafael Vidiella, a member at the time of the PSOE. Vidiella uncovered the whereabouts of Catalonian Communist leaders and introduced them to Péri.
52. *Historia del PCE,* p. 92.

11.
The Popular Front

The new line which Moscow had instructed the Communist parties of France and Spain to try out would eventually lead to what was called the policy of the Popular Front. It was successful in those countries where this new policy began to be developed and applied before being adopted by the Comintern. It failed wherever it was regarded as a result of the decisions made by the seventh congress of the Communist International which had officially adopted it. Of course in both instances it was a product of the decisions of the Communist International, but people did not understand that.[1] In putting the policy of Popular Front into effect in Spain, it is important to point out several stages: preparation and formation; triumph in the election; success of independent labor action; and repression of the same labor action at the hands of the Popular Front.

The French Model

After Hitler's rise to power, the Communist parties of some countries where there was general alarm, tried to capitalize upon it and made efforts to create associations and committees which, under hidden Communist leadership, attracted intellectuals, students, lawyers, and renowned scientists. They did not let this stand in the way of their anti-Socialist stance. They wanted to take advantage of the anxiety over Hitler's triumph to ensnare non-Communist elements which echoed Communist slogans and were sympathizers of the Soviet Union.

This occurred in France more than anywhere else. Henri Barbusse, the famous author of the novel *Le Feu* about World War I and editor of the weekly *Monde,* took the initiative of forming an Association of Revolutionary Writers and Artists (they were not yet called anti-Fascists). We already saw that Barbusse attended a ceremony of the Spanish association in Madrid. Likewise "around the middle of 1933 a delegate of the World Committee of Women against War and Fascism whose headquarters were in Paris, arrived in Spain. Her intent was to visit women's groups in Spain and see if it was possible to form a committee of Spanish women of the same nature as the World Committee."[2]

She interviewed Dolores Ibárruri who told her that "she would have no difficulty with communist women," as if in 1963 when she wrote her memoirs, it were not already public knowledge that those world committees against war and fascism were creations of the Communist parties, inspired and prepared by the genius of Comintern propaganda, the German Willi Münzenberg.[3] The French delegate was very interested in interviewing Socialist women, but "a lack of time" prevented her from doing so.

With the aid of Republican women "and some Socialist women too" the Spanish Committee of Women against War and Fascism was organized. The PCE controlled the committee, as was seen in August 1934 when it sent a delegation to the World Congress of Women against War and Fascism in Paris, headed by Dolores Ibárruri and made up of two Republicans and two Communists (Encarnación Fuyola and Irene Falcón). The repression of October of the same year put an end to this committee which was replaced by the Organización Pro Infancia Obrera (Organization for Workers' Children). Also in operation was an organization of Mujeres Antifascistas (Antifascist Women) likewise controlled by the PCE which considered it a seedbed for membership. MA held its first congress in Madrid in the summer of 1934. Proof of how this kind of organization attracted certain leftists who were always fearful of being labeled moderates lies in the fact that Victoria Kent, Isabel de Palencia, María Martínez Sierra, Luisa Álvarez del Vayo, and Matilde Cantos were part of it.

The list of names in the Spanish Committee of Intellectuals against War and Fascism, which grew out of the Association of Revolutionary Artists and Writers, a twin of the committee created in France during the same period, provides additional proof. Along the same lines, the PCE tried to attract students and formed BEOR (Bloque Escolar de Oposición Revolucionaria, Student Bloc of Revolutionary Opposition) in an attempt to win over FUE (Federación Universitaria Española) and UFEH (Unión Federal de Estudiantes Hispanos). It finally achieved its goal and in the process destroyed both organizations.[4]

All this followed the model established by the French Communist party which by 1933 had already formed organizations used as fronts. They suffered a setback when in February of 1934 the fascist Croix-de-Feu (Crosses of Fire) tried to storm the Palais Bourbon, seat of Parliament, and the Communist party ordered its militants to take to the streets to protest against the government. Twenty-four hours after this demonstration which was too much for the police of the Third Republic to handle, the CGT (not yet controlled by the Communists who had their CGTU) called a meeting which the Communist party did not attend.

At the meeting a democratic front in defense of the Republic was established with the Socialist and Radical parties. The Central Committee of the Communist party said that it did not want a front together with the leaders of the Socialist party. In April 1934 Thorez still said: "We have nothing in common with the Socialist party, the main support of the bourgeoisie."

A week after these statements, Thorez and the heads of the other European Communist parties were called to Moscow. There, on April 27, 1934 they received new instructions from the Comintern. It was then that the small movement got off the ground, emerging among intellectuals (among whom were several Communists who had Moscow's approval). It was called Amsterdam-Pleyel, because it was formed in August of 1932 on the eve of Hitler's victory at one meeting in Amsterdam and at another in the Pleyel Concert Hall in Paris. This movement, encouraged by the team from *Monde,* vegetated. After August 1934 it would receive support from the Comintern and its parties, it would have funds available, it would propagate organizations against war and fascism, and it would spread around the world founding several periodicals: *Vendredi* in France, *Futuro* in Mexico, *Claridad* in Buenos Aires. There was a congress of writers in Paris (during which André Gide, at the time a fleeting Communist, asked Stalin to free Victor Serge, who had been exiled to Siberia and who soon after would leave the USSR). No one in Spain raised his voice in defense of Serge despite the fact that he had lived a while in the country involved in Anarcho-Syndicalist circles, had been jailed in Barcelona, and wrote a novel about his experiences in Spain.

The International still did not see things clearly. The leading bureaucrats were used to the clichés of the policy of class against class. They could not get used to the idea of extending a hand to anyone who was not a Communist. It would be necessary to replace those leaders with Georgi Dimitrov, who was very popular because of his confrontations with Goering during the trial for the fire of Reichstag in which he was ultimately acquitted. Dimitrov, a Bulgarian, head of the Western European bureau of the Comintern in Berlin before Hitler, would be in charge of implementing the new policy which would reflect the new Soviet diplomacy as applied by Maxim Litvinov: entry of the USSR into the League of Nations, that "den of imperialist thieves" (as Lenin labeled it), Soviet participation in the disarmament conference, establishment of diplomatic relations with the United States and Spain (which took place in June 1933), Stalin's approval of Gallic rearmament which he gave during the visit to Moscow by the head of the French government, Pierre Laval (and therefore, the French Communist representative's vote in favor of that rearmament), and negotiations for an alliance with France and Great Britain against the Third Reich.

In Spain all this was expressed in the organization of associations and nominal committees. They required so much effort not only in work but also in adaptation that the organization did not pay the attention needed to what was going on in the country, and consequently, October of 1934 caught the party by surprise and it was not able to play any role in the events of that month.

Polarization of the PSOE

The first opportunity for recovery was offered by the PSOE. Aside from Thirdist dissidence, there had always been two well-defined tendencies in the Socialist party: one which favored the alliance with the Republicans and another which opposed it. That was before 1923. Then there was one favorable to discreet collaboration with the dictatorship and the other opposed to it. Once the Republic was proclaimed there were those who did not want Socialists in government and those who wanted to be in it. In 1933 Besteiro demanded that the party's ministers leave the government while Largo Caballero and Prieto wanted them to continue in the cabinet.

But when Azaña was removed from power in September 1933 through the maneuverings of Lerroux, who proposed a homogeneous Republican government as the first step in "widening the base" of the Republic toward the Right, the leftist Republican parties sent ministers to the new government without Socialists. This caused deep resentment among Socialists: they felt betrayed by their allies of the day before. While Prieto and his centrists were preparing what—as it slipped through their fingers—became the movement of October 1934, the labor wing, with Largo Caballero at its head, had become radicalized. They discovered Marxism, but an adulterated Marxism, in the manner the Communists interpreted it, the Marxism of proletarian dictatorship. Even before Largo Caballero this path was taken by Juventudes Socialistas.

By June 1933 the organ of the FJS, *Renovación,* had written that Russia was a formidable laboratory where a new economic order was being built. Not a few young Socialists joined Amigos de la Unión Soviética. In January 1934 the National Committee of the FJS suggested to the PSOE that it try to establish alliances with the Communists. Carrillo, secretary of the FJS, wrote: "The democratic minority rights of the masses are of no value for revolutionary reality; during the passage of the revolutionary period, and later during the dictatorship of the proletariat, democratic concessions would be suicidal."[5]

The Communists, still restricted by the straightjacket Moscow imposed on them, were unable to take advantage of these changes. They had to sing the old tune of "social fascism." Once they had discovered Marxism, the young Socialists looked for support among other Marxist organizations who would not attack them: Trotskyites, with whom they maintained good relations and with whom they made up in Madrid the local Alianza Obrera, and the BOC of Catalonia which in 1935 Carrillo proposed join the PSOE to strengthen its left wing. BOC turned down the offer.[6]

Already mentioned was the proposal of the united front which Juventudes Comunistas addressed to the FJS in June 1934, a proposal which really did not constitute a departure from the hard line, in view of the fact that it could be considered a maneuver to separate the FJS from the PSOE. Meeting together were Jesús Rozado, Fernando Claudín, and Trifón Medrano, representing Juventudes Comunistas, and Santiago Carrillo, José Laín, and Segundo Serrano Poncela, in the name of Juventudes Socialistas. The latter set as a preliminary condition that the JC join Alianza Obrera. The JC did not care for it because it did not give them the chance to approach the youth of the Republican parties and because the Trotskyites were in Alianza Obrera. They had to be satisfied with offering to stop their attacks on the PSOE and promising to study the possibility of taking part in joint action against fascist organizations.

To a certain extent the situation of 1919 between Juventudes Socialistas and the party was repeating itself. Juventudes in the summer of 1934 requested a "purge" of the party.[7] They thought that they, the JS, would lead the revolution (while the JC were satisfied with the PCE's leading it). Despite its failures, the JC did not let up. In September 1934 Dimitrov sent a letter to each of the Juventudes with the suggestion that they unify. In July the JC organized a Congreso Nacional de los Jóvenes de España in Madrid. They said that only 34 of the 326 delegates were Communists, yet the congress followed the party line. It elected a national committee composed of nine Communists, eight Socialists, three Republicans, two members of the UGT, two from the CNT, and four independents (which the Communists called "nonparty" as in the USSR). The congress was useless and the FJS did not officially join it.[8]

The Communist youths did achieve something. In a September rally of the JS in the stadium in Madrid, Medrano, representing the Communists, spoke and took a moderate stance compared with Carrillo's statement that the JS would take power and that Largo Caballero was the "Spanish Lenin." The Communists were scandalized by this epithet but when they saw that it caught on, they adopted it as a means, they thought, of flattering the Socialist leader.

Once out of government, Largo Caballero began to be radicalized along with some intellectuals (Luis Araquistáin, Carlos de Baráibar) and many union leaders. But the party's rank and file continued to be moderate and cautious; Besteiro and Prieto were enjoying positions of influence. Nevertheless, the members of what was gradually taking shape as the left wing acted with greater dynamism and got delegations on the national committees, which enabled Largo Caballero in 1934 simultaneously to be secretary of the UGT and president of the PSOE. He was leaning toward Alianza Obrera. For the Socialists the frustration of being removed from government and the worry over the rise of fascism were added to the general disappointment of the masses of workers and peasants who had gained relatively little under the Republic; less than they had hoped for, at any rate.

Araquistáin, in *Leviatán,* a monthly he founded to give direction to the Socialist Left, said that the Republic had been a "utopia of Azaña" which consisted of "believing that a Republic was possible for Spain, a Republic which, while maintaining private property, could give the proletariat permanent access to the government" and also in thinking "that it was possible to build a state that was not a class state as well as to transform a nation in which the idea of community . . . could overcome in the hearts of all the class struggle and the instinct for social war."[9]

Three party tendencies are readily apparent: Besteiro's, moderate and in favor of Socialism without alliances; Prieto's, who was resentful yet still willing to collaborate with the Republicans of the Left; and Largo Caballero's, who was beginning to talk of dictatorship of the proletariat. Each group had its organs: *Democracia* for Besteiro, *Claridad* for Largo Caballero, the old *Liberal* of Bilbao for Prieto, and *El Socialista* (because *prietistas* dominated the executive committee). Yet the Left gained positions, first in the UGT and later in the party. Radicalization became official to a certain extent with the editorial "Beware of the Red Light" which appeared in *El Socialista* on January 3, 1934: "Peace, no. Class war, yes. War to the death of the criminal bourgeoisie. Peace? Yes, but among proletarians of all ideologies who want to survive and free Spain from shame. Whatever happens, beware of the red light." In September *El Socialista* itself said: "All we need is power. We must take it, then."[10]

At the moment of truth the PSOE and the UGT failed. They were unable to maintain a national general strike (perhaps weakened by the failure of a general peasant strike in the summer which was poorly prepared and untimely). The only success the Socialists scored was through Alianza Obrera. October 1934, despite its failures, did not demoralize the labor organizations nor did the harsh and prolonged repression have that effect. The radicalization of the PSOE did not diminish; on the contrary, it increased. Largo Caballero, never one to theorize, said that "without power it is impossible to do anything. . . . Power does not consist of having a government of Socialists and a parliamentarian majority. If the Socialists rule over bourgeois institutions, the time will come when they will have to return power to the enemy."[11] There was a paradox: just when the Comintern was planning a change of policy toward the Right, in order to get the alliance of the very members from whom the Spanish Socialists (the bourgeois democrats) were separating, there began to arise among Socialist ranks interest and sympathy for the USSR.[12]

While the PCE continued to label Largo Caballero as the "supreme executioner of the Spanish revolution" and to say that the Socialists defended "not only the capitalists but also the privileges of the feudal masters," and that their role consisted of "paving the way for fascism,"[13] the Socialists began to attribute to the PCE an importance which was unjustified both for its volume and its influence. Doubtless it had a certain dazzle due to its radical tone and particularly because of the image, which, thanks to Willi Münzenberg's maneuvers, the PCE was creating for itself. Instead of trying to attract the CNT or BOC, which were more powerful organizations than the PCE, the Socialist Left sought the Communists' blessing and for several months displayed a novice's fervor; it was more Leninist than the PCE.[14]

Meanwhile the PCE was gradually increasing its means of propaganda. Some were illegal (such as *Bandera Roja*), others legal, and it had a series of periodicals in addition to the daily *Mundo Obrero: El Soviet* and *Frente Rojo* in Madrid, *Norte Rojo* in the North, *Lucha* in Valencia, *Bandera Roja* in Bilbao, *Catalunya Roja* in Barcelona, *Lucha Juvenil* for Juventudes Comunistas. Besides the fellow-traveler organizations, the party was preparing combat groups. Enrique Líster, upon his return from Moscow where he had been at the Leninist school and a military school, was put in charge and named instructor of Milicias Obreras y Campesinas (Workers' and Peasants' Militias) belonging to Juventudes.[15] Líster was also in charge of the "work" among the soldiers and of trying to establish contacts with the Unión Militar Antifascista (UMA) which later became the UMRA (Unión Militar Republicana Antifascista), which opposed the Monarchist UME (Unión Militar Española) in the barracks. Given its nature, this work was very superficial, yet lent itself to a certain propagandist boastfulness. For example the First Clandestine Conference of the Garrison of Madrid was held in January 1936.[16] At the moment none of that was important. But Juventudes Socialistas found it impressive in the same way that the party's methods of propaganda were impressive.

The present-day custom of decorating committee meetings, conferences, congresses, and rallies with flags, placards, and enormous portraits dates from that period. Prior to that the workers' movement had been much more sober. To a certain extent the Communists made fashionable the dramatization of political warfare. The consequences of this would be seen years later, especially in the period of opposition to Franco when dramatic gestures were more satisfying than acts which were truly injurious to France but were lacking in spectacle.[17]

The test was approaching its end. With all that had been gained thanks to it in France and Spain (particularly in France) Moscow was now determined to make a change in policy. José Díaz, in a rally on June 2, 1935 in Madrid, said: 'We are fighting and will always fight for our supreme program, for the dictatorship of the proletariat [but] in these times of danger, with Fascism as master of the inner workings of the state, we declare that we are willing to fight as one with all anti-Fascist forces based on a minimal program, a requirement for all those who take part in the popular concentration which we are calling for. ... We propose the formation of a provisional revolutionary government which will be satisfactory to the workers, to the popular masses, to all anti-Fascists, and which will be committed to carrying out the program approved by the anti-Fascist popular concentration."[18]

The Communist International's Seventh Congress

In the Communist International's seventh congress the green light for the trial run became a strict order from Moscow. It met in the Russian capital from the end of July to mid-August 1935. The Comintern bureaucrats did not dare to openly oppose the new policy. But it shocked them. Toward the end of 1934 when Hitler had already been in power for two years, Manuilski, the most important of all the Comintern bureaucrats, had written a pamphlet entitled "On the Threshold of the Second Cycle of Wars and Revolutions," in which he maintained that the bourgeoisie would look for a way out of the crisis by means of war against the Soviets and the proletariat by means of revolution. Stalin had said it; Manuilski quoted him. As the delegates began arriving, they interviewed Manuilski and Dimitrov individually. They did not know what to believe. Each leader told them something different. It was the first time the Comintern did not lead, but listened. The two leaders noted that despite the success of the new policy in France and Spain many delegations felt distrust. People had to change their way of thinking. The Germans in particular appeared in opposition to a change of policy since it would imply a censure of the one adopted by them in the past.

But the Germans would not be able to endure if they tried to oppose it because the new policy was implicit in the decisions made by the political board of the Russian party on July 1, 1934. It was an unusual meeting attended by the country's military leaders and leaders of the various apparats. The day before, Hitler had eradicated his opponents within the Nazi regime, namely Röhm and Strasser, in what was called the "night of the long knives." Moscow decided that it was necessary to seek an accord with Hitler. But how to make Hitler deal with Stalin? That tactic gradually took shape: pressure non-Nazi governments to ally themselves with the USSR. If this induced Hitler to deal with Moscow, so much the better; if not, at least there would be an anti-Nazi alliance. One form of pressure was to set up within each country fronts which would force the governments to declare themselves anti-Nazi. The Communist parties could not do this by themselves. So it was necessary for them to ally themselves with other forces, even with Catholics and local Fascists.[19]

The result was the diplomatic change, the political test of France and Spain, and finally the Communist International's seventh congress. In the congress Dimitrov gave a speech on August 2, the transcription of which goes on for sixty pages[20] and in which the secretary of the Comintern came out with the new line without breaking with the old. The Communists, as always, were looking for a unified workers' front, but it had to act as a mobilizing force for a more extensive front, the popular front of the Communists and all forces willing to confront Fascism. "Fascism is a fierce but precarious power because it drives the working classes to form the unified front which will conquer it." Wherever the Socialists were predominant, the Communists had to defend first the demands of the social democrats in order to then state their own. It was necessary to seek out trade union unity (dissolving the Communist-led confederations). The Communist party needed to fortify itself to form the united front and for the latter to form the popular front.

For eleven days delegation after delegation approved a report which contradicted everything the parties had been doing for ten years, ever since the fifth congress of 1925. But since many delegations were more insistent on the united workers' front than the Popular Front, Dimitrov spoke once again on August 13 to stress that both fronts "are connected" and that it was necessary to defend bourgeois democracy since it was a "working-class conquest." Nevertheless to avoid contamination of Communist militants as they entered into contact with other parties, they needed to improve the preparation of the militants. The transcription of the speech notes that following it there were shouts of "Hurra," "Rot Front," "Banzai," that the Germans cried out with particular zeal "Rot

Front," and that Manuilski shouted above the ovations: "Long live the faithful and proven battle comrade of the great Stalin, the helmsman of the Communist International, comrade Dimitrov!" followed by a "long and thunderous ovation which lasted for fifteen to twenty minutes." During the congress Togliatti was in charge of giving the theoretical justifcations of Stalin's new line. The latter, he said, showed that the USSR was so mighty that the capitalist nations were forced to sign agreements wth it.

The Spanish delegation, which took part in those ovations, spoke very little at the congress. It was much applauded because of the October 1934 movement in Spain, but it was not listened to since it did not say anything new. It played the role it was expected to: it acknowledged not having been Bolshevik enough, it promised to be so as it implemented the new line (without, of course, calling it that), and it extolled Dimitrov and Stalin. Díaz, Sesé, Arlandis, Hernández, and Ibárruri were its delegates. Incidentally, they had to leave Spain crossing the Pyrenees on foot, which was another indication of the organizational weakness of the party. Neither the *Historia del Partido Comunista de España* nor Ibárruri's memoirs say anything about its performance in Moscow. Anecdotally, Díaz went by "García" and Jesús Hernández by "Ventura." The speeches of the congress were published in part by *Información Internacional,* the periodical which, identical in format, replaced *Correspondencia Internacional,* suspended by the Spanish government. Dolores Ibárruri gave one of the four or five welcoming speeches; Díaz reported on the PCE in the eleventh session, and Hernández in the twenty-fifth session gave the PCE's support to Dimitrov's speeches.[21] José Díaz was one of the 47 members of the executive committee of the Communist International elected at the congress. Dolores Ibárruri was one of the 33 substitutes. Díaz was the third Spaniard on an executive committee of the International. Pérez Solís and Bullejos had preceded him.

In only three countries—France and Spain in 1936 and Chile in 1938—would the Popular Front be successful in a practical sense. In the rest of the world it never got beyond statements, manifestos, front organizations, but gained a climate of respectability for the Communists of which their previous policy had robbed them. The Spanish delegation returned via different routes. Díaz and Ibárruri went from France to San Sebastián as if they were crew aboard a yacht beloning to Luca de Tena, the owner of the Monarchist daily *ABC,* one of whose pilots was a friend of a local communist.[22]

The Popular Bloc

"In Spain the seventh congress [of the Communist International] had considerable and immediate repercussions . . . and caused deep political turmoil."[23] The seventh congress allowed the Communists to climb on the bandwagon of the Republican-Socialist electoral alliance which was already rolling when Dimitrov issued his slogan. Historians, blinded by the title the alliance finally received, as well as propagandists of one side or another who used this title, led people to believe that the Popular Front was initiated by the Communists. This pleased the Communists because it enhanced their influence, and it pleased the Right because they could blame everything on the Communists. The truth lies elsewhere.[24]

After several scandals involving members of the Center-Right government, it became evident that the dissolution of an ineffective Parliament and the call for elections would be inevitable. Center-Left Republicans began negotiations for an electoral accord. In January 1935 Madrid's newspaper *La Libertad* called a meeting of left-wing parties to study the situation. Negotiations began there.[25] Twelve years later Largo Caballero recalled: "The Republican parties and the Socialist party [and] General Union of Workers (UGT) agreed to form an electoral coalition. . . . I want to draw attention to the fact that it was just an electoral coalition, not a popular front, which was constituted quite a bit later."[26] This occurred in March and April 1935, prior to Díaz's speech about a "popular concentration" and before the seventh congress of the Communist International.

Upon its return to Moscow, the PCE delegation began to work on applying the tactic it hoped would remove the party from its position of isolation which it had barely begun to come out of with its first contacts with young Socialists. The party periodicals were "de-Communized"; associations, clubs, and centers were founded which did not appear to be part of the party but which were supported and led by it. The party financed new periodicals which were short-lived yet lasted long enough to popularize the slogan of Popular Front in the various groups in which they were circulated. At the same time the PCE tried to draw closer to the Socialists.

The first step was taken by the unions. In November 1934 the CGTU had proposed to the executive board of the UGT joint action against the antiunion measures taken by the government. The UGT's executive committee met in prison and agreed to accept the suggestion, and several liaison committees were formed in the few cities with both unions of the UGT and the CGTU.[27] A year later, on November 8, 1935, the executive committee of the CGTU proposed to the executive board of the UGT the entry *en bloc* of its confederation. On November 30, 1935 *Claridad* printed an account with the triumphant title "A Historic Date in the Unification of the Spanish Proletariat." An indication of the ideological confusion of the Socialist Left was the fact that its periodical listed as "historical" a date that with time would prove to be the beginning of a long process of Communist absorption of the UGT, which anyone familiar with Communist tactics could have foreseen. In an attempt to explain this naïveté, let us say that the leaders of the French CGT, headed by Léon Jouhaux, were also guilty since they had accepted the entry of the CGTU in their confederation without foreseeing that the Communists would absorb it after World War II.

The Communists proposed congresses of unification which would elect new union committees: the UGT agreed to allow joint assemblies to elect new committees only in those places where the CGTU was more powerful than the UGT.[28] The CGTU disappeared as an open entity. The UGT leaders' behavior was undoubtedly a result of the atmosphere as well as the belief that, if the unions were under their control, the new Communist members would not be able to do anything. They forgot that the worst enemy of an established bureaucracy is a bureaucracy looking to establish itself. This would be proven at their expense in less than two years.

Several months previous to this the BOC in Catalonia had invited the more or less Marxist Catalonian parties to negotiations for unification. These negotiations showed that, aside from the BOC and the Communist Left, everyone was following the orientation of the most moderate and least Marxist of them all, the Unió Socialista de Catalunya. The result was that both radical parties fused in September 1935 to form the POUM, Partido Obrero de Unificación Marxista (Workers' Party of Marxist Unification), while the moderates continued negotiating.[29] In Madrid the PCE took the initiative. On October 23, 1935 the Central Committee of the PCE sent an open letter to *Claridad,* proposing that the possibility of uniting the two parties be studied. *Claridad* answered unenthusiastically saying that first it was necessary to solve the Socialist party's internal problems and establish relations between Communists and Socialists. "There will be time to consider and discuss everything else." To begin, it was necessary to "strengthen the bases for common action."[30]

While the PCE maneuvered with Largo Caballero's supporters, Prieto did the same with his detractors. On December 17, 1935 at a meeting of the national committee, Largo Caballero only carried the minority and lost the presidency of the PSOE. In protest, the FJS declared itself "freed from all obligations with the party's current powers." Thus the road was opened for the Popular Front, since Prieto not only accelerated negotiations with the Republicans but also was inclined to accept the Popular Front's formula instead of merely an electoral coalition.

It might seem paradoxical that supporters of the Front were the Republicans and moderate Socialists, while the left-wing Socialists viewed it as unfavorable.[31] It is only an apparent paradox. Largo Caballero later explained his reasons for his lack of confidence in the Front: "Permanent political unions have never convinced me since they always end up toning down the significance of each party and [the parties] lose their political personality. People become confused, not knowing which of the parties is more suitable for the defense of their interests and ideas, and errors as well as right choices fall outside the direct responsibility of each party. And the error of one party can mean the downfall of all of them. For [working-] class parties it is suicide."[32]

It was the Republicans and Prieto who wanted a front instead of an electoral coalition (particularly the Republicans). Those Communists who were accepted in the discussion of the agreement of the Popular Front managed to have it presented as a permanent organization—without its being established explicitly—which would continue after the elections. The Republicans' reasons were evident: with the Popular Front they could hold the masses in check after winning the elections. The Communists' reasons were not as visible, but no less real: with a Popular Front which would support the future government they would be able to pressure that government to adopt the international policy which would suit the USSR. It was as if Stalin said to the Republicans: You can help me fight Hitler and I'll help you fight the revolutionaries.

POUM explained this clearly[33] and the left-wing Socialists had foreseen some of it. Thus, Araquistáin wrote that the concept of the popular front could make sense in some countries but that "this tactic makes no sense in other countries such as Spain. In Spain there is a petite bourgeoisie to win over but no large parties to represent it. When the Republic was installed, the Socialists, eager to consolidate the democratic revolution, took more care than anyone else to vitalize, encourage, and expand leftist parties whose mission was to represent the Spanish petite bourgeoisie. The Communists did not like this policy and fought it with determination, also fighting against the Socialists for collaborating with those parties and helping them grow. If we are not ill-informed, the Communists managed to retire from circulation a Spanish edition of Lenin's pamphlet "Two Tactics" which justifies the policy of Socialist participation in the provisional government of a new Republican regime. Deprived of Socialist support in the elections of 1933, those left-wing parties, an artificial creation of the Republic, were decimated, as could be expected; it was clear that they lacked strength of their own, an eloquent fact which cannot be forgotten in view of the diverse possibilities for future politics in Spain.

> Our problem, Spain's problem, is this: whether it suits the Socialists to go back to galvanizing and exalting, as in 1931, some bourgeois leftist parties, which will lead a precarious existence without daring to attempt a truly radical policy for fear of new attacks from the Right; or whether, on the contrary, it is more suitable for Socialists to devote themselves predominantly to the political and trade union unification of the proletariat and to directly winning over the rural and urban petite bourgeoisie, overlooking the intermediate petit bourgeois parties. The problem, of course, cannot and should not be resolved superficially and will have to undergo much meditation and discussion by the Socialists; but, for that very reason, it is not legitimate to offer definitive solutions, as some have tried to do, or to create situations which demand a popular or anti-Fascist front, as the Communists do, taking an initiative which, if seconded, would leave the Socialists without an option. In Spain at least the Socialists ought to be in control of their own destiny.[34]

Araquistáin had the habit of establishing a parallel between the Russian and Spanish Revolutions, and, basing himself on Lenin's pamphlet "Two Tactics," he justified the Socialist collaboration in Azaña's two-year governments. Vicente Uribe told him that the Socialists did not follow Lenin's principles and that if the Socialists were beginning to see things better now it was thanks to the PCE "which has not hesitated for a single minute in removing the blindfold from Socialist workers' eyes and showing them the way of true Marxism."[35]

Uribe also responded to the article about the Popular Front, affirming the commonality of interests between the USSR and the world proletariat. He pointed out that as far as the Communists were concerned, the united workers' front had priority over the popular front, which ought to be a result of the former: "We want every anti-Fascist, peasant, proletarian, urban petit bourgeois to participate in the fight under the leadership of the proletariat. Is that clear?"[36]

In a rally on November 3, 1935 at the Pardiñas Theater in Madrid, José Díaz proposed the constitution of a popular bloc. He said to the Socialists: "We want to march together with you until we become a single party."[37] This was possible because "the seventh congress of the Communist International was brazenly critical and self-critical regarding certain previously committed sectarian errors. It helped the Communists decisively to discard false and sectarian positions and slogans (such as calling the Socialists in general "social fascists") which had hampered their relations with a segment of workers and with nonproletarian sectors which nonetheless were likely to cooperate with the working class."[38] It was not enough to pacify the Socialists by talking of the workers' front. The Republicans needed to be reassured: "Comrades, we are not talking about assaulting the Republic; it is only a matter of the republicans' governing the second Republic."[39] Proletarian leadership was already fading from memory.

From the Pact to the Elections

The details of negotiations for the pact of the Popular Front are a mystery. No one, it seems, has left behind any information on it. So some may suppose that the inclusion of the Communists in the pact was done against the Republicans' will, and there are those who say that the moderate Republican leader Felipe Sánchez Román did not sign it because the Communists had signed it. This is not true. Sánchez Román opposed certain extremes of the pact proposed by the Socialists and wanted Juventudes Socialistas to dissolve its militias, yet "the only concession it made after long discussions . . . was to consider the Communist party as a member."[40] Others, basing themselves on Communist influence in the Marxist apprenticeship of the Socialist Left, believed that Largo Caballero was the one who introduced the Communists into the negotiations. Actually Largo Caballero was against the idea of the front and it was Prieto who influenced the Socialist position in this matter.

The Republicans wanted the Communists in the pact because they were the ones who favored the idea of having it become a postelectoral pact which would guarantee support and "order" for future Republican rulers. What opened the door for them was the "fireman" nature which the Republicans attributed to the Front, thanks to the Communist presence in it as well as their conception of it as a permanent pact. When POUM asked to be included in the pact, the Communists were secretly opposed, and when they could not get their own way, they acceded to POUM's entry. But when it was time to present a list of candidates, POUM got a position in Cádiz for Julián Gorkín and another in Teruel for Andrés Nin; then the Communists in Cádiz, with Republican support, vetoed Gorkín; and the Republicans in Teruel, aided by the Communists, vetoed Nin. Both lost the candidacy and POUM had to settle for Maurín's candidacy in the city of Barcelona.[41] Otherwise, the PCE did not let up in its campaign against POUM. The day before the pact was signed,

Mundo Obrero branded it the "vanguard of the counterrevolution," and five days before the elections it called POUM "the mastiff of fascism." The popular front in Barcelona was not called thus, nor was it called "popular bloc," the name it was officially given; it was simply referred to as Front d'Esquerres (Leftist Front) and was not intended to last after the election.

The Communists won the fight over the name. What Codovila failed to do in 1934 with the Alianza Obrera, the PCE managed to achieve in 1936: provide the coalition with the name adopted by the seventh congress of the Communist International. In this manner, the Communists could pretend to be the creators of the Front d'Esquerres. In reality they joined that bandwagon when it was already on its way and only after having gotten the green light from the Communist International.

"After long negotiations delayed by the conservative leaders of republicanism, a pact was worked out and signed in mid-January 1936. The fact that it was called the Pact of the Popular Bloc was an explicit admission of the overwhelming influence the politics of the Communist party had achieved,"[42] said the Communists themselves, boasting about it twenty years later. [43] It is not out of place to point out that it was the vote of the Unión Republicana, the most moderate bourgeois party, that decided the inclusion of the Communists, and that it was the Socialists of the Center (Prieto) who formally proposed their inclusion. The pact satisfied neither POUM nor the followers of Largo Caballero. Therefore Largo Caballero, at a rally in the Europa Theater on January 12, 1936, made a plea for unity with the CNT (which was going to vote for the Front in order to get its prisoners out of jail) and said that, following the elections, "we who will be free of all compromises, will have the opportunity to say to everyone, absolutely everyone, that we took the road we set out to take."[44] He added: "Prior to the Republic our duty was to bring about the Republic; now that this regime has been established, our duty is to bring about socialism."

Expressing a different viewpoint was *Mundo Obrero,* which reappeared with Jesús Hernández as editor: "The pact . . . is the weapon we need to open up our great forces to the development of democratic aspirations." They would hear nothing of socialism. Communists everywhere echoed what Díaz had said in a speech on November 3: "We need to make it plain and clear that the Popular Bloc should not be created only for electoral aims and functions."[45] Martínez Barrio described the objectives of the pact: "To legally channel the aspirations of the proletariat" but without "casting it out of constitutional coexistence into an angry pilgrimage along the revolutionary route."[46] Prieto wanted "the electoral alliance to be agreed upon in such a way that the instrument of government might spring forth from it if the results were favorable."[47] On the other hand Azaña confided to his brother in law: "The Communists are the ones who are most interested, of course, in taking as much advantage as possible of the Socialists and that is more to their detriment than ours. Not only do I not disapprove, but I think it is necessary for them to bring representatives to Parliament."[48] The Communists, according to Ibárruri, wanted the Popular Front to "represent something more than a simple electoral coalition. It was the instrument of unity of the workers and democratic forces in the electoral and postelectoral struggle for the development and consolidation of democracy in our country."[49]

The electoral campaign flew by; it was impassioned but generally peaceful. "Every leftist party was mobilized for the electoral campaign. The Socialist militias prepared themselves for battle, just in case. Actually we were only a couple hundred barely armed men, hardly enough to stand up against the threat of a military coup if the right wing lost the elections."[50] Finally, with a 72 percent voter turnout, on February 16, 1936 the right wing and the middle got 38.5 percent of the votes and the Popular Front received 34.2 percent. Because of the complexities of the electoral law approved by the right-wing Parliament of 1933, the Popular Front got 263 representatives, while the right wing and the middle had to be satisfied with 210. The PCE received 15 representatives,[51] and the PSOE 88. As soon as Azaña succeeded Portela Valladares and the political prisoners were released from prison, the PCE was faced with the dilemma of supporting or pressuring the government.

Support in the Streets and in Parliament

From February to July 1936 Spain lived through a period of increasing tension characterized by demonstrations, assaults, attacks on political party headquarters, assassination attempts, armed clashes, occupation of land, an average of ten to twenty strikes a day, and days in which half a million workers were on strike at one time. At the same time there were shutdowns of businesses, lands left uncultivated, flight of capital, and right-wing conspiracies. These conspiracies finally culminated in a single one, the strings of which were being pulled by General Emilio Mola.

The Republicans wanted a policy like that of 1931–32. The people in the street who thought they had won the elections—at least in the large cities and in radicalized towns—did not want another disappointment. They did not trust Republican governments, despite the fact that they were called Popular Front, and they tried to establish by themselves the order they wanted, which provoked the usual "breach of public order." The situation was made even more tense by the fact that electorally, rightists and leftists carried the same weight. The PCE was not involved in the tension. Like Prieto, who called for a return to peace and who like Azaña aspired to a legality which events proved to be outmoded, the PCE did not want a strain in social relations. A Spain in turmoil was of no use to the USSR. That is why Díaz said that the masses saw in the Popular Front "a front which was also extraelectoral,"[52] but that the leaders did not. He was mistaken, for what the masses were doing on their own account and at their own risk was going beyond the Popular Front.

Ibárruri, spokeswoman for the party in Parliament, asked the government to implement the program of the Popular Front and to squelch reactionary forces. At the same time the militants in the PCE had instructions to do whatever they could to stop the strikes. In a speech Díaz said: "Before calling a strike it is necessary to exhaust all possible means of fighting. And once it has been decided that only with a strike can the claims of justice be won, then it should be declared, but always under the sign of unity and strict control of the organizations."[53]

Previously isolated by its systematic radicalism, the PCE now was isolated by its insistence on limiting strikes to immediate demands and removing their political edge. Either the leaders or Codovila[54] realized this, because Díaz had to censure the Casares Quiroga government with these words: "The government which we are supporting faithfully, insofar as it fulfills the pact of the Popular Bloc, is beginning to lose the faith of the workers." The PCE criticized the Casares government which its representatives had helped establish in that they voted for the absurd discharge of Alcalá Zamora, president of the Republic, in order to leave room for Prieto to preside over the government by means of removing Azaña to the presidency of the Republic. So the PCE wanted Prieto. Although it flirted with the Socialist Left, at the moment of truth—of power—it supported Prieto. This would not be the last time that it joined the side of the Socialist moderates against the radicals. Finally, Prieto was not able to get the government because the Socialist parliamentary group denied him their support.

The PCE decided to change allies—move away from Largo Caballero, who wanted to go beyond the Popular Front, and draw nearer to Prieto who clung to it. In 1935 Hernández had said: "Behind Largo Caballero is everything that is healthy and revolutionary in the Socialist party."[55] But in 1936 the Communists began to cajole Prieto's follower, Ramón González Peña, calling him the hero of Asturias, and no longer would they call Largo "the Spanish Lenin." The Socialist veto to Prieto as head of the government moved the PCE to withdraw from the Largo

Caballero camp because "it rejected collaboration with the Republican parties in the name of an ultraleftist stance,"[56] since "the Communist party on several occasions had formulated the idea of a popular government in which the varied social forces which comprised the Popular Bloc would be represented," but the followers of Largo Caballero opposed it. For lack of a better government, "the Communist party gave its loyal support to the [Republican] government to put into effect the program of the Popular Front. The party defended the government in the streets and in Parliament against attacks by reactionaries and fascists."[57] At the same time the party emphasized the need to purge the army and repress Fascist elements. But it entrusted the defense of the Republic to the government without telling the organizations to prepare for it.[58]

The PCE grew although not necessarily among the workers. Its membership—in a country where there were scarcely any unorganized workers—went from 30,000 to 102,000 from February to July 1936.[59] The Executive Committee of the Communist International met in May 1936 and Hernández attended. The PCE, he said, was loyal in its support of the government and was striving to improve relations with the Anarchists (which was not true), was trying to attract unorganized workers to the unions, and was making "careful preparations to merge with the Socialist party." The Executive Committee of the Communist International approved the policy the PCE had been following.[60]

The proposals for a merger with the PSOE always contained one condition: membership of the future new party in the Communist International and acceptance of its line. "This unified party must be founded on the points discussed in the seventh congress of the Communist International," said Díaz in a speech on April 11. "To speed up and facilitate the political unity of the working class," he emphasized on June 1, "we must fight tenaciously against the degenerate sect of Trotskyism."[61] For the merger to come about it was necessary to adopt the International and the program of the weakest organization among those that were to merge. In a politically less irascible time the matter would have seemed absurd. Then it was almost accepted as logical. But the Socialists were beginning to feel mistrustful. Araquistáin wrote: "[The Communists] never want to collaborate with anything or anybody unless they can be absolute leaders."[62] What had snuffed out the ardor of the Socialist Left was the formation of the JSU.

Carrillo and the JSU

The capture of Juventudes Socialistas by the PCE was accomplished by means of two weapons in three moves. The weapons were the "verbal seduction" of the mass of members and the personal conquest of its leaders; the moves can be described as encirclement, separation from the rest of the Socialist forces, and occupation from within. We have already seen how the JS became radicalized before the Socialist party (or its left wing) and how the discovery of Marxism and the admiration of the USSR were simultaneous in both. But there was hesitation in the JS since many believed the Communists to be moderates. That is why Carrillo, secretary general of the FJS, and other friends of his flirted with the Trotskyists and BOC and formed with the former the Alianza Obrera of Madrid. At the outset the UJC (Unión de Jóvenes Comunistas, Union of Communist Youth) had problems with the Socialist youth over this. For example, in a meeting to form an Alianza Obrera Juvenil which was held at the Fomento de las Artes in Madrid—since the Socialist party headquarters was closed down—Medrano, representing the JC, requested the expulsion from the meeting of the delegate from the Communist Left. This was opposed by Juventudes Libertarias (Libertarian Youth) and more emphatically by Carrillo. The weekly *Espartaco,* a publication of Socialist youths, at times seemed more an organ of the yet-to-be-born Fourth International than of youths of the Second.

As a result of the murder of Juanita Rico, who belonged to the JS in Madrid, by Falangists, two meetings of the executive committees of the FJS and the UJC took place in July 1934, and simultaneously there were numerous joint rallies of both organizations. Following October, liaison committees between both youth organizations were secretly formed. That did not prevent Carrillo from seeking membership of BOC in the PSOE, as we have already seen.[63] Meanwhile, the FJS had withdrawn from the Internacional Juvenil Socialista (Socialist Youth International) after having censured its executive committee which it believed to be under the control of the reformists.

Because of that, many Socialist youths now felt a special attraction toward the Communist International. The Fourth International did not yet exist and Trotskyism had otherwise never managed to attract strong movements anywhere. The International Bureau of the Revolutionary Youth was made up of dissident organizations and was powerless. The Communist Youth International, on the other hand, was relatively strong and well off and shared some points of view with the JS: dictatorship of the proletariat to overthrow capitalism (which was on its death bed), and the fight against reformism. This seduction was accentuated after the seventh congress of the Communist International because each individual saw in it what he desired, and the Spanish socialist youths were more aware of the slogan of United Workers than of Popular Front.

That was evident in a letter which Justo Amutio, editor-in-chief of the Valencian *Adelante-Verdad,* wrote to Dimitrov and which Dimitrov answered. In his response he said that "the road to victory over fascism . . . lies in the unification of the Socialist and Communist Juventudes." The idea was not new. Some members of the JS had proposed it and many, perhaps infiltrated Communists, were propagating it. This infiltration was so strong in Valencia that Julián Gorkín of BOC denounced Margarita Nelken's helping Communist youth to get into the JS and he stated that as a Socialist representative she had been an agent of the Communist International for years. Then the fourth congress of the JS in Valencia in September 1935 declared "the incompatibility of young Socialists and Julián Gorkín because of his campaign against Margarita Nelken."[64]

More than a few of the PSOE watched with alarm the rapprochement of the JS with its Communist counterpart. Carrillo made note of it in a sarcastic article: "Terrified, they fear that we are a mob of crazy kids attempting to attack the party, impose a dictatorship on it, smother all internal democracy, and then assign the party to the Third International."[65] Ten months after having written these lines, those who felt that way had their fears confirmed by Carrillo himself since he was the main instigator in the PCE's capture of the JS. It is impossible to say whether he actually planned it, let himself be used, or whether he "converted." What is certain is that he was the instrument for the capture. Communist influence in Juventudes was increasing. The Juventudes of Murcia and Valencia proposed that the PSOE join the Communist International. For the old Socialists, it must have seemed like déjà vu of the events of 1919–20.

Just as Catalonia led the way for Marxist unification, it did so in the unification of Juventudes. Negotiations had begun there among the Juventudes of the Unió Socialista de Catalunya, the Federación Catalana del PSOE, and the PCC.[66] The latter two wanted to extend it to include middle-class Catalonian youth but nothing came of their efforts.[67] The sixth congress of the Communist Youth International in September 1935 guided the JC along new paths. Instead of imitating the Communist parties, they were to develop their own activity (always under the direction of the Communist International, of course) toward the middle class and labor youth organizations as well as cultural and athletic associations, etc. That is to say, they would achieve the formation of fronts which were more extensive than the Popular Front. They were to become, at least officially, mass organizations with no party affiliation.[68]

The UJC made an immediate proposal to the FJS for the unification of both organizations. A commission for unification was formed and a few days later a commission made up of both Juventudes went to Moscow. Carrillo and Melchor, representing the FJS, and Arconada and Medrano the UJC, met with Massie of the Communist Youth International and agreed upon the foundation of the merger: "To forge a new kind of extensive organization of working youth, as was indicated in the seventh congress of the Communist Youth International." The first two Spanish Communist parties had been unified in Moscow. The two youth organizations did the same. Early in May both executive committees appointed a six-member commission, three from each organization: Carrillo and Medrano were its chairmen.

Things were picking up speed. On April 4 Carrillo, recently back from Moscow, gave a talk at Socialist party headquarters in favor of unification. On April 5 there was a "rally for unity" at the bullring of Las Ventas. A ceremony of unity was held in Barcelona on April 12 in which Carrillo attacked POUM, calling it the "enemy of unity." The JC and the Juventudes of the Catalonian Federation of the PSOE joined together with an executive committee composed of the two previous ones. López Raimundo was the secretary general. Within two weeks provincial assemblies and congresses were called and they voted for unification. That was not necessary in the UJC. It was decided by the executive committee, and that was it. Juventud, an organ of the committee for unification, was published in May. There was no national congress of unification because of the Civil War. But there had already been common congresses of unification in the provinces which elected the provincial executive commissions. Things did not go smoothly in some places. In a JS assembly in Madrid at the Barbieri Theater there was shouting and opposition to unification. But the theater was taken over by the PCE militia and the dissidents were expelled.

Even though the FJS had some 200,000 members and the UJC some 50,000,[69] the committees on all levels were half and half, so that the Communists with fewer members controlled the new organization since, among the elected socialists, there was almost always an infiltrator or someone who had been "worked on" by the Communists. The instigators of unification among Socialist youth—Carrillo, Melchor, and Cazorla—officially joined the PCE after a trip to Moscow in October 1936 in the middle of the Civil War. About half the members of the FJS did not follow their leaders and most of them joined the PSOE. In short, of the 250,000 members which theoretially the new organization should have had, 150,000 were left, but the lure of unity attracted many youths who were not yet organized.[70] On the insistence of the Communists, the JSU officially joined the Socialist Youth International; being in it could be useful to Moscow. But practically speaking, they were in the Communist

Youth International. Between the PCE and Carrillo, they had taken 100,000 members away from the Socialists and, on the rebound, had strengthened the moderate wing of Socialism.

Fascination with the Falange

Gil Robles provided some facts in the Parliament which do not appear exaggerated to anyone who lived through those months: "From February 16 until June [1936] there have been 160 churches destroyed, 251 assaults or attempted assaults on temples, 269 people have lost their lives, 1,287 have been wounded, 215 cases of attempted personal assault, 138 robberies, 23 robbery attempts, 69 political centers have been destroyed, 312 have been assaulted, there have been 113 general strikes, 228 partial strikes, 10 newspapers destroyed, 33 assaults or attempts at assault of newspapers, 146 explosions, and 78 bombs defused before exploding."

The PCE was not involved in any of this (except for aggression and assaults on its quarters). People in the streets were becoming angry and the party could not control them. "To avoid 'disturbances' which are so annoying to Gil Robles and Calvo Sotelo . . . it is not enough to make a nobody like Mr. Calvo Sotelo responsible for what may occur; rather, the first step is to put in jail the employers who refuse to accept government decrees," said La Pasionaria in her last speech before July 18. Apropos of this, Franquist propaganda falsely claimed later that she had expressed threats against Calvo Sotelo in that speech. "At this stage . . . neither the government, the Parliament, nor the Popular Front has any significance in Spain. They are not in control," wrote Ossorio y Gallardo.[71] The party, with its 100,000 members— if indeed it had that many—was unable to vitalize the Popular Front or give the government authority.

Meanwhile, the party appeared to be obsessed and fascinated by the most spectacular but the least dangerous of the reactionary groups: the Falange. It was a strange fascination, which anyone familiar with the Communists or who read their press at the time could have sensed. The generals, the church, the powerful right-wing parties were dangerous, not José Antonio Primo de Rivera, the Falange's chief, who had few listeners in the nation. Yet the Communist newspapers were full of attacks on the Falange. Perhaps this fascination can be explained by certain similarities: both were small, new parties in a period of growth, dictatorial parties with hierarchies, with international liaisons, with the ambition for power in the near future, with powerful model nations, with active and illegal militias.

The objectives were different, but the mentality was not. Perhaps that was why the Communists understood the Falangists better than anyone else and therefore feared them, not because of what they were but because of what they could become. Perhaps that was a contributing factor in explaining why more than a few—yet not many—Communists went over to the Falange, in particular its new members who sought in the PCE what the traditional image promised: a place for protest, which the Popular Front policy prevented them from finding. Disillusioned but not appeased, they went to the other movement which appeared to be one of protest.

The street sale of *FE,* the organ of the Falange, and of *Mundo Obrero* provoked continual clashes, in which occasionally there were casualties. "Among the leaders of the Falange was a man named Mateos who had been a Communist and for a period of two years was the organizational secretary of the party local committee in Madrid. . . . He knew the party's system of organization, its conspiratorial methods, its tactics inside out. . . . What is the Falange doing? How does it do it? These two questions became an obsession for the Communist Party."[72] In the face of Fascism what could be done aside from the measures of repression which the PCE demanded from the government in vain? Would they have been enough? Was Fascism, on the increase throughout the world, a problem of simple policing? Had no one learned a lesson from France where the Rassemblement Populaire had won the elections and where the Blum government adopted some nonpolicing measures which had satisfied the people even if they were not revolutionary measures?

To these questions there were two answers which were being stated more and more emphatically. On the one hand there was that of the Socialist Left and POUM, each on its own account, who believed that the fight was between Fascism and Socialism: "The only way out of the situation is an unnatural, anti-Fascist, or a natural, historical, and decisive one: Socialism," said the Socialist association in Madrid.[73] "The alternative is Fascism or Socialism," said Maurín in Parliament amid "murmurs of approval in some parts of the chamber."[74] The dilemma for the Republicans was between Fascism and democracy. That is precisely why they were Republicans. In that position they found an unexpected ally: the PCE. A resolution by the plenary session of the central committee on March 1936 characterized the Popular Front as "an anti-Fascist organization of masses for the parliamentarian and extraparliamentarian fight of democracy against Fascism."[75]

Violence was on the increase. The murder of Police Lieutenant José Castillo on July 12 was followed by that of the leader of the Right José Calvo Sotelo on the following day, which some attributed to the Communists but which did not fit in with their methods or with party interests at the time. "We all . . . know that there was no premeditated plan and certainly no orders from the government. Castillo's death had created a great deal of disorder and no one had a clear idea of what to do. Gil Robles or any other right-wing politician could have just as likely been killed. But, objectively, Calvo Sotelo died as a result of the terrorist plan that his cohorts were implementing."[76] Four days later on July 17 a military uprising began and, with it, what no one predicted would turn into the Civil War and the PCE's big opportunity.

Notes

1. Little has been written about the Popular Front as a political tactic. There are some books about the one in France but only two about its Spanish counterpart. The reader may consult Víctor Alba, *Historia del Frente Popular,* Mexico City, 1959, and *El Frente Popular,* Barcelona, 1976. The former is about the tactic as such and the latter about its implementation in Spain. Javier Tusell analyzed the electoral campaign which proved victorious for the Spanish Popular Front in *Las elecciones del Frente Popular,* Madrid, 1971.
2. Ibárruri, *El único camino,* pp. 161–63.
3. Regarding this Communist expert in propaganda, refer to the book by his widow Babette Gross, *Willi Münzenberg: A Political Biography,* Lansing, Michigan, 1974. Münzenberg withdrew from the International at the time of the Nazi-Soviet pact and disappeared shortly thereafter. Many said that he had been liquidated by the NKVD. His widow relates that in 1934 Álvarez del Vayo who had met him in Berlin invited him to come to Spain. He took advantage of the cover which being a tourist gave him to explain his propaganda techniques to PCE leaders. In the summer of 1935 he visited Madrid again with a member of the International Red Cross, and used that trip to "attend conferences with Communist organizations and meet pro-Russian Socialist politicians" (p. 272). He also organized the solidarity rally in Paris which was so difficult for La Pasionaria to attend, as well as sending an international commission to Spain made up of British labor leaders Ellen Wilkinson and Lord Listowel to intercede for the Asturians who were under death sentences (p. 271). The Spanish committee against war and Fascism was founded during the course of a trip to Madrid by Barbusse, Lord Marley, and Münzenberg's associate, Louis Gibarti (p. 242).
4. In 1933 and 1934 the fights between Falangists, Socialists, and Communists began, particularly in the universities. The Communists were unable to take over FUE or UFEH by means of the work of its BEOR despite the fact that BEOR accepted non-Communist students. In the beginning this bloc was led by Tuñón de Lara, Tagüeña, and Claudín, who later went on to work permanently for JC, giving up his studies. At the UFEH congress in Valencia in February 1933 the members of BEOR were about to be thrown out and did not win a single post in the new board of directors headed by the Socialist Rufilanchas. But in the congress of 1935 in Madrid BEOR managed to achieve "absolute control for the Communists." At that time

FUE was "a mere shadow of what it had been." It is curious that when the government, in an attempt to avoid violent clashes between students of FUE and Falangists suspended both organizations in the university, the two got together to strike in protest of the measure. The Falange ended up dominating the University of Madrid after October 1934 while it failed to do the same at the Universidad Autónoma of Barcelona. UFEH, under the control of the PCE, then organized the Universidad Popular which was directed by Tuñón de Lara and Carmen Parga (Manuel Tagüeña, *Testimonio de dos guerras*, Mexico City, 1973, pp. 38, 60, 89). While the Falangists were struggling to attract Anarcho-Syndicalists, some Communist sympathizers among the students switched to the Falange and one of them, Matías Montero, died as a result of a violent clash. (Tagüeña, pp. 53–55). Another was José Miguel Guitarte, who had belonged to JC and had taken part in stoning the German embassy (ibid., p. 52). Although there were not too many of these switches, they are indicative of the little political training given in JC as well as of the ease with which loyalties could be transferred from one dogmatic and disciplined organization to another with the same characteristics although opposite in tendency.

5.   Ramon Casterás, *Las JSUC,* pp. 78–79. Carrillo's quote is in Ricardo de la Cierva, *Crónicas de la confusión,* Barcelona, 1977, p. 107.

6.   Carrillo was an occasional contributor to *La Batalla* and in August 1935 wrote a series of articles asking BOC to join the PSOE. These articles were responded to by Maurín. Both men's articles were gathered later in a pamphlet, "Polémica Maurín-Carrillo" (Barcelona, 1937) when Carrillo held a position which was diametrically opposed to the one of two years before. For information on the relations among Trotskyites (who were really no longer such since they had broken off with Trotsky), the young Socialists, and the left-wing Socialists, consult Pelai Pagès, *El movimiento trotskista en España,* p. 253ff.

7.   In a letter to *Claridad* of November 2, 1935 Álvarez del Vayo and José Díaz joined this plea for a purge. The position taken by JS is summed up in the pamphlet "Octubre: Segunda Etapa" published in mid-1935.

8.   Casterás, p. 83ff.

9.   Luis Araquistáin, "La utopía de Azaña," *Leviatán,* September 1934.

10.   *El Socialista,* Madrid, Spetember 27, 1934.

11.   A speech before the fifth congress of the FJS. *El Socialista,* Madrid, April 21, 1934. Other examples of Largo Caballero's stance and oratory are in G. Mario de Coca, *Anti Caballero,* Madrid, 1975, p. 87ff.

12.   Marta Bizcarrondo, *Araquistáin y la crisis socialista en la II República: Leviatán (1934–36),* Madrid, 1975, p. 87ff.

13.   Quoted by Santos Juliá, *La izquierda del PSOE (1935–36),* Madrid, 1977, p. 146. A collection of samples of the anti-Socialist prose of the PCE appears in J.M. Martínez Val, *Españoles ante el comunismo,* Barcelona, 1975, p. 107ff.

14.   The Spanish refugees in the USSR (almost all were Communists, but among them were the Socialists Margarita Nelken and Virgilio Llanos and the young Socialist José Laín), in an effort to apply sentimental pressure, wrote the executive committee of the PSOE from Moscow on May 16, 1936, echoing the Communist interpretation of the events of October and asking for unity of action with the Communists (text appears in Comín Colomer, vol. II, p. 474ff.).

15. Those militias were not very fearsome. The PCE had some thousand or so members in Madrid when it began to organize them. Training was done in a public park and consisted of loading and unloading a Browning pistol 7.65 Tagüeña had inherited from his father. "For a uniform we had a dark blue shirt and we saluted with a raised fist in the style of Rotfront." On several occasions the PCE tried to infiltrate the Socialist militias which were somewhat larger. For example, JC allowed some of its members to become part of the Socialist militias, such as Tagüeña, and a group of militias of the PCE, sent by Francisco Galán, joined their Socialist counterparts. This went on until the party decided that this infiltration was not profitable and ordered all Communists to return to the party militias. Tagüeña refused to comply with the order and was taken out of JC (Tagüeña, pp. 44, 61–62).

16. Enrique Líster, *Memorias de un luchador,* p. 55ff.

17. The *Historia del PCE* talks of Socialist radicalization (p. 100ff.) and says that although JS was sincere, "a series of leaders in the PSOE took leftist stances with very different aims: they were trying, in particular, to avoid having the Socialist working masses, where sentiments for unity ran very strong, leave the ranks of the PSOE and go over to the Communist party." It also says that in December 1934 a national liaison committee was created on the proposal of the PCE along with the PSOE, UGT, and CGTU but "for several months it was almost inert."

18. Ibárruri, *El único camino,* p. 191. The *Historia del PCE* (p. 98) says that at this rally Díaz "as secretary general of Spain's Communist party assumed the responsibility of the aforementioned movement [October 1934]" in which, as we have already seen, he did not have a leading role. It was a way of taking credit for what others had accomplished, which the PCC also did.

19. W.G. Krivitsky, *I Was Stalin's Agent,* London, 1939, p. 1ff.

20. Dimitrov, *Problemas del Frente Único y del Frente Popular,* Mexico City, 1939, pp. 7–67.

21. These reports are reproduced by Comín Colomer, vol. II, pp. 520ff., 545ff., 574ff. A curious detail is the fact that the speeches and resolutions of the seventh congress were also published under the title of *El comunismo al día,* with a translation and prologue by José Bullejos. It was published by the Partido Comunista Libre (Free Communist party) which Bullejos organized in 1935 but which never got off the ground. I suppose it was a delicious act of revenge for Bullejos.

22. Ibárruri, *El único camino,* p. 182.

23. *Historia del PCE,* p. 105.

24. The truth is found in detail in Víctor Alba, *El Frente Popular,* Barcelona, 1976, p. 277ff.

25. *La Libertad,* Madrid, January 16, 1935, editorial on p. 1.

26. Largo Caballero, *Mis recuerdos,* p. 149.

27. Amaro del Rosal, *Historia de la UGT,* vol. I, pp. 437–38.

28. Letters dealing with the negotiation of the collective entry are found in Comín Colomer, vol. II, pp. 650–57.

29. For information regarding the negotiations of unification in Catalonia see Alba, *El marxisme a Catalunya,* vol. I, p. 345ff. and Pagès, *Andreu Nin,* p. 179ff.

30. *Claridad,* November 16, 1935, in Comín Colomer, vol. II p. 657ff.

192   The Communist Party in Spain

31. Artola (p. 667) says that Largo Caballero was a supporter of the Popular Front. He is mistaken despite the fact that in appearance one would have to believe that, given the relations between the Communists and the Socialist Left, the latter must have supported the slogan of the former.
32. Largo Caballero, *Mis recuerdos*, p. 149.
33. Jordi Arquer, "Frente Popular Antifascista o Frente Único Obrero?" *La Nueva Era*, Barcelona, January 1939. POUM was in support of a united workers' list of candidates and of reviving the Alianza Obrera.
34. Luis Araquistáin, "La nueva táctica comunista," *Leviatán*, Madrid, August 1935.
35. Bizcarondo, p. 388ff.
36. Uribe's responses appeared in *Pueblo*, the newspaper which replaced *Mundo Obrero* which had been suspended.
37. Ibárruri, *El único camino*, p. 192.
38. *Historia del PCE*, p. 105.
39. Castro Delgado, *Hombres made in Moscú*, p. 237, quoting himself.
40. García Venero, *Historia de las Internacionales*, vol. II, p. 496.
41. Alba, *El marxisme a Catalunya*, vol. I, p. 368ff.
42. The pact can be seen in Alba, *El Frente Popular*, p. 353ff. The projects for the program proposed by the PSOE and the PCE can also be seen (p. 344ff.).
43. *Historia del PCE*, p. 107.
44. Reproduced in J. Simeón Vidarte, *Todos fuimos culpables*, Mexico City, 1973, p. 31ff.
45. "Discurso pronunciado por el secretario general del Partido Comunista de España, 3 de noviembre de 1935," Barcelona, 1935.
46. Diego Martínez Barrio, *Páginas para la historia del Frente Popular*, Valencia, 1937.
47. Indalecio Prieto, *Posiciones socialistas*, Madrid, 1935.
48. Cipriano Rivas Cherif, *Retrato de un desconocido (Vida de Manuel Azaña)*,Mexico City, 1961, p. 237.
49. Ibárruri, *El único camino*, p. 198.
50. Tagüeña, p. 90. For information on the campaign, see Javier Tusell, *Las elecciones del Frente Popular*, Madrid, 1971, vol. I. See vol. II of the same book for the results.
51. José Díaz for Madrid; Cayetano Bolívar for Málaga; Leandro Carro for Bilbao; Pedro Martínez Cartón for Badajoz; Bautista Gasset for Córdoba; Daniel Ortega for Cádiz; Eduardo Suárez for Las Palmas; Adriano Gachinero for Pontevedra; Florencio Sosa for Tenerife; Vicente Uribe for Jaén; Antonio Mije for Seville; Miguel Valdés for Barcelona; Juan Antonio Uribes for the province of Valencia; Dolores Ibárruri for Oviedo. On July 22, 1936 the Catalonian delegates who were elected as representatives of their respective parties in the Front d'Esquerres joined the above, and when these parties united in a Catalonian Communist party, the Communist minority swelled: Pedro Aznar, Jaume Comas, Pelai Sala, Ramón Pla Armengol, Joan Comorera. In 1937 the Socialist Félix Montiel joined the PCE. Margarita Nelken of the PSOE had already done the same.
52. Quoted by Claudín, *La crisis del movimiento comunista*, p. 133.
53. *Mundo Obrero*, Madrid, June 3, 1936. It is interesting to contrast this attitude with that of the leftist Socialists. Largo Caballero relates that Azaña

"called several times to tell me that the Unión General should advise the workers to be more patient and moderate. I told him that it was more urgent to require the bosses, even the so-called republicans, to be more prudent, less self-centered, and more respectful of the law" (Largo Caballero, *Mis recuerdos,* p. 150).

54.   "It is impossible not to remember the Argentine comrade Codovila who helped us enormously at that time and later on also to overcome our political gaps, to eliminate sectarian methods, and to organize the Communist party, the development and activity of which, in hard times, is intimately linked to the name and participation of Comrade Codovila" (Ibárruri, *El único camino,* p. 191).

55.   Degras, vol. II, p. 386.

56.   As proof of this verbal revolutionism, the Communists pointed to the resolution of the PSOE of Madrid of March 1936: "We have no other recourse but to establish revolutionary socialism which in some way or other must achieve political power to carry out the ideal of a classless democracy" (Contreras Casado, p. 214). This stance of the conquest of power must have necessarily alarmed the Communists who wanted, because it was in the interest of Soviet diplomacy, a Republican coalition government, but not a revolutionary one. *Historia del PCE* (p. 112) states that the Socialist Left "refused to take concrete steps in favor of unity. Its support of unity, like its leftism, was mainly verbal."

57.   *Historia del PCE,* pp. 114, 116. The text of the statement of the Communist parliamentary minority on the occasion of this crisis is in *Guerra y revolución en España,* Moscow, 1967, vol. I, p. 95.

58.   The CNT, at its May congress in Zaragoza, decided that if there were a fascist uprising it would declare a general strike at the same time it made an appeal to the UGT for unity of action.

59.   *Guerra y revolución en España,* vol. I, p. 87. The figures look exaggerated and no non-Communist source has confirmed them. The statement closest to the truth would be that in July of 1936 the PCE had some 10,000 members; this is the estimate given by Thomas (p. 99). According to a statistic from the Ministry of the Interior which Miguel Maura read in Parliament, as of May 1936 there were 1,447,000 dues-paying Socialist members (PSOE and UGT), 1,577,000 Anarcho-Syndicalists, and 133,000 Communists. Right-wing parties included 549,000 members.

60.   Degras, vol. I, p. 387.

61.   José Díaz, *Tres años de lucha,* Paris, 1970, pp. 143, 176.

62.   Quoted by Diego Sevilla Andrés, *Historia política de la zona roja,* Madrid, 1963, p. 246.

63.   Araquistáin related that Álvarez del Vayo was the go-between in the negotiations between the Socialist and Communist youths. Private, unofficial meetings were held at the home of Del Vayo with Codovila attending (Araquistáin, *El comunismo y la guerra de España,* Carmaux, 1939).

64.   The correspondence between Amutio and Dimitrov is in Dimitrov, *Los problemas del Frente Único y del Frente Popular,* p. 113. The incident with Gorkín appears in Alba, *El marxisme a Catalunya,* vol. I, p. 344.

65.   Carrillo, "La bolchevización del Partido Socialista," *La Batalla,* Barcelona, June 28, 1935.

66.   Casterás, pp. 92–94.

67. Casterás, ibid.
68. Ricard Viñas, *La formación de las Juventudes Socialistas Unificadas (1934–36)*, Madrid, 1978, p. 43ff.
69. Estruch (p. 90) gives some figures which are closer to reality: 80,000 members of the FJS and 5,000 of the UJC.
70. Hermet, p. 34. *Historia del PCE* devotes exactly eight lines to unification (p. 112).
71. *La Vanguardia,* Barcelona, quoted in Alba, *El Frente Popular,* p. 446.
72. Castro Delgado, *Hombres made in Moscú,* p. 241.
73. Artola, p. 668.
74. Alba, *El marxisme a Catalunya,* vol. I, p. 380.
75. *Guerra y revolución en España,* vol. I, p. 87.
76. Tagüeña, pp. 100–101. Tagüeña says that he knew that Calvo Sotelo's murderer was "Cuenca, one of the gunmen whom certain UGT unions paid to intervene in union struggles," and that Captain Condés "had tried to commit suicide, believing himself dishonored since Calvo Sotelo had confided in him under his word of captain of the civil guard" when he arrested him (p. 100).

12.
Winning the War

Even today the image created from 1936 to 1939 weighs heavily on the PCE, it determines its behavior and determines many people's opinion of it. Much has been written about the Spanish Civil War. Here an attempt will be made to synthesize. This synthesis will be facilitated by the fact that beginning in 1936 the party was monolithic to such an extent that it is sufficient to quote one leader on any matter without needing to add other quotes because everyone was saying the same thing, often with almost identical words.

Exacerbated Contradictions

The Civil War carried the contradictions implicit in the very nature of the PCE to their natural conclusions. When Gonzalo Sanz, of the first PCE, negotiated the merger of the PCE and the PCOE with Graziadei, he wrote some "notes to the rank and file" about the merger. In one of them he said: "In the Third International discipline is absolutely essential; the Committee of the International makes the decisions; others need only obey. Only in the congresses is discussion allowed. And the power to make decisions and the status of carrying out orders without objection comes down from the Executive Committee of the International by gradations, that is, by subordinate committees down to the lowest member."[1]

From 1921 to 1936 this system of discipline imposed from above which formed the backbone of the party had its ups and downs. Bullejos tried to achieve a certain amount of autonomy from Moscow, and that is why they removed him; it was not because of his political line (which was not his, but the Communist International's), since his successors also followed it. His successors gradually made the implementation of this internal standard more rigid. Owing to it, the great change of policy of 1934–35 could be carried out without losing old militants while still winning new ones. It was also the team of leaders which succeeded Bullejos who adopted one of Togliatti's observations, to the point of making it the compass of its politics: "As far as we are concerned, it

195

is absolutely beyond argument that an identity of objectives exists between the Soviet Union's policy of peace and the policies of the working classes and Communist parties in capitalist countries. That identity of objectives cannot be a cause for doubt among our ranks. We are not only defenders of the Soviet Union in general; we defend all its policies and each of its actions."[2]

On its way toward becoming internally monolithic, the PCE missed a series of opportunities to become powerful: the fight against the dictatorship, the proclamation of the Republic, October 1934, and the electoral victory of 1936. It had won members, but was far from being a decisive force in the nation. A labor leader, familiar with the PCE and the Communist International through personal experience, analyzed the causes of this systematic waste of opportunities:

A whole series of circumstances contributed to the rapid development of a great revolutionary Socialist party in Spain, which is to say, a Communist party. We were in a revolutionary period when the masses were in a state of plasticity and things were evolving rapidly.

The impossibility of a democratic revolution at the hands of the petite bourgeoisie, the failure of a socialism of collaboration, the chaotic and senseless performance of Anarchism—everything seemed to pave the way for the formation of that historically necessary party. . . . Moscow, nevertheless, ruined everything. It began by not recognizing the importance of the Spanish revolution in its incipient stage. . . . Then it ground up the germ that existed of the Communist party, splitting it down the middle, casting out left and right, when what was needed was to present itself as the center of attraction of the Spanish proletariat. Moscow's sectarianism was disastrous for the Communist movement and for the revolution. . . .

Because of its Russian policy, Moscow fears and shuns the workers' revolution in another European country for two reasons. One: a workers' revolution could destroy the current status quo and precipitate a war, something which Russia needs to avoid at all cost. Russia comes first, everything else is secondary. Two: the proletarian revolution in another European country would strike a fatal blow to the influence Russia has had on the proletariat up to the present. . . .

Moscow would like to have had strong sections of the Communist International in every country, including Spain, capable of fully monopolizing the leadership of the labor movement. But in Moscow's policies there is a fundamental contradiction. It claims to form parties which are, in appearance, revolutionary in phraseology and kinship with the Russian Revolution, but which in practice are demagogic, electoralist, and lacking in revolutionary substance and objectives.[3]

The PCE had not scored a single victory but it had grown. Maurín said:

> Following the elections of February 1936 in which the Popular Front claimed victory, labor parties and organizations showed a great influx of new members. The Communist party in its official *Historia* said: 'From February to March 1936 its (the Communist party's) total strength went from some 30,000 to some 50,000 members. By April it had 60,000; in June, 84,000. And on the eve of the Fascist uprising of July 18, it had in its ranks 100,000 members. . . .

> Let us assume that the official figures the Communist party gives in its *Historia* are essentially accurate: in February 1936 it had 30,000 members and that number grew to 100,000 by July.

> Where did the avalanche of neophyte Communists come from? From the Socialist party? No. The Socialist party grew in membership. From the CNT? No. The CNT also grew. Nor did they come from BOC which also grew considerably. . . . In revolutionary periods there is always a vacillating, politically backward mass of people seeking incorporation for protection, and they do it thoughtlessly, turning more often than not toward the group or organization which appears most radical and fluid. That vacillating and insecure mass, during the first months of the Republic, formed the foundation of the Radical Socialist party. It had 56 representatives in the Constituent Assembly and 3 representatives in the Parliament elected in November 1933. The politically vacillating mass had evaporated, or what is worse, it voted to the Right.

> The Communist party in 1936 was a radical socialist party: popular, demagogic, and communist in name only. The same politically immature mass which in 1931 was radical socialist, became communist in 1936. There was no difference between the Radical Socialists of the Constituent Assembly and the Communists of 1936: the specific weight was identical.

> Let us say that on July 18, 1936 the Communist party had 100,000 members. . . . These 100,000 Communists compared to the Socialists assembled in the Socialist party and the UGT (about 2 million), and to the Anarcho-Syndicalists in the CNT (about 2 million also) did not amount to much: 2.5 percent of the labor population. . . .

> Let us see what the status of the Communist party was as of July 1936: (1) mission: to make Spain dependent on Russia; (2) history: pitiful; (3) achievements: none with the exception of the Popular Front which was purely electoral; (4) union strength: none. . . ; (5) intellectual projection: null; (6) proportional labor strength: 2.5 percent; (7) representation in Parliament: 16 representatives in a house of 452, in other words, 3.5 percent. . . ; (8) leaders: Humbert-Droz (Swiss), Codovila (Argentine), Rabate (French), Stepanov (Bulgarian). . . . Then no one, and a little further on there were José Díaz, Dolores Ibárruri, and some others.

> As of mid-July 1936 the Communist party was a political hypothesis which did not deserve to be taken into consideration.[4]

The Civil War was going to transform that "political hypothesis" into tangible reality; especially for its rivals and critics. In the course of this process the contradictions between the interests of the USSR and Spanish national interests as well as those of the Spanish proletariat, between the party monolith and the ideological plurality in the Republican zone, between the loyalty of the leaders of Moscow and the aspirations of the members, were all going to cause not only personal heartbreaks among many Communists but also merciless divisions among anti-Fascist forces.

Uselessness of the Popular Front

The government, which a few days earlier had assured that the army was loyal, on July 17 said that the uprising was "an absurdity," did nothing to put it down, and asked for confidence in the inexistent "means of military strength of the state." But the people had gone out into the streets and were asking for arms. When Azaña asked Martínez Barrio to negotiate with Mola the formation of a conciliatory government, people in Madrid demonstrated against it. There were people of all parties, but the demonstration was not organized by any of them. Fighting had already begun in other places throughout the country. A new government presided over by José Giral, a man close to Azaña, who took over the following day, demobilized the troops and told the governors to give arms to the organizations of the Popular Front. But it was too late to snuff out the rebellion. However, where the civil governors had provided arms, the military failed; they were successful only where the people were unarmed.

Just before the uprising, through Communist initiative, the UGT, PSOE, JSU, and PCE met and wrote a note offering "the government aid and support of the masses so dear to it in defense of the regime and resistance against any attempts made against it." But the Popular Front was no longer of any use. It was not able to "put out the fires" of the people, which was the pretext for the coup. Azaña was not thinking of the Popular Front coup when he put Martínez Barrio in charge of mediating nor when he placed Giral at the head of the government. Giral spoke with no one other than Largo Caballero since behind him was the strength of the UGT and PSOE. Forgotten were the Popular Front and the Communists as well, since they had been of no use in stopping the masses, and since their policy of propaganda to infiltrate the army was so inefficient that there was not a single case of a soldier's refusing to follow his appointed officers. An attempt at resistance by the troops in Palma de Mallorca was paradoxically led by a militant of POUM who was sentenced to death because of it.

The UGT declared a general strike. The CNT did the same in accordance with its resolution at the congress of Zaragoza. The truth is that the workers had not waited for orders to strike. Fighting was not engaged in by the Popular Front but by the workers and in some places by the uniformed police, who would not have done it if they had not seen the workers in the streets. The Popular Front, which at the time was only the PCE and some Republican leaders, still published a statement: "The government is certain it has enough means to put down this criminal attempt. In the event that its means were insufficient, the Republic has the solemn promise of the Popular Front to intervene in the fighting the moment it is called to do so. The government gives the orders and the Popular Front will obey." First of all, prior to the uprising, the Popular Front offered to help a government which was not doing anything to stop the coup. When the coup broke out, it pledged obedience to a government incapable of giving orders.

Power is "in the streets."[5] And the PCE was trying to help the Popular Front regain it. On July 21 when fighting in the streets had ended, Dolores Ibárruri cried out via radio: "With the blood of the heroic militiamen and the armed forces loyal to the Republic, the government which grew out of the Popular Front, with the valor and spirit of sacrifice of all anti-Fascists and with the enthusiastic collaboration of the brave airmen, today there has been written one of the most glorious pages in our country's history." She was referring to the taking of De la Montaña barracks in Madrid. There was no mention whatsoever of the desires of the workers. Everything was the government, the Popular Front, the airmen, the nonexistent loyal forces, and almost in passing, the militiamen.[6]

Before, during, and after the fighting, the PCE tried to keep the Popular Front alive, follow the government, and put all its hopes in it (even though Communist members were out in the streets just like militants of all the other workers' organizations, and they gave their share of fighters and victims). This confidence in authorities who never deserved it explains the catastrophe in Seville, the stronghold of the PCE, where half of its leaders came from, and where since 1930 it had its largest base. Trusting the governor, the workers of Seville, paralyzed by the Popular Front, were on the defensive, and this allowed General Gonzalo Queipo de Llano, with audacity and few troops (130 soldiers and 15 Falangists, according to Ibárruri), to overtake the city and begin one of the most implacable massacres of the Civil War.

Committees cropped up in towns and provinces with aspirations far beyond those of the Popular Front. Later on Communists would label them as "committees of the Popular Front," yet they never were.[7] This interest in attributing to the Popular Front the spontaneous action of the masses is due to the desire to conceal the divorce of the PCE and those very masses. The PCE clung to the Popular Front even more than the Republicans, who felt overwhelmed and guilty. Because of this PCE obsession with the Popular Front they started talking about loyal forces instead of workers' forces, of rebels instead of Fascists, of loyal zone instead of revolutionary zone. It was not just to appease foreign opinion, as was claimed; rather it responded to the desire to keep things within Republican legality. From the beginning of the Civil War, even when it was not certain that it would turn into such or when people thought it would not last long, the PCE strove to maintain "Republican legality." This was more important than the people's aspirations as manifested in committees, confiscations, collectivizations, and militias."[8]

The PSUC

What the PCE had not previously gotten in Spain, it achieved in Catalonia thanks to the Civil War.[9] In 1935 when negotiations for Marxist unity in Catalonia divided, and BOC and the Communist Left formed POUM, the other organizations kept on negotiating. What kept them from reaching an agreement was the problem of international affiliation. Nobody, aside from the PCC, seemed enthused about the Communist International. But with the Civil War at hand and in view of the weakness of the four groups that were negotiating, an agreement was quickly reached and signed on July 23, 1936 to form the PSUC (Partit Socialista Unificat de Catalunya—Unified Socialist Party of Catalonia). Just as in the case of the JSU, the name "Communist" was dropped from the title and "Socialist" was adopted. Yet, at the same time, membership in the Communist International was decided upon. This membership was not formalized until 1939. The PSUC adhered to the International through the PCE whose directions it followed from the outset. There was never a delegate of the PSUC in the Comintern although the Comintern had one in the PSUC, the same one who had been in the PCC, the Hungarian Gerö ("Pedro"). There could no longer be any doubt about PSUC's dependency on the PCE, for a few months later Comorera and Vidiella were named members of the Central Committee of the PCE.[10]

The process of unification had bypassed all the usual stages. Up to July 1936 it had been confined to the establishment of a liaison committee of the four parties. But on July 21 the liaison committee, in a sudden move, agreed upon the merger, which the executive committee of the four parties ratified the following day. The provisional executive committee of the new party met at once and elected Joan Comorera as secretary general; he had formerly been the secretary general of the very moderate Unió Socialista de Catalunya (USC). Miguel Valdés, of the PCC, was organizational secretary. Also on the executive committee were Pere Ardiaca and García (Matas) of the PCC, Rafael Vidiella, Víctor Colomer (formerly of BOC), and Almendros, of the Catalonian Federation of the PSOE, Joan Carreras, Miguel Serra i Pàmies, and Pau Cirera, of the Unió Socialista de Catalunya, and Artur Cussó and Ramón Álvarez of the Partit Catalá Proletari. PSUC immediately expropriated the Christian-democratic daily *El Matí* and began to publish its organ, *Treball*. PSUC, in its initial stages, had 6,000 members (2,000 from the PCC, 2,000 from USC, 1,500 from the PSOE, and 500 from the PCP). The few unions of the UGT and the powerful Centro Autonomista de Dependientes del Comercio y de la Industria (Autonomous Center of Employees of Commerce and Industry, CADCI) were led by members of PSUC (but not of the PCC).[11]

The PCC probably would not have achieved the affiliation of PSUC to the Communist International, which means there would not have been a PSUC or that it would have been formed without the PCC if it had not been for the Socialist Comorera who played a role in this unification similar to that of Carrillo in the unification of Juventudes. Immediately following the seventh congress of the Communist International, USC's organ *Justicia Social* began to publish articles favoring the PCC and criticizing BOC (to which Comorera had privately proposed unification in 1933). In October the least "internationalist" members were removed from the executive committee of USC: Rafael Foch i Capdevila, Antoni Obach, and Joan Capdevila. They were replaced by individuals who all would have leading posts in PSUC in the future. From prison in Puerto de Santa María (where he was serving time for having been a member of the government of the Generalitat in October 1934), Comorera wrote several letters encouraging unification and criticizing BOC which was what the PCC required. The new party, he said, ought to be "the Socialist Party of Catalonia (Catalonian section of the Communist International)." Upon his return from Uruguay in 1931 Comorera had already removed from leadership of the USC its founders Rafael Campalans and Manuel Serra i Moret; he had been one of the most moderate elements within the USC and also most inclined to systematically collaborate with the Esquerra. It would seem that the 1935 line of the Communist International was befitting of its moderation.

The Catalonian Federation of the PSOE joined the unification process on the prompting of Rafael Vidiella, an ex-Anarchist who in the Socialist party sided with Largo Caballero yet without his cautiousness regarding the Communists. At any rate, the Catalonian Federation was so weak that it would have gone unnoticed during the events of July 1936 and would have perhaps lost the few small unions of the UGT that it controlled if it had not leaned on the PCC and the USC. Some members of BOC who refused to join POUM (some of whom became members of the PCC), others of the USC, and still others of the Catalonian PSOE, thus found themselves in PSUC with the moral consequences which will be seen later.[12]

What caused the doubts and the search for advantages in the negotiations to be forgotten was the fear of isolation in the face of pressure from the CNT and POUM which, in the days following July 19, were the dominant forces throughout Catalonia (obviously the CNT more than POUM). Comorera was the lifeblood of the unification and the one who made it possible by leaning toward the Third International; in March 1936 he had already told the press that only the merger congress would be able to decide international affiliation but that he would support the Communist International.[13] In a way, PSUC is an example of what might have happened in the event that the merger of the PSOE and the PCE had been achieved.

The policies of PSUC and the PCE did not differ at all. It was a single policy expressed in different languages, although PSUC had the harder part of the task because it was working in an area in which the CNT and POUM were more powerful than it was. It will soon be apparent that PSUC's leaders and "instructors" were not unskilled in the use of arms—in a metaphoric as well as a literal sense—which the Civil War placed in their hands. The first political measure PSUC took was to try to use the Esquerra, which until then had been the great party of the Catalonian middle class (and even of part of the working class), for the purpose of developing its own policy. It began by inducing the Esquerra to assemble the liaison committee of the Front d'Esquerres, which had not been in operation since the elections, its mission being only electoral.

In a meeting on July 22 Comorera proposed that all the components of the committee surrender to the discipline of the committee itself, that is, that it be transformed into a superparty. POUM refused; Comorera invited it to withdraw and it left. The committee never met again. Its aim had been to try to neutralize and subject POUM to the discipline of the committee, in other words, actually the PSUC.[14] PSUC deemed it necessary for the time being to verbally adapt to the general mood, for on July 28 it came out with a manifesto which said: "The revolution is winning. We must be alert, however, so as not to lose the conquests which have been won with our blood and sacrifices. This is not the time to respect classical law, classical justice. [The working class] must be triumphant in its revolution and it is prepared to defend with arms this right which it will not relinquish."

How to Win the War?

People took to the streets on July 19 to block a military coup. But three days later when they went back to work they found that, particularly in Catalonia and Valencia, many employers and managers had disappeared. To avoid not being paid on the following Saturday, the workers met in assemblies and agreed to "collectivize" those businesses, in other words, to appoint committees to run them. They might have been able to appeal to the government to extend them credit to pay the salaries, and indeed that was done in those places where unions, especially those of the CNT, were weak. But where unions were strong, the workers preferred to claim for themselves the responsibility of running the firms. Although it affected only large firms (and a limited number of them at that) and only in specific areas of the Republican zone, it signified a change in the system of ownership. A social revolution was superimposed on the Civil War. The military coup had unleashed the almost secular aspirations of the workers, it had given them the means to satisfy these aspirations, and had even made their satisfaction a prerequisite for the economy not to become paralyzed in the Republican zone.

The nature of the struggle went through a transformation which caused a collision of the two ideas about it. On the one hand were the Republicans who did not want social changes, only a speedy end to the Civil War with a Republican victory. But the Republicans, when it came time to take to the streets, were relatively few in number, and the fact that a Republican government had not known how to stop the coup made them lose credibility. On the other hand there was the CNT with its masses which had considerable strength in the streets, in the militias, in company committees, and in agrarian collectivizations; and next to them was POUM which, although it favored socialization, preferred collectivization to no social change; finally there was the Socialist Left, which even before the war maintained a position of "complete control of power" by the working class.

The Republicans believed that social experiments could alienate the democratic governments of Europe and isolate Spain, leaving Franco in an advantageous position. They used the reasoning of international politics to try to put an end to social change. This reasoning lost credibility when European nations stopped selling arms to the Republic. The CNT, POUM, and the Socialist Left thought that the people had neither an army nor military experts and that only with enthusiasm and a spirit of sacrifice could they overcome these disadvantages and win the war. One could not ask for enthusiasm and a spirit of sacrifice to defend a republic which had allowed the coup; rather they would only be obtained to defend the conquests made spontaneously by the people, that is, the collectivizations, committees, militias. To understand the significance of this reasoning, it must be emphasized that those conquests were really spontaneous and were not a result of union or party slogans; rather they confronted unions and parties with a fait accompli.

What position would the Communists adopt? At first nobody worried much about it because the PCE and PSUC were not strong enough— or so people thought—to decide in favor of one or the other. To understand the mechanism by which the PCE reached its position—or rather by which the Communist International reached it and transmitted it to the PCE—one must ask the question the leaders of the Communist International formulated before each new situation: what suits the USSR? What suited the USSR in the case of Spain in July 1936: a revolution or just the defense of the Republic? The USSR at the time had an alliance with France where there was a Popular Front government (although without the Communist party) which had accomplished some social reforms, but not a revolution, and that had alarmed its ally England which had a conservative government. In addition Moscow had reestablished relations with the United States, capitalist nation par excellence, and was looking for an alliance with Great Britain. So it did not want to put out the scarecrow of "Communist danger" and, above all, did not want any social change occurring in Spain to be attributed to the Communists or to the USSR's influence.

Consequently, the Communist International gave the PCE and PSUC the slogan that the war was being waged to defend the Republic and democracy and not to carry out social revolution. Later on when circumstances changed, that slogan was expanded—although not publicly—to: destroy the social changes which may have taken place. This was synthesized in the Communist cry of "First win the war." They wanted to make people think that the revolutionaries did not want to win the war, just the revolution. This was clearly absurd in view of the fact that what they were saying was that without a revolution the war could not be won. That the antirevolutionary slogan was readily accepted by the Spanish Communists is explained not only by its monolithic discipline and the prospects for recruitment it gave them, but also by the fact that for a Communist any revolution not led by the party was not a revolution and must be resisted, since the Communist party was the only representative of the working class and only the Communist party could make an authentic revolution. A revolution by the despised

Anarchists, the hated POUM, or the Socialist leftist renegades made the PCE sick to its stomach.

During the first weeks of the war this position, which the Republicans accepted as logical, was also accepted by the Communists—to many people's surprise—and only later would they realize its true causes.[15] In any event it was not a popular position at that time of creative, improvisational, destructive enthusiasm in which everything seemed possible and which André Malraux called "apocalypse of brotherhood." Having said this, one must recognize that Spanish Communists—or those of any country—were always perfectly capable of going against the current. Perhaps the isolation in which they had lived for fifteen years, until the Popular Front, had prepared them for it. It had been unpopular to ask for soviets when the Republic was proclaimed, to talk of social fascism and anarcho-fascism, to accuse Azaña of being a Fascist when General Sanjurjo was rebelling, to set the stage for the CGTU, to refuse to accept the Alianza Obrera, even to the capture the JS. Once again it was time for them to go against the current and they did it without batting an eyelash. It was a small party compared to the other labor organizations, with a small militia and mediocre leadership, but behind it in spirit was the enormous strength of the USSR, loyalty to "the fatherland of the proletariat," Stalin's infinite wisdom, and the habit of blind discipline.

The Defense of Property

What few Republicans dared do—defend the principle of private property—the Communists did with tenacity and a certain degree of daring which was a tribute to the democratic spirit of their adversaries, since they knew that nothing bad would happen to them by maintaining their positions despite the fact that they were a minority party. A few quotes will suffice to see the tone of the party's propaganda in those first weeks of the war:

> We are not making a social revolution today, we are developing a democratic revolution, and in a democratic revolution, the economy and production cannot take on socialist forms.—*Federico Melchor, leader of the JSU*

> We are fighting with sincerity for the democratic Republic because we know that should we make the mistake of fighting now for social revolution in our country—and even after our long struggle for victory—we would have surrendered to fascism.—*Santiago Carrillo, leader of the JSU*

> It is everyone's duty to respect the property of small businessmen and industrialists, for they are our brothers.—*Mundo Obrero*

As Communists, we defend a regime of liberty and democracy. . . . In these historic moments, the Communist party, faithful to its revolutionary principles, respectful of the will of the people, supports the government which is the expression of that will; we support the Republic and democracy. . . . The government of Spain grew out of the electoral triumph of February 16 and we support and defend it because it is the legitimate expression of the people who fight for democracy and freedom. Long live the democratic Republic!—*Dolores Ibárruri*

Our [Communist] sister party has repeatedly shown that Spain's current struggle is not between capitalism and socialism but between fascism and democracy. . . . The working class and all the people have one immediate, urgent task, the only possible task, and all the recent appeals of the Communist party reiterate and prove it: that of not realizing the Socialist revolution but rather of defending, consolidating, and developing the bourgeois democratic revolution.—*André Marty of the French Communist party and commissar of the International Brigades*

We cannot speak of proletarian revolution in Spain because historical conditions do not allow it.—*Jesús Hernández*

We wish to fight only for a democratic Republic with broad social content. We cannot speak now of dictatorship of the proletariat or of socialism but only of the struggle of democracy against fascism.—*José Díaz*

The Central Committee of the Spanish Communist party asks us to make public, in response to the tendencious campaigns and fantastic accounts of certain newspapers, that the Spanish people, in their fight against the rebels, are not trying to establish proletarian dictatorship but rather have only one aim: the defense of the Republican order and the respect of property.—*L'Humanité, Paris, August 3, 1936*

All these statements reflect the same thinking expressed in a letter from Stalin to the head of the government on December 24, 1936, as if it were a Christmas present. In it he gave some "friendly advice," such as that the government ought to attract the petite bourgeoisie, "protecting it against confiscation and ensuring its freedom of trade," and that the government ought to announce that it "would not put up with any interference in the property and legitimate interests of foreigners in Spain."[16]

The Central Committee of the PCE stated on August 18, 1936, scarcely a month after the war had broken out: "In its initial stages, the struggle could only be characterized as a fight between democracy and fascism, between reaction and progress, between the past and the future, but it has already gone beyond its limits and has been transformed into a holy war, a national war, a war in defense of a people who feel betrayed, who see their fatherland, their homes, the homes of their families in danger of being split up, leveled, and sold to foreigners."[17]

To put an end to the Republic, the right-wing forces adopted two successive tactics: first they tried to overcome it from within (Black Biennium, 1933–35), and when this failed they attacked it from without (coup of July 1936). To put an end to revolutionary conquests, the Communists would follow two successive tactics in accordance with what they deemed possible at the time: first, they would try to limit and undermine social change from within the revolution, and then they would attack the revolution from without, from a position of power.

From Giral to Largo Caballero

The Giral government was a collection of phantoms. No one paid attention to it. The initiative of the man on the street and the decisions of the organizations ran the country and the fighting. During the six weeks of this Republican government, the improvised militias prevented coups in Lérida and Valencia, conquered Albacete, Pozoblanco, Guadalajara, San Sebastián, Toledo, advanced through Aragon, put an end to the offensive against Madrid in the mountains to the north, and occupied Ibiza and Formentera. In Catalonia the committee of militias was organized and the industrial collectivizations were coordinated. The skeleton-like UGT and the minoritarian PSUC received representation disproportionate to their forces in the committee of militias. On July 31 Companys, the president of the Generalitat, tried to form a government made up of Republicans and members of PSUC (Comorera, Vidiella, Ruiz Ponseti). PSUC accepted but the government, with no authority whatsoever, collapsed within seven days and was replaced by another made up of Republicans only. There were, as a matter of fact, two powers in Catalonia. The same was true in Valencia, with a popular executive committee which on July 23 the delegate of the government, Diego Martínez Barrio, tried to dissolve. The Communists accepted the order, but the PSOE, UGT, CNT, and POUM refused, fortunately, because when the garrison attempted an uprising on July 25, had it not been for the committee which decreed the general strike and organized the fighting, the military would have taken over the city. In Asturias, Santander, Málaga, and Aragon the committees proliferated. Finally, on September 4 Giral resigned.

Azaña thought that Largo Caballero was qualified to replace him. With the responsibility that power carries, he would try to limit and channel the transforming forces. The Central Committee of the PCE refused to enter the government; it preferred Giral to a Socialist. But Largo Caballero did not want to give the Communists the privilege of not being in the cabinet and he required that in order for a government to be formed, the PCE must be in it. He also tried to get the collaboration of the CNT but the Anarchists refused. After the "instructors" consulted with Moscow, the bureau changed the decision of the central committee and it accepted. Jesús Hernández became minister of public instruction and Vicente Uribe, minister of agriculture. It was the first time that the Communists were in a government outside of the USSR. The party said that unity was necessary to fight Fascism, that the proletarian revolution had been completed, and that the government would be one of Popular Front. So it saved face for everybody.[18] Shortly thereafter the Communist party of Euzkadi was hurriedly formed to keep up with local events. Its leader, Juan Astigarrabía, joined the Council of Defense of Vizcaya and later the Basque government once the Parliament (on October 3) voted for a statute of autonomy.

In Catalonia a Council of the Economy was established to coordinate the collectivizations and a committee of war industry was created. On September 27, after a week of negotiations, Companys managed to form a new government of the Generalitat in which every organization which made up the committee of militias took part; then that committee was dissolved. The duality of power had disappeared. With the naming of three of its members to this government, this was the first time that the CNT and FAI accepted the fact that, given the circumstances, it was necessary to take part in power. Together with POUM they formed part of a government which in theory was a labor government, since the ministers of the UGT and PSUC were presumably such; in practice, they always voted with Republican middle-class parties, so the representatives of the CNT and POUM were in the minority even though in the streets they might have had an absolute majority, taken all the initiatives, and controlled the collectivized economy.

Meanwhile, things were happening which would have a decisive influence on the PCE. New delegates of the International arrived (although the exact dates of their arrival are not known). The principal delegate was Palmiro Togliatti (called "Ercoli" or "Alfredo"). Vittorio Vidali, besides being in charge of the Fifth Regiment, helped Togliatti when it came to shady business. Jacques Duclos came and went from Paris. Gerö continued as advisor to PSUC. At some periods Stepanov, and some say also Tito, acted as "instructors," although it seems to have been proven that Tito never went to Spain.

Togliatti provided the PCE with the theoretical arguments for its political stance. Toward the end of 1936 when there were numerous agrarian and industrial collectivizations and a collectivized and efficient industry of war in Catalonia, the Italian leader wrote an analysis, "On the Peculiarities of the Spanish Revolution." Note that, regardless of the PCE's orders, it was so evident that there was a revolution that neither could Togliatti ignore it nor did the PCE ignore it later on.[19] "Alfredo" said:

> The tasks which face the Spanish people are those of a democratic-bourgeois revolution. Reactionary forces, whose power the Fascist rebels tried to restore, ruled Spain in such a way that they made it the poorest and most backward country of Europe. . . . This means that in the interest of the country's economic and political development, it is necessary to resolve the agrarian question, destroying the feudal relations which predominate in the countryside. . . .
>
> What stands in the way of the solution to these problems by the democratic-bourgeois revolution? It is Fascism which in Spain not only is a form of capitalist reaction but also the champion of medieval and feudal vestiges, vestiges of the monarchy, of religious fanaticism, of Jesuitism and the Inquisition, champion of reactionary forces, of privileges of the nobility, of everything which, like a stone wall, stands in the way of the nation's progress and halts the development of its economy.[20]

So for the man who, under orders from Moscow, was going to be the inspiration of the PCE's policies, what was happening in Spain was a mere continuation of the democratic-bourgeois revolution of the period of the Republic. This was the reasoning used within the PCE to appease the old members who were growing impatient with the "softness" of party positions. Although the first government of Largo Caballero lasted only two months, one had the opportunity to see that "softness." For example, "the government had hardly been constituted . . . when Uribe on October 7 took to the meetings of the Council of Ministers a project of agrarian reform which responded to the needs of the peasants and of the whole country. . . . By this agrarian reform the peasants were given, for permanent use, the land of the large rural landlords involved in the uprising."[21]

This so-called agrarian reform which only affected the land of those who had rebelled (an even less drastic measure than that adopted by Parliament following the uprising of August 1932 when they expropriated the land of the Spanish grandees even though they might not have participated in General Sanjurjo's conspiracy), was a reflection of the Soviet model of not distributing land to be owned by the peasants or of forming voluntary collectivities but rather, of giving it for cultivation so that the peasants receiving it, out of sentiment or fear of having it taken away, remained politically tied to the very men who handed it over to them. The measure responded to the fact that "consistent in its position of defense of the Republic and of democracy, from the very beginning of the war the party had firmly opposed the FAI's and Trotskyites' distorting the nature of the war; it had opposed, in support of the very peasants, the pseudorevolutionary attempts of all those who dispossessed the peasants of their lands and wealth and made them join the anarchistic collectivities."[22]

In the first two and a half months of the Civil War, the Communist press did not print a single attack on the Nonintervention Committee of which the USSR was a part. *Correspondance Internationale*, wondering if the USSR could refuse to be part of the committee, finally said no because "France, with which the USSR was linked by a pact of mutual assistance, insisted on it." The article did not say that the USSR would have been able to insist on France's not forming part of the committee since France was linked to the Soviet Union by a pact of mutual assistance. But on October 7 Moscow declared that it would not feel obligated by the nonintervention accord if other members violated it, and that caused the Communist press to wake up to the fact of the committee's existence and the consequent attacks on it as well as praise for Moscow's new position.[23]

Up to that moment the USSR had not sent any arms or aid whatsoever to the Republic. The first fighting of the war was done with arms, aircraft, and munitions purchased in France and the United States as well as those made by the collectivized war industries. On October 15 the first Soviet ship, the *Zirianin,* arrived at the port of Barcelona. By that time the government had already made a decision which was in the process of being discussed on October 7 when Moscow made its declaration: send the Bank of Spain's gold reserves to the USSR. Negrín, minister of the treasury, held secret negotiations with some functionaries of the Soviet Embassy and in particular with Stachevsky (for in the meantime the two governments had appointed ambassadors for the first time since 1917). On Negrín's proposal, the Council of Ministers agreed to place the reserves of the Bank of Spain in a safe place where they could not fall into the hands of the enemy or be seized by some foreign tribunal under pressure by the rebels. Thus began the confusion regarding the Spanish gold. Members of the government have stated that although the Council of Ministers approved Negrín's moving the gold, no one ever said where it would be moved to. It seems dubious that no one asked Negrín where he was going to send the gold and that he did not volunteer the information. Be that as it may, what is certain is that the gold went from Cartagena at the end of October to Odessa and then to Moscow. Once the gold was en route to Russia, Moscow began sending arms. The first ship carrying Russian arms crossed the path of the Spanish ship with the gold in the Mediterranean. Although that gold probably did not comprise the entire treasury and although there were other minor stores in various countries, it is certain that as soon as the bulk of the Spanish gold was sent to the very country which was supplying the Republic with arms, the Republic surrendered with its hands tied to its supplier and even renounced the possibility of being able to request the kind and quantity of arms it wished to purchase, and it implicitly yielded to the political will of the trustee of the gold.

It is important to present the accounts clearly. Spain handed over to Russia gold worth some 550 million dollars of the time. In exchange for that sum it received arms and food. It will soon be seen that Moscow maintained that all the gold was spent on aid to the Republic (which therefore was not aid as such but rather a commercial operation). Franco received from Germany and Italy arms and supplies worth some 600 million dollars which were sent on credit instead of paid for in advance, as the Republic had to do. But in the battlefield the superiority of Franco's armaments over the Republicans was five to one or even ten to one, depending on the kind of weapons. So, for an approximately equal amount, Franco received five to ten times more arms than the Republic. Aside from any other consideration, the Russian arms then turned out to be five to ten times more expensive than those sent by the Italians or Germans. That difference in price cannot be explained by economic or technical reasons but rather only politically. And those political reasons were a decisive factor in the progress of the war.[24] Luis Araquistáin, confidant of Largo Caballero and his ambassador in Paris, said that the Russians were the ones who demanded the shipment of gold to Odessa and threatened to withhold the arms which already had been signed for until the gold was received. Incidentally, when Araquistáin in a conference in Barcelona in 1937 said that the arms from Russia were being paid for by gold sent to Moscow but without furnishing further details, the Communists asked for his imprisonment for "high treason and defamation."[25]

Finally, Moscow became convinced that what was happening in Spain was more than a mere sale of arms. On October 15 after a meeting of the political bureau of the Russian Communist party, Stalin sent a telegram to Díaz saying that "the cause of the Spanish people was the same as that of all advanced and progressive men." The telegram did not make any promises; nor did the Communists, who in Brussels in September 1936 organized a congress of the Rassemblement Universel pour la Paix (a continuation, four years later, of the conference of Amsterdam-Pleyel) make any promises. So that people of all ideologies could attend provided they were against the war, instructions were given to speak of nothing which could give rise to controversy. One of the taboos was the war in Spain.[26] Shortly thereafter orders were issued to the Communist parties to organize the recruitment of volunteers. Münzenberg took immediate charge of pro-Republic propaganda.[27] The phase of doubting which André Gide found so surprising was finally over:

> When I was in the Soviet Union, I was shocked that the press made no mention of the Spanish Civil War which at the time was causing a great deal of anxiety in democratic circles. I told my interpreter of my distress and amazement and I noted his embarrassment. But he thanked me for my observation and told me he would refer it to the appropriate individuals. . . . Jef Last, one of the members of our group, stood up and made a toast in Russian to the triumph of the Red cause on the Spanish fronts. It was met with cool and embarrassed applause and was immediately followed by a toast to Stalin. . . . Pravda had not yet made an official statement on the question of Spain and nobody dared show approval without official instructions or without knowing what he was expected to think. Just a few days later, when we arrived at Sebastopol, an immense wave of sympathy (for Spain) rose in Red Square in Moscow which Pravda helped spread throughout the entire country.[28]

Russian Aid

Largo Caballero had wanted his government to "combine Republican legality with the conquests of the revolution." To accomplish this double aim it had to rely on support of the CNT. When the CNT joined the Catalonian government, Largo Caballero succeeded in persuading the Anarchists to enter his government with two ministers from the CNT and two from FAI. This new government was formed on November 5. It continued to have PCE representation in the figures of Hernández and Uribe. What Largo Caballero wanted to achieve was ambiguous. This ambiguity—pleasing foreign interests as well as those of the people and satisfying legality as well as the need to change it—unavoidably helped those preferring legality over change, some out of class interests, others out of transferred patriotism. Things which exist have more weight than those which have yet to be created. That ambiguity favored the PCE because it allowed it to keep its members trusting in the revolutionary spirit which, after all, prior to February 1936, was what had attracted them to the PCE; at the same time that ambiguity allowed the PCE to serve the diplomatic interests of the USSR. The latter's interest in the Spanish Civil War had many facets. Although it took Moscow a while to notice it, as was normal for bureaucratic machines such as the Communist International and the Russian Communist party, that did not make it any less real. It can be summed up by the following:

1. In 1936 Russia, more than anything else, feared the Third Reich. Russian diplomacy consisted of isolating it by allying itself with Western nations. It already had a pact with France and was hoping for one with England. It wanted to avoid any situation which would weaken that alliance, incline any government toward Berlin, or give Berlin an excuse to draw any government to it. Therefore nothing must happen in Spain which would allow Berlin to talk about the "danger of Communism" or the "Red threat," or to have London grow close to Berlin.

2. Through the Communist International and its parties, the USSR was the agglutinant of forces which had been growing and which opposed Fascism. The Popular Front tended to give those forces a common platform (and to pressure Hitler to come to an agreement with Moscow if they could not contain him).[29] Moscow could not get rid of its facade of "fatherland of socialism" if it did not want to alienate the confidence of the most dynamic elements in the fight against Fascism. The Communist International and the Soviet government had to appear as firm supporters of the Republic if they did not want their anti-Fascism to lose credibility. But that support had to be given in such a way as not to aid the revolutionary forces in the Republican zone, rather just the conservative forces which would not alarm London and Washington. At the same time, that aid should not be so abundant as to allow the Republic to win the war quickly before the revolutionary forces could be annihilated.

3. Finally, Russia and the Communist movement had internal interest. It was two-sided. On the one hand the USSR did not look favorably upon an experiment in social transformation which, instead of following the Soviet model of dictatorship of the bureaucracy and of party technicians, was spontaneous, libertarian, and without a dictatorship over the revolutionary forces. To accept that was to lose the enormous advantage which was provided by offering the Soviet model as the only way and the Communist party as the only representative of the proletariat, socialism, and the revolution. On the other hand, shortly after the start of the Spanish Civil War there began in Moscow what was called the "witch trials" against the old Bolshevik friends of Lenin. By doing away with them, Stalin wished to eliminate any other possible alternative for power, and by forcing them to plead guilty to nonexistent crimes through use of torture, he could use them as scapegoats for the catastrophic consequences of his own politics. But, so that those trials were not viewed as one more aspect of the struggle to succeed Lenin, it was necessary to strip them of their Russian characteristics and present them as the inevitable consequence of any

divergence from the only way—Stalin's. Anyone who did not follow it ended up serving the Fascists. The evolution of events in Spain gave Stalin the opportunity to order the Spanish Communists to prepare trials like those in Moscow. That would "prove" that the treason of the old Bolsheviks was neither a Russian phenomenon nor one linked to Stalin, but rather a universal phenomenon related to Fascism.

Events proved that none of this was exaggerated, as incredible as an analysis of this kind might have then seemed to everyone (an analysis which not even POUM dared to consider despite its greater knowledge of Stalinism). And the events which shaped the history of the PCE from 1936 to 1939 would not be understood nor seen coherently if they were not examined in light of those Soviet interests. In no instance, no matter how anecdotal it was, did the leaders of the PCE find a lack of coincidence between these interests and those of the Republic; this fact seems proof enough that the point of view of the PCE's team of leaders was distorted by Soviet interests. This was otherwise common in all Communist leaders in any country. If that were not the case, the Communist International would not have put them in positions of leadership. Soviet aid existed. It is not necessary to enter into details, but it is fitting to relate its various aspects to that triple interest as well as to the PCE's policies. It was essentially made up of:

1. Aid in the form of armaments, paid for in advance with gold from the Bank of Spain. The Russians were always the ones to decide the amounts, the models, and the times when the shipments of arms would arrive. In this way they could test the arms they wanted and regulate the progress of the war. Shipments of arms began to arrive in October 1936 when gold had already been sent to Moscow. The first Russian tanks entered combat in Madrid on October 28 and the first Russian planes on November 11. The Francoists had Italian planes at their disposal by July 20. The Russian weapons and munitions never arrived in sufficient quantity to give the Republican forces superiority over the Francoists, but there were enough to keep the war going. There is no reason to believe that demand for advance payment in gold was only for commercial reasons (although that consideration was never absent from any Soviet agreement); it also assured the direct and inescapable control of Republican politics. There were other means of payment—unaccountable, naturally—such as the delivery of German or Italian planes downed in Republican territory to Soviet experts.

2. Aid in men. Shortly after October 15, 1936 the Communist International instructed the Communist parties to recruit volunteers. Men of all nationalities began arriving in Spain. The majority were idealistic, many were Communists, hardly submissive, whose parties got rid of them by sending them off to fight in Spain, as proven by the frequency of executions of members of the International Brigades for political reasons, not for reasons of military discipline. Long before they were organized, in Spain there were foreign Socialists, dissident communists, Trotskyites, anarchists fighting in the militias of their respective organizations. These non-Communist foreign volunteers later on became the target of numerous persecutions. Apart from that, although the officers in the International Brigades were Communists (André Marty was its commissar general), the majority of their members were not.[30]

3. Technical aid provided by members of the Soviet army. There were never any Russian soldiers in Spain (unlike the Francoist zone to which Mussolini sent several brigades and Hitler the Condor Legion). But there were military advisors of the General Staff and of some army corps sent by the Communists which on certain occasions threatened to suspend the Russian shipment of arms to carry out its plans. The purpose of this technical aid was for the Soviet army to learn from the experiences of the Spanish war, even though many of the advisors, upon their return to the USSR during the period of purges, were put to death. In all, there must have been 2,000 advisors.

4. Diplomatic aid was of little value, for although the USSR supported the Spanish delegation in the League of Nations, it never did so emphatically enough to have its support be of any use. Likewise, in the Nonintervention Committee the USSR never adopted a decisive position which could be useful to the Republic.[31]

5. Aid in propaganda was considerable, not only by means of the Communist parties but above all in the organizations as fronts. It is difficult to know whether the fact that the Communists defended the Republic helped win sympathy for it. The Republic financed a great deal of this propaganda especially the *Agence Espagne,* run by the Czechoslovakian Otto Katz, who signed as André Simone, and the daily *Ce Soir* of Paris (founded with Republican capital) which was under Communist control. Following the Civil War *Ce Soir* went over to the hands of the French Communist party which used its prestige and its title again after the liberation of Paris in 1944.

6. Financial aid. Soviet banks in France such as the Banque de l'Europe du Nord acted as depositories for Republican funds. Nobody knows where those funds ended up when that bank, at the beginning of

World War II, had to close its doors. In any event, in 1946, when the Republican government in exile was established, the bank did not give it a single penny.

7. Labor aid was nil. There were neither strikes, sabotage of the shipments of arms to Franco, nor strikes in the ports from which Franco's shipments left. At that time the Communists were in control of U.S. oil unions, yet they did not organize a single strike to prevent the shipment of oil to Franco. The Communist International proposed collaborating with the Socialist International, but it was refused because the proposal was seen as the utilization of circumstances in Spain for maneuvers of the Comintern against the Socialists. It must be said that the Socialists were no more enthusiastic than the Communists about converting sympathy for the Republic into practical solidarity. In the USSR and throughout the world, subscriptions were organized by Communists, Socialists, and Anarchists, but the result of these efforts were "cans of condensed milk": necessary, but not enough to win the war.[32]

As can be seen, Soviet aid was not negligible, but neither was it unselfish or unconditional, contrary to what Communist propaganda said.

Defense of Madrid

The first problem facing the second Largo Caballero government was the military situation in Madrid. On November 6 rebel General Enrique Varela's army arrived at Carabanchel Alto. The Council of Ministers judged it would be dangerous to leave in the capital files and ministries susceptible of being taken over or being cut off from the rest of the country. Consequently, it decided to move the seat of government to Valencia. The ministers of the CNT and PCE voted for the transfer. But during the first days of the uprising, the CNT had formed a Regional Committee of the Defense of Madrid which controlled the highways to the city and furthermore protected its members from what it considered to be threats by the Communists. Thanks to the contribution of the JS by means of the JSU, the Communists were in political control of the capital. At that time there were at Madrid's front about twenty Soviet tanks, the only ones to have arrived as of that date, as well as the CNT's Durruti column, several Catalonian columns, and Socialist and Communist columns. After Toledo fell into the hands of the Francoists, defending Madrid became very difficult.

The control points of the Regional Committee of the Defense of Madrid prevented the mass exodus of functionaries, political and union leaders, the middle class, and professionals and intellectuals who tried to leave with the government. They let government personnel pass—although not without a few scares—but made everyone else return to the city. Before the government left, it established a Junta de Defensa under the chairmanship of General José Miaja (who had belonged to the Unión Militar Española, as was discovered later when the files of this monarchist organization were found). As Largo Caballero told Miaja the post he was going to be given, Miaja stammered that he should take into account that his family and properties were in the rebel zone.[33] But he surprised everyone by his energy, and with the help of colonels Vicente Rojo and Manuel Matallana he organized the Junta de Defensa with representatives of all union parties and organizations. Santiago Carrillo was the delegate of Public Order of the Junta.

The Junta was dealing with a city which was prepared to offer resistance, a city strengthened, not weakened, by the government's departure. It was not just enthusiasm which inspired the fighting. There was also rebel General Emilio Mola's statement about the "Fifth Column" about to revolt in Madrid and which probably moved the Junta to order the execution of the political prisoners in Paracuellos (an act which was attributed to Carrillo, although this has not been proven). Finally, there was the rebels' announcement that behind their troops there were sixteen military tribunals, which was the equivalent of promising mass retaliations. Since the CNT's Regional Committee of Defense forced those who tried to leave the city to stay, and since there were many who wished to stay, they were better off defending themselves than waiting for the execution Franco promised. The discovery on the corpse of a rebel officer of the plan of operation against Madrid helped improvise the defense. Fighting went on for ten days on the outskirts of the city.

"Madrid suddenly became the center of the world. The best journalists from every country followed the fighting in the Casa de Campo and University City and, with the aid of binoculars, from their rooms in hotels near the Plaza de España. On the streets they could see for themselves the good humor, charm, and dignity of the city's defenders."[34]

The first of the International Brigades' batallions went into combat in Madrid. "Long live the Russians!" was the cry of the people. In a radio speech La Pasionaria's line, "Madrid will be the grave of Fascism" became a slogan.[35] The Communists had a lot to do with dynamizing the people of Madrid: they knew how to get to them, excite them, and organize great numbers of them. The Anarchists, who shunned the mass exodus of November 8, were as responsible as the Communists for the spirit of resistance in the people of Madrid. The Communists have always taken credit for Madrid's defense. They were certainly fundamental to it, but they were not alone. The Fifth Regiment and the International Brigades helped put a stop to the rebel offensive and later helped defend the city—an incredible feat for military experts who maintained that in modern-day war cities could not be defended. But they were not the only forces to do it; Durruti, of FAI, died in Madrid accidentally, and many others who were not Communists gave their lives in the defense of Madrid.

The PCE immediately capitalized on the situation. Russian tanks and the International Brigades impressed the people of Madrid and members of the Junta to such a degree that they no longer dared oppose any initiative of the PCE or JSU for fear that that would put an end to the shipment of Soviet arms. For example, in the middle of the air battle of Madrid when the city was undergoing daily bombardments and shellfire, the Communists put up posters saying, "If you see a Falangist, denounce him. If you see a member of POUM, shoot him." The Junta ordered the closing and seizure of POUM's radio station in Madrid and its newspaper, *El Combatiente Rojo;* the secretary of the local committee party, Enrique Rodríguez, protested to a Socialist member of the Junta who replied, "I know it is unjust, but between Russian aid and POUM we have no choice." By that time the "witch trials" had already begun in Moscow, POUM had denounced them in their press, and the PCE had begun a campaign against POUM, or rather it had intensified to the point of obsession a campaign which it had never stopped since Maurín left the PCE in 1930. The retaliation against POUM in Madrid showed what the Communists would do if they were in power.[36]

Pressure from the PCE

Largo Caballero was under constant pressure from the PCE and Soviet diplomats. After seven months, this pressuring met its objectives. The Communists found an ally inside the government. He was Juan Negrín. This tacit alliance—no one has been able to prove that there was complicity in that period—was due, more than anything else, to a coincidence of points of view. Negrín must have been seeking it, or at least accepted it at the time, when he decided the best place to deposit the Spanish gold was Moscow. He viewed the collectivizations unfavorably, as did the Communists. From his post as minister of finances (treasury) he did everything he could to sabotage them. Some of his measures were in support of Communist positions. For example he was opposed to organizations' removal of expropriated gold, jewels, etcetera to foreign countries for the purpose of buying arms on the international black market. These arms would not have been enough to win the war, but would have alleviated the situation on the Aragon front which did not receive Soviet arms. The USSR preferred to lose shipments of arms (of course, it was the Republic which was losing them since as soon as arms left a Russian port they were considered sold) to unloading them in Barcelona where they probably would have been used on the Aragon front. This front had a collectivized rearguard and was garrisoned mainly by members of the CNT and POUM (with a column of PSUC and another of the Esquerra).

Negrín obstructed as much as he could—which was a lot—the shipment of raw materials from abroad for use by the collectivized industries and, likewise, made it almost impossible for such industries to export their products. In other words, he would have rather seen shortages than the success of the collectivizations. To implement those measures, Negrín had new members recruited—up to 40,000 of them—for the corps of *carabineros* (armed customs police) who were dependent on the Ministry of Finances. Many of the new members were Communists. Negrín systematically refused to give credit to collectivized firms; he rejected every plan the ministers of the CNT devised to help them, and gradually suffocated them financially.[37]

In the councils of ministers, Hernández and Uribe tried to avoid creating conflicts. That is why little attention was given to Uribe's agrarian policy which tended to suffocate collectivizations and channel the peasants toward the PCE. There was hardly any discussion of Hernández's policy which essentially consisted of creating schools and then staffing them with teachers, licensed or makeshift, who were screened by the PCE. In the streets the party was carrying out a very active campaign in three basic directions.

One was the constant demand for the militias to become regular army (adding the name "popular" to sweeten the pill). The party foresaw that, if units composed mainly of people of a single organization had arms, the measures it hoped to adopt would cause resistance or might not be implemented for fear of provoking physical opposition. On the other hand, with a regular army it would be possible to dissolve the militias. The PCE at the time had little military force. Its Fifth Regiment performed well and was sizable (Moscow claimed it had 70,000 soldiers in January 1937), and the PSUC column in Aragon was also important and better equipped than the other columns of the same front. But the "heroes" of the popular army had not yet appeared; they would show up considerably later: Líster, Campesino, Modesto, Galán, Durán, Tagüeña. For the moment the forces under PCE control could not be compared to those of the CNT. If the PCE would gain control of the command positions of a popular army, it would control not only the people in the militias but the new recruits too and thus would have means of applying pressure which could not be ignored, especially in view of the fact that it would be bolstered by Russian weapons. The public reasoning of the PCE was that the army would be more effective than the militias, but the facts show that while there were militias, the Republic only had to withdraw in Extremadura and Málaga; however, it was able to contain the rebels in Madrid and advance in Aragon (and would have been able to reach Zaragoza and link up with the North if it had had Russian arms). Militarily, the volunteer militias made up for technical deficiencies and lack of arms by their enthusiasm, initiative, and spirit of sacrifice. A regular army, in order to equip itself, would have needed as many arms as the rebels or more, which was never the case.

At a rally at the Teatro Monumental in Madrid on October 22 Díaz had already asked for the transformation of militias into a regular army and creation of a war industry (which otherwise was already in existence in Catalonia but created by collectivized firms). Shortly thereafter, Comorera, in support of these demands, called the militias "tribes," which caused an angry rebuff. Prieto also wanted an army. Largo Caballero vacillated but finally approved of the army, and as of January 29, 1937 he began organizing it.[38] From the Communist point of view, the regular army had to follow these fundamental lines: "No revolution for the duration of the war; rigid discipline including the use of terrorist methods among army ranks; stiff political control of the army by means of a system of political commissars."[39]

The second front of the PCE's campaign was that of revolutionary economic measures. There was systematic criticism of collectivizations which never rose to the level of theoretical discussion but existed merely as rumors: that the control committees lived like kings, they stole, forced the peasants to join the collectivities, they concealed fascists, were responsible for the shortages which began to be felt early in 1937 (to a large extent because of Negrín's policy in the Ministry of Finances).[40] Those rumors were joined by others fed to the small shopkeepers and artisans leading them to believe that their businesses would also be collectivized despite the fact that the decree of collectivization of the Generalidad of October 1936 set as a limit for the collectivization of a business 100 employees as opposed to the 50 employees that the CNT and POUM wanted. In Spain's economy at the time, a business with 50 employees could not be considered small or even medium-sized. This decree had been prepared by the Economic Council, in which PSUC had little influence. It foresaw the formation of councils of industry and means of finance and credit for collectivized businesses. Neither of those essential points materialized until much later, when the Communists had already managed to corrupt the collectivizations and transform some of them—those having to do with the war—into nationalizations not unlike their Soviet counterparts (by which the sacrosanct Russian model was saved).

The third front, the one we could call Russian, was the campaign against POUM which the Communists called "Trotskyite," in spite of the fact that Trotsky criticized POUM more bitterly than he did the Stalinists and that POUM's positions had nothing to do with those held by the old Bolshevik. As soon as the Communists, by means of the Junta de Defensa and Soviet arms, managed to gain control of local power in Madrid, they began persecuting POUM. Despite the scant forces POUM had in the city, they organized a demostration which attacked POUM's headquarters.[41] Outside of Madrid, in Valencia and Catalonia where POUM was powerful, the assaults were, for the moment at least, merely verbal, yet very harsh. The Soviet consul in Barcelona, Antonov-Ovseenko, told a commission of the CNT that Stalin viewed with disfavor the presence of Nin and POUM in the government of the Generalidad.

In a rally in November Díaz said that "fascism, Trotskyism, and the "uncontrollables" are the three enemies of the people," at the same time that Hernández requested that churches be reopened and that Constancia de la Mora, head of censorship in Madrid, not only forbade the publication in the capital of criticism of the USSR and of the trials in Moscow, but furthermore opened Largo Caballero's mail. Koltzov, a correspondent for *Pravda,* wrote: "POUM is playing the part of a provocateur and demoralizer." This campaign was also backed up by the one against the CNT and the Anarchists.

Antonov-Ovseenko asked Companys to throw Nin out of the government. Companys staged a crisis and formed another government excluding Nin. Comorera let the truth be known while speaking with journalists who asked him why PSUC wanted to see POUM eradicated: "The reason is its unspeakable anti-Soviet campaign. ... To fight the USSR at this moment is to commit treason. And we are against traitors." (This "to fight the USSR" refers to the denunciation of the trials in Moscow by POUM's press.) On December 13, 1936 Nin was removed from his post as minister. On December 16 *Pravda* wrote that "in Catalonia the purge of Trotskyites and Anarcho-Syndicalists has begun; it will be undertaken with the same energy as in the USSR." *Soli* and *La Batalla* printed that pearl. The Soviet consulate replied that "it is not true that the entire Soviet press nurtures the hope that the purges begun in Catalonia against Spanish Trotskyites and Anarcho-Syndicalists will be carried out with the same energy as in the Soviet Union." True, the entire Soviet press did not say this; but *Pravda* did, and the consulate's statement did not mention *Pravda*.[42] Shortly thereafter, on January 9, Antonov-Osveenko, who had been a friend of Nin when they were both Trotskyites in Moscow, told a correspondent of the *Manchester Guardian* that "he categorically denies that Russia intervened in internal politics in Catalonia." On November 24 *La Batalla* had printed that "the situation is intolerable: by giving us a certain amount of aid, Russia tries to impose on us specific political models, to use the veto and, indeed, run Spanish politics." Twelve days later, the Soviet consulate in Barcelona, in a statement to the press, denied that the Russians ever intended such an interference and accused *La Batalla* of "supplying material for fascist insinuations."[43]

Pressure from the Soviets

What made the PCE's campaigns important was that they were supported by pressure from the Soviets based on the sale of Russian arms, a pressure which such campaigns echoed. In addition to the Russian ambassador, Marcel Rosenberg, his commercial attaché and right-hand man, Arthur Stachevsky, and the consul in Barcelona, Antonov-Osveenko, there were also other Russian subjects in the Republican zone. Those diplomats arrived in Madrid the day of the execution in Moscow of their former comrades Zinoviev and Kamenev and long before the new instructors of the Comintern arrived (although Togliatti made several trips before being sent permanently, it would seem, in June 1937). Alexander Orlov[44] arrived in September to establish a branch of the NKVD, the Soviet political police and espionage service.

There were also military advisors and some "honorary Russians" in the International Brigades. Those military advisors looked down their noses at the Republican officers to the extent that their leader Berzin (Goriev was his pseudonym) had to say that "our men treat the Spaniards as if they were from the colonies."[45] The attitude taken by the diplomats, alternately paternalistic and authoritarian, would have more important consequences. Stachevsky seemed to be flexible and it appeared that he had made the discovery of Negrín's political potential while Stachevsky was negotiating with him the shipment of gold to Moscow.[46] But Rosenberg was less subtle, and Antonov-Osveenko, perhaps to make up for his past as a Trotskyite, was frankly aggressive. It is possible that Antonov's aggressiveness was due to the fact that he saw in Companys and other politicians of the Esquerra much more adaptability than Rosenberg saw in Largo Caballero. Caballero finally grew tired of the ambassador's constant visits. A Socialist wrote:

> Those of us who were frequent visitors to the Ministry of War in the beginning were very much aware of, and finally got used to, the daily visits of the Soviet ambassador. . . . Although Largo Caballero spoke French fairly accurately, he always had an interpreter with him. But what an interpreter! It was not a secretary of the embassy but rather the very minister of foreign affairs, Julio Álvarez del Vayo. [One morning after a two-hour visit Largo Caballero was heard shouting through the office door.] Suddenly the door to the presidential office opened and the aged premier of Spain, standing before his desk with an outstretched arm and a quivering finger, was saying, pointing to the door, in an agitated state: "Get out! Get out! You must know, Mr. Ambassador, that we Spaniards are very poor, we are in great need of foreign aid, but we have more than enough pride not to permit a foreign ambassador to attempt to prevail over the head of the Spanish government. And as for you, Vayo, you had better not forget that you are a Spaniard and minister of the Republic, and not allow yourself to coerce its prime minister with a foreign diplomat.[47]

It was by no means certain that by being inflexible with the Russians and by not respecting their desires Soviet aid would have been withdrawn; at any rate, it was not certain that the loss of it would not be compensated by aid from other powers or the collusion of some government to provide arms. Looking at things in retrospect (which, of course, was not possible at the time), a Communist who separated from the party has written:

> To refuse aid to the Spanish proletariat, with the immense echo of sympathy which its struggle found even in the social-democratic labor movement, would have been the equivalent of striking a terrible blow to the prestige of the USSR among workers of every nation. And although Stalin's international strategy was based on the use of interimperialist contradictions—not on the development of the world revolutionary movement—it could not disregard the support of the labor movement. . . . But once the problem was seen in light of later events, the German-Soviet pact or the condemnation and abandonment of the Yugoslavian revolution of 1948 in particular, it is not absurd to suppose that Stalin would have reacted by denouncing our hypothetical unorthodox Spanish Communists, their alliances with Anarcho-Syndicalists, the followers of Caballero and POUM, as a sinister plot—set up by the Gestapo under Trotsky's leadership—against the USSR and Western democracy, for the purpose of preventing them from coming to the aid of the legal, constitutional, parliamentarian Spanish Republic.[48]

When it was apparent that Largo Caballero was hardly going to be accomodating, Stalin sent him the already mentioned letter of December 24, signed by himself, Molotov, and Vorochilov,[49] asking him what he thought of Rosenberg and the Soviet military advisors. It was necessary to consult a member of the Soviet Embassy because neither Codovila nor Rosenberg himself was sure of who signed the letter.[50] So that Largo Caballero would see things clearly, the Communist International, almost at the same time that Stalin's letter was mailed, published a resolution of its Presidium, dated December 28, in which it praised—it is not certain if ironically—"the sincere efforts of the party to strengthen fraternal relations with the Anarcho-Syndicalists," and said: "Since the Trotskyites, in the interest of fascism, are carrying out their subversive work in the rearguard, the Presidium approves the policy of the Spanish party which is aimed at the complete and definitive destruction of Trotskyism in Spain, essential to the victory over fascism."[51]

Against Largo Caballero

Toward the end of 1936 the Communist press began to talk of the need to unite the two parties, the PCE and PSOE. The negativeness of Largo Caballero was most likely due to his party patriotism more than to ideological considerations, even though he later wrote that he could not begin to think of uniting with those who six months earlier had asked him to break off relations with the Republicans, and for whom "the current slogan is to go back to pre–July 18,"[52] while keeping good relations with the bourgeois parties. In January 1937 there was a meeting of several members of the Socialist left wing. Rodolfo Llopis, undersecretary to the president, recalled that

> the conversation fell back to the loyalty of the Communists, the Communist campaigns on the fronts and at the rearguard, their desire to remove the Socialists from all kinds of organizations, taking advantage of the fact that our colleagues were committed to war work. We also spoke of their blatant proselytism, unscrupulously appealing to the most reprehensible techniques, and their constant disloyalty to us. There was also talk of the conduct of the young Socialists who had gone over to the Communist party. We spoke of the Communist "conquest" of two deputies elected as Socialists, Nelken and Montiel. . . . And in the meantime, our party did not show signs of life. The executive committee [presided over by Prieto] remained silent. Some members spoke. Caballero spoke, sparsely, precisely, and to the point: "Who is talking about absorption? I am not going to be absorbed by anybody. The party has a tradition and a potential which cannot be thrown overboard. The party cannot die. As long as I'm alive, there will be one Socialist."[53]

The fall of Málaga on February 8, 1937 increased the tension between the head of government and the PCE. In Málaga there had been riots, a sense of powerlessness, and mass exodus. The Communists took advantage of this setback to put the blame on Largo Caballero, for they had already arrived at the conclusion that he would not be malleable. He had to be replaced. But in order to do this he first had to be discredited. It would not be easy, since the Communists had lavished him with praise calling him the "Spanish Lenin." However, it was soon apparent that another campaign could destroy what had been accomplished by the first. Furthermore, the fall of Málaga could cause serious damage to the PCE because a Communist representative, Cayetano Bolívar, had been chief commissar of Málaga's sector. He never informed the minister of the chaos created while defending the city nor of the neglect of defense efforts, nor of the treason of two officers in charge of the fortifications (perhaps he kept silent about the latter because one of them had joined the party).[54] No action had been taken in response to the pleas for help of Coronel José Villalba, sent to Málaga when there was no longer any means of defending the city. If that had been common knowledge, the image of the PCE as effective and disciplined would have collapsed. It was necessary to immediately find a scapegoat who, in addition, would detract from Largo Caballero. Apparently, that scapegoat was Coronel Villalba, who indeed was put on trial (and absolved and reinstated eighteen months later). But that was not enough. A campaign began against General José Asensio, undersecretary of war. The ill will toward Asensio is explained not only by the trust the head of government had in him but also because he had ordered the transfer of some Communists who had important positions in the Ministry of War. Asensio's dismissal was precisely what Rosenberg had requested of Largo Caballero the day Largo kicked him out of his office. Finally, Asensio's dismissal was demanded by the Communist ministers in the Council of Ministers. Álvarez del Vayo supported them despite the fact that years later he wrote that he was "unquestionably one of the most intelligent and capable officers in the Republican army."[55] In addition to the two-facedness of the deceitful Socialist there was the indifference of the CNT which did not sympathize with Asensio because he was for the regular army. Finally, following an enthusiastic speech in his defense, Largo Caballero dismissed him on February 21, 1937. But he assigned him to Valencia so that he could continue to seek his advice.

Largo Caballero lost patience and began to clean out the Communists in his ministry. He assigned Antonio Cordón to the Córdoba front, which meant that there was no longer a Communist at the head of the technical secretariat of the undersecretary's office. He sent his own field aid, Manuel Arredondo, and the head of intelligence, Eleuterio Díaz Tendero, to the Northern front. These orders were issued the same day that Asensio's dismissal was made public. In addition he named some left-wing Socialists as inspectors of the army and of the war commissariat, specifying that among those to be inspected were Commissar General Álvarez del Vayo, Secretary of the Commissariat Felipe Pretel (both were socialists who worked for the PCE), and Undercommissar Antonio Mije, of the PCE. The Communist press did not even mention the dismissals. Díaz Tendero, whose Communist affiliation was not generally known outside of the ministry, used his relations with the Column of Iron, of the FAI in Valencia, to have *Nosotros,* its organ, print an attack against Largo Caballero which called him "the doddering old man." The Communists would subsequently use this epithet countless times against Largo Caballero: "The minister of war should keep in mind . . . that he is old, even more than just old, since he is falling into senility, and that the government cannot and should not be run by senile men."[56]

On February 14 there was in Valencia a demonstration of support for Largo Caballero who issued a manifesto in which he said: "Between this people and the government which I head there has been embedded, corrupting many consciences and encouraging turbulent passions, a plot which, in my estimation, acts against our cause both consciously and unconsciously. I believe there is a lot of both. But the practical result is . . . that the snakes of treason, disloyalty, and espionage are coiling about the feet of those who ought and are ready to lead the working and democratic people. I am not about to allow such a state of affairs to go on one hour longer."[57]

The campaign against Largo Caballero intensified in March, precisely during the Italian assault on the Guadalajara plains. The PCE asked for the dismissal of many officers close to Largo Caballero in spite of the fact that the PCE had sent representatives to a meeting of delegates of parties and unions to confirm their support of Largo Caballero. On the fifth day of the Battle of Guadalajara the Communist ministers demanded and were granted the dismissal of General Martínez Cabrera, head of the General Staff, and they managed to have named as his replacement Miaja's chief of staff, Colonel Vicente Rojo who, although this was not yet known, was a PCE sympathizer (not so much for ideological as for professional reasons and, as in the case of Miaja, possibly to be pardoned for having been a member of the Unión Militar Española).[58]

The new undersecretary of war, Carlos de Baráibar, editor of *Claridad,* who had just gotten over a serious illness during which he had not learned the details of what had gone on, was warmly received by the Russians and showered with praise. "He was being lovingly groomed to play the part of traitor with Largo Caballero." But he realized that in the Quartermaster Corps, the Medical Corps, and in War Transports there were Communists who manipulated the heads of those services, proselytized, and channeled the best materials to Communist-run units. Aware of the maneuver, Baráibar helped Largo Caballero to "clean out" the ministry with such vigor that the political bureau of the PCE printed a statement in *Frente Rojo* on March 29, 1937 which said that "the unity of all antifascists to win the war is obstructed by a series of events, especially during these last few days, such as the transfer or dismissal of top military leaders and commissars who have repeatedly given evidence of competence and ability—members of the Communist party, removed simply because they are Communists."

Baráibar realized that the war commissariat had become an instrument of the PCE. The decree which created it in October 1936 established that commissars would be named by the general commissar (Álvarez del Vayo) and approved by the minister of war. But Álvarez del Vayo delegated most of his duties to the subcommissar of organization, Mije, of the PCE, who appointed an endless number of Communists as "temporary commissars" with the result that they kept their jobs for weeks and even months without having been approved by the minister. Álvarez del Vayo himself later related: "The Communists . . . took more interest in its [the commissariat's] development and expansion than did other parties. The latter were content with just presenting lists of candidates. The Communists, on the other hand, sent their most active members from the very day of its creation. This difference became greater during the critical period of the defense of Madrid."[59]

On April 17 Largo Caballero issued an order which reduced the powers of the commissars and declared that those employed only provisionally who had not been confirmed by the minister of war would lose their jobs as of May 15. The campaign was stepped up in favor of "that group of heroes" because Largo wanted to "kill the initiative of the commissars." La Pasionaria advised: "Commissars, be firm in your posts." Only the CNT was pleased with the order which "brought to a grinding halt the activities by which the Communist party intended to gain political control of the entire army by means of a number of commissars who in no way were a match for the forces which said party has managed to carry to the front."[60]

The PCE was also alarmed by a decree which fixed the rank of major as the highest position anyone coming from the militias could aspire to (later Negrín annulled that decree), which obviously limited the possibility for Communist leaders to attain certain positions of leadership. The High War Council, in which the Communists and their friends were influential, retaliated and sent Hernández on a mission to Madrid and Uribe to the North where an offensive had been begun by the Francoists.

Both asked the Russian general Goriev to accompany them. No one ever found out what those missions were about. But Largo Caballero had to stifle his anger for he had something more important in the works: the offensive in Extremadura.

The General Staff had planned an offensive against Badajoz and Mérida (perhaps that is why the Communists had requested the dismissal of General Martínez Cabrera) which, if successful, would have divided the Francoist zone in two and possibly would have reached Seville. Parallel to those plans, Largo Caballero put friends of his (he no longer trusted Álvarez del Vayo) in charge of initiating negotiations with European powers to help put an end to the war (the USSR was not included nor was Rosenberg consulted). Victory in the operation of Extremadura could determine whether these negotiations would meet with success or whether the conflict would be ended and the Republic maintained.

But these were not such well-kept secrets that Moscow was left in the dark. Moscow did not want the war in Spain to end, and certainly not at the hands of a Socialist who in recent months had shown himself to be impervious to Soviet pressure. Hernández and Uribe were called by the Russian general Kulik who informed them that Moscow considered "the operation of Extremadura to be inappropriate . . . and should not be undertaken. You will find a way to manage." Instead of an offensive on Extremadura, Kulik proposed one on Brunete, which the Spanish military thought was absurd (it was later carried out when Largo Caballero was no longer in the government and resulted in disaster). Largo Caballero persisted but did not know how it would be possible to carry out the operation because the Russians informed him that they would not lend him the support of "their" planes, that is, purchased with Spanish gold. On the advice of his Russian technicians, Miaja refused to send troops from Madrid for this offensive.[61]

May 1937

Toward the end of February 1937 Stalin recalled Rosenberg and had him replaced by Leon Gaikins. He also recalled the generals and military technicians. They were all put to death. At the time the only man from Moscow was Codovila. But the PCE team of leaders by this time had grown so accustomed to guessing the wishes of the Communist International that it continued working without need for immediate instructions.

On December 15 *Treball*, the organ of PSUC, wrote: "Our stance regarding POUM is not a party stance. We are fighting against the provocateurs with the same tenacity and for the same reasons as we fight against fascists." Comorera, upon assuming his post as Catalonian minister of supplies, stated that food supplies were depleted and that his predecessor, Domenech, of the CNT, was incompetent. He suspended the rationing of bread which rose in price, and after a few weeks had to ration it once again and in smaller quantities. Of course, this made lines longer. But that price was too low to be able to accuse the CNT of high prices and food shortages. The newspaper of the Karl Marx Division of PSUC ran a cartoon of Nin arm in arm with Franco. POUM proposed the appointment of a commission to investigate PSUC's accusations, but PSUC did not respond. *Frente Rojo,* on the other hand, wrote in its February 6 issue: "[POUM] is a gang of bandits which fascism has left behind." *Mundo Obrero* asked for the trial of the "POUM riffraff." Carrillo, in a lecture of December 16, had said that "[the members of POUM] are nothing more than agents of international fascism." The campaign intensified when at the end of March POUM's press warned that a provocation against the revolutionary forces was being prepared and gave the alert not to respond to it.

La Pasionaria wrote in *Frente Rojo:* "There cannot be agreement or communication with them . . . for we must always remember that between us and the Trotskyites there is a chasm filled with blood."[62] In March Díaz said: "Our hatred is also directed, with the same degree of intensity, against that agent of fascism, POUM . . . which hides behind the slogans of self-styled revolutionaries for the purpose of carrying out its principal mission as agent of our enemy."

Pravda said that there were "enemies of the Spanish people who have infiltrated the ranks of anarchism." JSU's *Ahora* asked that "we liquidate once and for all this faction of the fifth column. The Soviet people . . . with their inexorable sense of justice will show us the way." Uribe said: "To win the war we must remove the cancer of Trotskyism." Carrillo said: "The policy of the Trotskyites, when it says that we are fighting for social revolution, is the policy of invaders, the policy of fascists." The CNT's *Solidarid Obrera* printed accounts of torture of members of the CNT in Murcia and Madrid by Communist police groups. In La Fatarella (in the Catalonian province of Tarragona) there was fighting between landowners who were members of the Catalonian UGT (Communist) and collectivized peasants. That was followed by disputes in workshops and small businesses where workers belonged to the CNT and employers to the UGT (in Catalonia the UGT and PSUC organized the GEPCI, the union of small businessmen). In March twelve tanks were stolen from an industrial war deposit (they later showed up in "Vorochilov's barracks," of PSUC). In an effort to counteract the

CNT and retain the middle class, which was deserting the Esquerra and going over to PSUC, Companys helped PSUC sabotage the implementation of the collectivization decree. "Friends of Durruti," a newly founded anarchist organization, denounced the Communist offensive against the CNT. The Council of the Generalidad proposed the suppression of the control patrols (which the right wing blamed for multiple crimes, but which in August 1936 during its formation, put an end to the activities of the "uncontrolled"). The council also proposed prohibiting police to belong to any organization. This, under the pretext of depoliticizing the police force, would subject it to PSUC, one of whose members was commissioner of police. The CNT opposed the move, there was a crisis in the Catalonian government, and another was formed without adopting any decision on the previous proposals. There was shooting between the CNT and PSUC in Vilanova, and the secretary of Juventudes Libertarias was murdered in Centelles. The Communist Cazorla suspended the CNT's newspaper in Madrid. On April 25 Roldán Cortada, a former syndicalist, Vidiella's secretary, and leader of PSUC, who apparently opposed the policy of pogroms, was murdered. PSUC turned his funeral into a demonstration against the CNT and POUM. On April 27 the police attacked Puigcerdá, a town controlled by the CNT, killing the local leaders. May Day was not celebrated to prevent clashes. The secretary of Juventudes Libertarias, Alfredo Martínez, called together the Catalonian youth organizations, warned them that danger was on the horizon, and suggested that they not take part in any of it. This proposal was rejected by Catalonian nationalists and the Communists.

Meanwhile in Valencia there were conflicts between the CNT-UGT—the agrarian committee—and Uribe, who wanted to let the orange growers export their produce by themselves. In Cullera, the orange growers, encouraged by Uribe's position, proclaimed the independence of the city and set bonfires to attract the attention of Francoist ships. In its May Day manifesto, the Communist International took advantage of Spain's situation to attack the Socialist International.[63] On May 3 the tension reached the breaking point. Eusebio Rodríguez Salas, the "One-Armed," ex-member of the CNT and the Bloc and then a member of PSUC and police commissioner of Barcelona, showed up at the telephone company with a group of police in order to occupy the building which was in the hands of the CNT. The CNT resisted, the police took the ground floor, and the CNT kept the rest of the building. As soon as news of what had happened in the telephone company spread, barricades were put up in many neighborhoods in front of party and union headquarters. If this had not happened because of the incident at the telephone company, there would have been some other reason to do it. Members of the CNT were realizing that they were being corralled and their leaders were not taking action. The rank and file, suffering under the weight of the Communist offensive in the committees, towns, and unions lost patience. They did not realize it was a provocation and took to the streets.

Throughout Barcelona there was fighting for six days. One faction was the rank and file of the CNT who were joined for reasons of solidarity by POUM despite the fact that they were aware that it was a provocation for which they, more than anyone, would pay the consequences. The other faction was the police and some armed Catalonian nationalist groups; PSUC stayed put garrisoning its headquarters and putting pressure on Companys. The ministers of the CNT travelled to Barcelona, and the regional committee of the CNT helped them to appease their own rank and file by means of radio broadcasts. Finally, because there was no way out of the situation, since the CNT was leaderless and did not dare try to seize power, the fighting stopped. There were 400 dead and 1,000 wounded. After the fighting, the special police sent from Madrid—5,000 attack guards under Communist command—and the PSUC groups initiated a period of arrests and murders. Alfredo Martínez, regional secretary of Juventudes Libertarias, was found dead. In Sardañola the mutilated bodies of twelve Libertarian youths were found. Several members of the CNT and POUM were murdered in the cellars of Pedrera, Gaudí's building which was used as offices of the Supplies Ministry under PSUC. The Italian Anarchists Camilo Bernieri and Francesco Barbieri were murdered a few steps from the palace of the Generalidad. Two or three Trotskyites who were not with POUM, the Socialist Marc Rhein, and others disappeared. Antonio Sesé, secretary general of the Catalonian UGT, member of the old PCC and PSUC, died when they opened fire on the car he was traveling in to assume his new post as minister of the Generalidad.

It was probably too late to change the course of events. But the labor protest failed, in addition, because it lacked clear objectives. It seemed futile to take to the streets demanding the replacement of a chief of police and a minister. The gesture was revolutionary; its execution turned out to be tragically banal.[64] There were some things that people were not aware of back then. For example, the government of the Generalidad requested planes of Valencia's government to bombard the CNT centers but they were denied. To have the 5,000 attack guards sent, Companys had to give Valencia's government the control of public order in Catalonia. During all these negotiations, Companys constantly relied on Comorera who did not leave the palace of the Generalidad all week long. Comorera persuaded Companys to accept Valencia's demand on public order.[65]

The first result of the events of May was that the Generalidad lost autonomy, which had been growing since the revolution. That is how, without foreseeing it, Catalonian nationalists, out of fear of revolutionary measures, had sacrificed the autonomy of their people. It would be much further reduced in months to come. The second consequence was that the PCE and PSUC blamed the events not on the CNT but on POUM. The CNT had been debilitated but it was still too strong to be attacked head on. POUM had come within range and the Communists never stopped firing at it. The following are some quotes to the point: "FAI, the protagonist in the events of May, was a dark force without conscience, manipulated by POUM," wrote the Communist journalist Manuel Benavides. The British reporter John Langdon-Davies wrote: "We are not dealing with an Anarchist uprising. It is a frustrated *Putsch* of the POUM." "POUM, acting in collaboration with well-known criminal elements and with certain misled individuals of Anarchist organizations, planned and led the attack on the rearguard in such a way that it coincided with the attack on the Bilbao front," said the *Daily Worker* (a London Communist daily) on May 11. The same paper printed: "The Monarchist flag flew next to the flags of the CNT and POUM." (Incidentally, Del Vayo tried to persuade Araquistáin to have the embassy in Paris issue this release, and failing to do so he issued it on his own even though he knew it was false.)[66]

The Communist press stated that forces of the CNT and POUM had withdrawn from the front leaving it stripped. This was not true. However, units of the International Brigades were sent to Tortosa to hold back the CNT from the region. But propaganda was so intense that even Azaña (who had begun to write his *Velada de Benicarló* during those days) wrote in his diary: "Most active in the rebellion were POUM, Estat Català [sic], the Ateneos Libertarios, and members of the CNT, although by no means all . . . but some columns of the CNT abandoned the front and went to Barcelona to help the rebels."[67] Following the custom of having stones thrown by organizations which did not officially appear as Communist, the Executive Committee of the Catalonian UGT gave an account of its decisions to the press:

> 1. To characterize the movement begun on May 4 as counter-revolutionary, aimed at furthering the disorganization and lack of discipline in the rearguard and at breaking the Aragon front. It is urgent to devise a speedy and energetic policy of public order throughout Catalonia, reestablishing the normalcy which currently exists only in appearance, putting an end to the intervention of "uncontrolled" members and Trotskyite instiga-

tors who still endure and who maintain their arms and militants intact.

2. To be ready to observe the decree of the Ministry of the Interior on the disarmament of the rearguard while ensuring the necessary disarmament guarantees for all organizations, especially all the known "uncontrolled" groups and members of POUM. . . .

3. To affirm that equal treatment cannot be given to the men or organizations which rebelledagainst the government and those individuals who were at its side defending the cause of antifascism. Therefore while ratifying their agreement to expel from the UGT members of POUM, this also requires the dissolution and declaration of illegality of said party in addition to the suspension of the daily *La Batalla* and its entire press and the confiscation of its printed propaganda, radios, etc. The same measures will be taken against organizations like "Amigos de Durruti," disallowed by the Regional Committee of the CNT.

4. To elaborate a new program of unity of common action between the UGT and the CNT. . . .

5. To urgently negotiate the organization of the War Industry Commission with the participation of all antifascist organizations which make up the government of the Generalidad which, under the direct control of the Republican government, will grade production, distribute raw materials, and guard against enemy sabotage and espionage by placing the war industries under custody of the army.

6. Mobilization of public services.

7. Militarization of transportation and communication services.

8. Immediate renovation of municipal councils.[68]

As can be seen, PSUC considered itself the victor and wanted to collect the bill. To impress people it took girls from its youth groups and photographed them dismantling barricades.

From "Spanish Lenin" to "Doddering Old Man"

"Soldiers on all fronts were demanding the punishment of those responsible for the counterrevolutionary uprising in Catalonia. The Minister of War refused to take action against them so as not to alienate the support of POUM and FAI, which he saw as suitable instruments for the struggle against the Communist party. There was general indignation. It was getting increasingly difficult for the Communists to continue participating in the government."[69] These lines by Ibárruri do not contain a speck of truth. Neither were the soldiers demanding anything—aside from more arms which Russia did not send—nor was the "uprising" in Catalonia either an uprising or counterrevolutionary, nor did Largo

Caballero see in POUM and FAI support for his fight against the Communist party since, in his opinion, he and the PSOE-UGT were enough to handle that. But it was true that it was increasingly difficult for the PCE to continue in the government. It was possible to foresee that Largo Caballero would ask the Communist ministers to leave any day. Therefore the PCE, the "instructors," and Moscow decided that the one who ought to leave was Largo Caballero.

The PCE by itself could not overthrow Largo Caballero, that is, could not oppose the UGT and CNT and the man it had established as the "Spanish Lenin." It needed allies. It did not have to look for them. Prieto was hardly speaking to Largo Caballero. He was president of the PSOE and from this position he tried to limit as much as he could the power of this old rival. Álvarez del Vayo's double-dealing had been discovered and he was ignored by Largo Caballero. The Republicans cut no ice, yet they were never sympathetic to a politician who for the last four years had opposed a Republican-Socialist coalition. Largo Caballero had to be removed from the pedestal on which the Communists had placed him. The PCE's press began a campaign of almost sympathetic criticism: Largo was old and tired, his prestige did not allow him to see that he was not prepared to handle military problems, he was surrounded by poor advisors, he was a tyrant, a bureaucrat, a saboteur of unity. At rallies and in conversations, in the militants' rumor mill, the "Spanish Lenin" had become a doddering old man. Aside from the Communists and a few of Caballero's devotees, nobody fell for the epithet of Spanish Lenin. So no one stopped believing in Largo just because all of a sudden he was no longer the "Spanish Lenin."

It was necessary to maneuver. Prieto was clever at this and had been planning for the moment when he would be able to intervene. Once an enemy of uniting with the Communists, he was now friendly to the Russians, to General Duglas, chief of the Soviet air advisors, and he even told Codovila that he viewed favorably a future merger of Communists and Socialists,[70] despite that El Socialista, run by a friend of his, Julián Zugazagoitia, repeatedly complained about Communist proselytism in the army.[71] In March in a letter to the Executive Committee of the PSOE, the PCE said that the Socialist party's hostility toward the Communist party was due to "some isolated members who misinterpret the feelings of the masses," and proposed the formation of liaison committees between the two parties "to facilitate discussion and adoption of measures conducive to unity of action and to the acceleration of unifying the Socialist and Communist parties into the great unified party of the Spanish working class." José Díaz and Ramón Lamoneda, secretary of the Executive Committee of the PSOE—the same Lamoneda who had been part of the first PCE and who had returned to the Socialist fold—made up the liaison committee which gave instructions for the creation of local liaison committees. The idea was not well received by the Socialist rank and file, but for the time being the liaison would be used not to form the unified party, but to replace Largo Caballero.[72] Lamoneda was a champion of the campaign against his colleague and said: "The people want and demand a government with authority on the fronts and in the rearguard, and, above all, they want swift punishment for the rebellious elements."

But the decision to eliminate the "Spanish Lenin" was not Prieto's; it had been made earlier when the merger was rejected, when the Ministry of War was "cleaned up," and when the plans for Extremadura were given the go-ahead. The decision was strengthened by the Republican victory in the Battle of Guadalajara. If Largo were also victorious in Extremadura, it would be impossible to overthrow him. Time was of the essence. The decision was made in March when Stepanov and Togliatti went to Spain and met with the PCE Executive Committee in Valencia. The meeting was attended by Gerö, Codovila, Gaikins—the Russian ambassador—Orlov, and Marty. Togliatti announced that the Communist International wanted Largo Caballero's dismissal. Díaz and Hernández said that Caballero must be replaced because he was a poor leader, not because Moscow ordered it. The other members of the bureau said nothing. Stepanov replied that it was not Moscow but history which condemned Caballero, and he was supported by Marty. The Spanish leaders were exasperated by Marty's dictatorial tone. Díaz, in a fit of anger, called Marty a bureaucrat and Marty retorted that he (Marty) was a true revolutionary. "We are all revolutionaries," replied Díaz. "That remains to be seen," Marty snarled. Díaz then said to him that he was a guest at the meeting and that if he did not like it he could leave. La Pasionaria began to shout to bring things to order. Codovila tried to calm down Marty. Togliatti, Orlov, and Gerö remained seated, unperturbed. Finally, once things had settled down, a vote was taken. Díaz and Hernández were the only ones to vote "no"—not so much out of disagreement as to protest what had gone on at the meeting. Togliatti suggested that the campaign against Largo Caballero begin at a rally in Valencia on May 9 where Hernández would give the opening speech. Hernández gave the speech.[73]

On May 15 the Council of Ministers met. Largo explained the Catalonian conflict and said that it had not been antigovernment, but between two union confederations. Without commenting on the head of government's statement, the Communists attacked Ángel Galarza, minister of the interior, calling him weak (perhaps because he had discovered the records of the Spanish Military Union in Madrid among which were the files of several pro-Communist military leaders such as Miaja and Rojo). When Galarza tried to defend himself, Hernández and Uribe proposed the dissolution of POUM. Caballero replied that legally it could not be done, and that if POUM had broken any laws it would be judged accordingly. Largo Caballero was backed by Montseny. Both ministers of the PCE then stood up and left the meeting. Largo Caballero wanted to continue but Prieto said that the departure of the two Communists meant that they had resigned and therefore the government had to be dissolved. Aside from the CNT and Galarza, no minister supported Largo Caballero. Caballero visited Azaña and handed him his resignation.[74] The first stage of the plan of the "instructors" of the Communist International had been completed. Russian arms, the Prieto rivalry, and the Republicans' fear of revolution had paved the way to power for the PCE. The only thing missing was the man willing to open the door to it.

Notes

1. *La Antorcha,* Madrid, December 23, 1921, quoted by Estruch, p. 32.
2. Quoted by Claudín, p. 148.
3. Joaquín Maurín, *Hacia la segunda revolución,* Madrid, 1935, p. 69.
4. Maurín, *Revolución y contrarrevolución en España,* p. 287 ff.
5. Quote by Dolores Ibárruri in Estruch, p. 94.
6. Quoted by Alba, *El Frente Popular.* In her memoirs Ibárruri says that she spoke on the radio on July 18. Actually it was July 19.
7. *Guerra y revolución en España,* vol. I, pp. 257–58.
8. That will to remain on the side of legal authority is shown even in small details. For example, the JS and JC, although officially unified, in Madrid acted independently, each with its own militias (Tagüeña, p. 120). Once the fighting had ended, the JC organized a column they called the Thirteenth Regiment—a traditional name, indicative of a regular army. The older Communists followed suit when, after the attack on the Montaña barracks, in which groups of all tendencies took part, the PCE managed to keep some of the arms and organized the Fifth Regiment (once again, an almost official name). It named as commanders Barbado and Castro Delagdo and as political commissar "Carlos Contreras" whose real name was Vittorio Vidali, an Italian from Trieste, who had been in Mexico involved in activities of a very suspicious nature (related to the murder of the Cuban student Julio Antonio Mella just a few days after he left the Communist party, a murder which was at the time attributed to henchmen of the Cuban dictator Gerardo Machado). Contreras-Vidali had arrived in Spain shortly before to strengthen the team of "instructors" of the Communist International and in particular of those in charge of organizing the People's Olympics in Barcelona, an idea Münzenberg devised to detract from the official Olympics which took place that summer in Berlin. The People's Olympics

were attended by many young Communists and Socialists as well as generally by athletes from all over Spain; those who came from areas under the control of the rebels had their lives saved thanks to the fact that they were in Barcelona. (On Vidali see Víctor Alba, *Historia del movimiento obrero en América Latina,* Mexico City, 1964, p. 231. On the Fifth Regiment in its beginnings see Castro Delgado, *Hombres made in Moscú,* p. 270 ff., 293 ff.)

9.   A leader of the former PCC, years later, commented that the PCE did not really wish to unite with the Socialists because the leaders of the PCE were highly bureaucratic and were afraid of losing influence, while in Catalonia the local Communist leaders "were a notable exception," were way ahead of the conclusions reached by the Seventh Congress of the Communist International, and to implement them "we rejected any notion of maneuvering" which met with "permanent, constant, and unwavering opposition by the political bureau of the Communist Party of Spain." (J. del Barrio, "XVI Aniversario de la constitución del Partido Socialista Unificado de Cataluña," *Acción Socialista,* Mexico City, July 1952. This weekly was published by Communist followers of Tito: Jesús Hernández, José del Barrio, and others.)

10.   Bolloten, p. 114.

11.   L. V. Ponamariova, *La formación del Partit Socialista Unificat de Catalunya,* Barcelona, 1977, translation of a work published in Moscow in 1963 and then published in Catalan by the PSUC in exile. The number of members is exaggerated. Anyone who lived through those times in Catalonia knows that neither the PCC nor the Catalonian PSOE had anywhere near half the forces which the Russian author attributes to them. At most, PSUC had at its creation some 4,500 members. There were a few who refused to unify and joined others parties (mostly from the USC who went over to the Esquerra Republicana de Catalunya, a party to which the USC was allied since 1931).

12.   Josep Lluís Martin i Ramos, *Els orígens del Partit Socialista Unificat de Catalunya (1930-1936),* Barcelona, 1977, p. 199 ff. This author finds Ponamariova's estimates of members satisfactory (p. 233).

13.   Alba, *El marxisme a Catalunya,* vol. II, pp. 18-19.

14.   Alba, p. 28.

15.   In March 1936 the Central Committee of the PCE proposed to the Executive Committee of the PSOE the merger of the two parties. The letter of proposal said that the new party ought to maintain "independence vis à vis the bourgeoisie with a complete break between social democracy and the bourgeoisie ... recognizing the need for revolutionary overthrow of bourgeois domination and establishment of proletarian dictatorship in the form of soviets." It was evident that this letter did not respond to the policy of the Popular Front, but rather was written in terms which the PCE thought could attract the Socialist Left. In the four months from March to July 1936 the PCE had completely changed its points of view (or at least those it admitted to) since, with the Civil War, it worked on forming a bloc with the petite bourgeoisie and wanted nothing to do with proletarian dictatorship, just when it was possible to attain it (*Claridad,* Madrid, March 12, 1936, quoted by Bolloten, p. 275).

16. Reproduced in *Guerra y revolución en España,* vol. II, pp. 100–101. Incidentally, no one of any tendency ever "made an attempt" against foreign possessions because it was evident to everyone that would have provoked intervention.

17. Quoted in Alba, *El Frente Popular,* p. 461; Estruch, p. 98 ff., and Bolloten, 1961, passim.

18. Hernández, who had been arrested in Bilbao in the PCE's early days for having organized an attempt on Prieto's life, sat next to him in government. In addition there was a pro-Communist, Álvarez del Vayo, in the Foreign Affairs Ministry and a right-winger of the PSOE who would later become pro-Communist, Juan Negrín, in the Treasury.

19. It is revealing that in the *Historia del PCE* the part about the Civil War is entitled "The National Revolutionary War," to tie together the reality of the revolution and the Communist slogan of "war for independence." It is also revealing that in Moscow when the leaders of the PCE attempted to put together a history of the Civil War, they called it *Guerra y revolución en España, 1936–39 (War and Revolution in Spain).* But for the duration of the war they refused to recognize its revolutionary nature. It was so evident, they could not go on denying it; it had become part of everyday speech to talk of the Spanish revolution.

20. Estruch, p. 96.

21. Uribe's decree was directed against the collectivities: "Although it appeared to the contrary, the decree was impregnated with an anticollectivist spirit and intended to demoralize the socialized peasants. It subjected the legalization of the collectivities to extremely rigid and complicated legal clauses. A strict time limit was imposed upon the collectivities. Those not legalized within this limit were automatically declared unlawful and their lands could be returned to the original owners" (Daniel Guérin, *L'Anarchisme,* Paris, 1965, p. 153). In addition, Uribe used their implementation to promote membership in a Peasant Federation of Valencia organized by the PCE. "The collectivizations in Valencia, which the decree on agrarian reform elaborated by the Communist minister Vicente Uribe had reduced to nothing," Ibárruri would say thirty years later (*El único camino,* p. 351).

22. Ibárruri, *El único camino,* p. 283. Of course, there is no mention of the fact that if the agrarian collectivization had been accomplished the way the author claims, it would have been an imitation of what Stalin had done less than ten years before with the forced collectivization of Soviet agriculture. Although there were cases of coercion, the great majority of collectivities were voluntary, for when the Communist party tried to destroy them as will be seen, the peasants organized them once again after the Communist forces that dissolved them withdrew.

23. Degras, vol. III, p. 397.

24. On the gold sent to Moscow see Ángel Viñas, *El oro español en la guerra civil,* Madrid, 1976. Viñas believes that the shipment of gold was justified and that it did not politically mortgage the Republic. If that were the case, those who, on the pretext of the gold and the "aid" purchased with it, yielded to the policy dictated by Moscow, would have an even greater responsibility. Regarding the friendly relations between Negrín and Stachevsky, who was in charge of Russian affairs, see Bolloten, p. 123, and Krivitsky, *In Stalin's Secret Service,* pp. 99–100. A few years later, Ángel

Viñas published *El oro de Moscú* (Barcelona, 1979), a highly documented book, in which he states that the Republic owed Moscow money by the end of the war and that the USSR's behavior was "generous," although he recognizes the political and police compensation which had to be paid for such generosity. The book does not contribute anything new to a polemic which goes beyond the limits of the perspective of an economist such as Viñas when one begins to make judgments of political and ideological values. But it will doubtless be used as an instrument for future propaganda when the PCE decides to write its own history. In mentioning foreign aid, one would have to cite the United States's contribution to Franco, particularly in oil, also sold on credit by that country's oil companies (likewise by England's). Despite the limited volume, Mexican aid should not be over-looked: arms were purchased from the United States as if for Mexico but were actually sent to the Republic.

25. Guelfo Zacaria, "I comunisti e la guerra di Spagna," *Correspondenza Socialista,* Rome, August–September 1961.
26. Gross, *Willi Münzenberg,* p. 287.
27. Ibid., p. 311.
28. André Gide, in *The God That Failed,* London, 1950, pp. 185–86.
29. It is not an exaggeration to say that Stalin saw aid to Spain as a means of pressuring Hitler to come to terms with Moscow. Louis Fisher, who at the time was an American journalist sympathizing with Moscow—and who continued to be so throughout the war in Spain—maintains that "Stalin had tried in 1936 to obtain a pact with Hitler who refused it" (letter in *Book World,* Washington, September 7, 1969). Documents on these frustrated attempts appear in Fisher's book: *Russia's Road from Peace to War: Foreign Soviet Relations, 1917–1941,* in which there is also information about Soviet aid to Spain. Regarding the Soviet position in the Civil War and its influence on the position adopted by the Communist International, see Dominique Desanti, *L'Internationale Communiste,* Paris, 1970, p. 239 ff.
30. In the texts cited in the bibliography, the reader will find documentation on those extremes.
31. Communist propaganda was so efficient that everyone was convinced that the Blum government had stopped helping the Republic because the con-servative British cabinet threatened him with not supporting France if the latter was implicated in problems (with Germany and Italy) due to helping the Republic. Something has been overlooked which is neither mentioned in Ibárruri's *Memoirs* nor in *Historia del PCE:* the Kremlin's response to the French government's asking how the Soviet Union would react if France were threatened for having aided the government in Madrid. The reply: "The Franco-Soviet Pact of 1935 obligates us to reciprocal aid in the event that one of us is attacked by another power, but not in the event of war caused by the intervention of one of us in the affairs of another nation." So Moscow adopted precisely the same position as the British conservative cabinet (quoted by Carlos Semprún Maura, *Revolució i contrarevolució a Catalunya, 1936–1937,* Barcelona, 1975, pp. 79–80). Documentation by Daniel Blume proves that French Socialists secretly and illegally helped the Republic ("Contribution à l'histoire de la politique de non-intervention," in *Cahiers Léon Blum,* Paris, 1977–78). Blum named Socialists as heads of certain customs offices through which material, not only from Russia

but also from France and other countries (purchased through France as if it were for itself) found its way to Spain. For that reason the French right wing attributed responsibility for defeat in 1940 to Pierre Cot (minister of the air force, 1936–37) for having "delivered all the French planes to the Republic," when actually he used the ministry to purchase arms for the Republic. For details on the methods of this "contraband" see Maurice Jaquier, *Simple Militant,* Paris, 1974. It is at least curious that every historian has remained silent about the aid of the French Socialists which shows the influence of Communist propaganda on those who it would seem ought to be immunized against it or know how to discern what is true and what is not.

32. The Soviet government used the Russian people's sympathy for the Republican cause to order a 1 percent cut of all salaries to aid the Republic. This order was issued on August 3, 1936, before the Communist International and the Communist party had adopted any public position on the war. The Republic did not receive any of the money from the cuts in salary since even the shipments of food made as a sign of solidarity were deducted from the Spanish gold. The war in Spain was used by the Soviet government to force the Russians to accept salary decreases. Some Russians took seriously what the Soviet press was saying about Spain and asked the party to send them to Spain to fight. They were arrested and deported to Siberia (Víctor Serge, *Memoires,* quoted by Semprún Maura, p. 79).

33. J. M. Gómez Ortiz, *Los gobiernos republicanos: España, 1936–1939,* Barcelona, 1977, p. 124.

34. Gabriel Jackson, *La República española y la guerra civil,* Mexico City, 1967, p. 277.

35. La Pasionaria was already popular. But her speeches during the Civil War transformed her into a figure whom propaganda draped in heroic robes. Actually, she was a leader who had been a worker, active in her youth, but as soon as she began her rise within PCE bureaucracy, she became a peculiar person, cold and calculating, who merely repeated what had been said by others, saying things like "They will not pass," and "It is better to die standing than to live on one's knees," both of which were of French patriotic origin. She had a maternal air. Those who knew her well agree on her total submission to the delegates of the Comintern and her extraordinary ability to maneuver. Teresa Pàmies's portrait of her in *Una española llamada Ibárruri* (Barcelona, 1975), while very apologetic, cannot conceal this aspect of her personality.

36. The American professor Robert C. Colodny's book, *The Struggle for Madrid,* New York, 1958, is an example of the methods used to promote the legend of Madrid having been saved by the PCE. This book is a web of lies of omission. Suffice to say that CNT's Cipriano Mera is not even mentioned. Regarding the Russian aid, Thomas (p. 309) estimates that in the decisive period of the Battle of Madrid, there were nine freighters en route holding 100 trucks, 25 tanks, 30 cannons, 1,500 tons of ammunition, 9,000 tons of food, and 1,000 tons of diesel fuel. A lot for a city under siege, but very little for a country which was "the land of the proletariat," covered a sixth of the globe, and had received 550 million dollars in gold to pay for its supplies. Regarding Carrillo and repression of the Francoists, consult Ramón Salas Larrazábal, "Santiago Carrillo y la represión republicana en Madrid,

1936," *Nueva Historia,* Madrid, June 1977. The author indicates that Carrillo could have prevented the massacres, "as Melchor Rodríguez palpably showed the following month the moment he took over as special prison delegate for the territory of Madrid." Thomas (p. 320) underlines that the Communists "took advantage of the opportunity when the government fled," and that while many officers hesitated to follow Miaja's orders, Antonio Mije placed the Fifth Regiment under his control and issued the call to defend Madrid house by house. Koltzov, a correspondent of *Pravda,* "seemed for a time the main source of inspiration in the junta," said Arturo Barea (*La forja de un rebelde,* Buenos Aires, 1951, p. 174).

37. Alba, *Los sepultureros de la República,* Barcelona, 1977, p. 220 ff.

38. It was logical for those who wanted a regular army to attract the sympathy of the career officers who were with the Republic and who felt uncomfortable with the militias. In that way, the PCE found many career officers among its ranks and managed to place quite a number of Communists in key positions in the Ministry of War, taking advantage of the good relationship with Largo Caballero in 1936. In the Central Staff there were two Communists: Antonio Cordón and Alejandro García Val. Largo Caballero's field aide, Colonel Manuel Arredondo, the head of the Department of Intelligence and Control, Captain Eleuterio Díaz Tendero, and the chief of Central Staff, Commander Manuel Estrada, were men who Largo Caballero considered to be loyal to his points of view but who had secretly joined the PCE or worked with it, so that the PCE was in on top military secrets (Bolloten, p. 227).

39. Franz Borkenau, quoted by Semprún Maura, p. 205.

40. The most visible aspect of the campaign against the collectivizations was the implementation of Uribe's so-called agrarian reform decree. In March 1937 Negrín lent his *carabineros* to Uribe to attack several collectivities in Valencia under the pretext of implementing the decree. This was the cause of four days of fighting in which many people were killed, peasant demoralization, and a rapid decrease in agrarian productivity in Valencia.

41. The Communists vetoed POUM's becoming part of the junta (Alba, *El marxisme a Catalunya,* vol. II, p. 140. Quotes given on the campaign against POUM come from this book which documents them).

42. A historian has written about this crisis in the government of the Generalidad: "There is sufficient circumstantial evidence that the Soviet Union set the following conditions for providing aid to Catalonia: that POUM not be allowed to continue being a member of the government of the Generalidad and that the latter submit to the general program established by the government of the Republic. Aid to Catalonia (in raw materials, not arms) began in December and immediately following, POUM's representative left the government of the Generalidad" (D. T. Cattell, *Communism in the Spanish Civil War,* Berkeley, California, 1956, p. 109).

43. Text of the announcement appears in Alba, *El marxisme a Catalunya,* vol. II, pp. 136–37.

44. Raymond Carr, *Spain, 1808–1939,* London, 1966, p. 662. It appears that there were two Orlovs, both in the NKVD, one in charge of directing the services of military counterespionage (against the nationalists and fascist spies) and another in charge of police operations against enemies of the PCE. The first went over to the Americans in the fifties. His physical

description did not agree with the one given by some (Jesús Hernández, for example) who knew the Orlov of political repression, who remained loyal to Stalin; no one knows if Orlov was his real name nor if he was a victim of the Russian purges which followed the Spanish Civil War.

45. Carr, p. 663.
46. Krivitsky, p. 99.
47. Ginés Ganga in *Hoy,* Mexico City, December 5, 1942. Quoted by Bolloten, p. 273. As to Álvarez del Vayo, Largo Caballero had his suspicions when Araquistáin, ambassador in Paris and a relative of del Vayo, warned him about certain facts he had discovered and which revealed a close relationship with the Russians. Largo Caballero informed Azaña, but he did nothing to eliminate him from the government. Once Prieto told del Vayo that he was behaving like a Russian, and the minister of foreign affairs resigned, but Largo Caballero refused to accept his resignation. He was probably afraid of irritating the Russians or of causing a crisis in the cabinet (Bolloten, p. 291).
48. Claudín, p. 195.
49. This letter was kept secret until 1939 when Luis Araquistáin, upon receipt of a copy from Largo Caballero, published it in *The New York Times,* June 4, 1939. It was later reproduced in *Guerra y revolución en España,* vol. II, pp. 100–102.
50. Thomas, p. 365.
51. Degras, vol. III, p. 398 ff.
52. Speech in Madrid in October 1937, quoted in Bolloten, p. 275. The allusion to the Communist demand for a break with the Republican parties referred to a letter dated March 1936 sent by the Central Committee of the PCE to the Executive Committee of the PSOE proposing a merger.
53. *Tribuna,* Mexico City, March 1949.
54. Araquistáin, *El comunismo y la guerra de España,* p. 28.
55. Julio Álvarez del Vayo, *Freedom's Battle,* New York, 1940, p. 126.
56. *Nosotros,* Valencia, February 25, 1937. Díaz Tendero was arrested and in his home were found 200 copies of *Nosotros.* When that paper's Anarchists found out, they were furious for having been had by a Communist in disguise. At the time Largo Caballero was 68 years old. It is an interesting technique: to have an accusation made by someone who apparently is not a Communist (in this case, the accusation was "planted" by a secret Communist in an Anarchist newspaper) to subsequently use it as "evidence" against the accused. Another example was the closing of the headquarters and press of POUM by the Junta of Defense of Madrid, controlled by the PCE (and specifically by its police delegate, Cazorla, of the JSU), and then present it as evidence that POUM was an enemy of the Republic, for if it were not, why would its headquarters in Madrid be closed? Asensio was tried when Largo Caballero was no longer head of government, but he was absolved and reinstated.
57. *Claridad,* February 27, 1937. The Communist press did not print this announcement by the head of a government in which there were two Communist ministers.
58. Bolloten, p. 243. The appointment of Rojo had to be revoked because it was not convenient at that time to remove him from the Madrid front. He was reappointed after the fall of Largo Caballero.

59.   del Vayo, *Freedom's Battle,* p. 127. The facts about Baráibar told by himself appear in Bolloten, p. 186 ff.

60.   During the last two weeks of April 1937, *Frente Rojo,* a Communist organ, and *Adelante,* Caballero's organ, argued around this subject, with comments from *Fragua Social,* organ of the CNT (quotes in Bolloten, p. 290 ff.).

61.   Hernández, *Yo fui un ministro de Stalin,* p. 80 ff.

62.   The Communists rarely called POUM by its name; instead they referred to is as the "Trotskyite group." They wanted to use against POUM the avalanche of false accusations that the USSR heaped upon Trotsky, although it was clear to anyone who was up on the situation that POUM never had been Trotskyite. Trotsky's brutal criticism of POUM can be found in Leon Trotsky, *La Revolución Española,* Madrid, 1977, esp. p. 160 ff.

63.   Degras, vol. III, p. 405 ff.

64.   No details have been given regarding those days in May because much has already been written about them. See: Manuel Cruells, *Els fets de maig,* Barcelona, 1970; Adolfo Bueso, *Recuerdos de un cenetista,* vol. II, Barcelona, 1978, p. 228 ff.; chapters in the books by Thomas and Jackson; and Alba, *El marxisme a Catalunya,* vol. II, p. 213, where there is documentation for all the sources of events referred to here. Not to be forgotten is *Homage to Catalonia* by George Orwell, a good deal of which is devoted to those days in May.

65.   These events are described in a document housed in the Hoover Institution of Stanford University. The document belongs to Jaume Antón Aiguader, nephew of the man who was minister of the government of the Generalidad in May 1937, who heard about them from his uncle. The document is signed by several Catalonian witnesses and dated in Mexico City on August 9, 1946. He adds that Artemi Aiguader kept all the documentation on the days of May in a safe in a French bank. It has never been published. What Togliatti had to say in a report to the Communist International on August 30, 1937 can be considered an a priori confirmation that the events of May had been hoped for by the Communist party. He relates that on the way from Valencia to Barcelona his friends told him that "the Anarchists have lost all their influence; in Barcelona there is not a single Anarchist worker left. Let's hope that they organize a second *Putsch* so we can really finish them off" (Palmiro Togliatti, *Opere, 1935–44,* Rome, 1979, p. 268).

66.   *Historia del PCE* attributes the responsibility for the events of May to POUM and cites a telegram from the Nazi ambassador in Burgos, according to which Franco had 13 agents in Barcelona, from which one could deduce that it was they who provoked the fighting in the city. *Historia del PCE* (p. 163) says that "the PSUC, members of the UGT, and youths incorporated in the JSU in Barcelona stood up to the insurgents without the slightest hesitation, in defense of Republican legality." Anyone who has lived through those times knows that, aside from Communists who defended their head-quarters from within, the police were the only ones confronting the CNT. Ibárruri blames the events not only on POUM but also on the CNT in general (p. 340 ff. in her memoirs).

67.   Manuel Azaña, "Memorias políticas y de guerra," in *Obras completas,* Mexico City, 1969, vol. IV, p. 582.

68.   *Las Noticias,* Barcelona, May 18, 1937.

69.   Ibárruri, p. 345.

70. Louis Fisher, *Men and Politics*, New York, 1941, p. 455. Fisher says that Prieto told him that at a certain moment he had been in favor of the merger.

71. *El Socialista*, January 14, February 20, 25, March 6, April 22, 23, 25, 1937, and a circular letter from the Executive Committee of the PSOE of March 28, 1937.

72. Bolloten, p. 301 ff.

73. Hernández, *Yo fui un ministro de Stalin*, pp. 61–70. *Historia del PCE* speaks of this rally (but not of the meeting of the bureau) and cites only Díaz as speaker (p. 164).

74. *Historia del PCE* (p. 164) says that the withdrawal of the Communist ministers occurred when "Largo Caballero did not accept the proposal the party repeatedly made for change in the government's policy." It makes no mention of the demand to dissolve POUM. Nor does Ibárruri speak of it in her memoirs (p. 347); it attributes the withdrawal of the Communists to a discrepancy in the council's agenda; Hernández in his book *Negro y Rojo* (Mexico City, 1949) written when he was still a member of the PCE) said that the Communists left because the ministers were arguing over "trifles," but in his other book he gives the same version as Largo Caballero in *Mis recuerdos* (p. 54), which was confirmed by Azaña in his *Memorias políticas y de guerra*, p. 595.

13.
Losing the War

For ten months, until the middle of May, the Republican zone had been ruled—with restrictions and pressures—by those who believed that the only way to win the war was the carry out the social revolution spontaneously initiated by those who bore the weight both of combat in the cities and fighting on the fronts during the first weeks. In May 1937 the relative predominance of that tendency ended. After Largo Caballero's fall from power, the government of the country would be entirely in the hands of those who said that the only way to win the war was undoing the revolution. They governed uninteruptedly for 23 months, without restrictions or pressures, until they lost the war and General Franco claimed victory.

Double Maneuvering

To set up that government, which with slight variants would last 23 months, two converging maneuvers were necessary: one to eliminate Largo Caballero and other to find a successor who would meet all the qualifications the lack of which had aroused in so many the desire to get rid of the old Socialist leader. In their own ways, taking part in those maneuvers were Azaña and the Republicans, Communists, and middle-of-the-road Socialists, despite the fact that no one knew all the details (the Republicans and Socialists, for example, did not know about the meeting between the bureau of the PCE and the delegates of the Communist International).

The Communists eventually confirmed Prieto's complicity. After eight years, Uribe wrote: "Prieto took part in the plan to replace Caballero as head of the government although without appearing to. We wanted to change what seemed a bad policy. Prieto wanted to take revenge on Largo Caballero whom he never forgave for, among other things, frustrating his ambition to be head of the government back in May 1936."[1] Prieto, in the Council of Ministers on May 15, 1937, jumped at the chance to provoke the crisis when the two Communist ministers slammed the door. Had he not done it, none of the other ministers probably would have dared. Prieto's supporters in the Executive Commission of the PSOE established good relations with the Communists precisely when Largo Caballero was trying to "clean out" the Ministry of War of infiltrators and had to resist pressures from Soviet diplomats and military men. Azaña did not allow any constitutional scruples to get in his way. On May 7, eight days before the crisis, he received, independently of one another, Socialists, Communists, and Republicans. They all said that they hoped to provoke this crisis. But "the council met . . . and nothing happened."[2] Azaña still had to wait one more week before they would present him with Largo Caballero's head.

The moment finally arrived, and Azaña cast aside his constitutional scruples and did not support a head of government who refused to dissolve a party because, according to the Constitution, that was a matter of justice, if it could be substantiated. Azaña did not have a single word of support to offer the head of government, yet several of ridicule for his Madrid accent. Caballero handed him his resignation. Azaña related that it was night and he asked him to give him until the following morning to decide whether to accept it or whether he could agree to have the two Communist ministers replaced. Then he called Prieto and Giral and on the following day he informed Largo Caballero that he had decided to accept his resignation and he began consultations.

The Communists realized that they had not sufficiently undermined Largo Caballero's prestige. They did not dare suggest another head of government. Azaña put Largo Caballero in charge of setting up a government. The Communists said that they would not participate in any government in which Largo was minister of war and operations were not conducted by the High Council of War, and in which the commissariat did not have autonomy. The Executive Committee of the UGT announced that it would not support any government in which Largo Caballero were not both president and minister of war. Caballero wanted to form a government with the CNT and UGT alone. Since it was already known that Caballero would fail, private negotiations were initiated. The Communists offered the Ministry of War to Prieto. Uribe explained it in this way: "By mutual agreement, Prieto was named minister of national defense (a new name for the ministry) and was committed to correcting Caballero's mistakes, strengthening the unity of the people, and improving relations between Communists and Socialists. I myself brought this up to Prieto on several occasions prior to his becoming minister of defense, and he always told me he agreed and that he would not do anything to jeopardize the unity of Communists and Socialists."[3]

The CNT supported Caballero because he intended to oppose the Communists and "he could only do this from within the ministry of war."[4] Largo Caballero's plan was rejected by Lamoneda representing the Socialists, Díaz representing the PCE, as well as by the Republicans; Caballero was forced to let someone else have the job of forming the government. But who? In the meeting between the executive committee and its "instructors" Togliatti had said that as successor to Caballero there were Prieto, but he was not pro-Communist, Del Vayo, who was a fool, and Negrín. Stachevsky had been in frequent touch with him over the matter of the gold. In February 1937 Gerö in confidence told some leaders of PSUC that Negrín could be the future head of government. Krivitsky commented: "Dr. Negrín was the man who suited Stalin: he had all the characteristics of a bureaucratic politician. Even though he was a professor, he was also a businessman. Of course, Dr. Negrín saw the close relationship with the USSR as his country's only salvation. It was clearly the only source of aid. He was willing to make all kinds of sacrifices and to follow Stalin to be assured of that aid."[5]

The PCE put Hernández in charge of offering Negrín the position before Azaña did or before Prieto suggested it to him. Prieto thought that he had "discovered" Negrín, and the Communists humored him in this illusion. The interview between Hernández and Negrín took place in Hernández's office while a Communist demonstration in opposition to Caballero's plan for a syndicalist government passed by. When Hernández told him that the PCE would propose his name to Azaña, Negrín did not appear surprised. His only objection was that he was little known. "Popularity can be made," Hernández answered laughing. Negrín added that he was not a Communist and Hernández replied that they did not want a president who was a Communist, just a friend of the Communists." Many aspects of the Communist party's policy seem fair and well-chosen," said Negrín. They agreed that Prieto would be minister of defense, thus taking advantage of his prestige and even his anti-Communism, which would seem to many a guarantee."[6]

When Azaña asked Largo Caballero, very constitutionally, what advice he would give to resolve the crisis now that he had already failed to do so, he replied: "Put the Communists in charge. Aren't they the ones who are bringing down the government? Well, let them govern." Azaña would follow that advice. Negrín offered the CNT two ministries, but it rejected them. On May 17, 48 hours after the resignation of Caballero, Negrín's government had already been formed. CNT's *Soli,* on the following day, ran an article with this headline: "A Counterrevolutionary Government Is Formed." The PCE had the same two ministries as in the previous cabinet.

The Government of Victory

"The formation of this government [Negrín's] was a victory for the policy of the Popular Front," said the Communists.[7] Spain's situation was very different from what it was in 1935, when the Popular Front was formed. But Moscow continued to adopt the Popular Front tactic and therefore the PCE had to make sure that whatever happened in Spain reflected this tactic. "Negrín was controlled, insofar as his frivolity allowed . . . by the Communist party—by the party directly as well as by two of Negrín's closest collaborators: one Benigno [Rodríguez, an ex-member of the CNT] who was editor of *Milicia Popular,* the [Fifth] Regiment's organ [and also Negrín's secretary in Valencia, Barcelona, and London] and by Sánchez Arcas, a fine architect and a marvelous person, who was blindly obedient to the party and who was undersecretary of propaganda."[8]

Negrín was a man of great vitality, with a voracious appetite. Azaña describes a meal he had with him in November 1937 when the country was totally rationed: "There were some big eaters there but the president of the government out-ate them all by a long shot . . . I have never seen anything like it."[9] He was not a Marxist; the inefficiency of the Republicans made him go over to the PSOE. But he certainly was a man of order. Although he felt no sympathy for the USSR or Communism, he admired the Communists for their discipline and sense of order. Since he possessed an extraordinary ability to double-deal and lie, perhaps he thought that, as a last resort, he would manipulate the Communists by letting himself be manipulated by them. He was not the only one to have the illusion. Prieto matched him in that. "Initially . . . his government was not dominated by the Communists," said a historian who often consulted with Negrín and who clearly was fond of him. "The party reflected the Soviet Union's belief that 'the establishment of a communist regime is not the solution to the problem of the war.' If dependence on the shipments of Russian arms excluded serious resistance to what the Communists considered the 'correct' policy, there were limits to what the Socialists in the cabinet called their 'sense of sacrifice.'"[10]

This sacrifice, which Negrín must not have felt as such since he never made any attempt to resist it, at times took on forms that bordered on farce. For example, the minister of the interior, the Socialist Julián Zugazagoitia, on August 14 gave orders to the censorship service not to allow "criticism of a certain exceptionally friendly nation for it could create difficulties." If any criticism was overlooked by the censors, the newspaper that printed it would be suspended indefinitely "even if it [the criticism] had been authorized by the censors," and the inattentive censor would be placed at the disposal of a special tribunal for sabotage.

I do not think that at the time people understood the mechanisms by which Communist influence was exercised. It was clearly not a matter of giving orders, although in extreme cases the "instructors," "military advisors," and the Communists did not hesitate to threaten to reduce the shipments of Soviet arms in order to discharge people from their positions or send them to prison. But generally slightly subtler methods were employed. So when the commissariat was without a commissar, Pedro Checa, Francisco Antón, and Castro Delgado met to study what commissar could replace del Vayo. "Pretel is a weak man, although he is in the hands of the party; Doporto is fairly appealing but has a bad temper; Crescenciano Bilbao is too much a Socialist to be useful to us; Inestal is an Anarchist who would not yield; the representative of the Republican Left is a decent person, bald and pleasant, but that is all." Suddenly, they remembered Bibiano Ossorio Tafall, former undersecretary of labor prior to the war, "a Republican from Galicia, a chatterbox and womanizer . . . who would not get in our way." Castro and Antón went to offer him the position. "It should be clearly understood that he owes the appointment to the party." Ossorio Tafall at the time was secretary of the Republican Left. "Ossorio Tafall was never an obstacle. He knew whom he had to thank for where he was."[11]

In May 1937 when the PCE began to popularize its ritornello of the Government of Victory, many people thought that Negrín would know how to use the Communists to keep the revolutionaries where he wanted them and then he would manage to tighten the reins on the Communists. "People breathed a sigh of relief. They look to him [Negrín] for energy, a will to govern, restoration of the normal methods of public order, the reestablishment of discipline."[12] When Azaña wrote this, he could not have suspected that he had discovered, 31 years *avant la lettre,* a use of the word *normal* which the Russians would turn into a verb, *normalize,* in Czechoslovakia in August 1968.

"Normalization"

"Normalization" consisted of: "reduction of workers' control in significant proportions; restriction of the importance of agrarian collectivities; centralization of state control over all important industries for the purpose of concentrating 'all the technical leadership in a single person with full power and responsibility to perform his work as it relates to production.'"[13] The government established a process by which owners of expropriated property could appeal the expropriation, and although few dared to do so, a fair amount of property was returned. Negrín announced that, once the war was over, those who had been expropriated would be compensated. The tendency was to return the management of many firms to their old managers or owners when the property itself could not be returned. A Catalonian Communist, Estanislao Ruiz Ponseti (coming from the moderate USC) said that that policy was like Lenin's NEP which in the future would allow the socialization of all property since that was "the quickest way of overcoming the principle of private property and of doing so with its own arms." Manuel Delicado said that "equal salaries promote irresponsibility and laziness which impede maximum efficiency in the workers."[14] In its March 30, 1937 issue *Frente Rojo* had posed the question: "Why have the workers fallen into that error [the craze to socialize and confiscate]?" And it gave the answer: "Because of ignorance of the political climate we are experiencing they think we are in the midst of a revolution." The Negrín government had come to redeem them from their error. It had a concrete mission: to impose order; and its theoretical justification: "A democratic-bourgeois revolution . . . is what is going on in our country, and we Communists are fighting at the vanguard against forces which represent the obscurantism of days gone by. . . . In these historic times, the Communist party, loyal to its revolutionary principles, respectful of the will of the people, is at the side of the government, which is the expression of that will, and at the side of the Republic and democracy as well."[15] This is the same thesis that Togliatti expounded five months earlier.[16]

In just over three months, things got back to "normal." The first thing the Negrín government did was to annul the Generalidad's collectivization decree of October 1936, alleging that the Generalidad did not have the power to regulate property (and, in effect, Article 44 of the 1931 Constitution stated that only the state has the right to expropriate property). On August 28, a decree gave the government the right to intervene in and control mines and mining industries. The Ministry of Defense only signed purchase contracts with noncollectivized firms, which was discrimination in favor of private property.

Then the government militarized war industries; indeed, it nationalized them. Since those industries were collectivized and their employees belonged to the CNT, they were punished by being deprived of their antiaircraft batteries which until then had protected them—that is, had protected production intended for the front. Now the level of production was irrelevant since purchases could be made from the USSR. The important thing was to humble the collectivized workers. The result of the measure was that when there were bombardments, the workers in the war industries suffered a higher percentage of casualties and the installations were dealt a powerful blow. The underground press—which had already begun circulation because there were certain things the legal press could not say—seemed to indicate that that measure might be due, in addition, to the fact that the lower the production of the war industries, the more Spain would have to purchase from the USSR, thus increasing dependency on Moscow.

There were other economic measures. In 1938, with funds derived from collectivizations, the Catalonian Credit Service, established in 1936 to help collectivizations, was required to return to the state the sums charged to collectivized firms as a share of the benefits, as admitted the secretary of the Council of the Economy himself, the Communist Ruiz Ponseti. But since collectivized firms continued to exist, the inspectors of the Treasury took to harassing them, even if by doing so their productivity was reduced. They imposed fines for abiding by the Generalidad's collectivization law instead of following the rules of the old corporation law.[17] So, ten months after assuming power, Negrín could declare: "To my knowledge the concept of private property has not been modified"; and Manuel Cordero, a friend of his, could write: "There are those who have misinterpreted the revolution, thinking that the expropriation of capitalists was done for the benefit of specific collective elements. They are mistaken. What the Republic's personal enemies have given up, which has been expropriated and which has yet to be returned to the state, will eventually have to be returned."[18]

On August 10, 1937 orders were given to dissolve the Council of Aragon.[19] This followed an intensive campaign by the Communist press backed up by the Republican Left organ *Política*, by *Claridad* which had fallen into the hands of Prieto and his men, and indeed by the entire press with the exception of the CNT. To make this measure look a little more "popular," representatives of the Republican, Socialist, and Communist parties met in Barbastro asking the government to appoint a general governor for Aragon. They did not have to ask twice. Ignacio Mantecón was appointed; up to then he had been the representative of Republican Left in the Council and shortly thereafter joined the PCE. The Líster, Karl Marx (of PSUC), and Number Thirty (of the PCE) divisions occupied the rearguard of the Aragon front, they arrested Joaquín Ascaso, president of the Council, and his friends, and suppressed the CNT press in Aragon. Ascaso and other Anarchists were accused of smuggling jewelry. With its Aragonese militants either in jail or dead (for said divisions murdered numerous members of the CNT), the CNT was in no position to fight back and could only give in, visit Azaña, and meet with the PCE and other parties (for which Ascaso was suddenly no longer a jewel smuggler). Negrín said that "the government believed it is following the right path."[20]

It was then that the Aragon front began to crack. The columns which had established it and made it advance during the first year of the war were dispersed in other fronts and replaced by Communist forces. To make people think that the Aragon front had been paralyzed because of the collectivizations (which had already been destroyed), the Battle of Belchite was begun on August 25 by the same forces that had "defeated" the Council of Aragon and the peasant committees. They could not defeat Franco's troops. The center of the revolution had been in Catalonia. In October 1937 the government was transferred there from Valencia despite the fact that the center of the war was in Valencia and the central plateau. Negrín's presence was an inspiration for PSUC. Comorera issued new orders to the Council of the Economy, converting it into an advisory body, and, by staffing it with technicians who were representatives of departments of the Catalonian government, its labor members were left in the minority. "Agreements on industrial groups [which would concentrate several enterprises into a single, more efficient one], which had been already approved by the Council, were permanently obstructed." Ruiz Ponseti proposed making the collectivized concerns cooperatives. The bank employees' union, in the third congress of the Catalonian UGT (Communist), proposed returning to the system of management of each enterprise by a single person: "They were labor representatives who denied the ability and right of their colleagues to run the economy, blaming them for all the defects inherent in any revolutionary upset and especially for the course of the Civil War."[21] This proposal would not have been made had it not had the approval of PSUC. But there was little enthusiasm for it even among delegates to the UGT congress.

One had to pay the price for a government which was at once unified and efficient and which attracted what in the nineteenth century were called the "respectable classes." The respectable classes felt so comfortable with Negrín and the PCE that Barcelona's hatmakers were smiling, for Negrín had ordered functionaries and their wives to wear hats to create an impression of normalcy. Tailors were also happy, because the new officers—mobilized, not volunteer—were placing orders for elegant uniforms so they could show off the regular army's gold stripes. A novelist friend of Negrín's wrote: "The government and the war machine worked as never before. And now there was an efficient army and administration, both necessities to run a modern war even though it be on a small scale. But the longing for freedom and the desperate efforts to build a new and better social scheme had been totally destroyed."[22] Enthusiasm had been replaced by fear.

Policy of Fear

At the beginning of 1938 an international delegation of revolutionary socialists visited the minister of justice and other authorities with the intention of bailing out the CNT and POUM prisoners; after a great deal of pressuring they got permission to visit the Modelo prison in Barcelona. They were greeted by the prisoners singing, not "Cara al sol," the Fascists' song, as they might have expected, but "The International." At the time there were more anti-Fascist prisoners than Fascist.[23] Indeed, just days after assuming power, Negrín created the Special Court of Espionage and High Treason, not against the "fifth column," but against the revolutionaries accused of "actions hostile to the Republic." In order for the unions to hold assemblies they had to have authorization from the police. Censorship was reinforced, and, as already seen, not only for military news. Antilabor repression, which began a few days after the establishment of the Negrín government and lasted until the last day of the war, was carried out by different organizations:

1. The "regular" police, almost entirely Communist-run, since Zuga-zagoitia, minister of the interior, met with a chief of security, Colonel Antonio Ortega, and a chief of police of Barcelona, Colonel Ricardo Burillo, both of whom were Communists and changed or ignored his orders. Police action against members of POUM and the CNT was almost always carried out by police who came from Madrid where the delegate of Public Order was Communist. Among the members of the police force who were noted for persecuting members of POUM and the CNT was Julián Grimau, a former Republican, son of a police lieutenant, a member of the PCE during the war, and who later became famous.

2. The SIM (Service of Military Investigation), created by Prieto in August 1937, quickly fell into Communist hands and installed *chekas* in various cities. Remembering the Bolshevik persecution of their Russian cohorts, the Anarchists gave that name to those almost private prisons. In them people were tortured, imprisoned without the judges' ever knowing, "disappeared," or were held indefinitely. There were *chekas* for both men and women, Fascists and anti-Fascists, in the suburbs and downtown, for Spaniards and foreigners. Each *cheka* had a group of guards and interrogators as well as a team of investigators who decided upon imprisonment. There were 6,000 agents in all. No one knew for sure who gave the orders for imprisonment. But it was known that certain *chekas* had foreign interrogators.

3. The Soviet NKVD, with Orlov at the head, also included Spanish and foreign assistants.[24] We know that José Peñarroya of PSUC and formerly of the PCE, who helped investigate the death of Casanellas and who on his own came to the conclusion that he had been a victim of the Soviet police, did not leave the party because of it; instead, when Antonov-Osveenko asked for someone to help a Russian general who had come to Barcelona to organize local services of the NKVD, Peñarroya volunteered for the job. He was part of the Russian team throughout the war.[25] Rodríguez Salas, who lost his position as chief of Public Order in Barcelona following the events of May 1937, was not given another post and was not employed by Soviet agents. On the other hand, working with them against POUM was Victorio Sala, who had been representative of the Cenit Publishing Company in Barcelona and a member of BOC from 1931 to 1932.[26]

4. The special groups of investigation in the International Brigades acted only among members of the brigades and their reports were the cause of some 250 executions. Those who were executed—among whom there were probably some Fascist spies—had been accused not of disagreeing with orders or political positions but of being spies or saboteurs (the majority of them were Communists who could not stomach the position of the PCE or the repression used to implement it). So not only did they take their lives but their honor as revolutionaries as well.

5. Finally, there were more or less secret groups of members of the PCE and PSUC in cities and on fronts. They tried to uncover—especially in Communist-run units—members of POUM and the CNT. Once they did, they murdered them and then said that they had gone over to the enemy or were killed trying to do so. They too not only lost their lives but their honor as well.[27] Prieto's inability to prevent the repetition of those instances led the CNT to form a secret committee to try to save those who had been threatened by moving them from Communist units to others run by Socialists or the CNT where they would be safe. Prieto issued several transfer orders but they were rarely obeyed; in certain cases the orders were the cause of execution when they were received and the answer was always: "Not carried out because he deserted to the enemy."

Although those party groups did not have a great deal of direct participation in police functions, they nonetheless were indispensable to the efficient performance of the Madrid police and the NKVD who did not know the militants they were persecuting. They pointed out those who would become victims. It must not be forgotten that following the events of May 1937, *Treball,* the PSUC organ, printed an incitement to inform on anyone who "jeopardized the Republic."

Non-Communist authorities looked unfavorably upon this repression—its lack of respect for legal methods in particular. But since they did not dare do anything to prevent it—for fear that, if they spoke out against it, they would be accused of being accomplices or harborers of those pursued and would be sought after themselves—they preferred to ignore what was happening. Zugazagoitia told Jordi Arquer of POUM, who visited him secretly, that he had ordered some prisoners to be freed on six different occasions and the order was never obeyed, and he complained that not even the janitors of the ministry paid any attention to him. Arquer himself, who wanted to go to Madrid to investigate the whereabouts of some of his comrades who had been arrested in Barcelona and transferred to Madrid, was advised by Irujo, the minister of justice, not to go "because no one would be able to protect you there."[28]

That the fear of being put in the same boat as those who were pursued was not unfounded was proven by José Bergamín, the Catholic writer who always, even before the war, collaborated with the PCE, in a prologue to a PCE book against POUM; in it he said: "Not long ago, some French intellectuals sent an urgent telegram to the People's Government of Spain asking for measures which would guarantee the defense of the accused [POUM]. They were asking for legal formalities from a government which, practically speaking, makes excessive use of them and, in this particular case, we would say to an exaggerated degree. . . . The warning is clear to everyone: to take on the defense of men accused of such a crime is something which no free man or party can do. Their lawyer is the one who must do it before the tribunal. But to defend the offender as such, as traitor or spy, is not to defend the man; it is to defend the crime. And in the case of this war, it is to totally identify with the enemy." Thus, Bergamín warned those who wanted to help the pursued that they would be accused of the same crime as the men they were trying to help. Faced with that, many chose to keep quiet or shut their eyes.[29]

That complicity out of fear was seen most clearly in the case of POUM and Nin. Negrín gave the PCE free rein to organize repression of POUM and he did what Largo Caballero refused to do: dissolve this party (even though it continued its operations underground and did not stop its now illegal press). On June 16, 1937 members of the executive committee of POUM were arrested in Barcelona by a team of police specially brought in from Madrid. Andrés Nin, political secretary of POUM, disappeared. It was learned that he had been taken to a private prison of the PCE in Alcalá de Henares but that was the extent of the information. When Negrín, under pressure from three international labor commissions which came to ask about Nin, in turn queried the Communists, he was told that Nin had been kidnapped from prison by agents of the Gestapo. Negrín dared to repeat that cock-and-bull story to Azaña who did not believe it. When members of POUM wrote on walls in Barcelona: "Negrín Government—Where is Nin?" members of PSUC during the night wrote beneath it: "In Salamanca or Berlin." There was no other choice: a special judge had to be appointed, and when he had a police commissioner of Madrid arrested, other (Communist) policemen freed him with a false warrant, and Negrín did nothing despite the fact that Azaña ordered him to punish those guilty of making threats to a judge.

In October 1938 the trial of the Executive Committee of POUM was held before the special tribunal. Federica Montseny, Largo Caballero, Julián Zugazagoitia, and Luis Araquistáin came out as witnesses for the defense; Antonio Cordón, Virginio Llanos, and a few other Communists were witnesses for the accused. The tribunal, which a few days earlier Negrín had asked to give the death penalty to the accused "because the army demanded it," instead found the accusations against the prisoners to be false, saying that they had never been in Franco's service, that they were proven anti-Fascists. They were sentenced to fifteen years in prison for having rebelled against the government during the events of May 1937. The tribunal also dissolved POUM and its Juventudes (which the government had dissolved fifteen months before without waiting for any judicial decision). POUM was vindicated. *L'Humanité,* a few days before the trial, had praised the Soviet judges setting them as examples for the Spanish judges, who were more independent than their Russian colleagues and did not give in to the orders of the PCE.

Those were brutal orders. In a rally Ibárruri said that it was "better to condemn a hundred innocent persons than let one guilty person escape." In a plenary meeting of the Central Committee of the PCE in Valencia it was decided to "teach the people to hate and be merciless with both their apparent and disguised enemies . . . the agents [of Fascism] disguised as 'revolutionaries' who work within anti-Fascist organizations. . . . We must fight to put an end to the tolerance and lack of surveilance of certain proletarian organizations which establish bonds of coexistence with counterrevolutionary Trotskyism and POUM, regarding it as a faction of the labor movement. Trotskyism, on both a national and international level, however it be disguised, has shown itself to be a 'counterrevolutionary terrorist' organization at the service of international fascism."[30]

Neither La Pasionaria in her memoirs nor the *Historia del PCE* make any reference to the persecution of POUM or Nin's disappearance. But as time went on some Communists began to have doubts, especially when they themselves suffered persecution (although not as harsh as what Nin had gone through). In 1970 Claudín wrote:

> The repression of POUM, the despicable assassination of Andrés Nin, in particular, is the blackest page in the history of the Communist party of Spain, which became an accomplice to the crime committed by Stalin's secret service. We Spanish Communists were without a doubt alienated—as were Communists throughout the world at the time and many years later as well—by the monstrous lies fabricated by Moscow. But that does not clear us of our historic responsibility. It has been 14 years since the twentieth congress (of the Soviet Communist party), and the PCE has yet to undergo self-criticism nor has it cooperated in helping to clarify those events. Even though current leaders of the PCE cannot add much to what we already know—and this seems fairly likely—they could require the Soviet Communist party to divulge information that only *it* possesses. The case of Nin belongs to the history of Spain, not just that of Russia.[31]

Arthur G. London wrote upon his release from many years of imprisonment in Czechoslovakia where he was tortured by Stalinists from his own country: "The influence of Stalinism made POUM face the consequences [of May 1937] on a totally disproportianate level. The presence of Soviet agents . . . caused such painful and tragic episodes for the labor movement as the disappearance and death of Andreu Nin who clearly must be rehabilitated as a labor militant. . . . It is obvious that we Communists who fought and died for Spain's freedom incurred a debt with the labor movement and anti-Fascist forces in general: that of reestablishing a number of truths which were disguised at the time. Nin was not an agent of the Gestapo or of Franco, and what should have been a discussion, albeit a difficult and rigorous one, became an authentic 'witch hunt' and Stalinism was to blame."[32]

Both authors failed to point out a fact which profoundly influenced the PCE: that repression and the murder of Nin and many others could not have occurred nor could the NKVD have been able to be so efficient if it were not for the collaboration of the party, its leaders, and its members. This was clear to a Communist historian who tried to let bygones be bygones when he wrote, "[Nin], who for so many years had devoted himself to the defamation of Russia and the policy of Popular Front . . . was perhaps a victim of Stalinism . . . but in the current state of investigations not even that vast appraisal can be supported; at any rate one thing is clear: the ignorance of Spain's Communist ministers."[33] More sincere was a female member of PSUC who, when she was older and looked back on the mood of that period—a mood created by party propaganda and by the training given its members—admitted: "If we militants [of PSUC] had been asked if Andreu Nin, 'leader of the Trotskyite-Fascist putsch' should be put to death, we would have said yes."[34] Even Santiago Carrillo admitted in 1974 in the film *Les Deux Mémoires,* that POUM "was not a party of provocateurs," but "a current in the revolutionary movement."

Finally, another kind of repression must be cited: by nonpolice authorities—although occasionally with the aid of police—against followers of Largo Caballero. After allowing him to give a lecture he was told to remain in his house, and they even tried to remove him from his position as representative of the Fundación Cesáreo del Cerro on the board of the Bank of Spain, but the director of this body, Lluís Nicolau d'Olwer, rejected that demand. Finally on October 17, ignoring orders from the government, Caballero went to Madrid and in the Pardiñas Theater (which was connected by loudspeakers to three other theaters) he explained his position and the reasons why he was no longer in power.[35] The government immediately expelled—at times *manu militari*—the editors and writers of Madrid's *Claridad* and Valencia's *Adelante* and *Correspondencia,* replacing them with supporters of Negrín.[36] A witness of the period admitted: "It is true that the Communists had their own parallel police organs in Spain, superimposed upon the organs of the state. That made relations with the other organizations difficult. Coalition policies become arduous if the whole is replaced by the part, particularly in police action, the most delicate of all human activities, where arbitrariness and error entail the gravest consequences."[37] How did it happen that a party—which in July 1936 played no more prominent a role than other labor organizations, which barely had 2.5 percent of organized workers (according to their own figures), which lost its stronghold in Seville, and which was going against the current among the workers—was able to use some means of action which under other circumstance would not have been tolerated?

Inflation of the PCE

The PCE went from 10,000, 30,000, or 102,000 members in July 1936 to 250,000 on the eve of the events of May 1937. PSUC went from 6,000 (or less) to 45,000 prior to the barricades of May. The Basque Communist party during the same period went from 3,000 to 22,000 members. So in all, the Communists had some 300,000 members at their peak. That was more than the PSOE, all the Republican parties, or the FAI and Juventudes Libertarias; but, of course, less than the CNT which must have had about two million members during the same period. There are no membership statistics for the period following May 1937; we might suppose that the CNT lost members, the UGT increased in membership, the PSOE also decreased, and the PCE grew even larger.[38]

According to a report Díaz presented to the central committee in March 1937, members of the party were categorized according to social background in the following way: 87,600 industrial workers; 62,250 agricultural workers; 76,700 peasants; 15,485 from the middle class; 7,045 intellectuals; and 19,300 women. The category of peasants included agricultural landlords, and industrial workers included technicians and employees. "It turns out that the number of members considered as workers totals close to 150,000, while the figure for members not connected with production nears 120,000."[39] These statistics are less revealing than the quotes of the period and the recollections of people who lived through those times, who knew that the PCE and even PSUC were middle-class parties; a substitute for the corpse-like Republican parties. This is confirmed by the following figures. In Madrid, where the PCE scored its maximum increase, only 10,160 of the 63,426 members were unionized, at a time when everyone wanted to have a union card in their pocket.

It must be kept in mind that in July of 1936 the percentage of organized workers was very high. There was little clientele available in the working class. Without a doubt the PCE attracted nonorganized workers and particularly young workers who, in the heat of the war, began to take an interest in politics. But, above all, it attracted the middle class, and not just those who felt disappointed by Republican parties, but those who had been left political orphans because of the defeat of the right wing at the beginning of the uprising. "The Republican middle class, surprised by the moderate tone of the Communist propaganda and impressed by the unity and realism of that party, greatly increased their numbers. . . . Both army officers and functionaries, who had never glanced through a pamphlet of Marxist propaganda, became Communists, some deliberately, others out of moral weakness, as well as those who were inspired by the enthusiasm which moved the Communist organization."[40]

A Canadian Communist recalled: "In Murcia and other places I saw that our poster and leaflets were seeking the membership of shopkeepers on the promise of absolute support of private property."[41] An American journalist who at the time was very close to the Communist International said: "The generals and bourgeois politicians as well as many peasants, all of whom approve of the policy of the Communist party regarding the protection of small property, have joined its ranks. I believe that those individuals have influence and are influenced. But in essence their recent political affiliation reflects their desperation over the loss of the old social system as well as their hope to salvage some part of it."[42] A friend of Negrín differed: "I tried to find out what their [the functionaries in the ministries] opinion was. I was surprised to learn that the majority were ambitious young people from the upper middle class. Unlike those of us in Madrid who joined the party because we saw it as the party of revolutionary workers, they joined because it was for them the same as joining the strongest group and sharing its disciplined power. They had skipped the rung of humanistic socialism; they were efficient and implacable."[43]

The intellectuals were very spoiled by the party. It took care of evacuating them, it found them lodging in Valencia and Catalonia, it helped them find jobs in many periodicals financed by the Ministry of Public Education (of which *Hora de España* was the best), and it maneuvered them in its Associations of Anti-Fascist Intellectuals. When the World Congress of Writers (one of Münzenberg's creations) was held in Madrid and Barcelona (with a final session in Paris), not one of the hundreds of Spaniards who participated protested the disppearance of an intellectual like Nin or the death of intellectuals like Landau or Bernieri. They did not even protest the fact that Spain was barely mentioned, and most of the conference was spent attacking André Gide who had been a fellow traveler and who, upon his return from the USSR, denounced what later would be called the "personality cult."[44]

In addition to shopkeepers and professionals, the PCE attracted many career army men. One of them wrote: "It cannot be denied that the Communists were masters in the art of propaganda. . . . It consisted mainly of saying that only they could defeat Franco and establish republican legality. To accomplish this it was necessary to organize an efficient and disciplined army. . . . Some professional military fell into the trap and quite a few, enthused by the communist propaganda, in a rash moment joined the party."[45] If these quotes do not suffice, here is another: "The Communist party today is, in the first place, the party of administrative and military personnel, in second place the party of the petite bourgeoisie and of certain well-to-do peasant groups, in third place the party of public employees, and only in fourth place the party of the workers."[46] Speaking of PSUC, the same observer pointed out: "Not many industrial workers are members of PSUC, nonetheless it has 46,000 members, the majority of whom are state or private employees, shopkeepers, merchants, officials, members of police forces, intellectuals, and there are a certain number of peasants."

In retrospect, Claudín verified: "Many members of the petite bourgeoisie joined the ranks of the PCE attracted by the renown the party had achieved as the defender of order, legality, and small property owners. And a large contingent of youths, still not affiliated with unions and traditional labor organizations, joined the PCE, or came under its control via the JSU. These youths were drawn by the party's militant virtues and by a simplified ideology in which revolution is identified with anti-Fascism mixed with patriotism."[47] The novelist Juan Agustín Goytisolo would recall that his father "leaned more toward the Right, but joined PSUC to defend himself against Anarchists who wanted to take over the factory where he was an engineer."[48]

Finally, a sentimental reference which clearly shows that what the PCE was seeking and managed to achieve was due to the efforts of the secretary of the Federación Campesina de Valencia (Peasant Federation of Valencia), organized by the PCE under the sponsorship of the Minister of Agriculture, Uribe, to fight against collectivities. He received the help of orange growers who, prior to the war, had formed the rank and file of the Derecha Regional Valenciana (Valencia Regional Right Wing) whose representative, Luis Lucía, was the only rightist in Parliament during the Civil War. At a meeting of its central committee, Mateu related: "There is so much sympathy for us in the countryside of Valencia that hundreds and thousands of peasants would join our party if we let them. These are peasants, many of whom believed and still believe in God, praying and secretly beating their breasts, who love the party as if it were something sacred. When we tell them not to confuse the Federación Provincial Campesina with the party and that one can be Communist even without the identification card of our organization simply by working for its policy, they respond: 'The Communist party is our party.' Comrades, they speak these words with such emotion."[49]

Nor should the appeal of Russian aid be forgotten. "Without it, the propaganda of the Communist party would have been less successful." Togliatti had foreseen it when he told Hernández that "Russian aid will be good not only for the Republican army, but also for the Communist party."[50] By changing its positions the party also changed its composition. It continued to serve the same supreme interest—the defense of the USSR—but to do so it had to serve other local interests and replace the working class with the middle class as its main component. That inevitably created internal tension.

Doubts and Fissures

The American writer Lillian Hellman visited Madrid during the Civil War. Otto Katz, Münzenberg's aide, was her guide. At the ruins of University City, Otto, panting, sat down and explained: "I've been sick for years. I'm an old man at forty." Hellman replied: "It must be hard to be a Communist." He said: "Yes. Especially here." And then, after explaining to her that he had been a Communist since his youth, he said: "Don't get me wrong. I owe [the party] more than it owes me. If I've been happy, it's been because of it. Whatever happens, I am grateful to it." To conclude this anecdote, Hellman said: "When I read the news of his execution in Prague in 1952, I recalled the passion with which he spoke that night and I hoped that it sustained him during his imprisonment and on the day he died."[51]

That same conversation could have taken place with many Communists during the Civil War, especially those, like Otto Katz, who had been in the party since adolescence. What they saw, read, and heard could not help but arouse suspicions in at least a few of them. These suspicions were occasionally expressed during the war. But the majority of those who were suspicious said nothing. That is why José Díaz could say: "In our country today there is more order and discipline than ever before. Our party, which from the very beginning proclaimed the need for republican discipline and order, recognizes the achievements made in this direction." And because he knew that what he was saying was more apparent than real, he added: "The government must give proof of relentless energy to crush all the enemies of the people."[52]

The party really did not feel quite secure yet. Its new members had never been in contact with workers. Díaz, in a plenary session of the central committee in Valencia in March 1937, complained that the party was cut off from the masses. For the purpose of reaching the masses, the only idea that Díaz came up with was, in the middle of the war, to request elections for a new parliament as well as municipal elections. The party had already had a great deal of power, and he hoped that the elections would give it complete power. Two months later Largo Caballero was replaced and the PCE got almost everything it wanted without need for elections; the matter was never brought up again.[53]

The PCE itself had doubts about the wisdom of the stance we could call "middle class." Madrid's *Mundo Obrero,* which was under less control since the executive committee was in Barcelona, slipped in an article which said: "One cannot say, as a newspaper does, that the only solution to our war is for Spain not to be Fascist or Communist because France wants it what way. . . . The Spanish people will be victorious in their opposition to capitalism." Díaz wrote an immediate reply in the executive committee's organ, *Frente Rojo,* of Barcelona: "To say that the only solution to our war is for Spain not to be Fascist or Communist is entirely accurate and corresponds precisely with our party's position. . . . To say that the Spanish people will be victorious in their opposition to capitalism neither corresponds to the situation or the policy of our party and the Communist International."[54]

By then the party had already launched its slogan of its fight for a "new kind of republic, one with deep social content,"[55] destined to appease the old members who were alarmed by the party line which they believed made excessive concessions. There was a time when they thought it was a trick to anesthetize the adversaries as they did with the Popular Front, as they would do later with the Nazi-Soviet pact, and are doing even today with Euro-Communism. But when they saw this policy resulted in things they thought the party could never do, they started to get nervous and, in cells or in private conversations, they expressed their doubts which must have been serious enough for the general mood to be felt by the bureau and to justify printing Díaz's reply to *Mundo Obrero* in its entirety in the twenty-seventh issue of 1938 of *Correspondance Internationale,* dedicated to Spain. The "new kind of republic" had to prevent from happening what Díaz denounced: "If it is true that today we are witnessing a magnificent awakening of the spirit of the people, it is also true that in that area there still exist weakness, black spots, and dangerous tendencies which must be counteracted and corrected. The past has not yet entirely disappeared and occasionally bad things from the past resurface in new and unexpected forms which can only do us harm because they tend to diminish the political activity of the masses and to place one part or another of the state outside of the people's control."[56]

There was also discontent in PSUC and the Catalonian UGT. Certain members of the UGT would have wanted their organization to have a greater role in the collectivizations, but they did not want these to disappear. For this reason in a plenary meeting of the Central Committee of PSUC in January 1938 Comorera had to say: "Unions cannot be separated from the economic leadership of the nation. In the first place, the government does not yet have an economic mechanism sufficiently well established to take on the responsibility by itself. On the other hand, Catalonia is a country of firmly rooted union tradition. We cannot rush or force the issue. Today it is absolutely necessary for trade unions to intervene in the economic leadership of the country."

The PSUC never became really homogeneous. It presented a facade of a unified party but there was inside fighting between the members of the different parties which merged in July 1936. A leader of Spanish Socialist origin related that in the first congress of PSUC, members of the former PCC "planned to gain control of the military secretariat and other important positions in the executive committee." Gerö, the Communist International's "instructor," maneuvered to calm people's emotions since "that was the closest they ever came to splitting apart." Here we have a clear case of old Communists clinging to their old ideas, not wanting to give their key positions to their present allies who followed the PCE line, although some (Estivill, Víctor Colomer, Cussó, Manuel Culebra, and A. García Cortada) were reluctant. There were attempts on the lives of those internal opponents. The source of this information, the military secretary of PSUC, is certain that he was shot at while sleeping in his office at the Hotel Colón; it was later reported that a gun which was being cleaned accidentally went off.[57]

Tension was also apparent in the JSU. Rafael Fernández, secretary of the Asturian chapter of the JSU, resigned from the national committee and signed a pact with Juventudes Libertarias; José Gregorio, secretary of the Valencian JSU, also resigned. Carrillo said that "they let themselves be manipulated by the Trotskyites." In the elections of the UGT in Asturias, the Communists received 12,000 votes and Caballero's faction got 87,000. There was much discontent when the Executive Committee of the JSU decided to abandon Marxism and in a rally in Valencia Carrillo said: "Our organization is neither Socialist nor Communist; the JSU is not Marxist." By then the JSU was the hub of an Alianza Nacional de la Juventud with youth groups from the skeletal Republican parties and FUE. The Alianza opposed the Frente de la Juventud Revolucionaria which was organized by Juventudes Libertarias and the JCI of POUM.[58] In any event, although some fissures appeared in the monolithic party, they were not serious enough to break it apart.

To the Conquest of the PSOE

The Socialist Left had allowed the Communist party to take over Juventudes Socialistas before the war; then the same happened to the Federación Catalana of the PSOE (which was absorbed into PSUC) and the UGT of Catalonia which was controlled by the Communists through PSUC; later, it was the war commissariat, thanks to the complicity of Álvarez del Vayo with the PCE; finally it lost the government. In losing the government it was left with just the UGT of which Largo Caballero was still secretary general with a majority of the national committee and the executive committee in the hands of the leftists.

The Executive Committee of the UGT had declared in May 1937 that it would not support any government which was not presided by Largo Caballero and in which he did not act as minister of war. Although this provided a great deal of pressure, it was not enough because Prieto and the Communists were hoping that if another government, different from the one desired by the UGT, was formed, the UGT would end up falling into their hands. The day after Negrín's government was constituted, the National Committee of the UGT met, and the Federations of Education, Graphic Arts, Oil, and Construction which were headed by followers of Prieto, criticized the executive committee and requested a special session to discuss the UGT's position during the crisis. In a six-hour report to the executive committee, Largo Caballero had said that the committee was a product of the last congress which met in 1933 and that the executive committee had always had the power to set the UGT's position in the event of a crisis in the government, and that it was the executive committee which in September 1936 had authorized Largo Caballero to form a government, to no one's objection, and therefore, the executive committee's mission still was to decide whether the UGT would support Negrín. The same was true of the executive committee of the PSOE which was elected in the congress of 1932 and in which Prieto held the majority.

These arguments, of a more administrative than political nature, were repeated in the plenary meeting of the national committee of the UGT of May 28, 1937, but in vain. A vote of 24 to 14 condemned the conduct of the executive committee during the crisis and a delegation of the national committee visited Negrín to offer him the backing of the UGT. On May 30 the executive committee resigned but the national committee did not accept the resignation.

Largo Caballero got carried away by his administrative ability. He found out that some of the 24 federations which had voted against him had not paid all their union fees, several of them having been remiss since 1933. In accordance with statutes, the executive committee suspended those federations who were behind in payment and in reaction to that the faction hostile to Largo Caballero requested a meeting of the national committee. The executive committee announced that for the time being the national committee would not meet. On October 1 the delegates of the federations supporting Prieto appeared at executive headquarters in Valencia, but they were denied entry. Then they went to the police, which had all doubtless been planned. The police claimed that the minister of the interior had authorized the meeting. On the steps of the building the delegates of the federations supporting Prieto along with Pretel, the UGT's treasurer, agreed to form a national committee and appoint a new executive committee with Ramón González Peña as president. José Rodríguez Vega was named secretary (he was a former founder of the PCE who went back to being a socialist). Felipe Pretel stayed on in his position. Amaro del Rosal, a Communist at the time, Daniel Anguiano (founder of the PCOE), and several followers of Prieto and Negrín rounded out the executive committee which Caballero called seditious. The committee declared its support for the Negrín government and offered to negotiate a pact with the CNT.

The liaison committee of the PSOE-PCE recognized the new executive committee. Censorship prevented supporters of Caballero from printing any comment. The minister of communications ordered the post office to deliver all the UGT's mail to the "staircase" executive committee, and the Bank of Spain refused to honor checks signed by Caballero's executive committee. The government agreed to recognize the "staircase" executive committee. Two delegates sent by the International Trade Union Federation, Sir Walter Citrine and Léon Jouhaux, were no longer able—nor did they try—to do anything. They were ideologically closer to Prieto than to Caballero but shared Caballero's mistrust of the Communists. Nevertheless, Jouhaux could not displease them because there were many Communists who had become members of his own French CGT when the Communist CGTU joined it in 1935.

At a meeting of the two executive committees and the national committee—but without Caballero—Jouhaux proposed the formation of an executive committee made up of members of the two rival factions. This was done, with González Peña as president, Rodríguez Vega as secretary, and also included Hernández Zancajo, Díaz Alor, and Pascual Tomás, all followers of Caballero. Largo Caballero did not recognize this new executive committee. That is how the UGT fell into the hands of Prieto's men. Rodríguez Vega, who apparently had returned to his first love, collaborated very actively with the Communists who, in a few months, had won key positions in UGT unions.[59] Now that the UGT was neutralized, the PCE could apply pressure to capture the PSOE. So far it had made several proposals for a merger, but it got nothing more than promises in return. One of the ways Prieto used to win the (relative) confidence of the Communists was to affirm his approval of the merger at precisely the time when Largo Caballero was beginning to become wary of it.

Prieto soon found himself in trouble. One night the Soviet ambassador appeared at the Ministry of Defense and said that some material which Valencia was impatiently awaiting had already left the Russian ports. Two days later he asked Prieto to propose the merger of the two parties. Prieto said: "I refused, and Gaikins repeated his plea almost threateningly. He was tenacious in his persistence insinuating that he was carrying out instructions from Moscow and that my stance would be either rewarded or punished there. He did not persuade me. In a third visit, and without making any mention whatsoever of that conversation, Gaikins told me that the long-awaited material which had been offered us would not be shipped out. There was the punishment."[60]

Lamoneda was to Prieto what del Vayo had been to Largo Caballero. He was secretary of the executive committee of the PSOE and, indeed, ran the party. Thanks to him, in June 1937 a national committee of coordination of both the Communist and Socialist parties was formed. The PSOE sent González Peña, Vidarte, Lamoneda, and Cordero to this committee; the PCE sent Díaz, Ibárruri, Cabo Giorla, and Checa. Part of its program was pressuring the Second and Third Internationals for common action (which was precisely what the Communist International had been after for quite a while and hoped to get with the lure of aid to the Republic).[61]

Only one of the federations of the PSOE, the Valencian, refused to observe the rules set up by the executive committee regarding the local liaison committees, and said that it would accept them when Hernández and Ibárruri apologized for their slander of Caballero. Minister of the Interior Zugazagoitia ordered the immediate seizure of the Valencian federation's headquarters. In Jaén, on the other hand, things moved forward: a Partido Socialista Unificado (United Socialist party) was formed and the executive committee of the PSOE had to expel the impatient socialists from Jaén.[62] But toward the end of October the PSOE ended discussions of unity between Socialists and Communists, saying that "such an inflexible framework was more appropriate for the Francoists than for a Republican Spain."[63] What happened between August and October? It looked like the Communists had gone too far too soon. Prieto wanted to stop them in their tracks. And naturally to do this he needed the PSOE. He realized that in the party rank and file, as in that of the UGT, there was serious discontent over so much collaboration with the same Communists who, in every other area, were pulling the rug from beneath the Socialists' feet.[64]

Tension in the Army

The line broke not at its weakest point but at its strongest: the army. As we have seen, Largo Caballero gave his support to the Communists in the beginning since, like them, he thought that it was necessary to form a regular army. But later he realized that they were taking advantage of that support not only to create units but also to try to gain some influence in military policy, run the Ministry of War, and give orders in the army through the commissariat and the International Brigades, which were established in opposition to the opinion of the minister of war and which in practice were always autonomous and more dependent on the party than on the government, even though the latter financed them.[65] When Madrid was under threat the government concentrated forces in the capital, but it did not send the International Brigades. That order came from the PCE.[66]

When Caballero realized that the PCE wanted to control the army and had a run-in with it over the matter concerning General Asensio, he began to dismantle the Communist machine from the Ministry of War, introduced changes in the commissariat, and transferred military leaders who served the PCE. That was one of the reasons why they decided to eliminate him. Communist propaganda seemed to indicate that all the battles which had been won were waged by Communist-controlled units and those which had been lost were waged by anarchistic "tribes." It even indicated that members of POUM's military units which had already been dissolved, were to be blamed for any defeat.[67]

The ascendancy of the Communists in the army was not due solely to their influence over the authorities or the ministry; rather it reflected two facts which their adversaries tended to ignore. On the one hand, the Communist units received the larger contingents of recruits and, on the other, the Communist units were efficient and disciplined—in the Spanish context—and full of fighting spirit as well. This was not because the Communists wanted to win the war or because the units of the CNT, Socialists, or those simply run by professionals without a party did not want to. After all was said and done, even though it might be because everyone would be risking their necks if Franco won, everyone was interested in victory, and not only because of the ideological motives, all of which were equally intense. So then, it was not a hypothetical greater degree of anti-Fascism that gave the Communists the advantage. It was their greater discipline and the fact that they were more powerful, for the Communist units received the best of Russian arms. The Communist units were sent on all the delicate operations. This resulted in a high percentage of casualties, but these were recruits and not necessarily Communists. The percentage of Communist casualties was neither smaller nor larger than that of any other organization. Only La Pasionaria cited more Communists than any other party or trade union when she published a list of commissars killed and chose to make a point of it.[68] Another reason for the advantage of the Communists was that many professional military men joined the party or agreed to follow its orders.

The party did not learn from the lesson provided by the comparison between professional soldiers and its militants. That lesson would have completely shot full of holes the thesis that war could only be won with a regular army. The Communists who headed military units turned out to be as efficient (if not more) as the professionals. No "hero" cropped up among the professionals, while among the militants of all organizations there were good leaders whom propaganda made sure to transform into mythical figures. Once removed from that pedestal, Líster, Durán, Modesto, El Campesino, Tagüeña—like Durruti, Mera, Rovira, and so many others—still stood as good leaders. That did not stop the recruits from despising some of those names—Líster and El Campesino, in particular—because of the brutal means they used to maintain discipline and efficiency in their units. Neither Líster nor El Campesino, in their respective memoirs, speak of their methods, which were common knowledge and doubtless responded to some temperamental shortcoming more than to necessity, since nothing to that effect was mentioned regarding Durán and Tagüeña whose units were equally efficient.

> Possessing many defects as well as attributes, Modesto, the former carpenter, was a true military leader and not a decorative figure prefabricated by propaganda. Furthermore, he had the support of the leaders of the Communist party who, because of his discipline, considered him the most trustworthy military militant. . . . He was not a man who knew how to attract those who had to work with him. He was sarcastic, not very sincere, despotic, and at times brutal. . . . Líster had a great deal of strength and vitality and a lively intellect. He was affable and had many fine human qualities and was a loyal friend. The Communist party was about to dismiss Líster from the army during the first months of the war due to the tumultuous way in which the new leader would enjoy life whenever combat would allow it. His leadership qualities were most influential in his military career.[69]

The party sent some of its second-rank leaders to the front, as did other organizations, but publicized it to a greater degree. Of them all it said that "they were first to advance and last to retreat," a slogan borrowed from the French Foreign Legion no less.[70] Its persistence in advocating a regular army prevented the PCE from defending a military policy implicit not only in the history of the Spanish people's fighting but also in the Soviet model, which is to say, a war sustained or aided by guerrillas. There were none to speak of aside from some which cropped up in Galicia, Asturias, and other places, made up of fugitives from Franco's massacres and whose objective was to join the Republican army. The other organizations share the responsibility for this deficiency with the PCE.

There were high-quality military men who joined the PCE or assisted it. But a good number of the professionals who participated in the PCE did so for shameful reasons, and the PCE used those reasons to attract those men to it. We have already seen how Miaja and Rojo managed to sweep under the carpet the fact that they had belonged to UME thanks to their submission to the PCE. There was another revealing case—that we know of at least—regarding General Sebastián Pozas. He had been director of the Civil Guard under the Republic. One sample of how he was regarded by his fellow officers: shortly after the elections of February 16, 1936 General Franco offered to deposit a sum of money abroad for him if he supported a "national government" which Franco and others were planning to establish to prevent the Popular Front from assuming power. Giral appointed him minister of the interior in July 1936. During his term in the Center front he was won over by the Communists and later, as head of the Aragon front, ended up joining PSUC. This caused Companys to protest to Azaña and Azaña to Negrín, but nothing came of it. Azaña noted in his diary in July 1937: "Yesterday I received a letter from Companys. . . . He said that he had sent two letters to the president of the council [Negrín], the first dealing with the arrest and trial of Nin and others from POUM, and the second with the fact that General Pozas, the chief of the General Staff Cordon, Llanos, the political commissar general of Catalonia, and police chief Burillo had attended the congress of PSUC." One of the causes of the violence of May 1937 was the fact that PSUC insisted on prohibiting the political affiliation of policemen, and yet scarcely two months after, the chief of police of Barcelona publicly declared himself a Communist.[71]

Hernández said the PCE recruited 50,000 new members in the army within three months because "on the front, in the barracks, hospitals, military staffs, our delegates were offering promotions in exchange for taking the party's or Juventudes' card. Whoever was reluctant knew that he was a candidate for the front line in special units and that he was in danger of losing his stripes."[72] High-ranking Communist posts proliferated. At the end of 1938 in the South-Central zone three of the four army corps were Communist-run. They controlled the commissariat almost totally and they were becoming more and more numerous in SIM, which they transformed from an intelligence service to a political police. Imitating the USSR, the Communists in SIM created concentration camps (Omells and others). The International Brigades were run by Communists with some secondary posts in the hands of Socialists.

The Communists in the Ministry of Defense had influence over dismissals and appointments and promotions; they refused to lend the support of their units and even planes which they controlled to the operations in charge of units of another tendency (especially in Aragon prior to July 1937). They also paralyzed operations of great importance that did not suit them (or Moscow), such as the Extremadura offensive planned by Caballero, and they imposed other offensives advised by the Russians (such as those of Brunete and the Ebro), despite the fact that they were not approved by the Spanish military. For all this they had not only the weight of the posts which they controlled but also—and more importantly—the possibility of opening or closing the spigot of shipment of Soviet arms.[73] The Communist contribution to the war effort was considerable, although it does not necesarily mean that it was greater than that of other organizations. But the methods employed, their underlying goals, and utilization of the effort for the benefit of the party and Soviet diplomacy could not be concealed for very long: only until Prieto himself, who had made all that possible, got fed up, just as his rival Largo Caballero had before him.

Elimination of Prieto

Prieto probably began to become aware of the mess he had gotten himself into shortly after taking over the Ministry of Defense when, on May 31, 1937 the Germans shelled the city of Almería in retaliation for two bombs dropped on their warship *Deutschland* off Ibiza. Álvarez del Vayo proposed bringing the matter before the Council of the League of Nations, but he did not persist when Litvinov, Russian commissar of external affairs, advised him not to do so. As for Prieto, he suggested bombarding the German fleet in the Mediterranean. Negrín said that Azaña would have to be consulted, which gave the Communist ministers time to inform Togliatti, who ran to see the Soviet advisors. They radioed "home," as they called Moscow. Moscow answered advising not to take the slightest risk of starting a general war. If Prieto did not give in, their advice was to go so far as to assassinate him to obstruct his plan. Azaña and Negrín were opposed and the matter went no further.[74] But it was a lesson to Prieto. He received many more which, as time went on, provided him with material for two pamphlets and numerous articles.[75]

Prieto began to act on his own the same way Largo Caballero had a year before. In November he dismissed 250 Communist political commissars[76] and demanded the resignation of the head of the comisariat, Álvarez del Vayo, for he realized, as Caballero had, that he was a Communist agent. The Communists succeeded in filling the position with a flexible Republican, Ossorio Tafall.[77] Russian aid was also a source of exasperation for Prieto. It was used, as already indicated, to try to force him to accept, among other things, the merger of the two parties. If at least it had been enough to win the war and had arrived on time . . . But no, it arrived piecemeal.[78] Sánchez-Albornoz, ambassador of the Republic, gathered some revealing facts about it:

> I've heard Gordón Ordás [Republican ambassador to Mexico] refer to the adventures surrounding his purchase of American airplanes for the government of the Republic in the beginning of the Civil War and how with

great zeal and difficulty he managed to have them flown to Europe toward their destination of Archangel. Gordón ended his story saying that the planes did not make it to Spain; the Russians kept them and sent on an equal number of old machines.

I heard from Giral that the Russian war material which, already paid for, slowly began to arrive in Spanish Republican ports, was not unloaded if the government did not agree beforehand to let Communists fill important police and military posts.

And I heard [Jiménez de] Asúa say that through German Socialists in Prague he became familiar with the negotiations between Stalin's and Hitler's governments which resulted in new dangers for the Spanish Republic. The Negrín government never believed Asúa.[79]

Then came the battle of Teruel, at the end of 1937. After two months of fighting, the Republican army had to abandon the city which it had taken in a surprise maneuver. The PCE ordered El Campesino to stay in the main square as much as possible to win prestige for one of its units and to show that Prieto had renounced victory. When he no longer belonged to the party, El Campesino maintained that the party, fearful that if Teruel was saved it would not be able to get rid of Prieto, decided to sacrifice Teruel to ruin Prieto.[80] He said that the russian General Grigorevich did not permit the arrival of sufficient ammunition to Teruel for it to defend itself.

After Teruel fell, the PCE then dared to attack Prieto. On February 20 the Francoists entered Teruel; on February 24 Hernández, who was in charge of getting Prieto just as he had done with Caballero, wrote an article in *Frente Rojo* denouncing the "defeatists." Stepanov had returned shortly before from a visit to Moscow. He told the political bureau that the USSR was preparing great shipments of arms, but first it was necessary to get rid of Prieto and then to embark on a policy of undying resistance.[81] The basis of the attack against Prieto was the accusation that he was a defeatist. It was true that he had shown himself to be a pessimist. Seeing the state of affairs in the military and knowing all the details of Soviet "aid," he understood that the war could not be won and leaned toward seeking mediation.

"Ever since the beginning of his service as minister of defense, Indalecio Prieto showed the same obsession that had characterized his predecessor's performance in the ministry: the destruction of the influence of the Communist party, even at the cost of diminishing the fighting spirit and effectiveness of the army's and rearguard's resistance. He did not miss a chance to interfere with military chiefs, especially if they were Communist."[82] Following this, Ibárruri showed the true colors of the old tactic of sectarianism: "The honest military leaders expressed their displeasure more than once" over the measures taken by Prieto. Those who did not were not being "honest."

The advance of Franco's troops along the Aragon front in March 1938 aided the campaign. By that time the government had already moved to Barcelona. Hernández's articles against Prieto, signed "Juan Ventura," appeared one after another. Negrín gathered the executive committee of the PSOE in his home and said that they could not disregard the Communists because of their efficiency, because of the USSR, and because they were the only ones outside Spain who were helping the Republic. But he added that he would not continue as president of the Council if Prieto was not in the Ministry of Defense.[83]

The situation was insane. One minister would publicly attack another. The colleague of the minister under fire who controlled censorship allowed the attacks to be printed. And a party that was in the government staged a demonstration along the Diagonal in Barcelona to Pedralbes Palace at a time when Azaña was meeting with the Council of Ministers there. "Down with the capitulating ministers!" "Get rid of the minister of defense!" "Long Live Negrín!" were the slogans being shouted. Azaña received thousands of telegrams from the fronts calling for Prieto's resignation. Of course, they were sent by Communists following party instructions. Negrín, who knew in advance about the demonstration, went out to talk with La Pasionaria who was at the head of it, and promised her that he would not tolerate the slightest gesture of capitulation.[84] Prieto told the Council that, given the situation on the Eastern front, he could not resign because that would be desertion, but that he would no longer have anything to do with Hernández.

That demonstration took place on March 16. On March 28 Negrín spoke out against the "defeatists" on the radio (echoing the Communist party's stance) and announced the recruitment of 100,000 volunteers (a campaign that did not succeed). Between those two dates Barcelona was under constant bombardment. The CNT sent a delegation to talk with Prieto. If he resigned, the confederate units would be at a greater disadvantage regarding the Communists. They feared a wave of terror which would force them to arm themselves. Prieto explained to them that he intended to resign because he no longer gave the orders in his ministry nor could he prevent the assassination of Socialists and CNT members at the hands of the Communists. He added that Negrín had become a prisoner of the Communists. The Russian arms were of poor quality (the ones sent to Communist divisions were good, and the ones which divisions of other tendencies got were mediocre). The CNT offered to back Prieto but the minister persisted in his determination to resign.[85]

On March 30 Zugazagoitia, up to that time one of Prieto's underlings, went to see him and told him, "The president of the Council called me and asked if you would be very angry if they took you out of the Ministry of Defense, and I went ahead and told him that you would not be. Was I right?" Prieto assured him he would not be angry and he wrote Negrín to this effect and refused another position as minister (of public works!). The Executive Committee of the PSOE adopted the following resolution: "Prieto's exit is almost an insult, but in the face of the present political situation we can do nothing but accept that sacrifice." On April 6 Negrín formed a new government. Entering it were the UGT of the "staircase," with González Peña, and the CNT with Segundo Blanco who replaced Hernández in public education. Hernández went on to be head of the South-Central Commissariat. Uribe was left in agriculture. There was a Socialist in the interior, Paulino Gómez. Negrín took the Ministry of Defense.

The Government of Victory of the year before had not achieved a single lasting victory. Negrín called this restricted cabinet a "war government." The undersecretaries of defense that Negrín appointed were Communist: Cordón in the army; Núñez Maza in the air force; Hidalgo de Cisneros, chief of the air force; Prados, chief of staff of the navy; Marcial Fernández, general director of Carabineros. In Catalonia, Pozas, an incompetent, was replaced by Coronel Juan Perea. The commissar was a new Communist, Ignacio Mantecón, who had distinguished himself in Aragon. Zugazagoitia was named secretary general of the Ministry of Defense. A few months later he complained that "when I want to find out something about the war, I have to buy a newspaper or ask a friend." The Communist Cuevas was appointed general head of security. On April 6 the political bureau of the PCE "approved without reservation the change which had taken place as a result of which the government of the Republic fully assumes the nature of a war government and National Union," and the bureau pointed out that "the Communist party of Spain has made every effort and sacrifice necessary for the formation of the present government." Actually those who had been sacrificed were the Socialists, because the second Negrín government was a Communist government with only one minister from the PCE. On April 15, ten days after the war government was formed, the Republican zone was cut in two when Franco's troops arrived at Vinaroz on the Mediterranean. Now it was the Generalidad's turn to be sacrificed.

Reduction of Catalonia

Prieto had planned on using the Communists against his rival, but ended up being used by them and being thrown out when he no longer was willing to serve them. In Catalonia Companys planned on using PSUC to check the CNT, but he was used by PSUC and made ceremonial president of a folklore autonomy when he refused to continue to yield. In 1873 and 1934 the Catalonian Republicans made the offer to Republicans from all over Spain to establish themselves in Catalonia and fight from there; the offer was finally accepted in 1938 but not for the purpose of fighting but rather to "put an end to autonomy."[86] The government had moved from Valencia to Barcelona to better control the revolutionary focus which was subdued but not dead. Companys finally realized that the rise of revolutionary forces had brought about the expansion of the functions of the Generalidad. When the forced decline ensued, that expansion was transformed into reduction. Several decrees of the Negrín government marked the legal stages of this retraction of autonomy: on January 6, 1938 he put the minister of finance in charge of supplies for Catalonia; on January 23 he dissolved the Commission of War Industries of Catalonia, whose functions went to the undersecretary of armaments, and on May 11 he ended the Generalidad's intervention in the banks. "With the opposition of the Anarchists who defended the primitive revolutionary conquests from the redoubt of the Council of Economy [of Catalonia], the Negrín government developed a policy of continued intervention and control of the Catalonian economy."[87] The result was that in 1938 Companys admitted in a letter to Prieto that from June to December 1937 production in Catalonia had fallen about 35 to 40 percent, and that Rodríguez Vega, at the third congress of the Catalonian UGT, reported that in some industries production was "half of what it normally was."[88] Keep in mind that, even though it was in a smaller percentage than today's, most Catalonian workers were not originally from Catalonia and decrease in productivity was not a Catalonian protest, but a result of a loss of enthusiasm for the policy "already initiated by PSUC to restrain labor control of the collectivized industry . . . and to defend the interests of the petite bourgeoisie and foreign companies affected by the collectivization."[89]

Catalonian intellectuals did not protest because, like those in the rest of the Republican zone, they were dazed, corrupted, and frightened by the Communists. But Companys, whose government did not include the CNT after June 1937, reestablished contact with the CNT, received a delegation of the illegal Executive Committee of POUM (and had this made public through the press office of the Generalidad), and made other gestures which marked his separation from PSUC. After all was said and done, he had to sign a decree on June 16, 1938 which rescinded another of August 28, 1936. The latter established "the normative principle of economic plentitude which in a sui generis sense could be considered the 'legal sovereignty' of the Catalonian Generalidad which had been born of the real sovereignty of the CNT and which had been used to defend it, in the beginning to a certain extent, from the centralizing policy in favor of the restoration of the bourgeois state established by Republicans, Socialists, and Communists."[90]

The final blow came from a decree of August 11, 1938. Using the battle of the Ebro as a pretext, Negrín militarized the war industry. Companys protested by ordering the resignation of Jaume Aiguader, minister of the Esquerra in the Negrín government. In a show of solidarity Manuel de Irujo, the Nationalist Basque minister, also resigned. When Companys explained this decision to the Council of the Generalidad, every member supported it (even though it was not a decision of the government but of the Republican Esquerra party of Catalonia) with the exception of the members of PSUC.[91] When those members returned to PSUC headquarters at the Hotel Colón, they found that there had been a call from Negrín asking a delegation to go to see him. Comorera, Valdés, Serra i Pàmies, and Vidiella went. "The crisis," he told them, "must be resolved immediately. Since Catalonia was represented by a member of the Esquerra, then it could also be represented by one of the PSUC." They wanted to consult with one another but Negrín said no. "Give me a name right away or I'll resolve the crisis without you." They suggested Comorera, but Negrín rejected him because he was too well known as a Communist. Then Comorera suggested Josep Moix.

"Who is Moix?"

"A UGT syndicalist."

"We'll take him."

And so PSUC agreed to give one of its men so that Negrín could claim he had a Catalonian minister.[92]

Negrín had taken advantage of Aiguader's and Irujo's resignations to get the resignation of his whole government. He suggested to Azaña that, since Companys was his main opponent, he ought to put him in charge of forming the government. Azaña thought for a moment of Besteiro who had just returned from London where he had represented the Republic at the coronation of George VI. Negrín announced that he would leave the country for a while. The PCE saw to it that a torrent of telegrams from the fronts fell on the presidency of the Republic and it organized a parade of Russian tanks along the Paseo de Colón. Azaña did not need any more hints, and Negrín once again became head of government. Moix replaced Aiguader, and Irujo was replaced by Tomás Bilbao of the Acción Nacionalista Vasca (Basque Nationalist Action, a small party), who was a personal friend of Negrín. There was no longer a minister from the CNT.

All this happened in August 1938 in the middle of the battle of the Ebro (one could wonder what the Russian tanks were doing in Barcelona). But the discontent of Catalonian Republicans had already been expressed on April 23, 1938 in a letter Companys wrote to Negrín in which he complained of the excesses of the Communist police citing concrete cases "which undermine," he said, "the morale and confidence of the Catalonian rearguard." The majority of the incidents cited were of CNT members murdered by Communists (mass murder in Siges, Igualada, Cervera, and Badalona). He also complained that, despite his position, he was not kept informed of the progress of the war.[93]

Negrín, Azaña, and the Communists said that Catalonia in no way supported the war effort and did not want to cooperate in the fighting. That was not true.[94] At that time Catalonia was providing more than 30 percent of the total strength of the army, more than 40 percent of the fire-line command, more than 60 percent of the Republican zone production. But to reach its goals, neither Negrín nor the PCE had any scruples in reviving one of the most deeply rooted prejudices of "semi-feudal Spain" which the new-style Republic had to destroy. It was clear that the new-style Republic had been put out to pasture.

Political Fiction

In 1937 Díaz had told the members of his party: "I want to call the attention of all comrades to the possibility that in our party which today is in a serious, difficult, and complicated situation there is a certain amount of impatience which endangers the unity of the labor movement and the development of the Popular Front. One must never forget that in our country there is neither a Soviet regime nor a regime of dictatorship of the proletariat and that our party does not have—nor can it have—all the power in its hands."[95] Within a year it did have all the power in its hands. Patience had been profitable, so much so that in time, following World War II, the behavior of the Communist parties of Eastern Europe would appear to be a copy of that of the PCE during the Civil War. Soviet arms played the same role in the Civil War that the presence of the Russian army did in Eastern Europe. The same "salami tactic" was followed, as the Hungarian Communist Matias Rakosi called it, that is, taking power slice by slice instead of swallowing it whole. In both cases there existed a political fiction based on fear—physical fear in Eastern Europe and fear of losing the war in Spain.

On April 30, 1938 Negrín had issued a program of thirteen points which he knew would not be accepted by the other side, but which he used to appease those who, thinking the war was already lost, were pressuring for mediation or settlement. In May the central committee of the party met in Madrid—a symbolic gesture—and came out with the slogan of National Union. This time the political report was left up to Ibárruri and not Díaz. Officially, Díaz was ill (indeed, he was suffering from tuberculosis and had had to go once or twice to the USSR for treatment), but it is possible that, according to Hernández,[96] Díaz came across as somewhat independent of Togliatti who may have decided to favor La Pasionaria over him as a means of bringing him to his senses.

The slogan of National Union was based on the asumption that Spain's independence was threatened and it was necessary to form that sacred union to defend it. The people were skeptical about this because they began to realize that Spain was only a pawn in the game of international politics. La Pasionaria said: "Our resistance is the point of departure of a new situation in the interior of the country whose essential characteristic is the unity of all anti-Fascist forces around the government of National Union. . . . A new kind of unity, greater, more solid, more efficient than what has existed up to now . . . one which allows us to mobilize, organize, and to bring new popular groups and new forces to fight the invaders." The war was no longer in defense of the Republic but of Spain's independence. And there was no longer a government of victory but a government of resistance. "To resist is to conquer," would be the slogan people would see on walls, hear over the radio, and read in newspapers.

The effort of winning over the middle class was increased precisely because it was clear that the working class was alienated. Díaz explained the meaning of National Union with these words: "What interest can Franco's victory hold for an industrialist, for example, who takes pride in his country and who knows that if the foreign invaders won, his factory would end up sooner or later in their hands? . . . What interest can men of Catholic ideology have in a foreign victory which would open up Spain to a bloody period of religious persecution of Catholics and against freedom of worship as is happening in Germany now? . . . The National Union is not just a political or parliamentarian formation: it is the association of all the people when the common good is in danger, as are the country's independence, territorial integrity, and the very existence of Spain as a nation."[97]

In November 1938 in the midst of military castastrophe, Díaz still said: "What do the petit bourgeois groups want, what do they need? They want greater liberty and initiative in the area of economics. That liberty can and should be given to them without bargaining, only being careful not to infringe on the principle of centralization of economic life in the hands of the state."[98] At the time a French journalist visited him and asked him why the PCE wanted the Popular Front to continue to exist once the war was over. He answered: "We cannot separate our problems from those facing the USSR and the working classes of the world. The alliance we are trying to consolidate here is no different from the one which, on a wider scale, the world Communist movement is attempting to bring about to stop fascism. . . . This alliance will not be easy to maintain but it must last for a fairly long period of time, both during the Civil War and after it. To view things differently is leftism; it is playing Fascism's game."[99]

That Popular Front, an echo of the worldwide Popular Front which Díaz wanted to see last beyond the war [a war which he was convinced was already lost], had been reconstructed on paper and at committee meetings but not in the streets. On April 2, the CNT and UGT officially entered the Popular Front—to sweeten the pill for the Anarchists, it was called the Anti-Fascist Popular Front—in which for the first time trade unions took part. Prior to that, on March 13, the CNT and UGT had signed a pact of unity of action which provided for a series of measures to strengthen the army, organize the war industry, and nationalize heavy industry and the banking system. The CNT naively believed it would protect what little remained of the July 1936 conquests. The Negrín government completely ignored the pact.[100] That Popular Front was unable to do anything when its delegation of the CNT presented it with the only survivor of a group of eight soldiers of the CNT who had been attacked and murdered by a Communist squad on the Eastern front. "Total silence was the reply; we recall that only one of the delegates, a Republican, said a few words in protest; the others remained quiet, almost indignant that we would disturb the sessions with such trifles. Seven soldiers murdered for belonging to the CNT—what did it matter?"[101]

Meanwhile, under the protection of the National Union slogan, persecutions, censorship, and pressure continued, all of which succeeded in bringing about the formation of other organizations as empty as the Popular Front—the Alianza Juvenil Antifascista, for example.[102] Above all, Prieto was the object of constant attacks. He wanted to leave the country but Azaña asked him to stay. He finally managed to have him sent as ambassador to the inauguration of the Popular Front candidate who had won the election in Chile. Prior to that, in August, Prieto had reported to the national committee of the PSOE on the circumstances surrounding the March crisis, but the public did not know anything about this report until after the war was over. At the meeting, and as a reply to the Communists, it was decided that followers of Caballero such as Zabalza and Largo Caballero himself as well as Besteiro and his friend Lucio Martínez should join the executive commission. The

Socialist party wanted to unite in order to withstand whatever it was dealt.

There were other kinds of measures. For example, after having created with Republican money the Compagnie France-Navigation for the purpose of transporting arms and other products to Spain—a company which later fell into the hands of the French Communist party and whose manager was Georges Gosnat, who later on became treasurer of the French Communist party—the government established a Mid-Atlantic Company, also for navigation, and in London it created several transport firms: Howard Tenens, Ltd., Prosper Steamship Co., Burlington Steamship Co., Southern Shipping and Karfish Co. In Marseilles an Entreprise Maritime was registered. After the Spanish war, these firms ended up in Russian hands through their own companies and after World War II Russian ownership of these firms was recognized. Some must still be in operation.[103]

Military Fiction

With Prieto out of the picture, the Communists quickly took over the army. High posts have been mentioned to which Negrín appointed Communists. Appointments of Communists proliferated in brigades, divisions, and army corps. From May to September 1938 there were 7,000 promotions, 5,500 of which went to Communists. Of the 27 brigades of the army of the Ebro, 25 were under Communist leadership, and its nine division commanders, three army corps commanders, and the chief commander (Modesto) were all Communists. In the six armies of the Republic, of the commanders of brigades, 163 were Communists and 33 belonged to the CNT; of the division commanders, 61 Communists and 9 CNT; of the army corps commanders, 15 Communists and 2 CNT. Of the six army chiefs, 3 were Communists, 2 were Communist sympathizers, and 1 was professional.[104] Prieto realized, much to his dismay, the meaning of such control:

> The risk of using Communists in military posts and any position whatsoever in public administration is in requiring of them the political discipline to serve their party's bureau before the government on which they depend. Such a procedure entails not only intolerable preferences but also diso-bedience, and at times disloyalty and even treason. It is difficult to take precautions against such duplicity because there are Communists in positions of trust who, to avoid arousing suspicions, are ordered to conceal their affiliation and even to camouflage it by making them join other parties.
>
> That, through such a system, the Communist bureau can have its hands in the most delicate of state affairs is already a very grave issue, but the

gravity reaches extreme proportions if that bureau blindly obeys instructions of a foreign government.[105]

This control was used not just to make the Communists obey; its weight was likewise felt by those named by the party and it made sure that orders given were not ignored. If they did so, retaliation was not far behind. For example, the subsecretary of aviation under Prieto's orders, Antonio Camacho, was a Communist but in some instances he obeyed orders from his minister which differed from those issued by the party. He received a warning: SIM arrested Camacho's wife and released her a few days later when it was learned that she was not guilty of what she had been accused. But Negrín, as minister of defense, replaced Camacho.[106] This incident is well known. There must have been many others which, because they affected mere officers and soldiers, never got beyond the circle of friends and family (who otherwise often did not even dare speak).

The Communist military men and party members sincerely wanted to win the war; they were sure that theirs was the only way to victory, and they believed that the methods used by those who made themselves executors were essential to win the war. The Communist units performed as well as those of other organizations and with the same spirit of sacrifice and probably with more mechanical discipline. The battle of the Ebro decimated those Communist military men as it did those of other organizations and the unaffiliated. Authors who have written about it have naively overlooked its political aspect. Hernández said—with confirmation from Castro Delgado—that starting with the Pact of Munich, Moscow was determined to reach an agreement with Hitler and so had to show the Führer that the USSR had no designs on Europe. So it was necessary to put an end to the Spanish Civil War. But neither the USSR, by refusing arms, nor the PCE could do it. It would have destroyed the prestige of the country and the party and without it Hitler would not have been interested in reaching an agreement with Moscow.[107]

The PCE received orders from Moscow, through Togliatti, to forsake Negrín by denying him the collaboration of the Communists. Without them Negrín would fall from power, that would be an excuse to send fewer arms, and thus the war would come quickly to an end. For the first and only time, the political bureau refused to obey an order from Moscow, or at least so said Hernández. Since none of this could be brought out into the open, Togliatti pretended to accept the bureau's decision and turned to the Russian military advisors to bring about an end to the war while the PCE continued its campaign of "to resist is to conquer."

It was then that Negrín was advised to accept the withdrawal of the International Brigades which would weaken the Republic much more than the hypothetical withdrawal of the Italian "volunteers" would weaken Franco. And it was then that the Russian generals informed the Republican General Staff of its plans for the battle of the Ebro (July-September 1938), which would inevitably be a battle of attrition, and even if it were victorious would not alter the course of the war. In this battle, the heroism, expertise, and efficiency of the soldiers were undeniable. But none of this could prevent the fact that of 90,000 soldiers, only 20,000 would return as the Russians had foreseen. When Franco's offensive against Catalonia began shortly thereafter, Catalonia had fewer than 60,000 rifles and 40 percent of the artillery was being repaired, according to reports by General Rojo himself.

Once the Republican army had been destroyed at the Ebro, the fall of Catalonia was inevitable. Miaja refused to provide troops for a hastily put together offensive in Motril and so a probably useless operation of relief for the Catalonian front could not even be carried out. Knowing that Catalonia could not resist, PSUC and the PCE started their members building trenches in the outskirts of Barcelona. The arrival of the Moors caught them unawares in their endeavor and they barely had time to flee.[108] It was important to maintain the image of the party as the last redoubt of resistance. The political fiction of the National Union was used to conceal the military fiction of "to resist is to conquer." This fiction led to ending the war.

Final Deceit

From May 1937 on, the people of the Republican zone were deceived. Negrín apparently thought that lying was normal political procedure. His vocation for lying was useful to the PCE which had to lie systematically, for it suited the interests of Soviet diplomacy. In that nearly two-year period, the political slogans were masks of reality. Communist party members believed what was repeated hook, line, and sinker. Even many of the leaders did not realize that what was being said and written did not reflect reality. But it is difficult to imagine that some leaders— especially those who had the trust of delegates of the Communist International—did not know the truth.

The campaigns against POUM, the CNT, the collectivizations, Largo Caballero, and Prieto were based on a system of lies that time has proved as such. Thousands of anti-Fascists lost their lives because of them. When one spoke of a "new type" of Republic, those who "invented" the slogan knew perfectly well that the Republic already existed thanks to the spontaneous action of workers on the days that followed July 18. In the same way, when one spoke of "to resist is to conquer," those who came out with the slogan knew that it was a matter of resisting in order for Stalin to gain time, but there was absolutely no possibility of victory. When those same individuals spoke of National Union, they knew that this expression concealed a monopoly of power by the Communist party.

Whenever Negrín would speak on the radio against those who wanted to negotiate a settlement, he knew that he was being hypocritical, for, as he himself later confessed, ever since August 1937 he had had "contacts, both direct and indirect, with the enemy: Spaniards, Germans, Italians, as well as neutral enemies."[109] When at the Parliament in Figueres at the end of January 1939 Negrín stated that "huge amounts" of arms were about to arrive, he was lying. *Frente Rojo,* printed in that almost border city, accused Largo Caballero and Araquistáin of being traitors, blaming them for the loss of Catalonia because their flight to France had "demoralized the fronts," but it hushed up the fact that the trip was per orders of Negrín and under police vigilance.[110]

The second to the last meeting, in Spain, of the political bureau took place in Figueres on January 30 and 31. It is amazing that the bureau, given that situation, dedicated its time to expelling from the party César García Lombardía, secretary of FETE (Federación Española de Traba-jadores de la Enseñanza—Spanish Federation of School Workers) and a member of the Executive Commission of the UGT. In another situation, the Executive Commission of the UGT, which also met and received a communiqué from the political bureau, probably would have suspended García Lombardía so as not to contradict the PCE, but now those who so far had been submissive felt brave yet did nothing. The expulsion was for personal reasons; no one ever doubted the man's loyalty.

One resolution adopted by the bureau said that "the unions of the UGT and CNT, in this decisive moment, cannot be divergent, for they will play an even more decisive role in that unity of the people for resistance and victory."[111] In those days when French concentration camps were beginning to receive refugees, to speak of resistance and victory was to lie. It had been like that for a long while, as proven by this anecdote: after the disaster of the Ebro, Negrín called together leaders of every organization to assure them that the "prospects were magnificent" and he invited everyone to toast with champagne. Both delegates of the CNT left in indignation. Negrín caught up with them and asked Santillán, "Why are you angry?" Santillán answered, "Because you are a miserable liar. The operation of the Ebro is the surrender of Catalonia." Negrín said, "If I told the truth, they would flee in all directions. But keep calm. I have resources abroad to help in the exile which is coming."[112] So Negrín, in November 1938, foresaw exile, not victory. When Negrín was claiming that he was willing to resist in the South-Central zone, not only did he know that resistance was not possible but also that he had no intention of leading it. Trifón Gómez, general intendant of supplies, asked Negrín in Le Perthus on February 9 if they ought to send supplies to the South-Central zone. If there was enough for about twelve days, no more was needed, was Negrín's reply.[113]

Regarding the PCE, although it continued to say that it was necessary to resist, it left in France the best-known leaders of the Central zone such as Carrillo, Mije, Antón, and Giorla, all of whom were members of the provincial committee of Madrid. The plane that took the Communist leaders from France to Valencia had 33 seats, but only 13 were occupied. So "those members of the political bureau and the executive commission of Juventud Socialista Unificada were doing the same thing as Azaña and Martínez Barrio and assumed that the war was lost and over with when Catalonia fell."[114] Díaz had had to be taken under emergency conditions to the USSR on November 10, 1938 due to a sudden relapse. The mission of Negrín and the PCE, which controlled all the machinery of the Republican state, was to evacuate from the South-Central zone those individuals in the greatest danger. But that was the same as saying that they ought to end the war. If they had wanted to do that, they would have concentrated the available ships which were the property of companies of the Spanish state to carry out the evacuation.[115] This was not done. What they did do was look for someone to whom they could pass the buck.

On February 13 Negrín issued a proclamation from Madrid calling for resistance and for everyone to bow to the will of the government. But the government was a ghost. It resided neither in Madrid nor Valencia; it moved from one place to another staying in hotels, military headquarters, or country houses. Communist "historians" claimed afterward that resistance was possible, that there were ten million Spaniards and from 500,000 to 800,000 soldiers. They did not say that there were only 95,000 rifles, 1,600 automatic rifles, 1,400 machine guns, 150 pieces of artillery, 50 mortars, 10 tanks, 40 planes, food for only twelve days, and gasoline for less than that.[116] Systematic deception finally lost its appeal. Referring to the PCE, Ibárruri said that "its influence in Madrid had weakened," and she attributed it to the political bureau's move to Barcelona.[117] There was more to it than that. "It has become an honor to be insulted by the Communists. They polarize every hatred, they represent every defeat; they truly are the enemy," wrote Zugazagoitia.[118]

On February 22, 1939, 250 leaders from the CNT met in Madrid and created a regional committee of defense. They were afraid that the Communists might take advantage of the situation and start a mass purge. They issued a manifesto saying that "either we all save ourselves or we all are finished." They foresaw that the PCE would prepare the evacuation of its highest-ranking militants and no one else. Delegates of this committee spoke to Socialists, Republicans, and members of the UGT who reflected their own anxieties. They also spoke with the local committee of the PCE: "We asked them to choose between peace and war, we warned that we would crush anyone who tried to crush us, and we frankly displayed our opposition to Negrín. They accepted the basis of resistance . . . but refused—without contradicting our accusations— to confront the government." This was subsequently related by García Pradas, editor of the CNT's organ in Madrid.[119] The Communists said that the professional military men were up to something. The CNT was not concerned since, without the forces controlled by the CNT or the PCE, they could not move anyone.

Colonel Segismundo Casado, who had taken part in plots against the monarchy, who had been head of the presidential escort, who had been in Largo Caballero's confidence, and who had to intervene in Brunete and Jarama to correct mistakes made by others, was also making moves. Negrín facilitated Casado's contacts with officers in the South and Central zones. He brought together several officers at the airfield at Los Llanos, listened to them talk of their pessimism, and instead of discharging them, as he would have had to do if he had really intended to resist, he allowed them to return to their posts. It was said that Casado was an agent of the British Intelligence Service. Thomas was convinced that he was not. In any event, Casado's plot, which almost could not be considered such because nothing was concealed, would not have been possible at all had Negrín not put CNT members, Socialists, and Republicans on Casado's side.

Negrín and Communist officers, as well as members of the bureau who had gone to the South-Central zone, finally settled in what was called the Yuste position, a country residence in Elda where there was an airfield and several planes which Communist militants jealously guarded. "Madrid was like a trap which everyone was trying to get out of when the door was still ajar." Líster thought that the fact that people were trying to get out of Madrid proved that the political bureau also thought the war was lost.[120] The bureau had informed Negrín that "if the government was willing to continue resistance, the communist party would support it. If it was willing to open peace negotiations, the Communist party would not be an obstacle."[121] But the bureau suggested changing some high-ranking military personnel and replacing Miaja and Casado. On March 3 Negrín promoted several Communists to generals and gave the high posts of the South-Central zone to Communists. Casado was also promoted to general but he, like Matallana, lost his command. On March 5 delegates from the regional defense committee interviewed Casado and representatives from several parties. Time was of the essence. Negrín called together Casado and other leaders to Elda. Only Matallana went and was arrested; the others smelled a rat and did not attend. That afternoon a National Council of Defense was formed by Republicans, the CNT, and members of the PSOE with Casado as president and Besteiro in charge of foreign affairs. Besteiro, in the appeal of the Council of Defense, after recalling Azaña's recent resignation in exile, said that "the Negrín government, with its veiled truths, its half-truths, its insidious proposals, cannot hope for anything except to gain time. . . . Republican opinion, without exception, is already supersaturated with the policy [Negrín's] of catastrophic fanaticism, pure submission to foreign orders, and utter indifference to the nation's suffering."

Casado thought that because the army corps were under professional military men, even though they were Communists, they would not rebel against the Council. Mera advised him to adopt precautionary measures, which he did not do, and on March 6, forces of the first and second army corps marched on Madrid abandoning the front. Mera, whose corps was off duty in Guadalajara, mobilized his forces. There was fighting in Madrid. There was fighting in Cartagena (which the fifth column took advantage of although it failed at the last moment), and in Valencia and other cities fighting never quite began, but forces were mobilized.[122] Negrín phoned Casado and proposed an official transfer of power which Casado rejected because "you cannot give what you do not have." Negrín became furious. Although La Pasionaria denied it, Modesto said that "up to its departure from Spain, the [Negrín] government continued parleying with Casado."[123]

Negrín, who had failed in his attempt to wash his hands of the war, went to Monóvar and took a plane. Five hours before, Togliatti had made La Pasionaria, Monzón, Stepanov, and others leave by plane while fighting was still going on in Madrid. But Togliatti and some others stayed behind and held the last meeting of the Central Committee of the PCE in Spain. "They simply told us of the accords," said Tagüeña whom Claudín had to join as a leading member of the JSU. Negrín had left, so the only authority was the Council of Defense, and even though it was illegal, to fight against it was to start one civil war within another, Togliatti told them. "The Communist champions of unity could not adopt that position. There was no other alternative than to try to save as many Communist militants as possible and leave the responsibility of ending the war in the hands of Casado's junta. Togliatti later asked Líster and Modesto if they thought the party had wasted a chance to take over power; they said no. The rest of us were not asked anything. This political line could not be a last-minute improvisation, but rather something that developed over time."[124]

Líster gives a somewhat different version. The central committee was made up of three members, the only ones who were there: Líster, Castro Delgado, and Modesto. All three gave their opinion of what had been agreed upon (which was what Tagüeña explained) and "afterwards they told us of their decision: all of us present ought to leave except Checa and Togliatti who would do so after implementing every measure to put into effect the agreements reached there." Líster commented: "The decision surprised me. It seemed normal for Checa, who was secretary of party organization, to stay, but I could not understand why Togliatti, member of the Communist International Secretariat would. I would understand it later as I began to find out what had happened to others when they returned to Moscow. Togliatti knew and was in no hurry to return."[125] Uribe, Castro, and others went to the planes. Uribe ordered the leader of the group of soldiers who was guarding the machinery, "Comrade, see to it that they depart. . . . Then, take to the mountains. The party will not forget you." And he gave him a wad of Republican bank notes: "Take these, comrade, just in case you can use them."[126]

At the meeting of the central committee no one had spoken of the fighting in Madrid. Tagüeña found out about it the next day in Paris. The play was complete. Others were now put in the position of taking on the mission of ending the war. Hundreds of soldiers and some professional officers who remained loyal to the party until the very end were sacrificed to make the PCE look like it had nothing to do with it. Even Negrín was blamed: "In his heart of hearts, Negrín himself was wishing for a catastrophe to free him from all state responsibility, and his conduct clearly showed that," wrote Dolores Ibárruri without adding that neither she nor the party opposed this conduct.[127]

Much later, Líster asked himself some obvious questions: "What instructions was Togliatti carrying out? . . . Why were the other members of the political bureau and the whole group of political and military party militants not made to go from France to the South-Central zone? Is it that Casado's uprising benefited only Negrín's plan to abandon the war or that at the same time it benefited other plans of putting an end to the war with our defeat? . . . Of all the dirty and shady sides there are to our war, this last part is the most suspect. I have not lost hope that many of those suspect aspects will gradually be cleared up."[128]

Notes

1. *Mundo Obrero,* Paris, September 25, 1947.
2. Azaña, *Memorias,* p. 591ff.
3. *España Popular,* March 11, 1940, quoted by Bolloten, p. 313.
4. Quoted by Bolloten, p. 314.
5. Krivitsky, pp. 100–102. The other quotes appear in Bolloten, p. 316.
6. Hernández, *Yo fui un ministro de Stalin,* pp. 86ff.
7. *Historia del PCE,* p. 165.
8. Castro Delgado, *Hombres made in Moscú,* p. 660.
9. Azaña, *Memorias,* p. 567. Togliatti (p. 348) agrees with Azaña. He says, "Negrín's style of working [was] that of a dissolute, boastful, disorganized, and bohemian intellectual, not without some signs of corruption (women)."
10. Thomas, p. 669.
11. Castro Delgado, *Hombres made in Moscú,* pp. 660–61.
12. Azaña, quoted by Juan Marichal in *La vocación de Manuel Azaña,* Madrid, 1968, p. 266.
13. Stanley G. Payne, *La revolución y la guerra civil,* Madrid, 1976, p. 89.
14. The quote from Ruiz Ponseti is in Payne, pp. 90–91; the one from Delicado is in Cattell, p. 175.
15. Dolores Ibárruri in a speech on May 25, 1937 quoted by Bolloten, p. 92.
16. On Togliatti consult Aldo Garosci, "Palmiro Togliatti," *Survey,* London, October 1964.
17. Albert Pérez Baró, *Trenta mesos de col.lectivisme a Catalunya,* Barcelona, 1970, p. 143ff.
18. *La Vanguardia,* Barcelona, October 21, 1938. Negrín's declaration of March 31, 1938.
19. It should not be believed that the PCE was the only one to destroy the Council of Aragon. Líster relates that Prieto called him at his office on August 5 and explained that in order to support the police in the dissolution of the Council of Aragon, he, Prieto, had proposed to the Council of Minsters that Líster's divisions help enforce order. "He told me that there would not be any wirtten order for the mission that they were giving me nor would there be communiqués on its enforcement. It was a secret matter between the government and myself: I should eliminate, without hestiation or legalistic or bureaucratic procedure, all those whom I felt had to be eliminated; I would have the full support of the government behind me" (Líster, *Nuestra guerra,* Paris, 1966, p. 152). As can be seen, Prieto, euphoric over having eliminated Largo Caballero and believing that he was going to manipulate Negrín and the PCE, wanted to use the PCE to carry out the dirtiest work. And Líster—clearly with his party in agreement since one could not imagine it any other way for an old member like himself— consented because this dirty work served the interests of the party.
20. The Aragonese peasants were more tenacious than the leaders of the CNT. As soon as the Communist troops left, they once again reorganized their collectivities which in many cases lasted until the arrival of the Fascists, although without their leaders who were in prison, and without the coordination and aid of the Council. Those who claimed that the collectivities were forced (even though in a few instances they were) were contradicted by the peasants' persistence in maintaining them.

21. Albert Pérez Baró, "El PSUC i el decret de col.lectivització," *Avui*, Barcelona, May 5, 1977.

22. Arturo Barea, *La forja de un rebelde*, Buenos Aires, 1951, p. 769.

23. For more on this visit see *Terror in Spain*, London, 1938, by John McGovern, British Independent Labor party representative. This pamphlet gives many details on repression of the non-Communist anti-Fascists.

24. Kritvitsky (p. 150) wrote about the NKVD in Spain: "Moscow put Slutsky, head of the Foreign Division of the GPU, in charge of inspecting the secret police who were a copy of the Russian model. He arrived a day or two after my departure. The GPU at the time was flourishing throughout the Republican territory, but it was more concentrated in Catalonia where independent groups were stronger and where also the true Trotskyites had their party's general quarters. Slutsky told me when he returned to Paris a few weeks later, 'They have good material there, but they lack experience. We cannot allow Spain to become a free territory and a camp for all anti-Soviet elements who have gathered there from around the world.'" Kim Philby, the Englishman who later was an agent of Soviet espionage, worked as a correspondent during the Civil War in Burgos for the *London Times* and was awarded a medal by Franco. It is not known whether at the time he was already working for the Russians or was a Franco sympathizer ("Philby," in *Historia y Vida*, Barcelona, May 1976).

25. R. Cabrer Pallás, "Ramón Casanellas i la rebotiga comunista."

26. One of the collaborators in the NKVD was the Catalonian Communist Caridad Mercader, who had begun to work as an agent in Paris in 1928 when she was infiltrated in the French Socialist party. During the war she received orders from Gerö (Prieto in *El Socialista*, Toulouse, September 27, 1951). Her son Ramón del Río Mercader, who belonged to Juventudes Comunistas (and was arrested following October 1934) was "handed over" by his mother toward the middle or the end of the Civil War to Russian agents of the NKVD who took him to Moscow and prepared him to assassinate Trotsky in 1940. By then he had assumed a false identity, going as a Belgian named Jacques Mornard. The assassin said that he was a "disenchanted Trotskyite," but following his 20-year prison sentence, he left Mexico, went to Cuba, and from there to Prague where he died. (Regarding Del Río Mercader, see Julián Gorkín, *El asesinato de Trotski*, Barcelona, 1971.) The assassin's mother lived in the USSR following the Spanish war and then in Paris after World War II. Both mother and son probably insured each other against any attempt to "discard" one or the other.

27. There were numerous cases but many of them are not known. A few were documented. See José Peirats, *La CNT en la revolución española*, vol. III, p. 260ff. for details.

28. There was incredible complicity—due in part to political naiveté, in part to the fascination of power, in part to propaganda—by the majority of press correspondents in the Republican zone. Herbert Matthews, of *The New York Times*, always echoed the views of the Communists and Negrín. While he was in Spain, Hemingway never spoke of the persecution of the CNT and POUM, although in his novel about the Civil War he portrayed André Marty as half mad and Koltzov, using another name, as a skeptic who did not believe in Nin's imaginary guilt. Gustav Regler, a German

Communist who worked as a political commissar with the International Brigades, knew of the executions which Marty ordered and spoke to Hemingway about them. Hemingway did not say anything in his press telegrams. Furthermore, he knew of other executions because José Robles, a professor at an American university and a volunteer in Spain, disappeared in December 1936, and his friend John Dos Passos asked Hemingway to investigate the matter. Hemingway told him that the head of counter-espionage had assured him that he would be judged impartially; Robles had already been murdered by the Communists by that time. When Hemingway found out about it, he assumed that they executed him because he was guilty. He never understood the indignation of Dos Passos who knew Robles well. Hemingway finally told everything in his novel *For Whom the Bell Tolls,* when the truth could no longer help to save anyone (Phillip Knighley, *The First Casualty,* New York, 1975, pp. 213–14).

29. Max Rieger, *Espionaje en España,* Barcelona, 1938, pp. 12–13. Max Rieger did not exist. The book was "translated" by Lucienne and Arturo Perucho and it was said that Professor Wenceslao Roces helped prepare it. When this same accusation was published in Mexico and Spain he did not protest. More information as well as documentation of the references made here are in Alba, *El Marxisme a Catalunya,* vol. II, ch. 2, and vol. III, ch. 6; Andrés Suárez, *El proceso contra el POUM,* Paris, 1974; Hernández, *Yo fui un ministro de Stalin,* ch. 5, and Gorkín, *Caníbales políticos,* passim. Togliatti found the "outcome of the trial scandalous" and blamed it on the fact that Minister of Justice González Peña "fell under the influence of Trotskyism during his trip to Mexico," and also on the fact that Paulino Gómez, minister of the interior, "during the trial forbade the press from undertaking any campaign against the Trotskyite traitors" (when in fact he had forbidden the publication of any information on the trial while it was going on) (Togliatii, p. 349).

30. Full plenary session of the Central Committee of the Spanish Communist party, Valencia, 1937, pp. 11–13.

31. Claudin, *La crisis del movimiento comunista,* p. 616.

32. Arthur London, *Se levantaron antes del alba,* Barcelona, 1978, p. 166. Despite the fact that his book is devoted to a large extent to the International Brigades of which he was a part, London does not talk about repression in the Brigades.

33. Tuñón de Lara, *La España del siglo XX,* Paris, 1968, pp. 568–69.

34. Teresa Pàmies, *Quan érem capitans,* Barcelona, 1974, p. 70.

35. Here are some of his explanations: "Largo Caballero did not want to be an agent of certain elements that were in our country. . . . Until shortly before the campaign [against me] was initiated, I was offered all that can be offered to a man who might have a sense of ambition and vanity. I could be head of the Unified Socialist party; I could be Spain's great politician. . . . But it had to be on the condition that I would follow the policy they wanted. And I said: no way" (Largo Caballero, *La UGT y la guerra,* Valencia, 1937, p. 5ff.).

36. The order for the seizure of those newspapers was given by Zugazagoitia, a follower of Prieto and minister of the interior, who in this instance managed to have it enforced. Cruz Salido was then the edior of *Adelante.* He was arrested in 1941 by the Vichy police and was handed over to

Franco who had him shot to death just as he did with Zugazagoitia, Peiró, and Companys.

37. Pietro Nenni, *Spagna,* Milan, 1958, p. 63.
38. Hermet, p. 46. The estimates are mine.
39. Estruch, p. 105.
40. Antonio Ramos Oliveira, *Politics, Economics, and Men of Modern Spain, 1808-1946,* London, 1946, p. 294.
41. Henri Scott Beatie, in April 1938, quoted by Bolloten, pp. 83–84.
42. Louis Fisher in *The Nation,* New York, August 7, 1937.
43. Barea, p. 737.
44. Gide's signature on a telegram sent by French intellectuals asking the Negrín government for legal guarantees for the accused of POUM (along with Paul Rivet, Roger Martin du Gard, Georges Duhamel, François Mauriac, and others) provoked the anger not only of José Bergamín but also of Ilya Ehrenburg, who engaged in a controversy with Gide. All details of the controversy are found in Gide, *Littérature engagée,* Paris, 1950. Ehrenburg referred to the signers of the telegram as "sensitive hearts, allies of the Moors and the Black Shirts." André Malraux did not protest either. When Victor Serge reproached him for it, he responded, "I accept Stalin's crimes wherever they are committeed," and Serge (who had just come back from Siberia), threw a cup of coffee in his face.
45. Jesús Pérez Salas, *Guerra en España,* Mexico City, 1947, p. 146.
46. Franz Borkenau, *El reñidero español,* Paris, 1971, p. 153. Togliatti admitted it in a report to Moscow in which, after pointing out what he called "weakness and gaps" in PSUC and the fact that Comorera "was not an inspiration but rather led in a bureaucratic manner," he noted that "the militants of the party were predominantly middle class" and that "said party leaders, on the local level, [were] former members of reactionary organizations, [who] speculated as much as the leaders of other organizations" (Togliatti, p. 301ff.).
47. Claudín, p. 186.
48. Suárez, p. 47.
49. Estruch, p. 107. Referring to this kind of evaluation of the influence of the PCE by its own leaders, Togliatti said "it led people to believe that the party could bring up the matter of its hegemony and openly fight for it in the government and in the nation" (Togliatti, p. 267).
50. Both quotes are in Thomas, pp. 360, 297.
51. Lillian Hellman, *An Unfinished Woman,* New York, 1969, p. 89.
52. Estruch, p. 112.
53. Full plenary session of the Central Committee of the Spanish Communist party, Valencia, 1937, and the *Communist-Party for the Liberty and Independence of Spain,* Valencia, 1937.
54. *Mundo Obrero,* Madrid, March 23, 1938; and *Frente Rojo,* Barcelona, March 30, 1938. This reply was doubtless inspired by Togliatti because it reflected what he reiterated in his reports to Moscow. The following is what the Italian leader thought of his colleagues the "instructors" and of the leaders of the PCE: "[In the Central Committee of the PCE] there is a great deal of disorder and improvisation. Our friends, the leaders, spend entire days arguing among themselves and with those who work in the ministries, the army, etc. . . . . All the leaders are tired, and sick from

overwork, as a result of the way they do things. . . . In their daily proceedings none of the party's political moves is based on or arises from a firmly established political plan; often decisions are made without examining their consequences. . . . I do not wish to hide my feeling that the responsibility for the shoddy work of the center in part falls to our 'advisors'. . . . Our Spanish comrades are adults; we must recognize this and let them proceed by themselves. . . . There is a group of colleagues (Uribe, Dolores, Hernández, Giorla) who are capable of leading the party and even doing it very well. But the advisors must not disorient those comrades by directing them along the wrong path either with the fabrication of improvised or erroneous theories or with a displaced political impatience, which along with that of our Spanish comrades, will end up by gradually phasing out the party's influence." Togliatti indicates that this tactic was applied by Codovila, Gerö, and the German Fritz Dahlem, who had to stop "considering themselves the owners of the party and thinking that the Spaniards are of no value." He adds that the Spaniards were unable to make a move without Codovila and that the advisors were in charge of relations with the government and other parties (Togliatti, pp. 271–72, 274).

55. That "new style" Republic was baptized by Díaz at the full plenary session of March 1937. "Its objective," he said, "is to destroy the material bases of semifeudal Spain by pulling up the roots of Fascism; in other words, we hope to overcome and consolidate what we were unable to do on April 14 [1931] and after the electoral victory of February 16 [1936]." He did not mention that in the weeks which followed July 19 the material bases of semifeudal Spain had already been destroyed by the same revolution which the PCE condemned. (*Guerra y revolución en España,* vol. II, p. 268ff.).

56. Estruch, p. 112.

57. Joaquín Almendros, *Situaciones españolas, 1936–39: El PSUC en la guerra civil,* Barcelona, 1976, p. 106ff.

58. A revealing sign of the mood of the JSU and also of the ease with which middle-class elements were accepted in its ranks was the case of Josep Casademunt, of the local committee of the JSU of Barcelona, who was expelled when it was learned that he had been a member of the Falange; he was later reinstated as a member and put back in his job by order of the Executive Committee of the JSU. Apparently the decision was made not to protect a Falangist, but rather because Casademunt was noted for his attacks on POUM and it was embarrassing to be found with a Falangist "in the front line of combat against Franco's Trotskyite agents." Therefore they preferred to hide the case which *Juventud Obrera,* underground organ of the Juventudes of POUM, uncovered in May 1938.

59. García Venero, *Historia de las Internacionales,* vol. III, pp. 310, 315; Amaro del Rosal, *Historia de la UGT,* vol. II, p. 645ff.

60. *El Socialista,* Paris, November 9, 1950.

61. London, *Se levantaron antes del alba,* p. 166, For information on these unsuccessful attempts by the Communist International to move toward the Socialist International and by the Profintern to move toward the International Trade Union Federation using aid to the Republic as a pretext, the reader may consult the documents of the Communist International. In each of the manifestos of May Day during the Civil War, the Communist International insisted on proposing unity of action in defense of the Republic to the other two Internationals. There were letters and negotiations but

nothing was accomplished because the distrust of the Socialists increased as they grew aware of what was going on in Spain. Those who did not want unity of action argued that the Republic could be defended equally well separately and that defense of the Republic on the part of Socialists would arouse more sympathy and less hostility than defense by Socialists and Communists together (Degras, vol. III, 409ff., p. 423ff.). The Prieto-Negrín PSOE sent several telegrams to the Socialist International urging it to accept Moscow's proposals, but the Socialist International was aware that Lamoneda was Negrín's man and therefore followed the PCE line and it paid no attention.

62. García Venero, *Historia de las Internacionales,* vol. III, pp. 349–50, in which the program of the national liaison committee appears, dated August 17, 1937.

63. Thomas, p. 491. Thomas, one of whose main informers was Negrín, blamed him for what really was Prieto's jurisdiction. The PCE used a trick to attract Socialists. As Basque and Madrid Communists who sought refuge in Barcelona joined PSUC, the PCE suggested to the PSOE that the Socialists who were in the same position also join PSUC since, upon being created, it had absorbed the Catalonian Federation of the PSOE. They did not listen to the PCE (Togliatti, p. 303). Togliatti does not mention a proposal but says that "the colleagues of the PCE put pressure on the PSOE."

64. The official version of the negotiations is in *Historia del PCE,* p. 165ff. It is perhaps the topic which the *Historia* dwells on the most. It says that the National Committee of the CNT had decided on June 1, 1937 to collaborate with the Negrín cabinet. That was not true. It was a matter of a visit to Negrín, upon his request, which Negrín presented as an offer for collaboration and which the CNT denied was such.

65. Caballero gave a cool reception to the Italian Communist Luigi Longo when he visited him to propose the creation of the International Brigades, perhaps because he already knew that the order for their organization had been given by the Communist International without first consulting him (Longo, *Le Brigate Internazionale in Spagna,* Rome, 1956, pp. 43–44).

66. Hermet, p. 41 quoting Longo.

67. The first part was reflected by the order for the General Staff to refrain from praising non-Communist units, given toward the end of 1938 by the minister of defense, Negrín. An example of the second part was Carrillo's statement according to which "Spanish youth points to the Trotskyites as the principal culprits in the retreat and rupture of the Aragon front." Therefore, "let us crush them without pity in order to strengthen our rearguard" (*Frente Rojo,* Barcelona, March 20, 1938). At that time there were only Communist-led units on the Aragon front; the units of the CNT had been transferred to other fronts and the unit of POUM had been dissolved and its members were scattered among other units.

68. *Frente Rojo,* Valencia, March 19, 1937.

69. Tagüeña, pp. 188–89. Togliatti told Moscow that he had had to take charge of the "discipline of the army's Communist militants. . . . They did not feel the central committee's authority. Thus arose an intolerable struggle among them which undermined discipline, self-control, etc. Intervention came in the form of a letter signed by the central committee to the military militants; there were other measures as well." He does not say what these other measures were (Togliatti, p. 278).

70. Ibárruri (*El único camino,* pp. 250–51), in a chapter significantly called "Fighting Members of Parliament," in which there appears a list of military men without including the name of Valentín González, "El Campesino," because he had left the party while in exile. On page 258ff. she speaks of the Fifth Regiment which was the nucleus of the first Communist units, but not of Castro Delgado who also had left the party in exile.

71. Azaña, *Memorias,* p. 699. Information on Pozas is in Bolloten, p. 243.

72. Hernández, *Yo fui un ministro de Stalin,* p. 122.

73. The CNT's press in Madrid in July 1938 reported that Margarita Nelken, openly a member of the PCE, was going through barracks offering promotions in exchange for taking the party card. It also reported that in towns of La Mancha the former political bosses, first of the monarchy and then of the Republic, had turned Communist and continued to dominate the towns after forcibly getting rid of the collectivizations which were created during the first days of the war.

74. Thomas, pp. 441–42.

75. *Entresijos de la guerra de España,* Buenos Aires, 1955; and *Cómo y por qué salí de ministro de Defensa Nacional,* Mexico City, 1940.

76. Since personal motives are influential in political stances and are not easily documented, there is no other choice here than to resort to hearsay. This decision of Prieto's "meant the transfer of Antón, Communist commissar on the Madrid front, to the head of a battalion. This young man was La Pasionaria's lover and shared a house with her and Togliatti in Madrid (her husband, a miner, was always at the front with their son). La Pasionaria consequently became a fierce enemy of Prieto" (Thomas, p. 492).

77. Prieto, *Cómo y por qué,* p. 84. On the differences between Prieto and the PCE consult Fisher, *Men and Politics,* p. 432.

78. Thomas (p. 442) says that Russia "presumably knew that if it sent Spain enough arms for the Republic to win the war, a world war would probably ensue."

79. Claudio Sánchez-Albornoz, *De mi anecdotario político,* Buenos Aires, 1972, p. 150.

80. Thomas, p. 670.

81. Hernández, *Yo fui un ministro de Stalin,* p. 159.

82. Ibárruri, *El único camino,* pp. 360–61.

83. García Venero, vol. III, p. 372.

84. Ibárruri (p. 362) and the *Historia del PCE* (p. 184) state that the CNT and FAI were part of the demonstration. This is not true. What the PCE did was to place some libertarians devoted to the PCE as representatives of those organizations.

85. César M. Lorenzo, *Les Anarchistes Espagnols et le pouvoir,* Paris, 1969, p. 313ff.

86. J.A. González Casanova, *Federalisme i autonomia a Catalunya, 1863–1938,* Barcelona, 1974, p. 408.

87. González Casanova, p. 409.

88. *Documentos sobre la industria de guerra en Cataluña,* Buenos Aires, 1939.

89. González Casanova, p. 409.

90. González Casanova, p. 410.

91. PSUC's Catalan ministers were Serra i Pàmies, Vidiella, and Comorera.

92. Montserrat Roig, *Rafael Vidiella, l'aventura de la revolució,* Barcelona, 1976, p. 135ff.
93. The complete text of this letter appears in Salvador de Madariaga, *España,* Buenos Aires, 1964, p. 697ff. Despite PSUC's collaboration with the Negrín government in the dismantling of Catalonian autonomy, Togliatti thought it was not enough and that PSUC collaborated too much with the Generalidad, whose leaders such as Tarradellas seemed to him to be "provocateurs of the capitulators." He reproached PSUC for not having been active enough in its criticism of the collectivizations and in its persecution of POUM, and in particular for not "knowing how to fight against the obtuse nationalism of petit bourgeois Catalonians." He even thought that in practice PSUC "had slipped into a separatist stance" (Togliatti, p. 302ff.).
94. Vicente Guarner (*Cataluña en la guerra de España,* Madrid, 1975) contributes a number of facts which refute the supposed indifference of Catalonia regarding the war. The estimates made are mine.
95. Estruch, p. 106.
96. Hernández, *Yo fui un ministro de Stalin.*
97. Estruch, p. 99. There was a large gap between Díaz's words and his personal feelings. The Austrian writer Manés Sperber, who at the time was a Communist, relates that on his way to Paris to visit a delegation of the JSU headed by Carrillo, who was en route from Moscow to Spain, he read in the papers about the bombing of Guernica. He found Carrillo and his colleagues in the hotel drinking champagne and he thought they must not have known about the destruction of the Basque city. He was mistaken; they knew all about it (Manés Sperber, *Au delà de l'oubli,* Paris, 1979, p. 120).
98. Estruch, p. 113.
99. Gilles Martinet, "Le Mouvement ouvrier peut-il avoir un programme 'constitutif?'" *L'Observateur,* Paris, May 5, 1955.
100. Its text is in *Unidad proletaria UGT-CNT,* Mexico City, 1938. Also see García Venero, *Historia de la Internacionales,* vol. III, p. 381ff.; and Del Rosal, *Historia de la UGT de España,* vol. II, p. 754ff.
101. Diego Abad de Santillán, *De Alfonso XIII a Franco,* Buenos Aires, 1974, pp. 499–500.
102. Regarding this organization, see Casterás, p. 262ff.
103. The enumeration of firms is in Thomas, p. 528.
104. Thomas, p. 550.
105. *El Socialista,* Toulouse, Feb. 19, 1953.
106. Prieto, *Cómo y por qué.*
107. Hernández, *Yo fui un ministro de Stalin,* ch. 7, esp. p. 175; Castro Delgado, *Hombres made in Moscú,* p. 672ff. Carlos Rojas ("Cartas abiertas a los vivos y a los muertos: a Víctor Alba," *Destino,* Barcelona, July 18, 1979) states that the battle of the Ebro was one of General Rojo's ideas which the Russian advisors considered "a blunder, and that is the way Lieutenant Colonel Lazarov had it stated." It might be that this opinion was expressed to cover themselves for the predictable failure of the operation, but it seems improbable that Rojo could have been able to carry through an operation of such importance against the opinion of the Soviet "consultants."
108. Teresa Pàmies, p. 150ff. These statements by a then young Catalonian Communist woman contradict what Togliatti told Moscow after the war

was over (pp. 361–67). For example, he said that "there were many local sections of PSUC whose behavior was not equal to the situation". And he added, "It was clear that the would-be control of Barcelona by PSUC was an illusion." Although recognizing his personal merit, Togliatti found Comorera weak, for he had allowed his party to be infiltrated by shady businessmen (as well as by nationalists and even Trotskyites) and he had not made certain that the finances of the central committee were clear. Togliatti did not find the other leaders any better. "A portion of the leading members showed themselves to be cowards. Valdés, the organizational secretary, had an embarrassing breakdown in the middle of the party headquarters and had to be taken to the border after having performed poorly for a few days (occupying himself more with the evacuation of families than with fighting) at a time when the city had begun to be bombarded every twenty minutes. . . . Ferrer and Molino, UGT leaders, stayed until the last day but were in no condition to work. . . . Ardiaca, secretary of the *agitprop* section, decided to go and live forty kilometers from the city when the situation got worse. He returned under orders from the Secretariat but was in no condition to guarantee the daily publication of the party's organ. Colomer acted like a Trotskyite and an enemy agent" (in January he published a theoretical periodical of PSUC which Togliatti would not allow to be circulated for he found it to be "Trotskyite in content"). On the other hand he praised the youths who were being counseled by Carrillo and led by Wenceslao Colomer. Once in Figueres the leaders of PSUC "hid out even more than members of the PCE" and "were overly occupied with the evacuation of objects of value." But "those days proved to us that the rank and file of PSUC was better than its leaders."

109. *Epistolario Prieto-Negrín,* Paris, 1939.
110. Rodolfo Llopis, "Memorias políticas," *Historia 16,* Madrid, June 1976. I do not mention the conduct of the Communist representatives in the four or five meetings which celebrated what remained of the Parliament during the Civil War. They only approved what the government had done, whatever that was, and Ibárruri or some other representative gave speeches out of necessity. The Parliament was so unrepresentative that no one paid any attention to it. It was another deception.
111. Del Rosal, *Historia de la UGT de España,* vol. II, pp. 879–80.
112. Diego Abad de Santillán, *De Alfonso XIII a Franco,* p. 504.
113. From a letter from Trifón Gómez to Fernando de los Ríos dated May 24, 1939, printed fragmentedly in José García Pradas, *La traición de Stalin: cómo terminó la guerra de España,* New York, 1939; and in Andrés Saborit, *Julián Besteiro,* Mexico City, 1961.
114. Enrique Líster, *¡Basta!* s.l.s.f., 1971, p. 116.
115. Ignacio Iglesias (*La fase final de la guerra civil,* Barcelona, 1977, p. 82) gives a list of ships belonging to Spain available at the time in Mediterranean ports which were not sent to Valencia's ports.
116. Thomas, p. 581. Those who said that resistance was possible were Ramón Tamames, *La República: la era de Franco,* Madrid, 1973, p. 322; and Manuel Tuñón de Lara, *La España del siglo XX,* p. 649.
117. Ibárruri, *El único camino,* p. 452.
118. Julián Zagazagoitia, *Vida y viscisitudes de los españoles,* vol. II, p. 247.
119. García Venero, *Historia de las Internacionales,* vol. III, p. 402ff.

120. Tagüeña, p. 301; Líster, *¡Basta!* p. 117. Togliatti said that party leadership was "demoralized, disoriented, and desperate." In his eyes, Ibárruri was the only one who was of any value. The government "deserted" in the face of Casado's coup. "The party's rank-and-file organizations have not responded well." Líster and Modesto told him that "the party could do nothing by itself without the support of the government" (Togliatti, pp. 324–32).

121. Ibárruri, *El único camino,* p. 461. The quotes from Ibárruri which follow are on p. 462ff.

122. Regarding these events which are still the object of controversy today, see Ignacio Iglesias, *La fase final de la guerra civil,* Barcelona, 1977; *Juventudes Socialistas Españolas en Francia; el último episodio de la guerra civil española,* n.p.n.d., 1939; Luis Romero, *El final de la guerra,* Barcelona, 1976; J. García Pradas, *La traición de Stalin: cómo terminó la guerra de España,* New York, 1939; Segismundo Casado, *Así cayó Madrid,* Madrid, 1968; Luis Romero, *El desastre de Cartagena,* Barcelona, 1971; Ángel María de Lera, *Las últimas banderas,* Barcelona, 1967. Only Iglesias and García Pradas analyze the political motives and question Negrín's explanations; the others accept them. Casado gives his own interpretation, which tends to be more military than political.

123. Juan Modesto, *Soy del Quinto Regimiento,* Paris, 1969, p. 285. Tagüeña corroborates Modesto's statement as does even Tuñón de Lara.

124. Tagüeña, p. 315.

125. Líster, *Memorias de un luchador,* pp. 431–32. After Negrín and La Pasionaria took off, Togliatti went to Alicante where he was arrested but was freed by a Socialist leader. He looked for someone to publicize a declaration of the Central Committee of the PCE but did not find anyone to do so until a Russian officer in Albacete who went by the name of Miguel Martínez agreed to do the job. Togliatti thought that "none of the party's organizations was able to defend itself. . . . The majority of those holding positions of power have failed." He thought that if the party attempted a coup the troops would not follow it nor would the masses respond. Therefore they had to settle for seeking the reestablishment of party legality. The declaration—made by Togliatti but signed by the party's central committee without consulting anyone—stated that "Casado's revolt is a product of a foreign conspiracy and of Trotskyite calumny"; he appealed to the Socialists to rebel against their leaders "who have handed the party over to Trotskyism" and to the CNT to rebel against FAI and to unite with the Communists because "by unity we are assured of victory." But in a letter to Ibárruri written three days before, he indicated that most probably there would be an offensive by Franco's troops which would break the fronts. All this occurred between March 12 and 18. On March 24, without having met any of his goals, Togliatti met Hernández and some others at the airfield at Totana in the province of Murcia and they left for Algeria (Togliatti, pp. 324–42). The Civil War ended six days later, April 1, 1939.

126. Castro Delgado, *Hombres made in Moscú,* p. 734.

127. Ibárruri, *El único camino,* p. 402.

128. Líster, *Memorias de un luchador,* p. 432.

14.
Period of Purges

From its foundation until 1935, the PCE lived in isolation, out of touch with reality and without influence over it, blindly implementing the slogans of the Communist International. From 1935 to 1939 it grew in influence until it finally became master of the government in the Republican zone, thanks to the insufficient and costly Soviet arms. After the war was over, for a period of two decades, the PCE went back to being a party without influence. From 1939 to 1956 the party was mainly devoted to internal affairs; there were numerous purges and frequent changes of policy.

The Triangle of Exile

The beginning period of exile was no different for the Communists than for those of any other organization: concentration camps, each man for himself, catch as catch can, obsession over *papiers*. . . Nor was it any different in appearance for the leaders: a privileged situation, a passport and material means to set oneself up in Paris or in other French cities. Shortly thereafter, as World War II approached, many leaders left for Latin America, a handful went to Moscow, and a few stayed in France. But unlike in other parties, that was not by individual decision but per order of the political bureau. Before leaving for Mexico, Mije wrote members: "You must remain in the concentration camps, comrades, to control the exile and to strengthen the party."[1]

In the concentration camps and in fields and harvests the Communists came out of the human isolation which the Civil War had imposed. The forced coexistence with people of other organizations made them aware of the hatred people felt toward them. Aside from the practical cases of sharing material goods, the other exiles wanted nothing to do with them. That and their habit of discipline caused the Communists to be the first to organize themselves in the camps. This tendency was reinforced by the Nazi-Soviet pact because they were forced to confront the verbal aggressiveness of their ideological adversaries, and they needed, at the very least, to talk to one another to find justification for what

299

seemed incredible. Líster went to Paris where in the Hotel Regine he came in contact with the political bureau. "Mije received us in a magnificent apartment. . . . In the dining room we saw Antón, Mije, and his wife and son as well as Giorla and Carrillo with their wives all seated at a table. The meal and the wine were exquisite and therefore extraordinarily expensive. The conversation had absolutely nothing to do with the war and concentration camps."

On February 10, General Rojo had given the heads of the large units "a certain amount of money to pay all the officers and commissars." Líster received 1,500 francs. Líster said that he later found out from Modesto that the money earmarked for the units of the Ebro and given to Santiago Álvarez for the Fifth Army "ended up in the hands of Mije, Giorla, Antón, Carrillo, and company. Several years later he learned likewise that Santiago Álvarez had greatly discriminated against the officers and commissars of the Fifth Army who did not belong to the party by not paying them their salaries and swindling those who belonged to the party by giving them much less than they deserved."[2] On the other hand, the ship *Cap Pinède* had arrived at Port-Vendres with boxes full of jewels and gold gathered by the Treasury from the time it left Madrid until the time it left Barcelona. Some of those boxes went to Odessa on board a ship that was no longer officially part of the France-Navigation fleet. Some were handed over to the French Communist party which put Charles Tillon in charge of them. This treasure was used during World War II to supply the French Communist resistance when it was organized after Hitler's attack on the USSR.[3]

These sordid maneuvers were the backdrop for the polemic which developed between Negrín and Araquistáin and later Prieto. Cases of murder, pressuring, and maneuvers at the hands of the PCE and the USSR came to light during the war; no one except POUM and the CNT had dared reveal them. On March 31 Negrín reported on his activities since the fall of Catalonia at the Permanent Commission of the Parliament, a meeting in which there was a violent argument between Araquistáin, Martínez Barrio, and Ibárruri. The yacht *Vita* left Boulogne for Mexico loaded with jewels; Líster suspected that Negrín had made the shipment to Prieto so that Prieto, thinking he was on top of things, could take possession of the treasure (actually, the government of Mexico controlled it) and so divert petitions for aid and the responsibility for the exiles' distress to Prieto.[4] Prieto got the Permanent Commission of Parliament, which established Negrín as head of the government, to found JARE (Junta de Auxilio a los Refugiados Españoles—Council of Aid for Spanish Refugees) which Prieto ran and which would help many to leave France for Mexico. Negrín founded SERE (Servicio de Emigración para Republicanos Españoles—Emigration Service for Spanish Republicans), which took charge, in particular, of financing supporters of Negrín in setting up companies. The two organizations sent some 150,000 exiles to Latin America.[5]

What the numerous books on the exiles have not mentioned is that during those agonizing times when World War II was about to or had already broken out, the Communists, by means of the complicity of some Mexican traveling companions, Fernando Gamboa and his wife Susana, whom the Mexican legation in Paris and later in Vichy put in charge of the embarcation of exiles, chose those who would receive a Mexican visa in accordance with the lists provided by the PCE. To be included in such lists, the PCE required that one sign the condemnation of the National Defense Council. Many signed just to conform, but many also refused and had to remain in France where quite a number were sent to Nazi camps or were shot to death or handed over to Franco's police.[6] This visa selection has never been mentioned nor has any mention been made of the fact that there were no Communists in the allied military units that took part in the beginning of the war, such as the Narvick operation. The PCE's stance at the time—like that of every Communist party throughout the world—was to call the war a war of aggression against the German people; the Allies were not to be aided but sabotaged. This was difficult for the Spanish Communists to digest for they had had the Condor Legion facing them and the German aircraft above them.

Nonetheless, the number of defections among the old members was low. On the other hand, there were defections in PSUC as soon as the exile had begun. Many who had been in USC and the Catalonian PSOE and now found themselves in PSUC did not dare leave it during the Civil War, but as soon as they were across the Pyrenees they separated from it. For practical reasons, others waited until they reached Latin America before separating from the party. Many who became members during the Civil War considered themselves detached from the party when it could no longer be of use to them. But on the whole, the militants in the PCE resisted (better than those in PSUC) the series of shocks caused by the loss of the war, the exile, the concentration camps, the flight of the leaders to the USSR and Latin America, and the Nazi-Soviet pact.

A Letter from Carrillo

While Franco's troops had not yet entered Madrid and the outcome of the war was still uncertain, the PCE and JSU exile in France kept up a bitter campaign against the National Defense Council. Carrillo distinguished himself in this endeavor. In March 1939 *Jeunesses du Monde,* printed by *Correspondance Internationale,* published an editorial signed by Carrillo on "Spanish Youth against Treason," in which he falsely claimed that the Council tried to arrest members of the government to hand them over to the executioner "hoping to win the sympathy of Franco, Hitler, and Mussolini." The other false claim was that the JSU and "the Communists were fighting as leaders of the patriots." Federico Melchor, in the April 15 issue of the same paper said that the Junta had "a political line lent by the Trotskyites." The May issue printed a document of the Executive Committee of the JSU which it said was written "days after the treason of Casado-Besteiro-Miaja." This statement, dated March 21, 1939 in Madrid, indicated that the JSU had publicly announced that it would support the National Defense Council on the condition that it abandon its "policy of division of the people and of persecution of anti-Fascists." Claudín, who had stayed behind, was now out of the country. Tagüeña, who also stayed behind with his troops, had departed on March 6. Carrillo never returned to the South-Central zone.

Here follows an episode in the history of the PCE which subsequently people tried to forget: it revolved around a letter from Santiago Carrillo to his father Wenceslao Carrillo, representative of the PSOE in the National Defense Council. This letter was printed in *Jeunesses du Monde* on June 6, 1939 and in *Correspondance Internationale* on June 3 of the same year as a model of an exemplary member who put serving the party above family ties. The letter was later forgotten until the Spanish Socialist Youth in Exile published it in 1946 in France (in exile the PSOE reorganized its own youth groups). In 1977 the libertarians in Madrid revived the letter and a spokesman for the PCE said it had been falsified. It was indeed authentic. Tagüeña speaks of it in his memoirs: "There was never any trust between Carrillo and myself, let alone friendship. I always believed he was ready to subordinate everything to his political ambitions. At the time he had just disowned his father, Wenceslao Carrillo. . . . As Spartan as the gesture may seem, no one doubted that he did it to appear before the Communist party of Spain as an upright member, able to sacrifice his family for the cause."[7]

Many years later when he was asked about the letter, Carrillo responded: "I realized that if I wasn't sent to Madrid it was so I wouldn't be in combat against my father or because I was a new member and they were wary of my political conviction. I don't know if there were comrades then who thought that. I admit that even if they were wrong, they could have doubts about me since I was a very young member. When I found

out about Casado's coup, I wrote a public letter which condemned my
father for treason, for I considered it such to negotiate with the Fascists
at the very moment when my comrades were fighting in the streets of
Madrid."[8] The letter was postmarked, not during the fighting in Madrid
but May 15, a month and a half after the end of the war. It was addressed
to Wenceslao Carrillo in London, who wrote a public letter to Stalin
naming him responsible for his son's letter, the text of which follows:

Paris, May 15, 1939
Mr. Wenceslao Carrillo
London
I have received the letter you sent me from London. I did not intend to
answer it. But later I thought it would be helpful for you to know the
reasons I decided to break off relations with you. The treason of Casado,
Besteiro, Miaja, Mera, Wenceslao Carrillo, and company has caused a
chasm so deep, on the one hand between the masses and the organizations
and the men faithful to the masses, and on the other the elements who,
during the course of the war, planned the surrender to Franco, that there
can now be nothing in common between the two factions.

The Spanish people have fought for thirty-two months with exemplary
heroism and courage. The men of Guadarrama, Brunete, Belchite, Teruel,
the Ebro, and the defense of Madrid recall for the anti-Fascists throughout
the world the magnificent struggle by a people endowed with a firm will
to defend democracy and national independence.

Throughout these thirty-two months of resistance, the Spanish people have
proven to the world that it is possible to stand up to the Fascist aggressors
with arms in hand. When capitulating pro-Fascist elements were proclaiming
throughout the world "slavery before death," the Spanish people raised
the flag of armed resistance against Fascism, and their example, together
with that of the admirable people of China, has moved millions of men
everywhere to confront Fascist piracy.

But your counterrevolutionary coup, your back-handed treason delivered
the heroic Spanish people, hands and feet bound, to Franco and to the
details of OVRA and GESTAPO. This occurred precisely at a time when
international solidarity for our people was on the increase; at a time when
pressure was being added by the working masses who, stirred by our
example, were forcing the reactionary governments of France and England
to lean more and more toward a policy of resistance to Fascist aggression;
at a time when our struggle stimulated workers and democrats from all
nations and made the capitulators retreat.

Your counterrevolutionary coup has been a great service not only to Franco
but also to the reaction and international Fascism; thanks to you one of
the main centers of resistance has fallen into their hands, and thus the
Fascists immediately felt much stronger and decided to occupy Bohemia,
Moravia, Albania, and Memel, and are threatening to provoke a general
war of which Spain will be the victim. To carry out your treason you

lured the people with the promise of peace; you led them to believe that you would put an end to the war, that there would be no retaliation, that national independence and the people's conquests would be safeguarded. And what have you given the people instead?

The war in the trenches ended only to give rise to a wave of persecution which caused in the ranks of the working classes and anti-Fascism— regardless of one's tendency—many more casualties than if resistance had continued; a period of repression has begun. Falangists, the Civil Guard, OVRA, and the GESTAPO hunt down anti-Fascists and murder thousands of them throughout the country. There is not an anti-Fascist family that is not bewailing the loss or imprisonment of a son, brother, or father who would now be alive and free had they not been placed in the middle of your vile treason.

The social victories of the workers have disappeared beneath the Draconian measures of Fascist authorities, faithful servants of management; the land which the Popular Front handed over to the peasants, thereby giving them freedom, has fallen back into the hands of the landowners.

Italians, Germans, and Moors do as they please in our territory which Fascist powers are trying to colonize.

That is what you, the Council of Treason, have given the Spanish people; that is what was concealed beneath your false promises of peace. Hundreds of thousands of Spaniards now verify with horror how much falseness and duplicity were concealed in your promises and how right we were to turn them against you.

Your whole band knew very well that in order to surrender to Franco a great and heroic people such as the Spanish people, it was necessary above all to discredit and disarm the Communists because we Communists who have always told the people the truth, we, the very flesh of the working class, were not going to allow such treason.

And everyone in unison—Casado, Besteiro, Miaja, Mera, yourself, and the press written by Fascist and capitulating cowards—began to sling mud at my party and its most beloved leaders; you insulted La Pasionaria, the woman whom all Spaniards considered a symbol in the fight for liberty, you sought her like wolves to have her arrested and handed over to Franco; you insulted Pepe [José] Díaz, the beloved leader of the Communists and the Spanish workers who led them through the difficult struggles of the last few years, who leads them today under foreign domination, and who will ultimately carry them to victory; you persecuted Jesús Hernández, Modesto, and Líster whom you also wanted to shoot down.

You have kept in jail numerous revolutionaries such as Girón, Cazorla, and Mesón, so that Franco would not have to bother going after them; you have murdered Conesa and Barceló and dozens of proven revolutionaries and fighters.

All the enemies of the people have united against my party and its men: officers from Fascist families, such as Casado, agents of international reaction, such as pro-Fascist Besteiro, ambitious military men like Miaja, adventurers of FAI, and followers of Caballero and Trotsky. And you are among them; you who, despite the fact that you are a worker, have not hesitated to betray your own class in the most despicable way.

Why did you all unite against my party? Because the Communist party fought for the victory of the people, and in effect, a truly honorable peace which would prevent terror and the slaughter of thousands and thousands of anti-Fascists and revolutionaries; because the Communist party made tremendous efforts to maintain unity without which such peace would be impossible, as has been proven.

Through this painful experience the Spanish people have deep in their hearts understood better than ever that behind the slogan of the fight "against Communism" is concealed the groundwork for the brutal reign of Fascism. The Spanish people have been able to see who their friends and defenders are as well as their disguised enemies.

And the Socialist workers who one day believed in the sincerity of the so-called leftism of Largo Caballero's group—your leader and main inspiration—have understood that the leftism-Trotskyism of Largo Caballero, Araquistain, Baráibar, Zancajo, and company, all agents of Fascism, has the same purpose as Besteiro's pro-Fascism. You all play the same role of treason in the service of Hitler and Mussolini. You all feel the same hatred for the great nation of Socialism, the Soviet Union, and for the leader of the world's working classes, the great Stalin, because they are the safeguard and the loyal friends of all peoples who fight for freedom; because they have consistently helped the Spanish people, and also because they were able to eradicate with an iron hand your twin brothers, the traitors, Trotsky, Zinoviev, and Bukharin.

All of you, followers of Caballero and Trotsky, Besteiro's friends, FAI, and other supernumeraries, you are all the enemies of the unity of the working class and the Popular Front. During the thirty-two months of fighting you have done everything possible to divide the UGT and JSU, to break the unity of the people, and abroad you are still dedicated to the same task of discrediting the heroic Spanish people and their staunchest leaders.

But you will not meet your goals. In light of recent experience the need for unity with the Communist party seems more clear to all socialist workers whom you have betrayed; all youth, all workers understand the need to maintain at whatever cost the unity of the UGT and JSU.

And the masses who saw that it was necessary to break the Popular Front to carry out the betrayal realize now better than ever that the Popular Front, freed from the ballast of the traitors who sabotaged it, is the weapon that will allow us to put up mass resistance to block the consolidation of Fascism in Spain and to lead us to victory.

Popular unity, without traitors, is absolutely essential in the fight against Franco and the invasion; and the Communist party, as always, leads the people in the struggle.

And I am a loyal member of the Communist party of Spain and the glorious Communist International. I feel ever more proud of my party which provides the example of self-denial and heroism in the fight against the invaders, the party which during the hard times of illegality did not strike its flag but, on the contrary, waged war against Fascism with determination and courage, the party which all Spaniards are counting on, and understandably so, for their liberation from the claws of Fascism.

I feel ever more proud to be a soldier in the ranks of the great Communist International which you and your friends hate so much and which has been able to raise throughout the world the flag of solidarity with the Spanish people while your friends from abroad, the leaders of the Second International, were doing everything they could to oppress us and were working and continue to work against unity, against the USSR using the same slogan as Hitler and Mussolini: "The fight against Communism."

My love for the Soviet Union and the great Stalin is constantly growing; they are the country and the man you all hate and slander precisely because they consistently helped Spain throughout our entire struggle.

The hatred that your gang of Trotskyites and followers of Caballero feel toward the Communist party, the Soviet Union, and the great Stalin is yet further evidence of the formidable role which they play in the struggle of the Spanish people for their freedom.

When you ask to get in touch with me you forget that I am a Communist and you a man who has betrayed his class, who has sold his people. No manner of relationship can exist between a Communist and a traitor. You remained on the other side of the trenches.

No, Wenceslao Carrillo, there can be no relationship between you and me because we no longer have anything in common, and I shall strive my whole life long, with loyalty to my party, my class, and to the cause of Socialism, to show that there is nothing in common between you and me but the same last name.

The Spanish Republic has been struck a blow because of your treason, but the fight is not over. The will of the people will bring Franco down, and the workers and peasants joined with all democrats headed by the Communist party will once again restore the people's Republic. But they will never—either under Fascist domination or after our victory—forget your infamous betrayal.

Santiago Carrillo[9]

The Interrupted Analysis

After any defeat, it is a tradition in the workers' movement to analyze the causes for the failure. The Socialists put all the blame for the loss of the war on the Communists, Soviet interference, and Negrín; the Republicans evaded the issue talking of "the atrocities committed by the Anarchists" (when in reality everyone, regardless of ideology, committed them). The Communists attempted to embark on an analysis which would justify them. The first attempt was a report from Comorera before the Central Committee of PSUC which met in Paris on March 2 and 3 before the National Council of Defense had been formed.[10] But a note, adjoined upon publication, said that "the treason of Casado-Besteiro . . . on express orders from Chamberlain-Deladier . . . is the best evidence of our party's clear vision in the analysis of the prospects of each new situation that arises." PSUC, said Comorera, "considering its mistakes and weaknesses, did its job until the very end." Later he indicated that resistance ought to be continued and the unity of the party strengthened. PSUC in occupied Catalonia should be "the only party of the working class" and it must make efforts to rebuild the Popular Front and the National Union. It was clearly not an analysis. PSUC and the PCE never made mistakes (he does not mention what the mistakes and weaknesses were aside from not having been hard enough on the "Trotskyites"). All the blame for the defeat went to the "traitors" in the Council.

The JSU did not even do that. Perhaps their leaders were too busy with the Sixth Congress of the Socialist Youth International which was held in Lille, France, in July 1939, and where it was agreed to expel the JSU because they were really a branch of the Communist Youth International. Carrillo spoke of the heroism of the Spanish youth—as if they all belonged to the JSU—but he did not analyze the reasons why this heroism was not sufficient to win the war. Tagüeña also spoke, saying that "to throw us out after having been defeated means joining the side of the victors. Of course the value of my arguments," he added years later, "dissolved in the face of the public and notorious fact that the JSU was under Communist discipline."[11] A discussion was begun among members under less comfortable conditions and was nipped in the bud in the camp of Argelés in October 1940; it was initiated not by the bureau but by Monzón and Trilla. It was decided to send members to Spain and to extend the party through the Midi of France.[12]

Among the leaders of the PCE in Moscow there were some discussions about the war. Togliatti said that the constitution of the Junta and Negrín's escape were tragic errors and so inexplicable that he suspected that Negrín was an accomplice of Casado, but Líster observed that Togliatti forgot to add that Togliatti himself had organized the Communist leaders' departure from Spain five hours before Negrín left. Togliatti made these statements in a letter of March 12, 1939 to the political bureau of the PCE. In the letter he "falsified certain facts in order to appear in the most advantageous position."[13] The Comintern tried to study what had happened: "In the spring of 1939 leaders of our party initiated in Moscow an examination of our war and particularly its outcome. Simultaneously we met with the Secretariat of the Communist

International to examine the same problem. But both our discussion and that of the Communist International were cut off shortly thereafter."[14]

Díaz presided over those meetings; doubtless he had gone to Moscow from his sanitarium. Líster took advantage of those discussions to point out that it was possible to continue the war and to accuse some leaders of remaining in France and others of leaving the South-Central zone too soon. He said that this behavior could be accepted only if the war was believed to have been lost in Catalonia. The war was too complex for them, and besides there was a tendency in some of the leaders toward "the good life" as well as toward mistrust of victory.[15] We do not know what Díaz's opinion was, although Tagüeña, who went to see him in his sanitarium in Moscow along with Castro and on Líster's insistence, related that Díaz "did not conceal his opinion that the party leaders who were in Spain in the final days of the war had made serious errors. He was indignant that they did not fight openly against Casado."[16] The Comintern could not criticize the party leaders because it always found their conduct "correct," since they had faithfully obeyed its delegates' instructions. Thus it did not want the discussions to continue. Any criticism at all would necessarily rebound on the Communist International. In the manifesto of May 1, 1939, the Communist International devoted exactly five lines to the "heroic struggle of the Spanish people" betrayed by the "capitulating leaders of the Second International."[17]

Several years would go by before the *Historia del PCE* appeared and Ibárruri wrote her memoirs for people to know what the PCE thought of the war and its own participation in it. Both those texts hold that the PCE's line was "correct," although La Pasionaria criticized its "lack of foresight." Aside from that, Casado and the Freemasons were to blame for the defeat. It seems incredible, but there was no doubt in attributing the failure of the war to the same people Franco had accused of having caused it: "Communist propaganda generally paid no attention to the role the Masonic organization played either openly or secretly in many of the political events of our days. . . . [The Masons] demanded the displacement of the labor representatives [read Communist] of the government [and] using the invisible threads of foreigners they wove the bloc of capitulation."[18]

The *Historia del PCE* is somewhat more coherent. The blame for defeat belongs to German and Italian aid to Franco as well as to the lack of unity among workers "to a great enough extent to have given the requisite firmness and range to national and popular unity." Nonetheless the PCE "did everything humanly and politically possible during the entire war to end it with victory for the people. It is the only Spanish political party that has no responsibility whatsoever for losing the war.

Such is the appraisal of all those who judged these events with a minimum of objectivity and sincerity. . . . The errors and inadequacies of the party bore no direct relation to the causes of defeat. . . . The Communists were the ones who, in defense of the people, gave the most evidence of self-denial and sacrifice."[19]

Stalin's Purges

In 1962 when Ilya Ehrenburg published his memoirs, taking advantage of the "thaw" of Khrushchev's time, in them he said that he was the only survivor of all the Russians who had gone to Spain during the Civil War. Tagüeña related that "the internationals who had gone from Russia to Spain to fight, as was expected, upon their return tried to contact their friends who had emigrated; from them we found out that the great majority of political émigrés had fallen in the latest purges. . . . For this reason the interbrigadiers called themselves Spaniards; it was the safest thing to do at the time. . . . We soon appreciated the danger involved in having or having had relations with an émigré. During the purges friendship or a casual relationship with any of the supposed members of the so-called opposition group was enough to cause one to 'drop out of sight.' On one occasion an interpreter from the International told me that the Spanish party had done well not to send Professor Wenceslao Roces to Russia because the police were well aware of his visits with Bukharin."[20]

Even before the end of the Spanish war, Ambassador Rosenberg and Consul Antonov-Ovseenko disappeared (the latter apparently was denounced by Gerö who survived all repressions but could not prevent Antonov's rehabilitation after the Twentieth Congress of the Russian Communist party in 1956). Further eliminations were Berzin (who used to give farewell parties for those who were called to Moscow to be executed), Stachevsky (who had participated in the transfer of Spanish gold to Moscow), General Grischin, Ambassador Gaikins, General Uritsky (in charge of arms shipment), *Pravda* correspondent Mikhail Koltsov, General Maximov, and Kleber. Many interbrigadiers also disappeared in Russia or in "liberated" countries after World War II: Rajk in Hungary, Walter in Poland, Copic and the Cvijic brothers in Moscow. London was tried in Prague and miraculously escaped with his life.

Other interbrigadiers later had important roles to play. Munch was president of the Popular Hungarian Republic; Szyr was vice-president of the Council of Poland; six members of the East German government had been in the Brigades. Twenty-four Yugoslavians became generals under Tito. Shehn was president of Albania's government, and Damianov became vice-president of the government of Bulgaria. De Vittorio was secretary of the Italian CGL. Longo became leader of the Italian Communist party; Malinowsky, a Soviet minister; Billoux, one of De Gaulle's ministers. André Marty and Auguste Lecoeur were not as lucky, having been thrown out of the French Communist party in 1952; Frantisek Kriegel was excluded from the Czech Communist party for refusing to sign while he was minister the treaty which allowed the occupation of his country by the Russians in 1968.

All the "instructors" died in bed. Togliatti was head of the Italian Communist party; Codovila, head of the Argentine Communist party; Vidali, head of the Communist party of Trieste, and Gerö called the Russians to occupy Hungary in 1956. Some of those executed were caught up in the machinery of Stalin's purges. But many died as a result of their relations with Spain. Stalin and the Communist International did not want any witnesses to their manipulation of the Spanish war. The last casualty was José Díaz, who died in a hospital at Tiflis on March 21, 1942 at the age of 47.[21] "He was a simple man, whom circumstances elevated to a position of excessive responsibility which he accepted with honesty and good will."[22] The rumor that he had committed suicide circulated among Spanish refugees; it was reinforced by some Spanish children who said they saw him throw himself from a balcony. It was learned that he had given several letters to an agent of the NKVD who was always at his side. They were never mailed. His wife denied that he killed himself. Bedridden since November 1938 with duodenal cancer as well as tuberculosis, Díaz hardly participated—and only from afar—in matters which the Spanish Communist leaders as refugees in the USSR had to deal with.

The Children and Karaganda

When the Communist leaders arrived there were a number of Spaniards in the USSR: children sent from Spain during the war along with their teachers as well as pilots who were studying in Soviet aviation schools and sailors from Spanish ships anchored in Russian ports. There must have been 300-400 adults and 2,000 children.[23] Since the country lived in utter terror of the police, those Spaniards inevitably had to be the object of suspicion. Nothing happened to them until the German invasion of the USSR. They saw the purges as an internal Russian problem. But as soon as Russia saw itself involved in the war, those Spaniards were asked if they wanted to go to Latin America, stay in Russia, or return to Spain. Almost all opted to go to Latin America. A few days later they were arrested and taken to Nova Sibirsk and finally in the winter of 1942 they ended up in the forced labor camp at Karaganda in the steppes of Kazajstan. Several of those Spaniards staged a hunger strike in 1946 and led the "inmates" in a strike in 1947. Of the 900 "inmates" at the camp, some 90 were Spaniards. Nothing was known of them until Francisque Bornel, a Frenchman at the camp, managed to get out in 1947 through action taken by his government, and he disclosed in Paris the existence of this group of Spanish Republicans in the Gulag.

Although it is difficult to believe, the leaders of the PCE were possibly unaware until that time of such a state of affairs, since those Spaniards were arrested in Moscow and taken to a rest home when the Spanish war ended. In any event, beginning in 1948 when Bornel made his disclosure, the Spanish Federation of Deportees of Paris initiated action and a press campaign was undertaken and the PCE of Moscow could not help but be informed. The Permanent Commission of the Spanish Parliament protested and ordered the Republican government in exile to take action. Mije was the only member of the Permanent Commission who was opposed. Referring to the Spaniards in the Gulag, he said: "Had they fallen into my hands, I would have executed them." At no time did the leaders of the PCE in Moscow defend those Republicans. They merely denied their existence.[24]

Nor did the PCE in Moscow do anything for the Spanish children who in spite of being minors were forced to become Soviet citizens, which placed them under Soviet laws which authorized the state to prevent any citizen from leaving the country. The children refused to become Russians and several members of the PCE were commissioned to persuade them. They were later placed in apprenticeship schools and were thereby dispersed.[25] Here is an example of how problems were "resolved." In an effort to achieve better living conditions for the Spanish Communists during times of very strict rationing, they were organized into a guerrilla battalion of the NKVD under Francisco Ortega. In this battalion many who had no desire or were in no position to fight but who agreed to it to survive lost their lives.

Living conditions were not good for Communists who were not in the higher echelons. There was one room per family. And when they differed with party leaders, even that was taken away and they were assigned to work in Central Asia or Siberia. One of the refugees, a Doctor Botet, was imprisoned and disappeared because when one of his sons was captured by the Germans in their advance through Russia, he was handed over to Franco and the Spanish government made him talk on the radio. Since he said things that did not please Moscow, his father paid for it. The NKVD made several attempts to recruit Spanish

Communists for the purpose of establishing espionage systems among the refugees. Díaz protested and many believed he was thrown over a balcony and was buried without a gravestone instead of having his body placed in the wall of the Kremlin as was done with other heads of Communist parties who died in the USSR. Now that Díaz was dead, no one took any action. It was a silence imposed by fear but also a product of indifference and the intrigues of party leaders.[26]

Díaz's Successor

From the beginning of World War II up to the Nazi attack on the USSR, the PCE was in political hibernation. In the USSR it was an association of mutual assistance to the extent it was allowed. When talking about Spain, so as not to annoy the Nazi ally, the Communist International ordered Spain to be referred to as the Francoist state and not Fascist state. A word to the wise. . . Díaz continued to be secretary general in name. His closest associates believed he had cancer. "It must have been very painful for José Díaz to see how they disputed over his inheritance without waiting for him to die. Dolores Ibárruri, because of her nature and her bond with Francisco Antón, lived a very isolated life as an émigré; on the other hand, Jesús Hernández was very active and his home was always full of people who sought his help and understanding. Although his marriage to Pilar Boves, who was divorced from Domingo Girón, had not been viewed favorably by the leaders of the party, the members did not hold it against her because she had won over many militants with her intelligence and ability."[27]

In the fight between the two clans, members who were in the Frunze Academy which moved to Tashkent when the Germans approached Moscow were with Hernández who was working in the Communist International and had contacts with important people. "Líster and Modesto openly sided with Hernández, and Dolores began to be the object of all sorts of disparaging epithets." Antón traveled to the cities where there were Spaniards to help them solve their material problems. He looked everywhere for members who would be willing to act as informers. At the time Dolores Ibárruri was living in Ufa and Hernández in Kuybishev with Dimitrov and functionaries of the Communist International.

In May 1943 Stalin decided to dissolve the Communist International. Members of its parties learned through the papers that the parties "had acquired the necessary maturity to function independently." With the dissolution Stalin was killing two birds with one stone: the appeasement of his allies and the direct dependence of all Communist parties on the

Russian Communist party. The dissolution resolution was signed by the members of the Executive Committee of the Communist International who were in the USSR and by several "representatives of the Communist Parties," among them Dolores Ibárruri. The last action the Communist International took was to order all Communist parties to favor the National Union and ally themselves with whomever they could. Although the offices of the Communist International continued to function as before, albeit assigned to the Central Committee of the Soviet Communist party, the Spaniards no longer had to worry so about getting in the good graces of Manuilski or Dimitrov.

With Díaz's death the PCE was left without a secretary general. By then Russia was in the war and it was necessary for the party to function politically. Its delegation had set itself up in the Marx and Engels Institute building. In Arbat Square there was another office which dealt with members' problems. Most members were with Hernández; it was he who had acted to solve their problems and it was known that he was in favor of having the majority of Spaniards leave the Soviet Union. On the other hand, aside from Antón, her secretary Irene Falcón, and Ignacio Gallego, there were very few who were whole-heartedly with Dolores Ibárruri. "The loss of her son Rubén on the Russian front had dealt her a severe blow and caused her to withdraw into herself to an even greater degree." Stalin had classified her as well as Díaz as a leader with a "Bolshevik temperament," and thus she believed she had the right to succeed Díaz. But no one had anything to be grateful to her for, since "she made the mistake of thinking that the complaints of the Spaniards about the general situation were exaggerated and were used by Hernández to gain popularity." Líster and Modesto were the most enthusiastic supporters of Hernández. In the fall of 1943 Hernández and Antón were ordered to go to Mexico and other places in Latin America where Ibárruri was more popular than Hernández. Why had Moscow decided on that maneuver which indeed eliminated Hernández? Possibly because it irritated the higher-ups that one of his promises was to have the Spanish exiles leave Russia.

The Valencian José Antonio Uribe remained in charge of the PCE in Russia. Castro Delgado, a staunch enemy of Ibárruri, stayed on in Moscow at the head of Radio Free Spain which called itself the Pyrenean Station. Ibárruri took advantage of Hernández's departure to come out of her isolation and began to concern herself with the problems of the émigrés. Now that the Germans no longer were a threat to Moscow, she managed to concentrate the majority of Spanish Communists in the capital. Since it was apparent that she would be Díaz's successor, Hernández's supporters began approaching her to tell her what action others had taken in opposition to her candidacy. Ibárruri was clever and extended a helping hand which Líster, Modesto, and others quickly reached for. Castro Delgado was the only one who continued to oppose her.

On the occasion of the promotion of Modesto, Líster, and Cordón as Soviet generals (which Ibárruri possibly got for them), a dinner was held in Kuntsevo, the summer residence of the leaders of the former Communist International. It was attended by Manuilski and Stepanov (Stepanov, as well as Orlov, had survived). It was clearly an occasion to give accolades to Ibárruri. In her speech, she "made unmistakable and harsh threats to those who continued to oppose her." Castro and Segis Álvarez, who continued supporting Hernández, were greeted by no one nor did they find a place to sit.

"The three generals said they were grateful for what they considered—with good reason—an undeserved honor. None of the speakers mentioned the other Spaniards who were in the Soviet army nor did they mention those who had won military ranks on the front (the three generals had not left the Frunze Academy at the time). Even less mention was made of those who had died as guerrilla fighters without any appointment whatsoever." That dinner was like "a reshuffling of the party roster." Beltrán burst into song in which he assured everyone that they would soon see the three generals as marshals. "This song would soon bring him profitable dividends." The generals were sent to beef up the ranks of the new Polish army which was being formed as a replacement for General Anders's army which had gone to Iran.

At the beginning of May 1944 at a partial meeting of the central committee made up of the members that were in Moscow and reinforced by three selected militants, it was reported that Hernández had been thrown out of the party in Mexico "on account of his divisionary efforts to take over the position of secretary general and his anti-Soviet activities, for he had suggested the departure from the USSR of the Spanish émigrés." So "he was automatically classified as a traitor and an enemy of the people." The central committee of Moscow decided to expel Castro Delgado from the committee and took away his job on the radio (and he was even deprived of his living quarters, although Castro wrote to Stalin and he got back the room in which he was living with three relatives). He was accused of being "coryphaeus" and Hernández's representative in Russia. However, he was not expelled from the party.

"The news and the subsequent terror spread among the émigrés: the former supporters of Jesús Hernández for having been such; those who had friendly relations with Enrique Castro for maintaining them; those who had lately come over to Dolores just in case they might be held accountable for their procrastination; even those who had taken no action at all just in case some personal enemy took advantage of the confusion to do them harm. . . . Everyone was at her [La Pasionaria's] mercy in the event she decided to bring up past activities." It is strange that Ibárruri was not named secretary general in that meeting of the central committee; however everyone began to call her that and that is how things remained.

Líster and Modesto, at a meeting of the Spanish collective of the Frunze Academy—before which they had often attacked La Pasionaria—asked that any fact which would help uncover those who had been expelled and other possible traitors be reported. "Since they were implicated and frightened, they would do almost anything to save themselves no matter whom they might ruin." Then a "traitor hunt" began. Those who had sympathized with Hernández and did not rush to get on Ibárruri's side lost their jobs and living quarters, and since the NKVD was always on the hunt for suspects, its agents began to ask Spaniards for names of possible "traitors." If they did not give any, they themselves became suspects. So to get out of it they would furnish names of supporters of Hernández. That is how a current Catalonian Socialist representative, Francisco Ramos, was sent to a camp where he spent ten years because a leader had given his name, a leader who in turn after a number of years was thrown out of the party. One of the victims of the period was Valentín González, El Campesino, who twice tried to escape from the Soviet Union and finally was successful in 1948.

Isolation in Spain

Several months after Franco's victory, in the summer of 1939, small, spontaneous, and isolated groups of resisters began to form in Spain. They gradually became coordinated, and traditional organizations began to appear secretly. PCE propaganda has listed this party as the pioneer of resistance to Francoism. Actually from 1939 to 1948 the CNT carried the weight of opposition and it was joined by POUM, the PSOE, and even some skeletal Republican groups as well as Basque and Catalonian nationalist organizations. Only in 1941 did there begin to be groups of the PCE that were not a result of police provocation.[28] The first attempt to reorganize the PCE was made in Madrid in July 1939. It was the work of Roberto Conesa, a member of the JSU who at the end of the war denounced his friends and began to work with the Francoist police. He organized the Socorro Rojo (Red Aid) with adolescents, mostly girls. Captured by the police on August 5, thirteen women from 18 to 21 years of age were sentenced by a court martial. The history of the PCE recognizes those first victims as "the thirteen roses."[29]

This loss—which like almost all those of the PCE was very large since there was always the tendency to include in underground activity new people, both unknown and inexperienced—momentarily paralyzed efforts to reorganize the party which were undertaken by members who had remained in Spain. Those in exile took a long time to establish contact with those first groups.[30] Distrust surrounded the Communists in jail. Their participation in the war was too recent for anybody to fraternize with them. They were kept in isolation—which increased their tendency to organize themselves in a closed circle. Without denying them basic, practical solidarity, they were not allowed to participate in activities which the opposition began to take on in the streets and jails (graffiti, manifestos, sabotage, pro-Allied propaganda). The opposition increased with the execution in October 1940 of Companys, president of the Generalidad.

Another factor that isolated the Communists as much as the memory of their activities in the Civil War was the Nazi-Soviet pact. The Communists themselves were disconcerted, and since they did not know what line to follow they merely reorganized the party, but it was devoid of any political activity. Nor at the time did they have anything to do with the guerrilla bands made up of survivors from the Civil War in which there were doubtless Communists but they acted independently. Spain at that moment appeared as a country of informers and those informed upon, of advocates and adversaries, with rationing, famine, a black market, safe-conducts for traveling, and a high percentage of the population in jail or in forced labor battalions. It was the time of executions by court martial five days a week and of individual cells occupied by anywhere from eight to twelve prisoners.

The entry of the USSR in the war removed the veil of silence from the Communists. France, the closest point of exile, had been almost completely abandoned by party leaders. There Jesús Monzón and Gabriel León Trilla took charge of reorganizing the party and placing it in the French resistance. The isolation was the cause for the weakness of the party and not, as the *Historia del PCE* alleges, because "hundreds of its members had been handed over by Casado's Junta to Franco's police," which was not true. Also false was that the party tried to reorganize the Popular Front and that the Socialists, Anarchists, etc. thought that it was not possible to fight against Francoism.[31]

Once the effects of Conesa's activities were no longer felt, a delegation of the party was set up in Madrid headed by José Cazorla, and a Madrid provincial committee was formed in which the soon-to-be-famous dramatist Antonio Buero Vallejo took part. There were arrests among both groups. Cazorla and Buero were condemned to death, but Buero's sentence was commuted. Groups also began to form in Euzkadi led by Realino and in Catalonia by Assa, a German-Turk from the Communist International. Acting as coordinator for these activities was Heriberto Quiñones, from the Canary Islands, who had lived in Argentina and who returned to Spain in 1932 as part of Codovila's team; he later worked with Gerö. Quiñones organized a political bureau. He maintained that the party had been abandoned by the central committee and that the party ought to be run not from exile but from inside Spain. He reduced practically all the party's activity to defending the policy of the USSR. He paid no attention to the instructions which began to arrive from Mexico, sent by means of sailors as well as messengers, the most important of whom was Jesús Larrañaga who arrived from Havana in 1941 accompanied by Manuel Asanta and Isidoro Diéguez. They established a "contact post" in Lisbon. But a slip-up in Madrid revealed their whereabouts to the Spanish police, and on Madrid's request, Portugal returned them to Spain where they were executed.

Despite Quiñones's obsession over security measures, he was arrested at the beginning of 1942 along with several of his friends and was condemned to death with Ángel Cardín and Luis Sendín. They were executed in October 1942. The *Historia del PCE* classified Quiñones as a "provocateur,"[32] and Carrillo intimated that he was an agent of the Intelligence Service. Actually he was a lesser agent of the Communist International who dared to improvise when the Spanish Communists had been left out in the cold, laden with all those epithets for having reproached the leaders for neglecting Spain.

The Asturian José Bayón tried to keep the political bureau active. The bureau agreed to eliminate the theoretical material published by Quiñones and Sendín and heed the directives coming from Mexico. Bayón and his friends were arrested in June just when they had handed over the bureau to Jesús Carreras, from the Basque region, who had arrived from France to take charge of the delegation. Carreras was arrested in 1943 while trying to go to France and was executed. At the end of 1943 Monzón sent to Madrid Gabriel León Trilla, a member of Bullejos's troika in 1932 who had rejoined the party and was Monzón's right-hand man in France. Trilla set up an office with a commercial front in Madrid. Thanks to him *Mundo Obrero* began to come out more or less regularly in mimeograph form and the party became more visible by means of regional and provincial committees but with few members. Of the entire opposition it was the weakest group. And it continued in isolation.

The National Union

The man in the street became aware that the Communists continued to exist through the adventure of the Arán Valley, the tragic expression of the establishment, finally, of a political line after several years of hesitation and the long silence of the period of the Nazi-Soviet pact. This line was decided upon in Moscow. Dimitrov had told Hernández: "The end of hatred must be proposed. . . . From now on [the Spaniards] must be grouped only in these two factions: first, those who are for the war, and second, those who are for neutrality; the traditional flags of leftists and rightists have ceased to exist only to give way to these two: patriots and antipatriots."[33] The PCE was against Spain's entering the war on Hitler's side, for that did not suit the USSR, even if to defend this position it would be necessary to shake hands with the Falangists and reactionaries who were supporters of neutrality. The Communist International wrote a draft for a manifesto: "The past should not be an obstacle to achieving unity in our struggle" for the purpose of realizing a "national union with even the most conservative forces" and "the formation of a government of national union" which, when able, would let the people decide the country's future.

This support of the USSR reached grotesque extremes. The PCE's organ in Mexico, *España Popular,* on June 24, 1941 ran this full-page title: "Workers, Spaniards, Defend the USSR! Fight Harder against Francoism and the Nazis. Not a Single Spanish Soldier Must Fight in the Anti-Soviet War." The new line was issued in a manifesto of the central committee (in Moscow) in August 1941: the forces opposing Hitler were greater than those which fought to defend the Republic. They had to be joined together. But Quiñones paid no attention and, for the time being, the only PCE in operation in Spain was his. Quiñones understood that in the midst of repression, with famine and the hope of Allied victory, the people would not accept the idea of shaking hands with the repressors who hoped for the defeat of the Allies. Since the slogan did not catch on, in September 1942 Moscow's central committee proposed a concrete program in hopes that it could regain support: the formation of a government of national union which would hold elections once the dictatorship was toppled.[34]

The result of this view of things was the establishment, in a meeting called the Grenoble Conference (although it met in Toulouse) on November 7, 1942, of the Spanish National Union. Shortly thereafter Radio Free Spain broadcast from Moscow that there were conversations with CEDA (conservative party under the Republic) and the Catholic unions.

In its initial stages the National Union had to use peaceful political measures. The Normandy landing changed the perspective. It was no longer necessary to worry about Franco's entering the war. The National Union, then, had to change its objective, not its composition and character: push Franco out of power. In November 1943 the Socialists and Republicans in Mexico had formed the Junta Española de Liberación (Spanish Liberation Junta) which attempted to negotiate with the Allies. In Spain the National Alliance of Democratic Forces was in gestation among the CNT, Socialists, POUM, and Republicans. The Communists were in neither; and so they said these two organizations were instruments of the Allies. The PCE should, therefore, have its own instrument. This was the National Union as it existed after the liberation of France.

The National Union was intended to include elements of all parties. Since the parties were in the Junta or the Alliance, they had to be divided, and "pro-Union" groups had to be formed in each of them: followers of Negrín in the PSOE and some Republicans and some members of the CNT in their organizations. The Spanish National Union was formed with names but without organizations. It was now an organization and not simply a slogan, and in Toulouse it began to issue manifestos and ended up constituting a Junta Suprema de Unión Nacional, which almost looked like a future government although no one knew who was in it. In November 1944, for example, a manifesto was followed by the usual cheers: "Long live the unity of the Spanish people to crush Franco and the Falange!" "Long live national insurrection!" "Long live the Junta Suprema de Unión Nacional!" "Long live free and independent Spain!"

To popularize this idea, the PCE spread the rumor that Stalin advocated it and had ordered the invasion of Spain. No one knows who relayed the hypothetical order or who heard it. But many members believed it. After Stalin's long years of silence on Spain it was a relief for them to hear that Stalin deigned to attend to their country. Monzón and Trilla had made concrete plans. The party was isolated and so were its leaders. They thought that the people would rebel at the slightest flare-up and they wanted the National Union to be the spark. Taking advantage of the units of the French resistance made up of Spaniards, they organized an invasion of Spain at three sites: the Basque region, Navarre, and the Arán Valley. The first two attempts failed within a few hours, having been crushed by the Civil Guard. In the Arán Valley there were more men and they managed to resist for a few days and called for the concentration of some of Franco's military forces. But they did not advance. All this occurred in October 1944. Carrillo, who had been in Moscow shortly before, returned to France; upon arriving at Toulouse he received the first news of the void in which the guerrilla fighters were moving. There had been a strenuous battle, with 248 casualties in the army (32 dead) and 599 among the guerrilla fighters (129 dead), in addition to 241 prisoners taken by the Civil Guard.[35]

Seeing it was impossible to score a victory, even a partial one, Carrillo went to the Arán Valley and gave the order to retreat. There was a stampede. Later, instead of telling the truth, Carrillo wrote: "The guerrilla fighters occupied sixteen towns. For those towns it has been the ten happiest days in the last six years. When, having met their objective, the guerrilla fighters retreated to another area of Catalonia . . . the clergy gave them their blessing."[36] At once Carrillo removed Monzón—who then went to Spain—and ended up as leader of the party in France. The National Union would be kept alive as a subject of propaganda, but as an organization and a tactic it was the first victim of that ten-day adventure which only becomes understandable if one recalls that the Communists, who always speak of the masses, have rarely been able to take their pulse. Many survivors of the adventure headed for the mountains. They were gradually joined by people being pursued as well as others who were already in the mountains. So, at the end of 1944, there were two guerrilla movements in the country: one, which had roots in the past, formed in particular around people from the CNT; and one which arose from the National Union around people from the PCE.[37]

A plenary session of the Central Committee of the PCE in Toulouse on December 5, 1945 determined that the guerrilla fighters would be the starting point for more extensive fighting by the people. But although they fought in some places effectively and in others desperately, although they received a small supply of arms from the French maquis, and although their members showed great fighting spirit, they were politically sterile. They were always kept in check by Franco's government and were never a source for concern except on a level of "public order" as is proven by the *Historia del PCE* which does not even devote a full page to them (only part of one) and this is filled with names of fallen fighters. Nevertheless, they were troublesome enough for there to be a special law in April 1947 "on the repression of crimes of terrorism and brigandage." To reinforce and control the guerrillas the bureau had sent Sebastián Zapiraín and Santiago Álvarez. They had to abandon their mission to devote themselves to reorganizing the party's delegation. A few months later, in August 1945, they were arrested and this caused the loss of seventy other members. Agustín Zoroa, a student in charge of the guerrillas, went on to head the delegation.

Although the fighting was between the guerrillas and the Civil Guard, clashes between guerrillas of the National Union and the CNT were reported—echoes of the Civil War. According to official reports, there were some 1,700 "bandits" of whom 570 were in the National Union and 260 were independent. There were 474 deaths. An officer of the Civil Guard stated that there were up to 8,000 guerrilla operations (Líster said there were 5,500), 2,116 "bandits killed," and 3,382 prisoners. In addition, 5,482 collaborators of the PCE's guerrillas and 1,086 of the CNT's guerrillas were arrested.[38] It finally became apparent that the man on the street was unaware of the guerrillas and that they would never meet any of their objectives. What should have been done during the Civil War was not done; it was done only when it would require futile sacrifices. Taking that into consideration, a delegation of the party made up of Ibárruri, Carrillo, and Antón interviewed Stalin in Moscow in 1948. "In the conversations Stalin intimated the possibility of giving up the guerrilla tactic as well as the need to promote the work of the organizations of the masses."[39]

The party immediately issued a communiqué dissolving the guerrillas, saying that this was a political necessity and that the only criticism that could be made was that it was not decided upon "a couple of years before" (during which time there were hundreds of deaths). Some agents were sent to Spain to help the guerrillas become part of the urban struggle.[40] They did not even consult General Manuel Riquelme who was the president of the National Union or Jesús Martínez who was the man to effectively lead it for the PCE. "It was a heroic episode but marginal, with few exceptions, to national life. Its extension beyond reasonable limits snuffed out the possibility of leading militants for the party."[41]

The Alliance and the Government in Exile

When in 1934 the tactic of the united front from below had failed and the Alianza Obrera, initiated by adversaries of the PCE had triumphed, the PCE decided to make a 180-degree turn and join the very alliance it had previously faulted. Twelve years later, in 1946, the same thing happened again. Now that the policy of National Union had failed, the PCE decided to join "that instrument of imperialism," the Alianza de Fuerzas Democráticas (Alliance of Democratic Forces). They used the Socialists who were undergoing an ideological crisis similar to the one twelve years before. The delegate of the PSOE in the Alianza managed to get its national committee—although reluctantly—to accept the PCE, but not before the PCE agreed to dissolve the Junta Suprema de Unión Nacional, a condition set by the Alianza which the party hastened to meet. In September 1946 *Nuestra Bandera* (the theoretical organ of the

PCE published in Toulouse) said: "The Alianza de Fuerzas Democráticas, together with resistance organizations like AFARE, the guerrilla groups, the Union of Free Intellectuals,[42] youth organizations, and Galician, Catalonian, and Basque anti-Franco forces, must be the foundation for the constitution of a Central Committee of Resistance . . . subordinate to and in close contact with the Republican government."

It was an attempt to change the name of the organization in order to make the PCE appear responsible for having initiated its creation. Likewise, it was a matter of subordinating the organization to a body alien to the opposition such as the Republican government in exile so that it might control it. None of that was achieved, not only because the committee of the Alianza paid no attention to those suggestions, but also because the Alianza broke apart shortly thereafter. This was due partly to loss of hope that the Allies would help overthrow Franco as well as hesitation on the part of the Monarchic generals to strike out against Franco (which the PCE and the Alianza were vaguely counting on), and partly because the very delegate of the PSOE who had proposed the PCE's entry turned out to be a police informer who provided the police with the necessary information to physically liquidate the Alianza.

The PCE's interest in having the Alianza "subordinate" to the government in exile is explained by the fact that the PCE had joined it after having criticized its constitution. That government was a result of a meeting in Mexico City of what remained of the Parliament elected in 1936; the meeting began on August 20, 1945. The Parliament appointed its president, José Martínez Barrio, as president of the Republic, and he put José Giral in charge of forming the government. This government did not have any Communists, but upon arriving in Paris it included two members of the CNT. Counting all its resources, it had some four million dollars inherited from JARE. SERE did not contribute anything, although Negrín acted as if he were in agreement with the formation of the government. The government was soon recognized by several Latin American countries (especially Mexico, which continued to recognize it until 1976) and by some "peoples' democracies," but not by the great powers nor the USSR. Russia, which had had the Francoist Blue Division fighting on its front, could have used this as a reason to declare war on Franco, thereby putting its allies in a bind, but it chose not to do so. Nor did it recognize the Republican government due to commercial reasons (trade with Francoist Spain through the Arabic countries had already begun) and because it would have had to account for the Spanish gold. Stalin took advantage of the conference at Potsdam to talk about Spain. He did not apply any pressure and so glossed over the fact that Moscow had opposed Churchill's idea of opening the second front with a landing in Spain which undoubtedly would have meant the end of Francoism. None of this was favorable to the PCE's image and even less so to the USSR's stance at the United Nations Security Council where Gromyko vetoed several resolutions to place the issue of Spain before the Assembly. Francisco Castillo Nájera, Mexican delegate to the Council, declared that the Soviet delegate had abused the right to veto and that the way in which he used it had doubtless "satisfied Franco." Gromyko was not trying to satisfy Franco but rather to block a precedent which some day could be used against the USSR.[43]

In April 1947 Carrillo was named minister, as were the Galician Alejandro R. Castelao and Rafael Sánchez Guerra, the latter arriving secretly from Spain. But while the government was maneuvering in the chancellories, Prieto tried to establish contact with the Spanish Monarchists. That caused a crisis in the Giral government and it was replaced on February 9, 1947 by one presided over by the Socialist Rodolfo Llopis with Vicente Uribe of the PCE as minister of the economy. Some months before, Uribe had called Llopis a "provocateur." That government intended to strengthen relations with the opposition in the interior of Spain in order to allow the Spanish people to freely decide their future. This last item was Prieto's hobby horse in his negotiations with the Monarchists. Franco counterattacked with a law of succession which he submitted to a referendum and which the PCE did not reject outright,[44] although later when it saw that all the opposition of the interior was opposed to voting in favor, it also adopted this same position. Meanwhile, Prieto's negotiations continued and in its congress of July 1947 the PSOE supported them and, in an effort to speed them along, it requested the dissolution of the Republican institutions. Furthermore, the congress was emphatically anti-Communist. In the face of all this, on August 5 Vicente Uribe wrote Llopis that the PSOE had violated the accords made when the government was formed and that the "Communist party, in keeping with its past, was and would continue to be the ardent defender of the unity of all Republican forces."[45] From then on there were no longer any Communists in the successive Republican governments in exile, nor were there any in Basque governments until much later, although the PCE of Euzkadi had been one of the signers of the Pact of Bayonne among all Basque forces in exile in March 1945.

These matters had little influence in Spain. After the break-up of the Alianza, the strictly labor opposition replaced the political opposition. The CNT stepped up its work in the illegal unions and ended up with numerous paying members (60,000 in 1946). There were spontaneous strikes, which were soon led by those illegal unions and in some places by those of the UGT: Manresa in 1946, Bilbao in 1947, Asturias,

Barcelona with the streetcar strike in 1951. The PCE and PSUC participated only minimally. Although the majority of its members were workers, the possibility of bureaucratizing by paying them a salary for their party activity put them in isolation. In the eyes of the workers the PCE was still the party of the middle class which had destroyed the collectivizations. The workers of that period were still the same who had fought before and during the Civil War. Nonetheless, in Vizcaya and later in Asturias and especially in Madrid the PCE was growing among the workers. For the time being this was a minority force and was not strong enough to take action on its own.

"Latin Americans" and "Russians" against Resisters

Since the beginning of the exile the PCE was divided into four groups: Moscow, the location of the major leaders; Mexico and other places in Latin America where the bulk of the minor leaders were; France, the site of the majority of its militants and some second- and third-rank leaders; Spain, where efforts were being made to reorganize again and again the party in the underground. Although the four groups followed Moscow's instructions, there was a fissure determined as much by geography as by living conditions between the leaders (Moscow and Latin America) and the rank and file (Spain and France). Since there were scarcely any leaders among the rank and file, it was the latter that produced the reorganizers: Quiñones and later Trilla in Spain, Monzón and Trilla in France. These reorganizers tended to separate themselves from those whom they saw as deserters—those who in the comfort of exile, where there was neither fighting nor danger, wanted to give orders. The leaders—especially those in Latin America—in turn tried to impose their policy and send messengers in charge of "whipping members into shape" to Spain and France, and, if necessary, to replace leaders who had come up from the rank and file. That would lead to a systematic— at times physical—elimination of rank-and-file leaders when, once World War II was over, "Latin American" and "Russian" leaders could gather in France and take over the entire party system.[46]

The "Latin Americans" and "Russians" found in France many Communists in the maquis (which formed the Fourteenth Corps of Spanish Guerrillas) and which the French Communist party had organized in its Franc-Tireurs et Partisans. These guerrillas took advantage of the opportunity to eliminate some Spanish political adversaries once France was liberated and before that time as well. That is how members of the CNT and POUM died. POUM's leader, Joan Farré, for instance, was murdered as he was escaping from a Nazi prison, and the Socialist

Auxiliano Benito, as well as the couple in the CNT, Francisco and Mercedes Miralles, also lost their lives. In addition, fighters from the National Union stormed rallies staged by the Socialists and the CNT, and they forbade any action that was not on the initiative of the National Union.[47] The bureau sent the resistance fighters on the adventure of Arán Valley. Those who were returning from deportation camps underwent interrogation and a purge on orders from Carrillo. Carrillo believed that any "inmate" of a stalag who had been saved owed his life to the fact that he collaborated with the Nazis. That is how the leaders of the Communist groups in Buchenwald were "purged" just as in the USSR prisoners of war and even the demobilized Russian soldiers were purged.[48]

Attached to the political bureau but not under its authority, Carrillo created a Commission of the Interior which controlled activities in Spain. Using security as a pretext, the actions of the commission were kept secret. In this way Carrillo controlled the party system in Spain. The political bureau set itself up in an apartment on the luxurious Avenue Kleber in Paris where it would remain until 1950. It had several publishing houses: Ediciones España Popular, Ediciones Nuestro Pueblo, Edicions Lluita, and publications like *Nuestra Bandera, Quaderns del Comunisme, Mundo Obrero, Lluita, Euzkadi Roja,* and *Juventud.* There were also publications of the party in Mexico City and other Latin American cities. The party controlled many Republican Centers and Casals Catalans. There were six to eight thousand members in its ranks, although no more than a thousand of them were militants.[49]

The leaders also undertook "purges" of those who during the war and the resistance were more independent not in political stance but in organization. They did not trust the resistance fighters. The *Historia del PCE* says there were "demonstrations of opportunism," an underestimation of the actions of the working class, contempt of the role of the masses, and that certain militants, "especially those who were working in France during World War II," underwent "intense pressure from the bourgeois ideology," an ideology which caused people to want to transform the National Union into a party in which the "PCE might lose its personality."[50] To justify those purges, Carrillo spoke in Toulouse on April 1, 1945 and presented an idea which he would not give up for more than ten years: the general political strike (HGP as it was called by the militants). The following are some quotes of his: "Glory to Marshal Stalin, to the Soviet Union, to the Red Army. The great Soviet Socialist state has carried the main weight of humanity's salvation. Spanish reaction is trying to save itself. Let's step up our surveillance of all spies. We must relentlessly combat the Fascist agents of POUM. If there is a person who represents the spirit of our nation it is our great comrade La

Pasionaria." The important decisions such as joining the Alianza Nacional de Fuerzas Democráticas, the elimination of the Junta Suprema de Unión Nacional, and the entry in the Republican government in exile were made by the bureau in whose discussions Ibárruri, back and forth to and from Moscow, participated less and less. Nonetheless in 1945 she was paid great homage with parties and pamphlets of her speeches on the occasion of her fiftieth anniversary.[51]

The plenary meeting of the central committee in Montreuil in March 1947 was very significant.[52] There Ibárruri presented the report of the political bureau. "Francoism is crumbling," she said. She spoke of the guerrillas, called for a Council of Resistance to replace the Alianza de Fuerzas Democráticas, and said, "Spain is falling apart in Franco's hands." Carrillo said that "strikes, demonstrations, and protest of every kind have battered all of Spain. . . . The regime has felt tremors in its very foundations"—and he concluded that it was necessary to show the working class that it had within its reach a decisive weapon, the general political strike. He said this when the party in Spain had been dismantled by the police, when discouragement in the opposition was becoming widespread, and on the eve of May 1, 1947 when the PCE called for everyone not to show up for work. As was to be expected, no one followed the order.

Finally, in October 1948 when the Cold War had already begun, a joint meeting of the PCE and PSUC decided to undertake a new tactic inspired by the visit to Stalin, which consisted of combining action in the streets and agitation with work in all official institutions wherever it was possible and particularly in the CNS, the Falange's "vertical unions." Thanks to that, some Communists, without declaring themselves as such although it was known that they belonged to the PCE, got elected in the "union" elections of 1950. They did not meet any obstacles because the Falangist leaders of the CNS were happy to be able to show off a few elected Communists as proof of how "clean" the "union" elections were. That realistic appraisal had very profitable results for the party, all the more so considering that the other labor tendencies, slaves of their principles, did not dare follow the same route. For the PCE there began "a tactic of patient accumulation of forces" and "the overcoming of a certain subjectivism which had previously existed in the appraisal of some of the issues facing the country."[53] The Communists later tried to make people believe that Barcelona's streetcar strike in the spring of 1951 was a result of this tactic; this implied that PSUC had led it. There is no truth to this. Around that time Gregorio López Raimundo and 27 Communists from Barcelona were arrested for running an illegal organization. Party propaganda presented this arrest as if it were the result of the strike and thus tried to take credit for the work of survivors of the Alianza de Fuerzas Democráticas.

How the Cold War Helped

In the long run the cold war was beneficial to the PCE. At a time when protest and opposition in Spain were on the decline, the cold war provided the PCE with a theme on which to act, and the Eisenhower Administration's foolish policy toward Franco made an excellent platform for propaganda for the PCE. By attributing to the Communists everything the opposition had done, Franco made the PCE look powerful in the eyes of the anti-Francoists in Spain and abroad, and he helped the PCE overcome its past. The Francoist press had made some mention of the guerrillas, of the adventure of Arán Valley, and of the strikes of 1947, attributing them to the influence of the leftists and even the masons. After 1950 everything was the fault of the Communists.[54]

But the PCE once again found itself isolated because Franco's government as well as the Republican government in exile and the bulk of those in exile began an "Atlantic" evolution. The PCE's isolation provided easy targets: Indalecio Prieto and his contacts with the Monarchists, the negotiations for a treaty between Madrid and Washington, and American aid to Spain. In September 1950 when the French government undertook police action to break up the operation it called the Communist Fifth Column of France, it told the Spanish Communist refugees in that country that they could choose between living in Corsica and other remote places in France or leaving for Eastern European countries. The leaders chose Prague but the militants received orders to stay in France at all costs. Two-hundred Spanish Communists were arrested and deported and 150 were moved to Oran.[55] It was the first time that the PCE suffered repression in France, albeit moderate and without physical harm. It no longer had the valuable support of the Communist ministers in the French government. The PCE's press was suspended and *Mundo Obrero* was printed in Prague, but after a short while it reappeared in Paris run by straw editors of the French Communist party as would later occur under De Gaulle with the press of the CNT and the PSOE. Shortly thereafter the border with Spain, which was closed in 1946, was reopened and that facilitated contact between the interior and those in exile. The party decided to send new militants to Spain almost at the same time that the United Nations lifted sanctions against Franco, and increased the circulation of his press by planting "tourists" and using new sympathizers unknown to the police. The party was gradually being rebuilt with an abundance of material means which no other opposition movement has ever had available. The strikes in Barcelona in 1953 as well as those in Bilbao allowed the Communists, if not to lead them, at least to be more influential than in previous strikes. Following the instructions set down at a meeting in October 1951 and in a letter from the central committee to members dated July 1952, contacts with Socialists and even Falangists were sought with great persistence. At this meeting the party's participation in the strikes was criticized, and it was pointed out that the party had not made any impact in the countryside and that it was not doing any work in doctrinal education.[56] Naturally this entailed eliminations and self-criticism which strengthened the political bureau's control over the party.[57]

At the same time the PCE was echoing the campaigns of the Stockholm Manifesto and the World Peace Committee and it organized delegations of Spanish exiles, under Communist control, to the different front organizations (of women, youth, students, lawyers, etc.) which were instruments of the cold war. A good part of the PCE's press in Spain, which was circulated with great risk to the militants, was devoted to this campaign which had little effect on Spaniards. The Spanish delegation to the World Peace Congress in 1949 said that the Spanish people would not take up arms against those ideologies and those countries that "have been, are, and will be on our side," it denounced the governments' passivity, and defended the United Nations' policy regarding Franco. That peace campaign managed to attract many of those intellectuals who, feigning naiveté and knowing that Western nations would not persecute them, systematically played the game of Soviet diplomacy.[58] Those not wishing to sign were called "lackeys of imperialism." Mije wrote in the Cominform's organ: "Our comrades have learned to isolate the lackeys of imperialism, the Socialist bosses, the Anarchists, and the right wing." These campaigns were pretty much damaged by the trials going on at the same time in the "peoples' democracies" against Communist leaders many of whom had fought in the International Brigades. Accustomed to accepting anything coming from Moscow and going against the current, the PCE blended its voice with the chorus against the accused. Some of its intellectuals stated very seriously that they knew from a good source, for example, that Rajk was guilty.[59]

The hardest test was the Cominform's (which the PCE was a part of) condemnation of Tito and his regime as well as the expulsion of Yugoslavia from the international Communist organization. The Spaniards who were in Yugoslavia had to choose between obeying the party and leaving or breaking with the party and remaining in Belgrade. Everyone chose the party despite the fact that quite a number sympathized with Tito who had given them a warm welcome and who had many interbrigadiers at the head of his army. In their new residence the Spanish Communists who had been refugees in Yugoslavia (sent there by the party) were the object of special investigation and interrogation to see if they had been infected by Tito's heresy. Vicente Uribe took charge of this inquisitional effort. Many were sent back to the USSR which "put a damper on their high spirits."[60] Although many years later Carrillo said, "We followed like sheep the denunciation of Comrade Tito"; the truth is that the bureau took advantage of Titoism to put that label on those who showed dissatisfaction with the party or who aspired to power. The party threw them out at the same time as it slandered them. In 1945 Tito was, in Ibárruri's eyes, "the glorious head of multinational Yugoslavia" and then became "the sabotaging traitor of the working class" as *Mundo Obrero* said on June 29, 1948, exactly twenty-four hours after his expulsion from the Cominform.

All this was punctuated by constant praise for Stalin, "the hope and light of the people" according to La Pasionaria whom in turn Carrillo called "teacher of the Marxist-Leninist science of historical development," pointing to her "critical and self-critical rigor which is characteristic of the great Stalinian proletarian leader." Boundless praise was even heaped on the past, as when *Nuestra Bandera* called Díaz "Spain's greatest politician."[61] The party had a considerable system of propaganda: periodicals in France (and later in Prague), underground printing shops in Spain, and Radio Free Spain, created in Moscow by Castro Delgado and later moved to Prague under the thirty-year leadership of Ramón Mendezona.[62] Although a few dared to listen to it during World War II, only the devotees of the party tried to pick it up afterward.

The Fifth Congress

Stalin had died in March 1953. The PCE's press showered him with praise. At the same time a good number of Franco's Communist war prisoners as well as some from the opposition were released from Spanish prisons. Many returned to their homes exhausted and disillusioned, but others persisted. They had made a considerable emotional investment in the party and they stayed in it. Some went to France, the majority stayed in Spain, and the party, having abundant material means, used them. It was an injection for the militants which could not but be felt by the upper echelons. For this reason the latter group resolved to call a congress (the fifth) far away from the rank and file in order to avoid dissension during the discussion of the new bylaws and the new program.

The drafts of the program and the bylaws were circulated through the committees. At the same time the congress was to issue the slogan of the Frente Nacional Antifascista (National Antifascist Front) in which Republicans, Monarchists, and disillusioned Falangists were to take part. Simultaneously there were attacks on Republicans and libertarians precisely because the PCE knew they would not accept giving up the Republic nor would they concede to a right-wing alliance. From the bureau's manifesto of August 1941 which proposed the unity of all groups in order to achieve a constitutional assembly, and from the original design of the National Union, that is, as a body of peaceful fighters,[63] to the National Front via the guerrilla National Union, the PCE discarded the issue of the regime and continuously made an effort to reach agreements with the Monarchists and the right wing without ever collaborating with Negrín's phantom government of which Uribe was a part. Even when the phantasmagoric Junta Suprema de Unión Nacional had been created, it was falsely reported that CEDA and the Catholic unions joined it. In 1945 La Pasionaria wrote a letter to many individuals in exile proposing constitutional elections in Spain, which is to say, without the establishment of the Republic as a prior condition.[64] Only after these tactics failed did the PCE resolve to enter the Giral government and consider the Republic as nonnegotiable, yet only on a temporary basis. Recall that the PCE was in the Alliance of Democratic Forces when it regarded that it was not suitable to consider the Republic a prior condition to negotiations with the Monarchists and the army. These antecedents must not be overlooked if the party's conduct after Franco's death is to be understood.[65]

The Communist press in Europe did not mention the fifth congress until it published its resolutions. It took place in Prague on November 1-5, 1954. Ibárruri read the central committee's report, Uribe presented the new program, and Carrillo presented the new bylaws. Following that the central committee was elected. There were representatives from the interior,[66] from the French, Russian, and Latin American groups, but they were limited in number. There was also a delegation of PSUC. The congress unanimously approved the party's new bylaws and La Pasionaria's report, the "Program of the Communist party of Spain in its struggle for the independence and democratization of Spain, for the radical improvement of the conditions of the Spanish people."[67] The program talked of the need to achieve the democratic revolution, to wipe out the vestiges of feudalism in the countryside, to terminate the treaties and pacts which tie Spain to the "plans of aggression of the American imperialists and alienate its sovereignty." It also talked of the need to reestablish democratic liberties and to improve the living conditions of the people as well as relations between the church and state, showing great respect for freedom of worship and the religious sentiments of a considerable portion of the Spanish population.

The central committee which was elected was composed of 29 members and 22 substitutes among whom there were 25 workers, 7 peasants, and 19 intellectuals. The new central committee chose Ibárruri as secretary general and a political bureau made up of Carrillo, Claudín, Cristóbal, Delicado, Gallego, Líster, Mije, and Uribe. Antón was no longer in the central committee or the bureau, although this was not mentioned in the Communist press. Nevertheless, moving into the central committee were "Federico Sánchez" (Jorge Semprún), Julián Grimau, Gregorio López Raimundo, José Moix, Wenceslao Roces, Rafael Vidiella, and Sánchez Arcas.[68] In her report La Pasionaria said that the party was "the only democratic force in Spain," she attacked the groups in exile that were not willing to deal with right-wing elements, and she advised that "when difficulties arise, when everything seems to be falling apart, we must not let ourselves become discouraged . . . but rather look to the Soviet Union with pride [proclaiming] that we are Communists, members of the Communist party of Spain, which is striving to learn from the revolutionary example set by the Communist party of the Soviet Union and which is fighting to establish Communism in our country."

The republican government in exile (headed at the time by Félix Gordón Ordás) shortly thereafter issued a statement commenting on the PCE's neglect of Republicanism and its "praise of the non-Republican ultra-Right." What bothered the PCE was that the statement revealed that some of the delegates to the congress proposed the eventual seizure of the Falange's assets and the elimination of subsidies to the clergy which the leaders opposed.[69] The party's bylaws, drawn up because the "previous ones did not fulfill the demands which the fight against Franco entailed for the PCE and had fallen into disuse," confirmed democratic centralism as a fundamental organizational principle, "the compulsory nature of the accords made by the upper echelons for the lower ones . . . , and the most emphatic denial of the existence of factions. The bylaws also proclaimed the principle of collective leadership," which had been implemented in the USSR after Stalin's death.[70] The fifth congress approved everything the bureau had done since the end of the war, it absolved the bureau of the failures of the National Union, prepared the way for what would soon be the new tactic of the PCE, and gave its blessings to a long list of purges.

Purges of the Bureau

At the plenary session of the Central Committee of the PCE in Montreuil in March 1947 Ibárruri, speaking of potential allies, had said: "The party has not excommunicated anyone nor has it declared itself incompatible with anyone but Franco." But that did not apply to the members of the party. Two years earlier in another plenary session of the central committee, Antón, who always agreed with Ibárruri, "with unusual persistence pointed out and condemned the mistakes and insufficiencies which militants in the party had committed. . . . This was an indication that the way was being prepared for the purges which ensued. On the other hand, you could see how the leaders who had arrived from Moscow tried to have the best militants coming up from France's maquis sent to Spain to lead the guerrillas or to take part in other missions. This cleared the way for giving posts [in France] to unprestigious and mediocre militants who were totally in the hands of La Pasionaria and Carrillo. . . . The phobia of persecution which overtook the leaders of the party was such that in the lists of 'traitors' which they prepared there was occasionally the name of someone who had died."[71]

There were numerous instances of purges. They even occurred in France when the resistance ended and they were not always nonviolent. The PSUC militant Llibert Estartús was murdered by his comrades, for example. On other occasions there were mainly exclusions such as the case of the Basque Communist Luis Bermejo who enjoyed a great deal of prestige in Toulouse. No one knows the number of individual tragedies—for it was considered as such for a militant to lose contact with the party—which caused this scramble for posts. Only a handful of known and proven instances can be cited here. One of them—transitory but revealing—is the case of Irene Falcón, Ibárruri's stalwart secretary. In exile she married the Czech Communist Geminder who was executed with Slansky and others. For this reason for several years Irene Falcón had no part in political activity and La Pasionaria did not call her to her side until after Stalin's death.[72]

In the silent, secret battle of "Latin Americans" and "Russians" against the resisters, the principal victims—but not the only ones—were Jesús Monzón and Gabriel León Trilla. Monzón who was from an aristocratic family from Navarre, had been such a fervent Communist that after the Civil War in devotion to the work of the party he forced his companion Aurora to have her infant son sent to Russia; he was never heard from again. Monzón had remained in France where along with Trilla he was the organizer of the National Union following Moscow's and Mexico's instructions. He was secretly in Spain when he received orders to return to France. He was arrested by the police while on his way to meet his liaison who was to serve as his guide. Líster believes that he owes his life to that arrest because the guide would have killed him. In retrospect, Carrillo explained that "in 1948 Monzón's case was made known to the party" (in an article by Carrillo himself appearing in *Nuestra Bandera*) and he accused him of having refused to go to Latin America and of staying in France "with the support of imperialist services and probably the Francoists." According to Carrillo, Monzón replaced his comrades in charge of the work in France taking advantage of their lack of initiative, which he called "action against the party." Monzón's stance, he added, was identical to Quiñones's: he wanted to place the party "at the rear of Monarchist and reactionary forces and to dissolve the party within the National Union headed by capitalists and Monarchist landholders." He also said that "behind Monzón are the services of American espionage and the Spanish Carlist agents." To prove it he said that Monzón was in contact with Noel Field who was reported, during Rajk's trial in Budapest, to have been an American agent. According to Carrillo, Monzón provided the "Carlist agents" with information on the guerrillas. In passing he said that in Northern Africa there were members at the head of the party who were in contact with American agents during the war. "Some of those responsible for this surrender were expelled, others made amends and were sent to the rank and file of the party" (that is, they were left without paying jobs).[73]

In a way what happened to Monzón and the "North Africans" was similar to what had befallen Marshal Tukachevsky whom Stalin put in charge of contacting the German Staff and whom Stalin later executed for doing precisely that. It was clearly a case of discrediting Monzón for having followed the party line set up in Moscow when this line failed. So the party had a scapegoat and it eliminated one of the leaders' rivals. Gabriel León Trilla worked with Monzón in Spain and France; his case was overshadowed when the member in charge of eliminating Trilla was arrested, sentenced, and executed for "Civil War crimes." He was Cristino García, a local leader of the French resistance. Trilla was in Madrid being pursued by the police. García told him to meet him in the Campo de las Calaveras where he was stabbed to death. García is said to have refused personally to be the murderer and he gave the "job" to one of his comrades. The party said that "Trilla acted on his own account as an authentic bandit; furthermore his work represented a risk for the underground organization and the security of many Communists. So he was executed by Cristino García's group."

The party did not say that García carried out orders because then it would have to say that those orders came from the bureau. Líster says that the comrade who received from Carrillo and Ibárruri the order to be relayed to García is still alive.[74] As a result of the execution by Franco of this maquis fighter, the French government closed the Pyrenean border in February 1946. Alberto Pérez de Ayala, a coworker of Trilla, was likewise killed by Carranqué, the man who carried out García's orders. Beltrán, another associate whose job was to cross the border, was accused of ties with Francoist authorities and orders were given to get rid of him. But he suspected as much and saved his life by being armed. Later he went to Mexico where he died.

The bureau privately took advantage of the Trilla case to terrorize certain individuals. Vicente Uribe said "categorically that the party had ordered the execution of León Trilla on a street in Madrid and Jesús Monzón escaped the same fate by being arrested by the police," and he also explained that he and Carrillo had gone to Moscow to "expel José Antonio Uribes and send him to do factory work for having permitted many Spanish [Communists] to leave [the USSR]. As leader of the JSU, Carrillo had the job of 'persuading' Spanish school-age youths not to meet with their parents even though they demanded it." All this was said before the Spanish Communists in Yugoslavia who were assembled to hear a report by Uribe whose brusqueness earned him the epithet of "the sergeant." Uribes was criticized for having allowed the Communists who had sided with Hernández to live in peace in the USSR; his only punishment for them was to send them to work in the factories.[75]

They could not send Hernández, Ibárruri's main rival, to work. As has already been explained, he was sent from Russia to Mexico and there was expelled from the party on orders from Moscow which preferred La Pasionaria. Hernández did not conceal his opinion of the National Union: "I cannot give my approval to the most reactionary forces in our country . . . which were the agents of the Fascist movement." In 1944 he wrote an open letter to the Central Committee of the PCE in Mexico in which he said: "Never has our policy been so confused and incoherent as it is today." He requested a conference of the party to correct the situation, "for you are not in touch with the feelings and concerns of the rank and file and you do not sense its discontent and sorrow over the isolation in which you have placed the party." The leaders answered: "Hernández has tried and is still trying to hoist a political flag against the party leadership . . . but Hernández's flag is not really political but one of personal struggle against the party leaders and its supreme leader, La Pasionaria." Uribe said this at the time that Felipe Arconada was spreading the rumor that Hernández was in agreement with the Trotskyites. Actually, Hernández had vindicated all actions of the party during the Civil War (and even wrote a book, *Negro y Rojo*, which was vehemently anti-CNT and filled with slander and lies), and he did nothing more than disagree with the party stance of the moment. In January 1944 in an effort to discredit him a supposed "self-criticism" was being circulated which Hernández himself denied having written; in it he retracted his accusations of the party leadership.[76] Only after having lost hope of replacing the leaders of the PCE and having been definitively expelled from the party did he decide to relate his true experiences in the book *Yo fui un ministro de Stalin* (*I Was Stalin's Minister*). By then he had joined members in France who, for other reasons, had also been thrown out of the party and were coming over to Titoism. Incidentally, it seems that Ibárruri vacillated a while before taking a position on the Yugoslavian issue; apparently Líster was tempted to adopt Titoism.[77]

José del Barrio and Félix Montiel did not hesitate to side with Tito. Thrown out of the party because of internal disagreements and rivalry in 1950, together with others who had been expelled they organized a new party, Acción Socialista, in defense of Yugoslavia and critical of PCE policy. This party broke up after a few years when it was unable to make an impact on the PCE rank and file although it did manage to attract quite a number of people in exile for the defense of Tito's cause.[78] By then the following individuals had already been expelled from the party: Ramón Pontones of the central committee; Manuel Tellado, police political commissar; Pedro Hernández Cartón, of the central committee and friend of Hernández; Antonio Hierro, secretary of the Communist parliamentarian minority; Antonio López, General Miaja's secretary during the war; Felipe Jiménez, Vicente Pueyo, Antonio Hernández, and Francisco Otero, of PSUC. Two had left silently: Manuel Tagüeña[79] and Gustavo Durán, chiefs of army corps. The latter was the model for Manuel in Malraux's *L'Espoir*, who got married in the United States and worked for the United Nations. Who knows for what mysterious reasons he was never attacked by the PCE?

Others surrendered, underwent self-criticism, and were "sent to the rank and file." Felipe Arconada was "tried" in Mexico and was sent to Russia where he worked many long years as a translator into Spanish of the texts of the Soviet Communist party. Wenceslao Roces was likewise "tried" and made a self-criticism. The Mexican press said that the "judges" in those cases and others of Communist exiles in Latin America were José Manso, Ángel Álvarez ("Angelín"), and Amaro del Rosal. Why they fell from grace was not known, but it was said—without confirmation—that it was because of financial reasons. Furthermore, they were charged with political accusations: they had subsumed the activities of the PCE in the Union of Intellectuals, the House of the Spanish Republic, and other front organizations. In his self-criticism Roces implicated Arconada and thus was allowed to stay on in Mexico. It is significant that it was considered a punishment to be sent to the USSR.[80] They could not try Castro Delgado. They could only expel him. Once in Mexico, he did not become a supporter of Tito but rather devoted his energies to writing about the PCE. He later returned to Spain and died shortly after arriving in 1965.[81]

Valentín González, El Campesino, neither underwent self-criticism nor declared himself a supporter of Tito. González's novelesque departure from the USSR—taking advantage of an earthquake which destroyed the gulag camp where he was being held—as well as his trip to Iran, his declaration in the Kravchenko trial in Paris in 1951, and his books written in collaboration with Julián Gorkín, for a while caused such sensation that the president of the French tribunal received a telegram from Moscow exactly 150 centimeters long signed by Pedro Prado and nine other Spanish Communists. The telegram said that El Campesino was "an old provocateur who slipped into the Spanish labor movement ...; he was a mythomaniac and illiterate in the service of the warmongers." They added that he had been expelled from the party in 1943, that he was a rapist, that his house was a center for orgies, that he beat his wife, and that he was a defeatist during the Civil War "in contact with Hitler's and Falangist elements." They went on to say that he had opened the front to the enemy, pushed his units to desertion, led his troops on hazardous operations to have them exterminated, and killed his best fighters (all of which were things the PCE was either not aware of or at least put up with). El Campesino answered, not without humor, that Ehrenburg had called him the "Spanish Chapaiev," saying that his picture was on matchbook covers and Soviet stamps and assured that he was being blamed for everything because his accusations could not be refuted. One of those accusations was that Moscow placed Modesto in charge of negotiating with Madrid the exchange of prisoners of the Blue Division for the Spanish mercury which Franco used to send to Hitler.[82] Less picturesque and dramatic, but politically more significant was the case of Comorera.

The Comorera Case

Juan Comorera, founder of the Socialist Union of Catalonia, secretary general of PSUC, and the man who did the most to subject it to Communist discipline, was not a Catalonian nationalist. During the war he did not hesitate to aid Negrín and the bureau in trimming the prerogatives of the Generalidad. He was an ambitious man who, having scarcely returned from exile in Latin America in 1931, managed to take over the jobs of the leaders of USC. He was very short-sighted, a poor speaker, and a mediocre writer, but he was brave in the style of the Communists, which is to say, he was not afraid of going against the current and being despised. Once the war was over, he was probably the most hated person in the Spanish labor movement.

Leaving Spain, his ambition took him to Moscow in order to transform PSUC from a member of the Communist International into "the Catalonian section of the Communist International." In doing so the issue of power, not nationalism, brought him into conflict with the bureau of the PCE. Later he went to Mexico where he worked like a confirmed Bolshevik. In a conference in 1944 Carrillo praised him greatly for having discarded "the reformist Trotskyite rubbish personified by Serra Pàmies, Del Barrio, Víctor Colomer, Estivill, and the rest of their riffraff"; because of this "there exists in Catalonia today a great organization of the PSUC joined to the party by bonds of blood and struggle." Nonetheless, Carrillo took advantage of the flattery to talk of the organic unity between PSUC and the PCE which had developed in France and which enabled the former, with less experience, to survive the persecutions. The time had come for PSUC to independently take on the work of the Catalonians in exile and the interior. This stance responded to the fact that the PSUC in Catalonia was not making any progress because it was considered a branch of the PCE. On the other hand, the same was not true of the Communist party of Euzkadi for, according to Carrillo, it was different in origin and composition from PSUC.[83] Comorera continued in his attacks on POUM and the CNT which had made him famous during the Civil War. He organized attacks on meetings of POUM in Mexico and there were insults and even assaults. He criticized everyone: Companys who "had mortgaged the freedom and the future of Catalonia" (said just a few weeks before his execution), Tarradellas "who followed in the tracks of Cambó." But he was willing, in accordance with the slogan of National Union, to "stick with them [Cambó's men] if they wanted him to." He also refused to bring up the issue of regime "because it was not a battle flag in the interior of the country,"[84] and he said that "PSUC and the PCE understood one another perfectly," although he repeated that they were two separate parties and he spoke of the "respective political lines."[85]

Comorera saw his base of power in PSUC and he did not want any interference from anyone. He adopted the same stance as the PCE since it came from Moscow, but he could not accept the PCE as leader of PSUC. Looking back, Ibárruri disguised this power rivalry calling it a result of "national and anarchic tendencies" that existed in the origins of PSUC and said that "Comorera was the perfect expression of those contradictions. While he proclaimed that the PCE was a Bolshevik party . . . he maintained that Catalonia, which had lived through the period of the Mancomunitat with Prat de la Riba, of the Lliga with Cambó, and of the Esquerra with Macià, was now going through the period of PSUC with Comorera."[86]

He returned to France. He felt isolated in Toulouse; accords were reached without his being consulted, militants were sent to Catalonia without his being told, and his reports and letters went unanswered. PSUC was economically dependent on the PCE. That caused many of Comorera's comrades to go over to Carrillo and abandon their own leader. Curiously, it was the former Anarchists that La Pasionaria spoke of who sided with the bureau: Vidiella and Moix. Comorera's influence had already been undermined when one day in March 1946 he received an invitation to attend a meeting of the bureau of the PCE. There was no agenda and Ibárruri opened the session saying: "We have met to answer two questions: where is PSUC going, and where is Comorera going?" And without waiting for Comorera to answer, she stated that PSUC had already accomplished its mission and that keeping it alive would be damaging to the democratic revolution and she proposed integrating it immediately in the PCE. But she added that that proposal should be made by Comorera. "You have all the qualities of a leader, not only a national one but international as well. If you make up your mind, we will help you along this path." Comorera refused. He did not want his power base to be taken away. With PSUC in the PCE, he would be left at the bureau's mercy. And the International to which he might have appealed no longer existed. In private Mije put things bluntly: "We've put up with him for thirteen years, and thirteen years and one day later we are ready to do away with him." When some of Comorera's friends went to see Moix he told them that he would respect whatever the bureau of the PCE decided because "after all, we are just ordinary functionaries."[87]

At first they invited Comorera to be part of the bureau of the PCE. That is how they thought they could gradually persuade him. But he disagreed with plans being made in the bureau for the future slogan of national reconciliation. Nor was he in agreement about talking about democratic-bourgeois revolution; he thought that the bourgeoisie had overly compromised itself with Franco and that therefore it was necessary to talk about democratic-popular revolution. Those in PSUC who were friends of the bureau went to committees and assemblies advocating changing PSUC to a Catalonian Section of the PCE. There was not much that Comorera could do to thwart those efforts. He was becoming more and more isolated. No one wanted to jeopardize daily bread. Finally in 1949 the secretariat of PSUC, with the votes of Moix, Vidiella, and Ardiaca, named José Moix—the inquisitor of Tagüeña and others— to replace Comorera in the general secretaryship of PSUC. Comorera appealed to Stalin without realizing he was cooking his own goose since there were men precisely in "popular democracies" who also wanted autonomy for their Communist parties.

He then wrote his defense which he addressed to the secretariat of PSUC. He justified himself for having taken over the party organ, *Lluita,* whose editor, Pedro Ardiaca, was "the author of the offensive to destroy PSUC" and he denied having planned a coup d'état and having kept the party funds. He reaffirmed that PSUC got itself accepted as an independent member of the Communist International but his enemies denied this. He reminded them that the slogans of "extermination" of Anarchists and members of the POUM were not his but the party's which his enemies also denied. He also reminded them that when four members of PSUC who had been arrested for opposition were shot to death in Barcelona (Valverde, Puig Pidemunt, Carrero, and Mestres), they shouted: "Long live Comorera!" He ended by requesting another round of discussions with the "brother party."[88]

The response to the document was a double statement. The secretariat of PSUC in one statement told of the expulsion of Comorera "for being a traitor to the party, the working class, and the people," and in another the Central Committee of the PCE expelled him from the committee for being "a traitor to the Communist party of Spain and the working class." That was in November 1949.

That was not enough. Wenceslao Colomer made his wife, Comorera's daughter, write a public letter to the secretariat of PSUC which outdid that of Carrillo to his father eleven years before:

Dear Comrades,

Until today I had not thought it necessary to write you a letter about Comorera's treason since you were aware of my position since the very beginning, which is to say, I am in total agreement with you, the party, the Communist party of Spain, and our dear comrade Dolores. Since my own father is speculating with hypocritical sentimentality, I want to put my position on record: every day I become stronger in my fidelity to the party and to its principles and its communist nature.

I have not been a member of the party for too many years but the short time I have been in its ranks has allowed me to understand the difference between serving the party and betraying it. To want to divide the party, to want to oppose it to the Communist party of Spain, and particularly at the present time is nothing but despicable treason.

Precisely because I know you all personally and because I also know the comrades in the political bureau, I could never tolerate the wretched attacks which Comorera has directed and is directing against all of you with the desire to serve the enemy. Precisely because I know Comorera and his bourgeois moral and family conduct, it has been easy for me to understand how right you are to expose him as a raving anti-Communist and anti-Soviet. Many things which I never understood, particularly in a leader, today are clear to me. His hypocrisy in covering up the treason committed has not impressed me. Now more than ever I see the reason why the party never tires of saying that a member's personal conduct, and particularly that of a leader, cannot be separated from his political conduct. Whoever in his private and family life has bourgeois concepts also has them in his political ideology.

I hold the party above all else, and when Comorera betrays it, choosing between him and the party is an easy decision.

I condemned his treason from the very first moment and now as each day goes by I become more and more convinced of how right our dear PSUC was to expel him from its ranks and expose him for what he is: an agent of reaction and imperialism.

His infamous speculation about me is one more demonstration of the vile methods which he and his cohorts use. Furthermore, I know all about a case where the relatives of one member of your group were provoked, relatives in Catalonia who, because they are there, are under close surveillance by Franco's police. I also know about the denunciation and provocation of one of your group. That is evidence enough to see the kind of person Comorera is and to feel the repugnance and hatred for him that every Communist feels for the police agents of the reactionary and imperialist enemy.

As a woman and a Communist, I rebel against the attacks of this little group of degenerates on comrade Dolores Ibárruri, for whom I have always felt deep admiration and respect and whose example, as a woman and a Communist, is for us a most precious treasure. Comorera's treason has only helped to deepen the respect that I have for that great leader of anti-Fascist women, head of all Spanish Communists.

For me, my father died the very day that the traitor Comorera was born.

Once again, dear friends in the Secretariat, accept my complete support and a warm embrace.

Nuri Comorera
Paris, March 21, 1950

Some seventy militants left PSUC with Comorera among whom were Josep Marles, Miguel Valdés, Emili Granier-Barrera, Andreu Bernardó, Tomás Molinero, and Agustín Cid. They tried to create a new PSUC, the "true one," but they were not successful. Then Comorera decided to go to Catalonia to "reconquer" the PSUC. To cut him short, *Mundo Obrero* printed a statement on September 15, 1951 which said: "Workers of Catalonia: Juan Comorera is a provocateur who conspired against the Negrín government in accordance with the French consul in Barcelona during our war. Juan Comorera is a provocateur whose function is to hand over Communists to the police. Juan Comorera is an enemy of the working class and as such should be dealt with wherever he appears." This incitement to assassination did not produce the desired effect. Líster said that executioners from the party were waiting for him at the border but that he, foreseeing it, hid in Bourg-Madame, grew a beard, and illegally entered Catalonia on January 31, 1951. He sought contacts, secretly published his own edition of *Treball*—thirty-two issues—with the assistance of his wife, Rosa Santacana, and the writer Ferrán Canyameras, a friend of his although not in ideology. One day in 1954 he was told that an agent from Moscow had invited him to a meeting. Comorera trusted that since Stalin was dead his case would be reviewed, and so he went. There was no meeting and he was arrested by the police. In 1957 he was court-martialed. The public prosecutor asked for a death sentence. He was defended by Josep Benet, who became a senator in 1977. He was sentenced to thirty years in prison. He was sent to the penitentiary in Burgos and died the following year. Jean Creach, correspondent from *Le Monde,* wrote that his being sentenced was due in part to the fact that the Communists arrested as a result of the Barcelona strike of 1951 had declared that it had been organized by Comorera; it was also due to the fact that Franco's government, which had just received prisoners from the Blue Division, having been graciously handed over by the USSR and whose trade with the Soviet bloc was on the increase, wanted to boast of its anti-Communism.

PSUC was gradually turning into a branch of the PCE, at least up to the seventies when the figure of Comorera began to become popular among younger members perhaps because they had never known him. When José Moix died in 1974, he was succeeded as leader of PSUC by Gregorio López Raimundo. In the new team, Vidiella specialized in casting aspersions on the CNT and POUM, López Raimundo in behaving cordially, and Moix, while he was alive, in threatening the members. Ardiaca was the confidant of the PCE.[89] Comorera was not the bureau's last victim. There were others, albeit less spectacular, in the same way that in post-Stalin USSR repression did not end but simply assumed a lower profile. In all, during the time of the purges hundreds of party members were expelled. Of the seventeen Communist representatives in 1936, four had been executed by Franco, one (Díaz) died under anomalous circumstances, and ten were expelled or voluntariiy left the party. The majority of members of the central committee elected in the fourth congress were no longer in the party.

Notes

1. José Borrás, *Política de los exilados españoles, 1944-1950,* Paris, 1976, p. 150. Mije did not go to Moscow because he had lost a package of documents with which he had been entrusted upon leaving Spain and he was afraid that he would be chastised for it in the USSR. The documents ended up in the hands of the French police.
2. Líster, *Memorias,* pp. 413-14.
3. Dominique Desanti, *L'Internationale Communiste,* p. 265.
4. Líster, *Memorias,* pp. 420-21.
5. Thomas, p. 605.
6. Patricia W. Fagen, *Exiles and Citizens: Spanish Republicans in Mexico,* Austin, Texas, 1973, pp. 51-52. This detail is mentioned but only in passing. The Spanish exiles, on the other hand, found out about everything and did not refrain from talking about it once they got to Mexico. Many POUM and CNT exiles who went to Latin America were indebted to the assistance of Quaker committees and the French Parti Ouvrier et Paysan. Others had to wait until 1945.
7. Tagüeña, p. 359.
8. Carrillo, *Demain, l'Espagne: entretiens avec Régis Debray et Max Gallo,* Paris, 1974, pp. 70-71. When the other Communist leaders went to the South-Central zone and Carrillo stayed in France, the National Council of Defense did not yet exist and therefore there was no fear that Carrillo would confront his father in a battle that had not begun.
9. The PCE's statement of the inauthenticity of the letter appeared in *Avui,* the Barcelona daily, as well as in other papers, on June 17, 1977. Regarding the letter's authenticity consult Víctor Alba, "Un enllustrador mal informat," *Avui,* Barcelona, August 9, 1977.
10. This report as well as a PSUC manifesto appeared in pamphlet form with the title of *Extracte de l'informe del company Joan Comorera,* n.p.n.d. (1939).
11. Tagüeña, p. 357. Comments on this meeting appear in *Jeunesses du Monde,* August 15, 1939, along with Carrillo's speech. Tagüeña relates that in Paris at that time the eternal Codovila, delegate of the Communist International, was advising the JSU on how to remain in the Socialist International.
12. Borrás, p. 150.
13. Líster, *Memorias,* p. 432. Togliatti's letter was kept secret until its publication in the seventies in the periodical *Rinascita* of the Italian Communist party.
14. "The strange part was that in the interminable meetings that went on during the course of a month [with the Communist International] we were not allowed to broach the subject of what had happened on the eve of Casado's uprising and certainly not to mention the events which took place at the airfield at Monóvar" (Hernández, *Yo fui un ministro de Stalin,* p. 261). Hernández wanted to talk about the latter, for unlike Ibárruri and other leaders, he had not left on March 6 but stayed and left later. In these discussions Manuilsky publicly defended Togliatti's position. He told Hernández that the Civil War was lost anyway and that it would not have been able to join World War II because the latter would not break out until the Spanish war was over. The important thing was to save the prestige both of the party and the USSR. Togliatti managed to do so by his tactic

of proclaiming resistance and allowing the Defense Council to end the war. Under Franco, the masses would become indignant toward the Socialists and Anarchists and would think that the Communists were right, that it would have been better to resist. The party would win out (Hernández, *Yo fui un ministro de Stalin,* pp. 254–55). The Communist International determined that the party's political bureau would be reduced to three people, Ibárruri, Checa, and Hernández, with Díaz as secretary general (he was never able to take part due to his illness). The three of them were meant to leave for France but were prevented from doing so by the outbreak of World War II. For the same reason other leaders who had gone to the U.S.S.R. to account for their actions had to stay in Moscow.

15. Líster; *¡Basta!* p. 114 ff.
16. Tagüeña, p. 344. The Spaniards did not know that the International had a report written by Togliatti upon his departure from Spain, dated May 21, 1939. No one knew of this report until 1979; it is about 100 pages long (Togliatti, pp. 344–410). It was said that the war was lost because of fighting against the Communist party and the popular front by defeatists, traitors, and enemy agents. The Negrín government was weak in spite of the fact that it worked closely with PCE leaders, for there was no homogeneity and all its ministers worked to thwart the PCE and Negrín. Furthermore, the fight "against the Trotskyites was weak, characterized by the scandalous outcome of the trial of POUM." It criticized Negrín for not having understood the problem of Catalonia and for having been influenced in his economic policy by bourgeois and corrupt elements. Nonetheless, it recognized that up to mid-January 1939 "Negrín was faithful to the party." The PCE was not active enough in working for unity and resistance, it was unable to prevent the break in the popular front and improve its relations with the Socialist party, although it managed to get the UGT to back its actions. Yet it did not move forward in the unification of the UGT and CNT and did not sufficiently control PSUC, which "displayed many more weaknesses and gaps than the PCE." He blamed the loss of Catalonia on military reasons and the weakness of the ties between PSUC and the masses. In conclusion, he found the PCE strategy to be sound and that the defeat ought to be blamed on the international situation, the worldwide treason of social democracy, and the democratic governments, but "had there not been internal weakness, the resistance could have been prolonged." Although the PCE grew a lot, it did not gain decisive influence in the key points of Madrid and Barcelona, did not Bolshevize its new militants, did not fight quickly enough against POUM, and was more proficient in the area of propaganda than in organization.
17. Degras, vol. III, p. 436.
18. Ibárruri, *El único camino,* p. 377 ff.
19. *Historia del PCE,* p. 203 ff. Much later, in 1960, a Russian author wrote a book about the Spanish war which did not follow word for word the official version and interpretation; it spoke of the war as a revolutionary movement and was severely criticized by the specialized Soviet press and did not receive extensive recognition. Claudín spoke about it in his book on the Communist movement (p. 606). It was called *The Spanish Proletariat in the National Revolutionary War,* by K. L. Maidanik, Moscow, 1960. This book is not included in the bibliography of this text since it was not consulted by the author.

20. Tagüeña, p. 341.
21. Teresa Pàmies, "Datos biográficos sobre José Días," *Nueva Historia*, Barcelona, May 1978.
22. Tagüeña, p. 344 ff.
23. The USSR never accepted non-Communist refugees and it accepted Communist refugees only in small numbers. Hernández (*Yo fui un ministro de Stalin*, p. 257) relates that he spoke with Dimitrov and asked him if a few boats could not be sent to France to pick up refugees. "It's not possible. We'd have one sticky problem after another in the USSR," was the response. Not even the wounded, disabled, or the sick? No, that was the concern of the International Red Aid. Hermet (p. 51) gives a summary of the various estimates of the number of Spanish refugees in the USSR: 4,000 of which 500 were party militants, according to Castro Delgado; according to Hernández, there were some 5,000 refugee children; according to El Campesino, there were 1,700 children, 102 teachers, 210 pilots, and 3,961 refugees. In any case, there were more refugees and even more Spanish Communists in any of the Latin American countries which accepted them than in the USSR. Even the United States and Great Britain accepted more refugees than the USSR.
24. *¡Karagandá! La tragedia del antifascismo español*, Toulouse, 1948. These Republican internees were thrown out of the USSR several years later when the prisoners of the Blue Division and the Spanish children were repatriated. The survivors went to Latin America. Mije's statement is in Borrás, p. 51.
25. Tagüeña, p. 408.
26. There are several books about the Spaniards in the USSR. They are all very impassioned; all were written by people who lost the "battle" over Díaz's succession. They clearly do not lie, but perhaps exaggerate. For this reason I have based my notes on Tagüeña, since he did not become involved with the internal fighting of the party and always showed great equanimity. The other books which can be consulted are: Jesús Hernández, *Yo fui un ministro de Stalin*, Mexico City, 1953; Enrique Castro Delgado, *La vida secreta de la Komintern: cómo perdí la fe en Moscú*, Mexico City, 1950; El Campesino, *La Vie et la mort en URSS*, Paris, 1950; Ettore Vanni, *Yo, comunista en Rusia*, Barcelona, 1950; José Antonio Rico, *En los dominios del Kremlin*, Mexico City, 1950; Lauro Cruz Goyenola, *Rusia por dentro*, Montevideo, 1946.
27. Tagüeña, p. 411. The other quotes on this issue are from the same book, pp. 440, 456, 465, 467-68, 471, 475.
28. On the opposition in this period consult Víctor Alba, *La oposición de los supervivientes, 1939-1955*, Barcelona, 1978. In that text more detail and the sources of documentation of the events described are given. One example of the PCE's tendency to present itself as the only opposition to Franco during those years can be seen in Pilar Gómez de Guzmán, "Historia del Partido Comunista de España: notas para una recuperación," *Tiempo de Historia*, Madrid, May 1977.
29. Gregorio Morán in *Diario 16*, Madrid, March 24, 1977 and following issues.
30. Ibárruri, (*El único camino*, p. 419) was aware of the "lack of foresight regarding the possibility of defeat. There was neither an underground press, radio communications, money, housing, nor illegal organizations. We had prepared nothing." She passes it off to the "obsession" of winning the war.

The other organizations were guilty of the same neglect, but none of them in 1938–39 had the material means the PCE had to plan for future underground activities. Líster underscored this deficiency and believed that it would have been possible to prepare for going underground if they had resisted for a few months longer (¡Basta! p. 115).

31. *Historia del PCE*, pp. 214–15. In her memoirs Ibárruri said that Cazorla was held in Madrid's prison where the Junta had thrown him and that the Fascists found him and shot him to death. Other versions indicate that he got out of prison before the end of the war, went into hiding and began to reorganize the party, was discovered and executed. The matter is still obscure.

32. *Historia del PCE*, p. 217.

33. Hernández, *Yo fui un ministro de Stalin*, pp. 331, 333.

34. Pilar González Guzmán, article quoted in which, without giving credit, large fragments of the *Historia del PCE* are printed.

35. F. Aguado Sánchez, *El maquis en España*, Madrid, 1975, p. 89.

36. Borrás, p. 156.

37. There are some books on the guerrillas; all are propagandistic and unreliable. Among those written by authors connected with the forces of repression of the period, the following can be consulted: F. Aguado Sánchez, *El maquis en España*, Madrid, 1975; Tomás Cossías, *La lucha contra el "maquis" en España*, Madrid, 1956; Ángel Ruiz Ayúcar, *El Partido Comunista: 37 años de clandestinidad*, Madrid, 1976. Of those written by Communists: Andrés Sorel, *Búsqueda, reconstrucción e historia de la guerrilla española del siglo XX*, Paris, 1970; José Antonio Vidal Sales, *Después del '39: la guerrilla antifranquista*, Barcelona, 1976; E. Pons Prades, *Guerrillas españolas, 1939–1960*, Barcelona, 1977 are more objective. J. M. Molina, *El movimiento clandestino en España, 1939–1949*, Mexico City, 1976 talks in particular of the guerrillas of the CNT, as does C. Damiano, *La resistencia libertaria*, Barcelona, 1978.

38. Ruiz Ayúcar, p. 244.

39. Pilar González Guzmán.

40. Sorel, p. 70.

41. González Guzmán.

42. These organizations existed only on paper, they had been formed by the PCE in exile with a few members and were used to make the PCE appear more influential than it was.

43. José María del Valle, *Las institutiones de la República Española en el exilio*, Paris, 1976, p. 185 ff.

44. *Mundo Obrero*, April 10, 1947.

45. *Mundo Obrero*, August 6, 1947. Tagüeña (p. 581) explained that the PCE delegate in Czechoslovakia, Velasco, got the Prague government to expel the representative of the Republic government in exile when there was no longer a Communist minister in that government.

46. Tagüeña related (pp. 506, 510, 545) that the Soviet authorities systematically opposed allowing the Spaniards who were not leaders of the PCE to leave the USSR. In order to get out of the country there were some who agreed to join the NKVD through Caridad Mercader. Among that group were Carmen Brufau and Carlos Díez, who ended up committing suicide (or who was murdered) in Venezuela. Later on, others were allowed to go to

a "popular democracy." In 1945 there was authorization for some Spaniards to leave on the appeal of their families. This is how Castro Delgado managed to get out of the USSR: the authorities grew tired of getting letters which Castro continually wrote to Stalin and Molotov. Those who had joined the battalion of the NKVD were allowed to leave for France in 1945. To leave the USSR one needed the approval of the PCE which had to be requested from its delegate in Moscow, José Antonio Uribes. Only through this channel could one get back the personal documents which had to be handed over to the authorities upon entering the country. The case of José Tuñon, pilot and long-time Communist, was tragic: having been refused permission to leave the country, he arranged with the labor attaché of the Argentine Embassy and tried to leave in a trunk which was part of the diplomatic corps' baggage. He was discovered and sentenced to twenty-five years on the gulag. Stalin's death and the thaw allowed him to get out and even finally to leave the "fatherland of the proletariat."

47. "L'arrestation d'assassins communistes espagnols dans l'Aude," *Beipi*, Paris, December 1, 16, 1953. This information includes the names of three victims: San Miguel of POUM, García of the CNT, and Geogeakopulus of the PSOE. They were the three from the maquis. Details on this are in José Borrás, p. 197 ff.

48. Líster, *¡Basta!* quoted by Jorge Semprún, *Autobiografía de Federico Sánchez*, Barcelona, 1977, pp. 111, 114. Semprún provides several names of those purged.

49. "L'Activité du PC Espagnol en France," *Beipi*, Paris, May 16, 1953. Regarding the maneuvers to win over those centers in Latin America and the use the PCE made of them, see Patricia W. Fagen, *Exiles and Citizens*, passim. What she explains about Mexico also happened in other countries.

50. *Historia del PCE*, pp. 226-27.

51. Dolores Ibárruri, *Por la libertad de España*, Mexico City and Toulouse, 1945. Carrillo's speech is in *Nuestra Bandera*, June 1945.

52. "Por una España republicana, democrática e independiente. Las sesiones del III Pleno del PCE en Francia," *Mundo Obrero*, March 27, 1947.

53. *Historia del PCE*, pp. 236-38. In support of this position, *Nuestra Bandera* (September-October 1948) printed an article by Lenin: "Should Revolutionaries Work in Reactionary Unions?" but without ever saying that Lenin was referring to the reformist unions and not the Fascist ones which did not exist in his lifetime.

54. This can be corroborated, for example, in *La España franquista en sus documentos*, by Guillermo Díaz Plaja, Barcelona, 1976, pp. 160, 191, 250.

55. Hermet, p. 61.

56. *Historia del PCE*, p. 243.

57. Ibárruri was the leader who deserved more blame than others. In October 1949 she had attacked *Mundo Obrero* for its stance on the issue of "vertical unions." This attack doubtless reflected a struggle among tendencies in the bureau which La Pasionaria tried to settle using her position of secretary general. The editors of *Mundo Obrero* immediately printed a self-criticism in the paper. But in the Cominform's organ of June 8, 1951 there appeared an indirect criticism of La Pasionaria. The Moscow paper printed in Bucharest maintained that "the heroic strikes by Spanish workers show that unity

can be achieved even under the terror of Fascism when Fascist and Falangist unions exist. . . . Communists must be everywhere where there are working masses and must work with them."

58. The Spanish delegates to the World Congress of Peace included: Manuel Sánchez Arcas, Manuel Martínez Risco, Salvador Bacarisse, José Quiroga Plá, Antonio Mije, Ignacio Hidalgo de Cisneros, Amaro Rosal, Daniel Anguiano, Federico Melchor, José Serrán, Luis Delage, Rafael Vidiella, Elisa Uriz, Ángel Galarza, A. Otero Seco, J. Antonio Ramírez, Cecilio Palomares, Manuel Núñez Arenas, Enrique Líster, Luis Fernández, Margarita Abril, Anita Martínez, María González, F. Olmo de Lada, Bertrand Reis, Luis Azcárate, José Moix, José Fontbernat, Armand Obiols, Elfidio Alonso, María Román, and Leonor Bornau. A message of greeting to the same congress was signed by Funes, Felipe M. Arconada, Tomás Bilbao, Adolfo Vázquez Humasqué, Pedro Carrasco, Arturo Mori, Moreno Villa, Ricardo Castellote, Arturo Souto, Bernardo Pizarro, Luis García Lago, Joaquín Arderius, Arturo Cortés, Urbano Barnés, Bibiano Ossorio Tafall, Trinidad Arroyo, Antonio Ramos Espinos, Manuel de Rivas Cherif, Manuel García Becerra, Antonio Pacheco, Víctor Basauri, José Carbó, Enrique Vega Trápaga, Rafael Guerra, Juan Rejano, León Felipe, Max Aub, Antonio Rodríguez Luna, José María Francés, Alfonso Pazos, Luis Salvadores, Emilia Elías, Navarro Costabella, José Diéguez, Rafael Trueta, Vicente Judez, Ricardo Vinós, Pedro Tomás Llinares, Francisco Matz, Félix Templado, Juan José Lastra, Antonio Espinosa, Antonio Ballesteros, Amalia Martín, Miguel Rengel, José Ignacio Mantecón, Julio Bejarano, Veneranda G. Manzano, Antonio Rallo, José Muni, Antonio Iturrioz, Juan Pedret, Gabriel Morón, Victoriano Rico, José Renau, Eduardo Serrano, Pedro Garfias, the widow of Bagaría, Vicente Gaspar, and Dionisio Nieto.

59. Jorge Semprún (p. 126) in reference to Manuel Tuñón de Lara whom he insinuates was part of special services. Semprún also recalls that in the trials in Czechoslovakia Josef Frank was accused of having been in the Gestapo in Buchenwald when he met him. In spite of knowing that the accusation was not true, he abstained from exposing the lie out of party discipline.

60. Tagüeña, pp. 553, 555–56, 565–66.

61. Hermet, p. 60. For Ibárruri's statement, see *Pour une Paix durable et une démocratie populaire,* Bucharest, December 27, 1949.

62. Teresa Pàmies, "Aquí Radio España Independiente, Estación Pirenaica," *Nueva Historia,* Barcelona, February 1978.

63. José del Barrio, after he had been thrown out of PSUC, said that this peaceful tactic of National Union responded to the British policy of letting the Spaniards overthrow Franco by peaceful means which was subsequently reflected in a three-part statement (United States, France, and Great Britain). He also said that if the PCE followed this line it was because when Churchill and Stalin partitioned Europe in Yalta, England got Spain (*Cuadernos de Política Socialista,* Paris, suppl. 1, 1950).

64. *Reconquista de España,* Toulouse, February-August 1944. Many announced that their names had been taken without their permission to support the National Union, among them Negrín, Nicolau d'Olwer, and Gil Robles. Ibárruri's letter appears in Borrás, p. 176 ff.

65. In January 1945 Carrillo had said: "The only possible way to reach an

agreement with the right wing and the Monarchists without whom the overthrow of Franco cannot even be considered, is to avoid for the moment raising the issue of regime, leaving it to the people to determine in democratic elections." A year and a half later he accused some sectors in exile of renouncing Republican legitimacy and said: "We Communists have never renounced that. Our position is to reach an agreement with forces not specifically Republican to organize an uprising against Franco" (Borrás, pp. 181, 187).

66. The representatives of the interior (Madrid, Valencia, Extremadura, Catalonia) were arrested upon their return to Spain. A police informer, infiltrated in the delegation from the interior and in attendance at the congress, gave them away. The novelist Luis Goytisolo was among those arrested.

67. The program was published in Spanish by the French Communist party in Nice in 1955.

68. Eduardo Comín Colomer, *La República en el exilio,* Barcelona, 1957, p. 567 ff.

69. The reply to this statement which it did not print appears in *Mundo Obrero,* March 31, 1955.

70. *Historia del PCE,* p. 248 ff.

71. Borrás, pp. 159, 161.

72. Semprún, p. 141.

73. *Nuestra Bandera,* February-March 1950.

74. Líster, *¡Basta!* p. 163. Attacks on Monzón and Trilla appear in *Nuestra Bandera,* no. 28. Manuel Azcárate, who was Monzón's companion in France and who was in contact with Field, never said anything about the issue, nor did he come out in defense of his companion in battle (Semprún, p. 120).

75. Tagüeña, p. 541. Tagüeña observes that "it was amusing that in a Socialist state a factory was considered a place of punishment, slightly better than a work camp."

76. This whole controversy, as well as the denial of having supported the National Union, are in Jesús Hernández, *Negrín contra la Unión Nacional Española,* Toulouse, 1945.

77. Jean Creach ("Le Parti Communiste Espagnol dans la stratégie soviétique. Repli vers le glacis," *Le Monde,* Paris, December 21, 1950) mentions the point about Ibárruri and says that Stalin had to reprimand her to pull her out of her hesitation. Without coming out and saying it, Carrillo suggests the point about Líster in *Demain l'Espagne* (Paris, 1974), saying that in an interview with Stalin, he said that Líster "does not have much affection for the Soviet Union" and Ibárruri replied, "He's getting smarter." This observation is somewhat mysterious and could have referred to something besides Líster's alleged inclination toward Tito which at any rate was quickly snuffed out.

78. Miaja, Rodríguez Vega, and César Falcón, among others.

79. Tagüeña, pp. 539, 542, 556, 608, 637. He explains the course of his disenchantment and separation and the efforts made to prevent him from leaving Prague. José Moix of PSUC was one of the men who put the greatest pressure on him and was sent from Paris just for that purpose.

80. *Zócalo,* Mexico City, January 14, 15, 1954.

81. The names given all those who had been expelled (except those who underwent self-criticism) can be found in Antonio Mije, "Defensa de la unidad de Partido," *Nuestra Bandera,* April 1970.

82. *La Monde,* Paris, January 6, 1951.

83. Carrillo, *Unidad y lucha,* Mexico City, 1944.

84. Comorera, *La batalla de la Pau,* Toulouse, 1945.

85. *Resolució de la reunió ampliada de la Delegació del Comité Central del Partit Socialista Unificat de Catalunya,* Toulouse, 1945. In 1938 Togliatti did not see this mutual understanding but rather complained in his reports to Moscow that Comorera paid more attention to his responsibilities in the Catalonian government than to those as secretary general of PSUC. He criticized the PCE for not having PSUC under better control and for not having sent their delegates to the meetings of the central committee of the Catalonian party. To get around this he proposed—and it was approved—that the military commissions, the war industries, etc. of both parties be joined together. He also criticized Comorera for "solving, by means of decree, problems which should have been solved through dialogue." Togliatti spoke in his report of January 1938 of the existence of Freemasons in the executive committee and in the secretariat of PSUC (there were three Freemasons in the executive committee and two in the secretariat). It is possible that one of them was Comorera "who dominated and terrorized the leaders." Togliatti wanted to replace him but could not find a replacement since the elders in the Catalonian Communist party (Ardiaca, Valdés) were suffering from "complete political inconsistency." In his analysis of the end of the Civil War, Togliatti underscored that PSUC had lent more support to the Generalidad than to the Negrín government and that there was a strong infiltration of Catalonian nationalists, Freemasons, and even Trotskyites in that party. Anyone who lived during that period knows that this is not true (Togliatti, pp. 302–8).

86. Ibárruri, *El único camino,* p. 387.

87. Evarist Massip, "Una altra resposta a Pere Ardiaca," *Serra d'Or,* Barcelona, September 1974.

88. "Los comunistas catalanes se dividen," *Historia Internacional,* Madrid, June 1976. It was the first time the document by Comorera was published; it was previously kept secret by PSUC. It was dated November 14, 1949. See also "Declaración del Secretariado del Partido Socialista Unificado de Cataluña sobre la conducta política de Juan Comorera," *Mundo Obrero,* November 10, 1949. Regarding the political—not nationalist—nature of the Comorera case, see L. Colomer and R. Viñas, "El PSUC a la Gran Enciclopedia Catalana," *Serra d'Or,* Barcelona, July-August 1978.

89. For information on PSUC's underground activity, see A. Ribas and J. Fabre, "El PSUC: quaranta anys de lluita política" and "La reorganizació del PSUC després de la guerra," *Avui,* Barcelona, July 23, 1976 and March 25, 1977, respectively. In 1949 eighty members were arrested at the same time. PSUC at the time had six urban terrorists in Barcelona. There were four executions and the "mystery" of those who had been arrested was never solved, according to one of the survivors, Carlos Martínez (*Treball,* July 21, 1978).

15.
Gaining Respectability

Following the fifth congress of the PCE two things happened which provided new perspectives for the party: the readmission of Spain in the United Nations and Krushchev's secret report to the twentieth congress of the Russian Communist party about the personality cult and subsequent de-Stalinization campaign. These two events were taken advantage of by the PCE in an attempt to gain "respectability." This lengthy process was headed by Carrillo who, with great bureaucratic aplomb, gradually took the party's inner working out of La Pasionaria's hands without a struggle or clash.

Franco in the United Nations

On June 13, 1955 the Soviet Communist party published a declaration accepting "pluralism as part of the way toward socialism." By doing so Moscow tried to make its control of the parties more flexible and to come to terms with Belgrade. This allowed the PCE, in its efforts to construct the Anti-Francoist Front proposed by the fifth congress, to be free to find its own way. It came across stumbling blocks in January 1956 when the USSR voted with the United States and other countries for the admission of Spain in the United Nations. The PCE would have to work hard—because it was less independent of Moscow than it claimed to be—to justify that vote. Released from prison after nine years and seeking refuge in Mexico, Santiago Álvarez would pick up the reasoning of the PCE (which was not even consulted by Moscow on this issue): "The entry of sixteen nations in the United Nations has meant a contribution to the cause of peace and peaceful coexistence. . . . Among those sixteen countries there are four popular democracies: Austria, which is neutral; Finland, supporting the cause of peace; and countries of Asia and Africa which are on our side, and even though Spain may be with them, it is a fact that the latest entry of sixteen countries in the UN favors the cause of peace."[1]

Eight days before the vote in the UN, the organizations of exiles in Mexico published a document opposing the admission of Spain in the UN. It was signed by the PCE. Eight days after the vote, the same organizations approved a protest of the admission of Franco. The PCE did not sign it because those who had drafted it refused to exclude the USSR in addition to the United States among those responsible. José Giral was one of the few who joined the side of the Communist delegates who were trying to suppress all mention of the USSR. Then a curious disagreement arose. La Pasionaria had just celebrated her sixtieth birthday in Bucharest, in the company of other leaders. And in Bucharest a statement was published lamenting the admission of Spain and defending Republican legality. At the same time, in Paris Carrillo's group had printed in *Nuestra Bandera* a statement saying that the admission of Spain would produce favorable results in Spain's journey toward democracy. To avoid a conflict, Carrillo sent Jorge Semprún to talk with Líster, Uribe, and Ibárruri. After listening to him, Ibárruri told him she had decided that the Bucharest group's declarations should be withdrawn (doubtless, although without admitting it, on orders from Moscow which of course was more comfortable with the Paris group's declaration which "whitewashed" the Soviet vote in the UN without even mentioning it). And she added that the entire matter would be discussed in a plenary meeting of the central committee. But before that plenary met, something happened that provided Carrillo with a powerful weapon.

De-Stalinization

The Twentieth Congress of the Russian Communist Party was convened in February 1956. Behind closed doors Krushchev read a devastating report about Stalin which could not be kept secret for very long. That report talked of the personality cult which Stalin had fostered and it blamed him for every mistake and failure made by the USSR. At first the PCE's leaders denied the report's existence; they later spoke of it as "attributed to Kruschev"; finally they decided not to ignore it and skirted the issue by praising Krushchev and talking about de-Stalinization but without doing anything about it. Ibárruri was at the Russian congress. Soon thereafter she was willing to "pardon" the expelled supporters of Tito (but not those members who had been expelled during 1942–44), when in the USSR there began the reinstatement of those who had been murdered under Stalin. Nonetheless no one in the PCE dared suggest the rehabilitation of Andrés Nin or that the circumstances surrounding his death be revealed.

It was then that the declaration of the Soviet Communist party regarding "pluralism as part of the way to socialism" was emphasized— as a result of Krushchev's visit to Belgrade. Regarding the declaration, Ibárruri said that it would help the Spanish Communists "to put an end to the narrow and sectarian concepts which hindered our activities." Carrillo silently prepared his part in the central committee's plenary. He saw that other parties were hurrying to de-Stalinize (Italy, for example) and that some (like France) resisted following the path indicated by Krushchev. He realized that things in the Communist movement would never again be exactly what they were prior to the secret report. *Mundo Obrero* was full of comments about "the victorious struggle against the personality cult" in Japan, Poland, Holland, but never in the PCE. Carrillo said later that after the dissolution of the Comintern "the Communist party of the Soviet Union had not previously been consulted on any change of policy or party decision; if by chance on any occasion, rather fortuitously—because it coincided with trips for other reasons— we had exiles there (in the USSR), we informed them a posteriori."[2]

Nonetheless, when in June 1956 the PCE issued a new slogan on the basis of a new political line, in a pamphlet entitled "Declaration of the PCE for National Reconciliation and a Democratic and Peaceful Solution to the Spanish Dilemma," it was a reflection of the new attitude coming from Moscow. National reconciliation was the Spanish version of peaceful coexistence.[3] According to the document, there had been an evolution in Spain, some Francoist forces were in disagreement with a policy which kept the spirit of the Civil War alive, and the Republican camp believed it was necessary to bury the hatchet. "A mood favoring national reconciliation is winning over the political and social forces that fought in opposing camps during the Civil War." It recalled that in 1938 the PCE had tried to end the Civil War with the thirteen points of the Negrín government. National Union (not referred to by name) responded to the same spirit. And as the twentieth anniversary of the start of the Civil War neared, the PCE "solemnly swore it was willing to contribute, without reservations, to the national reconciliation of Spaniards," and it called everyone, from Catholics and liberal Monarchists to Socialists and members of the CNT, to set as a common goal national reconciliation. At first nobody responded. But the PCE was already used to that.

The Plenary of East Berlin

In August 1956 the plenary of the Central Committee of the PCE met in the Edgar André military school in East Berlin. Ibárruri insisted on pointing out the shortcomings in the party's performance which she had underscored in the fifth congress. During the year and a half that the group of leaders in Paris carried the weight of activity in Spain, they did not manage to organize the Anti-Franco Front nor to establish relations with the Catholics, and they just barely began to have influence among students and intellectuals. It was a subtle way of making Carrillo look inefficient. As for Carrillo, he gave a report on "The Situation of Party Leadership and the Problems in Strengthening the Party."[4] It dealt with the "personality cult condemned by the twentieth congress and its repercussions in our party." It said that "we did not imagine" what Krushchev revealed in his report and explains it by pointing to the fact that Communist parties developed in bourgeois society "are not impervious to the vices and emotions of bourgeois society." Even before Krushchev's report the PCE made efforts to put an end to "the anti-democratic methods of order and command" and had challenged the idea that some comrades were irreplaceable, that "they were a sort of taboo that could not be touched," but "we have not been able to present in a serious, scientific way the roles of comrades José Díaz and Dolores Ibárruri in the formation of our party." Because of a lack of self-criticism, party leaders placed more importance on practical questions that ideological ones. The method of "unipersonal leadership" prevailed in all areas of activity. That "did not help to sustain an elevated political atmosphere in the political bureau." The secretariat had changed from an executive body into one which was superior even to the central committee.

To bring about national reconciliation it was necessary to avoid the personality cult and place more importance on ideological issues so that members would not be jolted, would not hold onto former concepts. And it all had to be done without "falling into the trap of breaking ties of proletarian internationalism with the Communist party of the USSR." The report was nearly eighty pages long and became the crux of the meeting. A resolution on it was adopted congratulating the CPSU for its criticism of the personality cult and expressing regret to the Union of Yugoslavian Communists over the break in ties. It also recorded the transformation of the secretariat into the supreme organ and cited the "exaggerated roles of the leaders [referring by name to Díaz and Ibárruri] as the authors of party victories, underestimating the role of the members themselves as a group," and said that those leaders were represented as heads of the Spanish people, which "contradicted reality." The central committee also recorded that Vicente Uribe was "reticent regarding collective leadership . . . and was inclined toward self-satisfaction, the use of unipersonal methods of leadership, pragmatism, and the underestimation of ideological work." And it added: "Comrade Uribe has admitted his faults and has made his self-criticism before the central committee." Mije was also rebuffed for his vacillation and so the central committee "hoped that this experience would be of use to Comrade Antonio Mije in the future."[5]

The central committee approved what had been accomplished since the previous congress, which must not have pleased Ibárruri, and it ratified the central committee's June declaration on national reconciliation and the possibility of replacing Franco through peaceful means. What national reconciliation meant in the spirit of the leading body was seen in a few comments in the central committee's meeting. According to Carrillo, one could be affiliated with the CNT and be a member of the PCE at the same time. Ibárruri maintained that "Falangists can defend the claims of the workers," and added that "one can be in the Falange and at the same time be useful to the cause of the working class." Carrillo indicated that "certain responsible workers in the 'vertical unions' assume at times progressive attitudes in defense of their comrades."

To administer the new policy the central committee chose Santiago Carrillo, Santiago Álvarez, Fernando Claudín, Manuel Delicado, Ignacio Gallego, Dolores Ibárruri, Enrique Líster, Antonio Mije, Vicente Saiz, Sánchez Montero, Federico Sánchez (Jorge Semprún), and Vicente Uribe.[6] There were a few militants, promoted from the central committee, and the same ones who had practiced personality cult. Just like in the USSR. Shortly thereafter PSUC convened its first congress, a meeting of no real importance, to back José Moix as secretary general, confirm support for the policy of national reconciliation, approve some bylaws taken from those of the PCE, affirm its Marxist-Leninist nature, and formalize relations with the PCE.

The Seizure of Protest

The East Berlin plenary not only helped to settle old accounts among the leading clans but also to examine the results of the first attempts at implementing the policy of national reconciliation made prior to June. In practice it was clear that the goal of such a policy was to allow the party to approach other forces and try to capture them. This was referred to as "the seizure of protest." The Franco regime realized this and was not very harsh with those who followed this line.

Now that there was clearly no longer any hope of overthrowing Franco through foreign activity, and since opposition on the part of survivors of the Civil War was exhausted and leaderless, and the CNT in the interior which had been supportive of it for years was decimated, it was now up to another generation to enter the struggle. It was the generation who were infants during the Civil War, who did not know the PCE from experience and were totally unfamiliar with it, since it was common in Spain for parents not to talk about the war to their children. So the PCE was able to get itself accepted by this generation at face value and without fear that old memories would cloud the image of the party as being sensible, unitarian and conciliatory. This generation's lack of political experience prevented it from seeing the maneuvers behind the slogans.

At that time there was no other organization in the opposition that was anything more than a powerless committee or a mere reflection of the exile. The police and a sense of disillusionment had taken care of destroying what had existed previously. The field was open for the PCE with its abundant means—money, militants, and press. The year 1956 was one of change for the opposition. Students in Madrid demonstrated on the occasion of José Ortega y Gasset's burial, there were clashes with the Falangists as well as fierce police repression. The first student democratic organizations appeared. In those groups of protesters there were many children from important families on the side of Franco. They had to go into exile.[7]

The PCE managed to infiltrate the students. It drew to it some of them who in turn controlled their almost spontaneous organizations because they were more disciplined and better prepared.[8] The majority of those who were indoctrinated withdrew later without even having become members of the PCE once they realized they had been manipulated by it. Examples of this manipulation were the "Encuentros de la poesía con la Universidad" (Poetry in the University), the Congress of Young Writers, and the University Manifesto of February 1956. Enrique Múgica was the man behind all those activities organized by the party, although many participants were not aware of it.[9] Of course, none of this reached the streets but remained in coteries. It not only helped to bring them out in the party press but also to penetrate the newly formed organizations and build bridges to other organizations of intellectuals and Catholics. There was a wide choice since the organizations were proliferating: the Unión Democrática de Estudiantes (Democratic Union of Students), composed of Catholics and Socialists, the Nueva Izquierda Universitaria (New University Left), the Assamblea Lliure d'Estudiants (Free Assembly of Students) in Barcelona, and many others.

The party used an old technique here: do not expend energy creating organizations but rather let other people form them (perhaps secretly pushing them to do so), allow the organizations to be put to the test and if they take hold, then mobilize a few members, put them to work in the organizations and gradually develop them until such a time when democratically or by other means they can be controlled. In this way the old organization provided the shell, at times prestigious and accepted by many, in which the party placed its own yolk for the more naive of them to hatch. This tactic had not brought them success in the unions of the UGT and CNT; during the party's early days it met with some success with the creation of PSUC and it was a failure in exile (where the Republican and Catalonian clubs created by the party were dissolved as of 1956 when the members of the clubs affiliated with non-communist clubs in hopes of taking them over yet rarely managing to do so and then for only a short time). But the tactic was somewhat successful in underground Spain. We will soon see how all the PCE's union machinery was formed in this way and how its support organizations were also created through the work of other people.

However, something happened to upset the arrangement for a while: the people's rebellion in Hungary of October-November 1956. The PCE had an old friend in Hungary, Gerö, who had been delegate of the Communist International to PSUC and who, while in Budapest, took it upon himself in the name of the party to ask the Russians to send in their tanks to occupy the country. The PCE sided with Moscow and echoed the insults directed toward the Hungarian revolutionaries. The university elements in the PCE, reinforced by some workers, came to blows with the students who wanted to demonstrate in support of Hungary. After this first resistance had been overcome, the pro-Hungarian students took to the streets and were beaten up by the armed police. The events in Budapest did not weaken the PCE nor did they cause it to lose intellectuals (as happened, for example, in France and Italy).

Moscow played a dirty trick on the PCE. Juan Negrín died in November 1956 and left the Franco government documents referring to the gold sent to the USSR in 1936. Although no claim was made as a result of this transference of documents, on April 11, 1957 *Pravda* printed an article entitled "The Spanish Gold Rush," which *Mundo Obrero* hastened to reproduce in its May 15 issue. The article said that the Spanish gold had all been used to purchase war material and that there was still a debit of fifty million dollars on the open credit extended to the Negrín government in 1938. The article underscored that none of the Spanish gold had been spent in support of the Spanish refugees and children since the cost of such support had been born by Soviet "unions."

The HNP

> The PCE lacked the intellectual subtlety necessary to analyze the new stage Spain was going through. It did not understand that economic development was possible and that large sectors of the population could feel tied to the regime by means of it. . . . The policy of national reconciliation was premature, because 1956 saw the first student protests as well as the passage of some important Falangists to the opposition. Then in 1957 there was a wave of strikes which extended from Barcelona to Madrid and the Basque region. The Communists were quick to take credit for those movements and to affirm that the strikes meant that the working class endorsed their policy. Since unaffiliated Catholics, Socialists, Anarchists, and liberals had taken part in the protests, the Communists eagerly announced that they were ready to make a pact with those sectors.[10]

Through intellectuals and professionals the PCE came in contact with scattered adversaries such as Dionisio Ridruejo whom it never managed to attract as well as with groups which began to form outside of the PCE and which could get in the way of its monopolizing the opposition. Some of those groups were larger and more active than the PCE, although they were less powerful, such as the Frente de Liberación Popular (Popular Liberation Front)—the FLP or Felipe, as it was called—the union-like ASO, and especially the IDC (Christian Democratic Left). Javier Pradera established most contacts; he even set up interviews between the PCE and Gil Robles and Giménez Fernández.[11] The contacts did not lead to anything concrete but once established, they paved the way for interviews, discussions of concrete action, and they even made those interviewed—especially if they were Christian Democrats—afraid of being considered moderates. What in other countries was called "intellectual terrorism" became widespread during that period; it was the fear that the Communists would label everyone: reactionary, imperialist agent, agent of the CIA, reformist, all of which would bring discredit before the opposition.

"Given the anti-Communist sentiments that exist throughout Spanish society, even among liberal groups, this call [for national reconciliation] cannot possibly be the point of departure for a regrouping," said a French left-wing newspaper remarking on the plenary of East Berlin. National reconciliation did not lead to reconciliation or any regrouping, to be sure. But these were not its objectives. What it proposed to do was eradicate the old mistrust and create a new image for the party. Progress was first made among intellectuals; then, more slowly, among Catholics, not only the Christian-Democrats whose guilt feelings could be manipulated but also those who were not politicized who used the pastorals of some bishops denouncing the living conditions of the proletariat as of some bishops denouncing the living conditions of the proletariat as an argument, and legitimately so.

When salaries were increased in 1957 followed by an even greater increase in prices, the Communists called not only the workers but also students, Catholics, and intellectuals to protest, while the other organizations continued their policy of only appealing to the workers. The protests were important in Barcelona and somewhat less so in Madrid and Bilbao. The PCE stated that the fact that different organizations came together in protest "indicated the possibility of great unitarian demonstrations." At the same time it took advantage of the occasion to slander its rivals by saying: "Under the pressure of American imperialism and other factors, a segment of the Socialist, Anarchist, Republican, Catholic, and liberal leaders are still in opposition to a formal political accord with the Communist party while at the same time recognizing the great degree of influence that this party has in the country."[12]

This was beginning to come true. "Communism, hardly noticeable in Spain several years ago, is now a well-organized underground movement with a new campaign plan," said a London paper printing as an element of this plan the fact that in his trial, Simón Sánchez Montero, delegate of the political bureau in Spain, instead of following Lenin's advice and concealing his political identity, declared himself a Communist, a member of the central committee of the party, and claimed responsibility for organizing several protests against the increase in the cost of living and in favor of national reconciliation. The latter claim was false since the party did not organize protests but rather tried to take control of them once they were in progress.

The non-Communist underground opposition rejected all collaboration with the Communists, but as soon as the non-Communists tried to organize a peaceful protest against the situation in Spain, the Communists not only joined in but also tried to appear as its real organizers.

But not taking into account to what extent the strikes had been a spontaneous reaction to harsh living conditions, the Communist Party called a Day of National Reconciliation on May 5, 1958 and a peaceful national strike [the HNP as it was called in the party] on June 18, 1958. Both were failures. Some Socialists and members of the newly formed Popular Liberation Front took part, but the PSOE officially condemned the initiative. In its optimism and eagerness to reach accords with other oganizations, the party tried to use the working class for spectacular mobilizations to show its appeal as an ally. This entailed a considerable amount of self-deception regarding the level of politicization of the workers and of the influence of the party. It was an approach which could only undermine the credibility of the PCE.[13]

With regard to the HNP, the police arrested Simón Sánchez Montero, Lucio Lobato, Abelardo Grimero, and seventeen other Communists and gave Sánchez Montero the opportunity to assume responsibility.[14] In Catalonia where the HNP met with no success whatsoever, a coordinating committee was formed with the Moviment Socialista de Catalunya and the Unió Democrática de Catalunya, the Front Obrer de Catalunya and PSUC. The first three organizations left the committee accusing PSUC of trying to take them over.[15]

A British ethnologist who was in Madrid during the HNP wrote that aside from the fact that the students, who were on vacation, could not participate in it, "the general attitude of the people was an almost frenetic desire to not get involved in hassles and even to avoid any discussion whatsoever."[16] The correspondent of *The New York Times* indicated that those who had planned the HNP had quite some freedom of movement—aside from the arrest of Sánchez Montero and his comrades—because Franco's police wanted to give credibility to the idea developed by the regime's propaganda that there existed a serious Communist threat.[17]

Despite their failure at mobilization, the HNPs had one advantage: they got some individuals to support them and when the support was withdrawn, seeing that the Communists were running everything, "the Communists looked like the only ones willing to confront the regime and could blame the Socialists and syndicalists for an imaginary fear of being discredited in the eyes of the Western democracies at a time when many Spaniards thought the United States was the only real support of the Franco regime."[18] A delegate to the International Confederation of Free Trade Union Organizations visited Spain at the time and informed his head office: "I heard the unanimous accusation that the embassy of the United States was publicly at the service of the current political regime. . . . The stance of those responsible at the American Embassy in Madrid, in my opinion, can only act to promote Communism in Spain. . . . One must be realistic and not allow oneself to believe that Franco is fighting Communism, because it is not true."[19]

The non-Communist opposition was aware of this but did not dare express it for fear of being accused of "systematic anti-Communism." An Italian journalist confirmed what the *Times* correspondent had said:

> The Communists in Spain had collaborated more or less closely with the other democratic underground organizations acting in the opposition (Socialists, liberals, left-wing Catholics, syndicalists) up until last May 5, but in the last two years and following the liberal anti-Opus manifesto which all parties with the exception of the Communists signed, the authorities had shown an unusual tolerance for the Communists.

In November 1956 in protest against Communist repression in Hungary, demonstrations were staged in Catalonia in which the police were greeted with the cry of "Beat the Russians!" There were arrests of Catholics, liberals, and Socialists. In the spring of 1957 there were further arrests of Catholics, liberals, and Monarchists. Socialists and Anarcho-Syndicalists were once again imprisoned in Asturias. And finally there were strikes in Barcelona last April. Four hundred of those arrested were put in jail: Anarchists, liberals, Socialists, and Catholics, and among them was the president of the Hermandades Obreras de Acción Católica (Labor Brotherhood of Catholic Action), Emilo Comas Franqués. There was only one Communist among the 400 arrested. The ILO and the ICFTU protested against Franco (protests which had great circulation in the democratic press). Yet the World Trade Union Federation, which is Communist, did not protest in the slightest.

There is no doubt that the care taken by the police not to take action against the Communists has helped enormously to arouse mistrust among the opposition which previously had accepted the Communists. The Communists modified their program. Until then they had tried to overthrow Franco relatively quickly and with help from democratic forces. For that moment on, the main objective was to destroy the democratic forces over an extended period of time and with Franco's help and then later to overthrow Franco and seize power.

It was a known fact that a month after the May disaster Santiago Carrillo, the secretary of the PCE in exile who enjoyed Moscow's complete confidence and who occasionally lived in that city as well as in Paris (La Pasionaria who lived in the Soviet capital was just a symbol), entered Spain with a safe-conduct granted by the minister of government, General Alonso Vega, known for having exterminated the Socialists in Asturias during the Civil War, and Carrillo met with him in the estate of [the bullfighter] Domingo Dominguín.

This was Carrillo's first trip. But later he made another and again met General Alonso Vega, this time in Barcelona. The accords reached in this meeting are not known, but the events which occurred as a result of it are, particularly the increase in trade between Spain and the iron curtain countries with ample credit for Spain.[20]

The party itself recognized this "soft treatment," especially with the delegates from the interior to the sixth congress who were arrested upon returning to Spain. In a speech in 1962 Carrillo evoked the sympathy of the Civil Guard toward the strikers and begged the army not to allow Franco to compromise its honor.[21]

The Sixth Congress

Whenever the Communists manage to come out of their habitual isolation what usually happens is that they commit sins of excess and try to be so affable, understanding, and tolerant that no one believes them. The tactic of national reconciliation was no exception. In Spain the anti-Communism of the rest of the opposition protected them somewhat from that danger, but in exile the tendency of the moderates (Republicans, the few supporters of Negrín that were left) to act as fellow travelers inclined the PCE toward "positions that were openly and radically contradictory to Marxism-Leninism, positions which meant deviation of an opportunistic, social democratic nature, a liquidation of the Marxist-Leninist party," as Carrillo said in a letter to the exiles in Mexico. He was referring to the desire to de-Stalinize the party, "an opportunistic interpretation of the twentieth congress [of the CPSU] which middle-class propaganda called de-Stalinization," since "on the pretext of 'freedom of speech' and 'discussion' in practice they wanted bourgeois ideology to achieve the right of free circulation among Communist ranks." He accused those who were of such a mind of wanting, on the pretext of "purging the Stalinists," to "move toward a 'national communism' which would liquidate proletarian internationalism," that is, to do away with submission to the USSR and even claim that "the historic conditions which made the Leninist type of party of the proletariat necessary have disappeared."[22]

The political bureau was entirely for "proletarian internationalism," as it proved by attending the Moscow Conference of Communist and Workers' Parties in November 1957. At the conference the PCE took a stand against revisionism, defended the unity of the Socialist camp based on Marxism-Leninism, and rose up against the "scandalous speculation that imperialism tried to make of the counterrevolutionary events in Hungary."[23] The PCE used the time not taken up with these attacks to plan the Day of National Reconciliation ordered by the plenary of the central committee in September 1957. The day was a failure for which the few workers who followed the order to stop work paid dearly. But the bureau saw it as a success because "Franco was unable to get any sector of the population out into the streets in protest against our Day."[24]

Carrillo was convinced that in the long run the tactic would be profitable. It is impossible to say whether at the time he was thinking about making all the revisions of which he accused the Spanish Communists in Mexico or if they were imposed upon him successively throughout the years by the very dynamics of his tactic of national reconciliation. In any case, he did not hestitate to implement it in spite of failures from the outset. A document issued by the central committee in April 1959, on the occasion of the twentieth anniversary of the end of the Civil War, made an analysis of Francoism blaming everything bad about it on the financial oligarchy, thus exonerating other forces and putting them in a position to be welcomed by the PCE.[25]

But in the party there were some who doubted, many who went overboard in "tolerance" and had to be contained or expelled, and there were others who suffered the same fate for being too rigid. Despite criticism of personality cult in the plenary of East Berlin, the rank and file of the party had no means of influencing the leaders. In an effort to put an end to the unrest, the sixth congress was convened in Prague on January 28–31, 1960. A conference of European Communist parties (the PCE was among them but PSUC was not) in Rome in November 1959 had affirmed that "the move toward socialism is inscribed within a perspective of democratic development." Thus began to take shape what with time would be the "Italian line." That helped give a certain credibility to the action of the PCE in Spain and strengthened Carrillo's position at the congress.

Ibárruri did not deliver the report of the central committee, as was her custom; it was read instead by Carrillo. How could Franco still hold power in the midst of an economic crisis? Repression and foreign aid were not the full explanation. The reason was division in the opposition. The PCE, then, had to try to bring together the opposition to stage a series of peaceful strikes nationwide and general political strikes in order to obtain amnesty, the reestablishment of democratic liberties, the improvement of living conditions, a foreign policy favorable to peaceful coexistence, and constituent elections. The "Socialist and bourgeois opposition" refused to take action against the dictatorship (actually it refused to ally itself with the PCE, but it did act on its own). The congress addressed a letter to those forces proposing a round table to reach a general agreement.

Carrillo heavily underscored the national strike, for "if it were achieved with the sympathy and support of the masses and the benevolence or neutrality of a sector of the machinery of repression, the dictatorship would not be able to survive and would crumble." It seems incredible to those who lived in Spain during that period, but that is what the Communists thought. So, on the basis of the analysis of Francoism contained in the document about the twentieth anniversary of the Civil War, the congress modified and softened the party program: expropriation with indemnity of the large absentee landlords but respect for large productive estates, maintenance of subsidies to the church, the democratic move toward socialism, gradual cooperativization of agricultural property, and plurality of parties. To achieve this program, the party, even in the underground, had to become a party of the masses, and some modifications in the bylaws were adopted toward this end: admission of secret members, flexibility in the admission of affiliates, presence of the party in all areas of activity even when not led by the party.

The congress elected a central committee and an executive committee (it was no longer called bureau) made up of Santiago Álvarez, Santiago Carrillo, Fernando Claudín, Manuel Delicado, Ignacio Gallego, Juan Gómez, Dolores Ibárruri, Enrique Líster, Ramón Mendezona, Antonio Mije, José Moix, Simón Sánchez Montero, and Federico Sánchez (Jorge Semprún). Substitutes were Gregorio López Raimundo and Francisco Marín. The secretariat included Carrillo, Claudín, Gallego, Mije, and Eduardo García (the latter, according to the rumor among leaders, was a member of the NKVD).[26]

Of importance was the fact that the congress elected Ibárruri president and Carrillo secretary general. La Pasionaria ended up being merely a decorative figure, not only because of her age, but because, despite her astonishing political flexibility, she did not seem to be the appropriate figure to "sell" the new line (with which, as Uribe, who no longer was on the central committee, she agreed only against her will).[27]

The accords of the sixth congress had Moscow's approval.[28] The PCE was so dependent on Moscow that despite the fact that the sixth congress had rejected violence as a tactic, in 1961 Carrillo proposed to the executive committee that, in view of the aggravated international situation, Líster and another comrade be put in charge of "planning the creation of detachments to attack the American bases in Spain." In a meeting of the executive committee, Líster suggested "a series of practical measures, among which as a first step, was the collection of data about the [US] base at Morón."[29] When relating this, Líster supposed that Carrillo had no real intention of forming guerrillas ever again but rather that he wanted to present to the next congress of the Soviet party which was to meet soon, proof of loyalty of the PCE. The following year, with no congress of the Soviet party in sight, the missile crisis, which was much more serious, broke out, but Carrillo made no proposal. In a meeting of the central committee in October 1961 Carrillo gave a report on the international situation which thoroughly supported the position of the USSR. At the same plenary, Ibárruri made a closing speech, one of her new ceremonial functions, which was even more passionately pro-Soviet than Carrillo's report. The same plenary decided to rebuild the Unión de Juventudes Comunistas, in acknowledgment that the JSU no longer existed and that the PSOE had again formed its own Juventudes Socialistas.[30]

There was some resistance among the rank and file in accepting the concessions made in the program, and Carrillo wrote a new pamphlet to justify them.[31] The PCE attended another conference of Communist and workers' parties and there La Pasionaria acknowledged that during the Civil War the party had not "cooperated sincerely and deeply enough with all the other popular forces which rose up against fascism," and so that mistake had to be corrected so it would not be made again. She also said that "the decisive and by no means easy participation of Comrade Krushchev in the struggle to reestablish Leninist norms in the Communist party of the Soviet Union . . . won him the respect, affection, and sincere admiration of the Communists and revolutionary workers of Spain."

The party's dilemma was how to combine the newer members' belief in the new position with the conviction of the older members that it was just a trick to attract more members. This kind of schizophrenia between members who were still Stalinist in heart and mind and "conciliatory" members would persist up until the present. Perhaps it was an advantage for the party which was milking two udders at the same time: the moderation and neophyte-like enthusiasm of the new members and the discipline, faith, and monolithic spirit of the older ones.

Hidden Victories

The sixth congress had not yet become aware that things in Spain were changing. It persisted in its vision of a country back in the thirties, at a time when the Opus Dei from within the government was artificially creating structures for a Spanish capitalism and conditions for improving the standard of living. As a consequence, the policy of national reconciliation was unsuccessful as an anti-Franco policy because new forces were on the rise which were affected by the changes made by Opus Dei, and these forces were not thinking of reconciliation but opposition to Franco. At the same time, the "nonmonopolistic middle class" with which the PCE wished to ally itself was drawn to the sphere of Francoism and the Opus Dei by the new policy of economic liberalization.

On the other hand, the PCE was making considerable hidden progress in having itself accepted as a "respectable" force, in infiltrating other organizations to win them over, and in taking over organizations which formed almost spontaneously under the protection of progressive Catholics. The machinery of the party was capturing, neutralizing, conditioning, and establishing foundations as well. Between the sixth congress of 1960 and the seventh in 1965 many things happened in Spain. The PCE was not always around and hardly ever acted of its own initiative, but almost always took advantage of events. The party was the only experienced organization which had militants trained before Franco. The other organizations were limited by their committees of exiles, old men now and without renewed vigor—like the CNT and PSOE—or they were paying for having been decimated in the first opposition—like the CNT and POUM—or they were almost improvised formations made up of people from after the war who had to start from scratch.

In its seventh congress in exile in 1958, the PSOE came out in favor of a unitarian formation which would exclude the Communists. The recently founded National Union, made up of liberal Monarchists, saw some of its leaders hold conversations with Communist leaders without producing any results. In 1961 a Union of Democractic Forces was formed in France and was composed of all the organizations in exile (excluding the PCE); its goal was to establish a short-lived regime of a noninstitutional nature. Pedro Ardiaca, Antonio Gutiérrez, and 27 other members of PSUC were arrested in Barcelona. In Barcelona there were clashes between students supporting democracy and those belonging to the Opus Dei. Some bombs exploded—without casualties—which the police attributed to the Communists. The Alianza Sindical Obrera (Labor Union Alliance) was formed. ETA made its first appearance in the Basque region. In July 1961 the PCE made another proposal for a peaceful national strike. There was a letter from Basque priests in defense of the strikers and a reaction from the hierarchy in favor of the regime. There were strikes in Barcelona, Madrid, and Valencia in September. In October a plenary of the Central Committee of the PCE was called. Carrillo said that all efforts to establish unity to the exclusion of the Communists had failed and he threatened that if an "accord from above was not possible, the PCE would take the initiative of the struggle to overthrow Franco and lead the new democratic situation." No one appeared to be frightened.

A Conference of Western Europe for Amnesty which was secretly organized by the PCE managed to surprise European Socialists and liberals and created problems for the Spanish prisoners because the Francoist press used the conference to accuse as Communists all those in prison or on trial who were not. As is customary in such proceedings, the conference did not produce anything positive, but allowed the PCE to pretend it was the center of opposition.

In 1962 the Hermandad Obrera de Acción Católica and its organ *Juventud Obrera* became active enough for the weekly to be suspended. Strikes ensued in Barcelona, the Basque region, Valencia, and Cartagena. And there were student arrests in Madrid and student strikes against the Opus Dei's university in Navarre. A laborers' strike took place in Jerez. The PCE organized a Conference for Freedom of the Spanish People in Rome. Once again many Socialists and liberals let themselves get roped in. There were mining strikes in Asturias and steel strikes in Vizcaya, strikes in Catalonia and letters of solidarity with the strikers from intellectuals (which were prepared by the PCE). The Catalonian and Basque clergy became radicalized.

The year's most important event was the colloquium in Munich in June 1962 convened by the European movement in which old enemies (Gil Robles, Madariaga, Llopis, Ridruejo) collaborated to write a proposal establishing the conditions for Spain's admission into the Common Market. So, national reconciliation was expressed in the absence of the PCE. The Francoist press called it the "collusion of treason" and the participants from the interior were arrested upon their return to Spain. The Executive Committee of the PCE on June 13 declared that "the Communist party on several occasions has stated its radical opposition to Spain's entry into the European Common Market, that it would put the Spanish economy in the hands of the great foreign monopolies," but it affirmed its agreement with the conditions established in Munich "which could constitute the fundamental basis for a political accord of the forces of the opposition from right to left." At the same time Carrillo, in a speech reprinted in *Mundo Obrero* in June, threatened: "What could exhaust the possibilities of political maneuvering of the middle class would be for the forces that appear as opposition to Francoism in the name of the middle class to embark on a dubious antipopular adventure—an operation controlled by the far right to replace Franco's dictatorship—which on the pretext of 'containing Communism' could in practice produce a policy similar to that of the current regime. . . . Then the working class and its Communist party would appear to all democratic sectors to be the only prospect for true liberation; then there would be objective conditions for a more radical and probably not peaceful solution."

In July there were many arrests of Socialists, Monarchists, and Communists. Among those arrested was Ramón Ormazábal who admitted he was a member of the Central Committee of the PCE and took responsibility for all protest activities in the Basque region. In his trial he said that if the strikes were not all Communist, they most certainly "reflected the policy of the Communist party." He along with Enrique Múgica and six others were sentenced to six years in prison.

In 1963 there were diverse acts of terrorism in Madrid for which the police blamed the PSOE, PCE, and the FLP. All three claimed that they were not responsible. Three libertarian youths were arrested, there were attempts to impose the death sentence, and they were given thirty years in jail. There was no international campaign on their behalf although Cardinal Montini sent Franco a telegram pleading for clemency. There were court martials against fifty members of the FLP and twelve Communist youths as well as the death sentence for Julián Grimau (who was arrested the year before) for "war crimes."

Grimau's trial caused the PCE to stage an extensive and clever campaign. Grimau became a Communist during the Civil War, he joined the police force as a Communist and although he worked against some men in the fifth column—for which he was tried in 1963—his main activity was against elements in the CNT and POUM. In exile he rose to the central committee of the party and was sent to Madrid despite the fact that on various occasions Carrillo and the executive committee were warned that, considering his background, it was not wise for him to be in Spain. Semprún reported that Grimau did not even take the most minimal precautions required in the underground.[32] Krushchev, Cardinal Montini, and many other notables sent Franco telegrams to no avail. Actually that kind of campaign forced Franco to execute him, considering his mentality and that of his regime.

There were some strange things about Grimau's case aside from the negligence or indifference of the executive committee regarding the special danger of sending him to Spain.[33] Apparently a Communist member named Lara informed on Grimau to the police. But "who instigated the denunciation? Was it police pressure or less admirable orders?"[34] A dissident *Mundo Obrero* said Grimau was sent to Spain as a "marked man." The PCE's *Mundo Obrero* asserted that this issue of the dissident *Mundo Obrero* was a falsification by the Spanish police. Líster does not mention Grimau in his accusations against Carrillo.[35] Grimau was the last Communist executed by Franco but not the last enemy executed by Francoism.

The syndical elections of the official CNS brought about an increase in the number of Communists elected. Since the government was allowing many exiles to return, the PCE issued the order, particularly in Latin America, for as many as possible to return to Spain. The PCE did not control the student organizations but it had enough influence in them to gain control of parasyndical student organs such as the Democratic Association of Catalonian Students, FUDE in Madrid, ADEV in Valencia, and CUDE (created in 1964) throughout Spain. Following the tactic used in infiltrating the CNS, the Communist students tried to infiltrate the official SEU, a tactic which students of other tendencies did not accept. Carrillo wrote in *Mundo Obrero:* "Any intelligently conservative person has to recognize that the guarantee of nonviolent transition lies in the first place in an accord with the Communist party."[36] Moscow censured Hidalgo de Cisneros for the passage in the Russian translation of his autobiography about the executions of the Russians who were in Spain.[37]

The executive committee replaced Semprún in Madrid with José Sandoval who had taken part in writing *Historia del PCE* and *Guerra y revolución en España,* and who had lived in Moscow for many years. A few months later he was arrested in Madrid along with a group of students. The weekly *Cuadernos para el Diálogo* began publication in Madrid. Although there was no formal pact between Christian Democracy which was the inspiration behind the magazine and the PCE, it was very common for contributors to *Cuadernos* to take the same position as the PCE, especially on international issues.

In November 1963 the central committee met to study the possibility of another general political strike. It stated that the strikes in Asturias the previous summer were led by the PCE. This was not true. It addressed the Chinese Communists saying: "Let's discuss whatever is necessary, but do not break the unity of the socialist camp, do not break the unity of the Communist and international labor movement."[38] In relation to this Carrillo said: "We will continue to fight on behalf of the purity of our theory and against the bourgeois and petty bourgeois influences which dogmatism and revisionism represent. . . . There are opportunists both on the Left and Right ... who criticize the Marxist-Leninists because, in order to combat modern capitalism, they are seeking the alliance of bourgeois and petty bourgeois social strata which historical evolution has condemned to disappear . . . and in the name of so-called progress of a dogmatic conception of Marxism, they consider this stance reactionary."[39]

The Defenestration of Prague

Carrillo's line was attacked from two directions. Some considered it out of touch with reality, based on an anachronistic view of Spanish society. Others accused it of being reactionary. This latter group was strengthened by Maoist positions which were becoming more and more emphatic. At heart it was the nostalgia of Stalinism; but strangely enough, it was not felt by the older Stalinized members who had been in the party for many years, but rather by the young who wanted a position more trenchant and less subject to doubt and hesitation. To a certain extent it was a search for psychological security.

The first evidence of these Maoist tendencies was a document written toward the end of 1963 by a group of Communist exiles in Belgium. It called Carrillo a revisionist and pointed to the tactical errors he made, in particular with regard to the unsuccessful general political strike. What is strange is that he was also criticized for using Stalinist methods to isolate whoever disagreed with him. Then other groups appeared: one which published *Mundo Obrero Revolucionario* and another which published *Chispa* (in memory of Lenin's *Iskra*). The latter was called Revolutionary Opposition of the Communist Party. There was also a group called Proletario, made up in particular by people who had not been in the PCE. In October 1964 delegates of those groups met and agreed to form a single organization which would be called Communist Party of Spain and which would have as its organ a new publication, *Vanguardia.*

Even more of a threat to Carrillo's line was opposition in the executive committee itself because it could represent a possible alternative to that line and thus to Carrillo's control of the party. It reflected the unrest in certain sectors of the party—especially among intellectuals and students—and it was manifested in three leaders: Fernando Claudín, Federico Sánchez (Jorge Semprún) of the Executive Committee of the PCE, and Francesc Vicens of the Executive Committee of PSUC (called Joan Berenguer in the underground). The press referred to that group as the "Italians," because they held opinions not very different from those of Togliatti in his "political testament" and because for a while they published a periodical in Rome called *Realidad* which was doubtless supported by the Italian Communist party. It was not an active group, simply three people who had the same outlook on the situation and who only expressed their points of view in the committees of which they were part; they did not argue with the militants nor did they try to cause schisms.

After presenting their positions in a lengthy document and discussing them in the executive committee in Prague in March 1964, the committee rejected them calling the authors "scatterbrained intellectuals," to borrow Ibárruri's phrase, and decided to relieve them of their positions. Then the central committee was consulted and the members who were in prison in Spain were polled. The central committee decided to exclude them from the committee and later from the party when they paid no attention to its calls to reconsider their position. Juan Gómez who briefly supported Claudín had a change of heart and made his self-criticism.[40] Early in 1965 Claudín circulated his document and then it was printed by *Nuestra Bandera* with some "critical notes."[41] The PCE's press said: "In the situation of extreme weakness in which the dictatorship finds itself, the conspiracy of Claudín and Sánchez represents a desperate attempt on the part of the oligarchy to prevent the crisis at hand from having the outcome it ought to have."

Besides expelling Vicens, PSUC made the same attacks on the dissidents, to which they added the names of "neocapitalists and revisionists." Carrillo pointed out that "there was no autonomy for the opposition on political stance and ideology," and added that Claudín and Sánchez had been taken in by neocapitalism to the point of losing faith in the people and believing that the only solutions were the ones proposed "by groups of monopolistic capitalism." What Claudín, Sánchez, and Vicens were talking about was never explained clearly to the militants. They were told that they wanted to destroy the party, that they had no faith in the proletariat, and they were assured that "they could have continued in the organization, expressing their opinions, in hopes that the situation in Spain and the struggles of the masses of students and workers would make them see clearly their reformist political stances. Instead they chose to fight against party policy."[42] It was not said that they could wait to see whom the evolution of the Spanish situation would prove right; it was taken for granted that it would be Carrillo.

Claudín had backed Carrillo in his fight against Uribe and Ibárruri (but Ibárruri, learning previously of the publication of Krushchev's secret report, changed her position and withdrew support from Uribe). Yet the Hungarian issue separated Claudín and Carrillo because Claudín thought the responsibility of the Hungarian Communist party should be considered and that imperialism should not get all the blame, while Carrillo stuck to the official Soviet explanation. Later Claudín went to Madrid and Bilbao on the occasion of the HNP and upon his return told the executive committee that the strike had been a failure. Carrillo, however, called it a success. Letters from members from the interior, especially from Javier Pradera and Manuel Sacristán, convinced Claudín that the executive committee had lost touch with reality. But how does one make an executive committee see this, a committee that in eight years had not made a single decision which did not first need Carrillo's approval excepting one occasion when Carrillo proposed going to Asturias and the executive committee agreed he should remain in Paris? Finally, since Claudín did not agree on a report of the executive committee to its president regarding the situation in Spain, it was agreed that he prepare his own report to be discussed in another session of the executive committee to be attended by Ibárruri and which would take place in Prague. That is where the "case" began in March 1964.

Claudín pointed out that the executive committee was the victim of subjectivism, that it saw things in Spain not as they were but as it wished to see them. Carrillo believed that Spain still had the same structural problems it had in 1931: a fragmented industry and semifeudal agricultural system. Consequently a democratic-bourgeois revolution was needed before socialism could be achieved. Claudín argued that the economy had reached a high level of monopolistic capitalism controlled by the state, making it fit for a transition to socialism, even though the political and social conditions needed for such a transition were quite a way off. Carrillo believed that a democratic revolution would do away with the controlling caste and the obstacles to the destruction of feudalism. Consequently, it would be easy to find allies in the bourgeoisie. Claudín pointed out that the economic need for a democratic revolution had already passed. Carrillo was convinced that Spain was on the threshold of catastrophe and that the bourgeoisie would hasten to join the proletariat to overthrow the regime. This would not happen, Claudín said, because neocapitalism was expanding and the bourgeoisie had no reason to overthrow the system. But since there were sectors of the bourgeoisie that wanted a liberalization of the regime, the search for allies among those sectors was appropriate; what Claudín disagreed with was Carrillo's optimism which made him push the PCE to work at a level of historical development lower than what Spain had already attained. Claudín agreed with Carrillo that the party needed to find a peaceful way of achieving socialism, but he insisted that the limits of any alliance with the bourgeoisie ought to be kept in mind. Given Spain's integration in international capitalism, it was the only option available, but the party had to steer clear of the upper bourgeoisie's game. Although in time Carrillo acknowledged that Claudín was right and that his error was "being right too soon,"[43] at first his reaction and that of the party were those which Claudín himself described at the end of his document:

> How is it possible that that overwhelming majority in the central committee, comrades who have proven themselves in fighting, in the decisions of the party, and who deserve all respect, and in some cases, admiration . . . how is it possible, I repeat, that those comrades have unanimously fallen into such astonishing Manicheism? . . .
>
> Behind that chilling fact there is an entire formation—to be more exact, deformation—which we have built up in the Stalinist period. United together with undisputed virtues of firmness, fighting spirit and self-denial, we have habits, concepts, methods which are completely foreign to the spirit of Marxism and Leninism. Under their influence, the discussion ceases to be a discussion; the difference of opinion becomes heresy; and heresy must be dealt with as the great protectors of faith in our national history taught us. Marx fades away in the presence of Torquemada.[44]

The Seventh Congress

Worried over the accusations of subjectivism made by Claudín and his friends, Carrillo justified himself before a gathering of members: "If in 1939 the party had said: it will be 1964 and there will still be Fascism in Spain, what would have happened? . . . They would have thrown us out, and I believe with good reason, as great demoralizers. . . . The members would have said to us: in this case, leave us alone, don't ask us for sacrifices, don't ask us to give up our lives and freedom; let us wait for better times when the struggle would be worth it."

This statement was indicative of the party's mentality considering the fact that no one protested it: if in order for the people to fight one has to deceive, one deceives; and for the people to fight they must see victory within reach. These two implicit statements, of a clearly elitist and paternalistic nature, cast aside the century-old traditions of struggle in the working-class movement as well as the motivation of those who fought in said movement—including the Bolsheviks. A new conception of the reasons for fighting was taking form: immediate victory. The line of national reconciliation was the first manifestation of this mentality, a direct descendant of the Stalinist mentality.

It is important to emphasize this, because otherwise the history of the PCE in the sixties and seventies will not be understood. A few more details, of an anecdotal nature, will help to depict this mentality. While the Asturian miners were on strike, Polish ships were unloading coal in Spanish ports and the PCE neither protested nor mentioned it in its press. Wenceslao Carrillo died (after his son visited him in the hospital in France on the advice of the PCE) and Ibárruri sent Santiago Carrillo a telegram of condolence; no one knows if it was to erase the letter written from son to father in 1939, to remind him of it, or to indicate to the Socialists that the past had been forgotten. The Cuban experience was a source of worry for the Spanish Communists in Latin America because it was incompatible with the line of reconciliation. Castro triumphed not by reconciling with Batista but by fighting him. Therefore, when Castro revealed that from the age of thirteen he had been reading *Das Kapital* and that he was a Marxist-Leninist, Ibárruri praised him and insisted that the experience of the Cuban Revolution was a "political phenomenon which was natural and logical in Latin America," but not exportable.[45] The Communist exiles in Prague saw how London, Clementis, and others who had been tried several years earlier were rehabilitated, and they compared this to the expulsions decreed by the Central Committee of the PCE. Ibárruri wrote a series of recollections of the seventh congress of the Communist International (that of the Popular Front) to stress that the alliances the PCE was seeking had precedents.[46]

Carrillo described the Twenty-Third Congress of the CPSU as a call to "rebuild the unity of the labor and Communist movement." That was the line the PCE adopted in the face of the Sino-Soviet conflict: calls for unity, but not an analysis of the Chinese positions, perhaps out of fear of finding that Mao's theory of the four classes was no different from the PCE's theory of national reconciliation.[47] Carrillo was aware that numerous youth organizations with revolutionary aspirations were cropping up in Spain. People began to write, talk, and think about the Civil War. It was then that the PCE tried to remake the image it had during those three years of war. In Moscow it published a history called *Guerra y revolución en España* (*War and Revolution in Spain*). Carrillo himself said that during the Civil War the "working class and the democratic forces transformed the state system through combined simultaneous action, from above, from the government by decrees, and from below by both creative revolutionary action and initiative of the masses. . . . The possibility of tackling the transformation of the state is inferred not be exclusively destroying the old state system by means of armed attack, but by democratic reforms imposed from above, from the government, and from below by movement of the masses."[48]

All this was probably discussed in the seventh congress which supposedly took place in Prague in 1965. It was surrounded by a "secrecy which was not just due to a need for security following the risks the [participants in the] congresses of 1954 and 1960 took,"[49] but also to the need to contain and conceal inner disputes. The year 1964 saw the beginning of the wave of schisms which would continue for ten years. Furthermore, Carrillo did what Stalin did after Trotsky: after eliminating his adversary Claudín, he adopted some of his positions but applied them to the extreme even to the extent of stripping them of their original intent.

Almost nothing is known of the seventh congress. *Mundo Obrero* printed a few statements, and that was the end of it. One result of the congress—which did not change the leading cadres—were two studies made by Carrillo which at once ratified the line of national reconciliation and incorporated some of Claudín's observations, of course without mentioning where they came from. He recognized, for example, that Spanish capitalism had changed in nature and had expanded from the days of the primacy of economic claims over political ones in the movement of the masses. He underscored the possibility of an alliance with Christian Democratic forces and spoke of the "job of raising the reconciliation of the people to a new level in order to make up for the time lost by the bourgeois democratic revolution which had been begun but not completed, as well as to carry out the technical and scientific revolution." He declared himself a pluralist and, naturally, repeatedly opposed the existence of American bases and supported trade with the "socialist countries." He insisted that "an understanding was possible among the evolutionist upper bourgeoisie, the working class, and the democratic movement . . . on the establishment of political liberties."

But he said that "our perspective will lead to the culmination and development of the system of political liberties along with the establishment of economic democracy toward socialism" "Antimonopolistic democracy" is a step toward socialism. He began to insinuate that the idea of proletarian dictatorship was the result of a specific situation, that of Russia, and he pointed out the difference between the party's having a leading role or a controlling one. It should have a leading role in the labor alliance and the "alliance of labor and cultural forces," a new formula devised in 1965.[50]

The culmination of those changes in nuance was the proposal, on the occasion of the thirtieth anniversary of the uprising of 1936, of the meeting of a "sort of preparliament, that is, of representatives of all tendencies in the country which recognized the need for democratic political changes to find a common program for survival."[51] The proposal did not meet with support and was not brought up again. Equally lacking in prominence was the second congress of PSUC, which also met in 1965, of which very little has been said; there were other factors which affected the life of the party more than a few phantom congresses. Khrushchev fell and Brezhnev rose to power in 1964, an item which Radio Free Spain did not broadcast for several days. And Spain witnessed the development of a series of movements, groups, and parties which declared themselves Communist—something that had not happened since the time of the BOC.

The Proliferation of Leninisms

With its open-door policy, the PCE was able to attract many young people, seduced by the name and the Francoist propaganda which blamed the party for all anti-Franco activities. The political training they received was not Marxist but rather could be called "administrative" and triumphant. Those new members worked in Spain and knew what was going on better than the leaders in exile. They saw two contradictions: one, what the PCE said was happening in Spain—the subjectivism Claudín spoke of—and what they were experiencing; another, the theory of unity and the actuality of maneuvers, the hand extended to the Catholics and the actuality of their winning over the Workers' Commissions (Comisiones Obreras), the proposals to the Socialists for unity and the constant hammering of anti-Socialist "training" to the members.[52]

That caused many to be disillusioned. The majority of the disillusioned retired from politics. In their work those members showed proficiency, a strong spirit of sacrifice, and unyielding devotion. For those very reasons their disillusionment was so great that they were discouraged from participating in any other kind of activity. Those who found that the party satisfied their personal needs stayed in it: camaraderie, community spirit, usefulness. Those were the individuals for whom the party became what the church was for the old-style Catholics. The party told them the right and the wrong, what their convictions and positions should be. To a certain extent it gave them peace of mind which they paid for with material and physical sacrifices, risks, and submission.

These members gradually acquired the mentality of the veterans, those who had lived through the Civil War. Without realizing it, they were becoming Stalinists to the extent that they accepted that the party was the representative of the working class and its vanguard, the only group to have taken action against Franco. It was the party which the establishment of socialism depended on, for all the others were potential traitors, reformists, parties which could be cajoled into manipulation but which sooner or later would be written off as enemies. The party's Soviet patriotism was very strong despite the growing coolness of the executive committee toward Russian propaganda.

At times there was discontent over what was considered excessive concessions. It was more common among the newer members—students in particular—who had been politicized before joining the PCE. The students protested most vehemently against the policy of the executive committee. Since those protests could not be expressed—the militants themselves squelched them—the result was constant separations, schisms, and the formation of small groups, parties, and movements which considered themselves to be the only authentic Communists. The Maoists began to speak out in 1963 and 1964. Later there were others who were not connected to existing international movements who formed parties, divided, and subdivided. Sometimes the cause for the separation was the coolness of the party on the national issue since it only seemed to take it into account, in practice, in Catalonia and, to a much lesser degree, in Euzkadi, but not in Valencia, the Balearic Islands, and other places where a certain national awareness was beginning to develop. The executive committee was afraid that by encouraging that awareness, even though it could be beneficial to the party for the time being, in the long run it would cause the creation of local Communist parties. It felt that one PSUC, submissive though it was, was enough. It did not want Comorera's experience repeated. Even in Euzkadi where there had been a local Communist party (a mere branch of the PCE as was proven when the Executive Committee of the PCE expelled Juan Astigarrabía, member of the Basque government during the Civil War), the Communists were being very cautious. For that reason ex-Communists founded the groups from which ETA was formed.

Other times the cause of dissension was the coolness of the party in social struggles or the absence of both revolutionary propaganda in the party press and Marxist education in its members' training. This last issue was important because Franco's government was allowing Marxist works to be published (as long as they made no mention of Spain) as well as works on the Spanish labor movement of the past. Furthermore, some groups of the opposition (that of Enrique Tierno Galván with the Seminar of Political Law in Salamanca, for example, or the periodical *Litoral* from Pontevedra),[53] were talking and writing about Marxism. Many young Communists, particularly students, devoured this literature and they could not help but see the enormous distance between a Marxist policy and PCE policy. Marxism met their concerns better than the PCE. For that reason, many left and formed Marxist groups: in 1963–64, the Communist party (Marxist), in 1967 the PCE (Leninist), and in 1968, Bandera Roja (Red Flag). These individuals were joined by groups and individuals from the FLP or from the Catalonian FOC, both of which at the time were fragmenting and disintegrating. This is not the place to talk about these minority movements, the complexity of their initials and schisms, or of the appearance among them of both Trotskyites and libertarian tendencies. But it should be pointed out that in those groups where members coming from the PCE were in the majority, the general orientation, especially when it came to putting things into practice, was toward Stalinism, authoritarianism, voluntarism, personality cult (no matter how insignificant the person worshipped was), and cynicism regarding methods of action (which did not preclude a spirit of sacrifice), all of which were like relics left over from the PCE. There were other cases—in the minority—in which Stalinism was replaced by terrorism, at times as a complement to political action, at times as a result of divisions between "politicians" and "military" militants. The Paris of May 1968 and the stance taken then by the French Communist party opened many sleepy eyes and strengthened the tendency to separate and form small groups. It is paradoxical that the PCE's condemnation of the Soviet invasion of Czechoslovakia in August 1968 reinforced the Stalinism of many of those who had separated. A simple listing of the names of those movements will give an idea of the fragmentation of those separated from the PCE and of the diversity of "Marxisms" and "Leninisms" which resulted from the lack of theoretical education of the PCE and the political autodidactism it led to: Acción Comunista, Bandera Roja, Círculos Obreros Comunistas, Front Obrer Català, Frente Revolucionario Antifascista y Patriota, Grupos Obreros Autónomos, Liga Comunista, Liga Comunista Revolucionaria, Movimiento Comunista de España, Organización Revolucionaria de Trabajadores, PCE (Marxist-

Leninist), PCE (international-proletarian), Partido Comunista Proletario, Partido Obrero Revolucionario, Partit Socialista d'Alliberament Nacional, Partit Socialista d'Alliberament Nacional (provisional), Unión Comunista de Liberación, and others.[54]

The PCE did not react to those schisms except for the traditional name-calling. However in the case of the Maoists, because it was the first schism and because Moscow was watching, it issued some violent attacks after "making efforts . . . to show them that they were pursuing an adventurous political policy [but] it was apparent that they were supported—as well as subsidized—to bring about schism in the party. . . . They did not stand for anything, they devoted themselves to libeling Santiago Carrillo and party leaders, at times using the same language the ultra-Falangists used to attack us."[55]

Regarding Carrillo, to those who "recall the venturesome qualities of his policy, because it was not based on the reality of events in Spain, he responded by recalling the 'encouraging' errors made by Lenin when he thought the German revolution was at hand. To those who accused him of using left-wing phraseology to conceal a muddled policy, he answered by saying that 'only trust in the virtues of the people' allows one to see things clearly. And to those who allow themselves to evoke experiences of other places, he answered by saying that the [PCE's] policy was made neither in Moscow, Peking, nor Rome."[56] Nevertheless, Carrillo himself who criticized Uribe in the plenary of East Berlin since he thought "it was truly insane to see the hand of the enemy and vile intentions behind any disagreement," adopted a policy of systematic suspicion, expulsion, and slander of anyone who separated from the party.

The important schisms came later and resulted in the formation of the ORT and PTE. The former, which attracted many Catholics, hung Stalin's portrait over the chairman's seat at the congress of 1977. The most colorful schism was Bandera Roja which occurred in PSUC in 1968 and was headed by Jordi Solé Tura, which in 1975 divided when Solé Tura went back to PSUC and others kept the name. The harshest attacks against PSUC came from Bandera Roja, and the most ardent supporters of PSUC, the most loath to accept criticism, were the ones in PSUC who came from Bandera Roja.[57] The fragmentation of the Marxist movement in Spain and its diversion toward terrorism is the responsibility of the PCE for not having educated its members and for having disappointed them. This responsibility is shared by the other major organizations of the opposition for not having been able to attract the disappointed by offering them a place from which to fight effectively.

The Abduction of Workers' Commissions

The trade union was the terrain where all those separated brothers of the PCE and the PCE itself confronted one another. In spite of the fact that it was called the representative of the working class, the proletariat was the sector of society where the PCE had least penetrated. The Communists participated in all the strikes and protests they could and tried to be in control of them. In some instances they managed to do so. But even after the seventh congress they were only slightly influential in the working class no matter how much its program of national reconciliation looked like it ought to draw a proletariat made up in huge proportion of people uprooted from rural areas. For those individuals the move to a city had been the beginning of liberation however precarious and deceptive it turned out to be.

When the CNT and to a lesser degree the UGT organized their underground unions, at the time of the first opposition, the Communists had no union machinery. In Catalonia where they had taken over the UGT during the Civil War, they saw how elements of POUM were reorganizing it. In a plenary meeting in March 1947 in Paris, the party decided to create its own unions. They would not be presented as new ones but rather as reconstructed from the UGT, taking advantage of the signs of exhaustion which the Socialists and the UGT of the interior were beginning to show. In that plenary Carrillo said that the workers understood the need for unions and they were already opposed to the bureaucracy of the official CNS. It issued orders to oppose the deduction in the "union fee" and to force the "union" delegates in firms to resign. The few Communists who dared put those orders into effect ended up in jail or were fired from their jobs.

It was then, while on a visit with Stalin, that the Russian leader suggested they work in "legal organizations of the masses" in addition to advising them to dissolve the guerrillas. The Communists "worked" in the "unions" of the official CNS from 1948 on. They scored a few successes: there were Communists elected in the "union" election of 1950 as well as in following years. By then what had not been true a few years prior had become a reality: the workers began to show their discontent over the official "union" machinery and opposed it.

The rest of the opposition foresaw this and renewed its free union activity. In 1959 the Alianza Sindical was founded, which joined the CNT, UGT, and STV, and later the ASO was founded, similar in nature but with the Solidaridad de Obreros Cristianos de Cataluña (SOC, Solidarity of Christian Workers of Catalonia) and with the backing of the Internacional de Trabajadores del Metal (Metal workers' International). Later in 1962 the USO (Unión Sindical Obrera), with Christian elements, was formed. In the face of all this, the PCE once again organized its own unions: the Oposición Sindical Obrera (Workers' Union Opposition), which wanted to be a united front to combat the official bureaucrats. None of those organizations made an impact, but they all reflected the great labor agitation of the early seventies in Catalonia, Asturias, the Basque region, Andalusia, and Navarre.[58]

The Oposición Sindical did not make any progress. Its delegates in some firms tried to establish relations with ASO and USO but nothing came of it despite the fact that the party said that "the development of worker unity and class consciousness is currently incarnated in the movement of Oposición Sindical Obrera . . . created by the proletariat itself within the framework of the 'vertical unions.' "

The Communists were trying in particular to make themselves attractive to the "Catholic current," considering that neither the Socialists nor the Anarcho-Syndicalists were paying any attention to them.[59] How were they supposed to do so if the plenary of the party central committee of November 1963 declared that the Spanish strikes had "confirmed that the prospect of a general strike was accurate and real" and affirmed "the leading role of the party in the strike in Asturias"?[60] Actually, the main work of the party—no mean task—was the preparation of a manifesto of the intellectuals in support of the strikes that year.

In the course of those strikes combat organizations were formed and negotiation was carried on outside of the official CNS; they were aptly named Workers' Commissions,[61] named in assemblies which the most active elements of each factory usually attended. These commissions first appeared in 1963 in Asturias and later in other strikes. They had no precise form, they responded to the needs of the period and their existence proved that strikes were not led by any party. "In the beginning the Workers' Commissions were nothing more than a rejection of the CNS and their irremovable and bought juries." Members of those commissions were being beaten, fired, and jailed. The workers did not trust the CNS. By working in it, the PCE removed itself from the workers even though it gained positions of power which were no longer effective.

Toward the end of 1964 the party realized that the Workers' Commissions were taking root and they decided to bring them under their power. The Oposición Sindical Obrera yielded to the Workers' Commissions (which would soon be designated as the CO). It is a known fact that an assembly is easily manipulated if a few well-coordinated elements take part in it. Communist members were experienced and disciplined and had trained leaders. With a vote by a show of hands they could easily intimidate. It was not hard for them to control assemblies and thus be elected to the commissions. The latter were essentially made up of Catholics who were the ones who developed the idea—for pragmatic reasons—without following anyone's instructions (although they were inspired by the JOC and the Jesuits). Gradually the Communists allied themselves with them within the CO and, by manipulating their sense of guilt and their fear of appearing as moderates, launched them into activity which was quite spectacular but which in the long run undermined the confidence of the workers in those commissions which were no longer spontaneous but organized and under strict leadership. In Madrid the alliance was all-inclusive: it went from the "left-wing" Falangists to the PCE via supporters of Tierno and the Christian Democrats. The CO in Madrid persisted for two years, became the center of the movement, and published two documents: "Ante el futuro del sindicalismo" which was dismissed as being too leftist, and "Declaración de las Comisiones Obreras de Madrid." Madrid is where Marcelino Camacho surfaced. He was a former member of the UGT who spent a year in prison in 1939, fourteen years in exile, and who returned to Spain as a Communist but without making it public, and who like dozens of other members of the commissions was eventually arrested.

The triumph in Madrid was not repeated in Barcelona where the ASO, USO, and SOC were stronger and kept away from the CO when they saw that the PCE was manipulating them with help from some Catholics; only in 1966 would they once again become active. In Bilbao the PCE collaborated with the USO. In Asturias the commissions continued to exist but independently and without centralization. There were official union elections in September 1966 and the PCE tried to get CO support. The candidates of the CO were victorious in Madrid, Barcelona, and the Basque region, but workers in Asturias showed a poor turnout. The PCE could now "contribute" the CO in its meetings with other groups of the opposition. It used the CO to mobilize, declare strikes, distribute propaganda, and recruit.

But the schisms of the PCE were transferred to the CO; those who had split were members of the CO. Dissension arose in the commissions: everyone was against the Communists. The Catholics, who began to realize they had lost a field of influence, withdrew. In Madrid the PCE managed to stay in power but it lost it in Bilbao and Navarre. The UGT resurfaced in Asturias. In Barcelona in 1969 there was a division and two different commissions. Other tendencies arose which were not a reflection of the PCE, as the group "What Is to Be Done?" in Catalonia which brought together those unaffiliated with parties and which held leadership of the Catalonian CO for a while. It was the period of the great strikes, like those by Harry Walker and Seat. The various Leninist groups put an end to this autonomy to be in turn replaced by the PCE (PSUC). Later there would be other crises, a reflection of those in the PCE. Just as ORT and the PTE arose out of the PCE, the CSUT and SU split the commissions after years of internal struggles, platforms, circles, and assemblies.[62] Those internal struggles were not without violence (particularly in Barcelona): there were attempts on lives, fighting, theft of records, destruction of duplicating machines, and the refusal to help prisoners who did not belong to the group. PCE members showed an unyielding tenacity and loyalty, and did everything they were ordered. Thanks to them the commissions emerged from Francoism as the strongest (or the least weak) union organization. Camacho declared himself a Communist (proving right those who had previously said so and who thus were labeled as "Francoist agents"). The PCE had finally gotten hold of an effective instrument in the labor field. After more than half a century without it, it now had its union "transmission belt."

A quote from "Ante el futuro del sindicalismo" will help in understanding why this pamphlet was barely distributed at all and will allow us to see the difference between the original commissions and the CO controlled by the PCE. "The Workers' Commissions, created by the workers themselves, are an independent movement, not subordinated to any ideological tendency. Capitalism has never given anything to the workers. The bylaws of the Workers' Commissions ought to be free and democratically agreed upon by the assemblies of workers."

Penetration on All Fronts

In 1966 an internal document of PSUC said that "the working class holds political leadership insofar as it is able to incorporate decidedly and loyally the other strata and sectors of society in the revolutionary struggle, and the best guarantee the working class has in achieving this is for the party to take on the political leadership of the *entire* popular struggle."[63] The word *entire,* emphasized in the original, marked the path that the PCE openly dared to follow. Now that there was a generation that had not lived through the Civil War and which lacked practical preparation in politics, with scant historical information and conditioned by the "anti-Communist" propaganda of Francoism, it could to a certain extent count on success.

Since the separated groups and others which arose outside of the PCE (but to a certain extent as a reaction to it) did not leave the PCE master of workers and students, the PCE did its best to cultivate a field which was still intact: the Catholics who had not been impervious to the diffuse influence of Marxism and whose guilt feelings over the past conduct of the church (and even the personal conduct of many individuals) did make them receptive to all that could wash away those sins. The PCE was the confessor that absolved and set the penance. The penance, of course, consisted of echoing the policy of the PCE.

Some Catholics had begun to oppose the bond between the church and Francoism in 1956 with the "Manifiesto de El Escorial" ("The El Escorial Manifesto") and later with "Catolicismo día tras día" ("Catholicism Day after Day") by J.L.L. Aranguren, and finally with the activities of HOAC and the CO. The FLP was Catholic in origin. *Praxis,* a periodical from Córdoba, was the first attempt to reconcile Marxism and Christianity. The Catholics were the only ones to take part in the HNP. In 1965 the PCE was able to say that there were "open and hidden alliances between Catholics and Communists" and that "the Catholics are our best allies." Manuel Azcárate was in charge of establishing and maintaining PCE relations with the church. By then there were a great many who had rebelled against their bishops, particularly in the Basque region and Catalonia. The sit-in of intellectuals and students in a Capuchin convent in Barcelona, the police beating of priests in the streets of Barcelona in 1966, and the refuge of labor assemblies and underground meetings in church sacristies were examples of the divorce between the clergy and its bishops.

This climate favored the Communists because their policy of national reconciliation made them acceptable. This acceptance, in turn, increased their respectability. Azcárate in several articles insisted on removing the dialogue between Catholics and "Marxists" (the name a number of individuals insisted on calling the Communists) from the philosophical to the practical sphere. He went so far as to say the Second Vatican Council had condoned class struggle and the participation of Catholics in establishing Communism. He met with a certain degree of success. Canon J. M. González Ruiz, for example, said that "the irrational rejection of Marxism is a sin against one's neighbor," and Carrillo praised "the loyalty and fighting spirit of our Catholic friends." The priest Francisco García Salve was elected to the party central committee. Periodicals like *Signo* and *Serra d'Or* tended to welcome Communist contributors and to disregard leftist anti-Communist ones.[64]

Those Catholic periodicals were not the only ones that played the game. The Communists were making headway in publications, newspapers, publishing companies (particularly in Catalonia), bookstores, art galleries, theaters, and in time even radio and television stations (even though they were very official and state-owned) as well as among university faculty (despite the fact that in order to be named one had to swear loyalty to the principles of the National Movement). There were colleges where activist students, belonging to groups which had split from the PCE, booed professors from the party. There were some left-wing writers who had difficulty publishing because of the black-balling by infiltrated Communists and particularly by the very publishers and editors who did not want to antagonize Communists by publishing authors who were not in favor with the PCE or who were critical of it. Of course, not everyone submitted to this self-censorship. But frequently editors who wanted to get rid of a reporter who used the paper to suppress information about the PCE's competitors and to play up the news that favored the PCE would be accused of obstructing freedom of expression of individuals who used their position to suppress the freedom of expression of non-Communists. That led to a kind of intellectual terrorism which caused, for example, non-Communist critics not to review books by left-wing authors who displeased the Communists, or seemingly impartial newspapers to welcome ill-intentioned reviews of books which attacked the PCE.[65]

That censorship often did not occur on party orders. It was enough to make an insinuation—that so-and-so was an agent of the CIA without any proof, for example—for the intellectual gossip mill, the *gauche divine* which began to spread in high-class bars during that time, to immediately repeat it. The PCE never responded to the few critical books published about it in the opposition; rather it cloaked them in silence or if it was not able to do so it blamed them on a "conspiracy." That is how phrases like "systematic anti-Communism" and "professional anti-Communism" became popular and replaced open discussion of ideas. Communists took advantage of the faulty reasoning that "to criticize the PCE was to play Franco's game," as if the same could not be said—and never was—of the PCE's criticism over a period of forty years of Socialists, Anarchists, and anyone else who disagreed with it. These were criticisms with names appearing in the Communist underground press which were followed by the arrest of those criticized, so graciously pointed out to Franco's police.

If the PCE was making progress among Catholics and the media, it was losing ground with students, perhaps because the splintered groups found there a more receptive audience and more militants. The PCE lost control of FUDE, it never gained control of the Student Democratic Union, and it formed some student commissions which were a copy of the Workers' Commissions but which did not carry any weight.[66] Several foreign Communist intellectuals traveling through the country did not help matters: Nicolás Guillén, Pablo Neruda, Miguel Ángel Asturias.

They made pro-Castro and pro-Soviet statements which Franco's press took great delight in printing.

Attempts to form alliances did not pan out. It was totally useless for an individual as discredited as Julio Álvarez del Vayo to organize a phantasmagoric Frente de Liberación Nacional (National Liberation Front) in Europe to oppose Spain's entry to the Common Market. In that sense the meeting in Munich was much more effective than any other campaign, and the Socialists, because of their contacts with their Dutch and Belgian correligionists, assured a permanent veto to the entry of Franco's Spain. Nonetheless, the PCE was with the rest of the opposition in the campaign against the referendum of 1966 but the days of national action or HGP (General Political Strike) decreed by the party on October 27, 1967 and May 14, 1968[67] were failures, although many Communists were elected in the union elections.[68]

By 1970 the PCE was the largest party in the opposition—the only to have a trained organization, professional militants, and abundant means.[69] But it was not the organization that got the most publicity. ETA had snatched the CO of the Basque region away from the Communists and undertook a series of actions which left the PCE in second place. Many people were mobilized, and many more uncommitted individuals were politicized than the PCE—with its HNP and HGT, its days of national reconciliation or the trials of its own members—ever managed to bring out into the streets, all in defense of the members of ETA who were court-martialed in Burgos in December 1970. Perhaps out of hope that there would be no more death sentences signed by Franco, the trial of Burgos stirred more emotions not only in Spain but throughout the world than the calculating propaganda of the PCE was ever able to arouse.[70]

Three Profitable Slip-ups

In 1964 Carrillo stated that "those who take for granted the relations between the Soviet Union and Spain are mistaken. . . . Comrades, I can assure you that the Soviet Union will not establish relations with Spain without taking into account the opinion of democratic and anti-Franco forces."[71] The fact that this had to be said indicates that the Communists and the Spaniards in general did not have much faith in the anti-Franco policy of the Soviet Union. The facts justified that skepticism: on December 19, 1967 Radio Free Spain broadcasted an editorial of *Mundo Obrero* which claimed that *Izvestia*'s statement that the monarchy could constitute an adequate transitional regime after Franco was erroneous and not well thought out. Radio Prague said that

Izvestia's stance should not be taken as a change in policy by the PCE. Then *Izvestia* wrote that the previous statements did not reflect the position of the CPSU. That did not stop a delegation of the PCE from attending the anniversary of the revolution in October in Moscow or Carrillo from ending his speech with "long live the Communist party of the Soviet Union and its Marxist-Leninist Central Committee!" or Ibárruri from saying on the same occasion: "We reaffirm our faith in communism and Lenin."[72]

Despite all of Carrillo's statements, Gregorio López Bravo, Franco's minister of foreign relations, went to Moscow and interviewed important officials, coal from Poland continued to arrive during mining strikes, the Moscow Circus toured Spain, the first Soviet tourist visited the Valley of the Fallen, the Tass Agency opened an office in Madrid, and the Falangist EFE opened one in Moscow. Carrillo foresaw that it would be impossible to attract non-Communist opposition without separating from Moscow. He made frequent visits to Rome and in 1966 went to Rumania on his way back from the USSR. In 1967 the issue of *Nuestra Bandera* devoted to the revolution of October 1917 stated that the Spanish Communists were the only ones responsible for Spain's move toward socialism. In 1968 there was another visit to Rumania and the first visit to Cuba.

In 1968 two events occurred which the PCE would take considerable advantage of. The riots of May in France, including the French Communist party's stance against students, threatened to destroy the less than solid influence of the PCE in the universities (and it actually weakened its hold considerably), but at the same time it gave the Communists an air of responsibility which increased its respectability in the eyes of the most moderate anti-Francoists. The Soviet invasion of Czechoslovakia which put an end to the "Prague Spring," and the attempt to establish a "socialism with a human face" allowed the PCE to make a gesture of independence regarding the USSR—made no less important by the fact that it coincided with a similar gesture by the Italian and French Communist parties. On May Day 1968 Santiago Álvarez wrote about the "great sympathy" with which the PCE viewed the Czech experience. In an interview on Radio Prague in July Carrillo said that the new Czech government did not pose a threat to the existence of the Socialist regime. On August 21, twenty-four hours after the Soviet invasion, Ibárruri protested in the Kremlin in the name of the PCE along with Carrillo, Longo, and Pajetta who were in Moscow at that time asking for an explanation from the CPSU. Without ceremony Suslov told Carrillo: "After all, your party is very small." On August 28 the Executive Committee of the PCE expressed its opinion which was "against the armed intervention of Czechoslovakia, considering that the solution to the country's problems belongs to the Czech people and their Communist party with the aid of the Socialist states and the parties of the world Communist and labor movements."

The committee pointed out that on August 22 the PCE addressed the CPSU proposing a formula which would simultaneously guarantee independence for Czechoslovakia and the strengthening of that country's socialist system. On September 15 *Mundo Obrero* stated that the Spanish Communists could not imagine or accept the hypothesis that following the Communist party's rise to power in Spain another socialist power could dictate its policy to them and intervene militarily.[73] In October the central committee approved this statement by a vote of 66 to 5.

Like the rest of the Western Communist parties, the PCE insisted that this criticism did not lessen its respect for the USSR. Carrillo and Ibárruri continued to attend Soviet functions following the invasion of Prague. But they kept their distance. In the conference of Communist parties in Moscow in 1969 the PCE was part of the group of twelve parties which criticized the document submitted to the delegations and signed it with reservations as did the parties from Rumania, Switzerland, Morocco, and Sudan. It did not dare go so far as the Italian Communist party which approved only one of the four chapters in the document. "We hold that the recognition of the plurality of parties is one of the characteristics of the Spanish revolution," said Carrillo.

This position entailed a certain degree of danger, even though its benefits more than made up for the risks. Had it not adopted the position, the PCE would have found itself isolated in Western Europe. Deciding to follow it, it ran the risk of having to abandon its base of operations in Prague, and therefore Carrillo tried to strengthen ties with Rumania and Yugoslavia. It is possible that if Soviet subsidies disappeared (which is doubtful, since the USSR did not retaliate in this way with the French and Italian Communist parties) the PCE might be able to rely on help from Bucharest and Belgrade and perhaps from the Italian Communist party.[74]

The greatest danger was in the interior. The members were mistrustful of the Francoist press and were in the habit of agreeing with Moscow. They suddenly found that its executive committee was criticizing Moscow. It was something that had never happened before and they were totally unprepared for it. Yet there were no defections among the militants. The habit of believing that the executive committee was infallible was hard to break and Soviet patriotism among the younger members was not so deeply rooted as among older ones. It was among the leaders that there was disagreement. Eduardo García, organizational secretary of the executive committee and Carrillo's confidant, and the engineer Agustín Gómez, member of the central committee who had lived in the USSR for many years, were not content with voting against the party's criticism of the invasion; they also tried to foment opposition to the criticism within the party. In April 1969 the central committee decided to expel them from the committee, but *Mundo Obrero* did not print the news until October. Then García wrote a circular-letter to the Spanish Communists who were still living in the USSR. As a result, the central committee expelled Gómez and García from the party.

Several members of the central committee opposed the expulsion. Enrique Líster who had voted in favor of the denunciation of the Russian invasion of Czechoslovakia was one of them. Actually, Líster had been upset over Carrillo's line for quite a while. He had written his book *Nuestra guerra* in 1966 to correct some interpretations given in *Guerra y revolución en España,* yet without mentioning that was the reason. The main difference of opinion was that Líster thought that the Civil War could have been prolonged by several months and he accused the leaders of the party of having given up when Catalonia fell.[75] Early in 1970 Líster spoke disparagingly of the "caricature of democratic centralism" Carrillo had established. He was no longer summoned to the meetings of the executive committee but he continued to be a member of the committee. Foreseeing a long and hard battle, Carrillo expanded the central committee by 29 new members and it was convened in September 1970. Realizing that nothing was going to come of it, Líster and two of his supporters (José Bárzana, in charge of party finances, and Celestino Uriarte, overseer of the Communist party of Euzkadi), withdrew from the meeting. Jesús Sanz and Luis Balaguer, both delegates in the USSR, joined them upon their arrival in Moscow. The central committee decided to expel them accusing them of "total duplicity" and of giving off "the repugnant odor of Beria."

Líster, Gómez, García, and some others—according to many, with the aid of the CPSU—published shortly thereafter their own edition of *Mundo Obrero* (with the title printed in red instead of black) and later tried to organize their own Communist party. They immediately attracted some of those who had separated and some malcontents (some over the weakness of the party line, others over separation from the USSR) and almost all those who were refugees in the USSR (which indicated that, in spite of everything, Líster was seen as a favorite of Moscow). Carrillo said that Líster withdrew from the PCE because he was opposed to its criticism of the USSR, and Líster stated that was only one of the reasons and not the most important one. That withdrawal hurt Carrillo, not because he took members (although not many) with him, but rather

because Líster knew a lot. He divulged some of it in a book entitled
¡Basta! (Enough!) in which he explained a series of dirty and bloody
deeds performed by the leading body of the PCE "for which it was hard
to believe that Carrillo was more to blame than Líster himself."[76] Carrillo
could count on Ibárruri's support not only for political reasons but,
given the lady's nature, probably also because she had not forgotten that
Líster had supported Hernández to succeed José Díaz thirty years earlier.[77]
In any event, the leaders of the PCE never have responded to the very
concrete accusation made by Líster; they merely slandered him and
recalled his brutality during the Civil War. An objective analysis of the
events leads to the conviction that Líster's accusations were accurate
but that he was not without fault for the events referred to since he
was part of the executive committee when they occurred.

At first it was believed by many, particularly people outside of Spain,
that Líster would take a large part of the membership with him. Carrillo
managed to keep it. And in hopes of gaining potential allies, he knew
enough to take advantage of Líster's pro-Soviet line. Líster, accusing
Carrillo of being anti-Soviet and a reformist, helped him gain respectability.

The Pact for Freedom

The USSR did not stop causing problems for the PCE which continued
to make the best of things. Gromyko and López Bravo held talks in
New York in October 1970. Leonid Kolossov, head of foreign policy of
Izvestia, vitisted Spain. A maritime delegation from the Soviet Union
began operations in Madrid. Carrillo took advantage of this rapprochement between Moscow and Franco to persist in seeking an alliance with
the Catholics: "We have often said that Spanish socialism marches
forward with the hammer and sickle in one hand and the cross in the
other," he told *Le Monde* on November 4, 1970. Then Rumania, Poland,
and Hungary established relations with Madrid. At the time Carrillo
wrote in *Información Española,* of Brussels, that when Bucharest formalized relations with Franco, the PCE was assured by the other satellites
that they would not do likewise. But they did not keep their word. "We
would have preferred that the European Socialists maintain their condemnation of a regime imposed with the aid of Hitler and Mussolini
until the very end; we would have preferred it on behalf of the prestige
of those countries as well as socialism."

Then the PCE criticized in a communiqué the unloading of Polish
coal in Spain during the mining strikes, something it had not done when
the same thing happened a few years before. Nevertheless, there was no

break in relations. In May 1970 Ibárruri and Carrillo met with Suslov, Ponomarev, and Kirilenko. Those discussions must have been laborious for it took four days for the communiqué to be published. The PCE agreed that the worldwide Communist movement "ought to be based on the principles of Marxism-Leninism and proletarian internationalism." The conversations "took place in a climate of sincerity, camaraderie, and mutual respect," said the communiqué.[78]

The PCE had initiated its new policy—a result of the national reconciliation line—prior to its visit to Moscow. It was the policy called "the pact for freedom." The first time it was spoken of was in *Nuestra Bandera* in April 1970. The PCE, in this statement signed J.S., said: "The naming of Juan Carlos [as Franco's successor] has been the hinge upon which the door of viability of the monarchy as a 'solution' has been closed. . . . In view of this door-slamming by the ultra-Right, there is the need to arrive at a pact among the political forces interested in opening a course of democratic development for the country [which] would offer it a democratic alternative. . . . It would not prejudge institutional or constitutional issues which only the people are entitled to judge. . . . It will possibly cause change with a minimal amount of violence and destruction for the masses and society as a whole."

The proposal was addressed particularly to those referred to as "evolutionists." The pact had to be settled immediately since it would be too late "tomorrow, when the movement of the masses puts an end to the Franco regime." The article said that the overthrow of Franco would not be the same as a democratic revolution because the Francoist oligarchy could continue to govern with a semblance of democracy. In the same issue of the party's theoretical organ Carrillo spoke of the Popular Front of 1936 which had failed because the church brought a sector of the population over to Franco's side. The policy of national reconciliation intended to correct this situation through dialogue with the Catholics. In the struggle for "an antifeudal and antimonopolist democracy" the attempt to revive the Popular Front would be utopian. But an alliance that was not merely electoral or parliamentarian was needed, one that had a common program, a certain amount of discipline, and unity of action. Carrillo acknowledged something that had always been anathema to the Communist movement: "In the foreseeable future of the revolution in Spain, the Communist party cannot be considered as the only revolutionary force and hardly as the only party of the revolution, all of which does not mean that the party backs down from assuming a leading role." The pact for freedom was "a coming together, a temporary alliance to ensure political freedom and amnesty."

These were the essential ideas of Carrillo's report to the plenary session of the central committee on September 1970.[79] He concluded his speech, which of course was favorably received, by exhorting "the unity of the [Communist] movement with respect for diversity as well as by working so that differences would not be an obstacle to solidarity and the unified struggle against imperialism." This goal was not met within the PCE since Líster convened in Paris in May 1971 what he called the eighth congress of the PCE which nominated an executive committee and other bodies.[80] This congress, which had little impact on the PCE, was preceded by the publication of *¡Basta!* Of real concern to the PCE was the party's financial situation in the event that Moscow decided to terminate aid and international support. The party leaders were accustomed to having withdrawal points in the satellites. Thus Carrillo made other trips—this time with Ibárruri—to Belgrade and Bucharest in 1971. Ibárruri, at the Twenty-Fourth Congress of the Soviet Communist Party, had advocated the unity of the worldwide Communist movement "on the basis of mutual respect, and an end to interference which would violate the solidarity and unity of Communist parties." Since the French Communist party was gradually approaching the positions taken by the Italians, it increased its aid to the PCE as a result of "the campaign for solidarity with Spanish democrats" in the summer of 1971, which ended with a rally in Paris headed by Jacques Duclos, Carrillo, and La Pasionaria. Given the friendly relations between Moscow and Paris, Duclos might possibly have had something to do with the order issued by the French government in August 1971 forbidding Carrillo to leave France, an order which was rescinded shortly thereafter.

There were also interviews with delegations of the Communist parties of nine countries, among them Japan, North Vietnam, Yugoslavia, and Rumania, and a trip made by Carrillo and others to Peking in 1971. Although there was little activity in Spain, 1971 was a dynamic year for relations with the Communist movement, and Carrillo played his cards right not to be left out. The Italians provided considerable aid. For example, Vidali (the "Contreras" of the Fifth Regiment and Nin's assassination) wrote an open letter to Líster saying that his line "was favorable to the class enemy." Vidali himself went to Cuba and spoke vehemently against Líster who had been to the island several times where he always met with great warmth. It was the French and Italian Communist parties which prevented Líster, taking advantage of his position as member of the Presidium of the World Congress for Peace in Bucharest, from having his party accepted as the representative of Spanish Communism with the aid of the Soviet delegation. Rafael Alberti, representing the PCE, refused, and although Líster kept his position, there was no Spanish Communist delegation at the congress. Azcárate wrote an article in *Mundo Obrero* which shot full of holes all the theoretical "justifications" of the Soviets for the invasion of Czechoslovakia, and upon Carrillo's return from China (in the company of López Raimundo, of PSUC; Exteberry, of the Communist party of Euzkadi; and Santiago Álvarez and Ester Blanco), *Mundo Obrero* said that there ought not to be "any guiding party or leading center."

To bring about the pact for freedom, the PCE first had to free itself from Moscow. This was clear, and Carrillo managed to give the impression that it was indeed doing so. He convinced many Catalonian petty bourgeois who, without realizing it was a maneuver of PSUC, agreed to be part of the Asamblea de Catalunya, created in November 1971 (which PSUC itself, along with other parties, finally tried to liquidate in 1974 and which died once and for all in 1977 once its official creators—Portabella, Xirinacs, Benet, and others—became senators).[81] It was less successful with labor forces. The UGT was reborn and made fierce attacks on the PCE early in 1971, pointing out that chief of government Carrero Blanco's criticism of Russia was hypocritical, that the USSR in fact aided Franco's regime, that the PCE never held a monopoly in the opposition, that the commutation of the death penalty in the trial in Burgos was not the work of anyone in particular (especially not of the PCE), and that the PCE did not defend the prisoners and those persecuted by other organizations unless it was politically advantageous to do so (and it gave examples of imprisoned members of the UGT who were never mentioned by the PCE).[82]

The intellectuals never paid any attention to these sorts of things. They were satisfied with a little flattery and the feeling that they were doing their "duty." They got that feeling—along with a lot of publicity—from the PCE. The PCE, in turn, was gaining respectability. So much so that it dared to appeal to the "honor of the military" to explain to them that it did not intend to "dismantle the army or by any means replace it with the former popular army," and it even offered to fight for them to improve their soldiers' income.[83]

So the PCE went into its new congress in 1972 in better shape than it had ever been before the previous congresses. It revived the labor movement at a critical moment (out of partisan interests, to be sure, but nonetheless the revival did exist), it brought out of silence many intellectuals who would never have risked being anti-Franco without the support of the party, and it gave the impression that for the first time in its history it dared act on its own without clinging to the medals of the leaders in the Kremlin.[84]

The Eighth Congress

The eighth congress was just as cloaked in mystery as the seventh. In spite of the fact that there was no longer the kind of persecution that had existed in 1965, it was held in October 1972 at a place that was not mentioned in any of the party's publications. There were 104 delegates in attendance and they elected a central committee of 118 members which in turn elected an executive committee of 24 members and a secretariat of seven. The names of the members of the executive and central committees were never given.[85] But it was announced that Ibárruri had been reelected president and Carrillo secretary general. Ibárruri gave a brief closing speech and Carrillo presented a report. The book with the various theses approved by the congress but which did not include the debates, was printed in Rumania.[86] Carrillo's speech was widely distributed in underground editions.

There was not much new in the resolutions and theses. Carrillo insisted that with a pact for freedom violence could be avoided in overthrowing Franco and that the general political strike could help attain that goal. He also spoke of the "centrists" who, instead of accepting the pact, came out in support of Franco. Manuel Azcárate took it upon himself to explain—without explaining anything—the conflict with the USSR and he made a plea for solidarity of the "socialist" nations and for the unity of the worldwide Communist movement "based on the respect and independence of each party [and] the noninterference, in words and deeds, in internal affairs." "The union of work and cultural forces" was called for and the existence of a "Spanish road to socialism" was proclaimed. Each participant began by praising Carrillo and quoting his report. The congress approved an eleven-point resolution which literally repeated as many sentences from Carrillo's report. The fundamental points were: solidarity with Vietnam (and not acceptance of the positions of the CPSU) was the touchstone of proletarian internationalism; the winning of political liberties in Spain was the party's immediate objective; opposition to the entry of Franco's Spain in the European Economic Community, but acceptance of Spain's entry following the fall of the dictator (this was the principal change of position which the congress made on Carrillo's suggestion); all anti-Franco forces ought to unify in a pact for freedom to form a provisional government and bring about amnesty, political liberties, and the election of a constituent parliament; the party ought to step up its work among Spanish emigrants in Europe; a "socialist" Spain would be based on party pluralism, fundamental political liberties, the freedom of information, criticism, and of artistic

394 The Communist Party in Spain

and intellectual creation, and the renunciation of any attempt to impose a given political philosophy. That support for the "bourgeois" concept of democracy was another change (albeit a relative one since it had been preceded by articles and talks which paved the way for the change in line).[87]

The congress received messages from 37 parties (including that of the USSR, but not China, Albania, or Czechoslovakia). The messages from pro-Soviet parties were cold and cautious, but in any event they recognized implicitly that the PCE was the legitimate expression of the Communist movement in Spain. Líster was thus removed as a rival. In its message the French Communist party gave as an example the pact that it had just signed with the Socialist party and the Radical Leftist party (and which the Communist party itself broke six years later).

The eighth congress was important in that it confirmed and gave official form to the positions which Carrillo, with the help of the elements that he led over to the central and executive committees, had been elaborating and which constituted actual verbal breaks with some of the principles of the traditional Communist movement. The people who knew about those turnabouts in tactic showed interest in the congress but also caution. It was left to be seen how the changes put down on paper would turn out in practice.

Notes

1. In *Mañana*, Mexico City, January 21, 1956.
2. Carrillo, *Eurocomunismo y Estado,* Barcelona, 1977, p. 165.
3. The documents must have been considered fairly important for the *Cahiers du Communisme* of the French Communist party to print them in their entirety in its October 1956 issue.
4. Published with this title by the French Communist party in Paris (1957), after the pamphlet came out in Prague with the *Informes y resoluciones del pleno del Comité Central del Partido Comunista de España* (August 1956), Prague, 1956.
5. Although sketched out seven years before, the elimination of the higher-ups reaching toward Ibárruri began when Carrillo managed to have the bureau, in a resolution of July 1953, remove Francisco Antón from the bureau and from the central committee as well as investigate its own political performance as a result of its "work against the party." In April 1954 the bureau sent Líster to Warsaw to inform Antón that he was being relegated to the rank and file, and in November 1958 the bureau confirmed this decision which it considered "entirely fair, as he himself acknowledged." His behavior, it added, had been characterized by "crude and brutal anti-Leninist means of leadership, as well as vanity and blind ambition" (Líster, *¡Basta!* p. 171). Before that, Antón (and through him, Ibárruri) had been allied with Carrillo in his rivalry with Uribe and Mije. One of the things for which Antón was criticized was his past as a Jesuit student, the same

Jesuits whose alliance the PCE would seek out a little later on the inspiration of Carrillo. The elimination of Uribe was more complex. He did not want to enter into discussions or talk to Ibárruri, so Carrillo was a mediator, or so he said. When Carrillo wanted to get La Pasionaria's support on the reconciliation line, to pay her back he presented her with Uribe's head. She accused him of being opposed to the frequent meetings of the central committee. Carrillo added: "Uribe is engaged in self-worship which has led him to establish a real personality cult . . . and he has nothing but scorn for the members of the political bureau." Following these attacks Gallego and Mije, who usually supported Uribe, went over to Carrillo (Líster, *¡Basta!* pp. 186–88).

6. The list for the new bureau appears in Comín, *La República en el exilio,* p. 618.
7. "Those incidents marked the beginning of activity in the university movement" (Enrique Palazuelos, *Movimiento estudiantil y democratización de la Universidad,* Madrid, 1978). This book was written by a member of the PTE who said he was "supervised by the central committee of the PTE," something along the lines of the *nihil obstat* in the works of Catholic priests. University students were bored and fed up with SEU's control—they were exasperated over the poor quality of instruction and its ideological limitations. The previous generation of students was noted for the brutality which members of SEU inflicted upon the few students who were not of the right wing. At the University of Barcelona the mere fact that one was Catalonian and not a Falangist was all that was needed to be the object of "attention" by SEU students. Later on, some of them rose to prominence as intellectuals belonging to the PCE or as their ideological friends.
8. Semprún (pp. 36–38) recalls the names of some prominent students at the time in Madrid: Carlos Semprún Maura, Enrique Múgica, Julián Marcos, Jesús López Pacheco, Julio Diamante, Javier Pradera, Fernando Sánchez Drago, Ramón Tamames, and Jaime Maestro. Juan Manuel Kindelán and Miguel Sánchez Mazas were also included.
9. Semprún, p. 95.
10. Paul Preston, "The Anti-Francoist Opposition: The Long March to Unity," in *Spain in Crisis,* London, 1976, pp. 139–40.
11. Semprún, p. 296.
12. *Cahiers du Communisme,* Paris, March 1957.
13. Preston, p. 140. Luis Ramírez, *Nuestros primeros veinticinco años,* Paris, 1964, pp. 169–71.
14. An account of this court martial appears in the *Boletín de Información* of the Basque government in exile, Paris, September 1, 1959. Santiago Álvarez reported on the same strike in "Situation et perspective de l'Espagne" (*Nouvelle Revue Internationale,* no. 6, 1959), which in its fourth issue of the same year printed an anonymous account on "Les enseignements de la grève nationale," which quoted the resolutions made by the bureau and the Central Committee of the PCE which met after the HNP. These resolutions stated that, in addition to the PCE, fifteen other organizations participated in the strike, which was not true.
15. J. Roig, "Veinticinco años de movimiento nacional en Cataluña," in *Horizonte español, 1966,* Paris, 1966, vol. II, p. 120.
16. M. Kenny, *A Spanish Tapestry,* Bloomington, Indiana, 1961, p. 140.

17. *New York Times,* June 1, 1959. The leaders of the PCE must have viewed matters more or less the same as the American journalist since when Semprún went to Paris to give a progress report on the strikes, in the summer of 1962, he found that the executive committee was on vacation at the Black Sea (Semprún, p. 253).
18. Esteban Gross, "Spain Reds Press Revival," *The Observer,* London, October 18, 1959.
19. *Ibérica,* New York, March 1958.
20. Silvano Villani, in *Corriere della Sera,* Milan. Articles reprinted in *Ibérica,* New York, December 1958. Carrillo's interview with Alonso Vega has never been confirmed although it was a hot item among the opposition.
21. Hermet, p. 71; and *Mundo Obrero,* December 15, 1960. Carrillo's speech appears in *Dos meses de huelga,* Paris, 1962, p. 114.
22. A letter written in April 1957 quoted by Líster, *¡Basta!* p. 169.
23. *Historia del PCE,* P. 260.
24. Ibid., p. 268.
25. *Bilan de vingt ans de dictature franquiste: les tâches immédiates de l'opposition et l'avenir de la démocratie espagnole,* Paris, 1959.
26. Semprún, pp. 240–42.
27. The elimination of La Pasionaria, which had begun in 1953 along with that of Antón, continued in the central committee in East Berlin, after which Ibárruri went to Moscow to live. There "she received only the news Carrillo wanted her to have and even then only upon occasion." In the central committee's plenary sessions her reports were replaced by others prepared by a commission appointed by the central committee. "She often spoke of jumping out of a window." During a visit which Carrillo, Semprún, and Líster made to Sochi, Ibárruri suggested creating the position of assistant secretary general for Carrillo. When he refused, she suggested he write a history of the Civil War. Later Carrillo told the bureau to propose the creation of the position of president and she finally agreed in 1959 during another visit by members of the bureau (Líster, *¡Basta!* pp. 188–89). The lists of delegates appear in *Historia del PCE,* p. 283. This "history" ends with the sixth congress. Its writing, in the hands of a group of members of long standing under the direction of Ibárruri, was one of Carrillo's concessions in order that her elimination not be interpreted as disapproval of her many years of work as a party leader, since the book essentially was a justification of the successive lines which Ibárruri defended from 1932 to 1960.
28. As proof of this, the accords were reprinted and glossed in an article by Claudín, "Grands Changements se preparent en Espagne," *Nouvelle Revue Internationale,* no. 4, 1960, which had replaced the Comintern's organ after it was dissolved and which consistently reflected Moscow's point of view.
29. Líster, *¡Basta!* p. 195.
30. Dolores Ibárruri and Santiago Carrillo, *Deberes del pueblo español en la presente situación internacional y nacional,* Montevideo, 1961.
31. Santiago Carrillo, *Sobre algunos problemas de la táctica de lucha contra el franquismo,* Montevideo, 1961.
32. Semprún, pp. 98, 200, 203, 206, 210–11; *Julián Grimau: el hombre, el crimen, la protesta,* Paris, 1963. Francoist reaction appears in *El Español,* Madrid, April 27, 1963.

33. Semprún, pp. 213–15.
34. Ruiz Ayúcar, *Crónica agitada de ocho años tranquilos, 1963–70,* Madrid, 1974, p. 46.
35. For information on these suspect matters, consult Amandino Rodríguez Armanda and José Antonio Novais, *¿Quién mató a Julián Grimau?* Madrid, 1976, pp. 159–61. A synopsis of the trial can be found in *Cambio 16,* Madrid, April 30, 1978.
36. Cedos, *Franquismo y lucha de clases: una aproximación histórica, 1939–1975,* Barcelona, 1977, p. 87.
37. Luis Galán Jiménez, "Un caballero del PCE: Hidalgo de Cisneros. Su muerte en el exilio," *Nueva Historia,* Barcelona, March 1978.
38. *Nouvelle Revue Internationale,* Paris, no. 2, 1964.
39. Carrillo, "La fuerza del marxismo creador," *Revista Internacional,* no. 11, 1964.
40. Hermet, p. 82.
41. Regarding this issue the fundamental documentation can be found in Fernando Claudín, *Documentos de una divergencia comunista,* Barcelona, 1978, and *Nuestra Bandera,* January 1950; "Notas críticas al documento-plataforma fraccional de Fernando Claudín," *Boletín de Información,* Prague, no. 23, 1965. A good explanation of the positions taken by the dissidents appears in Jorge Semprún, "La oposición política en España," and Fernando Claudín, "Dos concepciones de la via española al socialismo, 1956–1966," in *Horizonte Español, 1966,* Paris, 1966, vol. II. Semprún summed up the case in novelistic form in *Autobiografía de Federico Sánchez,* Barcelona, 1977, and the book's success sparked off a controversy in the press. The main characters (excluding Carrillo who claimed he had not read the book) summed up their points of view in *Opinión,* Madrid, October 28, 1977. Claudín spoke of himself to Álvaro Custodio in *Siempre,* Mexico City, March 17, 1976. Semprún depicted the psychological problems of a member out of step with the party's position in two films for which he wrote the screenplays: *La guerre est finie,* in 1966, and *Les routes du Sud,* in 1978.
42. Mije.
43. A summary of Claudín's position appears in Preston, pp. 147–48. Carrillo's statement appears in Carrillo, *Hacia el post-franquismo,* Paris, 1974, quoted by Preston.
44. Claudín, *Documentos de una divergencia comunista,* p. 216.
45. *Siempre,* Mexico City, July 17, 1963. In the same interview he said that the Franco regime was "on tenterhooks" and that ever since Grimau's execution "thousands of young workers have asked to be admitted into the Communist party."
46. Dolores Ibárruri, "Le 7è Congrès et l'expérience espagnole," *Nouvelle Revue Internationale,* no. 12, 1965.
47. Carrillo, "Acendrada fidelidad al marxismo-leninismo," *Revista Internacional,* Prague, no. 6, 1966. No similar statement was made regarding the 22nd congress of the CPSU, perhaps because it emphasized de-Stalination. Ibárruri was less cautious and more staunchly anti-Maoist than Carrillo in "Por la unidad del movimiento comunista" (*Revista Internacional,* Prague, no. 10, 1964), where epithets such as "intolerable arrogance" and "theoretical sophisms" abounded.

48. Carrillo, "La fuerza del marxismo creador," *Revista Internacional,* Prague, no. 11, 1964.
49. Hermet, p. 83.
50. Carrillo, *Después de Franco—¿qué?* and *Nuevos enfoques a problemas de hoy,* Paris, 1965 and 1967.
51. Carrillo, "Crece la oposición a la dictadura franquista," *Revista Internacional,* Prague, no. 1, 1966.
52. A good illustration of how those members were trained is in the collection of *Cuadernos de Educación Política* edited in the underground by the PCE. In this series there are more pamphlets on the functioning of the party than about the history of the labor movement (which was falsified after 1920), and there was more polemics against the Socialists than against Franco.
53. Hermet, p. 72.
54. Antonio Sala and Eduardo Durán, *Crítica de la izquierda autoritaria en Cataluña, 1967-1974,* Paris, 1975, p. xiii. For a better perspective of the unofficial communist movements, see *Los partidos marxistas: sus dirigentes, sus programas,* ed. F. Ruiz and J. Romero, Barcelona, 1977, and Julio Sanz Oller, *Entre el fraude y la esperanza,* Paris, 1972.
55. Mije.
56. Marc Etcheverry, "Les Espagnols sont-ils 'chinois'?" in *France-Observateur,* Paris, September 3, 1964.
57. Two studies of the policy of the PCE deserve to be mentioned; they are representative of the criticism which those groups issued: "Adulteraciones del equipo Santiago Carrillo," published by *Vanguardia Obrera* in 1969 and "El revisionismo en España," published in 1972 by *Bandera Roja.*
58. The PCE took advantage of the impression made by the recurrent mining strikes in Asturias to start a recruiting campaign it called "Promotion Asturias" (Álvaro Sanz, "La promotion Asturias," *Nouvelle Revue Internationale,* no. 12, 1963). This article makes no allusion to the unloading of Polish coal during the strike.
59. Santiago Álvarez, "Sobre el progreso unitario de la clase obrera española," *Revista Internacional,* no. 4, 1964; A.G., "Progrès de l'opposition syndicale en Espagne," *Nouvelle Revue Internationale,* no. 2, 1963.
60. *Revista Internacional,* no. 2, 1964, p. 63.
61. Paradoxically the PCE had no part in the birth of the Workers' Commissions, but in October 1955 in a manifesto it called on the workers to "form workers commissions to fight for the legal platform" of the congress of the official CNS.
62. Julio Sanz Oller, "La larga marcha del movimiento obrero español hacia la autonomía," in *Horizonte Español, 1972,* Paris, 1972, vol. II, p. 37ff. For information on the commissions see Nicolás Sartorius *¿Qué son las Comisiones Obreras?* Barcelona, 1976 (which says they were not formed until 1966 and thus attributes them to the PCE); José Antonio Díaz, *Luchas internas en las Comisiones Obreras, Barcelona, 1964-1970,* Barcelona, 1977; Marco Calamai, *Storia del movimento operaio spagnuolo dal 1960 al 1975,* Bari, 1975 (from the PCE's point of view); Julián Ariza, *Comisiones Obreras,* Barcelona, 1976; Julio Sanz Oller, *Del fraude a la esperanza: las Comisiones Obreras de Barcelona,* Paris, 1972. For more information on the labor movement during this period consult Cedos, *Franquismo y lucha de clases:*

una aproximación histórica, 1939–1975, Barcelona, 1977; and *Apuntes para una historia del movimiento obrero español de la post-guerra,* Barcelona, 1977. Regarding this stage of Spanish syndicalism in general: F. Almendros et al., *El sindicalismo de clase en España, 1939–1977,* Barcelona, 1978. Regarding the labor union elections of 1966; "En toda España, los resultados de las elecciones sindicales confirman: el triunfo del nuevo movimiento obrero ha sido aplastante," in *Boletíno de Información,* Prague, no. 21, 1966. In its propaganda the PCE refers to the Workers' Commissions as the basis for a new labor movement, and it assumed the CNT and UGT as well as the USO and all other organizations to be defunct. It was the party that established the "Bases programáticas del nuevo movimiento obrero," the title of one of the *Cuadernos de Educación Política* of the PCE.

63. Quoted in *Apuntes para una historia del movimiento obrero español de la postguerra,* Barcelona, 1977, p. 41.

64. Santiago Álvarez, "Sobre la unidad de católicos y comunistas," *Revista Internacional,* Prague, no. 6, 1965; M.A. (Manuel Azcárate), "Aspectos del diálogo católico-marxista," *Realidad,* Rome, November–December 1966; Federico Melchor, "Comunistas y católicos," *Nuestra Bandera,* 4th quarter 1967. One example of how successful these contacts were was issue no. 42 (April 1966) of the French Franciscans' periodical *Frères du Monde,* devoted to Spain, and whose Spanish contributors were Manuel Tuñón de Lara, Alfonso C. Comín, and J.M. González Ruiz.

65. One example, although it came from outside of Spain, was the film *La guerre est finie,* for which Jorge Semprún wrote the screenplay. It had been selected by France for the Karlovy Vary festival but it was withdrawn by the Czech Communist party on the request of the PCE (Semprún, p. 284). Arrabal has related several anecdotes about the poor reception given his works; even though they were famous abroad, they were not known in Spain where official and PCE censorship banished them (*Terrorismo intelectual y eurocomunismo: Arrabal en el banquillo,* Paris, 1977). For an idea of the political climate of the time see Carlos Semprún Maura, *L'an prochain à Madrid,* Paris, 1975.

66. Juan Díaz, "Le Parti Communiste dans les universités," *Nouvelle Revue Internationale,* no. 3, 1967.

67. Carlos Prieto, "La tactique du PC a contribué à l'affaiblissement des Commissions Ouvrières," *Le Monde,* Paris, February 18, 1970.

68. Santiago Álvarez, "Le Parti Communiste et le mouvement ouvrier," and Eduardo García, "Une avant-garde dans la lutte du peuple," *Nouvelle Revue Internationale,* no. 3, 1967.

69. "Por un Partido Comunista de masas: Resolución del CE del PCE," *Nuestra Bandera,* 2nd quarter 1967; "Más de 40 millones recaudados en la campaña de los treinta millones," *Mundo Obrero,* September 2, 1969.

70. The repression of the ETA drew attention away from the fact that there was also repression of members of the Workers' Commissions and of the several Communist parties (which the people saw as only one because they did not distinguish between the "M-L" and the "I's" which followed the name). Since many arrests were for acts of violence (which in 1969 led the government to suspend its hypothetical "constitutional guarantees"), this mishmash of Communist parties was damaging to the image that the PCE

wanted to create for itself with the line of national reconciliation. It is strange that the campaign in France in favor of the Communist Justo López de la Fuente was not taken up either by the PCE or by the French Communist party but rather by the PSU, a dissident socialist organization which was not on good terms with the Communist party. I have never been able to clarify the reason for this ("Un Lieutenant de Julián Grimau risque la peine de mort," *Tribune Socialiste,* Paris, February 20, 1965).

71. Semprún (p. 139) states that Carrillo said: "The Soviet Union will not establish relations with Spain until the party's central committee authorizes it," but that the written version gave the other text.

72. *Boletín de Información,* Prague, special issue, 1968.

73. All these quotes are from Hermet, p. 85ff.

74. Neil McInness, *The Communist Parties of Western Europe,* London, 1975, p. 147.

75. Líster, *Memorias de un luchador,* p. 8.

76. Preston, p. 150.

77. Ibárruri had not given up her pro-Soviet stance but it lost its "unconditional" nature (Teresa Pàmies, *Una española llamada Ibárruri,* p. 56).

78. *Washington Post,* May 5, 1970.

79. Carrillo, *Libertad y socialismo,* Paris, 1971.

80. In January 1973 the central committee of Líster's party expelled García, Gómez, and Álvaro Galiana for trying to "transform it into a pro-Soviet pressure group." These men, who published their own *Mundo Obrero* (the fourth periodical published at the time with the same name), accused Líster of being anti-Soviet. Toward the end of 1970 a congress of Líster's party changed its name to Partido Comunista Obrero Español (Eusebio M. Mujal-León, "Spanish Communism in the 1970's," *Problems of Communism,* Washington, D.C., March-April 1975).

81. "Judging by the underground propaganda it distributed and the identity of its 113 members which the police caught unawares at a church in Barcelona in October 1973, its scope appeared to be limited to PSUC and its sympathizers along with a certain number of well-known lawyers and professors of the nationalist Left such as Solé Barbera (who actually belonged to PSUC) and Jordi Carbonell and some radical priests like Xirinacs and Dou. The Catalonian Left and Right of center kept themselves apart from it" (Norman L. Jones, "The Catalan Question since the Civil War," in *Spain in Crisis,* p. 263).

82. Reprinted in *España Libre,* New York, January–February 1971.

83. Carrillo, *Nuevos enfoques a problemas de hoy,* pp. 123, 126. These statements constantly crop up in PCE propaganda.

84. A reflection of this increase in popularity is seen in the amounts (albeit undoubtedly exaggerated) of money brought in by the "campaign to aid the party." By the end it had amassed 46 million pesetas, 9.6 million in Spain, 400,000 in the central committee and its collaborators, and 31 million in the countries of emigration, in addition to 5 million brought in by PSUC (*Mundo Obrero,* September 17, 1971).

85. Mujal-León, by collating from works published after the congress, managed to compile the following names as members of the executive committee

who were elected or coopted in the years that followed: S. Álvarez, M. Azcárate, E. Blanco, M. Carmón, S. Carrillo, J. Calanda, M. Delicado, J. Díaz, K. Exteberri, H. Fernández Inguanzo, I. Gallego, J. Gómez, J.M. González Jerez, D. Ibárruri, A. López, G. López, L.L. Lobato, V. Martín García, F. Melchor, R. Mendezona, A. Mije, R. Oroneta, J. Pereira Riquelme, M. Pérez, E. Quirós, F. Romero Marín, and V. Suárez.

86. *VII Congreso del Partido Comunista de España,* Bucharest, 1972.

87. Shortly after the eighth congress of the PCE, PSUC celebrated its third congress which decided to try to widen its membership and reaffirm its identification with the policy of the PCE in international affairs (that is, with regard to Moscow) as well as in the thesis of the Spanish road to socialism. *La Nouvelle Revue Internationale* published a report by S. Zapiraín on the eighth congress in its first issue of 1973. There was no break with Moscow despite the congress's thesis.

16.
Back to 1936

Starting with Carrero Blanco's death in December 1973 what would become a consistent policy of the PCE began to take shape; until then it had been a series of zigzags. Starting in 1974 the PCE returned to 1936. The methods, vocabulary, and mechanisms were different, as were the motives. But the PCE's role in Spain after 1974 and that which it played in 1936 were identical. Then it was a matter of trying to prevent revolution in order to win the war; now it was a matter of avoiding pressure for social change in order to gain political change. Then it was at the service of the USSR; now it was at the service of the party. Then there was an alliance with the Republican right wing and Socialism; now the consensus. Then there was a demand for a government of "national unity"; now for a government of concentration.

Return to Isolationism

Following the partial triumphs of the tactic of the pact for freedom with Catholics and Workers' Commissions, the PCE once again found itself in isolation. There was a marked abstention on the part of workers in the official "trade union" elections. The Conferencia Democrática was created in Madrid inspired by Dionisio Ridruejo and without any input by the PCE. To put an end to this isolation Carrillo did something that ten years earlier he would have called "petty bourgeois intellectual masochism" (when Semprún spoke of the party's Stalinist errors before the executive committee): "rummaging around in the past."[1] He made no acknowledgment of political errors but he did refer to certain crimes as mistakes. For example, in Jorge Semprún's film *Las dos memorias* he admitted that POUM was not "a party of provocateurs [but] a current in the revolutionary movement."[2] Later he allowed himself to be interviewed by two accommodating writers who published *Demain, l'Espagne.*[3] The book is highly nostalgic and filled with half-truths and justifications based on a distorted view of Carrillo's political past. It attempted to present an image of the secretary general, and so of the PCE, which would have an appeasing effect and show that with the years

403

he and the party had settled down. It did not have much effect in Spain but in Western Europe the campaign turned Carrillo into a prominent figure in the opposition to Franco. Even when Salvador Puig Antich was executed in March 1974—for whom the PCE did not mobilize any of its considerable resources simply because he was an Anarchist—French newspapers ran Carrillo's picture instead of Puig Antich's.

The mistrust which arose from the ambiguity of relations between the party and Moscow lasted for some time. First there was the denunciation of what had happened in Prague, then a half-baked kind of reconciliation, followed by the affirmation of a "Spanish road toward socialism." Yet party leaders had attended the centennial of Lenin's birth as well as several "summits" of European Communist parties, in which the PCE rather cautiously aligned itself with the Italians.[4] It tried hard to overcome what some considered an image of weakness and vacillation and what others saw as double-crossing: it denounced the establishment of diplomatic relations between Madrid and Peking in April 1974, and at a plenary session of the central committee in September 1974 Azcárate delivered a report on "The Spanish Road to Socialism" and progress in the creation of a socialist Europe. Following that session, the PCE attended a conference of European Communist parties in Brussels. And scarcely a month after that conference which Carrillo found disappointing,[5] the Soviet periodical *Life of the Party* ferociously attacked Azcárate's report; the thesis that there could be contradictions between the interests of socialist nations and those of the revolutionary movement was absurd; the idea of autonomy of fraternal parties did not contain an ounce of proletarian internationalism; the hope for a socialist Europe was nationalism; and criticizing the Soviet system was the same as spreading lies about the USSR. What Moscow found exasperating was that a manifesto-program issued by the plenary of the central committee spoke of the "regional [Mediterranean] context of the struggle for socialism in Spain." This was followed by a visit by Carrillo, Ibárruri, Gallego, Azcárate, López Raimundo, and Melchor to Moscow in October 1974 to meet with Suslov and Ponomarev. The CPSU recognized the PCE as the official Spanish party and the PCE accepted the policy of peaceful coexistence—which until then had only earned, if not its reproval, at least its silence. The ambiguity continued. No one who has not been a Communist can understand the PCE's hesitation in separating from Moscow (aside from the financial reasons which could make that separation difficult).

Moscow might likely have been moved to greater tolerance by some international events which, to a certain degree, proved Carrillo right. Allende's overthrow in Chile proved that a more extensive alliance than that achieved by him was necessary to carry out reforms, regardless of how modest they might be. Carrillo took advantage of the Chilean experience to underscore his pact for freedom. He would later make use of what in appearance must have been unpalatable to him: the coup of the Portuguese armed forces and the ultra-Stalinist position of the Portuguese Communist party and its leader Alvaro Cunhal. The Chilean experience and more immediately the "open" policy of the Arias Navarro government in Spain and the union of non-Communist opposition in the Conferencia Democrática as well as the reconstruction of the PSOE (finally released from the straightjacket its leaders in exile had it in) all compelled Carrillo. By suspending the daily *Madrid,* the government handed him on a silver platter the key to expediting his policy.

The Junta Democrática

In March 1974, taking advantage of Puig Antich's execution, Carrillo declared that the regime was in crisis, that there was a need for a "convergence of all forces interested in achieving democracy, overcoming the Civil War, and creating a climate of civic coexistence," and in addition he asked for amnesty and the immediate release of Camacho and the other prisoners of the trial referred to as 1,001 for its number in the Court of Public Order. The hearing did not attract attention because it coincided with Carrero Blanco's death. If the ruling classes did not hear the "responsible voice of the Communist party," they would be "responsible to history for the period of violence that may overtake the country." In May Carrillo called a press conference in Paris and stressed the need to form a government of national reconciliation in which "several of Franco's ministers would no doubt have places" in order to plan for elections to a constituent assembly. He added that "even some [of Franco's] ministers have asked us for interviews because we Communists are now in demand as interlocutors." Shortly thereafter PSUC took advantage of a dinner colloquium organized by the magazine *Cambio 16,* which a member of PSUC and several bankers attended, calling it the beginning of an accord of the Catalonian opposition.[6]

The plenary session in September 1973 had authorized the executive committee to formalize alliances. In July 1974 the executive committee made use of the *pro forma* authorization and a so-called Junta Democrática was presented on July 30 at a press conference in Paris where, seated next to Carrillo, was Rafael Calvo Serer, member of Opus Dei and factotum of the daily *Madrid* until its suspension and advisor to Don Juan, Count of Barcelona.[7] The junta, they said, would have the following goals: the formation of a provisional government that would grant amnesty and establish political and trade union liberties and the right to strike; it would recognize the personality of the Basque, Galician, and Catalonian peoples; it would recognize the separation of church and state and would hold elections within twelve to eighteen months; it would integrate Spain within the European Economic Community, would respect international accords (the treaty of the American bases), and would recognize the principle of peaceful coexistence. Shortly thereafter Tierno Galván's Popular Socialist party, Prince Carlos Hugo's Carlist party, and later the Partido del Trabajo (Labor party) which arose from the Communist party (International) after having split from the PCE, as well as a Carlist princess and a handful of political adventurers all joined the junta.

The European press viewed the junta as a unified front of the opposition. The underground press in Spain was generally skeptical because neither the PSOE, which was in the process of illegal reorganization, the CNT, nor the Christian Democrats were part of the junta. In June 1975 the Christian Democrats, the PSOE, the Social Democrats, and some leftist groups (several of which came from the PCE) formed the Platform of Democratic Convergence, which excluded the Communists. So in the final year of Francoism there were two unitarian formations of the opposition: one of the Left and Center Left, and another of the PCE and the Right.

A number of statements issued by the junta or Carrillo insisted that Franco's regime was in crisis because "it lacked authority" and because "it was not in the best position to guarantee the interests and benefits of Spanish entrepreneurs." The junta was the last hope for the middle class "in the face of potential anarchic violence."[8] The PCE was the only real force behind the junta; it dominated it and was its spokesman. Tierno Galván himself recognized: "The PCE is more active and therefore in many cases has the priority in taking over positions effectively."[9]

The junta was for the PCE a way of playing Don Juan's card against that of Juan Carlos. It did not want a king who did not owe it something. The facts will show that once again the body of leaders was a poor judge of people, did not appreciate the interplay of forces, and did not understand the situation. But if the Junta Democrática never managed to qualify as a front, at least it gave the PCE a new shot of respectability: some right-wing elements took it seriously and once again began to remove it from its isolation. All this allowed it to take advantage of the narrow margin of tolerance that the Arias Navarro "opening" policy provided. Neighborhood Associations, for example, had been organized in the cities. The PCE took over many of them. It once again energized the Workers' Commissions (actually it used the old name for formations of Communist union militants who gradually separated from the official

CNS). In some places local "groups" were created for discussion as well as protest, and the PCE managed to lead a good number of them. Spontaneous strikes were once again on the rise and Communist members were always in view and managed to direct some of them in bitter competition with members of parties which had arisen out of the PCE.

The PCE had more abundant means, certainly much greater than the rest of the opposition. In 1974, for example, it had the following underground press: *Mundo Obrero, Nuestra Bandera, Realidad, Treball, Nous Horitzons, Euzkadi Obrera, Alkarriskera, Hemen eta Horain, A voz do Pobo, Nova Galicia, Horizonte, Nuestro Camino, Verdad, Acción, Joventut, Nuevo Amanecer,* and 32 local or company newspapers.[10] This press spoke little of the past. But the party needed to have its graves whitewashed. This was the task of some "historians" such as Manuel Tuñón de Lara who, referring to Nin, for example, said that although it was possible (but not certain) that he was assassinated by the NKVD, the Spanish Communists knew nothing of it[11]—an explanation which the Communists all reiterated. Another of those "historians," the new recruit Ramón Tamames, dared write a history of the Civil War without mentioning Nin's assassination.

The above-mentioned *Demain, l'Espagne* was Carrillo's contribution to this operation of wiping out memories which was completed by *Eurocomunismo y Estado,* where he repeated Tuñón de Lara's statement that the party had nothing to do with the assassination of Nin and added as "evidence" that he was a member of the bureau and knew nothing of it.[12] Some of the more stubborn members like Rafael Vidiella still nurtured their hatred; but others, like Teresa Pàmies, were more honest and did not conceal, for example, that they had had a fanatical adolescence in the party.[13] But neither the junta nor the platform could prevent the regime from showing enough strength in September 1975 to execute five political prisoners and resist extraordinary pressures from abroad.

The Disaster of the Rupture

Protest over the executions in September 1975 and the illness and death of Franco in November brought about the conditions that Carrillo had established for a national strike to be successful: the coalition of democratic forces (as was the junta, according to PCE propaganda); political organizational planning (which the PCE claimed to have accomplished); and favorable circumstances (Franco's death, the isolation of the regime in Europe).[14] But there was no general strike or any other kind of action capable of overthrowing a regime which had already lost its leader.

Things did not go according to the PCE's plans. In 1964 the PCE had said: "The transition will be achieved with a great struggle and mobilization of the people . . . even if it is achieved peacefully, [it will be] the opening of a revolutionary process." At the national conference in 1975 Carrillo said: "Despite every continuist formula, the democratic alternative continues to be our only solution. If it happens that Juan Carlos succeeds Franco, with the masses in the streets we will take advantage of the weakening of the entire power structure to meet the democratic objectives which Spanish society is demanding, culminating in the political resolution which will do away with the remains of dictatorial power."

But when the moment of transition drew near, the tone changed: "[To make the transition possible] the army will have to intervene as a regulatory agent to guarantee order, since the armed forces would be able to regulate the project of democratization to avoid dangerous upheavals."[15] The junta addressed a report to employers indicating that, on the road to democracy, "management . . . has one basic function: making their creativity and organizational talent work for the Spanish · people."[16] Carrillo had said that "the machinery of the state . . . is no longer the fascist machinery of the past. With slight alterations it might also suit a bourgeois democratic state. . . . There was a strong liberal current in the army, the police no longer gave orders to the judges, and ever since the change in Portugal, torture barely existed."[17]

The PCE declared itself anti–Juan Carlos: "What potential does Juan Carlos have? At most he would be king for a couple of months. If he had broken off with Franco in time, he could have found a base of support. Now he had nothing and is hated by everyone. I would just as soon see him pack his bags and leave with his father, saying: 'I return the monarchy to the people.' If he does not do it he will be in sad shape. . . . As far as the man in the street is concerned the only legitimate heir to Alfonso XIII is [Don Juan] the Count of Barcelona. If Juan Carlos takes his place he will betray his father. And in Spain, particularly in the eyes of the man in the street, whoever betrays his own father even to assume the role of king will never have credibility among his compatriots."[18]

When the platform invited the junta to an informational meeting in August 1975, the junta accepted and asked the platform to "try to publicly clarify" three issues: Juan Carlos's monarchy which the junta rejected because "it represented the continuation of the regime"; the formation of provisional governments of the state and autonomous regions; and the means of achieving the democratic rupture. As far as the junta was concerned, this last issue would be resolved by means of "hundreds of democratic juntas . . . with extensive mobilization of the masses which continue to manifest society's political power which must be a part of national democratic action to be led by the Junta Democrática of Spain."[19] The "peaceful national strike" was replaced by "national democratic action," but the methods remained vague and the same conditions that sterilized the opposition under Franco were still present: ineffectiveness in finding a way to overthrow him. Now it was the ineffectiveness of finding a way to break Franco's machinery. No more concrete was the plenary session of the Central Committee of PSUC, which still insisted on the rupture but without saying how to achieve it.[20]

Did these statements and those policy changes respond to a maneuvering spirit, to wishful thinking—being out of touch with reality—or to tactics? It might be thought that the orders for rupture the PCE issued were not sincere, because while they were imposed by the full weight of propaganda on the rest of the opposition which was fearful of being considered "soft," the above-mentioned statements were addressed to businessmen, the military, bureaucrats, and even the police force of the very state with which the rupture was being publicly proclaimed. Events would not contradict anyone who said that the PCE wished to involve the opposition in a hopeless policy in order to abandon it at an opportune moment and claim itself as the appropriate interlocutor. It is impossible to say whether that was its intention or whether it took advantage of what was going on, but those were the results.

This tactic was made possible in October 1975 when Franco became ill, by an agreement between the Junta Democrática and the Platform of Democratic Convergence which created the Democratic Coordination.[21] The Democratic Coordination not only gave the PCE a rostrum but allowed a group of adventurers who were staunch supporters of the junta to have a role in the series of maneuvers which had no practical results: what the people called the "Platajunta." Finally the PSOE threatened to leave if they did not stop listening to some of the most obvious adventurers. But this was an anecdote. Actually, everything was an anecdote because the Platajunta, although it made a lot of statements and managed to have the word *rupture* painted all over the country, was not successful in changing the course of events. What is curious is that the graffiti, demonstrations, and protests were mainly the work of the small groups which evolved from the PCE, not the PCE itself. The PCE tried to work exclusively through the Platajunta.

The tactic of rupture could not be successful. No one believed in it, yet no one dared to propose an alternative for fear of being accused by the PCE of "playing into Franco's hands." This left the field open for the PCE to choose the right time to break unity. As it became apparent that this tactic was not bringing results, there began to be talk of negotiated rupture and a rupture by means of a pact until finally the man in the street ended up sarcastically calling it "implored rupture."

Carrillo said it was necessary to reject the political reform because it did not return sovereignty to the people and also because it did not restore liberties and it replaced Franco's dictatorship with authoritarian monarchy.[22] But in April 1976 in Paris he said: "If King Juan Carlos accepts the democracy that the Spanish people wish to introduce in our country, the PCE will not oppose the monarchy." There was no longer talk of rupture. A Catalonian Communist acknowledged in 1979: "We were incapable of causing the rupture."[23]

That period of rupture and Platajunta gave the PCE, which was enjoying a wide degree of tolerance, the chance to strengthen its machinery. At Franco's death the party had 5,000 to 20,000 members (the lower figure was given by political observers, the higher by the PCE itself),[24] paid very little attention to women, and even exempted them from militant activity.[25] It also had recovered a part of its strength lost in the schism of Bandera Roja (readmitted at the plenary of the Central Committee of PSUC in 1975), it once again made the Communist party of Euzkadi a functioning body, it tried to foster the Galician Communist party, but it was not yet willing to allow the Communist parties of Valencia, the Canary Islands, etc. to organize.[26] In October 1975 Felipe González, secretary general of the PSOE, estimated that the PCE had 300 full-time salaried functionaries (as opposed to 7 in the PSOE).[27] Note that political parties were still illegal and clandestine.

Legalization

It would not take the PCE long to cash in on the disastrous operation of rupture which was possible thanks only to the lack of experience, political imagination, and intellectual courage of the rest of the opposition. And so we reach a period which cannot yet be considered historic because we are still too close to it. Nevertheless, it is essential to point out the most significant stages in order for the reader to have the necessary facts to formulate his own conclusions. A chronological outline will be followed.[28]

1976

January. Nicolás Sartorius, of the Workers' Commissions, spoke of the "new labor movement" in *Triunfo.* The Workers' Commissions of Madrid recommended that the 340,000 workers on strike in the capital return to work. They blamed the violence which accompanied the strike in Vitoria on inexperience. To "soften" the labor protest the tactic of a staggered return to work was used.

April. One of Carrillo's sons, Jorge, moved to Madrid and set up an import-export firm with the countries of the Soviet bloc.

May. Azcárate presented the PCE's economic program at the University of Madrid. He asked for credits from the International Monetary Fund and the European Economic Community.

July. Following a conference of Communist parties in East Berlin, Carrillo said that the USSR was not the "enemy." He did not view the newly-formed Suárez government with much enthusiasm. A group of 76 intellectuals issued a manifesto asking for legalization of the PCE. Half of them were not fellow travelers. A plenary session of the central committee to which the Spanish press gave extensive coverage took place in Rome on July 28 and 29 amidst great publicity. It elected a new central committee of which many Communists living in Spain became a part, using their real names. Thus it became evident that many who had denied being Communists actually were. The executive committee grew from 15 to 24 members. The central committee had 133 members, 49 of whom were over 60. There were 16 women (8 of whom were wives or relatives of leaders who had either died or been executed). The plenary emphasized the establishment of relations with the Catholics. Carrillo and Ibárruri were reelected—these were not really elections but rather appointments by general acclaim. Nor were resolutions voted upon; they were unanimously approved. Carrillo said that hopes for political reform had disappeared. "The opposition has a lot to offer. . . . It is committed to effecting democratic change within civil peace without revenge." It set the following as conditions for a "democratic transformation": amnesty, a democratic law of association, the constitution of a provisional government of national reconciliation, the beginning of a constituent period, and the formation of autonomous governments (but only in Catalonia, Galicia, and Euzkadi). An accord was also reached to strengthen the Democratic Coordination. A "democratic rupture according to pact" was insisted upon. The world Communist press gave extensive coverage of the plenary (*Revista Internacional,* no. 10, 1976, and *Boletín de Información,* no. 15, 1976). According to Carrillo, the PCE had 100,000 members. People who had been granted amnesty—and this included Communists—began to leave jail.

August. Carrillo questioned the existence of Valencian nationalist feelings; he was opposed to the formation of a Valencian Communist party (which was finally constituted the following year despite him). According to the press, Carrillo was secretly living in Madrid. "The PCE is becoming a party of support for right-wing positions," declared Salcedo, a Socialist. It acted openly and rented headquarters. Its papers were sold on the street, even though technically it was still illegal. People at Communist meetings would shout: "The PCE's strength can be seen and felt." In an interview with *The New York Times* Carrillo came out in support of keeping the American bases in Spain and of Spain's joining NATO.

September. Santiago Álvarez took charge of the Communist party in Galicia. In a radio interview in Paris Carrillo said that Juan Carlos was unwilling to allow the election of a constituent parliament but he agreed to an interview with the king.

December. Carrillo gave a press conference (technically clandestine) in Madrid. He announced that the PCE would recommend abstention in the referendum (called for six days later). The PCE, he said, did not belong to any International. The Spanish economy would not be able to become nationalized for many years. The market economy would last for a long time, but the PCE advocated planning for it. It opposed Spain's entry into NATO. The referendum gave an overwhelming victory to the "reformers": 94 percent in favor. The opposition, which had made extensive propaganda for abstention, was not able to achieve it to a politically significant extent, and it immediately began preparing to harvest the results of the political reform law it has opposed. On December 22, Carrillo was arrested. Apparently it was an uncontrolled police action designed to put the government in a bind. The French left-wing press called the jailing "the Carrillo operation" and said it was destined to force the government's hand. Carrillo was freed on December 30.

1977

January. An opinion poll indicated that 40 percent of Spaniards did not answer or did not know if they were for or against the legalization of the PCE; 35 percent were opposed and 25 percent were in favor. Carrillo was part of the commission made up of leaders of the opposition which was to negotiate the electoral system with Suárez.

February. On February 9 Spain reestablished diplomatic relations with the USSR.

March. Carrillo intervened in the controversy surrounding whether or not Suárez could run in the elections and decided in his favor, since he would help put "a halt to continuism." He later denied having supported that position. There was a meeting in Madrid between Berlinguer, Marchais, and Carrillo in which no criticism was made of the USSR.

April. The PCE proposed a "constitutional accord" among all the parties of the opposition. On April 9 after hearing the attorney general (in view of the Supreme Court's decision to keep out of the matter), the government decided to legalize the PCE. The High Council of the Army expressed its opposition. The minister of the navy resigned. The Central Committee of the PCE met on April 14. "Legalization represents an important break with the past," said Carrillo trying to semantically salvage the policy of rupture whose failure was confirmed by the legalization. "The Civil War is history now and we feel no hatred for those who fought on the other side." The elections "will not yet be totally free. . . . We are going into the elections with our own identity. . . . We are a Marxist revolutionary party." The PCE electoral campaign would be geared against Alianza Popular (a right-wing democratic party).

On April 16, at the conclusion of the central committee's meeting, Carrillo stated that "the Spanish flag will always appear at the side of the Communist party flag in all its rallies." If the monarchy continued to "work with resolve to fully establish democracy . . . our party would regard it as an institutional and democratic regime." On April 24 Carrillo appeared before the party's provincial committee of Madrid which viewed unfavorably the decision on the flag. "If the flag of the state which has recognized us is that of the king, then we accept it because the state is no longer Franco's. . . . Spain is not a word devoid of meaning for the Communists but rather a historic reality. We will be the first to defend its unity." The committee of Madrid approved the decision of the central committee on the flag and monarchy. The first legal rally of the PCE took place in Valladolid.

May. On May 13 Ibárruri arrived in Madrid in a Soviet plane with her two Russian decorations: the Lenin Prize and the Order of October. Carrillo was not there to greet her. It was rumored that Moscow hoped that she would apply pro-Soviet pressure within the PCE. Camacho visited the USSR and expressed great praise for the Soviet regime. On television Carrillo said: "Suárez is beginning to keep his word." The Workers' Commissions opposed the general strike in Euzkadi in protest of police violence during a proamnesty week. The Bank of Bilbao and the Banco Popular granted loans to the PCE for the electoral campaign. The Bishop of Guadalajara forbade the celebration of a mass arranged by the PCE for May Day. The charges against Carrillo for illegal association in December were dismissed. The PCE's militants assaulted members carrying Republican flags in a rally at Getafe. At a rally in Bilbao Ibárruri sang the praises of the USSR and the "socialist countries" which have "showed the world that workers have no use for capitalism." Ibárruri would rarely be heard in public again. On May 24 the electoral campaign began. Carrillo's book *Eurocomunismo y Estado* was published.

The Elections and the Ninth Congress

The electoral campaign gave the PCE the chance to strengthen the image of the party as level-headed, responsible, moderate, tolerant, and democratic.[29] The memory of the past still weighed heavily both on the extreme Right and Left, but the PCE managed to draw votes from the middle class and young Catholics. It used a good part of its persuasive powers on the latter. The campaign was intense, very costly, without histrionics or incidents. A sector of the militants was unhappy with the campaign because they thought there was too great a concession of principles as well as despotism at times on the part of leaders. Some anecdotes will help to convey the tone. The headquarters of the Civil Guard in Málaga rejected the local PCE's letter of sympathy over the murder of two civil guards. The executive committee issued the order that no Communist lawyer could defend the militant Justo Bello who killed a Fascist who insulted him while selling *Mundo Obrero* in Valdemoro. The day before the elections Carrillo told a French newspaper that the PCE was favorable to a government of national union in which he would be willing to participate and which could be possibly presided over by Suárez. In Catalonia, and particularly in the city of Barcelona, PSUC carried out a less appeasing campaign than the PCE; to a great extent it was designed to attract immigrant votes.

The results of the elections were disappointing to the party. It got twelve representatives which together with eight from PSUC formed a minority of twenty, which was slightly higher than Fraga Iribarne's Alianza Popular. It did not get a single senator. Of the 17.5 million votes, the PCE-PSUC received 1.5 million (the PSOE, 4.9 million; UCD, 6 million; Alianza Popular, 1.4 million). The PCE culled 9.02 percent of the votes (compared to the 33 percent for the PSOE and 47 percent for the UCD). It won seats in Madrid, Barcelona, Tarragona, Valencia, Alicante, Málaga, Cádiz, Seville, Córdoba, and Asturias. The fact that PSUC got higher percentages than the PCE could indicate that the tactic of appeasement was not the most appropriate. Nonetheless the PCE continued with it as can be seen in the following chronology.

1977

June. Carrillo stated: "We consider the success of the PSOE as positive and we lament the failure of the Christian Democrats." At a meeting of the executive committee Carrillo said: "The PSOE must take part in the government." On June 28 in a speech before Parliament Carrillo proposed the formation of a "government of national concentration."

October. Felipe González told *Le Monde:* "The Eurocommunist parties lack credibility because of the contradiction between the way they function and the model for society which they propose." In the same paper Carrillo responded that the PSOE was governed by a centralism even more rigid than the communists'. The PSOE was mistaken to consider itself the leftist alternative. "The leftist union in France is capital to the entire European Left." "Our participation in power will be made possible tomorrow." On October 25 the PCE signed the Moncloa Pact, supporting the economic and social measures of the Suárez government.

On the 27th Carrillo gave a talk at the Club Siglo XXI. He was introduced by Fraga Iribarne who, as minister of information, had led the campaign to justify Julián Grimau's execution. "The Moncloa Pact proved that we were right . . . it is a policy of democratic concentration." The third congress of the Communist party of Euzkadi and the fourth of PSUC took place. Antonio Gutiérrez replaced López Raimundo as head of PSUC's, whose program no longer included dictatorship of the proletariat. Roberto Lertxundi replaced Ormazábal in the Euzkadi Communist party. Both parties' attempts to achieve greater autonomy from the PCE failed.

November. Carrillo was not allowed to speak at the commemorative ceremonies of the sixtieth anniversary of the Russian Revolution which took place in Moscow. They said it was because he arrived late. The PCE publicized this incident as much as it could. Before his return to Spain, Líster, while still in Paris, attacked Carrillo saying that the incident in Moscow allowed him to go home "as a martyr of Eurocommunism."

Carrillo visited the United States just a few days prior to Felipe González's trip. At Yale University where there was a strike by non-instructional personnel he crossed the picket line and said that the picketers had been brought in from other places to create an incident (they were actually all strikers). Radio Liberty (which has a transmitter at Pals, in the province of Gerona) broadcast Carrillo's statements on Eurocommunism to the USSR.

Upon returning from the United States he announced that the PCE would no longer call itself Leninist and would be satisfied with being "revolutionary Marxist." He also said that German Social Democracy had an important part in Felipe González's trip to the United States and immediately added: "We are not at war with the PSOE." Nicolás Redondo, of the UGT, called Camacho a liar during a television debate. Upon his return from the United States, Felipe González said that Suárez could bring about a Popular Front by favoring the Communists on the trade union level and that he would thereby "jeopardize the future of the country."

December. The PCE proposed an electoral alliance to the PSOE for the municipal elections and spoke of forming "democratic candidacies." The PSOE was not interested. At the same time the PCE defended the Moncloa Pact and complained of the government's unilateral interpretation of it. The party also proposed periodical consultation with those who had signed it, which is to say, the establishment of a supragovernment. "It is not a good idea to involve the military in keeping public order," said Carrillo. He had just returned from a visit with Tito. He insisted that Spain not join NATO. An opinion poll indicated that only 38 percent of Spaniards knew what Eurocommunism was, and that of this 38 percent 57 percent did not believe in its sincerity. Of those who voted Communist, 26 percent did not believe in it and 31 percent did not know what it was about.

1978

January. The central committee determined that the representatives of the PCE would not discuss the monarchy in the drafting of the Constitution. On January 12 Carrillo said: "Felipe González would govern the same as Suárez." On the 17th he said: "Socialists and Communists will end up joining forces."

March. Carrillo came out in favor of nuclear plants.

April. Plans were made for the PCE's ninth congress. There were problems among the rank and file. Some of them were raised by the new members who were opposed to the excess of centralism; others by the elder members who opposed Carrillo's announcement that Leninism was going to be abandoned. As for PSUC—a party whose statutes defined it as "Marxist-Leninist"—*Treball* opposed the Leninist tendency but recognized that the weekly had a circulation of 10,000 as opposed to the 16,000 of the last days when it was semiunderground. Six members of the Central Committee of PSUC resigned, but an executive committee was reelected from which Gutiérrez and López Raimundo had previously resigned under criticism from the "White Flag" tendency. For the first time the PSUC Executive Committee was not elected unanimously. In Málaga the Leninists attacked Carrillo and 23 members were expelled. In Aragon those who supported abandoning Leninism were victorious as they were in other places, including Asturias where Leninists were powerful. One hundred and thirteen Asturian delegates walked out of the regional conference because of the antidemocratic procedures under which it was conducted. The Valencian and Balearic Communist parties approved Thesis 15 which proposed the abandonment of Leninism.

Carrillo had to attend some of the regional conferences and managed to have the local leaders win out over the militants everywhere. The people coming from the Workers' Commissions were the ones who gave him the victory.

The same would happen at the ninth congress which began in a luxury hotel in Madrid on April 19. The day before, the central committee, despite the Asturian Vicente Álvarez Areces's negative vote, had approved the report to be read by Carrillo. The press was frantic and provided the party with a huge amount of free publicity believing that there would be great debates. There were no debates but neither was there unanimity. With two votes against, not even the chairman was elected unanimously. Thirty-five delegates voted against the bylaws of the congress and 80 abstained. In his report Carrillo defended the Moncloa Pact, criticized the PSOE, did not mention the elections but said that what was important was the trade union elections, and he opposed Spain's entry in NATO. In the discussion of the report it was clear that the men of the Workers' Commissions controlled the congress. There was criticism of the "too close" relationship between Carrillo and Suárez as well as of "too harsh" attacks on the PSOE. The Andalusian delegation was the most bitter; it proposed removing the adverb *probably* from the sentence in the report that said "the party probably made mistakes." The discussion in commissions of the theses was heated, especially Thesis 15. Several theses were modified to the extent that by the time the congress closed Carrillo had become friendlier toward the Socialists and more aggressive toward Suárez. The discussion of Thesis 15 produced the statement that the removal of the word *Leninist* did not change anything and that the party was no longer the only working-class party in view of the fact that the Socialists were not "socialist democrats." A member of the Workers' Commissions from Catalonia spoke for the Leninists. When it came time to vote, there were 248 votes for Leninism, 968 for Carrillo, and 40 abstentions. La Pasionaria was absent from the discussion of Thesis 15 but she gave the closing speech. Carrillo and Ibárruri were reelected. A 160-member central committee was elected which in turn elected the executive committee which then chose the secretariat. The secretariat was made up of Ibárruri, Carrillo, Azcárate, Álvarez, Sánchez Montero, Brabo, Ballesteros, Lertxundi, Gutiérrez, Tamames, Camacho, Gallego, Romero Marín, Soto, Sartorius, Melchor, and Lobato. Marchais and Berlinguer were not among the many invited but Afanasiev, the editor of *Pravda*, was. He said that Marxism-Leninism was a "victorious doctrine" and that "Eurocommunism did not exist." He gave Carrillo a life-sized picture of Lenin. Incidentally, *Pravda* made no mention of Thesis 15. Unlike previous ones, the ninth congress was not unanimous.

The elements coming from the Workers' Commissions saved Carrillo in the regional assemblies and the congress and probably got paid back "administratively" (they already had a considerable number of posts in the central and executive committees as well as in the secretariat), but it seemed doubtful that they could modify the party line. Carrillo showed that he was in control of the party machinery and was still the boss. The congress did not modify the conduct of the party which continued to be one of "slow penetration" in the administration, publishing houses, education, television, and radio. There was no change in Carrillo's attitude toward the Socialists, which was to alternately criticize them and suggest unifying with them. Nor did the congress alter the tactic of the Workers' Commissions which consisted of (1) supporting the workers who wanted to strike in order to win them over, and (2) ordering the end of the strike upon achieving some minimum concession in order to make management see more clearly that it was easier to get along with the Communists than with the Socialists or Anarcho-Syndicalists. This line was seen more clearly in the discussion of the Constitution, during which the representatives of the PCE were the ones who least frequently disagreed and who more often used pressure to reach a consensus on all points. On April 26 Carrillo said: "There is no one in the Center that can govern better than Suárez." According to a PCE document the party could ally itself with the UCD in the municipal elections "wherever it was necessary to eradicate bossism."

May. In Gijón Carrillo said: "A Socialist government without Communists would not change things much." In Madrid he said: "This country will not be able to be governed without us." On May 30 there was a congress of the Union of Communist Youths. José Palau was elected secretary general. He declared his "independence" of the PCE. A Bulgarian guest who praised the USSR was booed. The Soviet delegation left having been booed with cries of "Freedom of expression is revolution too." Carrillo and Camacho spoke at the congress, which invited the Socialist Youths to work with the Communist Youths. On May 31 Carrillo said: "The country is disillusioned with the Socialists and the Center. . . . Either we have nuclear energy or underdevelopment."

June. In Bilbao Carrillo said: "There is no Communist solution for the Basque country." In a meeting with employers Carrillo said: "A government of concentration would solve the problem of low productivity, given the strength of the Communist party among workers." The Madrid police provided documents from their files for a historical exhibit organized by the Workers' Commissions. The central committee considered the constitutional project as "very positive." So it favored voting "yes" on the referendum on the Constitution. On June 20 the Communist representatives of the PCE and PSUC voted against the inclusion of the right of the regions to self-determination in the text of the Constitution. On June 23 the PCE joined the Federal Council of the European Movement. On June 26 the first congress of the Workers' Commissions was held. Camacho was reelected secretary general. It approved a "program of reconversion and economic recovery," a name given by the PCE to its social pact project. The PCE came out against nationalization of the pharmaceutical industry.

July. The Communist representatives voted in favor of the text of the Constitution.

Eurocommunism

What is called Eurocommunism[30]—a term coined by the liberal Italian journalist Indro Montanelli—is, in short, the elimination of some dogmas for tactical reasons. It responds to the discovery—made long ago by the Socialists—that in industrial societies the working class is not in the majority and coups to overtake power—unless one has Soviet arms or the Red Army behind him—are not possible. Consequently, ways had to be found to achieve power that were different from those of the Soviet model of 1917. For those Communist parties for which the possibility of gaining power was real—although not immediate—this turnabout took on the form of Eurocommunism, that is, the recognition of liberties which so far had been pejoratively called "formal" as well as the recognition of the mechanisms of "formal" democracy (including the plurality of political parties and the possibility of losing power through elections). It also entailed the subsequent renunciation, at least verbal, of the Communist party's monopoly of representation of the working class and of the dictatorship of the proletariat. In other words, Eurocommunism was an attempt to appear as a party just like any other.

On the theoretical plane, this was the equivalent of abandoning the Soviet model as well as—carried to its logical conclusion—Leninism which had inspired it. It was also becoming evident that the persistent loyalty to the USSR prevented the possibility of assuming power and destroyed Eurocommunism's credibility. It was necessary to become detached from the USSR. In 1968 Czechoslovakia provided the opportunity.

We have already seen how, beginning in 1956, the policy of national reconciliation was gradually watering down Leninism. Carrillo saw to it that this happened and is to be credited with the formulation of Spanish-style Eurocommunism. Azcárate was in charge of separating from Moscow. This was a long process whose highlights were the tactical dropping of dictatorship of the proletariat in the plenary of 1973 (which initiated the slogan of the "Spanish route to socialism") and the abandonment of Leninism in the ninth congress in 1978. This long process did not include a single theoretical essay or any factual analysis to support those changes in party stance and doctrine.

In the same way that Czechoslovakia was an excuse to draw away from the USSR (an excuse later repeated with the trials of the Soviet dissidents which the PCE criticized), Portugal's military escapade of 1974–75 (and the Portuguese Communist party's reaction to it) enabled the PCE, while criticizing the Stalinism of Alvaro Cunhal, to underscore the changes which they said had taken place in the Spanish party itself. Carrillo knew enough to take advantage of what could otherwise have been dangerous for Eurocommunism. "The Portuguese Communist party's maneuvering is a good example of how not to make a revolution," he said, and he condemned the occupation of Lisbon's Socialist newspaper *República* by its Communist employees: "Imagine if the typographers took over our *Mundo Obrero* and ran it themselves."[31]

He also managed to take advantage of a similar revision in the Italian Communist party for the same reasons but under other circumstances and with other slogans which Togliatti had initiated shortly before his death. Contact between the Spanish and Italian Communist parties became more frequent and closer. They collaborated in the conferences and meetings of the Communist parties which Moscow convened, in order to maintain a certain "independence" and claim the right of alternate channels to power. There were likewise special relations with the French Communist party, for the same reasons but to a lesser degree, since Marchais was more hesitant and less intense in his Eurocommunism.[32]

The theoretical bases for Eurocommunism appear in Antonio Gramsci's thesis of the "historical bloc." The elitist and paternalistic nature of this concept is evident although recently it has been disguised. In this sense, Gramsci was a Leninist, but he disagreed with Lenin in giving the intellectuals a more important role than "professional revolutionaries" in the party and in the "construction of socialism." The PCE transformed this into "the alliance of the forces of work and culture," together with the pact for liberty. Eurocommunism—like Spain's experience with political reform and transition to democracy generally—interested the Soviet and Eastern European dissidents because they saw hope for the evolution of their Communist parties as well as the transformation of their regimes. Furthermore, they found a defense, until now purely verbal, in the Eurocommunist parties.

In his book *Eurocomunismo y Estado,* Carrillo states that the dictatorship of the proletariat is not valid "for developed capitalist countries.

In those countries the forces of work and culture can exercise their hegemony by maintaining, increasing, and developing existent democratic liberties." But he explicitly adds that "if someone thought of implementing the methods and solutions of Eurocommunism in the Third World he would be irrevocably mistaken. What is called Eurocommunism is valid in the developed nations of Western Europe and other continents, but I do not consider it valid for the Third World."[33] In other words, liberty, democracy, a local approach to socialism, and pluralism woud not be accepted on principle because they are considered inherently good, but rather as a tactic since they could be profitable for a specific situation—the current stage of development of the capitalist world. For the people of Africa, Asia, and Latin America, Leninism, the Soviet model, the dictatorship of the proletariat, and other traditional dogmas are suitable. Eurocommunism, then, is not the result of revulsion toward the reality of Stalinism and Leninism, but rather an adaptation—as was the Popular Front, for example—to a given situation.

Transference of Loyalties

Separation from the USSR was the most difficult and essential part in moving toward Eurocommunism, since without it the evolution lacked credibility. The members, especially the older ones, the most solid support for the leaders, had been trained in blind, uncompromising loyalty to the USSR which outlived both the German-Soviet pact and de-Stalinization. There were also powerful material interests. The PCE survived thanks to aid from the USSR, and even though that aid might be substituted by aid from Romania, Yugoslavia, and the Italian Communist party, it could never be as considerable as Soviet aid.

Carrillo moved with lead feet. If it had not been for what happened in Czechoslovakia in 1968 he might not have gotten his own way. In 1964, speaking of de-Stalinization and in reply to Claudín and Semprún, he said that there had been police and concentration camps in the USSR, "but these institutions were necessary and I'm not sure that they aren't also necessary in other socialist revolutions even if under more favorable conditions. What alarms and disgusts me is not that police and camps, etc. existed, but rather the use that Stalin made of them during a given period."[34]

That he still considered those institutions to be necessary was, for example, proved by the fact that the PCE never had a word of criticism for Mao's China on his methods but only—and for a short time—on his separation from the Communist camp. Nor did he even criticize Fidel Castro's methods (Carrillo made another trip to Cuba in 1978.)

He justified the good relations between Castro and Franco saying that "he needed those relations to break the American bloc [sic]."[35]

Although the PCE criticized the arrival of Russian tanks in Prague and the trials against some of the dissidents, those statements were mere gestures which did not touch the real issue. For example, Spanish Communists evidently found Solzhenitsyn's remarks on Spanish television in 1976 very satisfying. He said that the Soviet regime was worse than Franco's, but the Communists called this remark (which was obviously true) a defense of Francoism as well as a discredit to one of Moscow's most bothersome dissidents. Carrillo said: "He has become a propagandist for the [Franco] regime. . . . I am afraid that the next time I see Brezhnev he'll say: 'Now you see we were right.' " In 1977 Amalrik invited Carrillo to a public debate on his interpretation of the Soviet Union but the invitation was turned down. The PCE has maintained positions in international politics which reflect the diplomatic interests of the USSR even if by doing so it damaged the image the Spaniards had of the party. For instance, when the party defended the Polisario Front (which was in obvious contradiction—although it was otherwise quite legitimate—to Spain's official policy). Another instance of this was when, at the risk of discrediting the Suárez government, for which Carrillo had such praise, the party at the Belgrade Conference on the implementation of the Helsinki accords denounced the treatment given Spanish émigré workers in West Germany. It did so for the obvious purpose of diverting criticism of human rights violations in the USSR or of giving Moscow the hackneyed line of "look who's talking."[36] Another example of the PCE policy's reflecting Moscow's interests was the fact that it did not say anything against holding the World Soccer Championship in Buenos Aires under General Videla's regime because that government was supported by the Argentine Communist party. But the most visible case of service to the USSR was Carrillo's change of policy on NATO: in Washington he came out in support of Spain's entry, but later opposed it and has since stood firm in his opposition.

Does all this mean that the separation from Moscow was propagandistic fiction? I think not. What it does mean is that the withdrawal is just a method of lending credibility to Eurocommunism and of forcing the Russians to accept it, but it is not a criticism or a radical condemnation of the Soviet system. The PCE has not made an in-depth Marxist analysis of the Soviet Union, the causes of Stalinism, how it came about, nor why the PCE from its very foundation always obeyed instructions from the Communist International. The explanation is the same as for France and Italy: Stalinism was a result of the backwardness of Czarist Russia, which does not explain why in more advanced countries there were also

Stalinist movements, nor the PCE's orthodox Stalinism. Here we are using the same argument Carrillo used when he said that Eurocommunism was not suitable for the Third World. Apparently it is not suitable for the Russians either since for example the PCE has never been critical of the fact that the USSR does not have a plurality of parties, free elections, and the other things that the PCE was demanding for Spain. Essentially it is a matter of unconscious racism: there are nations suited for freedom (Spain) and others that are not (USSR, China, Cuba).

The ambiguity the PCE felt toward the USSR was reciprocated by the Kremlin. Since the PCE went farther than any other Communist party in its commitment to Eurocommunism, Soviet criticism of the PCE has been stronger. But at no time has it exceeded the limits of "fraternal criticism" nor has it cut off the PCE's access to Moscow or Communist conferences. Moscow, in the conference of Communist parties of June 1976 in East Berlin, reluctantly agreed to have "proletarian internationalism" replaced by "international solidarity," and "Marxism-Leninism" by "scientific socialism." It also agreed to a discussion of "free choice of the various roads to a communist society."[37]

If it was indeed true that the "summit conference" of Eurocommunism in Madrid (the meeting of Marchais, Berlinguer, and Carrillo in March 1977) deserved criticism by some Communist parties (namely East Germany, Czechoslovakia, and later Romania), there was not a word of criticism of the USSR in the statement of the "summit." And if it is true that Carrillo said in *Der Spiegel* that the Soviets were ruled by a minority, although this minority "thinks it is acting in the name of socialism," and that the USSR "is not the socialist state that Marx, Engels, or Lenin" had proposed, it is no less true that he made this statement in reply to an essay by the Polish dissident Leszek Kolakowski on the definition of socialism. If one compares Soviet reactions to Eurocommunism and Maoism it becomes immediately apparent that the former is for show, open to arrangements and without rupture. Let us say that Eurocommunism has not established the PCE's independence from Moscow, just its autonomy. It is a considerable achievement, but less than the PCE wanted people to think.

It is not that Moscow viewed favorably the departure from the dictatorship of the proletariat and Leninism, and particularly separation from the USSR, but it accepted it and no doubt intended to take as much advantage as possible of a phenomenon it could not prevent from happening. There are enough means for Eurocommunist parties to continue supporting Moscow although in a less visible way. For example, there are numerous Soviet multinationals, some of which have roles in Eurocommunist parties (the Italian Communist party controls importation and exportation with the USSR; the French Communist party does the same; one of Carrillo's sons is an executive of a commercial firm that deals with Eastern countries). And there surely are other less-known links.[38] For a policy of coexistence, Eurocommunism with its open loyalty to the USSR, is probably more useful than traditional Communist parties. Besides, if Eurocommunism ever became powerful, it could provoke a serious crisis in NATO. The PCE's semicritical attitude toward the USSR, in any event, is a reality for party members, especially for young members not trained in Soviet patriotism. This presents a problem for the leaders: since the cement of party monolithism was Soviet patriotism—what is going to keep the party going in the absence of this patriotism? That is the real problem facing Eurocommunism.

From a Means to an End

The USSR is no longer the goal for Spanish Communists. For them the party was a means to this end. Thanks to Eurocommunism, the party has evolved from being a means into being an end in and of itself. How does the party see itself? "It is the only Spanish political party that had no responsibility in losing the Civil War."[39] "While the others retired to their winter quarters, so to speak, the PCE was alone in opposing, in a definitive way, Franco's dictatorship. . . . The Communists were the first and by far the greatest in number. . . . They are the representatives today of the basic political strength of the opposition."[40]

It is actually a monolithic party, although not as much as it used to be. Democratic centralism—the organizational system Lenin imposed on the Bolshevik party and which Stalin imposed on all Communist parties—remains the norm. Factions and dissidents are not allowed. We have already seen that the move toward Eurocommunism was made without consulting the rank and file; it was made by a decision of the leaders. The latter constitute a gerontocracy, even though in the last two years they have taken in new members. But decisions are still made by the older members. It is the only Communist party that has today the same leaders it had during Stalin's time. Marchais and Berlinguer were mere apprentices when Carrillo and La Pasionaria were leaders. It is leadership that did not accomplish anything, was out of touch with reality, and issued order after order without any apparent results. Only when it was backed by Soviet arms (during the Civil War) did it achieve real power (in the same way that only with the presence of the Red Army did the Communists take over Eastern Europe). It is a leadership that distrusts all criticism because it did not do a single thing that did not deserve it. At the ninth congress, professionals and intellectuals who

were more inclined to dissension were replaced by members of the
Workers' Commissions who were more disciplined. The professionals
had their own means of livelihood and so it was more difficult to subdue
them. Paid militants are economically dependent on party leaders. So
the party is a big bureaucratic machine. If it achieves power, so much
the better; if it does not, the important thing is for the machine to keep
on functioning. The French Communist party would have rather had
the Left lose the election of 1978 than for the party to lose influence
and for the Socialists to gain it.

Ideologically, the PCE is no longer a communist party in the traditional
sense of the term, but neither is it a social democratic party because it
lacks internal democracy and has too long a history. This "excess of
history" has determined its advance so far along the road to Eurocommunism, which has also involved a transference of loyalties to maintain
the monolithism and a means of erasing history. As much as Carrillo
justifies the past, he never makes a thorough study of it. When Semprún
wanted to talk about it, Carrillo snapped that "to rummage around in
the past is a petty bourgeois sort of masochism." This past was systematically falsified not only in *Historia del PCE* and in Ibárruri's memoirs
written fifteen years before, but also in *Demain, l'Espagne* and *Eurocomunismo y Estado* written within the last five years. Every word
written by Ibárruri and Carrillo is a lie. For example, in an interview
with Fallaci, Carrillo said: "for three years I was in the Civil War
shooting and killing, and I was even involved in guerrilla warfare . . .
and I don't know whether I'm a good shot, but I do know that I aimed
to kill and I did kill." This is pure fable. Carrillo went to the front only
to visit (besides, his nearsightedness would have kept him from fighting
on the front), and the closest he got to guerrilla warfare was in the Arán
Valley just in time to order a retreat.[41]

The PCE's Balance Sheet

The PCE was tied to the Communist International, and when the CI
disappeared, it was directly connected to the CPSU. The balance of its
work for sixty years can be no different from that of the international
Communist movement. This movement divided the labor movement;
it also corrupted it and submitted a portion of it to the interests of the
USSR, and in no way helped the workers or the Left generally. The
same can be said of its Spanish branch. The PCE says it is Marxist.
But it has not produced a single theoretician. Nor has there been a
single worthwhile book written by an active member of the party. Those
published were written after their authors left the party. Some economists

and historians who have written serious books have only produced propaganda since they joined the party. The PCE is considered part of the labor movement. Yet none of the progress made thanks to the movement can be credited to the PCE. When workers tried to join in the Alianza Obrera in 1934, the PCE fought it. On the other hand, the PCE arose from schisms in the PSOE and the CNT, it tried to divide the labor union movement with its CGTU, and then later divided it with its Workers' Commissions.

Whenever a Socialist or Anarchist is disillusioned with his party, he goes to another group. But whenever a Communist in disillusioned with the PCE, he usually heads home and is lost for the labor movement. Someone said that if all the ex-Communists got together they would make up the largest party in the country. But they do not unite, because they are so disillusioned that generally they refuse to continue to fight at all. The small number that do persist form the groups or "grouplets" that make up the mosaic of the nation's labor movement. They are usually groups which retain a Stalinist mentality; almost all are a product of PCE schisms. The PCE, on the rebound, has fragmented the labor movement and the Left. The PCE is to blame for some catastrophic attitudes in the labor movement and the Left. Chronologically, the first was the Popular Front. It prevented the formation of another Alianza Obrera, electoral in nature, which could have won in February 1936. The Popular Front at the time had brought the labor movement to a screeching halt. The second Communist initiative was the crushing of the revolutionary conquests of 1936. With its slogan of "Win the war first," the PCE—taking advantage of the purchase of Soviet arms which were paid for in advance—drew the conservative forces of the Republican zone to it. Under the pretext of winning the war, the PCE overthrew Largo Caballero's government, destroyed the collectivizations, persecuted, slandered, and murdered numerous Spanish revolutionaries and foreigners who had gone to fight in Spain, and finally it lost the war. We do not know whether the revolutionary strategy could have won the Civil War, but we do know that it was lost with the strategy of the PCE. In the first stage of resistance to Francoism, the PCE remained distant from opposition forces. It later sent many with high hopes on the bloody adventure of the National Union, thereby demoralizing and alarming a sector of public opinion which otherwise could have been drawn to active opposition.

In the second stage of the opposition—the period of "liberalization" of Francoism—the PCE issued slogans for national reconciliation which turned out to be ineffective. Stalin's advice guided the policy of the PCE from 1948 on; indeed, Eurocommunism is nothing but one method of applying this advice from "the helmsman of world revolution." The PCE did not create any organizations but it did take over several created by others (Workers' Commissions, student groups, and neighborhood associations) and used them for its own purposes. Before Franco died it divided the opposition with the Junta Democrática; upon Franco's death, with its slogan of "rupture," it isolated the opposition and deprived it of any influence during the transition to democracy.

So the PCE has a negative balance sheet. It is actually more negative than those of other Communist parties because they made no contribution at all, while the PCE dared to go further and actively and forcibly opposed, by means of slander and murder, a revolutionary experiment which, being different from that of the Soviets, was the first to take place after the Russian Revolution and perhaps could have brought victory to the Republic. Neither Marxism, the Left, nor the accomplishments of the labor movement were due to the work of the PCE. And the latter, with the aid of the sale of Russian arms and the Russian political police, caused the labor movement to lose what it had won in 1936.

The Reasons for Eurocommunism

The reasons for the Eurocommunism of the PCE must be looked for in its balance sheet. If the Italian Communist party was the first to begin to brighten up its facade, the PCE brought about visible changes in its own. Until several years ago the PCE was one of the parties most obedient to Moscow's policies. Why then, at least on paper, did it go so far that it could not be distinguished from the most moderate social democratic parties? Why had it gone so far that it adopted toward the USSR the position that Kautsky took in his polemic with Trotsky which was no different from the position held by Besteiro in the PSOE congress of 1921?

In politics things do not simply happen nor do they happen because of the whim of some leader or other. The "whims" of leaders are not without reason. The verbal evolution of the PCE has a reason and there must also be a reason for the fact that that evolution was more rapid and accentuated than that of other Communist parties. It is not that the PCE was more "diabolical and evil," corrupt, Stalinist, or brutal than other Communist parties. But the situations that the history of the country placed it in were such that they brought out all the negative potential of the party, the "best" of the Stalinist mentality. Out of loyalty to Moscow, it was required to show its worst side, and it did. Without the Civil War the PCE possibly would not have been Eurocommunist, or if the Civil War had occurred in another international context, at a time when it suited Moscow to foment a revolution in Spain, the PCE still would not have felt the need to change its direction or image. Present-day Eurocommunism is the result of the ultra-Stalinism of days gone by.

For the very reason that the PCE has much to forget and ask forgiveness for, its Eurocommunism must be more spectacular. Some PCE leaders have spoken of mistakes. None has spoken of crimes, and none has analyzed why those admitted mistakes happened. And there certainly has been no analysis of why those yet-to-be-recognized crimes were committed. What they have done is try to erase some of the mistakes and crimes from memory by appearing to be good, level-headed, responsible boys. It is a difficult task to use today's Communists to overcome the memory of yesterday's, especially when the same men are still leading the party. Only because so much time has gone by and there have been two generations which did not witness those days of hatred has the PCE been able to even hope that by changing its face people would forget or at least not notice. Is it not significant that of the great mass of literature on the Civil War very little has been written by people in the PCE? Is it not significant that the PCE so often mentions its opposition during the second stage of Francoism but hardly says a word about the first stage?

There is another reason why the PCE went so far. The country was modernized, clearly less than it would have been without Franco, but it was modernized nonetheless. The Soviet model is no longer of any use for a society and economy like Spain's. No Spaniard would want to live like Russians do today. The PCE's programs of the past no longer work. Eurocommunism is an attempt to adapt the underlying Stalinism of every Communist party to the realities of industrial society of the last quarter of the twentieth century. But in the same way that modernization of Spanish society does not make it less exploiting and capitalist, modernization of the PCE does not make it less Stalinist. The Eurocommunism of the PCE is not the result of a theoretical evolution, of reflection and recognition of errors and crimes, but rather the natural consequence of changes in society combined with the desire to forget the past of the PCE itself. This adaptation could have taken other shapes, for example, the return to a purist verbal radicalism. Why did the PCE choose to give in to the "social democratic temptation" instead of the "ultrarevolutionary temptation?"

Power for Power's Sake

Industrial societies have changed profoundly in the last half century. The working class is getting smaller and is no longer in the majority.

People employed in service occupations, with a middle-class mentality, are growing in number. Peasants are disappearing. Under these conditions the Communist party of industrial nations cannot remain faithful to their old slogans. The unified front from below is no longer viable since even if it came about, it would not form a majority. It would be absurd to talk of social fascism since fascism is not a threat, and so that slogan has been replaced by one that says "the Socialists want to manage capitalism." The middle class, executives, and university students must be won over in order to achieve power. To that end the PCE abandoned the slogans and theoretical positions that might have scared away those social groups (dictatorship of the proletariat and single party), but it kept what it needed to manipulate them: democratic centralism, Stalinist methods of action, intellectual terrorism, and amalgam and defamation of the competition and critics.

Changes in facade have not modified the essence of the party. It is no longer an instrument destined to achieve the goals of socialism or a classless society, but rather has become an end in itself. Today the party is a power machine. The Communists are the technocrats of power just as executives are the technocrats of profit. The ideas are the same; only appearances have changed. Eurocommunism is a cosmetic operation. If evidence were needed, it would be the Communists' persistence that the PCE is untouchable. When Jorge Semprún published his *Autobiografía de Federico Sánchez*, Carrillo complained: "We are no longer pointing the finger at anyone for responsibility for Franco's forty-year control of power; we are discarding the PSOE's historical criticism during that period (the Civil War and prior), and it appears that those who have been fighting the dictatorship will be put on trial. I think we are facing an anti-Communist trap in which various individuals are participating for various reasons."

Spanish Eurocommunists say: We will not criticize the Francoists or the Socialists on the condition that they do not criticize us. If we are criticized, it is not out of disagreement with our positions but because there is some mysterious sort of conspiracy. It is a matter of not doing one's duty—that of analyzing one's adversaries—in exchange for the adversary's not doing his: analyzing the Communists. If they do not follow suit, if they make an analysis, they are threatened with the old trick of the amalgam. All this is a replay of the way things were in the Spain of 1937. It is not a matter of revolution, socialism, or the working class. It is plainly a matter of power, of which the PCE wants a share. It wants to repeat its experience of 1937–39: to have a share of the power and gradually increase it until it is in complete control. In 1937–39 it was in service to the USSR putting an end to the revolution. Today it simply would be to serve the party. In 1937 they made use of the

blackmail of Russian arms. Today it is the blackmail of the Workers'
Commissions and the possibility of thereby manipulating a sector of
workers. If we are accepted in sharing power we will call a halt to the
strikes; if not, we will increase them.

Lenin is still very much alive in the PCE despite the ninth congress,
but it is a Stalinized and bureaucratized Lenin with large carpeted offices
in buildings purchased so that party bureaucrats could feel at home.
With the PCE in power—or with part of the power in the hands of the
PCE or simply with the PCE in power of its leaders—relations between
rulers and ruled would not change. In the name of change, the past is
relived; in the name of truth lies are repeated; in the name of freedom
there is coercion; in the name of equality favors are given to friends
whoever they may be. The "salami tactic" which had been tried out in
Spain in 1937–39 and which was successfully implemented in the "popular
democracies" of 1944–48 is once again being used in Spain. Eurocommunism is being used to disguise the fatty and rotten salami as a First
Communion meat pie.

The PCE has always been one to short-change by substituting slogans
for political analysis. In the past it was the inflammatory slogan which
rang of revolution and which never led to anything. Now—as during
the Civil War—it is the appeasing slogan which led to the Republican
defeat. Where it can lead today is anybody's guess. Precedents indicate
that the PCE has always had good leaders who have known how to
control the party and keep alive the patriotism of its members—formerly
Soviet patriotism, now party patriotism. But it has never had politicians
or statesmen. None of the party's slogans has ever been successful. I
repeat: never. The party has always been a political failure, but it has
survived and grown. That proves that its leaders are as good at party
machinery as they are bad politicians. That provides us with an en-
lightening bit of information: the party's best leaders have come from
Socialism: Carrillo, Comorera (as Gottwald in Czechoslovakia, for example.) And the double-dealers as well: Vidiella, López Raimundo,
Cazorla. Every time they have drawn Socialists to unify, it has been for
the purpose of absorbing them: the JSU, PSUC. Most of those who had
been expelled had Communist backgrounds: Monzón, Quiñones, Hernández, Del Barrio, Castro Delgado, Claudín, Semprún.

Since it became a reformist party through its propaganda, why does
it not call itself such? Because the party continues to be Stalinist. The
very way it changed its program was Stalinist. Carrillo said that the
difference between the PCE and the Socialists was that the latter wanted
to manage capitalism while the PCE wanted to establish socialism.

However, the party never explained what that socialism would consist of. At most, it said that it would not be like the Soviet brand (assuming it be socialism). But in none of its books or dealings did it explain how a nondemocratic party could respect and maintain democracy if it held power nor how its "socialism" would be different from the Soviet model aside from the promise that it would be democratic. It criticized the USSR but did not reject Soviet imperialism or refuse to play its game. It exalted democracy and freedom but never said why they were consubstantial with socialism; on the contrary, it explained and justified its failure in the USSR by historical reasons and did not deem them appropriate to the Third World.

In addition to what has already been said, Eurocommunism is a tactic of penetration. Carrillo saw that the Communists did not gain anything by force anywhere, and he also saw that wherever they were victorious—thanks to the Russians—they were unable to destroy the machinery of the bourgeois state but rather appropriated it themselves. Instead of a coup from without he wants to effect it from within. That explains the penetration in as many social sectors as possible and in particular the state machinery. The failure of the rupture was, in this sense, a bitter lesson which the PCE made better use of than anyone else. "The left wing [read the PCE] ought to take over the machinery of the state in order to transform it, for without it there is no revolution."[42] The policy of the PCE has been to proclaim at midnight that it was noon—and when there have been competent leaders they have said not only that it was noon, but three, six, and nine o'clock. The people thought they were crazy. But when it came to be three, six, nine, and then noon, it appeared that the PCE was right.[43] The terrible part is that it was not simply a matter of a play on words or political double talk, because there have been thousands of members and sympathizers who believed that it was noon at midnight because they adhered to their belief, went to jail, exile, or the gallows.

In this bloody game, the PCE is assisted by a poor collective memory. Franco, by preventing the study of the past, made things easier for the PCE. No one remembers, for example, the incident referred to when the JSU was formed. At the time, forty-five years ago, Carrillo wrote: "The fussy and addlebrained members [of the PSOE] live in mortal fear that we will try to attack the party to impose a dictatorship upon it as well as squelch all internal democracy and then assign the party to the Third International." Carrillo himself confirmed these fears with the JSU. Now the "fussy and addlebrained members" of other parties fear that the Communists are promising freedom in order to implant dictatorship, and affirm independence to later render submission to the

USSR. Experience reveals that this is what they did. And there is nothing to indicate that if they could they would not try to do it again.

Return to the Miniparty

Chances are slim for it to succeed, since the PCE is in the process of becoming again the miniparty it was until 1936. Not long after the ninth congress, dissenting voices surfaced inside the party from three tendencies: the Stalinists (thereafter popularly called *afganos*), anxious to eradicate Eurocommunism and encouraged by Moscow (where the failure of Líster's Workers' Communist party caused disappointment); the "renovators," who wanted more internal democracy and the end of Carrillo's reign, and which included mostly recent militants, contrary to the *afganos* made up mostly of old-guard militants; and disparate positions of many intellectuals (Ramón Tamames being the best known), popular singers, and artists who had infiltrated everywhere and served the PCE unconditionally, but started to abandon it when they saw the party stagnate. In the 1979 general elections, the PCE and PSUC maintained their positions (a total of 23 representatives). The same year, in the municipal elections, they succeeded in being present in a majority of municipal councils and frequently formed a coalition with Socialists in city governments.

But those accomplishments could not stop the party's internal decay. Conflicts erupted and expulsions took place in Asturias, Valencia, Andalucia, and finally in the Basque country, when the Basque CP (led by Roberto Lerxtundi) merged with a leftist nationalist group. The PCE refused the merger, expelled its partisans (but it took place anyway), and formed a new CP of Euskadi with old militants. Many intellectuals and militants with diverse responsibilities grabbed this opportunity to side with the Basques. They were expelled (Manuel Azcárate, Carrillo's right-hand man in international matters, representative Pilar Brabo, and several Madrid city councilmen). Their dissatisfaction arose from being unable to bring about the victory of the "renovating" tendency at the PCE's tenth congress (July 1981). The crisis erupted also in Catalonia, where, at the fifth congress of PSUC (January 1981), an alliance between *afganos* and Leninists (a tendency of young communists who viewed the party policy as too moderate) managed to displace the previous leadership, only to see it return to power during the sixth congress (March 1982). The *afganos* seceded and formed the Partit Comunista dels Catalans (led by Pedro Ardiaca), which does not seem to prosper despite abundant means at their disposal.

The results of regional elections for autonomous parliaments were disastrous for the PCE in Galicia and Andalucia, while PSUC held its positions in Catalonia. Confronted with this failure, Carrillo offered to resign, but the central committee asked him to remain in his post. For the dissatisfied, this was taken as proof that Carrillo controlled the apparatus and caused new desertions. The expelled militants and those who had left the party joined in a new Asociación para la Renovación de la Izquierda (ARI), which in the October 1982 general elections supported the Socialists.

The Socialists, whose influence grew during those years, were the target of constant verbal attacks from the Communists. Notwithstanding the coalition with them in municipal governments, the Communists did not abandon their old antagonism toward Socialists, accused of aspiring to administrate capitalism (an echo of a French CP slogan). This anti-Socialist campaign did not harm the PSOE which, in the October 28, 1982 general elections won an absolute majority in the Parliament, while the CP's 23 representatives were reduced to 4 (one of whom for PSUC) and a million of their voters did go to the Socialists. The PCE declared that, with its 4 representatives, it would support the 202 Socialists in Parliament and their government. Faced with the criticism of his leadership in the party's central committee, Carrillo resigned as general secretary on November 6, 1982, but managed to have one of his faithfuls, Gerardo Iglesias, to succeed him.

The PCE crisis has two aspects. The internal one is directly linked to Carrillo's dictatorship and with young militants' impatience at seeing their careers blocked by old ones. It is revealing that Carrillo, who took part in numerous shady affairs in the PCE's history, was not forced to resign for any of them but was for losing an election. The external aspect of this crisis is due to the fact that in the eyes of the Spanish people the PCE does not have any function as a party. The police function attributed by Carrillo during the electoral campaign (to "control the Socialists") does not seem to have attracted voters. "Communism in the world, and particularly in Spain, is like one of those stars, dead a million years ago, but whose light is still reaching us, although they no longer exist."[44]

Everywhere, Always

Not everything is negative in the Communist movement. Granted, it did not achieve anything for the workers, did not carry off any revolution—although it gained power in numerous countries—and did not make any contribution to the theory or practice of the liberation of human beings.

But at least its existence has some usefulness: it is a constant reminder of the fact that in each political militant, in each person there sleeps a Stalin. The French say that in everyone there is "a slumbering pig." Likewise it can be said that in everyone always, independent of ideology, there is a potential dictator, and that every movement in time of difficulty feels the temptation to resolve difficulties by force, imposition, and deceit. The lesson which the Communist movement provides—before, during, and after Stalin— is indispensable. Because it did not exist prior to 1917 the Russian Revolution was able to become what the USSR is today. The warnings of a few farsighted leaders were not sufficient because they were based only on theory. To give force to those warnings today we have the practice of the various Communist parties.

Nonetheless, one frequently finds attitudes of "Down with murder and long live the murderers," especially if the murderers have strength in unions and votes which they put at the disposal of those who, with a full knowledge of history, forget who made that history. Experience likewise shows us that force, dictatorship, imposition, and deceit solve nothing and end up destroying the very thing they were trying to defend by those means. Suffice to remember that the Communist movement has not won a single battle. All its victories have come about as a result of the failures of others. The Communists have only prospered where the labor movement was divided or had failed, where it did not do its job, where the Socialists, Anarchists, and syndicalists did not know how to achieve a policy which could get the approval not only of the working class but also of other social groups near it.

The Communist experience is a constant reminder of the difficulty of revolution and the dangers of undertaking it by imitating the enemy. The right wing is changing. The Left must change as well, and the Communist experience at least can show in which direction change should not be effected. One must go from a Left which is obsessed by the state to one that has faith in the participation, initiative, and responsibility of the common man. From a policy of productivity to one of austerity, from centralism to decentralization, from the desire for uniformity to the development of diversity. One must go from blind faith in indefinite progress to knowing how to establish priorities and disregarding apparent advances which, in practice, would be steps backward. One must also go from the concept of the future as something vague and hypothetical to a vision of what lies ahead as something real, immediate, concrete and yet still far off. One must create new images of the economy as distinct from property, and power as distinct from authority.

In sum, the Communists have shown us that only by removing the economy and power, wealth and authority from the sphere of the divine—in other words, by humanizing them—will the Left have the potential to be successful and to immunize itself, when the time comes, against the temptations of that dictatorial "pig" that sleeps in all of us. When Copernicus brought together sufficient evidence to prove that there were irregularities in the course of heavenly bodies if one accepted Ptolemy's idea that the Sun revolved around the Earth, he did not look for formulas that would make the hypothesis compatible with those irregularities but rather had the courage to wonder whether the hypothesis was not erroneous. The Communist experience, in the world as well as in Spain, puts us in the same position. It is not a matter of correcting the errors and irregularities to maintain a useless hypothesis (which is what Eurocommunism is trying to do), but of finding a new, useful hypothesis instead.

Notes

1. Semprún, p. 136.
2. Naturally he does not recall that in 1945 he himself said: "We must relentlessly combat the fascist agents of POUM," and that in 1954 Ibárruri cried out: "It's clear, then, that the foul-smelling, anti-Communist stench of POUM comes from the cesspool of Francoism."
3. Régis Debray and Max Gallo, *Demain, l'Espagne,* Paris, 1974. Regarding the false statements contained in these interviews and regarding Carrillo in general, consult the pamphlet of the Libertarian Front of Paris, "Autopsia de un oportunista" (Paris, 1976); it includes essays by Gómez Peláez, Semprún Maura, and Felipe Orero. Regarding Puig Antich and the PCE's indifference, consult Telesforo Tajuelo, *El MIL, Puig Antich y los GARI,* Paris, 1977.
4. Information on the PCE's presence in those "summits" appears in *Boletín de Información,* Prague, nos. 20, 23, 24, 1973, and 2, 3, 19, 20, 21, 23, 24, 1974.
5. Carrillo, *Hacia el posfranquismo,* Paris, 1974, p. 106.
6. Carrillo's conference is in *API Informaciones,* Barcelona, May 22, 1974. The dinner is in *Cambio 16,* Madrid, June 10, 1974. In support of the future junta, the PCE organized a rally in Geneva which thousands attended and at which a tape of Carrillo and Ibárruri was heard, for the Berne government had prohibited them from speaking in person.
7. It was not strange then that the movement's press printed statements which Calvo Serer had written in the same press twenty years earlier: "This is the dilemma: either [Catholic] catechism or civil war. . . . The ideal of the victors in 1939 ought to be imposed and in no way should we make concessions to the defeated. There is not need to resuscitate the political parties which have been so ill-fated. . . . Freedom of expression leads to demagogy, ideological confusion, and pornography." When Carrillo returned to Madrid and the PCE was legalized in 1977, Calvo Serrer also returned.

He was welcomed by some second-rank Communists and then was forgotten like all allies of the PCE in the past. So far he has been spared the insults that have been heaped upon some of the others. In 1976 he was still saying that the PCE was no longer totalitarian and internationalist (*La Vanguardia Española*, Barcelona, August 22, 1976). His recollections of this period are in *Siempre*, Mexico City, September 29, October 13, December 29, 1976.

8. Quoted by Aulo Casamayor, "Por una oposición que se oponga," *Cuadernos de Ruedo Ibérico*, Paris, November-December, p. 239.

9. Quoted by Martínez Val, p. 239.

10. *Nouvelle Revue Internationale*, no. 1, 1974.

11. Tuñón de Lara, *La España del siglo XX*, p. 569.

12. Carrillo, *Eurocomunismo y Estado*, p. 151.

13. Roig; Teresa Pàmies, *Quan èrem capitans*, Barcelona, 1974; and *Testament a Praga*, Barcelona, 1971. Pàmies was perhaps the only one to undertake this work of reestablishing the past, albeit within certain limits.

14. These conditions were set in the "Manifiesto-programa del PCE" approved in the second conference of the PCE (the first was in Pamplona-Bilbao in 1930), which met in September 1975.

15. Ramón Tamames, *Un proyecto de democracia para el futuro de España*, Madrid, 1975, pp. 10, 37.

16. Reprinted in *Cuadernos de Ruedo Ibérico*, Paris, November-December 1976, p. 85 ff.

17. Carrillo, *Demain, l'Espagne*, pp. 18, 19.

18. The first part of the quote is from Carrillo to Oriana Fallaci in *L'Europeo*, Milan, October 10, 1975. The second part is by Carrillo to José Luis de Villalonga in *Lui*, Paris, January 1975. The last sentence sounds paradoxical coming from someone who wrote his father a letter like the one of 1939.

19. *PCE en sus documentos*, Madrid, 1977, pp. 177–78.

20. Gregorio López Raimundo, *Cataluña y la ruptura*, Barcelona, 1975.

21. Prior to this accord Carrillo had said that the platform had been precipitously improvised, lacked a program, and did not intend a democratic change but rather the installation of monarchy of the movement as a motor of democratic change. None of this stopped the PCE from forming an alliance with the platform by means of the junta (Ramón Chao, *Après Franco*, Paris, 1975, pp. 250–52), as it did in 1934 with Alianza Obrera and in 1945 with the ANFD.

22. Carrillo, *PCE*, Barcelona, 1976, p. 91; *Cambio 16*, Madrid, April 19, 1976.

23. Teresa Pàmies, "Qui està desmoralitzat?" *Avui*, Barcelona, May 18, 1978. A chronology of the PCE, distributed by the party to the press in 1978, said that the PCE "elaborated [in 1976] the theory of democratic reform later agreed upon by pact." The break was such a failure that the PCE even wanted its name forgotten. It is astounding that the entire press printed this chronology without mentioning that it had been provided by the PCE and without correcting this and other "errors."

24. McInnes, p. 3.

25. I. Gallego, *El partido de masas que necesitamos*, Paris, 1971, p. 70.

26. A. Perezagua, "Le pays basque espagnol," *Nouvelle Revue Internationale*, no. 9, 1975.

27. Quoted in Ruiz Ayúcar, p. 415.

28. All the facts have been taken from issues of *La Vanguardia Española* of Barcelona, *Cambio 16* of Madrid, *The New York Times*, and *Le Monde* of Paris. For the sake of brevity, events referring to the government, the rest of the opposition, or Spanish politics in general are not cited, only those relating to the PCE.

29. Regarding the electoral programs, consult *Un hombre, un voto: guía electoral de 1977*, Madrid, 1977; and *Documentación Social: la realidad económica-social y los partidos políticos*, Madrid, 1977.

30. There are few analyses of Eurocommunism that are more than a mere collection of quotes. The most interesting is that of Fernando Claudín, *Eurocomunismo y socialismo*, Madrid, 1977. For documentation consult: N. Bosi and H. Portelli, *Les PCE espagnol, français et italien face au pouvoir*, Paris, 1975; Máximo Loizu and Pere Vilanova, *¿Qué es el eurocomunismo?* Barcelona, 1977; Gabriel Albiac, *El debate sobre la dictadura del proletariado*, Madrid, 1977; Alfonso Carlos Comín, "Liquider l'héritage d'une patristique marxiste," in *Il Manifesto: Pouvoir et opposition dans les sociétés post-révolutionnaries*, Paris, 1978; and Santiago Carrillo, *Eurocomunismo y Estado*, Barcelona, 1977.

31. "Carrillo contra Cunhal," *Cambio 16*, Madrid, September 22, 1975.

32. The most interesting texts of this evolution, aside from Carrillo's book, are: Berlinguer-Carrillo, *Una Spagna libera in un'Europa democratica*, Rome, 1975; *Manifiesto-programa del PCE*, Madrid, 1975; Azcárate, *Informe al CC del PCE*, 1973; "La victoria del Vietnam: eje de una profunda mutación histórica," *Nuestra Bandera*, nos. 79–80, 1975; and Carrillo's speech at the conference of Communist parties in Berlin, June 1976.

33. *Opinión*, Madrid, February 10, 1978.

34. Quoted by Semprún, p. 280.

35. *Informaciones Españolas*, Brussels, January 1970.

36. *El País*, Madrid, November 8, 1977. The accusation was made by a "provisional congress of Spanish emigrants," organized at the last moment in Kassel by the PCE.

37. Moscow has expressed criticism of the PCE on two occasions: once in *Tiempos Nuevos*, July 1977, and the other in the same magazine in January 1978 against Azcárate for his rejection of Leninism and his statement that the USSR was not really a socialist state. Although both criticisms appeared in relatively short articles and were not very severe, the PCE got as much propaganda out of them as it could. Carrillo, for example, said that they were "a pack of lies unworthy of a periodical belonging to a party that calls itself Marxist," and the uninformed reader got the impression that it was slightly less than an issue of excommunication. There was no excommunication since relations between the PCE and the CPSU were not broken off, and La Pasionaria went to Moscow during the summer of 1978, as was her custom. Shortly after the criticism of Russia, Carrillo and the Soviet ambassador in Madrid greeted each other effusively at the opening of *The Battleship Potemkin*, a few days after the sentencing in Moscow of the dissidents Orlov and Sharatsky.

38. The Canadian unionist Charles Levison in statements to *La Vanguardia Española*, Barcelona, June 25, 1978, and in his book *Vodkacola*, Paris, 1977, p. 359 ff.

39. *Historia del PCE*, pp. 206–7.

40. Ibárruri in *Interviu,* Barcelona, August 26, 1976.
41. These false statements were never corrected. In conversation with journalists about the past, leaders of the PCE systematically "forget" names like Líster, Claudín, and Semprún. It is the Soviet procedure of turning dissidents into nonpersons (Semprún, pp. 241, 243; he relates two instances of "forgetfulness" by Sánchez Montero and Romero Marín).
42. Carrillo, *Demain, l'Espagne,* p. 167.
43. The image belongs to the Hungarian poet Attila Joszef.
44. Ignacio Iglesias in a letter to the author, Paris, November 21, 1982.

Appendix A: Abbreviations

AEAR	Asociación de Escritores y Artistas Revolucionarios (Association of Revolutionary Artists and Writers)
ANFD	Alianza Nacional de Fuerzas Democráticas (National Alliance of Democratic Forces)
ARI	Associación para la Renovación de la Izquierda (Association for Renewal of the Left)
ASO	Alianza Sindical Obrera (Labor Union Alliance)
BEOR	Bloque Escolar de Oposición Revolucionaria (University Bloc of Revolutionary Opposition)
BOC	Bloque Obrero Campesino (Workers' and Peasants' Bloc)
CC	Comité Central (Central Committee)
CEDA	Confederación Española de Derechas Autónomas (Spanish Confederation of Autonomous Right-Wing Parties)
CGTU	Confederación General del Trabajo Unitario (General Unitarian Confederation of Labor)
CNS	Central Nacional Sindicalista (National Syndicalist Federation)
CNT	Confederación Nacional del Trabajo (National Confederation of Labor)
CSUT	Confederación de Sindicatos Unitarios de Trabajadores (Confederation of Unitarian Labor Unions)
ETA	Euzkadi Ta Askatasuna (Basque Country and Freedom)
FAI	Federación Anarquista Ibérica (Iberian Anarchist Federation)
FJS	Federación de Juventudes Socialistas (Federation of Socialist Youth)
FLP	Frente de Liberación Popular (Popular Liberation Front)
FOC	Front Obrer Català (Catalonian Labor Front)
FUDE	Federación Universitaria Democrática Española (Spanish Democratic University Federation)

FUE   Federación Universitaria Escolar
(University Students' Federation)

GES   Grupo de Estudiantes Socialistas
(Socialist Student Group)

HNP   Huelga Nacional Pacífica
(National Peaceful Strike)

IC   Internacional Comunista (Comintern)
(Communist International)

IDC   Izquierda Demócratacristiana
(Christian Democratic Left)

IJC   Internacional Juvenil Comunista
(Communist Youth International)

ISR   Internacional Sindical Roja (Profintern)
(Red Trade Union International)

JARE   Junta de Auxilio a los Refugiados Españoles
(Junta of Aid to Spanish Refugees)

JCI   Juventud Comunista Ibérica
(Iberian Communist Youth)

JL   Juventudes Libertarias
(Libertarian Youth)

JSU   Juventud Socialista Unificada
(Unified Socialist Youth)

MOC   Milicias Obreras y Campesinas
(Workers' and Peasants' Militias)

NKVD   Soviet political police

ORT   Organización Revolucionaria de Trabajadores
(Revolutionary Organization of Workers)

PCC   Partit Comunista de Catalunya
(Communist Party of Catalonia)

PCE   Partido Comunista de España
(Communist Party of Spain)

PCOE   Partido Comunista Obrero de España
(Communist Workers' Party of Spain)

CPSU   Communist Party of the Soviet Union

POUM Partido Obrero de Unificación Marxista
(Workers' Party of Marxist Unification)

PSOE   Partido Socialista Obrero Español
(Spanish Workers' Socialist Party)

PSUC   Partido Socialista Unificat de Catalunya
(Unified Socialist Party of Catalonia)

PTE   Partido del Trabajo de España
(Workers' Party of Spain)

SERE   Servicio de Emigración para Republicanos Españoles
(Emigration Service for Spanish Republicans)

SEU   Sindicato Español Universitario
(Spanish University Union)

SIM	Servicio de Información Militar (Military Information Service)
SOC	Solidaritat d'Obrers Cristians (Christian Workers' Solidarity)
SRI	Socorro Rojo Internacional (International Red Aid)
STV	Solidaridad de Trabajadores Vascos (Basque Workers' Solidarity)
SUT	Sindicato Unitario de Trabajadores (Unitarian Union of Workers)
UFEH	Unión Federal de Estudiantes Hispanos (Federal Union of Hispanic Students)
UGT	Unión General de Trabajadores (General Union of Workers)
UJC	Unión de Juventudes Comunistas (Union of Communist Youth)
UMA	Unión Militar Antifascista (Military Antifascist Union)
UME	Unión Militar Española (Spanish Military Union)
USC	Unió Socialista de Catalunya (Socialist Union of Catalonia)
USO	Unión Sindical Obrera (Labor Union of Workers)

Appendix B: Chronology

1919 (December) "Provisional" entry of the CNT in the Third International.

1920 (April) Foundation of the Spanish Communist party.

1921 (April) Foundation of the Spanish Communist Workers' party.
(November) Fusion of both Communist parties and formation of the PCE.

1922 The CNT withdraws its membership in the Profintern. Foundation of the Revolutionary Syndicalist Committees.
(March) First Congress of the PCE.

1923 (July) Second Congress of the PCE.

1924 First triumvirate (Maurín) and second triumvirate (Bullejos, Portela, Trilla).

1929 (August) Third Congress of the PCE in Paris. Bullejos as secretary general.
Separation of the Catalonian-Balearic Federation.

1930 (March) Bilbao-Pamplona Conference.
(August) The weekly *Mundo Obrero* appears. Foundation of the Workers' and Peasants' Bloc in Catalonia.

1931 (April) Proclamation of the Republic. "All power to the soviets."

1932 (March) Fourth Congress of the PCE. Purge of the troika of Bullejos-Trilla-Adame and its replacement by the troika Díaz-Ibárruri-Hernández.

1933 Foundation in Barcelona of Alianza Obrera. Revolutionary movement in Catalonia and Asturias.

1935 (August) Seventh Congress of the Communist International which issues the slogan of Popular Front.

1936 (January) Signing of the pact for the Spanish Popular Front in which the PCE participates. Formation of the JSU; Carrillo elected as secretary general.
(February 16) Elections. Sixteen Communist representatives elected on the Popular Front ticket. Support "in Parliament and in the street" for the governments of Azaña and Casares Quiroga.
(July 18) Military uprising.
(July 23) Formation of the Unified Socialist Party of Catalonia; Joan Comorera elected as secretary general. Position of the PCE: "Win the war first." Support for the Giral government. The PCE forms part of the Largo Caballero government. Letter from Stalin to Largo Caballero. Shipment of Spanish gold to Moscow by Juan Negrín.

1937 (May) Struggle in the streets of Barcelona. Campaign against the collectivizations, Largo Caballero, and POUM. Largo Caballero resigns. Prieto, with the support of Azaña and the PCE, has Juan Negrín named as head of government. Dismantling of the collectivizations. Communist control of the army and SIM. Restrictions of Catalonian autonomy. The "Government of Victory" loses the North and fails in Teruel. Persecution of POUM and the CNT; assassination of Andrés Nin and other revolutionaries.

1938 Fall of Lérida. Cut of the Republican zone at Vinaroz. Campaign against Prieto, his resignation, and Negrín's government of "resistance." Battle of the Ebro. Trial against POUM.

1939 Fall of Catalonia. Formation of the National Council of Defense in Madrid. The war ends (April 1).

1939–41 Party leaders seek refuge in Mexico. and Moscow. Members are ordered to remain in the French camps. Organization of the SRI in Madrid through police provocation. Trial of the "thirteen roses." Quiñones in charge of the Political Bureau in Madrid. Monzón and Trilla head the PCE's activity in France. Participation in the resistance after the German invasion of the USSR. Arrest and execution of Quiñones.

1942–43 (March 21, 1942) Death of José Díaz in the USSR. Struggle for succession in Moscow between Ibárruri and Hernández. Hernández is sent to Mexico and then expelled on Moscow's orders. Ibárruri elected secretary general. Spaniards in the gulag of Karagandá.

1944–48 Formation of National Union. "Invasion" of Arán Valley called off by Carrillo. Expulsion of Monzón and Trilla. Purge of those returning from Nazi camps. Attacks on the National Alliance of Democratic Forces and, finally, entry in it. Attacks on the Giral government in exile and finally entry in it with Carrillo as minister. Uribe as minister of the Llopis government in exile. Assassination of Gabriel León Trilla in Madrid by Cristino García. Dissolution of National Union. Guerrillas in Spain.

1948–53 Closing of the PCE's centers in France. Headquarters are transferred to Prague. Revelations of "El Campesino" who fled from the USSR. Conflict with Comorera and his consequent expulsion. Moix elected secretary general of PSUC. Expulsion of Tito's followers. Hernández publishes *Yo fui un ministro de Stalin.*

1954 (November) Fifth Congress of the PCE in Prague. New bylaws. Ibárruri reelected secretary general.

1956 Policy of "national reconciliation." "Peaceful national strike" fails time after time. Infiltration in the university. Congress of Young Writers. "Alliance of the forces of labor and culture." Carrillo's attack on the "personality cult" in the PCE following the Twentieth Congress of the Communist Party of the Soviet Union.

1960 Sixth Congress of the PCE in Prague. Ibárruri named president and Carrillo secretary general. The PCE is to become a party of the masses. Attempts to attract the Catholics.

1962 Julián Grimau's arrest in Madrid; his execution the following year.

1963 Scision which led to the Marxist-Leninist Communist party (Maoist).

1964 Expulsion of Fernando Claudín and Jorge Semprún. The PCE infiltrates the Workers' Commissions.

1965 Seventh Congress of the PCE (in Prague?).

1968 Condemnation of the Soviet invasion of Czechoslovakia. Expulsion of García Gómez.

1971 Policy of the Pact for Freedom. Expulsion of Líster. Numerous scisions which form Leninist and Stalinist groups.

1972 Eighth Congress of the PCE in Paris. Contacts with the Communist parties of Italy, Rumania, Yugoslavia; trip to China. Abandonment of the dictatorship of the proletariat, adoption of political pluralism.

1975 Formation of the Junta Democrática. Policy of rupture. Formation of the Platajunta (with the Platform of Democratic Convergence). Manifesto-program approved by the second conference.

1976 (August) Meeting of the central committee in Rome.

1977 (March) Carrillo in Madrid. "Summit" of Eurocommunism with Marchais and Berlinguer.

(April) Legalization of the PCE.

(June) Elections. The PCE gets 12 representatives and PSUC 8.

1978 (April) Ninth Congress of the PCE. Abandonment of Leninism. Ibárruri and Carrillo reelected.

1979 (March) Elections. Twenty-three PCE and PSUC representatives elected.

1980 Campaign against the Socialists.

1981 (January) Fifth Congress of PSUC in Barcelona. Victory of pro-Soviet faction.

(July) Tenth Congress of the PCE in Madrid. Failure of attempts to democratize the party.

(November) The CP of Euzkadi unites with other Basque nationalist groups and is expelled from the PCE. Members opposed to the unification form a new CP of Euzkadi. Several PCE leaders resign in solidarity with the Basque party. Azcárate is the best known.

1982 (March) The Communists separate from ARI.

(March) Sixth Congress of PSUC in Barcelona. The Eurocommunist faction recovers the leadership. The pro-Soviet faction leaves the party and forms the PCC.

(June) Failure of Communist candidates in regional elections in Andalusia. Carrillo resigns as secretary general of the PCE but the CC asks him to remain.

(October) Victory of the Socialists and failure of the Communist candidates in the general election. Only 4 PCE and PSUC representatives elected (instead of 23 in 1979). Loss of more than a million votes.

(November) Carrillo is forced to resign. Gerardo Iglesias is the new secretary general. Large numbers—artists, intellectuals, students—leave the party. The Comisiones Obreras try to keep their distance from the PCE.

Bibliography

History of the PCE

Acevedo, Isidoro, *Impresiones de un viaje a Rusia,* Oviedo, 1923.
Aisa, J., and Arbeloa, V.M., *Historia de la Unión General de Trabajadores,* Madrid, 1975.
Alba, Víctor, *Histoire des Républiques espagnoles,* Paris, 1948.
———. *Historia del Frente Popular,* Mexico City, 1959.
———. *El marxisme a Catalunya, 1919–1939,* Barcelona, 1974–75.
———. *Dos revolucionarios: Maurín, Nin,* Madrid, 1975.
———. *Els problemes del moviment obrer de Catalunya,* Barcelona, 1976.
———. *El Frente Popular,* Barcelona, 1976.
———. *Histoire du POUM,* Paris, 1976.
———. *Los sepultureros de la República,* Barcelona, 1977.
———. *La oposición de los supervivientes, 1939–1955,* Barcelona, 1978.
———. *Historia de la resistencia antifranquista, 1939–1955,* Barcelona, 1978.
———. *Transition in Spain,* New Brunswick, New Jersey, 1978.
Alcofar Nassaes, J.L., *Los asesores soviéticos en la guerra civil española,* Barcelona, 1971.
Alexandre, Philippe, *Le roman de la gauche,* Paris, 1977.
Allen, David E. *The Soviet Union and the Spanish Civil War,* Stanford, 1952.
Almendros, Joaquín, *Situaciones españolas, 1936–39: el PSUC en la guerra civil,* Barcelona, 1976.
Almendros Morcillo, F., et al., *El sindicalismo de clase en España, 1939–1977,* Barcelona, 1978.
Álvarez, Ramón, *Eleuterio Quintanilla,* Mexico City, 1973.
Álvarez, Santiago, *El Partido Comunista y el campo,* Madrid, 1977.
Álvarez Suárez, Maximiliano, *Sangre de octubre: UHP,* Madrid, 1936.
Álvarez del Vayo, Julio, *Freedom Battle,* New York, 1940.
———. *La nueva Rusia,* Madrid, 1932.
Andrade, Juan, *La burocracia reformista en el movimiento obrero,* Madrid, 1935.
———. "La fundación del Partido Comunista de España," *Tribuna Socialista,* Paris, May-June 1977.
Araquistain, Luis, "La nueva táctica comunista," *Leviatán,* Madrid, August 1935.
———. *El comunismo y la guerra de España,* Carmaux, 1939.
———. *Mis tratos con los comunistas,* Toulouse, 1939.

———. "La intervención de Rusia en España," *Cuadernos*, Paris, March-April 1958.

Arnau, Roger, *Marxisme català i questió nacional catalana*, Paris, 1974.

Arquer, Jordi, *Los comunistas ante el problema de las nacionalidades ibéricas*, Barcelona, 1932.

———. "Frente Popular Antifascista o Frente Único Obrero," *La Nueva Era*, Barcelona, January 1936.

Arrabal, Fernando, *Carta a los militantes comunistas españoles*, Paris, 1978.

Arrabal en el banquillo, Paris, 1977.

Artola, Miguel, *Partidos y programas políticos, 1808-1936*, Madrid, 1974.

L'assassinat d'Andrés Nin: ses causes, ses auteurs, La Guépeou, Paris, 1938.

Autour du procès du POUM, Paris, 1938.

Aubin, C.V., "Manuel Núñez de Arenas y de la Escosura (1886-1951)," *Bulletin Hispanique*, Paris, vol. LIII, no. 4.

Autopsia de un oportunista: Santiago Carrillo y su mundo político, Paris, 1976.

Azaña, Manuel, *Obras completas*, Mexico City, 1967.

Azcárate, Manuel, *Crisis del euro-comunismo*, Barcelona, 1982.

Bahne, S., "Origine et débuts des Partis Communistes des pays latins," *Archives de Jules Humbert-Droz*, Dordrecht, 1969.

Balbontín, J.A., *La España de mi experiencia*, Mexico City, 1952.

Balcells, Albert, *El sindicalisme a Barcelona*, Barcelona, 1965.

———. *El arraigo del anarquismo en Cataluña*, Barcelona, 1973.

———. *Crisis económica y agitación social en Cataluña de 1930 a 1936*, Barcelona, 1971.

Barea, Arturo, *La forja de un rebelde*, Buenos Aires, 1951.

Barril, J. del, "El XVI aniversario de la constitución del Partido Socialista Unificado de Cataluña," *Acción Socialista*, Mexico City, June 1952.

Barrot, Jean, *Le mouvement communiste*, Paris, 1972.

Benavides, Manuel D., *Guerra y revolución en Cataluña*, Mexico City, 1944.

Berlinguer, Enrico, and Carrillo, Santiago, *Una Espagna libera in un'Europa democràtica*, Rome, 1975.

Bernieri, Camilo, *Petrogrado 1917-Barcelona 1937*, Milan, 1964.

Bilbao, Esteban, *La unificación comunista*, Madrid, 1932.

Bizcarrondo, Marta, *Araquistáin y la crisis de la II República: Leviatán*, Madrid, 1975.

Blumé, Daniel, "Contribution à l'histoire de la politique de non-intervention," *Cahiers Léon Blum*, Paris, 1977-78.

Bolloten, Burnett, *The Grand Camouflage*, New York, 1961.

———. *The Spanish Revolution*, Chapel Hill, N.C., 1979.

Bonamusa, F., *El Bloc Obrer i Camperol, 1930-1932*, Barcelona, 1974.

———. *Andreu Nin y el movimiento comunista en España, 1930-1937*, Barcelona, 1977.

Borkenau, Franz, *The Spanish Cockpit*, Ann Arbor, 1963.

Borrás, José, *Política de los exilados españoles, 1944-1950*, Paris, 1976.

A Boss for Spain, Madrid, 1964.

Brennan, Gerald, *The Spanish Labyrinth*, Cambridge, 1950.

Brockway, Fenner, *The Truth about Barcelona*, London, 1937.

Brome, Vincent, *The International Brigades*, New York, 1966.

Broue, P., *Trotsky y la guerra civil española*, Buenos Aires, 1966.

_____. *La révolution espagnole, 1931-1939*, Paris, 1973.

Broue, P., and Temime, E., *La révolution et la guerrre en Espagne*, Paris, 1961.

Buber-Neumann, Margarete, *La révolution mondiale*, Paris, 1971.

Buenacasa, Manuel, *El movimiento obrero español, 1888-1926*, Barcelona, 1928.

Bueso, Adolfo, *Recuerdos de un cenetista*, Barcelona, 1976.

Bullejos, José, *Europa entre dos guerras*, Mexico City, 1945.

_____. *España en la segunda República*, Mexico City, 1967.

_____. *La Comintern en España: recuerdos de mi vida*, Mexico City, 1972.

Cabrer Pallas, R., "Ramon Casanelles i la rebotiga comunista," *Xaloc*, Mexico City, July-August 1977.

Calamai, Marco, *Storia del movimento operaio spagnolo dal 1960 al 1975*, Bari, 1975.

Camacho, Marcelino, *Charlas en la prisión*, Paris, 1974.

Carr, Raymond, *Spain, 1808-1939*, London, 1966.

_____. (ed.), *The Republic and the Civil War in Spain*, New York, 1971.

Carrillo, Santiago, *Après Franco, quoi?* Paris, 1966.

_____. *Demain, l'Espagne*, Paris, 1974.

_____. *PCE*, Barcelona, 1976.

_____. *Eurocomunismo y Estado*, Barcelona, 1977.

_____. *El año de la Constitución*, Barcelona, 1978.

Carrillo, Santiago, and Berlinguer, Enrico, *Una Spagna libera in un'Europa democràtica*, Rome, 1975.

Carrillo, Wenceslao, *A propósito del Consejo Nacional de Defensa*, Mexico City, 1943.

Casado, Segismundo, *The Last Days of Madrid*, London, 1939.

Castellas, A., *Las Brigadas Internacionales en la guerra de España*, Barcelona, 1974.

Casterás, Ramón, *Las JSUC ante la guerra y la revolución, 1936-1939*, Barcelona, 1977.

Castro Delgado, Enrique, *Mi fe se perdió en Moscú*, Mexico City, 1950.

_____. *Hombres made in Moscú*, Mexico City, 1960.

Cattell, D.T., *Communism and the Spanish Civil War*, Berkeley, 1956.

_____. *Soviet Diplomacy and the Spanish Civil War*, Berkeley, 1957.

Cazcarra, Vicente, *Aragón: el regionalismo de los comunistas*, Zaragoza, 1977.

CGTU, *Hacia el Congreso de la CGTU*, Madrid, 1934.

_____. *Plataforma de lucha aprobada por el primer Congreso de la CGTU*, Madrid, 1934.

Claudín, Fernando, "Dos concepciones de la vía española al socialismo," *Horizonte Español*, Paris, 1966.

_____. *La crisis del movimiento comunista: de la Komintern a la Kominform*, Paris, 1970.

————. *Eurocomunismo y socialismo,* Madrid, 1975.

————. *Documentos de una divergencia comunista,* Barcelona, 1978.

Coca, G. Mario de, *Anti-Caballero,* Madrid, 1975.

CNT, *Memoria del Congreso celebrado en el teatro de la Comedia de Madrid de los días 10 al 18 de diciembre de 1919,* Barcelona, 1932.

Colodny, Robert G., *El asedio de Madrid,* Paris, 1972.

Comín, Alfonso C., *Cristianos en el Partido, comunistas en la Iglesia,* Barcelona, 1977.

Comín Colomer, Eduardo, *La República en el exilio,* Barcelona, 1957.

————. *Historia del Partido Comunista de España,* Madrid, 1967.

Comorera, Joan, *Socialisme i qüestió nacional,* Barcelona, 1977.

El comunismo al día, Madrid, 1935.

El comunismo en España, Madrid, 1953.

Congreso Extraordinario del PSOE, 1921, Madrid, 1974.

Contreras Casado, M., "El Partido Socialista: la trayectoria de un conflicto interno," in *Estudios sobre la II República Española,* ed. M. Ramírez, Madrid, 1975.

Conze, Edward, *Spain Today,* London, 1936.

Cordón, Antonio, *Trayectoria,* Paris, 1971.

Crime ou châtiment? Documents inédits sur Julián Grimau, Madrid, 1963.

Cruells, Manuel, *Els fets de maig,* Barcelona, 1970.

————. *El 6 d'octubre a Catalunya,* Barcelona, 1970.

————. *Salvador Seguí, el Noi del Sucre,* Barcelona, 1974.

Cruz Goyenola, Lauro, *Rusia por dentro,* Montevideo, 1946.

Cuadrado, Miguel M., *Elecciones y partidos políticos de España, 1868–1931,* Madrid, 1969.

Chao, Ramón, *Après Franco,* Paris, 1975.

Chapaprieta, Joaquín, *La paz fue posible,* Barcelona, 1971.

Damiano, Cipriano, *La resistencia libertaria,* Barcelona, 1978.

Davis, Daniel, *The Spanish Civil War: The Last Great Cause,* New York, 1974.

Debray, Régis, and Gallo, Max, *Demain, l'Espagne,* Paris, 1974.

Degras, Jane, *The Communist International: Documents,* London, 1961 ff.

Delperrie de Bayac, Jacques, *Les Brigades Internationales,* Paris, 1968.

Desanti, Dominique, *L'Internationale Communiste,* Paris, 1970.

Díaz, Elías, "La filosofía marxista en el pensamiento español actual," *Cuadernos para el Diálogo,* Madrid, December 1968.

Díaz, José, *Tres años de lucha,* Paris, 1970.

Díaz, J.A., *Luchas internas en las Comisiones Obreras,* Barcelona, 1977.

Díaz del Moral, J., *Historia de las agitaciones campesinas andaluzas,* Madrid, 1923.

Díaz Nosty, B., *La comuna asturiana,* Madrid, 1974.

Dimitrof, J., *Problemas del Frente Obrero y del Frente Popular,* Mexico City, 1939.

East European Fund, *Soviet Shipping in the Spanish Civil War,* New York, 1954.

Ehrenburg, Ilya, *España: república de trabajadores,* Madrid, 1932.

Epistolario Prieto-Negrín, Paris, 1939.

Erroteta, Peru, and Vega, Pedro, *Los herejes del PCE,* Barcelona, 1982.

España hoy, Paris, 1963.

Estivill, Ángel, *6 d'octubre, l'ensulciada dels jacobins,* Barcelona, 1935.

Estruch, Joan, *Historia del PCE (I), 1920-1939,* Barcelona, 1978.

———. *El PCE en la clandestinidad, 1939-1955,* Madrid, 1982.

Fagen, Patricia W., *Exiles and Citizens: Spanish Republicans in Mexico,* Austin, Texas, 1973.

Falcón, César, *Crítica de la revolución española (desde la Dictadura hasta las Constituyentes),* Madrid, 1931.

Fejto, François, *Dictionnaire des Partis Communistes et des mouvements révolutionnaires,* Tournoi, 1971.

Ferri, Llibert, et al., *Las huelgas contra Franco,* Barcelona, 1978.

Fisher, Louis, *Men and Politics: An Autobiography,* New York, 1941.

———. *Russia's Road from Peace to War: Soviet Foreign Relations, 1917-1941,* New York, 1969.

Flores, Xavier, "El exilio y España," *Horizonte Español, 1966,* Paris, 1966.

Freymond, J., *Contribution a l'histoire du Comintern,* Geneva, 1965.

Fuentes, Enrique, "La oposición antifranquista de 1939 a 1945," *Horizonte Español, 1966,* Paris, 1966.

Fusi, Juan Pablo, *Política obrera en el País Vasco, 1880-1923,* Madrid, 1975.

Gabriel, Pere, "Socialisme, sindicalisme i comunisme a Mallorca," *Recerques,* no. 2, Barcelona, 1972.

———. *El moviment obrer a Mallorca,* Barcelona, 1973.

Gallo, Max, *Histoire de l'Espagne franquiste,* Verviers, 1969.

Gannes, Harry, *How the Soviet Union Helps Spain,* New York, 1936.

García Palacios, L., *Los dirigentes del PC al desnudo,* Madrid, 1931.

García Pradas, J., *¡Teníamos que perder!* Madrid, 1974.

———. *La traición de Stalin: cómo terminó la guerra de España,* New York, 1939.

———. *Rusia y España,* Paris, 1948.

García Venero, Maximiano, *Historia de las Internacionales en España,* Barcelona, 1957.

Garmendía, J.M., et al., *Eurocomunismo y Euzkadi,* San Sebastián, 1977.

Garosci, Aldo, *Gli intellettuali e la guerra di Spagna,* Turin, 1955.

———. "Palmiro Togliatti," *Survey,* London, October 1964.

Gide, André, *Littérature engagée,* Paris, 1950.

The God That Failed, London, 1950.

Gómez, Manuel, "From Mexico to Moscow," *Survey,* London, October 1964.

Gómez Casas, Juan, *Los anarquistas en el gobierno,* Barcelona, 1977.

———. *Historia del anarcosindicalismo español,* Madrid, 1968.

Gómez Ortiz, J.M., *Los gobiernos republicanos: España, 1936-1939,* Barcelona, 1977.

González, Valentín, *La vie et la mort en URSS,* Paris, 1950.

González Casanova, J.A., *Elecciones en Barcelona, 1931-1936,* Madrid, 1969.

———. *Federalisme i autonomia a Catalunya, 1868-1938*, Barcelona, 1974.

Gordón Ordás, Félix, *Mi política en España*, Mexico City, 1962.

Gorkín, Julián, *Caníbales políticos*, Mexico City, 1941.

———. *España: primer ensayo de democracia popular*, Buenos Aires, 1961.

———. *El revolucionario profesional*, Barcelona, 1975.

———. *El asesinato de Trotsky*, Barcelona, 1971.

Gorkín, Julián, and Sánchez Salazar, L.A., *Murder in Mexico: The assassination of Leon Trotsky*, London, 1950.

Gross, Babette, *Willi Münzenberg: A Political Biography*, Lansing, 1974.

Grossi, Manuel, *La insurrección de Asturias*, Barcelona, 1935.

Guarner, Vicente, *Cataluña en la guerra de España*, Madrid, 1975.

Guérin, Daniel. *L'anarchisme*, Paris, 1953.

Guerra y revolución en España, 1936-1939, Moscow, 1966.

Hemingway, Ernest, *For Whom the Bell Tolls*, New York, 1940.

———. *The Fifth Column and Four Unpublished Stories of Spain's Civil War*, New York, 1969.

Hermet, Guy, *Les communistes en Espagne*, Paris, 1971.

Hernández, Jesús, *Negro y Rojo*, Mexico City, 1946.

———. *Yo fui un ministro de Stalin*, Mexico City, 1953.

Hidalgo, Diego, *Un notario español en Rusia*, Madrid, 1930.

Historia del Partido Comunista de España, Paris, 1960.

Horizonte Español, 1966, Paris, 1966.

Horizonte Español, 1972, Paris, 1972.

Humbert-Droz, Jules, *Archives de . . .* , Dordrecht, 1970.

———. *De Lénine à Staline: Dix ans au service de l'Internationale Communiste*, Neuchâtel, 1971.

———. *Dix ans de lutte antifasciste, 1931-1941*, Neuchâtel, 1972.

Ibáñez, Jesús, *Memorias de un muerto*, Mexico City, 1945.

Ibárruri, Dolores, *El único camino: Memorias de La Pasionaria*, Mexico City, 1963.

———. *En la lucha: Palabras y hechos, 1936-1939*, Moscow, 1968.

Iglesias, Ignacio, *Trotsky et la révolution espagnole*, Lausanne, 1974.

———. *La fase final de la guerra civil*, Barcelona, 1977.

La insurrecció d'Octubre a Catalunya, Barcelona, 1935.

Izcaray, Jesús, *Las ruinas de la muralla*, Paris, 1965.

Iztueta, Pablo, et al., *El marxismo y la cuestión nacional vasca*, San Sebastián, 1977.

Jackson, Gabriel, *The Spanish Republic and the Civil War, 1931-1939*, Princeton, 1965.

———. (ed.), *The Spanish Civil War*, Boston, 1967.

Jacquier, Maurice, *Simple Militant*, Paris, 1974.

Johnson, Verle, *Legions of Babel*, London, 1967.

Juliá, Santos, *La izquierda del PSOE, 1935-1936*, Madrid, 1977.

Julián Grimau: El hombre, el crimen, la protesta, Paris, 1963.

Kenny, Michael, *A Spanish Tapestry*, Bloomington, 1961.

Kern, Robert, *Red Years, Black Years: A Political History of Spanish Anarchism*, Philadelphia, 1978.

Knighley, Phillip, *The First Casualty*, New York, 1975.

Koltzov, Mikhail, *Procés de la traició trotskista*, Barcelona, 1938.

────. *Diario de la guerra de España*, Paris, 1963.

Krivitski, Walter, *In Stalin's Secret Service*, London, 1939.

La Cierva, Ricardo de, *Crónicas de la transición*, Barcelona, 1975.

Lamberet, Renée, *Les mouvements ouvriers et socialistes—chronologie et bibliographie: L'Espagne, 1750-1936*, Paris, 1953.

Landau, Katia, *Les stalinistes en Espagne*, Paris, 1938.

Landis, Arthur, *The Unfinished Revolution*, New York, 1972.

Largo Caballero, Francisco, *Discursos a los trabajadores*, Madrid, 1934.

────. *Mis recuerdos: Cartas a un amigo*, Mexico City, 1954.

────. *La UGT y la guerra*, Valencia, 1937.

Lazitch, Branko, *Les partis communistes d'Europe, 1919-1955*, Paris, 1956.

Lera, Ángel María de, *Ángel Pestaña: Retrato de un anarquista*, Barcelona, 1978.

Levinson, Charles, *Vodka-Cola*, Paris, 1977.

Líster, Enrique, *Nuestra guerra*, Paris, 1966.

────. *¡Basta!* Paris, 1971.

────. *Memorias de un luchador: Los primeros combates*, Madrid, 1977.

London, Arthur, G., *Espagne*, Paris, 1966.

────. *Se levantaron antes del alba*, Barcelona, 1978.

Longo, Luigi, *Las Brigadas Internacionales en España*, Mexico City, 1966.

Lorenzo, César M., *Les anarchistes espagnols et le pouvoir*, Paris, 1969.

Lozano, C. M., *¡Hasta nunca! Fermín Galán*, Barcelona, 1976.

Llopis, Rodolfo, *Cómo se forja un pueblo: La Rusia que yo he visto*, Madrid, 1929.

Lluelles, Víctor, *Diccionari polític de Catalunya*, Barcelona, 1977.

Macià: La seva actuació a l'estranger, Mexico City, 1952-55.

Madariaga, Salvador de, *Spain: A Modern History*, New York, 1958.

Malo Molina, José, *Los comunistas y la crisis de la universidad*, Madrid, 1977.

Manifestes, thèses et résolutions des quatre premiers congrès mondiaux de l'Internationale Communiste, Paris, 1934.

Martín Maestre, J., *La caída de Kruschev y la crisis del comunismo*, Madrid, 1965.

Martín i Ramos, J.L., *Els origens del Partit Socialista Unificat de Catalunya, 1930-1936*, Barcelona, 1977.

Martinet, Gilles, *Les cinq communismes*, Paris, 1971.

Martínez Bande, José, *Brigadas Internacionales*, Barcelona, 1972.

────. *Los cien últimos días de la República*, Barcelona, 1973.

────. *Por qué fuimos vencidos*, Madrid, 1974.

Martínez Barrio, Diego, *Páginas para la historia del Frente Popular*, Valencia, 1937.

Martínez Prieto, Horacio, *Facetas de la USSR*, Madrid, 1933.

Martínez Val, J., *Españoles ante el comunismo*, Barcelona, 1976.

Matorras, Enrique, *El comunismo en España: Sus orientaciones, sus organizaciones, sus procedimientos,* Madrid, 1935.

Matthews, Herbert L., *A World in Revolution,* New York, 1973.

Maurín, Joaquín, *El sindicalismo a la luz de la revolución rusa,* Lérida 1922.

———. *La crisis de la CNT,* Barcelona, 1924.

———. *Los hombres de la dictadura,* Madrid, 1930.

———. *El Bloque Obrero y Campesino,* Barcelona, 1932.

———. *Revolución y contrarrevolución en España,* Paris, 1966.

———. "Hombres e Historia," *España Libre,* New York, February 19, 1960ff.

McGovern, John, *Terror in Spain,* London, 1938.

McInnes, Neil, *The Communist Parties of Western Europe,* London, 1975.

McKenzie, Kermit E., *Comintern and World Revolution: The Shaping of Doctrine, 1928–1943,* New York, 1964.

Meaker, Gerald H., *The Revolutionary Left in Spain, 1914–1923,* Stanford, 1974.

Miralles, Rafael, *Españoles en Rusia,* Madrid, 1947.

Miravitlles, Jaume, "The Man Who Denounced Antonov-Ovseenko," *The New Leader,* New York, August 6, 1956.

———. *Episodis de la guerra civil espanyola,* Barcelona, 1972.

Modesto, J. *Soy del Quinto Regimiento,* Paris, 1969.

Mola, Emilio, *Lo que yo supe,* Valladolid, 1940.

Molas, Isidre, "Les eleccions parcials a Corts Constituents d'octubre de 1931 a la ciutat de Barcelona," *Recerques,* no. 1, Barcelona, 1970.

Molins i Fábrega, Narcís, *UHP: La revolució proletària d'Astúries,* Barcelona, 1935.

Mont-Fort (Joaquín Maurín), *Alianza Obrera,* Barcelona, 1935.

Moreno Hernández, Ramón, *Rusia al desnudo: Revelaciones del comisario comunista español Rafael Pelayo de Hungría, comandante del ejército ruso,* Madrid, 1956.

Morrow, Felix, *Revolution and Counter-Revolution in Spain,* New York, 1939.

Munis, G., *Jalones de derrota, promesa de victoria,* Mexico City, 1948.

Nenni, Pietro, *La guerra de España,* Mexico City, 1956.

Nin, Andreu, *El sindicalismo revolucionario y la Internacional,* Barcelona, 1923.

———. *Lo que son los Soviets,* Madrid, 1931.

———. *Las organizaciones obreras internacionales,* Madrid, 1933.

———. *Els moviments d'emancipació nacional,* Barcelona, 1935.

———. *Los problemas de la revolución española,* Paris, 1971.

Novais, J.A., and Rodríguez Armada, A., *¿Quién mató a Julián Grimau?* Madrid, 1976.

Núñez, Mercedes, *Cárcel de Ventas,* Paris, 1967.

Núñez de Arenas, Manuel, *Historia del movimiento obrero español,* Barcelona, 1970.

Ollivier, Marcel, "La nueva táctica comunista," *Leviatán,* Madrid, September 1935.

———. *La Guépeou en Espagne,* Paris, 1946.

Orlov, Alexander, *The Secret Story of Stalin's Crimes,* New York, 1953.

Orwell, George, *Homage to Catalonia,* London, 1938.

Padilla, Antonio (ed.), *El movimiento comunista español,* Barcelona, 1979.

Pagés, Pelai, *Andreu Nin: Su evolución política, 1911-1937,* Madrid, 1974.

_____. *El movimiento trotskista en España, 1930-1935,* Barcelona, 1977.

_____. *Historia del Partido Comunista de España (desde su fundación en abril de 1920 hasta la caída de la Dictadura en enero de 1930),* Barcelona, 1978.

Palazuelos, Enrique, *Movimiento estudiantil y democratización de la Universidad,* Madrid, 1978.

Pàmies, Teresa, *Testament a Praga,* Barcelona, 1971.

_____. *Quan érem capitans,* Barcelona, 1974.

_____. *Una española llamada Dolores Ibárruri,* Barcelona, 1976.

Paniagua, Xavier, "La visió de Gaston Leval de la Russia Soviética el 1921," *Recerques,* no. 3, Barcelona, 1974.

Payne, Stanley G., *Franco's Spain,* New York, 1967.

_____. *The Spanish Revolution,* New York, 1970.

El PCE en sus documentos, Madrid, 1977.

Peirats, José, *La CNT en la revolución española,* Buenos Aires, 1955.

_____. *Los anarquistas en la crisis política española,* Buenos Aires, 1964.

_____. *Los anarquistas en la guerra civil española,* Madrid, 1976.

Peiró, Juan, *Problemas y cintarazos,* Rennes, 1946.

Pérez Baró, Albert, *Trente mesos de col.lectivisme a Catalunya,* Barcelona, 1970.

_____. *Els "feliços" anys vint,* Palma de Mallorca, 1974.

Pérez Salas, Jesús, *Guerra en España,* Mexico City, 1947.

Pérez Solís, Óscar, *Mi amigo Óscar Perea,* Madrid, 1929.

_____. *El Partido Socialista y la acción de las izquierdas,* Valladolid, 1918.

Pestaña, Ángel, *Memoria que al Comité Nacional de la CNT presenta de su gestión en el II Congreso de la III Internacional, su delegado,* Madrid, 1921.

_____. *Consideraciones y juicios acerca de la Tercera Internacional,* Barcelona, 1922.

_____. *Setenta días en Rusia,* Barcelona, 1924.

_____. *Trayectoria sindicalista,* Madrid, 1974.

Pike, D.W., *Conjecture, Propaganda, and Deceit in the Spanish Civil War,* Stanford, 1968.

_____. *Les Français et la guerre d'Espagne,* Paris, 1975.

Pla, José, *Historia de la segunda República española,* Barcelona, 1946.

Polémica Maurín-Carrillo, Barcelona, 1937.

Ponamariova, L.V., *La formación del Partit Socialista Unificat de Catalunya,* Barcelona, 1977.

Pons Prades, E., *Guerrilla española, 1936-1960,* Barcelona, 1977.

Portela, Luis, "Vida y muerte de la Agrupación Comunista de Madrid," *La Batalla,* Barcelona, April 21, 1932 ff.

_____. "Presentación" to *Los hombres de la Dictadura,* by Joaquín Maurín, Barcelona, 1977.

––––––. "El nacimiento y los primeros pasos del movimiento comunista en España," Ms., Barcelona, 1978.

Preston, Paul (ed.), *Spain in crisis,* New York, 1976.

––––––. "The Origin of the Socialist Schism in Spain, 1917–1931," *Journal of Contemporary History,* vol. 12, no. 1, London, January 1979.

Prieto, Carlos, "La tactique du Parti Communiste a contribué à l'affaiblissement des comissions ouvrières," *Le Monde,* Paris, February 18, 1970.

Prieto, Indalecio, *Posiciones socialistas,* Madrid, 1935.

––––––. *Cómo y por qué salí del Ministerio de Defensa Nacional,* Mexico City, 1940.

––––––. *Entresijos de la guerra de España,* Buenos Aires, 1955.

––––––. *Yo y Moscú,* Madrid, 1955.

––––––. *Convulsiones de España,* Mexico City, 1967–69.

––––––. *Dentro y fuera del Gobierno (discursos parlamentarios),* Mexico City, 1972.

Puzzo, Dante, *Spain and the Great Powers, 1936–1941,* New York, 1972.

Qüestió nacional i lluita de classes, Barcelona, 1977.

Rabasseire, Henri, *España, crisol político,* Buenos Aires, 1966.

Ramírez, Luis, *Nuestros primeros veinticinco años,* Paris, 1964.

Ramírez Molina, E., "¿Anticomunista, el cristiano?" *Cuadernos para el Diálogo,* Madrid, April 1968.

Rama, Carlos, *Crisis española del siglo XX,* Mexico City, 1960.

Ramos Oliveira, Antonio, *Nosotros, los marxistas: Lenin contra Marx,* Madrid, 1932.

––––––. *Politics, Economics, and Men of Modern Spain,* London, 1946.

Regler, Gustav, *The Great Crusade,* New York, 1940.

Renaudel, Pierre, *L'Internationale à Berne,* Paris, 1919.

Resnais, Alain, *La guerre est finie,* Paris, 1966.

Reventlow, R., *Spanien in diesen Jahrhundert,* Frankfurt, 1970.

"La révolution espagnole," *Études Marxistes,* nos. 7–8, Paris, 1969.

Rico, José Antonio, *En los dominios des Kremlin,* Mexico City, 1950.

Richards, Vernon, *Lessons of the Spanish Revolution,* London, 1953.

Rieger, Max, *Espionaje en España,* Barcelona, 1938.

Rienfer, K., *Comunistas españoles en América,* Madrid, 1953.

Ríos, Fernando de los, *Mi viaje a la Rusia sovietista,* Madrid, 1935.

Rivas Cherif, Cipriano, *Retrato de un desconccido: Vida de Manuel Azaña,* Mexico City, 1961.

Robinson, R.A.H., *Los orígenes de la España de Franco,* Barcelona, 1974.

Rocker, R., *Extranjeros en España,* Buenos Aires, 1938.

Rodríguez Armada, A., and Novais, J.A., *¿Quién mató a Julián Grimau?* Madrid, 1976.

Rodríguez Castillo, E., *Communist Offensive against Spain,* Madrid, 1949.

Roig, Montserrat, *Rafael Vidiella: L'aventura de la revolució,* Barcelona, 1976.

Rojas, Carlos, *¿Por qué perdimos la guerra?* Barcelona, 1970.

––––––. *La guerra civil vista por los exiliados,* Barcelona, 1975.

Rojo, Vicente, *España heroica*, Mexico City, 1961.

Romero, Joaquín, and Ruiz, Fernando, *Los partidos marxistas: Sus dirigentes, sus programas*, Barcelona, 1977.

Romero, Luis, *Desastre en Cartagena*, Barcelona, 1971.

——. *El final de la guerra*, Barcelona, 1976.

Romero Solano, L., *Vísperas de guerra en España*, Mexico City, 1947.

Rosal, Amaro del, *Los congresos obreros internacionales en el siglo XX*, Mexico City, 1963.

——. *Historia de la UGT de España*, Barcelona, 1977.

Rosmer, Alfred, *Moscou sous Lénine*, Paris, 1953.

Rossif, F., *Mourir à Madrid*, Paris, 1963.

Roy, M.N., *Memoirs*, Bombay, 1964.

Ruiz, David, *El movimiento obrero en Asturias*, Oviedo, 1968.

——. "Escritos juveniles de Santiago Carrillo," *Historia 16*, Madrid, July 1977.

Ruiz, Fernando, and Romero, Joaquín, *Los partidos marxistas: Sus dirigentes, sus programas*, Barcelona, 1977.

Ruiz Ayúcar, Ángel, *Crónica agitada de ocho años tranquilos, 1963-1970*, Madrid, 1974.

——. *El Partido Comunista: Treinta y siete años de clandestinidad*, Madrid, 1976.

Saborit, Andrés, *Julián Besteiro*, Mexico City, 1961.

——. *Asturias y sus hombres*, Toulouse, 1964.

Sala, A., and Durán, E., *Crítica de la izquierda autoritaria en Cataluña, 1967-1974*, Paris, 1975.

Sánchez-Albornoz, Claudio, *De mi anecdotario político*, Buenos Aires, 1972.

Sánchez Montero, Simón, *Qué es el comunismo*, Barcelona, 1976.

Sánchez Salazar, S., and Gorkín, J., *Murder in Mexico: The Assassination of Leon Trotsky*, London, 1950.

Sanromá, José, *Marxismo, eurocomunismo y estado*, Madrid, 1978.

Santiago de Pablo, Luis, "El marxismo en los exilados comunistas españoles," in *Situación y revisión contemporánea del marxismo*, Madrid, 1966.

Santillán, Diego Abad de, *Por qué perdimos la guerra*, Buenos Aires, 1940.

——. *Contribución a la historia del movimiento obrero español*, Puebla, 1971.

——. *De Alfonso XIII a Franco*, Buenos Aires, 1973.

Sanz, Miguel Ángel, *Los guerrilleros españoles en Francia, 1940-1945*, Havana, 1971.

Sanz Oller, Julio, *Entre el fraude y la esperanza: Las Comisiones Obreras de Barcelona*, Paris, 1972.

Sartorius, N., *El resurgir del movimiento obrero*, Barcelona, 1976.

Schwartz, Fernando, *La internacionalización de la guerra civil española*, Barcelona, 1971.

Semprún, Jorge, "La oposición política en España, 1956-1966," in *Horizonte Español, 1966*, Paris, 1966.

——. *Autobiografía de Federico Sánchez*, Barcelona, 1977.

Semprún Maura, Carlos, *Revolució i contrarrevolució a Catalunya, 1936-1937*, Barcelona, 1975.

_____. *L'an prochain à Madrid*, Paris, 1975.

Serge, Víctor, *Mémoires d'un révolutionnaire*, Paris, 1951.

_____. *Le Tournant obscur*, Paris, 1972.

Sevilla Andrés, Diego, *Historia política de la zona roja*, Madrid, 1963.

Solé Tura, Jordi, *Diccionario del comunismo*, Barcelona, 1977.

Sonadellas, Concepció, *Clase obrera y revolución social en España, 1936-1939*, Madrid, 1977.

Sorel, Andrés, *Búsqueda, reconstrucción e historia de la guerrilla española del siglo XX*, Paris, 1970.

Soria, Georges, *Guerre et révolution en Espagne, 1936-1939*, Paris, 1975.

Sperber, Manés, *Au délà de l'oubli*, Paris, 1979.

Suárez, Andrés, *El proceso contra el POUM*, Paris, 1974.

Tagüeña, Manuel, *Testimonio de dos guerras*, Mexico City, 1973.

Tamames, Ramón, *Un proyecto de democracia para el futuro de España*, Barcelona, 1975.

_____. *La República: La era de Franco*, Madrid, 1973.

Termes, Josep, "Repercussions de la revolució d'octubre a Catalunya," *Serra d'Or*, Barcelona, December 1967.

Thomas, Hugh, *The Spanish Civil War*, New York, 1961.

Torralba Beci, Eduardo, *La nueva senda del comunismo*, Madrid, 1923.

Trevisano, Giulio, *Piccola enciclopedia del socialismo e del comunismo*, Milan, 1958.

Trotski, León, *Ma vie*, Paris, 1953.

_____. *Escritos sobre España*, Paris, 1971.

_____. *The Spanish Revolution, 1931-1939*, New York, 1973.

_____. *La revolución española*, Madrid, 1977.

Tuñón de Lara, Manuel, *La España del siglo XX*, Paris, 1966.

_____. *El movimiento obrero en la historia de España*, Madrid, 1972.

_____. *Luchas obreras y campesinas en la Andalucía del siglo XX*, Madrid, 1978.

Tusell, Javier, *La segunda República en Madrid: Elecciones y partidos políticos*, Madrid, 1970.

_____. *Las elecciones del Frente Popular*, Madrid, 1971.

_____. *La oposición democrática, 1939-1962*, Barcelona, 1977.

El último episodio de la guerra civil española, Paris, n.d. (1939).

Un hombre, un voto: Guía electoral de 1977, Madrid, 1977.

Valle, José María del, *Las instituciones de la República española en el exilio*, Paris, 1976.

Vanguardia Obrera, "Adulteraciones del equipo de Santiago Carrillo," Madrid, 1971 (Ms.).

Vanni, E., *Yo, comunista en Rusia*, Barcelona, 1950.

Vega, Pedro, and Erroteta, Peru, *Los herejes del PCE*, Barcelona, 1982.

Venegas, José, *Andanzas y recuerdos de España*, Montevideo, 1943.

Vidal Sales, José, *Después del 39: la guerrilla antifranquista,* Barcelona, 1977.
Vidarte, Juan Simeón, *Todos fuimos culpables,* Mexico City, 1973.
Vidiella, Rafael, *De París a la cárcel de Madrid,* Barcelona, 1932.
Vilar, Sergio, *La oposición a la dictadura,* Paris, 1969.
_____. *El disidente,* Barcelona, 1981.
Viñas, Ángel, *El oro de Moscú,* Barcelona, 1979.
_____. *El oro español en la guerra civil,* Madrid, 1976.
Viñas, Ricard, *Las Juventudes Socialistas Unificadas, 1934–1936,* Madrid, 1978.
Voros, S., *American Commissar,* Philadelphia, 1961.
Welles, Benjamin, *Spain: The Gentle Anarchy,* New York, 1965.
William, G., *First Congress of the Red Trade Union International at Moscow, 1921,* Chicago, 1922.
Yagüe, María Eugenia, *Santiago Carrillo,* Madrid, 1977.
Zugazagoitia, Julián, *Guerra y vicisitudes de los españoles,* Paris, 1968.

Public Documents: PCE, PCC, PSUC

Acta de acusación contra los agentes de Trotsky, aliado del fascismo alemán, Valencia, 1937.
Adame, Manuel, *El CN de Reconstrucción y la política del Partido,* Barcelona, 1931.
_____. *Qué es el Bloque Obrero y Campesino,* Madrid, 1932.
"La agresión israelí-imperialista a los pueblos árabes," *Nuestra Bandera,* Spring 1967.
Álvarez, Santiago, "Le Parti Communiste et le mouvement ouvrier," *Nouvelle Revue Internationale,* March 1967.
_____. "L'Alliance des catholiques et des communistes," *Nouvelle Revue Internationale,* September 1968.
_____. "Del encuentro de Budapest a la Conferencia de Moscú," *Nuestra Bandera,* Summer 1968.
Ana, Marcos, *Si mil veces volviera a nacer, mil veces volvería a ser comunista,* Prague, 1963.
Antón, Francisco, "El programa de la victoria sobre el franquismo," *Mundo Obrero,* April 13, 1950.
Ardiaca, P., *Por un partido marxista-leninista,* Barcelona, 1937.
Arlandis, Hilario, *Los anarquistas en Rusia,* Barcelona, 1924.
Azcárate, Manuel, "Práctica y teoría del diálogo católico-marxista," *Realidad,* July 14, 1967.
_____. "Realidades españolas en el diálogo cristiano-marxista," *Nuestra Bandera,* Spring 1967.
Le Bilan de vingt ans de dictature fasciste: Les tâches immédiates de l'opposition et l'avenir de la démocratie espagnole, Limoges, 1959.
Bullejos, José, "Le mouvement des mineurs espagnols," *Internationale Syndicale Rouge,* April 1925.
_____. *El Partido Comunista y el trotskismo,* Madrid, 1932.

460   The Communist Party in Spain

Carrillo, Santiago, *Conferencia de . . . secretario de la JSU en el Teatro Apolo de Valencia, el 16 de diciembre de 1936,* Valencia, 1937.

―――. *Somos la organización de la juventud,* Madrid, 1937.

―――. *La juventud, factor de la victoria,* Barcelona, 1937.

―――. *El deber de la JSU,* Mexico City, 1945.

―――. *Por la República y la legalidad constitucional, todos unidos a la lucha,* Montevideo, 1945.

―――. *Los niños españoles en la URSS: Conferencia del día 6 de septiembre de 1947,* Paris, 1947.

―――. *Informe sobre problemas de organización y los Estatutos del Partido: V Congreso del PCE,* 1954.

―――. *Sobre algunos problemas de la táctica de lucha contra el franquismo,* Montevideo, 1961.

―――. *La situación en el movimiento comunista (pleno ampliado del PCE, noviembre de 1963),* Paris, 1964.

―――. *Discurso ante una asamblea de militantes del Partido (19 de abril de 1964),* Paris, 1964.

―――. *Después de Franco ¿qué? La democracia política y social que preconizamos los comunistas,* Paris, 1965.

―――. "Coloquio sobre los problemas de la universidad," *Realidad,* June 1966.

―――. "Contra la agresión de Israel: Solidaridad con la justa causa de los pueblos árabes. Declaración del Partido Comunista de España," *Nuestra Bandera,* Spring 1967.

―――. *Nuevos enfoques a problemas de hoy,* Paris, 1967.

―――. "Cuba, marzo de 1968," *Nuestra Bandera,* Spring 1968.

―――. "La lucha por el socialismo hoy," *Nuestra Bandera,* June 1968.

―――. "Une déclaration du Parti Communiste d'Espagne," *L'Humanité,* Paris, September 7, 1968.

―――. "Conférence de presse de Santiago Carrillo à Rome," *L'Humanité,* Paris, February 14, 1969.

―――. *Los problemas del socialismo hoy—más problemas del socialismo: El conflicto chino-soviético. Discurso pronunciado en la Conferencia de los partidos comunistas y obreros de Moscú,* Paris, 1969.

―――. "La democracia en el partido leninista," *Mundo Obrero,* April 5, 1970.

―――. *Libertad y socialismo,* Paris, 1971.

―――. *Hacia la libertad,* Paris, 1972.

―――. *Hacia el posfranquismo,* Paris, 1975.

―――. *Las tareas del movimiento obrero para que el franquismo desaparezca también,* Barcelona, 1975.

―――. *Hacia un socialismo en libertad,* Madrid, 1977.

―――. *La propuesta comunista,* Barcelona, 1977.

Colomer, Wenceslao, *Per una joventut culta, lliure, i feliç,* Barcelona, 1937.

Comorera, Juan, *Cataluña en pie de guerra,* Valencia, 1937.

―――. *Discurs pronunciat al miting del Gran Price, el 1 de juny de 1937,* Barcelona, 1937.

———. *La batalla de la pau,* Mexico City, 1945.

Comunistas y anarcosindicalistas: Las tácticas de la CNT y la Internacional Sindical Roja, Madrid, 1932.

Conquistemos a las masas: La acentuación de la crisis revolucionaria y las tareas del PCE, Madrid, 1933.

Contreras, Carlos, *La Quinta Columna: Cómo luchar contra la provocación y el espionaje,* Valencia, 1937.

Cuarto Congreso del Partido Comunista de España (Sección Española de la Internacional Comunista): Tesis Sindical, Madrid, 1932.

La cuestión nacional y el movimiento nacional-revolucionario en España, Madrid, 1932.

Checa, Pedro, *Qué es y cómo funciona el Partido Comunista (algunas normas de organización),* Madrid, 1936.

Deberes del pueblo español en la presente situación nacional e internacional, Montevideo, 1961.

Díaz, José, *Discurso pronunciado por el Secretario General del Partido Comunista de España el 3 de noviembre de 1935,* Barcelona, 1935.

———. *Nuestra bandera del Frente Popular,* Madrid-Barcelona, 1936.

———. *Qué somos y qué queremos los comunistas,* Valencia, 1937.

———. *Tres años de lucha por el Frente Popular, por la libertad, por la independencia de España,* Paris, 1939, 1970.

Dimitrof, J., *Las lecciones de Almería,* Barcelona, 1937.

———. *En el segundo aniversario de la lucha del pueblo español,* Valencia, 1938.

Diz, Juan, "Le Parti Communiste dans les universités," *Nouvelle Revue Internationale,* March 1967.

Dos meses de huelga, Paris, 1962.

Estatutos y tesis aprobadas por el I Congreso Nacional celebrado en Madrid en marzo de 1922, Madrid, 1922.

Un futuro para España: La democracia económica y política, Paris, 1967.

Gallego, Ignacio, "Salvaguardar al Partido de los zarpazos del enemigo," *Mundo Obrero,* April 13, 1950.

García, A.M., "Los anarquistas y las alianzas obreras," *Revista Internacional,* Barcelona, May 17, 1935.

García, Eduardo, "Une avant-garde dans la lutte du peuple," *Nouvelle Revue Internationale,* March 1967.

———. "En torno a una auténtica política de reclutamiento," *Nuestra Bandera,* Winter 1967.

———. "Le Parti Communiste consolide ses rangs," *Nouvelle Revue Internationale,* August 1968.

Guerra y revolución en España, 1936–1939, Moscow, 1962.

Hacia la unidad de la lucha de clases, Madrid, 1932.

Hernández, Jesús, *El Partido Comunista antes, durante y después de la crisis del gobierno Largo Caballero,* Valencia, 1937.

Historia del Partido Comunista de España, Paris, 1960.

Hurtado, Manuel, *Normas de organización y estructura del Partido Comunista,* Madrid-Barcelona, 1932.

Ibárruri, Dolores, *Una necesidad internacional: Ayudar al pueblo español a liberarse de la tiranía franquista,* Montevideo, 1945.

————. *Por la libertad de España,* Mexico City, 1945.

————. *Informe del Comité Central: V Congreso del Partido Comunista de España,* Prague (?), 1954.

————. *España, Estado multinacional,* Paris, 1971.

Informes y resoluciones del Pleno del Comité Central del Partido Comunista de España, Prague, 1956.

Izcaray, Jesús, "30 días con los guerrilleros de Levante," *Mundo Obrero,* May 6–August 26, 1948.

————. "Las guerrillas de Levante," *Mundo Obrero,* October 1–November 13, 1947.

Lang, P., *La alianza del trotskismo y el fascismo contra el socialismo y la paz,* Madrid, 1936.

Las lecciones de los combates de octubre en España, Madrid, 1936.

Líster, Enrique, *El pueblo español lucha por la paz,* Paris, 1968.

López Raimundo, Gregorio, *Por una acción democrática nacional de Cataluña,* Barcelona, 1975.

Losovsky, A., *Programa de acción de la Internacional Sindical Roja,* Barcelona, 1923.

————. *Los partidarios de la ISR en la revolución española,* Barcelona, 1931.

La lucha por la bolchevización del Partido, Madrid, 1932.

Llamamiento del Comité Central del Partido Comunista por el triunfo del Bloque Popular: A luchar y a vencer, Madrid, 1935.

M.A., "Aspectos del diálogo católico-marxista," *Realidad,* November-December 1968.

Marty, André, *España, donde se juega el destino de Europa,* Barcelona, 1937.

"Más de 40 millones recaudados en la campaña de los treinta millones," *Mundo Obrero,* September 2, 1969.

Melchor, Federico, "Comunistas y católicos," *Nuestra Bandera,* Fall 1967.

Mije, Antonio, "La educación y la práctica internacionalista del Partido Comunista de España," *Nuestra Bandera,* Winter 1969.

Modesto, Juan, *Progreso y perspectivas del movimiento guerrillero,* Paris, 1947.

Montiel, Francisco F., *Por qué he ingresado en el Partido Comunista,* Barcelona, 1937.

Noveno Congreso del Partido Comunista de España, Barcelona, 1978.

"Nuestro programa: Por una república democrática," *Mundo Obrero,* December 31, 1954.

Octavo Congreso del Partido Comunista de España, Bucharest, 1972.

El Partido Comunista ante las Constituyentes, 1931.

El Partido Comunista y la revolución española, Barcelona, 1932.

El Partido Comunista por la libertad y la independencia de España, Valencia, 1937.

Pla, Nuria, "Juventud: lo prosoviético y lo antisoviético," *Nuestra Bandera*, Summer 1968.

Pleno Ampliado del Comité Central del Partido Comunista de España, Valencia, 1937.

"Por una España republicana, democrática e independiente. Las sesiones del III Pleno del PCE en Francia," in *Mundo Obrero*, March 27, 1947.

"Por un Partido Comunista de masas. Resolución del CE del PC de España," *Nuestra Bandera*, Spring 1967.

El POUM en el banquillo, Barcelona, 1938.

El problema agrario y las luchas de los campesinos, Barcelona, 1932.

Los problemas de la revolución española: Los renegados del comunismo, Barcelona, 1932.

Programa del Partido Comunista de España frente a las próximas elecciones, Madrid, 1931.

Programa del Gobierno Obrero y Campesino: Partido Comunista de España, Madrid, 1932.

Programa del Partido Comunista de España: V Congress del PCE, Paris, 1955.

Los progresos en la organización del nuevo movimiento obrero, 1965-1967, n.p., 1968.

PSUC, "Declaración del Secretariado del Partido Socialista Unificado de Cataluña sobre la conducta política de Juan Comorera," *Mundo Obrero*, November 10, 1949.

_____. *Aportació a la histórica social i nacional de la classe obrera de Catalunya*, Paris, 1955 (?).

_____. *Una proposta democràtica i socialista per a Catalunya*, Barcelona, 1976.

_____. *Informe del Comité Central al VI Congrés*, Barcelona, 1982.

"Qué hay tras la inmolación de Jan Palach?" *Mundo Obrero*, February 5, 1969.

"Resolución del Comité Ejecutivo del Partido Comunista de España," *Mundo Obrero*, March 24, 1969.

Resolución del Pleno del Comité Central del PCE sobre la situación política y las tareas del partido, Madrid, 1932.

La revolución española, por el Dr. I. Kom, Barcelona, 1932.

Rosal, Amaro del, "Anécdotas y recuerdos," *Nuestra Bandera*, Fall 1970–Winter 1971.

"Sangre obrera sobre el Amur," *Mundo Obrero*, April 3, 1969.

Sanz, Gonzalo, "Recuerdos de aquellos días," *Mundo Obrero*, April 13, 1950.

Los sindicatos en la revolución española y las tareas sindicales de los comunistas españoles, Barcelona, 1932.

El socialfascismo, Barcelona, 1933.

Soria, Georges, *L'espionage trotskyste en Espagne*, Paris, 1938.

Suárez, Víctor, "Les Commissions Ouvrières en Espagne," *Nouvelle Revue Internationale*, February 1969.

Los sucesos de Barcelona, 1937.

Tareas de organización, Madrid-Barcelona, 1932.

464   The Communist Party in Spain

Togliatti, Palmiro, *Opere, 1935-1944*, Rome, 1979.

───── . *Sobre las particularidades de la revolución española*, Barcelona, 1936.

Uribe, Vicente, *La política agraria del Partido Comunista*, Valencia, 1937.

───── . *Todos unidos por la reconquista de la República*, Paris, 1945.

───── . *Informe sobre el programa del Partido: V Congreso del PCE*, Paris, 1954.

Name Index